*"I love your book. As a UNIX geek with SS7 telco background, I have had a fledgling NT 4.0 system plopped in my lap. The fellow who built the two servers and Exchange has left and the Mucky Mucks have decided I will be the MS systems administrator. Humph, now I have to learn THIS?! I bought your book and it has warmed my heart to Microsoft NT 4.0 and Exchange Server. Thank you for a well-thought-out endeavor. I look forward to the Exchange Server 5 book you will write.*

*P.S. I bought your book because of the* Mastering NT Server *and* Mastering NT Workstation *books by the same publisher."*

**GEORGE F. MISHLER**
**SYSTEMS ADMINISTRATOR**
**TELESERV CORPORATION**

*"I would like to thank you for writing such an informative book. We have been able to utilize your material to set up our own Exchange organization."*

**IAN D. CARLSON**
**A. O. SMITH AUTOMOTIVE**

*"I referenced your book many, many times during our migration to Exchange Server. Keep up the good work."*

**DAVID MISTRETTA**
**NETWORK ENGINEER**
**HARBINGER CORPORATION**

*"Your latest book,* Mastering Exchange Server, *is the greatest of help to me in the administration of an Exchange setup on two NT domains. Just about everything I have done comes from reading your excellent book."*

**BILL CARN**

# Mastering™ Microsoft ® Exchange Server 5.5

# Mastering™ Microsoft® Exchange Server 5.5

## Fourth Edition

Barry Gerber

SYBEX®

**San Francisco • Paris • Düsseldorf • Soest • London**

Associate Publisher: Guy Hart-Davis
Contracts and Licensing Manager: Kristine O'Callaghan
Acquisitions & Developmental Editor: Maureen Adams
Editors: Susan Berge and Donna Crossman
Project Editor: Chad Mack
Technical Editor: Donald Fuller
Book Designer: Kris Warrenburg
Graphic Illustrator: Tony Jonick
Electronic Publishing Specialist: Kris Warrenburg
Project Team Leader: Shannon Murphy
Proofreaders: Nelson Kim, Teresa Trego, Jennifer Campbell,
Dave Nash, and Patrick J. Peterson
Indexer: Ted Laux
Cover Designer: Archer Design
Cover Photographer: FPG International

Screen reproductions produced with Collage Plus.
Collage Plus is a trademark of Inner Media Inc.

SYBEX is a registered trademark of SYBEX Inc.
Mastering is a trademark of SYBEX Inc.

TRADEMARKS: SYBEX has attempted throughout this book to
distinguish proprietary trademarks from descriptive terms by following the capitalization style used by the manufacturer.

The author and publisher have made their best efforts to prepare
this book, and the content is based upon final release software
whenever possible. Portions of the manuscript may be based upon
pre-release versions supplied by software manufacturer(s). The
author and the publisher make no representation or warranties of
any kind with regard to the completeness or accuracy of the contents herein and accept no liability of any kind including but not
limited to performance, merchantability, fitness for any particular
purpose, or any losses or damages of any kind caused or alleged
to be caused directly or indirectly from this book.

Library of Congress Card Number: 99-67587
ISBN: 0-7821-2658-8

Manufactured in the United States of America

10 9 8 7 6 5 4 3 2

*To Jane, my wife and best friend,
for reminding me in so many ways
that technology should serve
and not control humanity*

# ACKNOWLEDGMENTS

**M**icrosoft's Exchange Server has come a long way since its first release in 1996. Keeping up with all of the changes and tracking through all of the beta and pre-release versions of Exchange 4, 5, and 5.5 was an adventure with all of the peaks and dips of a world-class rollercoaster ride. Equally adventuresome was the production of this edition, which includes updates since the release of Exchange Server 5.5 and a whole new look at the Outlook clients. Without the help and support of a number of fine people, this fourth edition of *Mastering Microsoft Exchange Server* would never have happened.

Deepest thanks to the marketing folks at Microsoft and Microsoft's public relations support firm, Waggner Edstrom, for their early encouragement and continuing assistance in opening doors I never even knew existed.

Words really cannot express both my indebtedness to and respect for the Exchange Server 4, 5, and 5.5 development teams. I'll never forget the patience they showed with my seemingly endless and not always well-articulated questions, especially as product delivery deadlines approached. My *Exchange Book* e-mail folder overflows with helpful, timely, and just-in-time responses from them all: Behrooz Chitsaz, August Hahn, David Johnson, Bill Kilcullen, Eric Lockard, Mark Ledsome, Steve Masters, Tom McCann, Ramez Naam, Jim Reitz, Todd Roberts, Rob Sanfilippo, Elaine Sharp, Rob Shurtleff, Aaron Snow, Bill Sorinsin, Paul Waszkiewicz, Jeff Wilkes, and Rusty Williams.

Finally, my heartfelt and everlasting thanks to the team of editors who kept me honest and articulate through all editions of the book. John Read at Sybex listened to my ideas for the first edition and helped shape them into a book. Peter Kuhns very ably picked up the ball for the second edition, as did Neil Edde for the third edition and Maureen Adams for this edition. Maureen Adams, who recently received a well-deserved promotion, with help from Lorraine Fry, shepherded my first edition draft manuscript through all the highs and lows of the production process. Ben Miller took over for the second and third editions and made me look like the most articulate technoid ever to come down the pike. Chad Mack, Susan Berge, and Donna Crossman ably took over these tasks for this edition. I'd also like to thank the production team of Shannon Murphy, Kris Warrenburg, Nelson Kim,

Teresa Trego, Dave Nash, Patrick J. Peterson, and Jennifer Campbell. And last, but far from least, Eric Lockard (first edition), Rob Sanfilippo (second and third editions), and Don Fuller (current edition) were the very best technical editors I've ever been privileged to work with. They all read every word and looked at every diagram and screen capture in an effort to ensure that what you read here is both accurate and understandable.

Thanks to everyone for all your help. Whatever errors of fact or judgment remain are mine and mine alone.

Barry Gerber
bg@bgerber.com
www.bgerber.com
Los Angeles, California

# CONTENTS AT A GLANCE

# TABLE OF CONTENTS

## Part VI    Connecting to Other E-Messaging Systems

### 15   External Links Using Exchange Connectors    579

## Appendixes

# INTRODUCTION

**I** wrote this book because I want to share the excitement I feel about the future of electronic messaging in general and about Exchange Server in particular. I also want to help you determine if there is a place for Exchange in your organization and, if so, to provide the information you'll need to set up an Exchange system of your own.

Your explorations of Exchange Server will open many new doors in the area of electronic communications. In addition, your work with this exciting product will afford you a peek at Microsoft's next iteration of NT Server. Exchange Server implements much of the object-oriented structure of Microsoft's Windows 2000, formerly known as NT 5. *Mastering Exchange Server 5.5* will, at the very least, give you a leg up when you tackle Windows 2000 Server.

# What's So Exciting about Exchange Server 5.5?

While this book covers all aspects of Exchange Server 5.5, it is still pertinent to Exchange Server 4 and 5. Exchange Server 4 was one of the most powerful, extensible, scalable, easy-to-use, and manageable electronic messaging back ends on the market. Exchange Server 5 retained all of 4's features and added extensive support for a range of advanced Internet communications protocols. Version 5.5 adds new Internet protocol support plus a few features we've all been wanting for some time.

Version 3 of the Post Office Protocol (POP3) enables nonproprietary, lightweight client access to Exchange Server messages. Version 4 of the Internet Message Access Protocol (IMAP4) adds key features missing in the POP3 protocol. Microsoft's Exchange and Outlook clients for Windows and the Macintosh are full-featured and very easy to use, but they only run on those operating systems and they require large amounts of workstation disk and memory resources. Any POP3 or IMAP4 client, whether running in MS Windows, Macintosh, any flavor of UNIX, or another operating system, can access Exchange Server to send and receive messages. Furthermore, POP3 and IMAP4 clients such as Qualcomm's Eudora, Microsoft's Internet mail client, Netscape's mail client, the University of Washington's Pine, or Microsoft's Outlook Express demand fewer workstation resources. So, they can run on those lower-end workstations still in heavy use in corporate America.

The Hypertext Transfer Protocol (HTTP) makes possible Web browser access to Exchange Server–based mailboxes, public folders, and schedules. Like POP3 and IMAP4 clients, Web browsers are both nonproprietary and lighter in weight than the standard Exchange clients. So users and their organizations realize the same benefits they get with POP3 or IMAP4 clients, while using a client that is on virtually every desktop. HTTP support also enables controlled and selective access to Exchange Server environments by anonymous users.

The Lightweight Directory Access Protocol (LDAP) opens the Exchange Server directory of user e-mail addresses and other information to Internet users. Exchange Server users with LDAP-enabled POP3 and IMAP4 clients can find e-mail addresses in the Exchange directory from anywhere in the world. This adds an unprecedented and most welcome level of user friendliness to the POP3 and IMAP4 world. The Exchange directory also can be made available to anonymous non–Exchange Server users armed with LDAP clients.

The Network News Transfer Protocol (NNTP) brings those popular USENET newsgroups to Exchange Server public folders. An Exchange server can function as a full-fledged NNTP server. Users of Exchange clients, Web browsers, or standard newsgroup reader software can participate in all or a select portion of the newsgroups hosted on an Exchange server.

In addition, Exchange 5.5 raises the maximum database size from 16GB to 16TB, adds Outlook 98 and 2000 clients that bring many new features to the table, and lets you retain users' "deleted" messages on your Exchange server for easy end user recovery.

With these and an impressive array of other features, Exchange Server 5.5 can help your organization move smoothly and productively into what I like to call "the e-messaging decade."

# What You Need to Run Exchange Server

Exchange Server is a complex product with a remarkably easy-to-use interface for administration and management. All of this complexity and parallel ease of use requires an industrial strength computer. The minimum server computer suggested below is for testing, learning about, and evaluating the product. It's also enough for a small, non-critical installation. However, as I discuss in the book, when the server moves into critical production environments where it will be accessed by large numbers of users, you'll need to beef up its hardware and add a number of fault-tolerant capabilities. On the client side, with the broad range of clients available for Exchange, the lower-end machines now on desktops in most organizations should be more than adequate.

At a minimum, to test, learn about, and evaluate Exchange Server you'll need

- Microsoft Exchange Server 4 or later

  - Exchange Server 4: Microsoft NT Server 3.51 or later (upgraded to NT 3.51 Service Pack v.4 or later)

  - Exchange Server 5: Microsoft Windows NT Server 3.51 (upgraded to NT 3.51 Service Pack v.5 or later) or NT 4 (upgraded to NT 4 Service Pack v.2 or later)

  - Exchange Server 5.5: Microsoft NT Server 4 (upgraded to NT 4 Service Pack v.5 or later)

- A 400MHz Pentium II–based PC with 64MB of RAM and one 1GB disk drive

- Tape backup hardware

- A local and/or wide area network

- At least one 200MHz Pentium II or equivalent computer with 32MB of memory running Microsoft Windows, Novell NetWare, or Apple Macintosh networking and a Microsoft Exchange or Outlook client, or a POP3 or IMAP4 client or Web browser

# How This Book Is Organized

I've divided this book into 7 parts and 19 chapters. As you proceed through the book, you'll move from basic concepts to several increasingly more complex levels of hands-on implementation.

I'd prefer that you step through each chapter before going on to the next. Understanding the concepts and planning carefully are central to implementing a sophisticated electronic messaging system like Microsoft Exchange.

However, if you're in a hurry to get your hands dirty, start with Chapters 6, 7, 8, 9, 11, and 12. They'll help you get an NT server, an Exchange server, and some clients up and running quickly. As long as you're not planning to put your quickie server into production immediately, there should be no harm done.

Before going live, however, I strongly suggest that you take a look at Part I; it will help you fix up any "little" problems that crop up and guard against a lot of future headaches.

# Conventions Used in This Book

There are many notes in this book. Generally, they are positioned below the material to which they refer. There are three kinds of notes: Note, Tip, and Warning.

**NOTE**   Notes give you information pertinent to the procedure or topic being discussed.

**TIP**   Tips indicate practical hints that might make your work easier.

**WARNING**   Warnings alert you to potential problems you might encounter while using the program.

Remember, Exchange is designed to help your organization do what it does better, more efficiently, and with greater productivity. Have fun, be productive, and prosper!

# PART I

# Exchange Concepts, Basics, and Design

This section focuses on the concepts and features of Microsoft's Exchange client/server electronic messaging system. It's designed to prepare you for installing, administering, and managing small and large Exchange Server systems.

Chapter 1 explores the role of Exchange in the "e-messaging decade" and looks at some of the things you can do with Exchange. Chapter 2 looks at the basic structure of Exchange Server and how it relates to real-world business and social structures. Chapter 3 focuses on the components of Exchange Server. Chapter 4 looks at Microsoft Windows NT Server—how it works and how it integrates with Exchange Server. Chapter 5 addresses the complex process of planning for the implementation of an Exchange system.

# Introducing Exchange

■ Exchange and the "e-messaging decade"

■ Exchange applications; e-mail and way beyond

■ Exchange basics

**M**icrosoft's Exchange client/server electronic messaging system is a major player in what I call the "e-messaging decade." It lets people work together in a variety of productivity-enhancing ways. The Exchange system is one of the most exciting, innovative, and promising software products I've ever seen. I can't wait to get started, so let's go to it.

# Exchange and the E-Messaging Decade

Electronic messaging is more than e-mail. It is the use of an underlying messaging infrastructure (addresses, routing, and so on) to build applications that are based on cooperative tasking, whether by humans or computers. We can expect the years 1996 to 2005 to be the decade of electronic messaging *(e-messaging)*, when store-and-forward–based messaging systems and real-time interactive technologies will complement each other to produce wildly imaginative business, entertainment, and educational applications with high pay-off potential.

Microsoft's Exchange Server will play a key role in e-messaging. Exchange Server is one of the most powerful, extensible, scalable, easy-to-use, and manageable e-messaging back ends currently on the market. Combined with Microsoft's excellent Outlook clients, Internet-based clients from other vendors, and third-party or home-grown applications, Exchange Server can help your organization move smoothly and productively into the e-messaging decade.

In writing this book, I was guided by three goals:

- To share the excitement I feel about both the promise of electronic messaging and the Exchange client/server system

- To help you decide if there's a place for Exchange in your organization

- To provide the information and teach you the skills you'll need to plan for and implement Exchange systems of any size and shape

The rest of this chapter introduces you to the Exchange client/server system. We start with a quick look at several of the neat ways you can use Exchange for e-mail and more, then focus on some of Exchange's key characteristics and capabilities.

This is just an introduction, so don't worry if you don't understand everything completely by the end of this chapter. All that we discuss here we will cover in more detail later in the book.

By the way, when I use the word *Exchange* or the words *Exchange system* from here on, I'm talking about the whole Exchange client/server system. *Exchange Server* means just the server product, and an *Exchange server* is any computer running the Exchange Server product. *Exchange client* refers to any client that lets you access all the features of Exchange Server, for example, Microsoft's stable of Outlook clients. *Exchange client* does not refer to general-purpose clients like IMAP4 or POP3 clients or to Internet browser–based clients that provide limited access to Exchange Server's features. When I talk about these, I'll use either their commercial or generic names or both, for example, *the Eudora POP3 client*. Got that? Okay, explain it to me.

# Exchange Applications

I dare you not to get excited about electronic messaging and Exchange as you read this section. Just look at what's possible and imagine what you could do with all this potential.

## E-Mail Is Only the Beginning

Together, Exchange Server and its clients perform a variety of messaging-based functions. These include e-mail, message routing, scheduling, and supporting several types of custom applications. E-mail is certainly a key feature of any messaging system. And the Outlook Calendar is far and away better than previous versions of Microsoft's appointment and meeting–scheduling software. (Figures 1.1 and 1.2 show the Outlook 2000 client Inbox and Calendar for Windows in action.) Take a look at Figures 1.3, 1.4, and 1.5 for a glimpse of the Internet-based POP3, IMAP4, and Web browser clients you can use with Exchange 5 and above.

**FIGURE 1.1:**

The Outlook 2000 client for Windows Inbox

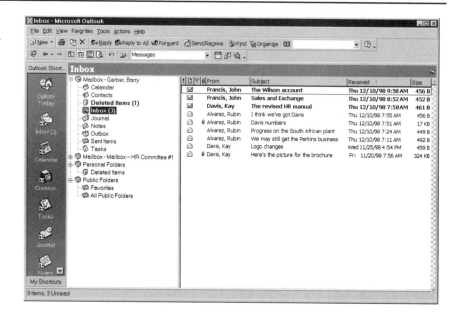

**FIGURE 1.2:**

The Outlook 2000 client Windows Calendar

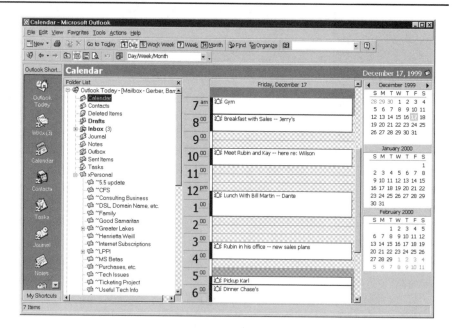

**FIGURE 1.3:**

Qualcomm's Eudora Pro 3 POP3-compliant client accesses mail stored on an Exchange server.

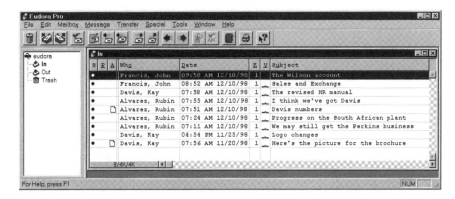

**FIGURE 1.4:**

Microsoft's Outlook Express IMAP4 client function accesses messages and folders on an Exchange server.

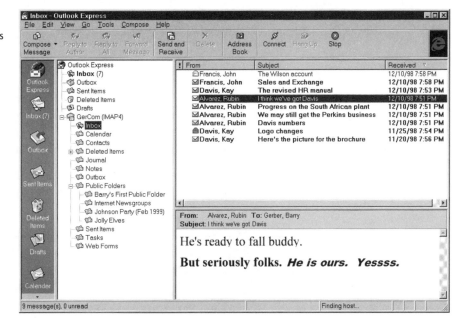

**FIGURE 1.5:**

Microsoft's Internet
Explorer Web browser
accesses mail stored on an
Exchange server.

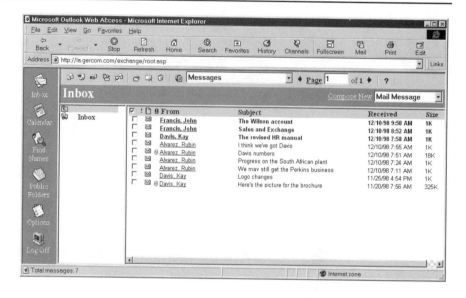

E-mail clients are exciting and sexy, but to get the most out of Exchange, you need to throw away any preconceptions you have that messaging packages are only for e-mail and scheduling. The really exciting applications are not those that use simple e-mail or scheduling, but those that are based on the routing capabilities of messaging systems. These applications bring people and computers together for cooperative work.

So what do these hot apps look like? Let's start with the simplest and move toward the more complex.

## Change Is the Name of the Game

Some of the marvelous user interfaces you see in Figures 1.1 through 1.5 may look different by the time you read this book. Software development and marketing, especially in the world of electronic communications, is running at hyperspeed. Updates and even major revisions hit the market at a breakneck pace. The Internet makes it even easier for vendors to market and deliver their wares. New pieces and parts of applications appear almost daily for manual or totally automatic download and installation.

The basic architecture of Exchange Server and its clients is unlikely to change much over the next year or so. The outward appearance of user interfaces is much more likely to

*Continued on next page*

change. As far as Exchange goes, plan for change as a way of life. Keep an open mind and at least one eye on Microsoft's Exchange-oriented Web pages.

In the long run all this hyperactivity will prove a good thing. Our requirements will find their way into and bugs will find their way out of products faster. I will admit, however, that I sometimes long for the days of yearly or less frequent updates on low-density 5¼-inch floppies.

## Just a Step beyond Mail

You're probably familiar with e-mail *attachments*—those word processing, spreadsheet, and other work files you can drop into messages. Attachments are a simple way to move work files to the people who need to see them.

Sure, you could send your files on floppy disk or tell people where on the network they can find and download the files. But e-mail attachments let you make the files available to others with a click of their mouse button: They just double-click an icon, and the attachment opens in the original application that produced it (if your correspondent has access to the application, of course).

Using attachments has the added advantage of putting the files and accompanying messages right in the faces of those who need to see them. This leaves less room for excuses like "Oh, I forgot" or "The dog ate the floppy disk."

As great as attachments can be, they have one real weakness: The minute an attachment leaves your Outbox, it's out of date. If you do further work on the original file, that work is not reflected in the copy you sent to others. If someone then edits a copy of the attached file, it's totally out of sync with the original and all other copies. Getting everything synchronized again can involve tedious hours or days of manually comparing different versions and cutting and pasting them to create one master document.

Exchange offers several ways to avoid this problem. One of the simplest is the *attachment link* or *shortcut:* Instead of putting the actual file into a message, you put in a link to the file (see Figure 1.6), which can be stored anywhere on the network. The real kicker is that the file can also be stored in Exchange public folders. (More about these later.) When someone double-clicks an attachment link icon, the linked file opens. Everyone who receives the message works with the same linked attachment. Everyone reads and can modify the same file.

FIGURE 1.6:

Exchange links keep
attachments alive.

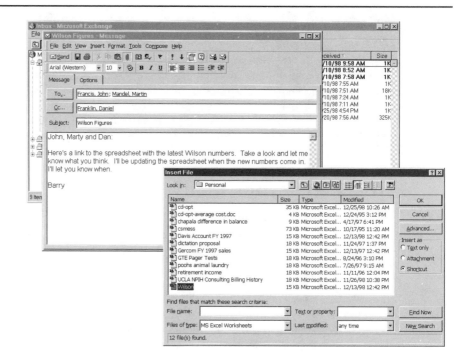

## Off-the-Shelf Messaging-Enabled Applications

Here's another way to guard against dead work files: Microsoft Windows enables messaging in many word processing and spreadsheet applications. For example, when you install the Exchange client on your computer, Microsoft's Office products like Word and Excel are e-messaging enabled. You can select Send or Route options from the apps' File menu; this pops up a routing slip. You then add addresses to the slip from your Exchange client's address book, select the routing method you want to use, and assign a right-to-modify level for the route. Finally, you ship your work off to others with just a click of the Route button.

Figure 1.7 shows how all this works. Though it's simple, application-based messaging can significantly improve user productivity and speed up a range of business processes.

FIGURE 1.7:

Microsoft Word 97 includes messaging-enabled Send and Route functions.

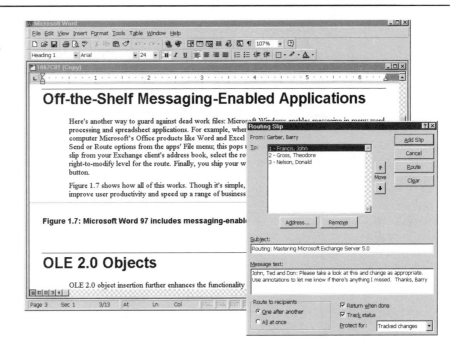

## OLE 2 Objects

OLE 2 object insertion further enhances the functionality of the Exchange messaging system. Take a close look at Figure 1.8. Yes, the message includes an Excel spreadsheet and chart. The person who sent the message simply selected Object from the Insert menu that appears on every Exchange message. The Exchange client then inserted a blank Excel spreadsheet into the message as an OLE 2 object. Having received the message, we can see the spreadsheet as an item in the message, as shown in the figure. When we double-click the spreadsheet, Excel is launched and Excel's menus and toolbars replace those of the message (Figure 1.9). In essence, the message becomes Excel.

**FIGURE 1.8:**

With OLE 2 objects, sophisticated messaging-enabled applications are easy to build.

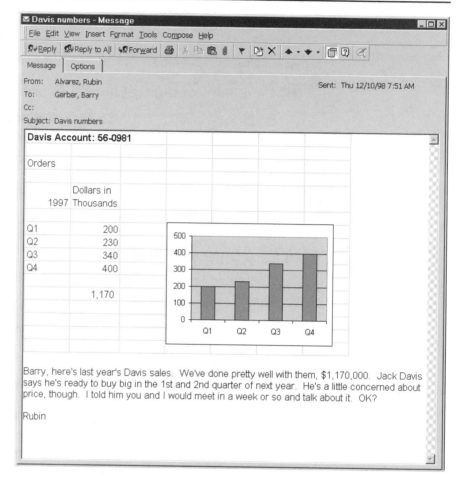

The Excel spreadsheet is fully editable. Though Excel must be available to your recipients, they don't have to launch it to read and work on the spreadsheet. Even if your recipients don't have Excel, they can still view the contents of the spreadsheet, though they won't be able to work on it. (That is, even if they don't have the application, they can still view the object when they open the message.)

**FIGURE 1.9:**

Double-clicking an OLE 2–embedded Excel spreadsheet in a message enables Excel menus and toolbars.

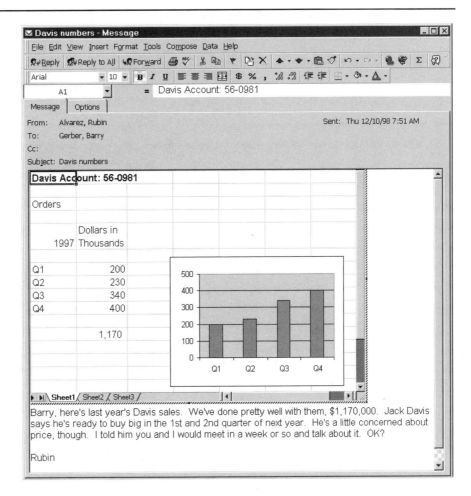

## Electronic Forms

Exchange Server 4 and 5 come with the Exchange Forms Designer (EFD) that is based on Microsoft Visual Basic. You can use the Forms Designer to build information-gathering forms containing a number of the bells and whistles you're used to in Windows applications. These include drop-down list boxes, check boxes, fill-in text forms, tab dialog controls, and radio buttons.

EFD, which is easy enough for nontechnical types to use, includes a variety of messaging-oriented fields and actions. For example, you can choose to include a preaddressed To field in a form, as shown in Figure 1.10, so users of the form can easily mail it off to the appropriate recipient. Once you've designed a form, it can be made available to all or select users, who can access the completed form by simply selecting it while in an Exchange client or Outlook (EFD forms work in both).

**FIGURE 1.10:**

Electronic forms turn messages into structured information-gathering tools.

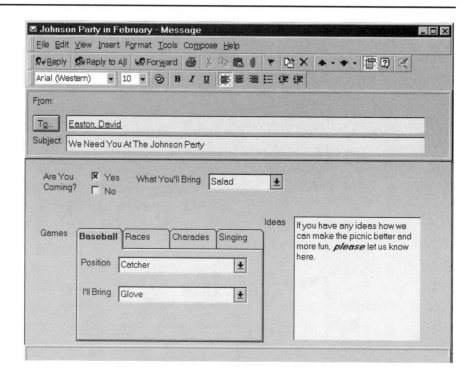

Exchange 5.5 adds Outlook Forms Designer (OFD). This Visual Basic Script–capable application opens many new doors, especially when linked with Exchange 5.5's groupware-enabling server scripting features. OFD forms work only with Outlook clients.

## Applications Built on APIs

If all this functionality isn't enough, you can go to the heart of Exchange Server and use its Application Program Interface (API). Exchange Server supports both the Simple and Extended versions of Microsoft's Windows-based Mail Application Program Interface (MAPI). It also supports the X.400-oriented, platform-independent Common Mail Call (CMC) APIs, which have functions similar to those of Simple MAPI. Using Simple MAPI or CMC, you can build applications that use e-messaging addresses behind the scenes to route data between users and programs. Extended MAPI lets you get more deeply into Exchange's storage and e-messaging address books to create virtually any messaging-enabled application you can imagine.

These custom-built applications may involve some level of automation, such as regular updates of your company's price lists for trading partners or sending a weekly multimedia message from the president to employees at your organization. Building apps based on MAPI or CMC requires someone with programming skills in languages like Visual Basic or C++.

## Applications Using Exchange Public Folders

As you'll discover later in this chapter and chapters to come, Exchange Server supports mailboxes, private folders, and public folders. All of these can hold messages and any kind of computer application or data file. Mailboxes and private folders are where Exchange users store and manage their messages and files. Public folders are used for common access to messages and files. Files can be dragged from file access interfaces like the Explorer in Microsoft's Windows 95/98/NT 4 and dropped into mailboxes, private folders, or public folders. If you begin thinking of mailboxes, private folders, and public folders as a messaging-enabled extension of Explorer, you'll have a fairly clear picture of Microsoft's vision of the future in regard to how an operating system organizes and displays stored information.

You can set up sorting rules for a mailbox, private folder, or public folder so that items in the folder are organized by a range of attributes, such as the name of the sender or creator of the item or the date the item arrived or was placed in the folder. Items in a mailbox, private folder, or public folder can be sorted by conversation threads. You can also put applications built on existing products like Word or Excel or with Exchange or Outlook Forms Designer, server scripting, or the API set into mailboxes and private or public folders. In mailboxes and private folders these applications are fun for one, but in public folders, where many people access them, they can replace the tons of maddening paper-based processes that abound in every organization.

If all this isn't already enough, Exchange is very much Internet-aware. With Exchange 5.*x*, you can publish all or selected public folders on the Internet where they become accessible with a simple Internet browser. You can limit Internet access to public folders to only those who have access under Exchange's security system or you can open public folders to anyone on the Internet. Just think about it: Internet-enabled public folders let you put information on the Internet without the fuss and bother of Web site design and development. Any item can be placed on the Internet by simply adding a message to a public folder. Figure 1.11 shows a public folder–enabled price list for the one product produced by my favorite fictitious company, GerCom, which you'll learn more about later.

**FIGURE 1.11:**

Using Exchange public folders to publish a price list on the Internet

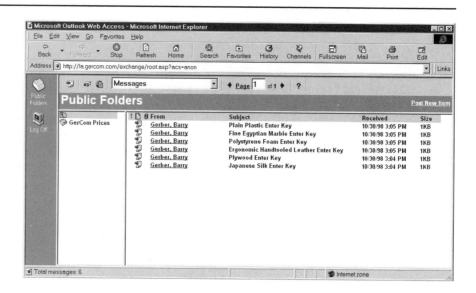

Before we leave public folder applications, I want to mention one more option. Exchange Server 5 and later lets you bring any or all of those devilishly delightful USENET Internet newsgroups to your public folder environment. With their Outlook clients, users then can read and reply to newsgroup items just as though they were using a standard newsgroup reader application. Exchange Server comes with all the tools you need to make it so. All you need is an Internet connection, access to a newsfeed provider, and a set of rules about which groups to exclude. Remember, this is where the infamous alt.sex newsgroups live.

# Some Exchange Basics

It's important to get a handle on some of Exchange's key characteristics and capabilities. Once you do, you'll better appreciate the depth and breadth of Microsoft's efforts in developing Exchange, and you'll be better prepared for the rest of this book. In this section, we'll take a look at

- Exchange as a client/server system
- The Exchange client
- Exchange Server's dependency on Microsoft's Windows NT Server
- Exchange Server's object orientation
- Exchange Server scalability
- Exchange Server security
- Exchange Server and other e-messaging systems

## Exchange as a Client/Server System

The term *client/server* has been overused and overworked. To put it simply, there are two kinds of networked applications: shared-file and client/server.

### Shared-File Applications

Early networked applications were all based on *shared-file* systems. The network shell that let you load your word processor from a network server also allowed you to read from and write to files stored on a server. At the time, it was the easiest and most natural way to grow networked applications.

Microsoft Mail for PC Networks is a shared-file application. You run Windows, OS/2, DOS, or Macintosh front ends, which send and receive messages by accessing files on a Microsoft Mail for PC Networks post office that resides on a network file server. The front end and your PC do all the work; the server is passive. Figure 1.12 shows a typical Microsoft Mail for PC Networks setup.

Easy as it was to develop, this architecture leads to some serious problems in today's networked computing world:

- Changing the underlying structure of the server file system is difficult, because you have to change both the server and the client.

- System security is always compromised, because users must have read and write permissions for the whole server file system, which includes all other users' message files. Things are so bad that a naive or malicious user can actually destroy shared-file system databases in some cases.

- Network traffic is high, because the front end must constantly access indexes and hunt around the server's file system for user messages.

- Because the user workstation acts directly on shared files, these can be destroyed if workstation hardware or software stop functioning for some unexpected reason.

Shared-file applications are in decline. Sure, plenty of "legacy" (that is, out of date) apps will probably live on for the data processing equivalent of eternity, but client/server systems have quickly supplanted the shared-file model. This is especially true in the world of electronic messaging.

**FIGURE 1.12:**

Microsoft Mail for PC Networks is a typical shared-file e-messaging system.

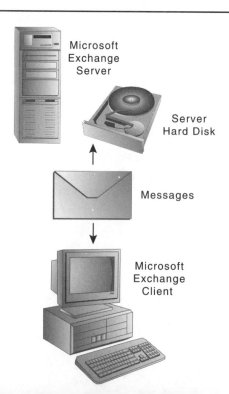

Microsoft Exchange Server

Server Hard Disk

Messages

Microsoft Exchange Client

## Client/Server Applications

Today, more and more networked applications are based on the client/server model. The server is an active partner in client/server applications. Clients tell servers what they want done, and if security requirements are met, servers do what they are asked.

Processes running on a server find and ship data off to processes running on a client. When a client process sends data, a server receives it and writes it to server-based files. Server processes can do more than simply interact with client processes. For example, they can compact data files on the server or—as they do on Exchange Server—automatically reply to incoming messages to let people know, for instance, that you're going to be out of the office for a period of time. Figure 1.13 shows how Exchange implements the client/server model.

Client/server applications are strong in all the areas in which shared-file apps are weak:

- Changing the underlying structure of the server file system is easier than with shared-file systems, because only the server processes access the file system.

- System security can be much tighter, again because only the server processes access the file system.

- Network traffic is lighter, because all the work of file access is done by the server, on the server.

- Because server processes are the only ones that access server data, breakdowns of user workstation hardware or software are less likely to spoil data. With appropriate transaction logging features, client/server systems can even protect against server hardware or software malfunctions.

As good as the client/server model is, it does have some general drawbacks. Client/server apps require more computing horsepower, especially on the server side. With Exchange, plan to start with very fast Pentium machines, lots of RAM, and plenty of hard disk capacity—and expect to grow from there.

Client/server applications are more complex than shared-file apps. This is partly due to the nature of the client/server model and partly due to the tendency of client/server apps to be newer and thus filled with all kinds of great capabilities you won't find in shared-file applications. Generally, you're safe in assuming that you'll need to devote more resources to managing a client/server application than to tending a similar one based on shared files.

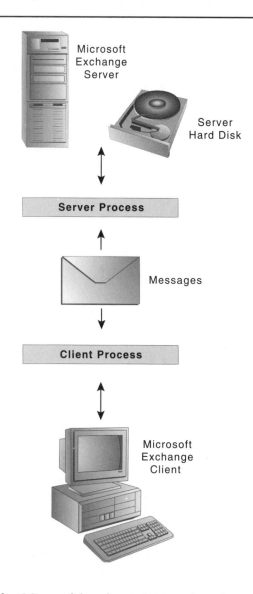

The good news is that Microsoft has done a lot to reduce the management load and to make it easier for someone who isn't a computer scientist to administer an Exchange system. I've looked at many client/server messaging systems, and I can say without any doubt that Exchange Server is absolutely the easiest to administer. Exchange Server's administrative front end, called the *Exchange Administrator,* organizes the management processes very nicely and provides an excellent system based on a graphical user interface (GUI) for doing everything from adding users and network connections to assessing the health of your messaging system (see Figure 1.14).

**FIGURE 1.14:**

The Exchange Administrator makes management easier.

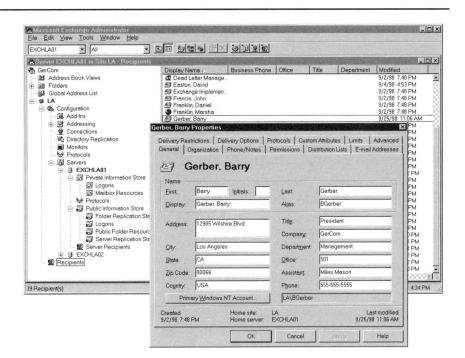

## A Quick Take on the Exchange Client

As should be clear from our look at some of its applications earlier in this chapter, the Exchange client is the sexy part of Exchange. It's where the action is—the view screen for the backroom bits and bytes of Exchange Server. While this book is mostly about Exchange Server, you can't implement an Exchange system without the clients. So we'll spend some time on the Exchange client, currently incarnated under the rubric *Outlook,* in various places throughout this book. Meanwhile, let's discuss some client basics.

## Information Storage

The client stores information in one of two places—private and public information containers. Each has a different purpose and function.

**Private Information Containers**    Though you can share some of their contents with others, private information containers generally hold items that you and you alone have access to. There are two basic kinds of private information stores: mailboxes and personal folders. You access mailboxes and personal folders using an Exchange client or Internet-based clients such as the POP3 and IMAP4 clients built into Outlook Express.

Mailboxes can send and receive messages. You can add folders to a mailbox to help you organize your messages. If you have the rights to other mailboxes, you can open them in your Exchange client as well.

Personal folders may or may not have the send and receive capabilities of mailboxes. You can create as many personal folders as you desire. A private folder can hold as many subfolders as you wish. Like the folders you add to mailboxes, personal folders help you organize information. You can drag and drop messages between folders. Using *rules* (discussed below), you can direct incoming mail into any of your personal folders.

The contents of mailboxes are stored inside the Exchange Server database. Personal folders are stored outside of Exchange Server on private or networked disk space.

**Public Information Containers**    Public information containers are often called *public folders*. Let's use that term here. Public folders hold items that you want others to see. Users whom you authorize can create public folders and drag and drop anything they wish into them. Public folders can also be nested and rules can be applied to them.

Public folders are stored inside the Exchange Server database. They are key to the organization-wide implementation of Exchange. Some, all, or none of an Exchange server's public folders can be automatically replicated to other Exchange servers. This lets you post items to public folders on one Exchange server and have them quickly and painlessly appear on any combination of the Exchange servers in your system. Even without replication, users all over your organization can access public folders.

## Sharing Information

You can share information with others by sending it to them or placing it in public folders for them to retrieve on their own. You can drop messages, word processing documents, and other work files—even whole applications—into public folders. You can use public folders to implement many of the kinds of applications I talked about at the beginning of this chapter.

For example, instead of electronically routing a draft of a word processing document to a bunch of colleagues, you can just drop it into a public folder. Then you can send e-mail to your colleagues asking them to look at the document and even to edit it right there in the public folder.

## Organizing Information

Creating a set of personal and public folders and dropping messages in them is a simple way to organize information. More sophisticated approaches include the use of rules, views, and the Exchange client's Finder.

**Rules**    As a user, you can set up a range of *rules* to move mail from your Inbox into personal or public folders. For example, you might want to move all the messages from your boss into a folder marked URGENT. Rules can be based on anything from the sender of a message to its contents. Depending on its type, a rule may run on the Exchange server or on the client. The Exchange client doesn't have to be running for server-based rules to execute.

**Views**    Exchange messages can have numerous attributes. These include the obvious, such as sender, subject, and date received, as well as less common information, including sender's company, last author, and number of words. You can build views of messages using any combination of attributes and any sorting scheme. Then you can apply a particular view to a folder to specially organize the messages it contains.

**The Finder**    You can use the Exchange client Finder to search all folders or a single folder for messages from or to specific correspondents, messages with specific information in the subject field or message body, and even messages received between specific dates or of a specific size.

## Exchange Server's Dependency on NT Server

Exchange Server is a component of the Microsoft BackOffice suite. Like Microsoft's SQL Server and Systems Management Server, Exchange Server runs only with Windows NT Server. It won't run on top of NT Workstation or on Windows 95/98; even though both are 32-bit operating systems, they can't host Exchange Server.

Among operating systems, NT is the new kid on the block. As a longtime Novell NetWare user, I initially faced NT with not just a little fear and foreboding. That was then. Now I am a confirmed NT user and supporter. My personal workstation is an NT-based machine, and all my servers but one run NT. (The one holdout is a NetWare server I use to ensure that NT- and Windows-based software works with Novell's IPX/SPX.)

It took me two weeks to get comfortable with NT and a month to become totally productive with it. What sets NT off from all other operating systems for workstations and servers is Microsoft Windows. NT, whether the workstation or server version, *is* Microsoft Windows. If you can use Windows, you can use NT. Networking with NT is a breeze, and running apps on top of NT Server is a piece of cake. Figure 1.15 shows one of my NT/Exchange server desktops with some NT and Exchange management applications running. This shouldn't be foreign territory for any Windows aficionado.

NT is chock-full of features that make it an especially attractive operating system. One of these is its very usable and functional implementation of Microsoft's domain-based security system. Domains have names—one of mine is called LA for my hometown, Los Angeles—and include NT servers, NT workstations, and all flavors of Windows- and DOS-based machines. Though there are a number of domain security models, the general rule is that the members of a domain can use any resource they have been given permission to use—disk files, printers, and so on—in the domain without having to enter a password for each. Exchange Server depends on NT domain security for a good deal of its security.

Later in the book you can read a whole chapter on NT and what you need to know about it to run Exchange Server. There's also a chapter on installing NT Server.

**FIGURE 1,15:**

On the surface, NT Server is just plain old Microsoft Windows.

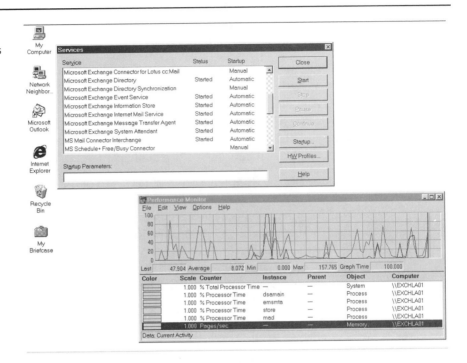

## Exchange Server's Object Orientation

Exchange is a classic example of an *object-oriented* system. Take another look at Figure 1.14. See all those items on the tree on the left-hand side of the Exchange Administrator menu, such as GerCom, LA, EXCHLA01, EXCHLA02, and Recipients? Each of these is an *object*. Each object has attributes and can interact with other objects in specific ways. Exchange objects can hold other objects, serving as what Microsoft calls *containers.*

*GerCom* is the name of the fictitious organization I created for this book; it is the equivalent of a company name like IBM or TRW. (People often ask if I'm related to the baby-food Gerbers. I'm not, but GerCom at least lets me dream. Want to buy some stock?) Microsoft refers to this object as the *organization.* The GerCom organization contains all the objects below it.

*LA* is the name of a physical site in the GerCom corporate hierarchy, Los Angeles. It is also a home for Exchange servers. The GerCom/LA hierarchy has two servers, named *EXCHLA01* and *EXCHLA02*.

The Recipients object way down at the bottom of the hierarchy is a container for Exchange Server recipients. *Recipients* are objects that can send or receive messages. Among other things, recipients include user mailboxes and distribution lists. Each recipient object can contain a large number of attributes. The tabbed Properties dialog box in Figure 1.14 should give you some idea of the breadth of attributes that can be assigned to a mailbox.

Notice that the Recipients container is a part of the LA site hierarchy. *Sites* are the most important containers in Exchange. They hold configuration information about recipients and how to reach them, as well as information about servers and other Exchange objects. This information is stored in what Microsoft calls the *Exchange Server directory*. Though specific instances of the directory are stored on the servers in a site, any instance of the directory actually contains information about all the servers in an organization.

Object orientation makes it easy for Microsoft to distribute Exchange Server's functionality and management, and it makes it easy for you to administer an Exchange Server environment. For example, based on my security clearances I can manage any set of recipients—from those in only a single site to all the recipients in my organization.

## Exchange Server Scalability

Exchange Server scales very well both vertically and horizontally. NT runs on top of computers based on single and multiple Intel and DEC Alpha processors, so it's very easy to scale an Exchange server upward to more powerful hardware when increased user loads make additional computing power necessary. Since you'll be taking both Exchange Server and NT with you, you really won't have to learn much more about your new machine than the location of its power switch.

If vertical scalability isn't what you need, horizontal scaling is also a breeze with Exchange Server. You can set up a new Exchange server and quickly get its directory and public folders in sync with all or some of your other servers. You can even move mailboxes between Exchange servers in a site with a few clicks of your left mouse button.

How do you know if it's time to scale up or out? Microsoft has an answer for this, too: You can use the LoadSim application included with Exchange Server to simulate a range of different user loads on your server hardware. By analyzing the results of your LoadSim tests, you'll get some idea of the messaging loads you can expect a server to handle in a production environment.

## Exchange Server Security

Exchange Server security starts with NT's security system. Several different NT security models are available; the one that's right for you depends mostly on the size and structure of your organization and the department that supports Exchange Server. In all cases, the idea is to select a security model that puts the lightest burden on users and system administrators while still appropriately barring unauthorized users from messaging and other system resources. (More on this in Chapter 4.)

NT also audits security. It can let you know when a user tries to add, delete, or access system resources.

The security of Exchange Server is enhanced in several ways beyond the NT operating system's security. Access to Exchange Server objects such as public folders can be limited by the creator of the folder. Data encryption on the server and client protects messages and other Exchange resources from eavesdropping by those with server or workstation access. Digital signatures prove the authenticity of a message. Even traffic between servers can be encrypted.

## Exchange Server and Other E-Messaging Systems

The world of electronic messaging is far from a single-standard nirvana. A good e-messaging system must connect to and communicate with a variety of other messaging systems. Microsoft has done a nice job of providing Exchange Server with key links, called *connectors,* to other systems. The company has also built some cross-system message-content translators into Exchange Server that work automatically and are very effective. With these translators, you're less likely to send a message containing, say, a beautiful embedded image that can't be viewed by some or all of the message's recipients.

In the case of Microsoft's legacy messaging systems—Microsoft Mail for PC Networks and Microsoft Mail for AppleTalk Networks—you have an option beyond connectivity. You can choose to migrate users to Exchange. Migration utilities for other messaging systems like Lotus cc:Mail are also provided with Exchange.

## X.400

A fully standards-compatible X.400 connector is built into Exchange Server and can be used to link Exchange sites. The 1984 and 1988 standards for X.400 are supported. The connector also supports attachment to foreign X.400 messaging systems.

## SMTP

As with the X.400 connector, a Simple Message Transfer Protocol (SMTP) connector is built into Exchange Server. Unlike the old Microsoft Mail for PC Networks SMTP gateway, it is a full-fledged SMTP host system capable of relaying messages and resolving addresses, while supporting several Enhanced SMTP (ESMTP) commands. UUencode/UUdecode and MIME (Multipurpose Internet Mail Extensions) message-content standards are also supported. So, once you've moved your users from MS Mail for PCs to Exchange, you won't hear any more of those vexing complaints about the meaningless MIME-source attachments users get because the SMTP gateway was unable to convert them back to their original binary format.

## Microsoft Mail for PC Networks

A built-in connector makes Microsoft Mail for PC Networks 3.x (MS Mail 3.x) post offices look like Exchange servers to Exchange clients and vice versa. If connectivity isn't enough, you can transfer MS Mail 3.x users to Exchange with a supplied migration tool. If all this is too much, Exchange clients can directly access MS Mail 3.x post offices. So you can keep your MS Mail 3.x post offices, at least until you've got Exchange Server running the way you want and have moved everyone off the legacy mail system.

## Microsoft Mail for AppleTalk Networks

Connectivity for Microsoft Mail for AppleTalk Networks systems is also provided by a connector built into Exchange. When connectivity isn't enough, Mail for Apple-Talk users can be migrated to Exchange Server.

### cc:Mail

If Lotus cc:Mail is running in your shop, you'll be happy to hear that Exchange 5.*x* comes with tools to connect and migrate users to Exchange. Never let it be said that Microsoft doesn't care about users of IBM/Lotus products. At least there's a way to pull them into the MS camp.

### Lotus Notes

Exchange 5.5 adds a connector for Lotus Notes. With this connector, Exchange and Notes clients can see each other's address directories and exchange mail.

### Other Messaging Systems

Gateways are available for links to other messaging systems such as Notes, PROFS, SNADS, fax, and MCI Mail. Both Microsoft and third parties build and support these gateways. You can even extend the benefit of these gateways to your MS Mail users.

### The Wonderful World of Exchange Server Third-Party Applications

At various places in this book, I'll spend some time discussing one neat third-party application or another. For example, in Chapter 17, I'll focus on apps for controlling those pesky viruses right inside of Exchange Server. Appendix C contains a fairly exhaustive list of third-party apps for Exchange Server.

# Conclusion

In this chapter you learned about some of the exciting things you can do with Exchange. You also had a first look at some key aspects and characteristics of the system. The rest of this book is devoted to helping you understand Exchange—how it works and how you can implement some of the nifty applications I've only hinted at in this chapter.

# The Exchange Hierarchy

■ A conceptual view of the Exchange hierarchy

■ A practical view of the Exchange hierarchy

■ Exchange organizations

■ Exchange sites

■ Exchange servers

■ Exchange recipients

■ How Exchange hierarchy design affects server administration and e-messaging addressing

**M**icrosoft has built Exchange around a set of four key elements:

- Organizations
- Sites
- Servers
- Recipients

The relationship between these elements is hierarchical. The organization is at the top of the hierarchy, and recipients are at the bottom. The Exchange hierarchy imposes an organizational structure on both the real world and the Exchange world. The hierarchy also determines at least the defaults used to construct e-mail or, even better, e-messaging addresses for Exchange users.

# A Conceptual View of the Hierarchy

The four key elements in the Exchange hierarchy stand for two conceptually different but related realities. First, the elements represent real people, places, and things. An *organization* is a collection of people who have some reason for associating with each other. An organization can be a business, an academic institution, a club, or some other entity. A *site* is a sub-organizational unit like a geographical location or a department. *Servers* are computers running Exchange Server software. And *recipients* are the people and things that can send or receive mail. In the real world, each of these elements includes all the elements below it: Organizations include sites, which include servers, which include recipients.

The four key Exchange elements represent a second set of realities: Exchange *objects*. Remember when I talked about Exchange's object orientation in Chapter 1? I noted that each of the four Exchange objects serves as a container for the objects below it. Organizational objects include site objects, which include server objects, which include recipient objects.

In this latter case, the language of object orientation replaces the language of social organization, but the effect is the same. The Exchange hierarchy orders the way we think about both the real world and Exchange itself. Take a look at Figure 2.1 to see how the Exchange Administrator brings these two conceptual views together in a single, easy-to-use interface.

**FIGURE 2.1:**

The Exchange Administrator makes it easy to deal with Exchange's hierarchy.

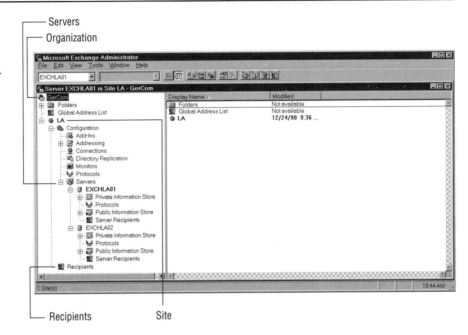

Servers

Organization

Recipients     Site

While there are four key elements in the Exchange hierarchy, other significant elements are contained within each of the four elements. We'll talk about these later in this chapter.

# A More Practical View of the Hierarchy

Concepts are important, and I'll assume you're comfortable with the ones presented above. However, we "systems" types can't live by concepts alone. We need to move quickly from concepts to designing, installing, and running systems.

So let's look at the four elements in the Exchange hierarchy from a more practical perspective. As you read on, you'll begin to see where you'll have to make some very specific design decisions related to the four elements before you can even think about installing an Exchange server. You'll also begin to see just how central the Exchange hierarchy is to setting up and managing an Exchange environment.

## Organizations

By now it should be pretty clear to you that an Exchange organization can be all or part of a company, a school, a club, or another entity; it's the master container in the Exchange hierarchy. Examples of organizational names include IBM, IBMUSA, and IBMENG.

In Figure 2.1, GerCom is the organization. The name GerCom represents *all* of the fictitious little company I created for this book. That means I can include all the subdivisions of my empire within this particular Exchange hierarchy.

## Sites

Sites are subdivisions of the organization. Generally, they encompass geographical or business divisions. Examples include Engineering, NY, and SFO. Currently, GerCom has only one site, LA (see Figure 2.1).

For fault tolerance and faster performance, a good deal of key information is replicated automatically and frequently between all the Exchange servers in a site. That can make for some heavy-duty network traffic. Sites should be geographically contiguous enough that Exchange servers within them can be connected at reasonable cost by higher-bandwidth (128Kb/sec or greater) wide area networks (WANs).

Sites are usually connected by slower WANs, since replicating information between sites is usually done in a more selective way and at a more leisurely pace. Sites include a range of sub-elements or objects. For example, Exchange connectors let you link sites together and to the outside world. Exchange contains tools for setting up and administering these objects, including tools for administering and managing Exchange connectors. Figure 2.2, another view of the Exchange Administrator, shows the tool for the Internet Mail Service (IMS), which links my LA site to the Internet mail system and can even be used to link my LA site to other sites in my Exchange hierarchy through the Internet.

The IMS tool has a number of what Microsoft calls *property pages*—so called because this is where you set the attributes, or *properties*, of the service. Figure 2.2 shows the Internet Mail property page of the IMS tool, as you can see from the tab at the top of the page. The IMS tool has a total of 12 property pages, as indicated by the 12 tabs. Each tabbed page covers a different set of properties required to administer and manage an Internet mail link.

**FIGURE 2.2:**

Working with the Internet
Mail Service in a site

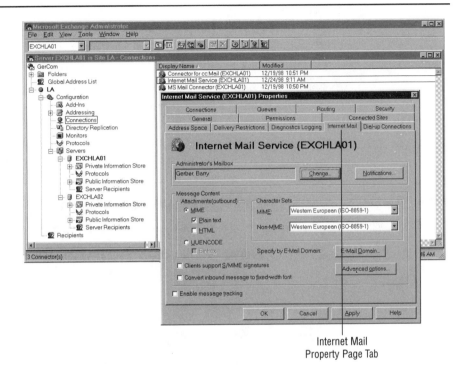

Internet Mail
Property Page Tab

## Servers

Servers are the physical Exchange servers within a site. At the moment, there are two Exchange servers in the LA site. They're called EXCHLA01 and EXCHLA02, which stand for "Exchange [Server] in Los Angeles #1" and "Exchange [Server] in Los Angeles #2." You'll find the servers toward the bottom of the Exchange hierarchy tree in Figure 2.1; notice that they are in the Servers container.

Some organizations like to base their Exchange server names on departments, such as engineering or marketing, within a geographical site (for example, site = LA; server = Marketing). Working with my imaginary MIS department, I've decided to use a different naming scheme for GerCom. To start, I put all my LA employees on one server, EXCHLA01. As I ran out of capacity on EXCHLA01, I added EXCHLA02. As GerCom grows—and I know it's going to grow—I'll add more servers, called EXCHLA03, EXCHLA04, and so on. (There's nothing inherently good or bad about my naming scheme; I just think it's better for GerCom than a scheme based on department names. My company is relatively small right now, so two servers are enough for all employees. I don't want to pop for servers for each department, and I'm willing to tolerate Exchange servers with "meaningless" names. So there!)

As with sites, a number of tools are available for administering and managing server-based Exchange objects. Among other things, each server has tools for managing local message storage and for replicating public folders between servers. In Figure 2.3, the Exchange Administrator is used to set some default limits for EXCHLA01's private information storage area.

**FIGURE 2.3:**

Exchange servers include tools for managing private information storage areas.

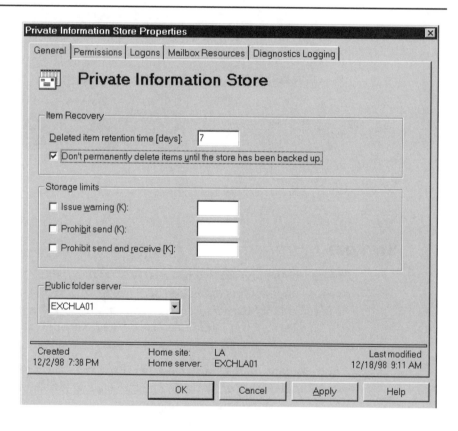

## Recipients

Exchange has four major types of recipient objects: mailboxes (the most widely used of which is the primary mailbox), public folders, custom recipients (essentially aliases for addresses outside an Exchange organization), and distribution lists. Each of these plays a different role and can be used to good advantage depending on the needs of your organization. As with other entities in the hierarchy, Exchange has tools for administering and managing recipient objects.

### Mailbox Agents: Recipient Objects That Serve the System

There is a fifth kind of recipient object, though it's one you have little control over. It's called a *mailbox agent*. Mailbox agents are generally created by the system and used to support system-level information passing. Developers can write programs that implement mailbox agents. I'll talk in a bit about one of these mailbox agents, the Schedule+ Free/Busy mailbox agent.

Recipients live in recipients containers. In Figure 2.4, which is a view from the Exchange Administrator, recipients containers show up five times in the GerCom tree. The Folders container near the top of the hierarchy holds, among other things, public folders. The Global Address List, down a bit from the Folders container, holds **all** recipients for an organization. Each of the two servers in the LA site has a recipients container named *Server Recipients*. And there is a site-level recipients container, named *Recipients*, at the bottom of the hierarchy.

Each of the four types of recipients containers—Folders and the Global Address List at the organization level, Server Recipients at the server level, and Recipients at the site level—plays a special role in Exchange Server.

- The Global Address List holds all the recipients in an organization. It is used by Exchange clients to address messages and can be used by Exchange administrators to administer and manage recipients. For reasons of corporate policy or for the purpose for which they were created, some recipients may be hidden from the Global Address and other address books. Exchange administrators with the proper rights can readily access hidden recipients and even unhide them if necessary.

- The Public Folders container holds all the public folders in an organization. Even hidden public folders are visible in the Public Folders container, which is available only to Exchange administrators with the proper access rights.

- The messages in each Exchange mailbox are stored on one and only one Exchange server. However, the attributes of the mailbox (for example, the name and street address of the mailbox user) are or can be replicated on other Exchange servers in the site and organization.

- Site-level recipients containers hold all mailboxes on all servers in a site, as well as the three other types of recipients for a site. A good deal of recipient administration and management is done in site-level recipients containers.

**FIGURE 2.4:**

A site-level recipients container includes all five recipient object types.

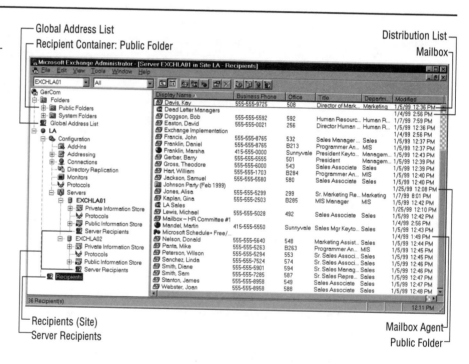

Figure 2.4 shows what's in the site-level recipients container for GerCom. As you can see, all five of the recipient object types are included in this container. Distribution lists, public folders, and custom recipients appear only at the site level. That little icon marked *Microsoft Schedule+ Free/...* is a mailbox agent. It represents the Microsoft Schedule+ Free/Busy Connector for the LA site. The connector lets

users of Schedule+ for Exchange Server see the schedules of users of Schedule+ for Microsoft Mail for PCs, and vice versa.

Now just to verify that server-level recipients containers hold only mailboxes and, to be totally correct, mailbox agents, take a look at Figure 2.5. There's not a distribution list, custom recipient, or public folder to be seen—just a sea of mailboxes. Well, almost. Our old friend the Schedule+ Free/Busy Connector is there, too. It's there because, although it serves the whole LA site, it lives on my server EXCHLA01 or, in Microsoft-speak, it is *homed* on EXCHLA01. (That is, mailbox agent recipients appear in the Server Recipients container of the server they're homed on.)

**FIGURE 2.5:**

A server-level recipients container includes only mailboxes and mailbox agents.

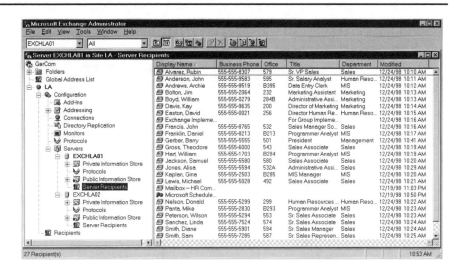

Let's take a closer look at each of the four major Exchange recipient objects.

## Mailboxes

*Mailboxes* hold private messages and other objects such as word processing documents or spreadsheets that belong to individual Exchange users. Any mailbox may contain folders created by the system or users. There are four system-created folders in Exchange: Inbox, Outbox, Deleted Items, and Sent Items. Generally, messages are received in the Inbox folder, sent from the Outbox folder, moved into the Sent Items folder after transmission, and held in the Deleted Items folder after deletion

Other folders may be created in an Exchange mailbox by a specific Exchange client. For example, the Outlook 2000 client creates Calendar, Contacts, Drafts, Journal, Notes, and Tasks folders in an Exchange mailbox when it initially accesses the mailbox.

Users can create as many folders in a mailbox as they wish and can give the folders any name they choose. Users can delete folders they create, but they cannot delete system-created folders. Any folder, whether system- or user-created, can have folders nested below it.

All mailboxes are stored on the user's Exchange server in an Exchange database called the *private information store.* You must be connected to your Exchange server to access your mailbox on Exchange Server. Figure 2.6 shows my own Exchange client and its mailbox; my Inbox is open.

**FIGURE 2.6:**

An Exchange client with its mailbox

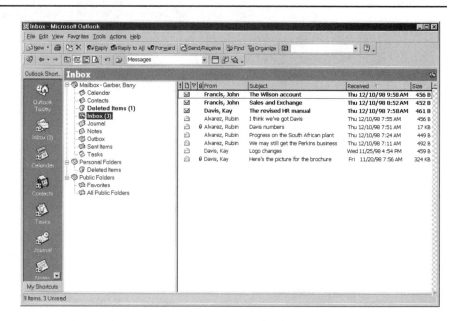

You can give others access to your mailbox. This lets them see and, if you wish, respond to your messages, as a secretary might do for a boss. You can also create mailboxes just to support specific activities or projects. By assigning certain people the rights to these kinds of mailboxes, groups can work cooperatively without turning to the public folders I'll discuss later. If you have rights to multiple mailboxes, they can all be made available simultaneously in your Exchange client. Figure 2.7 shows that my colleagues and I are using a shared mailbox to plan our Exchange system.

Notice that the shared mailbox has not been accessed by an Outlook 2000 client. You can tell this because the mailbox only has Deleted Items, Inbox, Outbox, and Sent Items folders.

**FIGURE 2.7:**

An Exchange client with access to multiple mailboxes

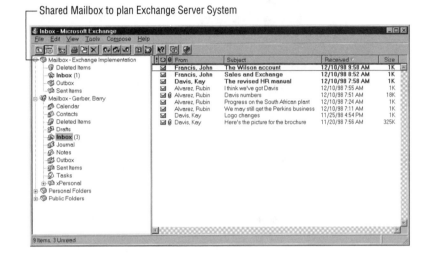

─ Shared Mailbox to plan Exchange Server System

# Personal Folders

To hold messages outside the Exchange server environment, Exchange users can create personal folders. Unlike mailboxes, which are stored in a specific Exchange database called the *private information store*, personal folders are stored, at least initially, as standard files on a local or networked disk. When created, personal folders have only one system-created folder, Deleted Items. Personal folders can help you organize information in special ways. As Figure 2.8 shows, I'm using a personal folder named *Exchange Book* to isolate and manage messages and other information related to this book. In the folder named Chapter 1, I've dragged and dropped the items with .TIF and .DOC extensions into the folder using the Windows NT Explorer. The item from Rubin Alvarez, which is flagged with an envelope icon, is a message I dragged and dropped into the folder from my mailbox's Inbox.

You can tell that my Exchange Book personal information store is stored on a local or network disk (and not inside the Exchange private information store database) because it's not in either of the two mailboxes in my Exchange client. To move folders or items in the personal information store into my Exchange server, all I have to do is drag them into one of the two mailboxes.

**FIGURE 2.8:**

An Exchange client with a
personal information store
for a special project

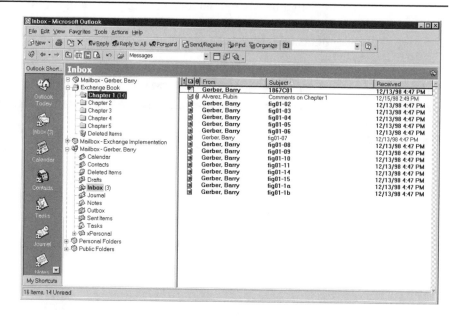

## Public Folders

Though public folders can originate messages, most of the time you'll use them to receive messages. They're created by users and allow groups of users to share data. When you create a public folder, you can choose who has access to it—all users or only some. When you use a public folder, you can mail or directly post messages or files to it or simply drag and drop them into the folder. (Remember that messages can be anything from simple text to application files.)

## Custom Recipients

When Exchange Server users need to communicate with people outside your Exchange system, you can add these "foreigners" to your directory as custom recipients. Then Exchange users can pick them from directory lists just as they would select any internal Exchange recipient. You'd do this, for example, with someone who has an SMTP mail account on another system.

You don't have to create a custom recipient for every foreigner, however. If only a few Exchange users need to access a particular outsider, they can create an address for that person in their own contacts lists or address books or do "one-off" addressing on a per-message basis (one-off addressing is a one-time, manually typed address).

### Distribution Lists

Distribution lists let you group together recipients, including other distribution lists. They make it easy to send a message to lots of people and places using a single address.

### Hiding Recipients

You can hide any of the four recipient objects. Hidden recipients can send and/or receive mail, but they don't show up in address books. You can use them, for example, to protect the anonymity of specific recipients or to support applications.

# Reasons to Be Careful about Exchange Hierarchy Design

The Exchange hierarchy does a nice job of imposing an organizational structure on both the real world and Exchange's own little world. If that were all it did, we could stop right here. But the hierarchy plays two more significant roles: It shapes the way you manage your Exchange system, and it defines the default e-messaging addresses of everyone inside it.

## The Exchange Hierarchy and Exchange Management

Look at Figure 2.1 once more. No matter how much GerCom grows as a real company, I'll always be able to easily think about and manage all the sites, servers, and recipients inside it from the same Exchange Administrator session.

Furthermore, if I had more than one Exchange organization, I'd have to treat the organizations as foreign to each other when I linked them together. That could significantly increase the networking and administrative cost of operating my Exchange system. For example, I'd have to set up and manage separate Internet links for each organization.

It's not all that easy to fix problems like the one I'd create by dividing my company into a bunch of sub-organizations. You'll welcome the ability to bring together Exchange organizations when your real-world organization changes—for example, when it merges with another organization. Still, it's better not to rely on futures. Define your organization as broadly as you can from the start, unless you've got some social, political, or economic reason for doing otherwise.

## The Exchange Hierarchy and E-Messaging Address

In Figure 2.9, you can see how my default cc:Mail, Microsoft Mail for PC Networks, SMTP, and X.400 addresses are dependent on the way I've named the first two elements—organization and site—in my Exchange hierarchy. Server names are not included in addresses. Once a message gets to its destination site, the servers in the site are "smart" enough to get the message to the appropriate server, wherever it is located in the Exchange organization.

**FIGURE 2.9:**

The Exchange hierarchy defines everyone's default e-mail addresses.

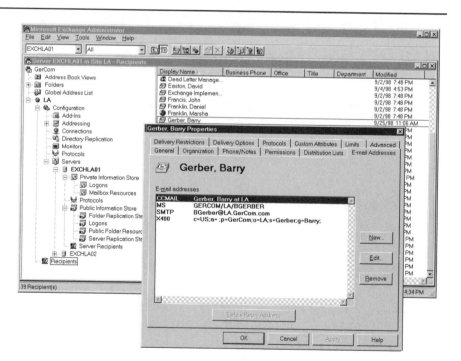

It's quite easy to change the default addresses that Exchange Server assigns to one or more recipients or even to add more addresses of a given type for any recipient. This way you're not trapped by your original Exchange hierarchy naming scheme. Still, it's best to get everything as right as possible from the get-go.

Although a variety of social and political barriers can get in the way of doing so, it's best to make your Exchange organization as all-inclusive as possible. Try to include the whole company, university, club, or whatever. If you don't, you may end up with a bunch of folks running around with addresses like jones@marketing.*acmela*.com and smith@marketing.*acmeny*.com.

One of the few times that centralized MIS or general management should rear its sometimes ugly head is in the early stages of Exchange hierarchy design. If yours is a decentralized organization, you can get back on your own horse as soon as this phase of the design process is finished.

# Conclusion

In this chapter, you learned about the Exchange hierarchy. You saw how the objects in the hierarchy organize both the real world and Exchange itself. You learned key terms that you'll see again and again throughout this book. And you learned to be careful in designing the key elements of your Exchange hierarchy. How you define and name these elements will determine both how easy your Exchange system will be to manage and what your default Exchange e-messaging addresses will look like.

**3**

# The Architecture of Exchange

■ Exchange Server's four core components

■ Optional Exchange Server components

■ Exchange client components

**E**xchange is a client/server electronic messaging system. In this chapter, we'll take a close look at the architectures of both the Exchange server and client. We'll also see how the Exchange client and server interact from an architectural perspective, as illustrated in Figure 3.1.

This is an important chapter. It exposes you to a range of Exchange terminology that you'll find useful later on, and it gives you a sense of how the whole Exchange system hangs together and works. Remember that virtually all of the architectural components we discuss here are, in whole or in part, real program code running somewhere on an Exchange server or client machine. We'll revisit all of these components later in the book.

**FIGURE 3.1:**

The architecture of Exchange

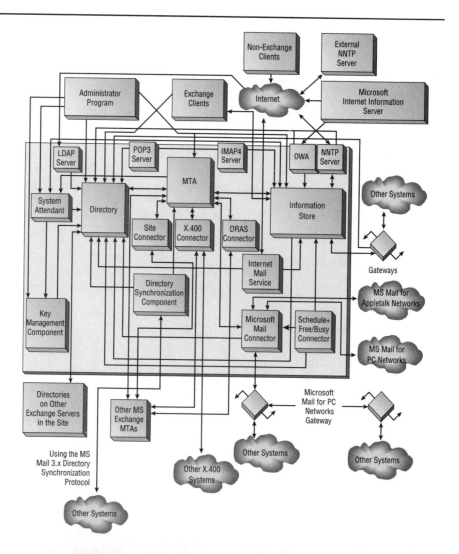

No, Figure 3.1 isn't a bird's-eye view of a spaghetti factory; rather, it's more or less a complete diagram of the Exchange hierarchy based on a diagram originally developed by Microsoft. It shows the components in the hierarchy and how they relate to each other. Everything inside the large, heavy-lined rectangle is part of a single Exchange server running all the required and optional Exchange Server components. Everything outside the rectangle is external to the server itself. The lines indicate communications between components. All communications are two-way; where there is only one arrowhead, the arrowhead points away from the Exchange component that initiates communications. A line with an arrowhead at each end indicates that either of the two components can initiate communications at different times, depending on the function being carried out.

Don't get too hung up with the details of Figure 3.1. It's here partly to give you a sense of the complexity of Exchange and partly to get you thinking about Exchange as a set of real processes that do real work. We won't go through every line and arrowhead of the figure in gory detail. However, when you come to the end of this chapter you should have a pretty good idea of how the various components in the Exchange hierarchy work, both alone and in league with their fellow components.

# Exchange Server's Core Components

Exchange Server cannot provide messaging services to users unless all its core components are up and running. Core components include the

- Directory
- Information Store
- Message Transfer Agent
- System Attendant

Let's take a closer look at each of the core components.

## The Directory

The Exchange Server directory functions as both a database and a service. The directory is a container holding information about all of a site's objects that are required to send and receive messages within and to the site. These include recipients (as defined in the previous chapter) as well as servers and all kinds of message-routing information. Copies of the directory for a site are stored on all Exchange servers in that site. If an organization includes multiple sites, information for all sites is included in every site directory.

The directory service (DS) is the access point for the directory database. Other processes on the Exchange server and on Exchange clients talk to the DS to provide and obtain information.

One of the key functions of the DS is to send and receive directory update information. Within an Exchange site, the DS sends this information directly to and receives it directly from the DSs on other Exchange servers. Across Exchange sites, the DSs send and receive directory update information as standard messages through the message transfer agent (MTA) on each Exchange server. The Exchange Server directory uses this update information for regular intrasite and intersite replication of directories across an Exchange organization. (More about all this in later chapters.) The DS can also exchange directory update information with "foreign" e-messaging systems. The optional directory synchronization component does this.

Note that I use the term *replication* to describe the directory update process inside an Exchange organization, while I use *synchronization* to describe updates with foreign e-messaging systems. Though the processes are similar, Microsoft has chosen to use different terms to describe them. Remembering the differences in meaning between the two words will make your hands-on experience with Exchange Server much easier.

In addition to cross-server and cross-system updates, the DS is responsible for such tasks as managing and presenting system address books to Exchange users and enforcing security on all recipient objects. Figure 3.2 shows how the directory and the DS work together to present address information to users. Figure 3.3 shows some of the major functions of the directory in graphical form.

## FIGURE 3.2:

The directory service process accesses the directory database.

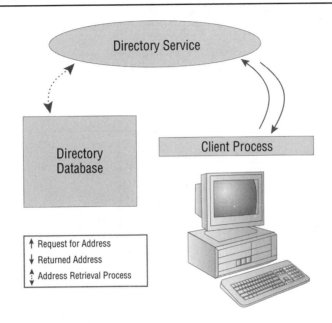

## FIGURE 3.3:

Major functions of the directory

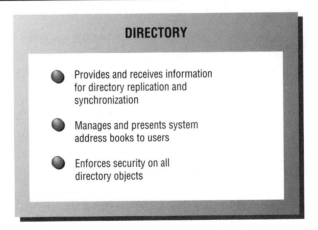

## The Information Store

Like the directory service, the information store (IS) functions as both a database and a service. Each Exchange server contains one IS, which can, at your pleasure, contain one or two databases. One database, the private information store, holds user mailboxes. The other, the public information store, holds public folders. Figure 3.4 shows the basic structure of the Exchange Server IS.

**FIGURE 3.4:**

The Exchange Server information store

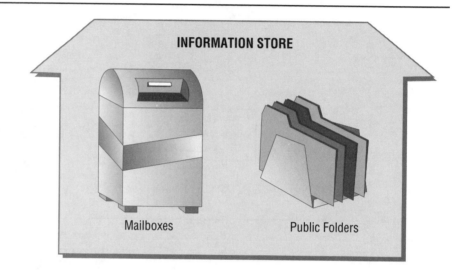

Incoming messages are placed in the Inbox, which, as I noted in Chapter 2, is a special folder in a mailbox. Public folders are used to give all or some recipients in an Exchange system access to specific messages.

To balance network loads and reduce access costs, public folders can be replicated in whole or in part to other Exchange servers, either in the same site or in remote sites. Additionally, to lighten the load on servers with mailboxes, you can place public folders on separate Exchange servers and direct clients to those servers when they need access to public folders.

The *IS service* is a buffer between the IS databases and other components of Exchange Server. It performs a number of functions. Among other things, it receives incoming mail from and delivers outgoing mail to the message transfer agent, notifies clients of the arrival of new mail, looks up addresses in the directory, and creates directory entries for public folders. Figure 3.5 shows some of the major functions of the IS service.

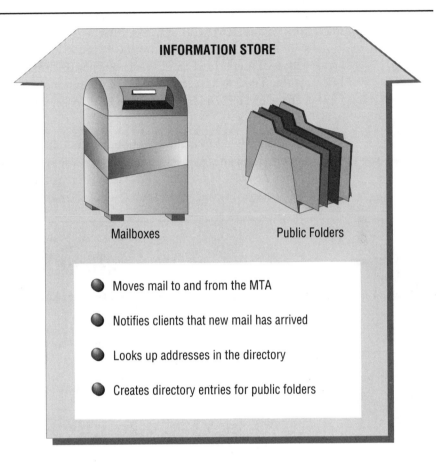

**FIGURE 3.5:**

Major functions of the IS service

## The Message Transfer Agent

The message transfer agent (MTA) routes messages between its server's IS and other Exchange systems. Within a site, the MTA routes messages directly to the MTAs on other Exchange servers. When it routes messages to Exchange servers located in different sites in the same organization, the MTA gets help from other Exchange components called *connectors*. Back in Figure 3.1, you can see three of these connectors—Site, X.400, and DRAS (Dynamic Remote Access Server)—directly below the MTA. I'll discuss these in more detail later in this chapter.

The MTA also routes messages to certain foreign e-messaging systems, including legacy Microsoft Mail 3.*x* systems, Internet systems, and those based on the X.400 standard. As with inter- and intrasite routing, when routing to these foreign systems the MTA gets help from special Exchange connectors, such as the Microsoft Mail and X.400 connectors, and the Internet Mail Service. For other systems such as IBM's SNADS or Novell's GroupWise, gateways are used. (Refer back to Figure 3.1.)

The MTA has one other major function: When X.400 systems are involved, the MTA converts messages in Exchange's default Microsoft MAPI format to native X.400 format, and vice versa. This allows Exchange Server to readily trade messages with X.400 systems. Figure 3.6 presents the MTA's major functions graphically.

**FIGURE 3.6:**

The MTA is a message router and format translator

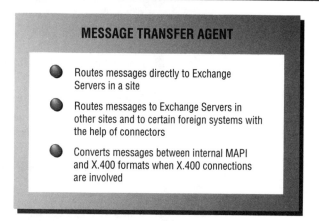

## The System Attendant

Other Exchange Server components cannot run without the system attendant (SA); it's the first Exchange component to activate on start-up and the last to stop on shutdown. The SA performs a range of functions, six of which are key to Exchange Server's operation. Let's take a closer look at each of these functions, as shown in Figure 3.7.

## The SA Helps Other Servers Monitor Network Connections to Its Server

The system attendant receives and replies to network link integrity messages from other Exchange servers. These servers know that something is wrong—either with the network link or the system attendant's own server—if they fail to receive these replies.

**FIGURE 3.7:**

The system attendant performs six key functions for Exchange Server.

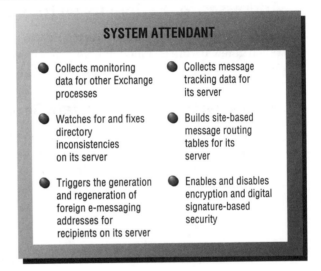

**SYSTEM ATTENDANT**

- Collects monitoring data for other Exchange processes
- Collects message tracking data for its server
- Watches for and fixes directory inconsistencies on its server
- Builds site-based message routing tables for its server
- Triggers the generation and regeneration of foreign e-messaging addresses for recipients on its server
- Enables and disables encryption and digital signature-based security

## The SA Monitors for and Corrects Directory Inconsistencies on Its Server

The SA automatically checks the consistency of its copy of the directory against those of other Exchange servers in its site. If it finds inconsistencies, the SA attempts to reconcile and fix them.

## The SA Collects Message-Tracking Data for Its Server

The SA logs data about sent messages, which can be used for tracking a message's status and the route that it traveled once sent. This capability is especially useful when used in conjunction with similar data gathered by the SAs on other Exchange servers.

### The SA Builds Site-Based Message Routing Tables for Its Server

Like any network, an Exchange Server network needs *routing tables,* which are used specifically for routing messages. The SA interacts with the directory to build tables that the MTA uses to route messages to servers in its site.

### The SA Triggers the Generation of Foreign E-Messaging Addresses for Recipients on Its Server

The SA generates X.400, SMTP, Microsoft Mail, and cc:Mail addresses by default. When gateways are installed, the SA generates gateway-specific e-mail addresses for users. When creating addresses, the SA interacts with the directory.

### The SA Participates in Certain Security Functions

Security in Exchange is very good. An Exchange mailbox can use both digital signatures and encryption. The SA is involved in enabling and disabling these two components of Exchange security. To do this, it interacts with the *Key Management Component,* which is discussed later in this chapter.

# Optional Exchange Server Components

Exchange Server comes with all the following optional components except gateways. These components are "optional" not because you always have to pay extra for them, but because Exchange Server can run without them. Optional components include

- The Exchange Administrator program

- The Directory Synchronization Agent

- The Key Management Component

- Exchange Internet protocol servers:

  - Web Service

  - Post Office Protocol 3 (POP3)

  - Internet Message Access Protocol V4 (IMAP4)

- Network News Transfer Protocol
- Lightweight Directory Access Protocol
- Exchange connectors:
  - Site Connector
  - X.400 Connector
  - Dynamic RAS Connector
  - Internet Mail Service
  - Microsoft Mail Connector
  - Schedule+ Free/Busy Connector
  - cc:Mail Connector
- Exchange gateways

You might find it helpful to refer back to Figure 3.1 as I discuss each component.

## The Exchange Administrator Program

You've seen examples of the Exchange Administrator program in action in Chapters 1 and 2, and you'll get to know it very well as we move along. The main point I want to make here is that the Exchange Administrator is *home*. It's where you go whenever you need to do almost anything with Exchange Server—from creating and managing users to linking with other Exchange servers or foreign mail systems to monitoring the activities on your server. The Administrator is the single point from which you can manage anything, whether it's one Exchange server or your entire Exchange organization.

The Administrator is home in another way, too: It's easy. Soon after you start using the Administrator, you'll feel about it the way you feel about that comfortable old chair in the den. Really!

## The Directory Synchronization Agent

The Directory Synchronization Agent (DXA) lets you create address books that include addresses from outside your Exchange system. It also allows you to send Exchange Server address information to other e-messaging systems. It sends directory update information to and receives it from Microsoft Mail for PC Networks 3.*x* and Microsoft Mail for AppleTalk Networks systems.

The DXA uses the Microsoft Mail 3.*x* Directory Synchronization Protocol, so any foreign, non-Microsoft e-messaging system that is compatible with this protocol is fair game for cross-system directory synchronization.

## The Key Management Component

Exchange supports RSA public key encryption and digital signatures within an Exchange organization. These help ensure the authenticity of a message and the person sending it. Exchange Server's Key Management Component supports these services. With this component in place and running, Exchange client users can create secure messages.

## Exchange Internet Protocol Access Components

Exchange 5.5 comes with a set of five Internet protocol servers. These let you extend the reach of Exchange users beyond Microsoft's very good but proprietary electronic messaging protocols. The five components are Outlook Web Access (OWA), the Post Office Protocol (POP3) server, the Internet Message Access Protocol (IMAP4) server, the Network News Transfer Protocol (NNTP) server, and the Lightweight Directory Access Protocol (LDAP) server. If you try really hard, you'll find all five of these in Figure 3.1's spaghetti factory.

### Outlook Web Access

Outlook Web Access (OWA) lets users access everything in their Exchange or Outlook mailboxes as well as items in public folders using a Web browser like Microsoft's Internet Explorer or Netscape's Navigator. Outlook Web Access components work in conjunction with the Active Server (AS) subsystem of Microsoft's Internet Information Server.

### POP3 Server

Exchange Server's POP3 server gives users with standard POP3 e-mail clients, like Eudora or the mail clients in both Microsoft's Internet Explorer and Netscape's Navigator, limited access to their Exchange mailboxes. Users can download mail from their Exchange Inboxes, but that's all. Users have no direct access to other personal or public information stores or to their schedules. This is due to limitations in the POP3 protocol itself, and not in Microsoft's implementation of the protocol.

### IMAP4 Server

The Exchange IMAP4 server goes POP3 one better, adding access to folders in addition to the Exchange Inbox. With IMAP4, folders and their contents can remain on the Exchange server.

### NNTP Server

The NNTP server lets you bring all those exciting USENET newsgroups into your Exchange server's public folders where your users can read and respond to them with the same e-mail clients they use to read other public folders.

### LDAP Server

Exchange Server supports the Lightweight Directory Access Protocol (LDAP), a protocol that works with X.500-compatible directories. Exchange Server security willing, any client with LDAP capability can access information in the directory on an Exchange server via the Internet. Thus, users of non-Exchange e-mail clients can use the Exchange directory to find the addresses of people they wish to send mail to. LDAP also opens the Exchange directory to other exciting things like communications applications (e.g., Web browser–based paging or faxing apps) that use the directory to get the information they need to reach a particular Exchange user. LDAP is a neat way to open the Exchange directory to the non-Exchange world. Exchange 5.5 provides full LDAP version 3 compatibility.

## Exchange Connectors

You use Exchange connectors to link Exchange sites to each other and to connect them to foreign e-messaging systems. You link Exchange sites to each other so that they can exchange user messages and cross-replicate their directories and public folders. You link Exchange sites to foreign systems primarily so that Exchange users can trade messages with users of those systems and/or synchronize directories with them. As an added bonus, you can also use connections to foreign sites to link Exchange sites to each other; more on this in just a bit.

Exchange connectors run on—surprise—Exchange servers. You can run one or more instances of any Exchange connector within a site; one instance can service all the Exchange servers in a site or even all the sites in an organization.

Before we dive into the connectors themselves, we need to talk a bit about an impressive feature of Exchange Server, *indirect site links.* When Exchange servers connect sites, they conduct their business using standard messages; that is, they move user-to-user communications as messages. And they replicate directories and public folders by means of system-generated messages. Users generate user messages, but directory and public folder replication messages are generated by the Exchange Server system itself. Directory and folder replication messages are marked as system messages to indicate their special content. Figure 3.8 shows how this works.

When an Exchange server sees a system message, it treats the message differently from a user message, using it to update directory or public folder information.

Because site links are message-based, you can connect Exchange sites *directly* (point-to-point) and/or *indirectly* (through foreign e-messaging systems). Direct site links are easy to understand: You just run a connector on an Exchange server in each of two sites and tell the connectors to link to each other. Direct site links are done in real time without any intervening systems between the Exchange servers. (Figure 3.8 shows a direct site link.)

**FIGURE 3.8:**

Site links are based on the exchange of messages.

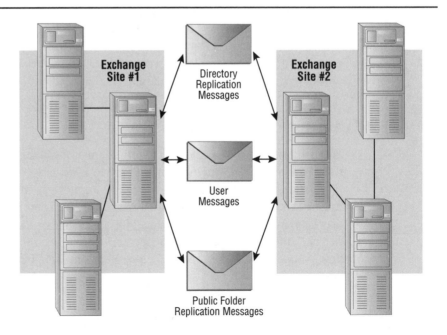

Indirect site links are a bit less self-evident. When two or more Exchange sites are connected to a foreign e-messaging system such as the Internet or a public X.400 system, not only can users trade messages, but the servers in the sites can also exchange system messages that let them cross-replicate directories and public folders. Indirect site links are not done in real time. An Exchange server in one site sends its user and system messages to an intervening e-messaging system such as the Internet. The intervening system then passes these messages on to the Exchange server in the other site. The effect is the same as a direct link, though the process is different.

That wasn't so bad, was it? Take a look at Figure 3.9 if you're still a bit in the dark.

Okay, now we can talk about the Exchange connectors. There are a number of different Exchange connectors, including Site, X.400, Dynamic RAS, Internet Mail Service, Microsoft Mail, cc:Mail, and Schedule+ Free/Busy. Let's look at each of these connectors.

## Intrasite Communications: Two Out of Three Ain't Bad

Exchange servers in the *same* Exchange site require no special connectors. They're linked to each other automatically as soon as they are up and running. Connections *between* sites require that you set up direct or indirect links through Exchange connectors. User communications and public folder replication are message based, whether two Exchange servers are talking intrasite or intersite.

However, as we've already noted when talking about the directory, Exchange servers in the same site don't use message-based communications to cross-replicate their directories. Instead they communicate more directly with each other. Direct communication is necessary because the servers in a site can't send messages until they have a copy of the directory, so they can't use messages to replicate directories. It's a chicken-and-egg problem.

**FIGURE 3.9:**

Linking Exchange sites
indirectly through foreign
e-messaging systems

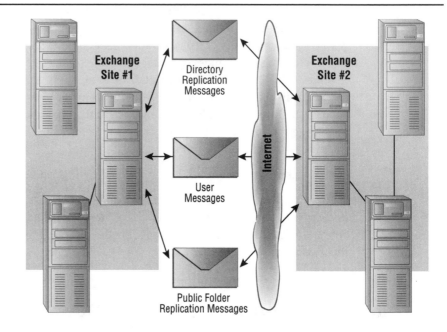

## Site Connector

The Site Connector is used for direct links only. It requires synchronous (continuous) connections between sites. The Site Connector is the fastest, least complicated route to intersite connectivity.

## X.400 Connector

Despite its name, the Site Connector is not the only way to directly link Exchange sites; the X.400 Connector also performs this function. Again, you need a synchronous network connection for direct links. In addition, the X.400 Connector can indirectly link Exchange sites through foreign X.400 systems and it can be used to link Exchange sites to foreign X.400 systems just for user message exchange. Indirect or mail-exchange–only links can be implemented with either a synchronous or an asynchronous (non-continuous) connection. The X.400 Connector is fully compliant with all the 1984 and 1988 X.400 transport and message content standards.

## Dynamic RAS Connector

You'll learn more about NT's Remote Access Server (RAS) in the next chapter. Exchange's Dynamic RAS Connector (DRASC) lets you set up direct links between Exchange sites in a way similar to the Site Connector, but it operates over cheaper, lower-bandwidth voice, ISDN, and X.25 lines. An asynchronous connection is all you need for a DRAS connection.

## Internet Mail Service

The Internet Mail Service (IMS) is your Exchange server's link to SMTP mail systems. It can issue and respond to SMTP and several ESMTP commands and can do both MIME encoding and decoding and uuencoding/uudecoding of messages. The IMS can be used only to exchange mail with Internet mail users or to directly or indirectly link Exchange sites.

Microsoft changed the IMS a bit in version 5 of Exchange Server. Its original name, *Internet Mail Connector*, was changed along with the way you install the IMS. There are also a number of improvements in the IMS, like its ability to route Internet mail from non-Exchange clients or servers.

## Microsoft Mail Connector

You have two post office–wide options for dealing with legacy systems running Microsoft Mail 3.*x* for PC Networks and Microsoft Mail 3.*x* for AppleTalk Networks. Either you can move entire post offices and their user mailboxes to Exchange Server using migration tools that come with Exchange Server or you can link the legacy systems to Exchange Server, providing recipients on all sides with transparent access to each other. The Microsoft Mail Connector (MMC) supports the latter option.

The MMC creates and interacts with a shadow (emulated) Microsoft Mail post office on the Exchange server. Exchange sends and receives mail through the MMC using this shadow, which looks like an Exchange server to users on the Exchange side and looks like a Microsoft Mail 3.*x* post office to users on the MS Mail side. Microsoft Mail's EXTERNAL.EXE program or a version of EXTERNAL .EXE that runs as an NT service is used to transfer mail between the shadow and the real MS Mail post office. Connections can be either synchronous or asynchronous. If it can bear the traffic, you need only one MMC to link all your MS Mail post offices to the Exchange world.

Users of Microsoft Mail 3.*x* for AppleTalk Networks are linked in a similar manner. Once the connection is in place, the MMC gives AppleTalk Mail recipients full access to Exchange recipients, and vice versa.

Before we leave the MMC, I want to be sure you're aware of a third option for users of legacy Microsoft Mail for PC networks systems. This one requires neither whole post office migration nor use of the MMC. On a user-by-user basis, you can connect a user's Exchange client directly to both the user's Microsoft Mail and Exchange mailboxes. This lets the user send and receive messages from both the Microsoft Mail and Exchange systems. This option is best when you haven't got the time or other resources to migrate everyone in a Microsoft Mail post office to an Exchange server or to deal with the intricacies of the MMC.

### cc:Mail Connector

The cc:Mail Connector works a lot like the Microsoft Mail Connector. It allows Exchange Server users to continue accessing messages in their Lotus/IBM cc:Mail post office. Like the Microsoft Mail Connector, the cc:Mail Connector is ideally suited to keeping access to a legacy mail system alive during migration to Exchange Server.

### Schedule+ Free/Busy Connector

Microsoft Schedule+ lets users set up meetings with each other. It uses a graphical user interface to show, in aggregate fashion, the times available to users selected for a meeting. This information is available on Exchange servers and in Microsoft Mail for PC Networks post offices. The Free/Busy Connector, which is an extension of the MMC, lets Exchange servers and Microsoft Mail post offices share schedule information. You *can't* use the Free/Busy Connector for Exchange site connections, either directly or indirectly.

## Exchange Gateways

Exchange Server supports X.400 and SMTP mail natively; to access other systems, you'll need *gateways*. Exchange Server gateways don't resemble the clunky DOS gates used with Microsoft Mail 3.*x*. Like the rest of Exchange Server, they run as processes on NT Server. As long as gateway developers know what they're doing (and that's sometimes a big assumption), gateways tend to be stable, robust, and fast.

Gateways are available for such services as Notes, PROFS, SNADS, and fax, as well as for pagers and voicemail. Microsoft produces some gateways, and third parties offer others. Keep in touch with Microsoft and the trade press for details.

# Exchange Client Components

As I've noted before, the real fun of Exchange is on the client side. That's where you get to see the business end of Exchange—from "simple" e-mail to complex, home-grown messaging-enabled applications. Exchange client components include

- The Exchange client (currently incarnated as the *Outlook client*)
- POP3 and IMAP4 clients from Microsoft
- Schedule+
- The Microsoft Exchange and Outlook Forms Designers
- Microsoft Exchange and Outlook Forms Designer forms
- Other client-based applications

Here's a quick look at the Exchange client components from an architectural perspective. Figure 3.10 shows the clients and their functions graphically.

## The Exchange Client

You receive, transmit, and access messages in the *Exchange client*. It's your window on your mailbox and on personal and public folders. The Exchange clients work with all versions of Exchange Server up to and including 5.5.

Exchange Server ships with clients for Macintosh, Microsoft/PC DOS, Windows 3.1*x*, and Windows NT and with an upgrade for the Exchange client that ships with Windows 95 (aka the Inbox or Windows Messaging). The upgrade adds a range of new features to the Windows 95 Exchange client, including out-of-office messaging, auto-signatures, and free-form rules.

**FIGURE 3.10:**

Exchange client
components

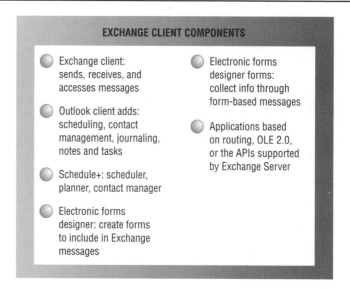

**EXCHANGE CLIENT COMPONENTS**

- Exchange client: sends, receives, and accesses messages
- Outlook client adds: scheduling, contact management, journaling, notes and tasks
- Schedule+: scheduler, planner, contact manager
- Electronic forms designer: create forms to include in Exchange messages
- Electronic forms designer forms: collect info through form-based messages
- Applications based on routing, OLE 2.0, or the APIs supported by Exchange Server

**TIP**   Don't try to use the original Windows 95 client to access Exchange Server. It doesn't work. Upgrade to the Exchange Server version of the Windows 95 client. Trust me, it'll save you a lot of grief.

The Outlook clients are Microsoft's most current Exchange clients. They ship with Microsoft Office 97 and 2000 and, for some operating systems, with Exchange Server. Outlook nicely integrates electronic messaging, scheduling, and contact and task management with a whole bunch of other functions like electronic journaling of every message you read or file you open. Take a look at Figures 1.1 and 1.2 in Chapter 1 for a refresher on Outlook's user interface. Outlook accesses the same directory and information store as the Exchange client. It does modify your Exchange mailbox, adding new folders for things like your schedule, contacts, and tasks. More importantly, it uses a differently structured schedule database, so you have to decide whether you're going to use the older Schedule+ or Outlook for scheduling and contact/task management.

## POP3 and IMAP4 Clients from Microsoft

Microsoft Internet Explorer 4 and later come with Outlook Express. This lighter-weight client supports both POP3 and IMAP4 server access. Outlook 2000 includes support for both POP3 and IMAP4.

## Schedule+

Schedule+ is a messaging-enabled application that includes scheduling, planning, and contact-management features. Version 7.5, the version that comes with Exchange Server, is a serious update of the original version, which was labeled "version 1.0" (Microsoft has a knack for skipping version numbers). Most of the improvements lie in the way it handles features such as schedule viewing, printing, and to-do lists, and less in the program's already pretty decent collaborative-scheduling function.

---

**TIP**    Again, don't try to use the 7.0 version of Schedule+ that comes with Microsoft Office 95. Upgrade!

---

## The Microsoft Exchange and Outlook Forms Designers

Users and developers can create forms with the Microsoft Exchange or Outlook Forms Designers. Forms created with the Designers can be used for a range of tasks, including the collection of data, and can have drop-down pick lists, multiple-choice selections, action buttons, and other useful attributes.

## Microsoft Exchange and Outlook Forms Designer Forms

Forms created in the Microsoft Exchange and Outlook Forms Designers can be stored on servers and made available to all or select users, who can send them to specific recipients as messages or post them in folders for others to access. Users can manually collate data collected in forms; or, with the right programming, data can be automatically extracted from forms and processed. (Look back at Figure 1.10 for a glimpse into the wonderful world of electronic forms.)

## Other Client-Based Applications

Aside from the Microsoft Exchange and Outlook Forms Designers, there are a variety of ways to build client-based applications using Exchange Server's messaging capabilities:

- Microsoft's version 95 and 97 stable of applications (Word, Excel, and so on) include some nice collaborative tools and easy-to-use routing-slip capabilities based on Exchange messaging. Applications from other vendors also incorporate these capabilities.

- You can turn an Exchange message into any OLE 2–compliant application just by inserting an object from the app into the message.

- You can write programs that use Simple and Extended MAPI or the X.400-oriented Common Mail Call APIs supported by Exchange Server.

> **NOTE**
>
> Exchange is a complex product. The cost of an Exchange installation will, of course, depend heavily on licensing fees imposed by Microsoft. Check with the company for all pricing details.

# Conclusion

In this chapter, you got a grounding in the architecture of Exchange. You learned about the core and optional components on both the Exchange server and client sides. You also had a chance to learn how the components interact with each other. The knowledge you've gained here has more than theoretical value: It will help immensely as you move toward installing and managing a real-world Exchange environment.

# Exchange and Windows NT Server

- Why Exchange Server runs only on top of NT Server

- NT Server is easy to install and use

- Key features of NT Server and their integration with Exchange Server

**E**xchange Server is part of Microsoft's BackOffice suite of products. Like other BackOffice applications—SQL Server and Systems Management Server, for example—Exchange Server runs only on top of Microsoft Windows NT Server. You can install Exchange Server's very nice Administrator program on an NT Workstation, but not Exchange Server itself. Windows 95, Windows 98? Forget it!

# Why NT Server?

NT Server has two key features not available in other Microsoft operating systems. The lack of these features does not make it impossible to run Exchange Server on, say, NT Workstation or Windows 95/98. Together, however, these features make NT Server the best platform for Exchange Server and Microsoft's other BackOffice products.

The key features? First, NT Server is optimized for lots of users. Second, it has some nice extended tools for ensuring the integrity of your disk system. Let's look at these features in more detail.

## What about Windows 2000?

As I write, Microsoft's Windows 2000 is going through Beta testing. 2000 is an exciting and innovative operating system with all the features of NT 4 and lots more. However, I strongly urge you to stick with NT 4 until Windows 2000 has had a complete version 1 shakedown. I remember with much dismay those scary blue screen crashes that killed NT 4 when Service Pack 2 was installed and a SCSI disk or tape device was accessed. If e-mail is a mission-critical application for your organization, don't tempt fate by using a brand new OS.

## NT Server Can Handle Heavy Multiuser Loads

Servers tend to support lots of users. Server users make major demands on CPU, disk, and network resources. NT Server is optimized to move data within and between these resources even under heavy loads.

Because of this optimization, NT Server can handle a large number of simultaneously connected users—just how many is limited only by your hardware configuration and the number of connect licenses you've bought.

Because it lacks server-oriented optimization and because it *is* optimized for workstation functionality, NT Workstation is limited to a maximum of ten users. Some claim that this limitation is artificially low and designed to force users to buy NT Server so that Microsoft can make more money. I have to disagree. The price difference between NT Server and NT Workstation isn't great enough to justify such an argument.

Windows 95 and 98 are also optimized for workstation functionality, but I'm uncomfortable with their continued reliance on MS-DOS to support older hardware technologies. Windows 95/98 are great for user workstations running newer hardware and faster, more stable 32-bit applications; however, they do not have the stability to function as a platform for critical applications such as e-messaging.

## NT Server Supports RAID Levels 1 and 5

Systems using redundant arrays of inexpensive disks (RAID) protect data by writing all or part of it to two or more drives. This ensures that the data can be recovered in case of a drive failure. When the bits in a byte of data are written to two or more drives, data is said to be *striped across* the drives.

There are at least five levels of RAID:

- *Level 1* mirrors data stored on one disk onto another disk and provides 100 percent duplication of data. The system usually has to be shut down to replace a failed mirrored drive with the mirroring drive; however, a shutdown isn't required with NT's level 1 RAID.

- *Level 2* uses data disks and extra check drives; data bits are striped across these drives *(bit striped)*, along with information that allows 1-bit data errors to be fixed and 2-bit errors to be detected (though not fixed) on the fly. Level 2 RAID offers the best performance with large data blocks.

- *Level 3* uses a single redundant check disk for a group of data drives. Data is bit-striped across the data disks, and XORed (exclusive ORed) parity information for the data is stored on the check disk. If any drive fails, its data can be reconstructed from the remaining drives and the check disk.

- *Level 4* is similar to RAID level 3, but data is block- or sector-striped—instead of bit-striped—across disks. Level 4 is best for transaction processing.

- *Level 5* doesn't use dedicated check drives; rather, it distributes regular and check data over the drives in the array, based on an algorithm that allows data to be recovered when a failed drive is replaced. Level 5 RAID allows for simultaneous reads and writes of data to disks and is most efficient when handling small amounts of information.

If you show just about anyone these definitions of the various RAID levels, they'll probably tell you I'm all wet. But actually I'm quite dry; the problem is that specific RAID implementations never fully adhere to all the details of these general definitions. Don't worry, though: These definitions are more than adequate to help you understand how NT Server handles RAID.

RAID can be implemented in hardware or software. NT Server supports software-based disk mirroring and disk duplexing (RAID level 1) and disk striping with parity (RAID level 5).

Under *disk mirroring* you create a constantly updated copy of all or part of one hard drive on another drive; both drives are connected to the same disk controller. The copy lets you recover from a drive failure. With *disk duplexing* you do the same thing, but the drive being copied is connected to a different disk controller than the drive holding the copy. This eliminates the single point of controller failure you have with disk mirroring.

*Disk striping with parity* involves creating stripes on up to 32 drives, preferably connected to multiple disk controllers. Data is written in ordered bits across the stripes. Parity information lets you recover data stored on a failed drive using the remaining good drives. Depending on hardware, you can often swap out a bad drive with a good one without even turning off the computer's or drive system's power.

Another benefit of RAID, especially level 5, is better disk performance. A RAID system can improve disk access speeds by splitting reads and writes over multiple drives and multiple disk controllers. (In fact, Microsoft recommends using RAID level 5 disk striping to improve Exchange Server performance. More about this later.)

## Consider a Stand-Alone Hardware RAID System

You can purchase stand-alone hardware RAID systems for NT from a variety of third-party vendors. Third-party hardware RAID solutions won't let you run Exchange Server on top of NT Workstation or Windows 95/98, but they might give you better performance than NT Server's built-in software-based RAID functionality. This is especially likely if you run NT Server on a single-processor computer. Stand-alone hardware RAID systems don't eat up your computer's CPU time doing RAID.

Exchange is likely to be considered a critical application in your organization. You probably won't want to run it without the benefits of at least RAID level 1.

**NOTE**   You manage NT disks in general and RAID systems in particular using NT's Disk Administrator, which is located in NT's Administrative Tools program group. For more on the Disk Administrator, see the Sybex book *Mastering Windows NT Server 4*. And for more on mastering Windows NT Server 4, see the sidebar in this chapter brilliantly titled—yep—"Mastering Windows NT Server 4."

# NT Server Is a Piece of Cake

If you haven't had much (or any) experience with NT Server, don't let that bother you. It is quite simple to install—not much harder than installing Windows 95/98, in fact. We'll look at basic NT Server installation in Chapter 6.

Once installed, NT Server is very easy to use. It comes outfitted with the complete Microsoft Windows graphical user interface (GUI) suite that is the spitting image of Windows 95/98. If you're comfortable with Windows 95/98, you'll be just fine with NT Server. Trust me.

Applications for NT—Exchange Server included—tend to build on the Windows GUI. Remember the neat GUI administrative front end for Exchange Server we looked at back in Chapters 1 and 2? With their GUI front ends, NT apps let you focus on the substantive task in front of you. That way, you don't have to spend all your time editing cryptic text files or cobbling together makeshift system monitoring or administration commands in the wide-open spaces of the operating system. (If it's not obvious, that last sentence was referring to UNIX.)

# NT Specifics for the Exchange Server Crowd

NT Server is a bundle of nifty components. To understand how NT Server and Exchange Server work together, you'll need a basic grounding in eight of these components:

- NT services

- NT networking

- Microsoft network domains

- NT User Manager for Domains

- NT Server Manager

- NT and multiprocessing

- NT Event Viewer

- NT Performance Monitor

Some of the eight key NT Server components are also available in NT Workstation. That's a nice plus. If you're not already an NT aficionado, by the time you're finished setting up NT Server and Exchange Server, you'll probably be ready to make NT Workstation your desktop operating system. I've even gone a step further. My office, home, and laptop workstations run NT Server. I'll wait while you get back up off your knees after paying homage to yours truly. Anyway, for you NT converts-in-the-making, the following detailed discussion of the eight components is a kind of two-for-one deal: It'll help you get comfortable with both NT Server and your future NT Workstation machine at the same time. And just so you know when a particular component is available only in NT Server, I'll use the words *NT Server* as opposed to *NT* when discussing it. (I'm just loaded with brilliant ideas.)

## Mastering Windows NT Server 4

The eight NT Server components discussed in this chapter are far from all you'll ever want or need to know about NT. For the definitive word on NT Server, get a copy of Sybex's *Mastering Windows NT Server 4*. The authors—Mark Minasi, Christa Anderson, and Elizabeth Creegan—manage to make learning about a complex operating system both relatively painless and, believe it or not, fun.

I decided to have Sybex publish my book partly because I liked *Mastering Windows NT Server 4* so much. The deal was cinched when the company assured me that I'd have the same stylistic freedom given to Minasi, et al. I got that freedom, and I hope you'll like this book as much as I enjoyed *Mastering Windows NT Server 4*.

## NT Services

NT is a full-blown, preemptive, multitasking, multithreaded operating system that's able to run many tasks or processes simultaneously. Many of the processes that run on NT are called *services*. Services can run all the time the computer is on, or they may be started and stopped manually as needed by those with the appropriate rights. Network protocol services, the computer's login services, and many applications, such as client/server databases and tape backup and virus protection programs, run as NT services. And—you guessed it—Exchange Server is a set of NT services as well.

The NT Control Panel includes a little Services icon. When you double-click it, an applet starts up with a window that displays all available NT services. Within this window you can check to see if a service is running, stop and start services, and set a service's default configuration (that is, whether it starts on boot-up, can be manually started, or is disabled). Figure 4.1 shows the Services applet in action on the GerCom Exchange server.

Don't worry about how services get created or integrated into the operating system; it's the responsibility of the application provider to make sure this happens. And don't get the idea that the NT Services applet is the only way to monitor Exchange services. No way. As you'll see, Exchange comes with a bunch of its own service monitoring tools.

**FIGURE 4.1:**

The NT Services applet is
used to monitor and
control Exchange Server
components.

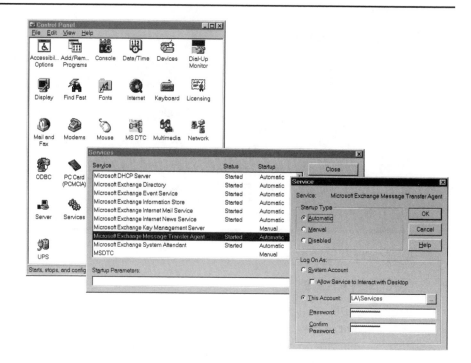

## NT Networking

NT provides support for a range of networking protocols. These include IPX/SPX, NetBEUI, TCP/IP, and (with optional software) SNA networks. Third parties provide other networking protocols for NT Server, including DECnet and XNS.

NT also supports a set of standard remote procedure calls (RPCs) that enable client/server communications between programs running on the same or different computers. RPC-based communications move with equal ease across hardware platforms, operating systems, and networking protocols.

All Exchange client-to-server communications and some Exchange server-to-server communications—intrasite directory replication, for example—are based on the RPCs. The RPCs support only direct links between Exchange servers (as *direct* was defined in Chapter 3). The RPCs can run on top of IPX/SPX, NetBEUI, TCP/IP, or SNA. The RPCs can also work over other network layers that are not transport protocols—for example, Named Pipes or Sockets. In Figure 4.2 you can see how the RPCs work in an Exchange system and use the networking protocols supported by NT. See the sidebar "NT's RPCs and Exchange" for more on this RPC set, which is so central to Exchange.

**FIGURE 4.2:**

How NT's RPCs and Microsoft networking support Exchange Server

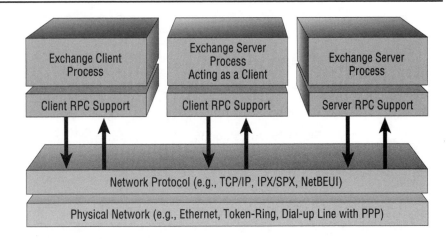

One of the really impressive parts of NT networking is the Remote Access Server (RAS). The RAS supports client-to-server and server-to-server links based on slower connect options. It works with standard phone lines, ISDN, X.25, and RS-232C null modems. Key supported protocols include NetBEUI, TCP/IP, and IPX/SPX—all on top of the Point-to-Point Protocol (PPP). One NT Server can have up to 256 RAS connections. (For the record, NT Workstation supports only one RAS connection.) As you'll see later, the RAS is a key part of Exchange's connectivity options.

NT networking, like Microsoft networking in general, is quite simple. If you've got a network adapter in your computer, you're asked what kind of networking you want when you install NT Server. If you understand basic networking concepts—for example, how to set up a TCP/IP node—you'll have little if any trouble with NT networking. (We'll come back to networking issues constantly throughout the rest of this book.)

## Microsoft Network Domains

Microsoft network domains both organize and provide centralized administration and security for groups of resources. Resources include computers, the programs running on them, and the peripherals attached to them. Windows and DOS workstations integrate best into Microsoft networks.

Computers in Microsoft networks can include

- Windows NT servers

- Novell NetWare servers

- Windows NT workstations

- Windows 95 workstations

- Windows 3.11 workstations

- MS-DOS workstations

- Apple Macintoshes

Peripherals include disk drives and the files on them, as well as printers.

## NT's RPCs and Exchange

Exchange relies heavily on Microsoft's implementation of the OSF's DCE RPC API. Talk about alphabet soup! Translation: Exchange depends on Microsoft's version of the Open Software Foundation's (OSF's) Distributed Computing Environment (DCE) remote procedure call (RPC) application programming interface (API). That's quite a mouthful, so I'll use the term "OSF RPCs" from here on to avoid drowning you in a sea of acronyms.

In general, remote procedure calls support client-server computing. The OSF RPCs aren't suitable for all client-server applications, because to work they require direct, synchronous (continuous) connections between clients and servers. You can't use the OSF RPCs in a situation where you want to assign a task to a server, disconnect from the server, and then go about your work until the server contacts you to return the results of the task you assigned it. You've got to remain linked to the server during the entire process. So the OSF RPCs are not well suited to things like client-server databases; in fact, Microsoft uses other RPCs to support its SQL Server database.

There are OSF RPCs for clients as well as servers. NT Server, NT Workstation, and Windows 95/98 support both the client and server RPC sets. The other Microsoft operating systems support only the client RPC sets.

Client and server versions of the OSF RPCs are available for a wide range of operating systems, which means that Microsoft can more easily write Exchange clients and servers for non-Microsoft operating systems. This is key to the company's development of Exchange clients for the Apple Macintosh.

**NOTE**    Microsoft's NT Server Enterprise Edition adds new stability and reliability to NT. Servers can be clustered so that if one fails, the other can take over.

Microsoft networks are built around *domains*. A Microsoft network can have one or many domains, each of which is a logically separate entity. A resource in a Microsoft network can belong to one and only one domain.

Generally, domain users log in to domains, not to the individual machines in a domain. Domains can make life easier both for users and for system managers. Users don't have to remember more than one password to access any resource in the domain (unless it is protected by a special password). System managers can centrally create and administer user accounts for the domain.

Domains also make interserver communications easy. If servers live in the same domain, each has to log in to the domain only once in order to communicate with all other servers in the domain—unless, of course, a special password is required for specific communications.

Domains require *domain controllers*, which is where

- NT administrators:
    - Create and manage accounts for domain users
    - Set access rights for domain resources
- The NT Server operating system:
    - Stores user account information for the domain
    - Stores resource access rights for the domain
    - Authenticates domain users
    - Enforces access rights for domain resources

Of all the resources in a Microsoft network domain, only NT servers can be domain controllers; while every NT server needn't be a domain controller, every domain controller *must* be an NT server. Exchange Server can optionally be installed on an NT server that is a domain controller. That way, you can set up a simple Exchange system using just one NT server.

It's considered good practice to have at least one backup controller in each domain. Backup domain controllers stay in sync with the primary controller and take over if the primary controller fails. They can also perform authentication in parallel with the primary and other backup domain controllers. This helps balance the load in systems with large numbers of users.

As you'll see later, domains are key to using and administering Exchange. Domain and Exchange security are tightly integrated—to see just how tightly, take a look at Figure 4.3, which shows the Exchange Administrator being used to create both a new Exchange mailbox and a new domain user account for the mailbox.

**FIGURE 4.3:**

The Exchange Administrator creates a new Exchange mailbox and domain user.

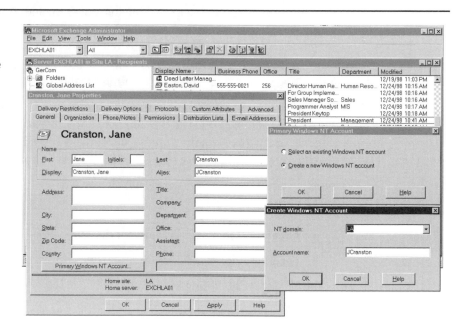

## Cross-Domain Trusts

When one domain (called the *trusting* domain) trusts another (the *trusted* domain), it accepts the other domain's authentication of a user or server. The user or server doesn't have to log in to the trusting domain to access its resources; one login to a trusted domain is enough to access all available resources in a trusting domain, unless access to a resource is specifically limited by a special password.

Figure 4.4 shows how cross-domain trust relationships make it easier for users and servers to access resources across a network. The users and servers in domain B (the trusted domain) can access resources in domain A (the trusting domain) without using additional passwords. Note that the figure's arrowhead points to the trusted domain and away from the trusting domain.

Trusts are not only good for users, they're just what the doctor ordered for busy system administrators as well. Trusts expand the reach of administrators in creating and maintaining user accounts. After setting up a trust relationship between domains, an administrator can in one fell swoop create a user in one domain and give that user access to all other trusting domains.

**FIGURE 4.4:**

Trust relationships open a network to users.

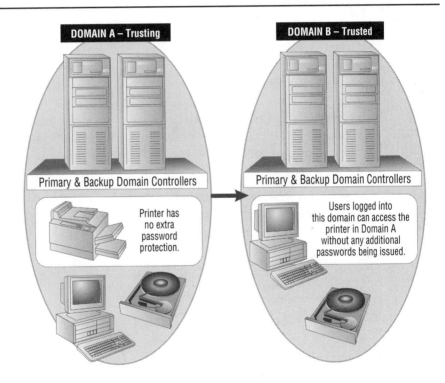

Trust relationships have all kinds of implications for the way users and systems managers operate day to day. For example, with the right kind of trust relationship and security rights you can administer Exchange not on a domain-by-domain basis, but from a multidomain or network-level perspective.

Also, trust relationships are key to cross-domain interaction between Exchange servers. With the appropriate trust relationships and rights in place, Exchange servers in different domains can interact to exchange messages and cross-replicate directories and public folders.

## Domain Models

There are four domain models for Microsoft networks:

- Single-domain model

- Master-domain model

- Multiple-master domain model

- Complete-trust domain model

Let's look at each model in detail.

**The Single-Domain Model**     Single-domain systems have no need for trust relationships because there is only one isolated domain. See Figure 4.5 for a graphical depiction of a network with a single domain.

The single-domain model is best in situations that have no organizational or technical need for a segmented network. The maximum number of users in a domain is limited pretty much by the hardware your domain controller runs on. The more users you have, the larger your domain security tables become; in addition, you'll need more powerful hardware (CPU, RAM, and disks) to plow through the tables when authenticating users. Depending on the hardware you use and based on hardware capabilities current as of December 1999, you can expect to support up to 26,000 users if all users are using NT Workstation and/or NT Server in a domain.

Once you're running your primary and backup domain controllers on the most powerful hardware you can find or afford, the only way to support more users is by moving either to the multiple-master domain model or the complete-trust domain model. I'll discuss these two in just a bit, but first let's look at the master-domain model.

**FIGURE 4.5:**

A network based on the
single-domain model

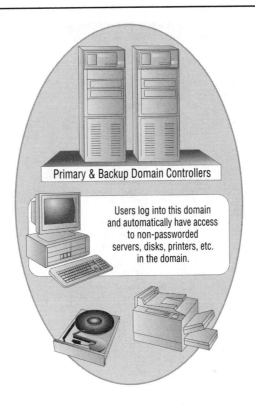

**The Master-Domain Model**   Master-domain systems include one administrative domain and one or more resource domains where servers and workstations are located. The master domain handles all security tasks. It is a trusted domain, while all other domains are trusting. See Figure 4.6 for a diagram of a master-domain system.

The master-domain model is most appropriate in organizations that need to segment resources (say, by department or geographically) and that have a centralized MIS department. Each department or geographical unit can have its own domain, while MIS administers from the master domain. Note that even though this model has multiple domains, there is only one administrative domain—so you're still limited to 15,000 to 40,000 users per domain.

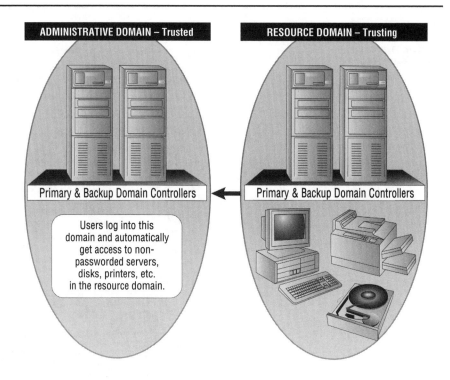

**The Multiple-Master Domain Model**    Multiple-master domain systems have two or more master domains and two or more resource domains. Each master domain is responsible for some portion of users based on a logical segmenting factor—for example, the first letter of the user's last name, or the geographical breakdown of the company. Each resource domain trusts all the master domains. Figure 4.7 depicts the multiple-master domain model. Here the master domains trust each other and are trusted by both of the resource domains. This is not required, however; each master domain can be trusted by either one or a set of resource domains. In the figure, for example, Administrative Domain #1 could be trusted only by Resource Domain #1, while Administrative Domain #2 could be trusted by both resource domains.

In many cases, you'll also want two-way trusts between the master domains. That way, system administrators with appropriate rights can create new users, and so on, in any master domain as needed.

The multiple-master domain model works best for larger organizations that need to segment both resources and MIS administration. Resource domains are often based on departmental divisions.

Multiple-master domains are a way around limits on the maximum number of users per domain. So if your domain controller hardware limits you to 40,000 users per domain, *each* master domain can handle up to 40,000 users. With two domains you're up to 80,000 users, and so on.

Multiple-master domains also allow MIS administration to divide the task of managing domains into smaller units. This tends to reduce the likelihood of error and lets large multinational organizations spread the management tasks across geographical and sociopolitical boundaries.

**FIGURE 4.7:**

A network based on the multiple-master domain model

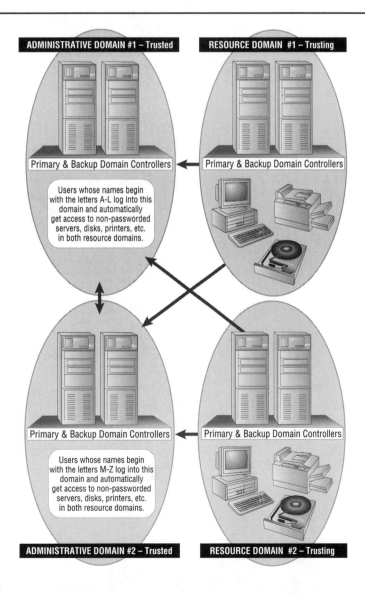

**The Complete-Trust Domain Model**    Complete-trust domain systems consist of several domains; each domain handles its own security administration. Since this model has no master domains, all domains must be both trusted and trusting. Figure 4.8 shows a system based on the complete-trust domain model.

**FIGURE 4.8:**

A network based on the complete-trust domain model

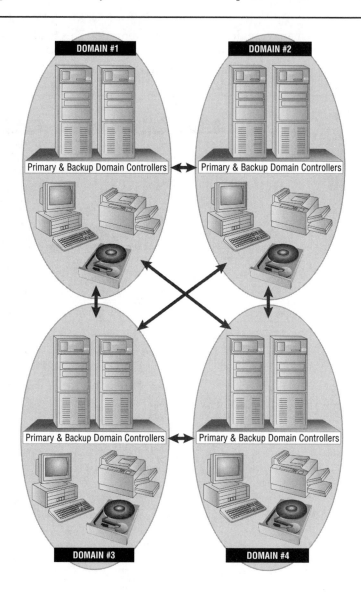

Complete-trust domain systems are appropriate when an organization lacks central MIS administration and is segmented in some way—by department, for example. Each department is a domain, and control of the domain is in the hands of the department. Each domain can have up to the maximum number of users its domain controller hardware will support. The major drawback of complete-trust domain systems is the number of trust relationships that have to be set up and maintained in organizations with lots of departments.

## User Manager for Domains and Cross-Domain Trusts

You set up cross-domain trusts in NT's User Manager for Domains. From the Policies menu, select Trust Relationships. From there it's a no-brainer, as long as you've really got other domains and they're on the same continuous local or wide area network. You can set up both trusted and trusting relationships for the domain you're running the User Manager for Domains from. We'll get into all this in hands-on mode later in the book.

## The NT User Manager for Domains

So you've got one or more domains—now what? Well, first you'll want to create user accounts and user groups in your domains and give them rights. Even though you can create domain users and Exchange mailboxes with the Exchange Administrator, you'll still need to know how to create and manage domain accounts and groups. For example, as you'll see later—even before you install Exchange Server—you'll want to create a domain-based user group to administer and manage your Exchange servers.

NT Server includes a nice interface, called the User Manager for Domains, for administering and managing domain accounts and groups. Figure 4.9 shows how User Manager for Domains can be used to add a new user account to a domain. Just to prove that the tight integration between NT Server and Exchange security is a two-way street, take a look at Figure 4.10. As soon as I click the Add button in the New User dialog box, Exchange—through User Manager for Domains—brings up a standard set of mailbox-creation property pages. I fill in these pages as needed, then click OK in the mailbox's Properties dialog box, and I've created a new domain user and an Exchange mailbox all at once.

Though the actual domain account information is stored on an NT server, you can run the User Manager for Domains on an NT workstation as well. (I'm running it on my NT workstation in Figures 4.9 and 4.10.) This is just one of the ways you can manage an NT server remotely. As you'll find out later in this chapter, Exchange Server also supports a lot of remote management functions. In fact, remote management is one of the most impressive features of both products.

**FIGURE 4.9:**

Adding a user to a domain with the User Manager for Domains

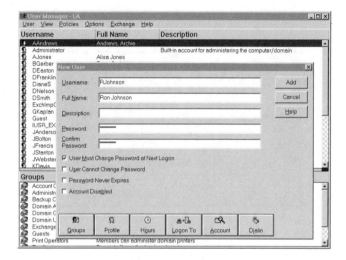

**FIGURE 4.10:**

The User Manager for Domains lets you set up an Exchange mailbox for a new user.

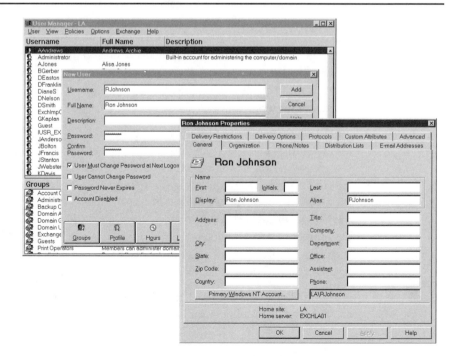

**NOTE**    Although it runs on NT Workstation machines, User Manager for Domains comes only with NT Server. You can borrow it from one of your NT servers, or you can use the copy of the User Manager for Domains that's included in Microsoft's optional NT Resource Kit. The kit, worth its purchase price even if you don't need a copy of the User Manager for Domains, is available from a variety of sources. Check with Microsoft for more information.

## The NT Server Manager

The Server Manager is another one of those wonderful NT management tools that can run remotely. It lets you see what's happening on other servers and allows you to make certain changes on those servers.

In Figure 4.11, I'm running the Server Manager from my NT workstation. You'll notice that we're looking at the domain LA; the servers and workstations in LA are listed on the upper left-hand side of the screen. Here I'm using the Server

**FIGURE 4.11:**

Using the Server Manager to remotely monitor shared resources

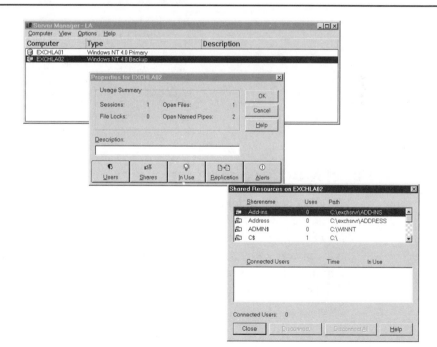

Manager to see what's up resource-wise on my Exchange server, EXCHLA02. You'll notice that I have the option of disconnecting one or more of the shared resources. I might choose to do this if a problem occurred with a resource that I couldn't fix any other way.

Do you remember our earlier discussion of the Control Panel applet for monitoring and administering the services running on an NT machine? Wouldn't it be neat if we could use the applet for remote computers, too? Well, we can't. But not to worry: We can use the Server Manager instead. While at my NT workstation (shown in Figure 4.12), I can stop an Exchange Server process on EXCHLA02. I love it!

**FIGURE 4.12:**

Remotely administering
Exchange Server services
using the Server Manager.

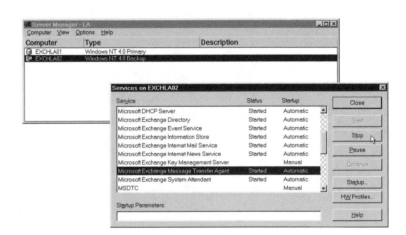

## NT and Multiprocessing

As users begin to take advantage of the great features built into Exchange and as you add new users and tasks—an Exchange connector, for example—to an NT/Exchange server, you'll find yourself scrambling to find the computing horsepower you need to keep everyone and everything happy. You can often pep up a server by adding more RAM and/or a RAID level 5 disk system. If that isn't enough, the next best bet is to add processing power.

When you know the load on an Exchange server will grow significantly in the span of a year or so, you should seriously consider buying a multiprocessing system, even if you don't outfit it with a full complement of CPUs at the outset. That way, you won't have to upgrade to a whole new machine—you can just add processors when demands increase. A number of vendors now offer computers that support multiple-CPU configurations. To show you that my money or at least my clients' money is where my mouth is, I've taken to insisting on a minimum dual-processor Pentium machine for the Exchange Server installations I set up.

## The NT Event Viewer

Like all good operating systems, NT logs a variety of things that happen as it runs. In NT parlance, these "things" are called *events*. Event *logging* is just another NT service.

Three kinds of events can occur in NT: system, security, and application. *System events* include activities centering around disk drives, network adapters, serial ports, mice, and other peripheral hardware. *Security events* are attempts by users and NT processes to enter the system. *Application events* can be anything that the authors of an application that runs on an NT machine choose to log.

You use the NT Event Viewer, which you can find in NT's Administrative Tools program group, to look at events. You pick the kind of event—system, security, or application—that you want to look at from the Event Viewer's Log menu. To see details about a particular event, you double-click on the event. Figure 4.13 shows the Application Log for the NT/Exchange server EXCHLA01.

Each event shown in the Event Viewer is given what might be called an "attention level." Events included solely for informational use are flagged with a little blue icon that has a lowercase letter *i* inside it. Events that require some attention are marked with a yellow exclamation-mark icon. Events that have failed or for some other reason require serious attention are flagged with a red stop-sign icon. Events marked with a little key are about application-level security. Figure 4.13 shows the successful loading of a component of Exchange Server's Web service, which lets users access their mailboxes and schedules with a Web browser.

You can do lots of other useful things with the Event Viewer, such as applying filters to check only some events. For now, though, we'll focus on another of the Event Viewer's great capabilities: You can use it to look at other computers in domains you have access to. In fact, although we're viewing the NT server EXCHLA01 in Figure 4.13, the Event Viewer is actually running on my NT workstation.

**FIGURE 4.13:**

The Event Viewer shows the Application Log for an NT/Exchange server.

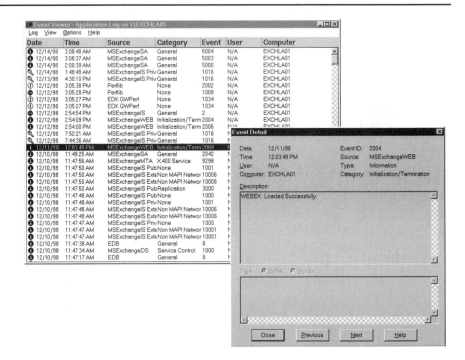

## Keep Those Icons in View

I keep shortcuts for User Manager for Domains, Server Manager, Event Viewer, and Performance Monitor on my desktop. A shortcut for Exchange Administrator also occupies a place of honor on my desktop. I use these five apps so often that it's a pain to have to navigate NT 4's Start menu to find them.

## The NT Performance Monitor

NT's Performance Monitor is a graphically oriented application that lets you monitor hundreds of activities on an NT machine. Like other NT management tools, the Performance Monitor can monitor one or more machines at the same time.

Though you'll find the Performance Monitor useful for a variety of tasks, it's especially helpful in planning and managing your Exchange Server system. Exchange Server comes with LoadSim, a planning application that simulates various user loads on an Exchange server and a supporting network. The Performance Monitor is one way to measure the impact of these loads. Load-measurement parameters for e-messaging are added to the Performance Monitor when you install LoadSim. Figure 4.14 shows the Performance Monitor and LoadSim in action.

**FIGURE 4.14:**

The Performance Monitor and LoadSim help in planning an Exchange system.

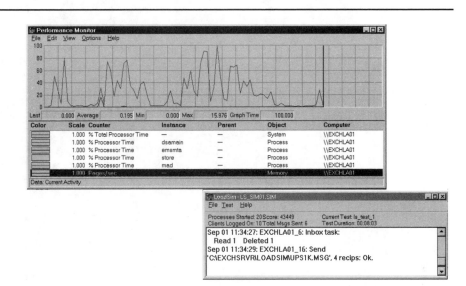

Exchange Server also adds several measurement parameters of its own to the Performance Monitor, letting you monitor certain aspects of the performance and health of an Exchange server. For the record, you'll also use the Exchange Administrator program for some monitoring tasks.

# Conclusion

In this chapter you learned why Exchange Server runs only on top of NT Server and how easy NT Server is to use. You also had a chance to become familiar with a number of NT Server components and to see how important they are to Exchange Server. This information, combined with what you've learned in previous chapters, will help you in planning and implementing your Exchange system.

# Designing an Exchange System

■ An 11-step process for designing an Exchange system

■ Entertaining detailed examples as well as abstract concepts

■ Technical details on a number of Exchange components found nowhere else in this book

**W**hether your system will be based on a single Exchange server in a single site or hundreds of Exchange servers spread out over multiple sites, you need to consider a number of design issues before implementation. This chapter presents a planning model based loosely on an 11-step process developed by Microsoft. Tracking and re-tracking through these steps will help your organization decide where it wants to go with electronic messaging and how it can get there with Exchange. I can tell you from lots of experience that the 11-step process really works. Generally, I've found I can gather any required information and generate a fairly complex first-draft plan, complete with a most convincing executive summary in a week or less.

This chapter isn't just about design, though. It also offers practical information about Exchange and how it works. Here, for example, you'll find detailed information about Exchange's seemingly endless network connection options: what they do and which networking topologies and protocols support them. Information like this is central to designing and implementing an Exchange system, and it's not found anywhere else in this book. If you're going to skip a chapter, please—not this one. This is a long chapter covering a great deal of information in detail. Just as you wouldn't try to implement a complex Exchange system in one day, you shouldn't try to plow through this chapter in one hour.

Here, then, with more than a little poetic license, is a list of Microsoft's 11 steps to designing an Exchange system:

1. Assess the needs of users in your organization.

2. Study your organization's geographical profile.

3. Assess your organization's network.

4. Establish naming conventions.

5. Select a Microsoft networking domain model.

6. Define site boundaries.

7. Plan intersite links.

8. Plan servers and internal connections to them.

9. Plan connections to other systems.

10. Validate and optimize your design.

11. Roll out the plan.

Now let's discuss each of these steps in more detail. This discussion builds upon the 11-step process presented by Microsoft in the Exchange documentation and other Microsoft publications, but it is far from a word-for-word regurgitation. Therefore, you should blame me—not Microsoft—if you encounter any problems from following the advice I give in this chapter. (Of course, if this stuff helps in any way, you should send the fruit baskets and such to *me*.)

## Exchange Design Is Iterative, Not Linear

Throughout this chapter, remember that designing an Exchange system is not a linear process, it's an iterative one. You'll find yourself coming back to each of the steps to gather new information, to reinterpret information you've already gathered, and to collect even more information based on those reinterpretations. New information will likely lead to design changes and further iterations. Even after you've fully implemented Exchange, you'll return to steps in the design process as problems arise or as your organization changes.

Within reason, the more iterations you go through, the better your final design will be. But take care not to use iteration as a route to procrastination. Whatever you do, start running Exchange—if only in a limited test environment—as soon as you can.

# Assess User Needs

Here you're interested in who needs what, when they need it, and how you'll provide it. You'll want to get a handle on the programming, software, hardware, MIS systems, systems support, and training resources that will be required to satisfy user needs.

Remember that Exchange is an e-messaging package, not just an e-mail product. Users may need specific e-messaging–enabled applications. Depending on what they have in mind, application development can be a real resource hog. Also remember that, in some cases, hardware and software may require new workstations, not just new servers.

Be prepared to give users a clear idea of what Exchange can do. You don't need to get technical with most users; just give them a view of Exchange from the end user's perspective. Take another look at the first two sections of Chapter 1 to see how you might organize your presentation.

One of the biggest mistakes most people make when implementing a system is to ignore or give only passing attention to the assessment-of-user-needs step. Knowing as much as you can about what the users require up front means you'll have an easier time during implementation.

For example, imagine that you don't know from the get-go that your organization could benefit significantly from a particular custom-programmed e-messaging–enabled application. You'd go ahead and implement Exchange as an e-mail system with only the resources such an implementation requires. You'd get your Exchange system up and it would be perking along just fine when suddenly—maybe three months later—some user comes up with this great idea for an e-messaging–enabled app.

Boink! Suddenly you have to tell management that you need a few programmers and maybe more hardware to implement this—"er, um, idea nobody thought of four or five months ago." I'll leave the rest to your imagination.

> **NOTE**      Whatever you find out in your user-needs assessment, add a fudge factor in favor of more hardware and support personnel. Exchange has so many fantastic capabilities that you can be sure your users will find all kinds of ways to challenge whatever resources you make available. Depending on your users and their ability to get away with unplanned demands for resources, fudging by as much as 25 percent is reasonable.

Suffice it to say that a user-needs assessment is the single most important part of the Exchange design process. Because it is, we'll cover it in more detail than the other 10 Exchange design steps.

## Questions to Ask

There are a number of questions you'll want to answer during your user-needs assessment. Here are the major ones:

1.  What kinds of users (for example, managers, salespeople, clerical staff, lawyers, doctors) does my organization have, and what do they think they want from the new Exchange system?

2. What sorts of e-messaging services are different groups of users likely to need (for example, e-mail, calendars and scheduling, public folders, specially designed applications)?

3. Which specially designed applications can be developed by users, and which must be developed by MIS personnel?

4. Do all users need every capability from day one, or can implementation be phased in—perhaps based on user groupings from question 1, above?

5. What sorts of demands are users (or groups of users) going to put on your Exchange servers? Much of the information in this category can be used with Exchange Server's LoadSim program to simulate expected server load and thus project server hardware and networking requirements.

   - How many users will there be per server?

   - How many sent messages will there be per user per day?

   - How many received messages will there be per user per day?

   - How frequently will users send messages:

     - to others on their server?

     - to others in their site?

     - to others at each of the other sites in your organization?

     - to others outside your organization? Be sure to break this down by the different kinds of external connections you'll have (see steps 7 and 9).

   - How often will users read messages in their mailboxes?

   - How often will users read messages in public folders?

   - How often will users move messages to personal folders stored locally and on the network?

   - How often will users move messages to public folders?

   - How big will the messages be? What percentage will be 1K in size, 2K, 4K, 10K with attachments, or 100K with attachments?

6. What level of message delivery service will users want and need? This should be stated in hours or minutes between the time a message is sent and received. You'll need to specify this for both internal and external communications.

7.  What sorts of hardware and software resources (for example, computers, operating systems, Exchange client licenses) will different groups of users need to implement Exchange on the client side?

8.  What kinds of training will be required for users or groups of users?

9.  What sorts of MIS resources will be required to support user needs?

# An Example: Assessing GerCom's User Needs

Throughout this chapter we'll use a set of examples based on GerCom, the fictitious little company I created for this book. Though the examples are not real, they are based on my own experience in implementing e-messaging systems, including Exchange. The examples are illustrative, not exhaustive; they don't cover every conceivable issue you might encounter in designing your own Exchange system.

Tracking through Microsoft's 11 design steps can be interesting, exciting—even exhilarating. It also can be as boring as watching glue dry. So I'll try to leaven my GerCom examples with a bit of humor. Hey, it's my company; I can do as I like with it, right? Anyway, as you read along, please keep in mind that I'm not making fun of a very important process—I'm just trying to keep an artificial example from becoming dried glue.

## What GerCom Users Need to Do

In our user-needs assessment, we at GerCom uncovered several user groups with different needs. Here are some highlights of our assessment.

Our top-level execs, led by little old me, are small in number but big in ideas when it comes to Exchange. We want to do e-mail and apps based on the collaborative tools built into Exchange and both Word and Excel 2000. Our controller has this great idea about building a system in Exchange-enabled Excel that lets employees act on their stock options. This system would play against our financials, which run on an Oracle database on a UNIX server. The controller would also like to use an Exchange-Excel system to collaboratively develop annual budgets. And he and I are thinking about more elaborate, custom-programmed Exchange-enabled workflow apps for things like purchasing. Again, there would be a lot of interaction with our Oracle financials.

Our vice president of human resources is one of those power users—always coming up with ideas that no one else ever thought of. She wants to put, say, the personnel manual and all the forms we use into public folders. Then employees could read the latest copy of the manual or get a form they need. Some forms, like those for our internally administered health insurance, would be full-blown Exchange or Outlook Forms Designer forms. People would select one of these while in their Exchange client, fill it in, and send it off using the default address built into the form. Forms like all those "W-something" whatsits from the IRS would just be legal electronic copies that people can fill in, print, sign, and return by—gag—our internal snail-mail system.

## Why Not the Internet?

You might be wondering why GerCom doesn't just put all its forms and such on the Internet. Well, while I'm the last one to disparage the Web, I don't believe it's the best place for all internal business processes. People work in their e-mail all the time. They usually have to start their browsers to go after Web stuff. Not only can users easily find what they need in public folders, they can easily interact with corporate staff and processes simply by filling in an e-mail–enabled form.

GerCom execs travel a lot (too much if you ask the board of directors or other employees), so we want to be able to dial in to send and pick up our Exchange messages and use those Exchange-based applications we've come up with. There are several ways to dial into an Exchange server from Microsoft's Exchange client, using either the company's Remote Access Server or the Internet. However, the Exchange client is a bit of a disk- and RAM-resource hog for less well-endowed portable PCs. So for our road warriors, we're strongly considering standardizing on the Internet-based IMAP4 client that comes as part of Microsoft's Outlook 2000 or Internet Explorer 5 Outlook Express application. We'll also take advantage of the Web browser–based access to Exchange server that's been around since Exchange 5.

We execs want our clerical staff to do e-mail and to be able to create forms with Outlook Forms Designer. My secretary came up with a great idea for using an e-mailed form to collect personal information about employees. No, we're not one of those super-snooper kind of companies; we just like to recognize things like spouses' and kids' birthdays and such. The clerical staff also came up with the idea of using Microsoft Outlook's e-messaging–enabled Calendar capabilities to do group scheduling and room reservations. They hate the combination of phone tag and written messages now used to set up meetings.

Our systems people expect the executive suite to be a heavy user of Exchange. I haven't seen all the numbers they've come up with from LoadSim yet, but rumor is they're considering giving us our own Exchange server. Since I know the boss intimately, I'm sure I can get him to sign off on that one.

The salespeople have some big ideas, too. They want in-office and remote e-mail like the top execs, but they also want to use Exchange for customer ordering and to keep copies of our price lists stored on customers' computers automatically updated. We're still not quite sure how we'll do it—heck, this is only Chapter 5—but we do know we'll need some way of linking to those customers. The sales staff also wants to build an e-messaging–based system in which customers can place orders and pay for purchases. That would involve our Oracle-based ordering and payables systems. As president, I like that one, especially the payment part.

GerCom's marketing folks mainly want e-mail so they can send press releases to all those magazine editors who would rather never see another press release. We showed them some of the other stuff you can do with Exchange, but they couldn't seem to come up with any apps. So we told them that unless they could make a good argument for other apps over the next few weeks, they'd have to live with only e-mail for a while. They seem happy.

The manufacturing people are really excited about Exchange. I never mentioned it, but GerCom makes Enter keys—you know, the little key on your computer keyboard marked ↵. (Hey, it's a really specialized world out there.) Anyway, the manufacturing folks figure Exchange will give them a good way to link their production plans and inventory to the sales department's customer ordering system. Manufacturing wants to be able to send customers automatic updates on shipping dates. A copy will go to sales, of course. Manufacturing figures this will both keep customers happy and keep our aggressive salespeople out of their faces. We accepted this proposal, though we know it's going to take some custom programming involving our Oracle data. Of course, manufacturing also wants in-house e-mail.

For some reason, GerCom's engineering department hasn't been able to come up with a use for Exchange other than in-office e-mail. Well, what do you expect from a bunch of people who spend most of their working hours trying to improve the Enter key?

The MIS department wants in-house and remote e-mail, and it has a bunch of ideas of its own about Exchange. For example, it's tired of printing and routing all those Oracle reports most people ignore. MIS wants to develop an app that downloads electronic copies of those reports to the NT environment, puts them into specific Exchange public folders, and then sends out an electronic form telling recipients that the latest report has arrived.

Why a form and not a message? There'll be a field on the form where recipients can indicate that they don't need the report anymore. The form will be programmed to automatically remove those recipients who don't want the report from its Exchange distribution list. There'll also be a place to put ideas about changing the report or new reports. Pretty neat. The MIS people have not only eliminated a lot of increasingly expensive paper, they've also come up with a way to keep the reporting process alive and responsive to changing needs.

## Supporting GerCom's User Needs

Whew! Our users have a lot of great ideas. Now we should begin laying out some specific things we'll need to support their needs. We won't go into detail on things like network connections, server hardware needs, or systems support personnel; those come later. For now, we just need to cover things like acceptable message delivery performance, end-user support personnel, and end-user hardware.

A lot of the apps we're planning are going to be pretty critical to GerCom's bottom line. We've decided we want messages to move between our offices and to our trading partners at a good speed—within ten minutes, if at all possible.

We already know it'll take about six new MIS people just to serve the needs of our 2,500 employees. Two of these will be involved in initial training and then in supporting users who want to develop their own apps. The other four will focus on programming custom apps. We've got plenty of space for these new folks, so we won't have any serious added costs on that front. We will, however, have to buy these new employees some hefty hardware. And we'll have to outfit our training rooms with beefier systems.

We've also decided to hire a corporate Exchange manager who will report to the director of MIS. The six people I mentioned above will report to the Exchange manager, along with any other Exchange-related personnel we add.

We're also trying to decide what to do about user workstations. Someone suggested we cancel all executive travel to pay for new machines for everyone. (I can't imagine where they got that idea.) We probably won't do that, but I'm working with the controller to try to figure out how we can upgrade everyone who needs a new computer (about 75 percent of our employees) in the next year and a half. It will involve lots of bucks, but GerCom's going to gain a great deal from this system, and the Enter key business is really hot right now. That year-and-a-half time frame, by the way, ties in closely with our rollout plans, which you'll read about at the end of this chapter. Are you beginning to see why I included the sidebar "Exchange Design Is Iterative, Not Linear" in this chapter?

I'm very happy with GerCom's needs assessment. Since we started the process, I've seen the LoadSim numbers for the whole organization. Though they're just rough estimates, they look pretty good; we can refine them later. We're off to a good start.

# Study Your Organization's Geographical Profile

You need a list of all the geographical units in your organization. Here you should think not only in terms of cities, states, and countries but also in-city and even in-building locations. Start at the top and work your way down. At this point, diagrams are important. Draw maps and building layouts.

This is the time to gather information on the workstations and servers you've got in each location. You'll want to know how many run each of the different kinds of operating systems in your organization. Operating systems you should watch for are Windows NT Workstation and Server; Novell NetWare 3.x and 4.x Servers and NetWare IPX/SPX workstations; Banyan VINES servers and workstations; Windows 95/98; Windows 3.1x; MS-DOS; Apple Macintosh; UNIX workstations by type of operating system; and workstations used remotely. If you've got hardware and software inventories for these machines, your job will be a lot easier. If you're looking for an automatic inventorying system, check out Microsoft's Systems Management Server. Not only can you use it to gather workstation and server hardware information automatically, it can help you install Exchange clients throughout your organization. You can use all the information you collect about workstations and servers to determine who's ready for Exchange and who isn't and how many Exchange client licenses you'll have to buy.

As you gather information in other steps, begin to look at it in the context of your geographical profile. For example, you'll want to meld geographical information with what you've found out about user needs and user groupings.

## More on User Workstations

"Yes, I know that our users are working on ancient desktop computer systems. But we just don't have the money to buy them what they really need." I wish I had a dollar for every time I've heard that one; why, I'd be able to buy decent systems for most of those poor users. I've always wondered why companies that have money to burn on fancy cars and trips to expensive and often useless meetings and employee seminars can't seem to find the two or three thousand bucks it takes to upgrade a user's workstation.

I limped along for quite some time on a substandard 200MHz Pentium II workstation with 64MB of memory. Then I moved up to a 500MHz dual Pentium II processor and 512MB of RAM. Yes, 512MB of RAM. When I ran NT on my old, underpowered sleepwalker, it was all I could do to keep my word processor, a spreadsheet, and my e-mail software open at the same time. If I opened anything else, the machine started thrashing around so much between RAM and virtual memory that it slowed to a nearly useless crawl.

With my new system, I can run word processing programs, spreadsheet programs, and Exchange together without wasting precious time to switch between them. And I still have plenty of horsepower left for all those tasks I used to do with paper because I couldn't bring up the applications fast enough when I needed them. At will, I can now simultaneously open (or keep open) such apps as an accounting package and Microsoft Word, Excel, Project, Outlook, and PowerPoint. With all that computer power, I'm also no longer reluctant to run other key programs—say, Internet Web browsers or NT Control Panel applets—at the drop of a hat.

Bottom line: I've had my new system for less than a year; by my estimates, the productivity increase I've experienced in that time has already paid back the cost of the system's purchase.

Maybe all of your users don't need a dual 500MHz Pentium system with NT and 512MB of RAM. However, as you start assessing user needs, don't let the dismal state of your organization's stable of workstations stop you and your users from reaching for the stars as you think about potential applications for Exchange. Who knows—you just might come up with a next-generation business-computing model for your organization. And that might get you a corporate car or a trip to Hawaii for that conference on the role of MS-DOS and the 486 PC in modern corporate computing.

*continued on next page*

You'll notice I talk here about my NT desktop system, not my Windows 95 or 98 system. I strongly urge you to consider starting with or moving to NT Workstation for desktop business computing. Sure it doesn't always let you use some of the neat pieces of hardware that no home should be without, e.g., some digital scanner or camera products. But, business is about platform stability, not trivial fun and games. If you need that other stuff, run one or two 95 or 98 machines to support it.

## An Example: GerCom's Geographical Profile

As you can see in Figure 5.1, GerCom has grown by leaps and bounds since earlier chapters. It now has offices in Chicago and New York City—Figure 5.2 shows just how much we've grown. Hey, we've got two buildings in the "City of the Broad Shoulders." Now aren't you sorry you didn't buy stock when you had a chance?

GerCom's top executive staff, marketing, and most of MIS are in Los Angeles; sales has people in all three cities. Manufacturing and engineering are in Chicago, the Enter key capital of the world. We've got 1,500 people in LA, 800 in Chicago, and 200 in New York.

All but two of our network servers run NetWare 4.x. The operating system on the two maverick servers, which support our Oracle database, is Sun Solaris (UNIX). We lucked out when it comes to user workstation types and operating systems: Except for five workstations, they're all Intel-based, almost all run Windows, and all but a few are linked to our NetWare servers using either Novell's ODI or VLM IPX/SPX stack.

We have five Windows NT workstations, and three are in the executive suite. They belong to me, our controller, and our head of human resources. At my insistence, MIS started learning NT about a year ago. Two of our midlevel MIS staff use NT workstations for everything they do. All five workstations are linked to our Novell servers using NT's built-in IPX/SPX networking capabilities.

Because we're a young company, most workstations are Pentium-based or better, though a lot of the Pentium systems have only 16MB of memory. Still, as I noted in the sidebar "More on User Workstations" in this chapter, we've got a lot of upgrading to do before we can fully implement Exchange.

**FIGURE 5.1:**

GerCom, an Enter key manufacturer with a national presence

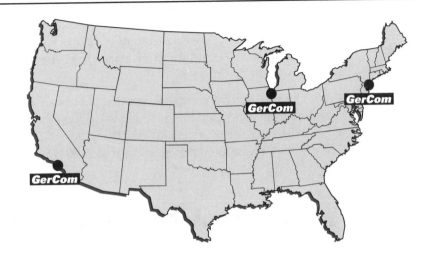

**FIGURE 5.2:**

Two—count 'em, two—locations in Chicago

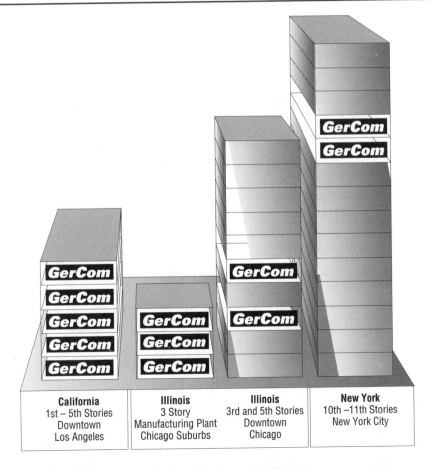

| **California** | **Illinois** | **Illinois** | **New York** |
|---|---|---|---|
| 1st – 5th Stories | 3 Story | 3rd and 5th Stories | 10th –11th Stories |
| Downtown | Manufacturing Plant | Downtown | New York City |
| Los Angeles | Chicago Suburbs | Chicago | |

Our year–to–year-and-a-half goal is to move all our users from Windows 95/98 to NT workstation. NT Workstation is a real business operating system without the system-destabilizing weaknesses of Windows 95/98. We're seeing our competition moving in that direction and we need to go there too. Yes, there is competition in the Enter key business.

With information from the first iteration of our user-needs and geographical assessments in hand, GerCom's MIS folks are already beginning to think about who's where, and how to structure the company's NT and Exchange hierarchy. They've also started lobbying me and our controller for user workstation upgrades.

# Assess Your Organization's Network

In this step, you just want to know what your network looks like now. This isn't the place to get into what kinds of networking you'll need; that comes later. You need to answer four key questions here: What's connected to what, and how? (If you're counting, that's two questions.) How much bandwidth have we got on each network? And, finally, how reliable are our networks?

## What's Connected to What, and How?

Generally, in answering the first question, you should start at the top of your organization and work down to the domain or server level. For each link, name the physical connection, the networking topology, and the networking protocols running on the connection. For example, physical connection = local hardwire, networking topology = Ethernet, networking protocols = IPX/SPX, TCP/IP, SNA. This information, especially when combined with the information you've collected in steps 1 and 2, will prove invaluable as you start to plan for the Exchange connectivity you'll need.

In looking at your organization's network, don't forget about connections to the outside world. Do you have connections to the Internet, to X.400 messaging systems, to trading partners? If you've got such connections, pay particular attention to existing naming conventions. They may limit your choices in naming the key entities in the Exchange hierarchy.

# How Much Bandwidth Have We Got on Each Network?

To assess the bandwidth on each of your networks, you'll need some help from a network monitoring tool. If your networks are NT-based, you can try using NT's Performance Monitor to get a handle on traffic. Microsoft's Systems Management Server has some pretty good network monitoring capabilities, too. For NetWare systems, try one of the many software-based network traffic monitors out there. A lot of modern network hubs, switches, and such also come with excellent network monitoring software. If you're flush with cash, go for a hardware-based monitor, such as Network General's Sniffer.

What you want here is a chart that tells you, on average, how much of a network's bandwidth is available during each of the 24 hours in a day. You'll have to take several samples to get reliable data, but it's worth it. A warning light should go on in your head if you're already using more than, say, 40 percent of the available bandwidth on any network during daytime hours and you're not already running a heavy-duty messaging system like Exchange. With that kind of scenario, you just might have to make some changes in the network before installing Exchange. We'll talk about those changes later; for now, be sure to collect this data on available bandwidth and incorporate it into your organizational maps.

# How Reliable Are Our Networks?

Having a reliable network is an important issue. More and more in corporate America, there is strong pressure to centralize network servers. Centralization makes good economic sense. If all network servers are in one place, one set of staff can support and monitor them, assuring 7-day-a-week, 24-hour-a-day uptime.

That's quite true. However, 7-day × 24-hour server availability is useless if the networks people use to get to the servers are unreliable. I've seen this little scenario play itself out in several organizations: centralize the servers, the network fails, users can't get to their now mission-critical e-mail and other data, responsible IS planners are roundly criticized, lower-level IS personnel are even more heavily criticized or fired. Grrr!

Bottom line: Don't make your users work on unreliable networks. If your networks can't come close to matching the reliability of your servers, put the servers closer to their users. The little extra it costs to manage decentralized servers is worth the access insurance it buys. Sure, get those networks up to par, but don't risk your Exchange implementation on centralized servers before the reliable network is in place to support them.

## An Example: GerCom's Networks

Figure 5.3 shows the GerCom map with some higher-level connectivity information added. In Los Angeles, GerCom has a dedicated T1 TCP/IP link to the Internet. By the way, the registered Internet domain name is "bgerber.com." GerCom's four office buildings are connected in serial fashion through NetWare servers, using a networking topology consisting of non-dedicated, asynchronous dial-up lines and the Point-to-Point Protocol (PPP). We run both IPX/SPX and TCP/IP on the dial-up network.

**FIGURE 5.3:**

GerCom's existing cross-country links

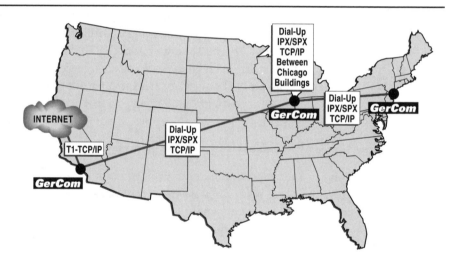

You can see in Figure 5.4 that NetWare servers and user workstations in all GerCom buildings are linked by Ethernet and IPX/SPX. We also run TCP/IP to support workstation connections to our Sun UNIX servers, where e-mail and our Oracle databases reside.

**FIGURE 5.4:**

GerCom's existing
in-building networks

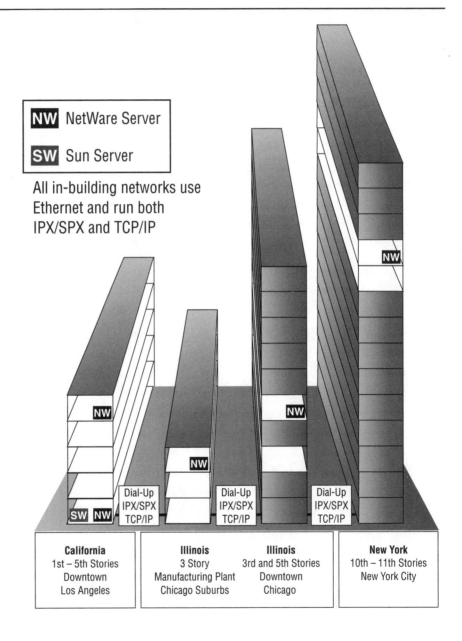

NW  NetWare Server

SW  Sun Server

All in-building networks use
Ethernet and run both
IPX/SPX and TCP/IP

Dial-Up
IPX/SPX
TCP/IP

Dial-Up
IPX/SPX
TCP/IP

Dial-Up
IPX/SPX
TCP/IP

| **California** | **Illinois** | **Illinois** | **New York** |
|---|---|---|---|
| 1st – 5th Stories | 3 Story | 3rd and 5th Stories | 10th – 11th Stories |
| Downtown | Manufacturing Plant | Downtown | New York City |
| Los Angeles | Chicago Suburbs | Chicago | |

# Establish Naming Conventions

It's time to set some criteria for naming the four key elements in your Exchange hierarchy: the organization, sites, servers, and recipients. Your goal here is to establish a logical and consistent set of naming conventions that fit in well with your real-world organizational structure and culture.

As I pointed out in Chapter 2, the choices you make for Exchange organization- and site-naming conventions—at least at the outset—influence both the ease with which you'll be able to manage your Exchange system and the default e-messaging addresses assigned to users. It's true that, at any time, you can change your naming conventions and even the names you've assigned to specific instances of any of the four elements in your Exchange hierarchy. Some of these changes are easy to make, while others are much more difficult. For example, to change your organization or site name, you must reinstall Exchange Server. But why put yourself in the position of having to make a bunch of midcourse corrections? Do your best to get things right on take-off.

## Naming the Organization, Sites, and Servers

Here's one easy and usually safe naming convention you can use:

- Organization = master company name

- Site = a geographical location

- Server = departmental names

Names for organizations and sites can be up to 64 characters long, but I'd suggest keeping them to around 10 characters out of respect for people at "foreign" sites who may have to type in these names as part of a recipient's e-messaging address. Server names are limited to a maximum of 15 characters.

For most names, almost any character is permitted. However, for organization, site, and server names I strongly suggest you use only the 26 upper- and lower-case letters of the alphabet and the numerals 0 through 9. Don't use spaces, underscores, or any accented letters.

If you don't follow this convention, I guarantee that sometime, somewhere, you'll get into trouble. For example, I named a site "LA_HOME" in an early test implementation of Exchange. The underscore became a question mark when the site name was used to construct X.400 addresses. The question mark was technically okay, but it threw users who sometimes had to give their address with an underscore and sometimes with a question mark, depending on the type of address it was. Bottom line: Don't get fancy when naming organizations, sites, and servers.

## Naming Recipient Mailboxes

You'll also need some criteria for naming mailboxes. There are four key names for each Exchange mailbox: the first name, the last name, the display name, and the alias name. Exchange administrators create and modify these names in the Exchange Administrator program. You enter the first and last names, and by default, Exchange constructs the display names and alias names from the first and last names. You can change the rules for constructing default display names and alias names, and you can also alter these manually once they've been created. In Figure 5.5 you can see the different names for my Exchange mailbox.

**FIGURE 5.5:**

Exchange creates display and alias mailbox names using first and last names.

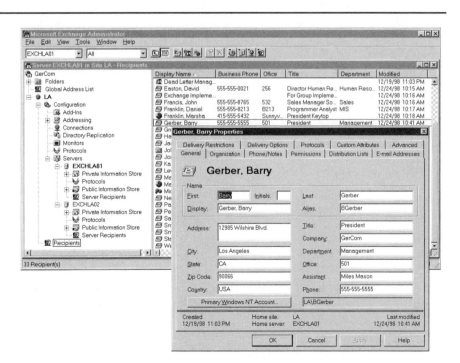

## Display Names

The Exchange client global address book shows the display name for each mailbox (see Figure 5.6). You'll need to decide on a convention for display names. You've got two basic options: first-name-space-last-name (John Smith) or last-name-comma-space-first-name (Smith, John). You can also set up custom defaults. You can change the defaults at any time, but the change applies only to newly created mailboxes. Fortunately, there's a fairly easy way to automatically change the display names of old mailboxes as well. See the sections in Chapter 17 on importing from and exporting to the Exchange directory.

Display names can be up to 256 characters long. Display names are only a convenience—they're not a part of the mailbox's e-message address. They are, however, the way in which Exchange users find the people they want to communicate with—so don't scrimp when setting them up. You might even want to include department names and/or titles in display names so users aren't faced with ambiguous selections, as they might be if they encountered a list of 25 recipients named John Smith.

Practically speaking, display name lengths should be limited only by your users' willingness to read through lots of stuff to find the mailbox they're looking for.

**FIGURE 5.6:**

The Exchange client global address book shows each mailbox's display name.

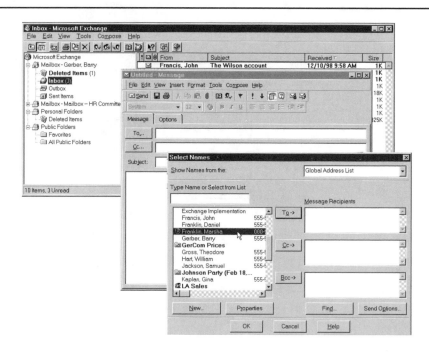

Full-blown religious arguments have sprung up around the metaphysics of display name conventions. I'll leave the decision to you (though, as you'll see, I do have my own preference).

## Alias Names

For some messaging systems, the user's mailbox is identified by an alias name, which is part of the mailbox's address. Either Exchange itself or the gateway for the foreign mail system constructs an address using the alias. For other messaging systems the mailbox name is constructed from other information. Figure 5.7 shows the four addresses that Exchange built for me for cc:Mail, Microsoft Mail for PC Networks, the Internet, and X.400. My MS Mail and Internet addresses use the alias "bgerber". cc:Mail and X.400 addresses do not use the alias. Rather, they use the full first and last name attributes of the user.

Aliases can be up to 64 characters long. That's too long, since some people in foreign messaging systems will have to type in the alias as part of an e-messaging address. Try to keep aliases short—10 characters is long enough.

**FIGURE 5.7:**

Exchange Server uses mailbox alias or the first and last names to construct e-mail addresses.

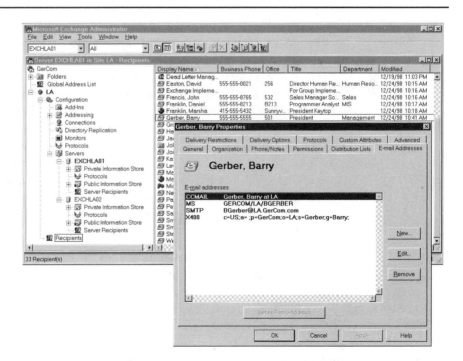

For some foreign messaging system addressing schemes, Exchange must remove illegal characters and shorten the alias to meet maximum character-length requirements. Remember my example about a site "LA_HOME"? It can be just as bad with aliases. Do all you can to ensure that aliases are constructed using less-esoteric characters.

As with display names, you can set default rules for the aliases that Exchange assigns newly created users. There are several options for these defaults, including full-first-name-first-letter-of-last-name (JohnS) and first-letter-of-first-name-full-last-name (JSmith).

Alias naming conventions are a religious issue, too, so you'll get no recommendations from me.

## An Example: GerCom's Naming Conventions

GerCom chose to follow the simple guidelines listed above for naming its organization and sites. The organization name is "GerCom." Site naming is based on geography (cities): "LA," "NY," and "Chicago."

We did run into one problem in selecting an organization name: You'll remember from the GerCom network assessment that our registered Internet domain name is "bgerber.com." My current Internet address for GerCom is bgerber@bgerber.com. (Don't try to send anything to that address; remember that all this GerCom stuff is fake.) Given the name I chose for my organization (*GerCom*), the Internet address that Exchange will construct for me by default will be bgerber@LA.gercom.com. Take another look at Figure 5.7, if you don't believe me. We could have used "BGerber" for our Exchange organization name, but we like "GerCom" too much. No accounting for taste. We also could have tinkered with DNS MX records on the UNIX side to redirect mail sent to bgerber.com over to gercom.com, but since our Internet mail flow is limited right now, we decided to go whole hog and de-register the name bgerber.com and instead register gercom.com as our Internet domain name.

We nonconformists at GerCom didn't follow the guidelines for server naming, though. As I mentioned in Chapter 2, rather than create separate departmental servers at each site, my MIS department and I prefer to create one Exchange server, fill it up with users, and then set up a new one. This is a nice approach for smaller organizations that don't want to invest in lots of hardware at the outset. Many large organizations also like this approach, since there's often not much to be gained in identifying different Exchange servers with different departmental units.

GerCom servers get names based on this convention: EXCH + *SITE* + *an order-ing number.* The first server in the site LA is EXCHLA01, the second is EXCHLA02, and so on.

GerCom display names use the last-name-comma-space-first-name (Smith, John) convention. Remember that the display name is what people see when they go looking for a mailbox in the Exchange client. I just think it's easier to find people by their last names (all the Smiths) rather than by their first names (all the Johns). For similar reasons, alias naming at GerCom is based on the first-letter-of-first-name-full-last-name (JSmith) convention. Since Exchange and NT security are so tightly integrated, we'll use the same first-letter-of-first-name-full-last-name (JSmith) convention for NT usernames. I should note that I had no trouble imposing these conventions on my very compliant and, it should be noted, imaginary MIS department.

# Select a Microsoft Networking Domain Model

You've got four networking domain models to choose from. Which is right for your organization? Here you should think about both today and tomorrow, because it's not easy to change a domain model. Moving to a new model often involves changing server and domain names and moving users and resources to different or new domains, and neither of these is pleasant to do with NT. As with Exchange naming conventions, the best way is to get it right the first time.

Go back to Chapter 4 and take a look at the section on the four domain models. Decide how your organization is structured and pick the model that best fits that structure.

## An Example: The GerCom Domain Model

At GerCom we've decided on the multiple–master domain model. Look how much we've grown in five chapters: Though we have only 2,500 employees now, we're already in three cities. We're gonna be *big,* and we need to think seriously about exceeding those users-per-domain limits I discussed in Chapter 4.

Figure 5.8 shows how we'll structure the domains. We'll have a master domain for each city, as well as a single-resource domain in each of the four buildings we now occupy. Right now only the Chicago master domain will be responsible for multiple-resource domains—one for each of our two Chicago buildings. As we add cities we'll add master domains and appropriate resource domains. As we add buildings in cities we'll add resource domains.

**FIGURE 5.8:**

GerCom's implementation of the multiple–master domain model

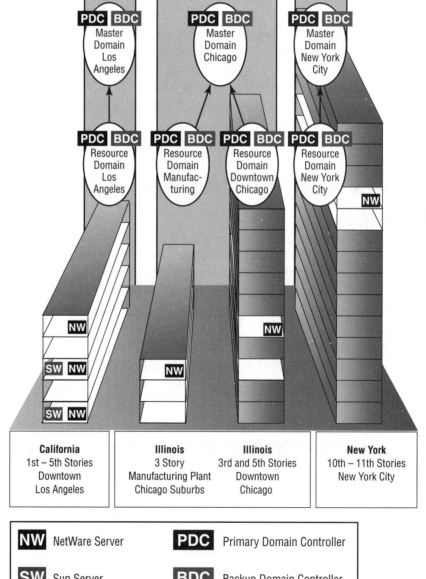

GerCom doesn't have a lot of NT expertise in-house. (I'm probably the most knowledgeable employee right now.) We're planning to hire an NT networking guru right away, and once that person is in place we'll determine how many more NT support staffers we'll need. With the ability to remotely manage NT, we should be able to stay light on the NT support side, at least until we get more deeply into programming Exchange-enabled custom applications. For now, the NT people will report to the Exchange manager we decided on in step 1. That's kind of unusual, but for now we primarily need NT support staff to implement Exchange.

# Define Site Boundaries

When defining site boundaries you have to remember a couple of things. First, Exchange sites and Microsoft network domains are related. Second, all the Exchange servers in a site must have certain networking capabilities.

## Exchange Sites and Domains

One domain may include one or more sites. In addition, one or more Exchange sites can cross two or more networking domains (see Figure 5.9). If you want your Exchange system to be easy to administer and manage, I strongly suggest you stay away from multiple sites in a domain and sites that cross multiple domains. Stick with the one-site, one-domain model.

All of the Exchange servers and users in a site must be able to communicate freely, without issuing passwords each time they need to access each other. As I noted in Chapter 4, Exchange server freedom of speech is tightly linked to domain security.

**FIGURE 5.9:**

The three ways that Microsoft networking domains and Exchange Server sites can relate to each other

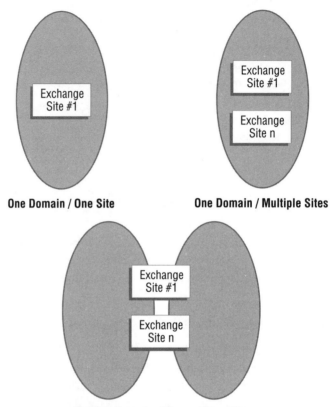

One Domain / One Site

One Domain / Multiple Sites

Multiple Domains / One or More Sites

## Required Networking Capabilities

With the right security in place, the moment an Exchange server starts running it automatically begins communicating with other Exchange servers in its site. You don't have to do a thing to start these communications—they just happen. The first time this happens, you'll literally jump for joy, especially if you're used to those old fashioned e-mail systems like Microsoft Mail for PCs with all their gizmo gateways, dirsync machines, and such.

When communicating with each other, Exchange servers in a site automatically swap user messages and frequently update one another's directory information. Optionally, they can also cross-replicate all or part of their public folders. As noted in Chapter 3, intrasite cross-server directory replication not only helps keep directories up to date on all Exchange servers, but it also brings a degree of fault tolerance to Exchange. As long as you have one good copy of the directory on one Exchange server, the others can reconstruct a good portion of their directories from it. Don't let this lull you into thinking you don't need to do regular backups. There is some server-specific information in each server's directory that can only be protected with a backup. It can't be reconstructed from the copies of the directory on other servers.

Frequent intrasite directory replication increases network traffic a bit. Also, since users in a site often have some affinity for each other, you can usually expect higher user messaging and folder replication traffic between servers in one site than between servers in different sites.

All of this intrasite interserver network traffic requires that Exchange servers in a site be connected by a high-bandwidth dedicated network, but high bandwidth isn't absolute. For example, from Exchange's perspective, a 155Mb/sec ATM link isn't high-bandwidth if you're eating up 154.9Mb/sec sending continuous streams of video images. There are no hard and fast rules here, but any physical network that can provide Exchange with 512kbps of bandwidth most of the time should be adequate. Lower bandwidths can work in cases where directories change very little and public folder replication is nonexistent or kept at a bare minimum. Physical networks capable of delivering at least this kind of dedicated bandwidth include (in increasing bandwidth availability) faster Frame Relay and satellite, full T1, microwave, DSL, T3, Ethernet, Token Ring, Fast Ethernet, FDDI, ATM, and SONET.

## Consider DSL

Digital Subscriber Line (DSL) networking is finally available in many locales in the United States. DSL is a variable bandwidth networking topology. Bandwidth ranges from as little as 64kbps through T1. Compared to most other higher bandwidth technologies, DSL is inexpensive. In the real world, I currently pay $199 per month for a 384kbps always-on DSL Internet link. This link supports my Exchange Server connection to Internet mail as well as a lot of other Internet-based functionality, like an FTP service, a Web server, and a time sync service. As we'll see in Chapter 15, always-on links have distinct advantages when you're connecting Exchange Server to the Internet using the Internet Mail Service.

Intrasite communications between servers is based on the remote procedure calls (RPCs) discussed in Chapter 4. Networks must run networking protocols that support the RPCs; these include IPX/SPX, NetBEUI, TCP/IP, SNA, NetBIOS, Windows Sockets, and Named Pipes. For the best overall performance, I've found TCP/IP is generally the best option, though NetBEUI/NetBIOS can be quite impressive in smaller, non-routed nets.

A good deal of the information that moves between Exchange servers in a site is transmitted in Exchange's native MAPI-based format. As you'll see later, when information leaves an Exchange site it isn't always possible to transmit it in MAPI format.

## An Example: GerCom's Site Boundaries

As you'll remember from its geographical assessment, GerCom is located in three cities: Los Angeles, Chicago, and New York. It has more than two physical locations only in Chicago. Though you already know this from GerCom's site-naming conventions, the company will have Exchange sites in each city.

Except in Chicago, our existing Ethernet-TCP/IP-IPX/SPX networks are all we need for intrasite connectivity. We'll have to add a higher-bandwidth connection between our two buildings in Chicago, and we're planning to use a T1 connection for that. Figure 5.10 shows the GerCom building diagram with this new site boundary information imposed on it.

We plan to station an Exchange administrator at each GerCom site. These three MIS employees will be responsible for Exchange installation, testing, implementation, and management. They'll also provide NT system management backup. To do these things, we feel that the three employees must be on-site. We think that one person at each site will be enough, but we're open to adding people if more are needed. The Exchange administrators will report to GerCom's new corporate Exchange manager, mentioned in step 1.

With Exchange Server's great remote management capabilities, the Exchange administrators in each city will be able to help out at other sites when needed without leaving their offices. And when we add administrators, they won't have to be assigned to a specific site—they can remotely go wherever their Exchange administrative skills are required.

**FIGURE 5.10:**

GerCom's site boundaries

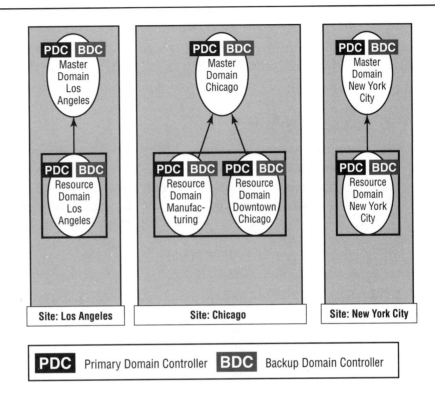

The four end-user–oriented Exchange training and app-development staffers mentioned in step 1 will be distributed among the sites as well. Two will be in Los Angeles, one in Chicago, and one in New York. In addition to their main responsibilities, these folks will also back up the Exchange site administrators. Because of the remote management capabilities built into NT Server and Exchange Server, the backup function won't require full knowledge of NT or Exchange Server. These folks will mainly be ready to help when a local hand is physically required.

# Plan Intersite Links

As you'll remember from Chapter 3, you link sites by running one or more Exchange connectors on Exchange servers in each site. There's no need for each Exchange server in a site to run its own connectors; one Exchange server can serve all the intersite needs of all Exchange servers in a site. However, if a site has two or more Exchange servers, it often makes sense to run site connectors on multiple servers. This improves performance and, if you use different network links for each connector, allows for redundant links between sites. Figure 5.11 should make this a bit clearer.

## Site Link Options

In Chapter 3, I noted that you can connect sites either *directly* or *indirectly.* Direct connections are point-to-point between servers; indirect links pass through foreign e-messaging systems. Both direct and indirect connections use messages to move user communications and directory and public folder replication information between Exchange servers in different sites. With direct connections the servers talk directly to each other. With indirect connections the servers communicate by sending messages through a mediating system, such as a public X.400 service or the Internet.

**FIGURE 5.11:**

Making the Exchange inter-site connection

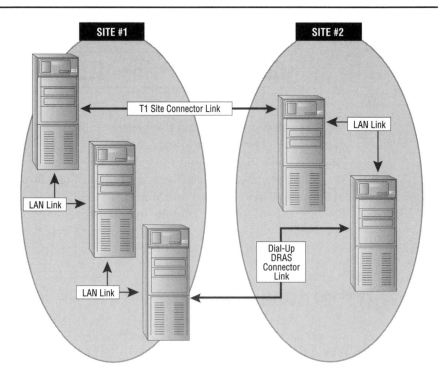

---

**NOTE**    I use the terms *connection* and *link* to refer to two very different things. In the paragraph above, they refer to the way servers *communicate* with each other, be it directly or indirectly. In other places in this book, *connection* and *link* refer to actual *physical and protocol-level networking options*, such as Ethernet, TCP/IP, and X.400. I tried without success to find another word to modify the terms *direct* and *indirect*.

---

When connecting Exchange sites, you get to choose between four connector options:

- Site Connector (direct link only)
- X.400 Connector (direct and indirect links)
- Dynamic RAS Connector (direct link only)
- Internet Mail Service (direct and indirect links)

Let's look at each of these in more detail.

## The Site Connector

Of all the Exchange connectors, the Site Connector is the fastest and simplest to set up and manage. And of all the ways to link sites, the Site Connector is most similar to the automatic, built-in links between Exchange servers in the same site. It moves messages and directory and folder replication information between Exchange sites using the Open Systems Foundation (OSF) remote procedure calls. The only difference is that the Site Connector uses standard messages for all three functions, while Exchange servers within a site perform directory replication more directly.

The Site Connector requires a continuous network. It doesn't support dial-up links, and it's best suited to Exchange intersite connections with heavy user loads and directory and public folder replication message duties. If you already have a wide area network with adequate bandwidth in place, the Site Connector can be especially attractive, because you don't need to add any networking infrastructure to support the connector. Of course, if you're expecting heavy cross-site network loads, you'll need high-bandwidth network connections like those provided by topologies such as T1, Ethernet, Token Ring, T3, Fast Ethernet, FDDI, ATM, and SONET. When you begin considering the higher-capacity networking topologies listed here to link sites, you might want to go one step further and merge the sites to take advantage of Exchange Server's higher performance intrasite communications.

## The X.400 Connector

When used for direct site links, the X.400 Connector works a lot like the Site Connector. It sends and receives user communications and directory and public folder replication information as messages. It doesn't use RPCs, however. The X.400 Connector can move messages between sites in X.400 format or, like the Site Connector, in native MAPI format. If you choose to use the X.400 format, the messages will have to be translated into X.400 before they leave the originating site and then translated back into MAPI after arriving at the receiving site.

The X.400 Connector runs on top of a special physical transport stack that supports TCP/IP, OSI TP0 (X.25), and OSI TP4/CLNP networking protocols. If you're into the OSI world, these protocols will be familiar to you. If not, you can find info on them in any of a number of fine books on OSI-based networking. Like the Site Connector, in direct link mode the X.400 Connector can handle heavy intersite loads given adequate bandwidth.

The X.400 Connector is a bit slower than the Site Connector, both because it has to translate to and from X.400 format when that format is used for intersite communications, and because there's some networking overhead involved in X.400 communications. However, the X.400 Connector gives you more control than the Site Connector over a site link and what passes over it. For example, you can schedule X.400 site connections, restrict the message size, and specify which sites you'll accept messages from. The Site Connector doesn't support restrictions of this sort. The X.400 Connector allows direct server-to-server links over dial-up lines using X.25, for example. The Site Connector doesn't support dial-up links.

You can also use the X.400 Connector for indirect Exchange site links. In this case you connect each Exchange site to a public X.400 provider's network. The sites can be connected to the same provider network or to different ones. Of course, if different providers are used, they must be able to communicate with each other. You can use any of the networking protocols noted above to make these connections.

Cost considerations lead most organizations to opt for lower, sub–local area network bandwidth links to public X.400 providers. That's fine, but it means that indirect site links should be used mostly for low-traffic site connections and to provide redundant links for sites already connected by higher-bandwidth direct links.

### The Dynamic RAS Connector

Unlike the Site Connector and like the X.400 Connector, the Dynamic RAS Connector (DRASC) lets you link sites that don't have full-time networks between them. You can use the DRASC for ad hoc asynchronous links using voice, X.25, and ISDN physical connections. Exchange servers talk directly to each other over the DRASC, so DRASC connections support RPCs. As should be obvious from its name, the DRASC is based on NT's RAS (Remote Access Server), which I talked about in the last chapter. You'll remember that RAS provides NetBEUI, TCP/IP, or IPX/SPX protocol support on top of PPP.

With the DRASC you get many of the controls that the X.400 Connector delivers without all the complexities of X.400. Exchange data is always moved in native MAPI format, though you won't see any great speed advantage since you're connecting at ISDN bandwidths at best. So, as with low-bandwidth, indirect X.400 site links, use the DRASC for low-traffic or redundant links.

### The Internet Mail Service

The Internet Mail Service lets you link sites directly and indirectly. I won't spend a lot of time on these here; each gets coverage in later chapters. For now, suffice it to say that the caveats about low-speed links also apply to the use of these two connectors.

## An Example: GerCom's Intersite Connections

So how about GerCom? What is that paragon of Enter key manufacturers going to do to connect its three sites? Well, as president I've had to swallow hard a couple of times, but we're going to pop for T1 links between our three sites and use Site Connectors. The main reason for this decision is the amount of cross-site traffic we expect our neat but demanding applications to generate in the form of public folder replication and cross-site movement of larger messages. Figure 5.12 shows the GerCom building diagram with our planned intersite connections in place.

Those T1 lines aren't going to be cheap, but we have high hopes that Exchange will revolutionize the way we do business. As you'll see later in this chapter, we're also planning to do some indirect links. These will add important redundancy to our Exchange network.

**FIGURE 5.12:**

GerCom's intersite
connections

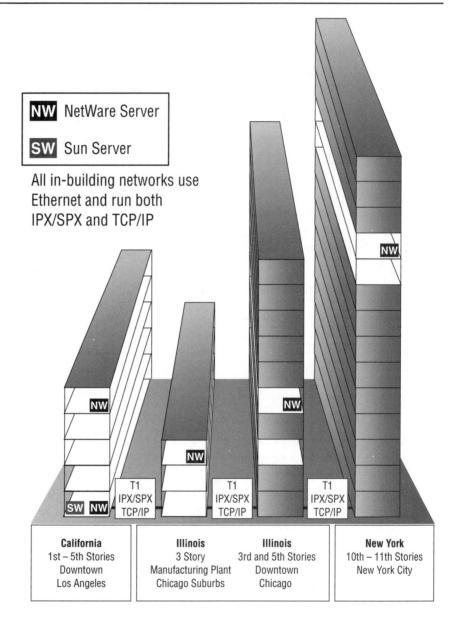

NW  NetWare Server

SW  Sun Server

All in-building networks use
Ethernet and run both
IPX/SPX and TCP/IP

T1
IPX/SPX
TCP/IP

T1
IPX/SPX
TCP/IP

T1
IPX/SPX
TCP/IP

**California**
1st – 5th Stories
Downtown
Los Angeles

**Illinois**
3 Story
Manufacturing Plant
Chicago Suburbs

**Illinois**
3rd and 5th Stories
Downtown
Chicago

**New York**
10th – 11th Stories
New York City

# Plan Servers and User Links to Them

There's quite a bit to do in planning your servers and user links. You need to decide what kinds of hardware to use for each of your Exchange servers. After that you have to figure out how to back up the servers. Then you have to make sure you've got adequate bandwidth on your local networks to keep Exchange happy; if you don't have it, you've got to decide how to get it. Finally, before you go on to the next step in the Exchange design process, you have to think about remote users and how you'll connect them to Exchange.

## Designing Your Exchange Servers

The intricacies of Exchange Server design and fine-tuning could occupy a whole book; you'll have to experiment here. Install NT Server and Exchange Server, then run the optimization app that comes with Exchange Server. (We'll talk more about installation and optimization in Chapter 6.) Next, take out that set of user-demand numbers you put together when you did your user-needs assessment. Plug those numbers into LoadSim and run it against a reasonable Exchange server machine—say, a 500MHz Pentium II with 256MB of memory and at least two 4GB SCSI hard drives. Don't run LoadSim on your Exchange server. Instead, run it on a separate 400MHz or better Pentium-based NT workstation with at least 128MB of memory. And don't try to simulate more than 200 users on one LoadSim machine. If you don't follow these guidelines, LoadSim may not be able to generate the loads you've asked it to, and you could be led to believe that your Exchange server hardware is adequate when it's not.

## SCSI, Not Enhanced IDE

Enhanced IDE drives are nice, but for production Exchange Servers I prefer SCSI drives. They're fast and tend to be more reliable than IDE drives. If you're going to use a hardware RAID configuration, you won't have much choice other than SCSI, because SCSI drives are used in most hardware RAID products. For best performance, choose wide or ultrawide SCSI drives.

If LoadSim indicates that you've got too little computing power for your needs, start by moving Exchange's transaction logs to another disk drive (this is covered in Chapter 9). If this doesn't solve your problem, you'll need to run NT's Performance Monitor to locate any bottlenecks. (See the Sybex book *Mastering Windows NT Server 4*, by Mark Minasi, Christina Anderson, and Elizabeth Creegan, for more on using the Performance Monitor.)

Look at the obvious culprits: server hard disk capacity, memory, and CPU. Based on the results you get from the Performance Monitor, you can decide what to do. Distributing Exchange database files differently—for example, putting the server's public folders on a different drive, RAID array, or server—can significantly improve an Exchange server's performance in some situations. Adding RAM to an Exchange server can make a world of difference in performance, because it allows the server to do more work without having to waste time paging RAM segments out to disk. Adding more processors to multiprocessor machines, or moving to more powerful processors like those from Digital Equipment, can be a quick route to improved performance. However, be careful here: Focus on disk capacity and RAM before turning to CPU power. More or faster CPUs can indeed improve performance, but they're not going to fix performance problems originating from poorly optimized disks or too little RAM. If all this vertical scaling can't solve your problem, consider going horizontal and splitting users across multiple Exchange servers. Exchange makes horizontal scaling very easy.

## Server Fault Tolerance

As you're designing your servers, don't forget the whole issue of server fault tolerance. Multiprocessor machines are starting to show up with processors that can back each other up in case of failure. You'll need a version of NT that can handle this sort of processor redundancy. In addition to processor redundancy, look for systems with error-correcting memory. On the disk side, consider multiple controllers and nicely redundant RAID level 5 technologies. Remember, NT Server can do software-based RAID level 5. Many machines are now available with two or more redundant power supplies. Don't forget uninterruptible power supplies (UPSes). More about them later in this chapter. In some cases, you can swap out failed RAID drives and power supplies without even bringing down your system. And, be sure to consider the new technologies like Microsoft's NT Server Enterprise Edition that lets you set up multiple NT/Exchange servers that mirror each other, with server A generally able to quickly and automatically replace server B in case server B fails.

You'll need to start thinking now about how you'll manage user storage on each server. Storage management gives you more control over how much of what is stored on Exchange server disks, and it helps you remain within your server disk budget. There are several disk management questions you'll want to answer here, including

- Do you want some or all of your users to store messages in personal folders on a workstation or non-Exchange networked disk drives, instead of in their Exchange server–based mailboxes? (See Chapter 2 for more on these two options.)

- For those who will use their Exchange server mailboxes, do you want to limit the amount of storage they can use?

- Do you want to impose limits on the storage used by public folders?

- If you have public folders containing messages that lose value with time— for example, messages from Internet lists or USENET news feeds—do you want Exchange to automatically delete messages from these folders based on message age?

- Will you implement Exchange Server's ability to save deleted messages for a designated period of time? This is a neat capability, because users can recover messages they accidentally deleted. However, all those "deleted" messages can take up tons of disk space.

You can base your answers to most of these questions on the results of your user-needs assessment, though you're bound to make adjustments as you pass through iterations of the design process. And, do note that while it's tempting to force users to store messages in personal folders on local or non-Exchange net-worked disk drives to save on Exchange server disk, you then run the risk that key user messages won't get backed up. As the ever-present "they" say, "You pays your money and you takes your chances."

Once you're comfortable with the basic design of your servers, you need to plan for uninterruptible power supplies (UPSes). I consider a UPS to be part of a server, not an add-on. UPSes are cheap, given the peace of mind they can bring. In spite of NT's and Exchange Server's ability to recover from most disastrous events, you don't want to tempt fate and risk damage to your organization's precious e-messaging data. Get enough UPSes to serve the power needs of each server, and get a UPS that comes with software to gracefully shut down your servers if power stays off for an extended period.

# Backing Up Your Exchange Servers

When you know what your Exchange servers and networks will look like, you can begin thinking about backing up your servers. You need to use backup software that is especially designed for Exchange's client/server architecture. Such software lets you back up an Exchange server's directory and information store without shutting down Exchange processes and, thus, closing off user access to the server. The software communicates with Exchange's directory and information store services to ensure that the databases they are responsible for are fully backed up. I'll talk more about the fine points of Exchange backup in Chapter 10.

NT's own Backup program has add-ons to do a proper backup of Exchange servers. Other NT backup vendors, such as Computer Associates's ArcServeIT (`http://www.cai.com/`) and Veritas Software's Backup Exec (`http://www .veritas.com/`), have released add-ons to their products that can properly back up Exchange Server.

You can back up an Exchange server either locally or over the network. When you back it up over the network, you can run the backup from another NT/Exchange server or from an NT-only server.

For Exchange servers with lots of disk space (5GB or more) and slow network links to potential backup servers (less than 100Mb/sec), I strongly suggest that you bypass the networked server backup option and do the backup locally on and from the Exchange server itself. You'll have to spend some money on a backup device and software for the Exchange server, but you'll get it back in available bandwidth and faster backups. Available bandwidth means that other network-dependent tasks—and there are lots of those on an Exchange network—run faster. And faster backups mean shorter periods of that awful feeling you get when important data is not yet on tape.

Whether you back up over the network or locally, don't skimp on backup hardware. You're going to *add* hard disk storage to your Exchange server, not take it away. Go for high-capacity 4mm, 8mm, or DLT tape backup systems. Think about tape autoloaders—those neat gizmos that give one or more tape drives automatic access to anything from a few tapes to hundreds of them.

Don't forget those personal folders stored on user workstations. You have to decide who will be responsible for backing them up—Exchange staff, other MIS staff, or users themselves. The technology for centralized workstation backup is readily available. For example, agents are available for most third-party NT backup products that let you back up all or part of specific user workstations.

While you're at it, don't forget NT server backup. If you have NT servers that don't support Exchange, you'll need to back them up, too. You can back up an NT server over the network, but if the servers have lots of disk space, consider the same local backup strategy for non-Exchange NT servers that I suggested for Exchange servers.

## Networking Your Exchange Users

Once you've got your server design down, you'll need to think about how to connect users to your Exchange servers. It's usually a no-brainer for local connections, though you'll want to be sure you've got enough bandwidth to move the stuff that Exchange makes available to your users. For example, a message I put together with a very simple embedded color screen capture is 855K. The graphic looks impressive, and it let me make a point that I never could have made without it. Still, I wouldn't want my recipients to get it over a 33.3 or 56Kb/sec connection.

If you're concerned about LAN bandwidth, there are a couple of things you can do. First, get rid of those slower networks. Dump 4Mb/sec Token Ring and Arcnet networks. Second, segment your LANs to reduce the number of users on any segment. In this situation you might even put multiple network adapters in your Exchange server, one for each segment or group of segments. And do take a look at faster networking technologies like 100Mb/sec Ethernet; those really neat networking switches that can replace routers and significantly improve network backbone performance; and the latest in neat stuff, switched fast Ethernet hubs that bring switching to workstation connectivity. Yes, any of these options will cost your organization some bucks, but they're likely to be bucks well spent. It's just like the way it is with user workstations: Slow technologies don't get used, and the benefits of the applications you're trying to run on top of them are lost.

Don't forget remote Exchange users. Many users need to keep in touch when they're away from the office, whether at home or on the road. Remote users can connect to an NT server by way of its Remote Access Server. The RAS gives users the equivalent of a hardwired connection, so for them it's more or less like being on the office LAN. The major difference is that they probably won't stay connected all the time—they'll connect to send and receive messages, and the rest of the time they'll work offline.

Remote users also can connect to their Exchange servers by way of direct TCP/IP links through an Internet Service Provider (ISP). And don't forget the Internet-based POP3, IMAP4, and Web browser–based client options that are supported by Exchange Server. With their lighter-weight demands on workstation resources, they could be just what the doctor ordered for your remote users.

We'll talk more about how to implement remote Exchange links in a later chapter. At this point you need to think about how many users will likely need a RAS connection to each site at one time. If it's just one or two, you can set up a couple of modems on an Exchange or NT server and let users dial in to those. If you expect lots of users you might want to consider setting up a separate NT server dedicated to dial-in connections. Remember, one NT server with the right hardware can support up to 256 dial-in RAS connections.

If users will be connecting to their Exchange servers over the Internet, you'll need an Internet connection of adequate bandwidth to support them. Unless you have few users who need Internet access, think T1.

## An Example: GerCom's Servers and User Links

With one exception, we GerComites are pretty sure from our LoadSim tests that the "reasonable machine" I described above—a 500MHz Pentium II with 256MB of memory and two 4GB SCSI hard disks—will work for now for each of our four Exchange servers. The exception? The LA server. With the heaviest staff load and an Internet connection to boot, we've decided to buy a four-processor capable 500MHz Pentium II machine and put 512MB of RAM and 32GB of hardware-based RAID level 5 disk space on the LA server. (We bought the LA machine with only two processors; we'll add more as needed.)

Remember how the GerCom executive suite was possibly going to get its own server? MIS overruled the idea. They really don't want the responsibility of administering two Exchange servers in LA, at least at the outset. Instead they opted for LA's special powerhouse server. Of course, as soon as it looks as if we execs (or any other group, for that matter) need it, we'll get our own Exchange server.

We'll try to limit all but select users to 10MB of mailbox storage. Select users will be those heavily involved in building, testing, or using some of those e-messaging–enabled apps we're planning to do; they'll get as much as 200MB to play with. Since most users won't have write access to public folders, at least at the outset, we're not going to impose any limits on storage there. We will, however, set Exchange to automatically delete messages older than two weeks in those public folders that contain e-mail from Internet lists and older than five days for USENET newsgroups stored in our public folders. And, we'll only let deleted messages hang around for seven days. Most users know almost immediately that they've deleted something they need. Seven days should be more than adequate for GerCom's fast-fingered delete key pushers.

Just from thinking through all the storage issues, there's one thing we know for sure: We won't get far on the 4GB or 32GB of disk space we put in our servers. We're already planning for increased storage needs.

Each server will have a UPS with orderly shutdown software. We'll back up for now with those neat little Hewlett-Packard DDS-3 SureStore tape autoloader units (`http://www.hp.com/storage/surestore/`) that let us put six 4mm tapes' worth of storage—up to 144 compressed GB—online. We plan to put one Sure-Store on each Exchange server. For now, to save some money, non-Exchange NT servers acting as primary or backup controllers will be backed up by the tape units on the Exchange servers.

As you'll remember, all but one of GerCom's networks had adequate bandwidth available; only the Engineering network had less than 60 percent of its bandwidth available during most of the day. We're planning to split the Engineering network into three nets: Two will support our two CAD groups, and the other will be for Engineering's clerical and administrative staff.

For remote users, we'll run the RAS dial-in on all our servers. To start, there will be two standard voice-line–based RAS links on each server except the one in LA. (The large number of users in LA dictates that we start with six voice-based RAS lines.) In LA we'll also have a 128kbps ISDN RAS connection for us execs who just can't tolerate those "creepy" 56kbps modem links. We expect ISDN use at GerCom to grow considerably over the next few years, unless a better option comes along.

We decided that, for now, we can get the most reliable remote connectivity with RAS, as opposed to TCP/IP or the new Internet-based client connects. However, we'll also test Outlook client TCP/IP links through an ISP and Exchange's Internet-based Web browser and POP3 and IMAP4 clients. If they work well, we'll start moving remote users over to them. Heck, if they work well, we might even have some of our users with lower-powered workstations use them instead of the resource-hog Outlook clients.

# Plan Connections to Other Systems

As John Donne almost said, "No organization is an island." In fact, today not only is no organization an island, but no organization can *afford* to be an island. With the e-messaging decade upon us, electronic messaging will increasingly become the primary means of communicating and doing business. Consider connections to systems outside your organization to be necessities, not niceties.

## Connection Options

Exchange sites can be connected directly to foreign X.400 systems, Internet mail systems, and legacy Microsoft Mail for PC and AppleTalk Networks systems and cc:Mail. Legacy system links can include not just message exchange but synchronization of Exchange and legacy address directories as well. With optional gateways from Microsoft and third-party vendors, you can connect to such systems as IBM PROFS, Verimation Memo, MCI Mail, and fax devices.

Exchange connections to foreign X.400 systems use the X.400 Connector. Such connections can be either continuous and permanent or dial-up, and they can use any of the X.400 Connector networking options listed above in step 7 (designing site links). The Internet Mail Service can use a continuous and permanent or dial-up TCP/IP link to the Internet. Third-party gateways use a range of networking protocols; contact your gateway vendor for specifics. The Microsoft Mail Connector can run on top of almost anything, including TCP/IP, IPX/SPX, NetBEUI, X.25, voice lines, and the RAS. The Exchange Directory Synchronization Agent mentioned in Chapter 3 lets you keep Exchange and legacy Microsoft messaging systems in sync. It uses the same networking protocols as the Microsoft Mail Connector.

## Connect or Migrate?

Now is the time to decide if it's better to migrate users from legacy systems to Exchange Server or to wait and just link them to Exchange Server using various connectors, gateways, or even direct individual workstation connects in the case of Microsoft Mail for PC Networks or cc:Mail. The number of users to be migrated, the kinds of messaging systems they use, and the size of your own technical and training staff will play a big role in this decision. (Migration from Microsoft's and other messaging systems gets a whole chapter of its own later in this book.)

*continued on next page*

If you do decide to migrate users, you need to determine exactly which messaging systems you'll be migrating your users from: Microsoft Mail for PC Networks and/or AppleTalk Networks, Lotus cc:Mail, IBM PROFS, Verimation Memo, DEC All-in-One, and so on. Next, you need to figure out what kinds of tools, if any, exist that can help you migrate users from each messaging system to Exchange. For example, Exchange includes a nice migration application for Microsoft Mail users. Once you know what kinds of migration tools are available, you have to set a timetable for migration. Finally, you have to determine whether, based on your timetable, you should link other messaging systems to Exchange before you've migrated all users in them over to Exchange.

If you choose to migrate users to Exchange, be aware that Exchange can create new user accounts from text data files. If your legacy messaging system lets you output user information to a file and you've got someone around who can write a program to assure that all the information Exchange needs is in the file in the right format and order, you should certainly consider using this nice, time-saving Exchange migration option. I'll talk more about migration in a later chapter.

In planning, don't underplay the importance of X.400 connections, especially if your company communicates with organizations outside the United States. The X.400 suite includes the Electronic Document Interchange (EDI) standard, which supports electronic commerce by providing secure communications when you use your messaging system to, say, purchase products and services. Yes, you can secure your Internet mail communications, but X.400 is catching on, even in the United States. Keep it in mind.

As with intersite links, you need only one Exchange connector to link an entire site to a foreign messaging system. And as long as intersite links are in place, a single foreign messaging system connector can send and receive messages for an entire organization. As with intersite connections, though, you might want more than one connector to balance network traffic loads and provide redundancy.

## An Example: GerCom's External Links

GerCom will stick with its T1 Internet connection, moving management of the e-mail side of its Internet domain from our Sun systems to the Exchange server in Los Angeles. For the time being, at least, domain name service will continue to be handled by GerCom's Sun systems, though we're looking seriously at the DNS software available for NT.

We're also going to set up T1 Internet connections for our other two sites—for intersite redundancy, not direct delivery of Internet mail. Internet mail will still come into the LA Exchange site and be delivered to Chicago and New York through the Exchange system. Those T1s will put us in just the right position bandwidth-wise if our tests of remote access for Exchange users via the Internet are successful and we move most users from RAS to Internet-based Exchange client links.

To support the customer purchasing and payment applications that our salespeople want to build, we'll be using X.400 connections to six of our trading partners—two inside the United States and four outside. This will let us develop the app using the X.400 EDI standard. We'll have one T1 link to a public X.400 provider in Los Angeles. (Yikes, another T1!) Figure 5.13 shows all of GerCom's external links.

**FIGURE 5.13:**

GerCom's connections to the outside world

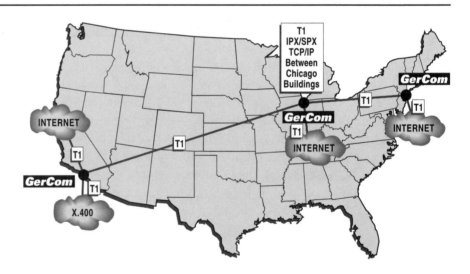

We don't have any legacy Microsoft Mail systems; we've been using our Sun systems to support the Simple Message Transport Protocol (SMTP) on our UNIX system. Users have a bunch of POP mail clients for e-mail. As indicated above, we want to close down our UNIX-based mail system. So, we'll have to migrate our UNIX mail users to Exchange and deal with that e-messaging address change brought about by changing our registered Internet domain name from "gerberco" to "gercom." We'll use comma-delimited files from the UNIX system to create Exchange user accounts, so we should be able to set up all our user accounts easily.

I'm less sure about migrating messages and any storage folders our users may have. We may just leave that up to users; most have reported that much of what's in their folders is no longer of use to them anyway.

# Validate and Optimize the Design

*Validation* means ensuring you've got a system that guarantees message delivery, integrity, and security. It also means making sure the system you've designed is versatile enough to handle the range of documents, messaging formats, and applications your organization needs. *Optimization* is a balancing act in which you try to build the fastest, most stable and reliable systems you can while still meeting organizational requirements and keeping costs down.

## Guaranteed Delivery

Guaranteed message delivery comes with reliable NT and Exchange servers and reliable internal and external networks. To increase the likelihood of guaranteed delivery, go for as much server fault tolerance and networking redundancy as your organization can afford. Use high-quality server and networking hardware and software inside your organization; buy outside networking services from stable, experienced, and well-established providers. Monitor the health of your networks, and be prepared to fix problems quickly. During the validation phase, send messages of all kinds through all of your connections, and then check to see if they arrive intact. When problems arise, use Exchange's own message-tracking tools to catch up with wayward messages, and take advantage of Exchange's network and system-monitoring tools to discover why a message didn't get through.

Reliability is only one side of guaranteed message delivery. You also need Exchange servers that are sufficiently fast and networks that have the bandwidth to move messages quickly enough to meet maximum delivery time parameters. If you've specified that all messages should be delivered to all internal users within five minutes, for example, now's the time to see if your Exchange system is capable of performing up to spec. If not, you have to either increase your permissible maximum delivery times or, depending on the source of the problem, come up with speedier servers and/or higher-bandwidth networks.

## Message Integrity

*Message integrity* means that messages arrive in the same form as they were transmitted. Problems with message integrity often can be traced to mismatched binary message-part encoding and decoding. For example, a binary attachment to a message bound for the Internet is uuencoded by the sender, while the receiver expects MIME encoding. As you'll see later, there are lots of ways to set coding parameters in Exchange to help avoid problems like this.

## Message Security

In Exchange 5 and greater, RSA encryption and public keys work both within a single Exchange organization and can be enabled to work across Exchange organizations. For messages defined for foreign e-messaging systems, Exchange Server implements a set of encryption and authentication standards: NTLM encryption, TLS encryption, SASL clear text authentication, and Secure MIME. More on these in later chapters.

You can try to validate message security on your own or with the help of a certified electronic data processing auditor. If security is important to your organization, I strongly recommend the latter.

## System Versatility

Exchange's internal message formatting, along with formatting available in X.400 and Internet Mail, means that you'll be able to send documents of almost any type, containing virtually anything from text to last night's Letterman show. But be sure to validate that everything you need is there and works.

On the applications side, you've got all the app development environments I mentioned in Chapter 1, as well as applications like Microsoft's Schedule+ and Outlook. Exchange Server is a very popular product, so plenty of Exchange-based e-messaging–enabled applications are already available from third-party vendors, and there are many more in development. Keep your eyes open for the latest "killer" Exchange apps.

## Optimization

When you've done everything to ensure guaranteed message delivery, message integrity, and security, as well as system versatility, it's time for *optimization*. You optimize your design by checking out alternatives that may help improve your Exchange system. The basic question is, Can you do it better, faster, easier? For example, you might want to consider implementing support for X.400 messaging, even though your organization has no current need for it, simply because competitors are moving toward it.

Optimization can also focus on reducing costs without compromising the quality of your system. For example, you might want to come up with lower-cost options for connecting Exchange sites or for realizing network redundancy.

## An Example: Validating GerCom's Design

GerCom's design validates very well. Based on tests we've done, our system seems quite reliable, and we're meeting our ten-minute message-delivery maximum. Our certified data processing auditor says our messaging security looks good.

We've covered the message format bases by including native Exchange, X.400 Mail, and Internet Mail capabilities. We've found nothing that we can't dump into a message and move through and out of our system with integrity. That includes everything from text to a full-color animated "film," complete with sound, showing our exclusive high-end, Fine Egyptian Marble Enter key in action.

On the applications side we've started working with Schedule+ and both Exchange and Outlook Forms Designer. Both are performing as expected so far. Our development people are quite happy with the custom programming APIs available in Exchange. They're sure they can put together any of the applications our users have requested so far.

We put together and evaluated one alternative networking option, using the Dynamic RAS Connector in place of a Site Connector to link our Exchange sites. I continue to worry about the cost of those T1 connections in our original plans for intersite links, but in our tests the DRASC was just too slow to handle the traffic we expect. So we're now wedded to those T1 lines.

# Roll Out the Plan

*Rollout* doesn't mean dropping a whole Exchange system on your organization all at once. It means making Exchange available to specific systems people and users according to a carefully thought-out schedule. You should also go through a testing phase with specific users.

You might start your rollout in MIS—maybe just with yourself, if you're part of MIS. Next, you might move on to samples of users based on the groupings you uncovered in your user-needs assessment. Then move steadily onward until all users are up and running in Exchange. The key is to get Exchange out to all users as fast as possible without crashing your organization. (Here I'm referring to your *real* organization, not your Exchange organization.)

Remember that rollout is an integral part of the Exchange design process. As you step through your rollout plans, be ready to change your design. If something doesn't work, change it now. Don't let things pile up to the point that change becomes virtually impossible.

Whether you're in a test or production rollout phase, be sure to keep users in the loop. Get them committed to Exchange. Let them know if and when they're going to see the new Exchange client or other clients supported by Exchange Server. Explain to them how they can use whatever client you plan to provide them both to do what they're already doing and to get other tasks done. This is where user training comes in.

Keep MIS staff involved and informed as well. An Exchange installation and implementation is a big deal for an MIS department. Over time, I'll bet that just about everyone in MIS will get involved with Exchange. MIS staff should understand and welcome Exchange, not see it as a threat to their jobs. Train MIS personnel as data processing colleagues rather than just end users. You don't have to tell everyone in MIS everything there is to know about Exchange—they can buy this book for that purpose (hint, hint). But be sure to talk to them about both server and client basics from a more technical perspective.

## An Example: The GerCom Rollout

The GerCom Exchange rollout is a two-year project, and we're about six months into it. (How time flies when you're having fun.) The rollout is a very detailed and complex process; I can only touch on key highlights here. I've got to keep that glue from drying, you know.

We decided to start with a basic Exchange installation for use by our 11 new Exchange MIS employees and the executive suite. If our executive staffers weren't so computer literate I'd never have approved this part of the rollout plan, but we execs have all lived with computers and new system rollouts for a long time, and I know we're a good and safe starting point for Exchange. And what better way to get upper management behind Exchange and the rollout?

The first phase of GerCom's Exchange rollout went pretty smoothly, though we were surprised at how poorly the Outlook 2000 client performed on anything less than a 200MHz Pentium machine with 32MB of RAM. We're pushing hard to find the resources to upgrade user workstations to at least this level.

We allowed two months for phase one of the rollout. As a condition of employment, all of GerCom's new non–Los Angeles Exchange staff had to live in LA for these two months (at great but justifiable expense, I might add). Exchange site administrators participated in the setup of the LA site and then helped bring up the servers for the Chicago and New York sites. The servers were linked by local networks for the test phase, and we were able to proof out the entire GerCom Exchange system right in LA.

During this period our Exchange training and applications development staff went through training of their own. I was happy when, to a person, they came out of training as enthusiastic as I am about end-user and MIS Exchange application development. They did remind us that we had to make a commitment to buy the latest version of Microsoft Word and Excel for our users. We did. Staff also suggested that we buy some evaluation copies of Microsoft's Access database product. We did.

When our trainers finished their own training we had them do some test training with the MIS staff. That turned out really well; everyone seemed genuinely enthusiastic. No one openly expressed opposition to Exchange or the kinds of applications we plan to develop with it. I've asked our MIS director to talk to his staff to be sure that what we saw on the surface is real.

At the end of the two-month period the Chicago and New York Exchange staff returned to their respective cities. There they set up their servers and connected them to the T1 lines we had installed. Our LA Exchange site administrator is specially skilled in Internet and X.400 connectivity, so we sent her to Chicago and

New York to help with those connections. Hey, these Exchange folks are traveling as much as we execs are.

Bringing site administrators to Los Angeles worked very well. It concentrated them for training, let them learn from each other as they did real tasks, and helped them build important relationships that would make their jobs both easier and more rewarding. We'll get these folks together on a regular basis, and we'll use this same plan when we implement a new site.

With all sites up and running, the second phase of the GerCom Exchange roll-out focused on bringing all of our departments into Exchange for e-mail only. This involved a lot of training and no small amount of Exchange system administration. We were able to create most of our user accounts from comma-delimited files produced on our UNIX system, but that information wasn't enough to fill in all of the blanks on those 11 property pages available in Exchange Administrator's user administration and management tool. We exported more information from our Oracle human resources database in comma-delimited files and imported it into our Exchange servers, but our Exchange administrators still had to fill in information we didn't have in electronic form. They also had to create accounts for employees who didn't have UNIX mail accounts (mostly recent hires).

During phase two we brought the LA and New York sales staffs into the loop first, because they're the biggest contributors to GerCom's bottom line. Then, in order, came Chicago Sales, LA Marketing, Chicago Manufacturing, and Chicago Engineering.

Our Exchange training/end-user application development staff was stretched to the limit a few times during phase two of the rollout. The Exchange site administrators also felt a lot of pressure as they worked to add users and tune their systems. Probably at least in part because of the LA training, they all supported each other both technically and emotionally—face-to-face, on the phone, and through our growing Exchange system.

Our hardware and networking projections are holding pretty well, though I have to tell you that our servers' disks are filling up fast. And Performance Monitor tests are indicating that we may soon need to add more processors and memory to our LA machine. (It's either that or cut back on our expectations.)

Phase two lasted four months, though we thought we could finish in three. The final phase of our Exchange rollout involves the creation of end-user and custom-programmed applications. We've allotted 18 months to complete this phase, and we're going to start it now.

We'll work on the two kinds of applications in parallel. We'll start with some of the end-user apps our controller wants to implement, then we'll move on to the human resources apps. Our first custom-programmed application will be the customer notification system that our manufacturing people came up with. Once that's in place, we'll move on to the customer ordering and payment system that sales wants. We figure that we should start easy and work up to the more difficult tasks.

Of course, now that we're into the implementation phase we're hearing new ideas from all quarters. I've asked MIS to work with users to quickly understand what they have in mind and determine if it can be implemented in Exchange— and if it can, what it might cost. The exec staff will look at these proposals with MIS and determine where they should fit into our current implementation plans. Of course, as you might imagine, some of our hotshot users are already coming up with their own Exchange applications based on the user-oriented app tools we've talked about.

Because we execs and MIS worked closely together, there was no finger-pointing when these surprise apps popped up. We gave everyone an opportunity during the early phases of the design process. We told everyone that we couldn't guarantee implementation of ideas that came in late, but we quickly came up with a way to filter new ideas that surfaced during rollout. No one panicked. No one screamed. All is well.

Right now, things look good. A reasonable amount of planning, coupled with an openness to change, has gotten our Exchange rollout off to an excellent start. I can't wait to see what the system looks like in 18 months.

# Conclusion

In this chapter you learned the 11 steps involved in designing an Exchange system. You also learned that the Exchange design process is an iterative one in which you constantly revisit steps to refine your design. This is true even for the final step—Exchange system rollout, where you test and modify your design in the real world.

Now we're ready to move on to the hands-on part of the Exchange experience. The remainder of this book is devoted to showing you in detail how to bring up an Exchange system. We'll start by installing an NT server and then an Exchange server. Before we finish we'll cover every one of the concepts and realities we've touched on already, and even more. Let's go!

# PART II

# Installation

Microsoft Exchange Server runs on top of Microsoft's Windows NT Server. In this section, we'll install both products, protect them and their users against hardware crashes, and build a basic networking environment to protect them.

Chapter 6 focuses on installing NT Server, setting up an uninterruptible power supply, backing up, security, and networking. Chapter 7 provides details on Exchange Server installation and security.

# Installing Windows NT Server

■ Installing Windows NT Server software

■ Installing uninterruptible power supplies

■ Setting up NT Backup

■ Giving domain access to NT servers and workstations

■ Setting up NT Server clients

**H**ave you ever gone on the Alice in Wonderland ride at Disneyland? It starts by taking you down a rabbit hole, with Alice saying, "Here we gooooooooooooo." That extended "go" fades away toward the end, adding to the ride's excitement and sense of entering the unknown. Like Alice, we're about to embark on a wild and exciting adventure. I promise to do all I can to make our hands-on trip through Exchange interesting, productive, and fun—but a little less bumpy, arbitrary, and confusing than Alice's sojourn in Wonderland. Let's go.

# Installation: An Overview

In this chapter, I'm presuming you'll be installing NT Server on a computer with nothing on it that you wish to preserve. For example, I assume you don't need to update a Windows for Workgroups machine to NT Server and preserve the software you've installed under the existing operating system. This seems a reasonable assumption, since you're preparing a machine for Exchange Server and are unlikely to be using an existing workstation or server.

If you're going to install NT Server on top of DOS, Windows 3.1*x*, or LAN Manager 2.2, you should back up your existing system before installing NT Server. If you need help with backing up and restoring or other issues related to installing NT Server over an existing operating system, take a look at *Mastering Windows NT Server 4* (Sybex, 1996), by Mark Minasi, Christa Anderson, and Elizabeth Creegan. It can also help you troubleshoot installation problems, deal with NT Server reinstallations, and handle a host of other things I just don't have the space to cover here. (See the sidebar "Mastering Windows NT Server 4" in Chapter 4 for more about this book and why I think it's so neat.)

NT Server installation is a six-step process. These steps include

- Setting up the server hardware
- Installing NT Server software
- Installing an uninterruptible power supply
- Setting up NT Backup
- Giving domain access to users and NT systems
- Setting up NT Server clients

Let's look at each of these steps in more detail.

**WARNING**    Microsoft had to do a number of things to NT Server to make it compatible with Exchange Server. Some of these involved new functions required by Exchange Server, while others fixed bugs that emerged when NT Server was stressed to its limits by Exchange Server. These modifications are available in what are called *service packs*. You need to upgrade NT Server 4 to Service Pack 3 or later to make it ready for installation of Exchange Server 5 or later. Exchange Server 5.5 can run only on NT 4 with NT 4's service pack 3 or greater. Got that? Good. There'll be a test tomorrow at 5 P.M. As I mentioned in Chapter 1, things are likely to change by the time you read this book. The Internet and high-speed, high-pressure marketing and software delivery channels it has fostered make unending, unpredictable, and incredibly quick software modification not only possible but also economically necessary for vendors. Check the Web sites at `www.microsoft.com/ntserver` and `www.microsoft.com/exchange` for updates.

# Setting Up the Server Hardware

Setting up the hardware is a pretty straightforward process. First, you pick a server platform and outfit it with various components. Then you test out its memory, disk drives, and other hardware to ensure that everything is working well.

## Getting Server Components in Order

In Chapter 5, I wrote of a "reasonable machine" for running Exchange Server: a 500MHz Pentium II with 256MB of RAM and two 4GB SCSI hard disks. Let's assume you're starting with this PC or its Digital Alpha equivalent.

## A Lower-Powered Test Machine

If you're just going to test Exchange Server and promise not to put your test configuration into production, you can use a somewhat lesser hunk of hardware than the "reasonable machine" I tout. I'd recommend at a minimum a 200MHz Pentium PC with 64MB of RAM and a 4GB IDE hard disk.

I suggest that you outfit your system with a SCSI peripheral controller, a super-VGA display adapter, at least a 15-inch monitor, a 24*x*-speed or faster CD-ROM drive, two or more serial ports, a mouse, and one or more network adapters. Let's look at server components in a bit more detail.

### Peripheral Controllers

Peripheral Component Interconnect (PCI) SCSI controllers are the best choice for modern server hardware. Of all currently available controllers, they can move the greatest number of bits in the shortest time. You'll use them to connect both hard disks and tape drives to your server.

You should buy PCI SCSI controllers with a right-to-return guarantee, since not all controllers run properly in all computers with PCI slots. This is due to some vagueness in the Intel PCI spec and to the resulting differences in implementation by various computer and component manufacturers. Things have gotten better over the past year or so, but play it safe; be sure you have that guarantee.

### Display Adapters and Monitors

Exchange Server is loaded with applications that use a graphical user interface (GUI). A super-VGA display adapter and a 15-inch or larger monitor let you keep multiple GUI apps open and available.

### CD-ROM Drives

NT Server is a software monster, but a fast CD-ROM drive makes NT Server installation and modification almost fun. The NT Server installation program can automatically detect and enable most CD-ROM hardware, including both Enhanced IDE and SCSI devices.

## What to Buy

NT Server comes with a little manual titled *Hardware Compatibility List*; it lists the components that work with NT. You can also find the *List* on the Web at `http://www.microsoft.com/hwtest/hcl/`. Before you buy anything, consult this guide. 'Nuff said.

## Serial Ports

You'll need one serial port to interface your NT Server to an uninterruptible power supply (UPS). Also, you'll probably want to use a serial port for a mouse. However, if you plan to provide Microsoft's Remote Access Server (RAS) connections for your NT Server users, use a PS/2 or mouse port to free a serial port for RAS. If you need a lot of RAS ports, look at multi-port boards from companies like Digi International (`http://www.dgii.com/`).

## Mice

Pick either a PS/2 or mouse port or serial mouse depending on serial port availability.

## Network Adapters

Based on the Exchange network design you came up with in Chapter 5, you'll need one or more network adapters in your server. Again, PCI adapters are the best choice. As with PCI SCSI controllers, you should buy network adapters with a right-to-return guarantee.

# Setting Up Adapters

Be careful how you set up network adapters, especially ISA bus cards. Otherwise, if you get the settings wrong, you may have to reinstall NT Server software all over again. Once you've got an adapter set up the way you want it, write down the settings. You'll need them when you get into the NT Server's network installation.

If you use PCI SCSI controllers and network adapters, you shouldn't have to worry too much about setting I/O addresses, DMA channels, or interrupts (IRQs). If you don't use PCI cards, be sure to select IRQs that don't conflict with those of other adapters. Good IRQ options are 5, 10, 11, and 15. If you're using a bus mouse, you'll probably use IRQ 5 for that. So that leaves IRQs 10, 11, and 15 for your controller and network adapter.

Be sure to pick nonconflicting I/O addresses and DMA channels for those adapters that require them. Adapter manuals will give you the basics on configuration methods and parameters. The setup programs that come with individual adapters make it pretty easy to spot conflicts. Don't forget to write down all of the settings you choose. Tape copies of this information both inside and outside the computer.

# Testing Key Components

E-messaging is a critical application. As I noted in earlier chapters, you're best off when you run e-messaging on fault-tolerant hardware. But even before you consider this option, you should be sure that everything in your server is working properly. You'll want to test five key components as soon as your server is in-house: memory, hard disks, CD-ROM drives, SCSI controllers, and network adapters.

Good memory and disk tests are time consuming: Testing out the "reasonable machine" I recommended for Exchange Server could take between six and seven days. Don't let that deter you, though. You want to be sure you've got a solid platform under your organization—if for no other reason than you'll sleep better at night.

During NT Server installation, the system is automatically configured for a variety of hardware options. So all your hardware should be working during the installation process. For this reason, you'll want to test your CD-ROM drive, SCSI controllers, and network adapters before installing NT Server. Be sure to test all of these together to be sure that no IRQ, I/O address, or DMA conflicts occur.

It should go without saying, but I'll say it anyway: Don't consider your testing phase finished until all components pass the tests you set out for them. Now let's start testing.

## Testing Memory

Because the quick boot-up memory test on Intel-based PCs cannot find most memory problems, use Touchstone Software's Checkit (http://www.checkit .com/) or DiagSoft's DiagSoft (http://www.diagsoft.com/) to test memory. You should run either of these programs from DOS with no memory manager present, and run the complete suite of tests in slow rather than quick mode. (Similar memory-test products are available for non–Intel-based machines.)

A good memory-test program on a fast machine will take around four hours per 16MB of RAM. So plan to settle in for a long nap after you start testing the 128MB of RAM on your server.

## Testing Hard Disks

There are two kinds of software-based hard disk testers: those that write one pattern all over the disk and then read to see if the pattern was written correctly

(MS-DOS's SCANDISK is such a tester), and those that write a range of patterns and test to see if each was properly written. You'll want a multipattern tester because it is more likely to find the bit-based problems on a disk. Spinrite's Spin-Rite (`http://www.spinrite.com/`) is a good multipattern tester that can find and declare off-limits any bad areas on disk that the manufacturer didn't catch. Unfortunately, disk tests are even more of a snoozer than RAM tests. Plan a nap of three days or so around the testing of one 4GB drive.

## Cheap Is Cheap

The newspapers in Los Angeles and most big cities are full of ads for what seem to be unbelievably inexpensive components like SIMMS, DIMMs, disk drives, motherboards, and CPUs. Don't bite. Trust me on this one: I've been through the mill with cheap, flaky components. NT Server all by itself can beat the living daylights out of a computer. Add Exchange Server and you'll pay back in your own sweat and time every penny and then some that you saved by buying cheap. Buy from stable, long-lived vendors at reasonable but not fairy-tale prices. RAM for an NT Server should always be ECC type. They cost a little more but are worth the money.

If you've got enough hardware, you might want to run your RAM and disk tests simultaneously. This will cut down on your nap time, but it will get you up and running with Exchange before the dawn of a new century.

### Testing CD-ROM Drives

I test my CD-ROM drives in DOS using MSCDEX.EXE and the DOS driver for the drive. If I can do a directory on a CD-ROM in the drive I'm testing and copy a file or two from the CD-ROM, I assume that it's working well enough to move on to NT installation.

**TIP**    Newer Pentium II and III motherboards don't work all that well with older IDE CD-ROM drives under NT 4. Spend a little more and get a modern CD-ROM drive. I've had great experience with Creative's 48x Blaster CD-ROM drive (www.soundblaster.com).

### Testing SCSI Controllers

If you've tested your hard drives as suggested above, you've also tested their controllers, at least in isolation from other adapters. Just be sure to run your tests again with active CD-ROM drives and network cards to ensure that no adapter conflicts are lurking in the background just waiting to mess up your NT Server installation.

### Testing Network Adapters

I never install a machine that will be networked without making sure that it can attach in MS-DOS mode to a server. Use whatever driver you're comfortable with, Microsoft's NDIS drivers or Novell's ODI or VLM drivers.

# Installing NT Server Software

As with setting up hardware, installing NT Server is fairly straightforward. If you've read Part I of this book, you should encounter no surprises. We'll go through all the steps you'll take to get NT Server up and running.

I'd love to show you all the screens you'll see during installation; however, since no operating system is yet in place, there's no way to capture these screens. Rest assured that each step discussed here parallels one or another screen you'll see during installation. Later in this chapter—once we've got NT Server installed—I'll show you enough setup screens to make up for the early deficit.

## Starting the Installation

I'll assume from here forward that you're going to install NT Server 4, not 3.51. Release 4 comes on three diskettes and a CD-ROM. To start installation, put the diskette labeled "Setup Disk 1" into your start-up drive and boot the system. The installation program will start, and you're off to the races. The first notable thing you'll see is a message telling you that NT Setup is checking out your system's hardware configuration. This will take a while.

---

**TIP**     Most modern Pentium II and III motherboards support boot-up from a CD-ROM drive. The NT 4 CD is fully bootable. So, check out the BIOS on your motherboard. If it supports CD-ROM boot-up, set it to so boot and you won't need to mess with those ancient installation diskettes I mention in this section.

---

In the unlikely event that you have problems at any point during the installation, check out *Mastering Windows NT Server 4*. This wonderful tome also includes information on alternative ways to install NT Server 4.

Once you've gotten through the hardware configuration detection part of the installation process, your screen turns blue and displays in white letters the words `Windows NT Setup`. At the bottom of the screen you'll see the message `Setup is loading files (Windows NT Executive)`. (What's in the parentheses will change as each new file is loaded.) All of this takes some time, so be patient.

## Detecting Mass Storage Devices

Next, you'll be prompted for Setup Disk 2; put it in and press Enter. You'll see info about what's being loaded at the bottom of the screen. After a fair amount of time, Setup gives you a list of options. Press Enter to begin installing NT. Setup will then tell you it's ready to begin detecting storage devices like hard disk, CD-ROM, and diskette drives. Detection can be automatic or manual. Unless you've got some pretty weird storage hardware, go ahead and tell Setup to do an automatic detect by pressing Enter.

As soon as you press the Enter key, you're prompted for Setup Disk 3. The detection phase won't actually begin until you insert the diskette and press Enter again. Setup now loads a series of device drivers and tests them to see if it can detect a range of popular SCSI controllers, disk drives, and SCSI or IDE CD-ROM drives. The program reports the SCSI and IDE CD-ROM mass storage devices on your system as it finds them. When it finishes, Setup offers you the opportunity to have it load SCSI drivers that you have for devices not supported by NT Setup's repertory of drivers.

If all goes well and Setup has found your SCSI devices and/or IDE CD-ROM drives, press the Enter key to proceed. Don't worry if you don't see your IDE hard disk drives at this point. Setup will take care of them as soon as you press the Enter key.

If a mass storage device in your computer wasn't automatically detected and the NT Server hardware compatibility list says that drivers for it or its controller ship with NT Server, then you've probably got a problem with the hardware itself. Go back and test the device as indicated earlier in this chapter.

If an undetected device isn't supported in the off-the-shelf NT Server package and you have specific drivers for it from the manufacturer, you can manually load them at this point. To do so press the S key.

Setup next looks for IDE drives. If it finds any that have over 1024 cylinders, it warns you of this fact and notes that under certain circumstances all of the space on the disk may not be available. If you're using a modern Pentium motherboard with built-in IDE support, you can pretty much ignore this warning and press the Enter key to continue the NT installation. Otherwise, read the warning in full and do as advised.

## Insert the NT Server CD-ROM Disk

Next, the CD-ROM file system is loaded. Then, if the NT Server CD-ROM disk isn't in the CD-ROM drive already, Setup asks that you insert it in the drive and press the Enter key.

## Licenses

When the licensing dialog box pops up, page down through the licensing agreement and then press F8 to agree to the conditions of the license. F8 doesn't show up on the screen until you've paged all the way down to the end of the license.

## Checking for Software and Hardware

Setup will look for previous versions of NT on your computer. If it finds one, it will offer you the opportunity to upgrade the existing version or install a new one. That's your call. (If this is a fresh install, you won't see this message.) Setup will also detect other known operating systems and offer you an opportunity to upgrade or install a new version where appropriate. For example, because of differences in the registries of the two operating systems, you can't install NT over Windows 95/98. However, you can install the two operating systems in parallel on the same machine and Setup will offer this option if appropriate.

If you're installing NT on a computer without a previous version of NT, Setup shows you the basic configuration of your hardware, e.g., PC, keyboard, and mouse type. Change anything that isn't correct and accept the displayed configuration.

What follows assumes you're installing on a fresh computer with no previous version of any operating system installed. If you're upgrading NT Server or installing it over another operating system, you should already know enough about NT installations to handle the minor differences in the installation process from this point on.

## Preparing Disk Partitions

At this point, Setup shows you the unpartitioned space on the hard disk drives it detected and asks where you want to install NT Server. If you've worked with DOS disk partitions, what follows should be pretty familiar. You can choose to set up partitions of any size up to the capacity of a disk drive. Assuming you've got two fresh disk drives in your computer, I recommend setting up a partition of around 1024MB for the NT Server operating system.

At this point, you only need to worry about the primary partition NT Server is to be installed on. You can take care of other partitions later using NT's Disk Administrator applet. I'll talk more about Disk Administrator later in this chapter.

Now comes the $64,000 question: Do you want to format the partition as a FAT (File Allocation Table) or NTFS (NT File System) partition? FAT partitions are compatible with MS-DOS. You can boot an NT server under DOS and read what's on the server's FAT-formatted partitions. So, you might want to format your operating system in FAT partitions. I myself have pretty much given up on DOS, so I tend to format my NT Server operating system partitions in NTFS format. Why NTFS? NTFS has always been more fault-tolerant than FAT and, in today's incarnations, performance differences between it and FAT are usually hard to detect. Choose the format you want and press the Enter key. Setup puts up a little gauge showing formatting progress.

## Copying Files from the NT Server CD-ROM Disk

When formatting is finished, Setup asks for the directory that NT should be installed in. Accept the default \WINNT by pressing the Enter key.

Setup then asks if you want a basic or a basic and exhaustive examination of your hard disk for corruption. It's best to do the basic and exhaustive test, though it takes a while.

Upon completion of the examination, Setup begins copying files from the CD-ROM to the partition you designated. After copying the files, Setup tells you it has finished this phase of installation and asks you to remove diskettes and CD-ROM disks from their drives so it can reboot your computer. Follow this advice religiously. Even leaving the CD-ROM disk in its drive can mess up the next phase. When you have removed the floppy disk and the CD-ROM, press the Enter key to embark on the next leg of your journey to NT Server.

## Setup's Installation Wizard

Upon reboot, NT Setup runs through some basic text startup screens. During this time, it fully formats the disk partition NT server will be installed on and reboots the machine once more. Have patience here; pretty soon Setup goes into graphical user interface mode and asks you to put the NT Server CD-ROM disk back in the CD-ROM drive. Do so and click OK.

Then Setup brings up a Wizard to guide you through the next phase of NT Server installation. The Wizard looks a lot like the installation Wizards that come with a range of products designed for the Windows 95 and 98 operating systems. It leads you through further hardware detection, the installation of Windows NT Networking, and a bunch of other housekeeping chores.

The sections below guide you through the various phases of NT Server installation. They're keyed to the installation Wizard. Click Next on the Wizard to move on to the next phase of installation.

### Ownership and Licensing

After the hardware detection phase, the Wizard asks you to enter your name and the name of your organization. This is not necessarily the name of your Exchange organization. This information is just used to identify who installed NT Server and the organization claiming ownership of this copy of the product. Enter that information and click Next.

The next Wizard screen asks for the CD key that appears on the back of the jewel case your NT Server CD-ROM came in. Enter the key and click Next.

Next, the Wizard requests licensing information. Select the licensing type you've paid for and enter any required values. Heed the Wizard's warning to use the License Manager in the Administrative Tools program group to set the number of client licenses purchased, once your NT server is up and running. If you don't, users and other systems won't be able to connect to the server.

## Naming Your NT Server

The Wizard next asks you to name the NT server. This name should follow the Exchange Server naming scheme you developed based on discussions in the first part of this book. As you'll recall, I named my first NT server EXCHLA01.

Next you're asked whether this NT server is to be a primary or backup domain controller or stand-alone server. If this is the first NT server you're setting up, make it the primary domain controller. If not, select one of the other options. Because of the load that domain controller status tends to put on an NT server, it's best not to make your Exchange servers do double duty as NT domain controllers. However, in the early phases of Exchange server installation, testing, and evaluation, you should be able to get away with assigning domain controller and Exchange server status to a single computer.

## Creating an Emergency Repair Diskette

The NT emergency repair diskette is used to recover operating system information in case of a partial hard disk failure. The Wizard next offers you a chance to make such a disk. Jump at it. I can't tell you how many times I've been able to recover a seemingly dead server by using its emergency repair disk.

## Selecting Components for Installation

The good old Wizard now offers you a list of components you can install. Decide what you want. Don't bother to install Windows Messaging. It'll be wholly overwritten later when you install an Exchange client on the server.

Also, don't bother with the fancy graphically based screen savers. They just eat up CPU. It's better to use NT Server's console-lock command for security, rather than a screen saver. Once you've got NT Server running and you're logged in, you can activate the command by simultaneously pressing the Ctrl, Alt, and Delete keys and clicking Lock Workstation in the Windows NT Security dialog box that pops up. While the screen is locked, press the Ctrl, Alt, and Delete keys for a password-prompt dialog box. Enter the password for the administrator or your own password, and you're back in business.

## Installing Windows NT Networking

NT Server is nothing without networking. The Wizard now takes you into the network installation portion of the Setup process. When the Wizard shows you a dialog box with 2) Installing Windows NT Networking highlighted, click Next.

First, the Wizard asks if you're wired to the network or will connect by a Remote Access Server dialup connection. Though you can connect Exchange servers using dialup connections, any Exchange server's primary connection should be through a hardwired, permanent link. So, select that option and click Next.

## Installing Internet Information Server

The Wizard's next question is key to your Exchange server installation. You're asked if you want to install Microsoft's Internet Information Server (IIS). If you want Exchange users and/or anonymous individuals to access your Exchange server using a Web browser, you'll need an Internet Information Server somewhere on your network.

The IIS doesn't have to be installed on an Exchange server. Again, if you're in the early installation, testing, and evaluation stage with Exchange Server, go ahead and install the IIS on this soon-to-be Exchange server. Later you can set up a separate server to support Web access for all your Exchange servers.

## Installing Network Adapters

The Wizard will now offer to auto-detect any network adapters in your computer. Automatic detection is generally pretty reliable, so I suggest you click Start Search and let Setup find your adapter or adapters. However, Setup can't detect information about I/O addresses, Interrupts, and DMA channels for a lot of older ISA bus cards, so verify what Setup says about these settings and enter the correct information, if necessary.

If Setup is unable to detect your adapter or adapters, click Select from list and find your adapter or adapters on the list that the Wizard brings up. You may have to use a diskette from your adapter's manufacturer, if drivers for the adapter aren't included with NT Server. NT Server's hardware compatibility list can help you here.

## Selecting Networking Protocols

Life is full of choices and so is NT Server installation. Your next set of choices is extremely important. The Wizard presents several networking protocol options. TCP/IP protocol installation is selected by default. If you've got Novell NetWare users, you'll also want to install IPX/SPX protocols. If you can at all avoid it, don't install NetBEUI, because it's an unrouteable protocol that's useful only in smaller networks. With your NT network properly set up, you'll have no need for it.

When you've finished selecting networking protocols, click Next. The Wizard next presents you with a list of requested and suggested networking services. Unless you have a strong reason for doing otherwise, accept the suggestions and click Next. If you want to get more deeply into networking options, click Select from list and make still more choices. For more details on networking protocols, see *Mastering Windows NT Server 4*.

## Installation at Last

The networking installation portion of the Wizard next warns you that it's about to actually install something. If you're ready, click Next. If not, move back through the Wizard's screens to correct or change anything that needs to be altered.

Installation begins, and you're almost immediately offered a dialog box with such things as the I/O port address, interrupt number, and transceiver type (e.g., 100BaseT) that will be assigned to your network card or cards. Select the default settings or, if offered, change the parameters as needed. Remember what I said above about problems Setup has auto-detecting these parameters on ISA bus adapters; the Wizard will warn you about this. Make sure these settings are correct. If they're not, you're going to have to do quite a bit of manual configuring of your server later on.

The Wizard next asks if there is a DHCP (Dynamic Host Configuration Protocol) server on your network. If there is and you answer yes, the DHCP server will assign an IP address to your computer automatically and give it other information necessary for TCP/IP networking. Unless you instruct otherwise, DHCP will usually give the server a different IP address every time the server's old IP address expires (every three days by default). That can wreak havoc on Internet mail and other TCP/IP related services on your server. So, even if you've got a DHCP server, it's best to assign a permanent IP address to the computer.

The Wizard next brings up a TCP/IP networking dialog box. For details on configuring TCP/IP networking, check out *Mastering Windows NT Server 4*. It's chock-full of useful stuff on the subject.

One thing to be sure to look into is Microsoft's Windows Internet Name Service (WINS). WINS lets you automatically or manually associate an NT networking computer name like EXCHLA01 with an IP address. Then, when a workstation or server comes looking for another workstation or server with a specific NT networking name, the WINS server tells it the associated IP address. With that address in hand, the workstation or server is able to quickly establish communications without the aid of slower, more limited protocols like NetBEUI.

When you've finished setting up TCP/IP networking, click OK. The Wizard next presents a dialog box that lets you review the binding of the networking services, protocols, and adapters that will be set up on your NT server. You can disable some of these if you wish, but for now I suggest you let them be.

Finally, the Wizard tells you that it is ready to start the network so you can continue configuring the network. Click Next to move along.

## Welcome to the Network

Assuming you're installing this server as a Primary Domain Controller, if all goes well network-wise, the Wizard asks you to specify the name of the domain you want to create and the administrator name and password for the domain. Since you're creating a new domain, you'll be creating a new administrator name and setting a password for it. Enter this information and click Next. In my case I entered **LA** as my domain name. Remember from Chapter 5 that this is the name of the Exchange site this server will support. I entered the name **administrator** and a password of my choice in the administrator name and password fields presented by the Wizard.

If you don't get the dialog box discussed in the paragraph above and you're using an ISA network adapter, it's most likely because one or more of the default parameters offered by the Wizard for your adapter—the I/O address port, interrupt, or DMA channel—is incorrect. In such a case, NT Server is unable to talk to the network adapter and set up network communications. Verify these parameters and rerun NT Server installation. Remember how I noted the importance of getting those adapter parameters right? Now you know why.

## NT Servers and Workstations Need Special Rights to Enter a Domain

NT is very security-conscious. NT servers and workstations can't enter a domain unless they've been given permission to do so by an NT account with sufficient rights. This permission is given using an NT application called *Server Manager*. When you first set up a domain, you obviously can't get permission to enter it from anywhere. So entering an administrator name and password creates the first account in your NT domain and gives that account the rights to enter your server into the domain. You can then use Server Manager with that same account or another account that is granted similar rights to grant other servers and workstations permission to enter the domain. I'll talk more about all of this later in this chapter.

## Installing Internet Information Server

After Setup does its thing for a bit, the Wizard presents you with a dialog box with one option remaining, Finish. Click Finish to complete the NT Server installation.

If you've asked to install the Internet Information Server, you're then presented with a list of IIS options. At this point, just accept them all and click OK. Answer the typical installation questions that come next and when you're finished, IIS installation begins. For help installing the IIS see Sybex's *Mastering Windows NT Server 4* and Peter Dyson's *Mastering Microsoft Internet Information Server 4* (Sybex, 1997).

## Finishing Up

To complete NT Server installation, you're asked to set the correct time, time zone, and date to configure your display adapter. When you've finished with these, Setup copies files from the CD-ROM disk to your hard disk drive and then prepares your computer to run NT. If you asked to create an emergency repair disk, you'll be offered the opportunity to do so now.

When all else is done, Setup brings up a dialog box that lets you reboot your computer and start NT. Do it! NT Server boots up and asks you to log into your newly created domain. Enter the administrator name and password you provided during installation; you're now running NT Server.

At this point, you can fiddle with your display adapter's video resolution, if necessary, and do any other housekeeping chores you'd like. To play with the display adapter resolution, right-click the desktop and choose Properties.

At last, you get your reward. It may seem anticlimactic, however. All that work and what do you get? Microsoft Windows, that's what! Heck, you've probably seen that a hundred times. No bells? No whistles? No dancing bears? Nothing— just plain vanilla Windows front-ending one of the most powerful multitasking, multithreaded operating systems in the world. Enjoy!

Oh yes, if you're offered the opportunity to back up the previous version of NT so you can recover in case the Service Pack install doesn't work, jump at the chance. I can't tell you how many times some little thing went wrong in an upgrade and how returning to the previous service level saved my life.

## Upgrade Time

Now that you've installed NT Server 4, don't forget to bring it up to at least Service Pack 5. Service Pack installation is easy. Get the Service Pack off the Internet or from Microsoft on a CD-ROM disk. Before running a Service Pack update, be sure to shut down all running programs. If you've downloaded the Service Pack update, you'll find that everything you need for the update is compressed into a single self-executing file. Find this file with NT Explorer and double-click it. The installation process starts automatically. Follow the instructions. If you got the Service Pack on a CD-ROM, insert the disk into your NT server's CD-ROM player. If the update shell starts automatically, just do as asked. If not, find and run the file UPDATE.EXE. When the update is finished, your computer is rebooted and you're good to go.

**WARNING**   As of this writing at least, Microsoft's Internet Information Server is one of the most volatile pieces of software in the world. If you have an earlier version of NT Server 4, IIS version 2 is included. You need at least version 3 of IIS and an IIS component called "Active Server Pages" to access Exchange servers through the Internet, for example, to see your mail or schedule with a Web browser. So, after installing IIS, check its version number. If it's less than 3, get your hands on and install IIS 3 or later. If you aren't offered the option of installing Active Server Pages when you install IIS 3, get and install them, too. IIS upgrades and Active Server Pages come with Service Pack 3 and higher.

# Setting Up and Formatting Other Disk Partitions

If you installed more than one hard disk drive in your computer or if the partition you installed NT Server on is smaller than the disk drive the partition resides on, you're not quite done yet. You'll need to use NT Server's Disk Administrator applet to set up and format one or more additional disk partitions. Here's how to do it.

---

**WARNING**    The built-in IDE controllers on most modern Pentium II and III motherboards require special drivers. NT will boot-up and you'll be able to start NT's Disk Administrator, but things could go wrong. You need to replace the IDE drivers installed by NT before you start setting up and formatting additional disk partitions. If you don't, NT could fail during drive setup. Check out the driver diskette that came with your motherboard for the correct software and instructions on installing it.

---

To get to the applet, click the Start menu icon on the NT Server Task Bar at the bottom of your screen. Next select Programs from the Start menu; then select Administrative Tools from the Programs menu and finally select Disk Administrator from the Administrative Tools menu. (See Figure 6.1.)

---

**FIGURE 6.1:**

Starting NT Server's Disk Administrator applet

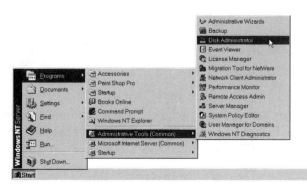

In Figure 6.2 you can see that half of Disk 0 in my server is formatted NTFS style. That happened when I installed NT Server. The other half hasn't been partitioned or formatted. Disk 1 is totally unpartitioned and unformatted. To partition a drive, click it in Disk Administrator's graphic presentation of your disk drives. Then select Create from the Partition menu. This brings up a dialog box like the one in Figure 6.3. Set the partition size you want in MB. When you're done, click OK.

Disk Administrator's graphic presentation of your disk drives now changes to show that the partition exists but isn't yet formatted. To format the partition, select Format from the Tools menu. Use the Format dialog box that pops up to select such things as NTFS or FAT formatting and click Start. You'll next see a little dialog box warning you about all the terrible things you can do to your drive by formatting it. Click OK, and formatting begins.

**FIGURE 6.2:**

Disk Administrator ready for some disk partitioning and formatting

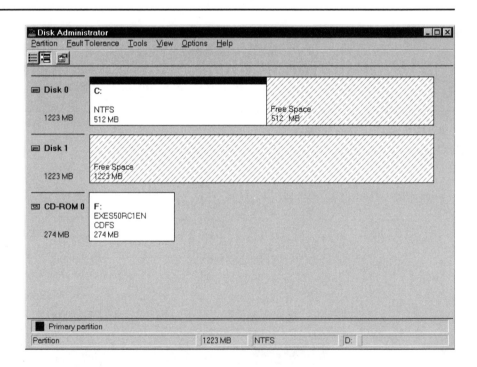

After a partition is formatted, Disk Administrator's graphic presentation of it changes. In Figure 6.4 I've formatted the rest of Disk 0 as a FAT partition and all of Disk 1 as an NTFS partition. Why? Glad you asked.

**FIGURE 6.3:**

Using Disk Administrator to set the size of a disk partition

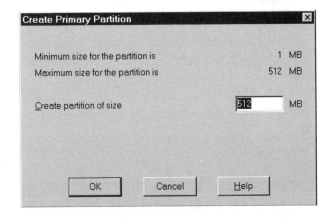

**FIGURE 6.4:**

Two disk drives as partitioned and formatted using Disk Administrator

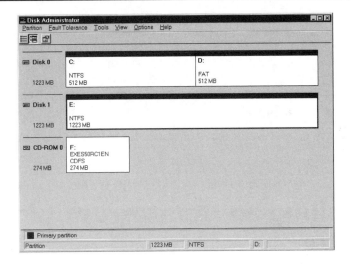

In some cases, access to FAT partitions is quick and dirty, while access to NTFS partitions is a bit slower. Because FAT partitions offer some speed advantages over NTFS when transaction logs are written, Microsoft advises putting Exchange Server's temporary transaction logs on a FAT partition. We'll talk more about these logs later. Put simply, these logs hold data that Exchange Server must quickly dump from memory when it's too busy to write the data to its permanent directory and information store databases. Later, at its leisure, Exchange Server moves data from its transaction logs to the databases. That 512MB FAT partition on Disk 0 will be reserved for the transaction logs.

As mentioned earlier, though they're a bit slower to access in some situations, NTFS partitions are more fault tolerant and secure than those of the FAT persuasion. Microsoft strongly suggests that you put your Exchange Server databases on NTFS partitions. That's why the NTFS Disk 1 has one NTFS partition.

We've only touched the surface of Disk Administrator in this section. Take a look at *Mastering Windows NT Server 4* for more on this very useful NT Server applet.

## Don't Forget Shutdown

Like all good operating systems, NT Server must be shut down; you should never just turn off an NT server. NT Server buffers a lot of data to RAM before writing it to disk. Though the writes from RAM are done quickly, on a busy server there's always data waiting in the buffers. A graceful shutdown ensures this data is all written out to disk. To shut down a server, click the Start menu icon and select Shutdown. You can select from three options: Shutdown the Computer, Restart the Computer, or Close All Programs and Log On as a Different User. If you pick Shutdown the Computer, don't turn off the computer until you see a message telling you that it's okay to do so.

# Installing an Uninterruptible Power Supply

An uninterruptible power supply (UPS) takes power from the wall socket and feeds it to a battery to keep it charged. The UPS continuously feeds power from its battery to your computer through internal power-conversion circuitry. When power from the wall socket fails, the UPS battery continues to supply power to your computer, letting it run at least until the battery is exhausted and, if so configured, shutting down the computer before UPS battery power is exhausted.

As I noted in Chapter 5, a UPS should be considered part of your NT Server installation. Let's install one right away.

# The UPS Itself

Buy a UPS with "online" circuitry; these tend to be the best and most responsive in power outages. Also, it should be one that can be controlled by an NT server, so it should be equipped with an RS-232 port that you connect by a cable to one of the server's serial ports. Get the RS-232 cable from the UPS's vendor if at all possible; then you won't have to mess with that old devil known as RS-232 interfacing.

NT Server's built-in UPS software talks to the UPS and can shut down the server gracefully, just as if you'd done it manually. Get a UPS that can detect and signal both a wall socket power failure and a low battery (which usually means about two minutes of power left in the battery). With low-battery information available, NT Server doesn't have to begin a shutdown immediately on power failure. If wall-socket power returns before the low-battery signal, no shutdown needs to occur at all.

For more on selecting a UPS, see *Mastering Windows NT Server 4*.

# Configuring UPS Support

Figure 6.5 shows NT Server's UPS setup screen; to get to it, just double-click the UPS icon in the Control Panel. To get to the Control Panel, click the Start menu icon at the bottom of the screen, then point to Settings on the Start menu, and finally point to Control Panel. In the figure, the UPS is connected to the second serial port. I've told the setup program that my UPS sends positive voltages to indicate power failure, low battery, and remote UPS shutdown, as indicated on the screen under UPS Configuration. (The best source of information as to whether your UPS's signaling voltages are negative or positive is the UPS's manual or manufacturer.)

By checking the Remote UPS Shutdown box, I'm telling NT that it can shut off the flow of power to the server. NT would take this action if it detected very erratic power-failure or low-battery signals, which can indicate battery problems and the need to devote all power in the UPS to recharging the battery.

Under Execute Command File, I've told NT to execute a batch file, END.BAT, on shutdown. This particular file deletes some temporary files that one of my applications writes and closes but leaves on disk until the application itself is closed. This ensures that the files are cleaned off the disk, even though the application will remain open if the server is shut down due to a power outage.

**FIGURE 6.5:**

NT Server's UPS
setup screen

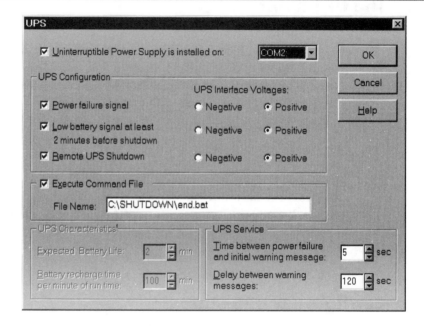

I've accepted the default values in the UPS Service area located in the lower-right corner of the configuration window. This means that when a power failure occurs, the UPS service will send a message to users five seconds after it happens and then every 120 seconds thereafter until power is restored or the server is shut down.

The UPS Characteristics area in the lower-left corner of the window applies to UPSes that don't provide a low-battery signal. Since you'll be sure to buy a UPS with such a signal, you won't even get an opportunity to fill in this information, right?

## Testing the UPS

Of course, you need to test your UPS regularly. Do the tests during off-hours and warn users that you'll be taking the system down. Testing is simple: Just cut power to the UPS and make sure everything goes as expected. Be sure to let the test go far enough for battery power to run out and for the UPS service to shut down the server.

## UPSes with Special Software

Most good UPSes come with special software for NT. This software replaces the basic UPS software that comes with NT, providing such enhanced features as scheduled periodic testing of the UPS and monitoring of power quantity and quality over time. This software doesn't add much to the cost of a UPS, and it's well worth having.

# Setting Up NT Backup

As I mentioned in Chapter 5, a variety of products are available for backing up NT. NT comes with its own backup software, which is quite functional if you're not using a tape autoloader. It's important to get some sort of backup going immediately on your NT server, so let's get NT's own backup program up and running right now.

## Hardware

Okay, let me say it right at the start: Please don't use anything other than 4mm, 8mm, or DLT SCSI–compatible tape drives. Forget those awful third-floppy mini-cartridge thingies that take forever to back up a byte of information to low-capacity tape cartridges. And don't mess with those fancy new units that use gigantic but relatively low-capacity (and high-priced) 3M cartridges. Stick with the proven, working, relatively inexpensive 4mm, 8mm, or DLT tape technologies. If you go with 4mm, be sure to get a DDS3 or DDS4 unit that can handle 12GB or larger tapes.

Installing a SCSI tape backup unit is easy. Just plug it in and be sure that your SCSI chain is terminated at both ends. You can use the same SCSI controller you use for your disk drives, though you'll get better backup throughput if you use a separate controller for the tape drive. Also be sure to use the shortest SCSI cables you can: When a SCSI cable chain (including the cable inside your computer that supports internal disk drives) gets too long, you'll start experiencing some pretty crazy data glitches on your disks and tape drives.

## Installing Tape Device Drivers

NT comes with device drivers for a wide range of tape drives. To install the driver you need, find the Tape Devices icon in the Control Panel and double-click it. This brings up the Tape Devices dialog box shown in Figure 6.6. Click the Drivers tab to move to the Drivers property page and click Add. (See Figure 6.7.) Select the driver you want and click OK. The driver will then be installed.

If you're using a SCSI 4mm tape drive, your life should be quite easy. The generic driver for 4mm devices (shown in Figure 6.7) will work with any SCSI 4mm drive, unless the drive's manufacturer has done something weird with the unit's interface. Even if this is the case, drivers for those units are either included in NT Server or are available from the tape unit's vendor. NT Server comes with drivers for Exabyte 8200 and 8500 8mm drives, which are also quite generic.

**FIGURE 6.6:**

Add a new tape device driver using the Windows NT Tape Devices applet.

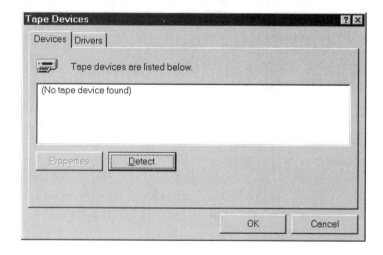

FIGURE 6.7:

Select the right driver from the Install Driver dialog box.

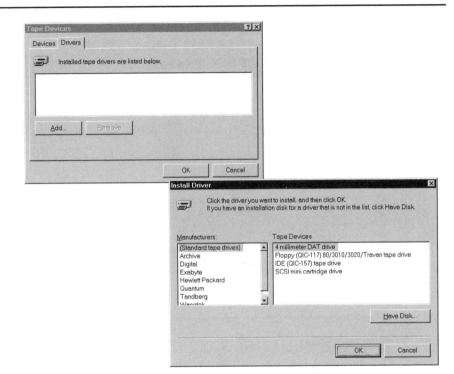

## Setting Up a Basic Backup

The real lessons we can learn about backups have to do with Exchange Server—but we're not ready for such a lesson right now. Nevertheless, you should have a backup in place immediately. So right now I'll take you through a simple backup scenario using NT's Backup program. In a later chapter, I'll show you how to back up Exchange Server.

To open NT's backup program, click the Start menu icon, point to Programs, then point to Administrative Tools and, within Administrative Tools, point to Backup. This opens a window like the one in Figure 6.8. In the Drives window, click the little box next to the drives you want to back up. I've chosen to back up both the C and D drives on my computer.

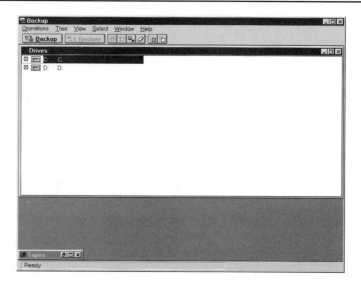

## Selective Backups

If you want to back up only some directories or files on a disk drive, double-click the icon for the drive. This opens a typical directory tree from which you can choose what you want to back up.

Next, double-click the Tapes icon at the bottom of the Backup window to open the Tapes window. If you've put a blank cartridge in your tape drive, your Tapes window will look like the one in Figure 6.9. The only time the window *won't* look like this one is when you've cheated and installed one of those infernal minicartridge tape units. In that case, you'll see something—though I have no idea what, because I refuse to get mixed up with the things—telling you the tape isn't formatted. To format it, click the Operations menu and select Format Tape from the menu.

Backup's Tapes window
indicates that a blank tape
is installed in the drive.

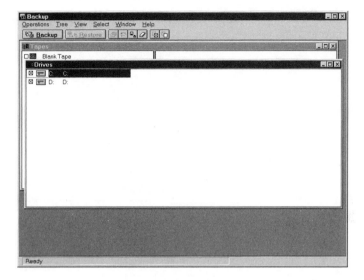

When everything is ready, with your blank tape in the drive, click the Drives
window. Then, click the Backup button located on the toolbar (in the top left-
hand corner of the Backup window). This brings up the Backup Information dialog box (see Figure 6.10). In the figure, I've left the default Tape Name intact. I've
also instructed Backup to verify the backup and to back up the server's Registry—which, among other things, replaces such files as SYSTEM.INI and
WIN.INI on NT servers.

I've left the Hardware Compression box unchecked, since choosing that option
would mean that the tape won't be readable if I ever use a piece of equipment
with a different compression scheme. Under Backup Set Information, I've added
my own description for the backup. I'll hold on to this backup for a while, since it
will let me restore my system to the pristine way it was just after I installed NT
Server. I'm doing a normal (full) backup as opposed to a differential or incremental backup, and I've accepted the default Log Information parameters. The little
scroll bar on the right-hand side of the Backup Set Information area of the Backup
Information dialog box indicates that I'm backing up more than one disk drive.
Scrolling down lets me put in backup set information for my D drive. That's it.
Now just click the OK button to start the backup.

**FIGURE 6.10:**

Setting up a backup using the Backup Information dialog box

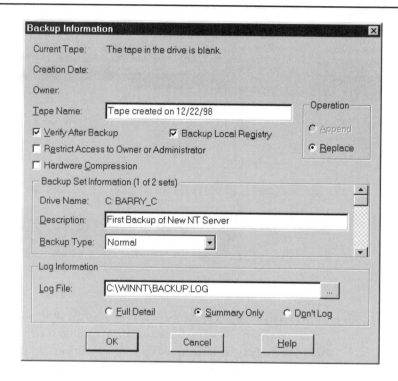

Restoring files is just as easy—you use the same interface. And as with backing up, you can restore all or only some files. I could say a lot more about backups, but I'll save it for a later chapter when I discuss backing up Exchange Server.

# Giving Domain Access to Users and NT Systems

You can log into a domain on any Windows-based computer simply by entering a valid domain username and password. As noted previously, Windows NT workstations and servers can enter a domain only after they've been given explicit permission to do so. Here's how to create domain users and permit NT systems to join a domain.

## Creating Domain Accounts and Groups

An NT/Exchange user must log in to a domain using an NT security account. Each account is created in a specific domain and may be given rights in other domains through trust relationships. Each Exchange user has a mailbox on a specific Exchange home server. Though there are some exceptions, which I'll discuss in a later chapter, to access their Exchange home server, users must be logged in to the same domain as the server or into a domain that is trusted by the home server's domain.

You'll remember from Chapter 4 that you can set up an NT security account at the same time you create a new Exchange mailbox. Unless you have a specific reason for doing otherwise, you're best off letting Exchange create new NT security accounts. It will give users the rights they need in the domain and configure them properly for Exchange.

Though you'll often create Exchange mailboxes and NT security accounts at the same time, there will be times when you'll have to create new accounts or groups outside of Exchange. Since we'll need to set up a new account and group before we install Exchange Server in the next chapter, here's a brief, basic tutorial on creating accounts and groups in a domain.

Figure 6.11 shows the User Manager for Domains, which you use to create and modify domain users and groups. You'll find this app in the Administrative Tools program group on your NT server.

Make sure you're working in the right domain. The domain name appears at the top of the dialog box, right next to the words "User Manager." (Notice that in Figure 6.11 I'm in my LA domain.) If you've got more than one domain and you're not in the right one, click the User menu and then choose Select Domain. You'll see the dialog box shown in Figure 6.12. Click the domain you want, then click OK to return to the User Manager screen. The domain you chose will now be listed at the top of the screen.

**FIGURE 6.11:**

The User Manager for Domains

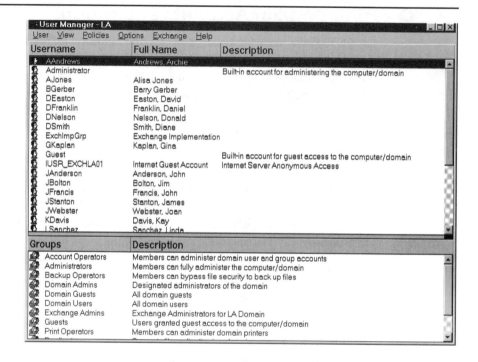

**FIGURE 6.12:**

Selecting the correct domain

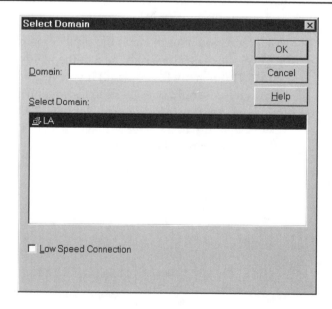

To add a new user, select New User from the User Manager's User menu; the New User dialog box will pop up (see Figure 6.13). Here you'll give the user a user-name (alias), a full name, and a password, and you'll set rules about passwords.

**FIGURE 6.13:**

Creating a new
domain user

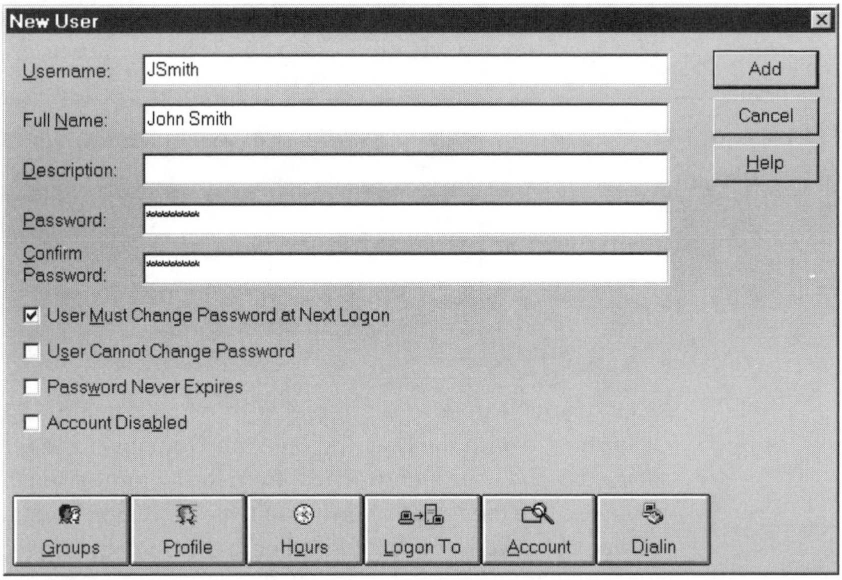

Using the large buttons at the bottom of the dialog box, you can add a user to different user groups, specify a script that runs on login, set valid domain login hours for the user, specify whether the user can log in to all workstations or just specific ones in the domain, and specify the type of account being used. These custom user options come into play as you begin to implement a range of applications in your domain. For more on these options and creating domain users in general, see *Mastering Windows NT Server 4*.

NT security groups allow you to give specific rights to a set of NT security accounts. Think of them as shortcuts. Instead of assigning rights to each account separately, you give them to the group, and then all members of the group inherit the rights. I'll save the specifics for the next chapter, when we'll set up a group for Exchange Server administrators.

## Giving Domain Access to NT Servers and Workstations

You'll need to grant an NT server or NT workstations access rights to a domain in two situations: before you install them and if you need to move them to a new domain. You grant access rights using the Server Manager program, which is in the Administrative Tools program group on your NT server. Select the Server Manager icon to get started. Figure 6.14 shows the Server Manager dialog box.

**FIGURE 6.14:**

The Server Manager

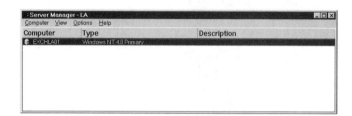

Once you've opened the applet, if the right domain isn't already selected, select it as you did with the User Manager for Domains (using the Computer menu instead of the User menu). Then, from the Computer menu, select Add to Domain. Use the Add Computer to Domain dialog box to add a new workstation, server, or backup domain controller to the domain (see Figure 6.15). Click Add when you're done. Now, when that new or wandering NT server or workstation shows up, the domain will welcome it with open arms. As you'll remember from my NT Server installation instructions, if you forget to grant domain rights prior to installation, you can actually grant them during an NT server or workstation installation. Microsoft put this capability into the installation program for those of us who can't remember what we ate for dinner last night.

**FIGURE 6.15:**

Using the Server Manager to give domain access to an NT system

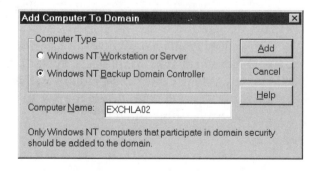

# Setting Up NT Server Clients

I'm going to cover Windows 95/98 networking in a fair amount of detail, and I'll give less attention to networking the other Windows-based operating systems. When push comes to shove, Windows networking is pretty much the same no matter which flavor of the OS you're using—Windows 95, Windows 98, Windows NT Server or Workstation, or Windows for Workgroups. There are minor differences in the graphical interfaces for each OS, but that's about it.

## Windows 95/98

During installation of Windows 95/98, if the computer you're setting up has a network adapter, you'll have the option to set up networking components. You'll go through a process very similar to the one for setting up NT Server networking at the product's installation.

To install and configure networking after a Windows 95/98 installation, start by double-clicking the Add New Hardware icon on the Windows 95/98 Control Panel. This brings up a Wizard that will attempt to detect anything new you've put into the computer since installing the OS. Track through the Wizard's screens; if the adapter is detected (and it very likely will be), the Wizard will install the proper driver for it. If the adapter isn't detected, you can either try adding it manually using the Wizard or wait until the next step.

When the Wizard is finished, double-click the Network icon in the Windows 95/98 Control Panel. This brings up the Network dialog box (see Figure 6.16). Here's how to set up the Network dialog box.

**FIGURE 6.16:**

Windows 95's Network
dialog box

## Configuration

Configuration includes the installation and setup of network adapter drivers,
Windows network client software, network protocol support, and network-
oriented services.

**Installing Adapter Drivers**    If you weren't able to install a driver for the
computer's network adapter, you'll need to do it here. Click Add in the Network
dialog box, then double-click Adapter in the resulting Select Network Component Type dialog box. This brings up the Select Network Adapters dialog box (see
Figure 6.17). If your adapter is listed, double-click it. If it isn't listed, you'll need a
driver on diskette from the manufacturer. Click Have Disk and tell Windows 95
which drive the disk is in. Once the driver is installed, click OK to return to the
Network dialog box.

Setting up a network
adapter

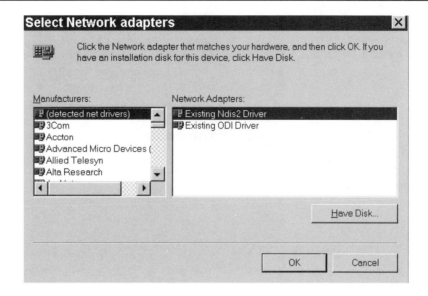

**Installing Windows Client Software**   Next, you'll install one or more Windows clients. Click the Add button in the Network dialog box and then double-click Client in the resulting Select Network Component Type dialog box. As you can see in Figure 6.18, you can install clients for Microsoft and other network manufacturers. Install the Microsoft network clients by clicking Microsoft in the Manufacturers area of the screen and then double-clicking Client for Microsoft Networks in the Network Clients area. Repeat this to install each of the client types needed on the computer.

If the computer you're setting up needs Novell NetWare 3.*x* support, I strongly suggest you use client NetWare support from Microsoft rather than from Novell—unless, of course, there's some reason the computer needs Novell's ODI stack or can't use Microsoft's substitute. If the computer needs NetWare 4.*x* support, you'll have to use Novell's own shell support. Novell's and Microsoft's support for each other's networks is constantly changing; stay in touch with the vendors for news on the latest and greatest.

**FIGURE 6.18:**

Selecting the network
clients to install

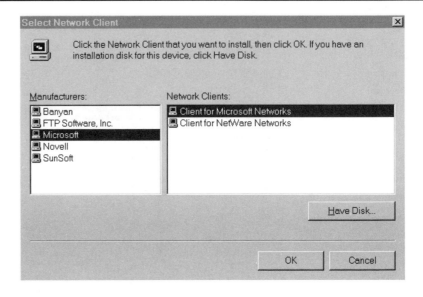

**Installing Network Protocols**    When you finish adding clients, you're ready
to add any network protocols the computer needs. Back in the Network dialog
box, click Add, then double-click Protocol. This brings up the Select Network Protocol dialog box shown in Figure 6.19.

Depending on the clients you've added, you will already have installed some
protocols. For example, if you've added Microsoft's support for its and Novell's
networks, you've already installed the NetBEUI and IPX/SPX protocols. In the
Select Network Protocol dialog box, add TCP/IP support. I prefer Microsoft's
implementation of TCP/IP. To install it, just select Microsoft from the list on the
left and TCP/IP from the list on the right. You'll be taken through a standard
TCP/IP installation process.

**FIGURE 6.19:**

Selecting the network
protocols to install

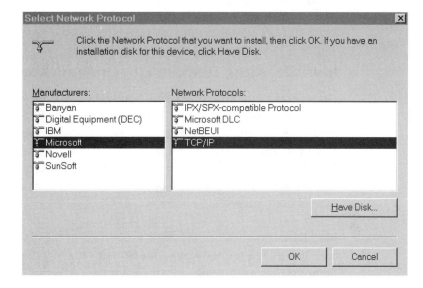

**Installing Network Services**    You can add some special network-oriented services to the computer you're setting up. From the Network dialog box, click Add, then double-click Service in the resulting Select Network Component Type dialog box. This brings up the Select Network Service dialog box shown in Figure 6.20. Services include file and printer sharing for Microsoft and NetWare networks, as well as some backup agents.

**FIGURE 6.20:**

Selecting which networking
services to install

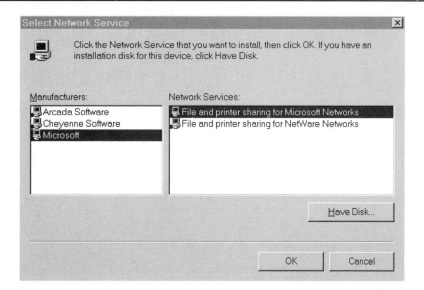

File and printer sharing let the computer share its resources with others in its domain. The agents allow backup software that's running on another computer to back up all or part of the machine you're setting up.

## Identification, Domain Log On, and Access Control

Before you set up any networking parameters, the Network dialog box has only one property page, Configuration (see Figure 6.16). Once you've added network components, two more property pages are added to the Network dialog box: Identification and Access Control. The Identification page lets you enter information about the computer and the login domain. The Access Control page is for setting resource-sharing security options for the computer. Let's take a brief look at each of these pages.

**Identification**    Click the Identification tab at the top of the Network dialog box. You'll see a property page like the one shown in Figure 6.21. Type in the name you want to give the computer you're installing. You can optionally type in a description of the computer.

**FIGURE 6.21:**

Identifying the computer

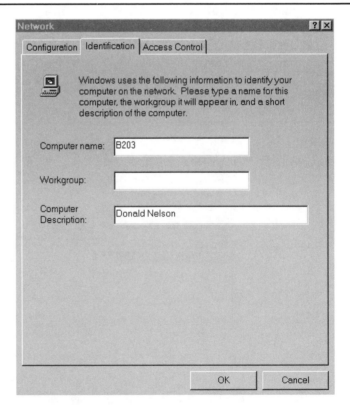

**Domain Log On**   Now you need to set up for the domain you want to access. Click the Network dialog box's Configuration tab (see Figure 6.22). Then double-click Client for Microsoft Networks to bring up the dialog box shown in Figure 6.23. Select Log On to Windows NT Domain. Type in the name of the domain you want to log into; in my case, LA. Select Quick Logon or Logon and Restore Network Connections, depending on how much network traffic you want to generate at initial logon and whether you're willing to wait a bit when you connect to a network resource for the first time.

**FIGURE 6.22:**

Preparing to configure the Client for Microsoft Networks

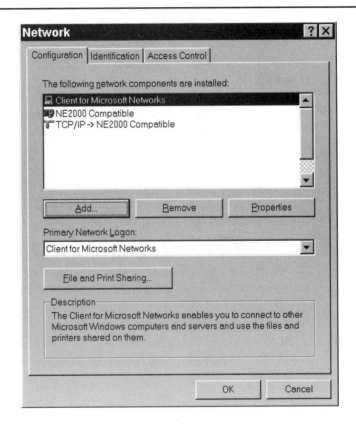

**FIGURE 6.23:**

Setting domain logon information for the Client for Microsoft Networks

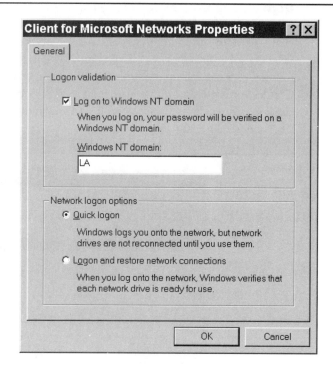

**Access Control**  Next, click the Access Control tab in the Network dialog box to bring up the Access Control property page (see Figure 6.24). Here's where you set security for the computer. With share-level access control, anyone who logs in to the domain will have full access to any disk files or printers shared out on the computer, unless they are password-protected. If you select the User-Level Access Control option, you will be able to specify which domain users and groups will be able to access each resource shared out on the computer.

FIGURE 6.24:

Setting access parameters
for shared resources

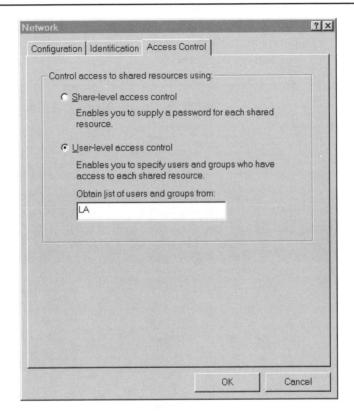

## Rebooting to Implement Changes

When you're done with network configuration, click OK in the Network dialog
box. You'll be told to reboot your computer for the changes you've made to take
effect; go ahead and reboot now. When the Windows 95 or 98 screen comes back
up, you should be able to see your NT server when you double-click your desktop's Network Neighborhood icon.

# Windows NT Workstation

Like NT Server, NT Workstation lets you do network configuration at the time
you install it. And as with NT Server, if you need to do a network configuration
after installing NT Workstation, you can do it by double-clicking the Network

icon in the NT Workstation Control Panel. This brings up the Network dialog box shown in Figure 6.25. You may have to fish around a bit, but you should be able to find the NT Workstation equivalents of all the buttons and pick lists we just covered for Windows 95.

**FIGURE 6.25:**

NT Workstation's Network dialog box

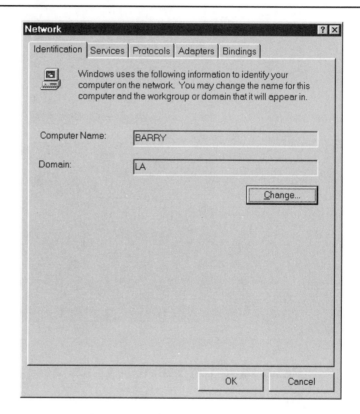

## Windows for Workgroups

I won't even mention Windows 3.1. In my opinion, Windows for Workgroups is *the* only choice if you want to network Windows and you're not ready for Windows 95/98 or NT Workstation. You can upgrade existing Windows 3.1 installations to Windows for Workgroups for a modest sum, then use Windows for Workgroups for all new installations.

As with the other Windows operating systems, you can do a networking setup when you install Windows for Workgroups, as long as the computer has a network adapter. If you need to mess with networking after installation, click the

Network Setup icon in the Network program group; this opens the Windows for Workgroups' Network Setup dialog box (see Figure 6.26). As with NT Workstation, you should be able to determine very quickly how to do all the network setup tasks I've already discussed in detail for Windows 95/98.

**FIGURE 6.26:**

Windows for Workgroups' Network Setup dialog box

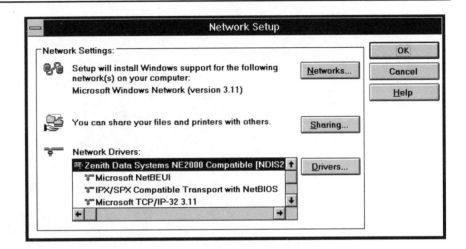

## Novell NetWare and Other Clients

If you have clients that run NetWare drivers, there are a couple ways you can give them general access to NT servers. You can read about these in *Mastering Windows NT Server 4*. In addition, if you need to link DOS or OS/2 workstations to NT Server, check out *Mastering Windows NT Server 4.*

# Conclusion

In this chapter you learned how to install a Windows NT server: preparing hardware, installing software, hooking up and configuring UPS and backup protection, giving domain access to users and NT systems, configuring networking, and setting up different kinds of clients.

With NT Server in place, we can now move on to installing Exchange Server itself. Here we goooooooooooooooooooooooo (fade toward the end). You didn't think our trip to Wonderland was over, did you?

# Installing an Exchange Server

- Getting ready

- Installation

- Preparing to run Exchange Server

**T**his will be a fun chapter because, after all the theory and planning and installation of NT Server, we're actually going to get an Exchange server up and running. Installing an Exchange server is a three-step process. First, you go through several operations to prepare for the installation. Second, you run the Exchange Server Setup program. And third, you do a few minor housekeeping chores once installation is complete. Let's get to work.

# Getting Ready

Before installing an Exchange server, you'll need to ensure that your hardware is properly set up. Then you'll have to pull together some key information about your NT server, a couple of user accounts, and your soon-to-be Exchange server. Finally, you'll set up security for your Exchange server.

## Verifying Server Hardware Setup

If you've read the previous chapters, you're more than ready now. Unless you're running a really basic test machine, I'm assuming you've got that 500MHz Pentium system with 256MB of RAM and two 4GB SCSI drives that I recommended back in Chapter 5. You should also have installed a good UPS and a 4mm, 8mm, or DLT SCSI tape backup device.

## Gathering NT Server Information

You'll need to assemble information on the domain system that Exchange Server will be installed into, as well as the type of NT server you'll be installing it on.

### The Domain Model

If you're installing Exchange Server in a single-domain system as defined in Chapter 4, you won't have to take any special steps before installation. If Exchange Server will operate in domain systems based on any of the other three domain models defined in Chapter 4, or if your Exchange site will cross domains, I assume you've already set up the required cross-domain trusts.

## The NT Server's Role

As I suggested earlier in this book, you'll normally want to run Exchange Server on an NT server that is neither a primary nor backup domain controller. This is to ensure that Exchange Server and domain-controller functions, both of which can place a heavy load on your server, won't have to compete with each other on the same server.

In addition to potential performance issues, running Exchange Server on a primary domain controller can slow the time it takes the server to come back up after a crash and recovery from a tape backup. Also, if you ever have to move an Exchange server to a different domain, you'll have to do a fair amount of additional work if the server is also a primary or secondary backup controller.

All this having been said, you should always have at least one backup domain controller. So, if you're running a small network, placing your Exchange Server on a secondary domain controller won't cause the world to end. Users on a small network will place limited demand on server resources, and the risk of a major server crash is probably worth the cost of maintaining a separate secondary domain controller.

This, of course, is the ideal. Since this is your first Exchange server installation, you'll probably use the NT server you set up in the last chapter. And since it's probably the first NT server you've set up, it's also acting as a primary domain controller. Not to worry—just don't expect to run a monster production Exchange server on this kind of setup.

All of the above goes double for the Internet Information Server (IIS). If you want to access your Exchange server from the Internet, for example, to work with mail in your Exchange mailbox, you'll need to be running IIS. IIS can be an even bigger resource hog on an NT server than domain controller support. For early testing and learning it's fine to run Exchange Server and IIS on an NT server that is also a domain controller. I do strongly suggest, however, you use that 500MHz Pentium jobbie I've been touting.

## The NT Server Name

Be sure you've set the NT server computer name to the name you want Exchange Server to use when referring to the third item in the Exchange hierarchy, the server. If it's not set to the desired name, *change it now*. To change the name after Exchange installation is difficult to impossible.

# Gathering Account Information

To install Exchange Server, you'll need info about the NT server's Administrator account. You'll also have to come up with names for an NT account and group you'll create later in this chapter.

### The Administrator Account for the NT Server

When you installed NT Server you created an account (probably named "Administrator") and entered a password for it. Be sure you've got the password on hand.

### The Username and Password for the Site Services Account

In a minute, you'll create a special domain-based Windows NT security account that will be used by all Exchange servers in a site to run Exchange Server processes. Without this account, Exchange Server processes can't run—which means that Exchange Server itself can't run. The account also ensures that unauthorized Exchange servers can't be introduced into an Exchange site.

Pick a username and password for this account (the name "Services" is a good if unimaginative choice). You'll create the Site Services account shortly.

### The Name of the Exchange Server Administration Group

It's a good idea to set up a domain-based group that has specific rights to administer an Exchange server. Then, when you need to give someone these rights, all you have to do is add them to the group.

You'll create the Exchange Server administration group in just a bit. Right now, you just have to pick a name for it. A good choice is "Exchange Admins." My creativity zooms.

# Gathering Exchange Server Information

The Exchange Server Setup program will give you a number of options. To respond to some of these options, you'll need some specific information, including the names of your organization and site, the path where Exchange Server is to be installed, and a list of the Exchange Server components you want to install.

## The Organization and Site Names

The organization and site names represent the top two items in the Exchange hierarchy. You should have these ready from Chapter 5.

## The Installation Path

The Setup program defaults to the path C:\EXCHSRVR. Unless there's some reason that you don't want to use this path (e.g., to install Exchange Server on another drive), accept the default.

## What Will Be Installed?

As with most programs installed in Microsoft Windows environments, you'll be able to choose which Exchange Server components you want to install. Options include Exchange Server itself and the Exchange Administrator program. Within the Exchange Server option you can choose whether to install specific subsets of components. For your first installation, you'll probably want to install everything—which is *a lot* of stuff; that's one reason for the high-capacity drives.

---

**NOTE**    Exchange client software can be set up so users can install it from a server. This is done in a separate step that we'll cover in Chapter 11.

---

# Setting Up Security

As I noted earlier, Exchange security is based on an NT security account (Site Services) and administration group (the Exchange Server administration group). We're now ready to set these up.

## Creating the Site Services Account

To set up the Site Services account, log in to the domain in which you'll be installing Exchange Server. Log in as Administrator, then open User Manager for Domains in the Administrative Tools program group. (Go back to Chapter 6 if you need background on the User Manager for Domains.)

From the main User Manager for Domains window, click the User menu and select New User. Next, fill in the New User dialog box that pops up (use Figure 7.1 as a guide). Be sure to deselect the User Must Change Password at Next Logon box and to select User Cannot Change Password and Password Never Expires. When you're done, click Add and then click Close. (The Cancel button turns into a Close button after you click Add.) On installation, Exchange Server Setup will grant any required rights to the account you've just created.

**FIGURE 7.1:**

Setting up the Site Services account

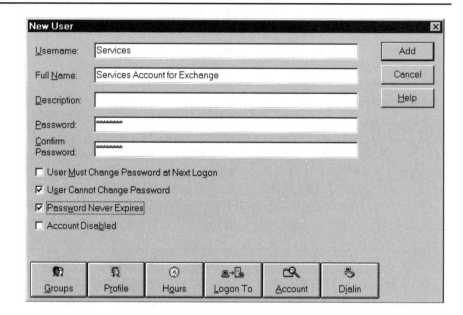

Remain in the User Manager for Domains for the next step.

If you haven't already done so, create an account for yourself. We'll use the account in just a second.

---

**WARNING**   Be sure to record the username and password for the Site Services account; you'll need them when you install Exchange Server.

---

## Creating the Exchange Server Administration Group

From the User menu in the User Manager for Domains, select New Global Group and enter a group name and description in the dialog box that pops up (see Figure 7.2). Then, from the Not Members box, select the users to be added to the group and click Add. (Add the account you created for yourself to the group.) Finally, close the User Manager for Domains applet by clicking the Close button.

After Exchange Server has been installed, you'll be able to grant your group the proper permissions. I'll cover that process later in this chapter.

**FIGURE 7.2:**

Setting up the Exchange Server administration group

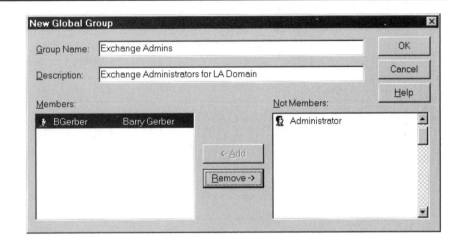

# Running the Exchange Server Setup Program

At last! Insert the Exchange Server 5.5 CD-ROM into your CD-ROM drive. A hyperlink application should start up. You can use the application to do various things including installing Exchange Server. Or, if you prefer, you can navigate the CD-ROM with NT Explorer, finding and running the programs you need as described in this section.

If the hyperlink application doesn't start automatically, use Windows NT Explorer to find the Exchange Server Setup program for your processor. You'll find it under the SETUP directory on the Exchange Server CD-ROM. When you've located the program, double-click its name to start it up. Let's discuss some of the screens you'll see once Exchange Server's Setup program is up and running.

Be sure to pick the directory on the CD-ROM with the correct processor version (Alpha or Intel) and language (English, French, and so forth) for your installation environment. Remember, you're choosing the language that such things as event logs will appear in—not the languages Exchange clients will support.

---

**WARNING**  The first thing you'll see when the Setup program starts running is a dialog box like the one in Figure 7.3. If any programs are running on the server, close them. Lots of stuff gets updated by Setup, so take this warning seriously. When you're done reading the licensing information in the dialog box, click Accept.

---

**FIGURE 7.3:**

Setup's technical and legal warnings

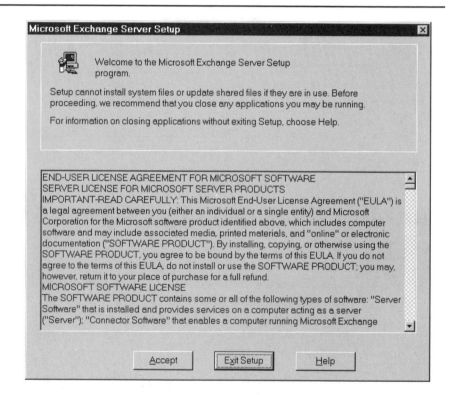

## Selecting Installation Options

Setup will now tell you that it's searching for installed Exchange Server components. When the search is done, you'll need to pick the installation mode you want and set the directory in which Exchange Server will be installed (see Figure 7.4). Again, I suggest accepting the default directory for this first Exchange Server installation.

## Batch Mode Installation

You can actually install Exchange Server in a non-interactive batch mode, which can be especially useful when you're installing remotely. You'll need a program that lets you do software distribution, such as Microsoft's NT Server–based System Management Server.

Check out the Exchange Server documentation and the sample batch files on the Exchange Server CD-ROM for more on batch installations. Though not required, a program that lets you do software distribution, such as Microsoft's NT Server–based Systems Management Server, can help make batch installations easier.

Next, click Complete/Custom for the type of installation. This brings up a dialog box like the one in Figure 7.5, which offers you the option of installing four sets of Exchange Server components: Microsoft Exchange Server, Microsoft Exchange Administrator, Books Online, and the Outlook Web Access components. By now you should be pretty clear on what the Server and Administrator components are. Books Online are Exchange Server's online documentation. Outlook Web Access components support Internet browser access to Exchange Server for such things as reading mail and looking up addresses.

**FIGURE 7.4:**

Choosing installation options

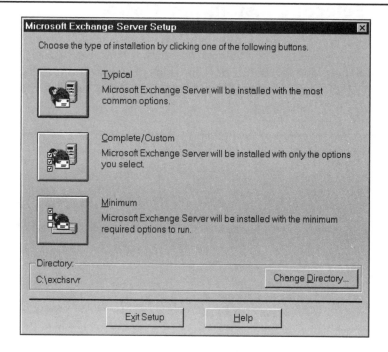

**FIGURE 7.5:**

Selecting the Exchange Server components to be installed

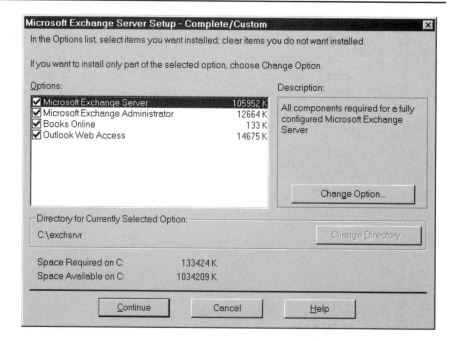

# Refining Installation Options

During a Complete/Custom install, you can change the options for the Microsoft Exchange Server portion of the Exchange Server installation. Highlight Microsoft Exchange Server as I have in Figure 7.5 and click the Change Option button. A window like the one in Figure 7.6 pops up. Use it to select the Exchange Server components you want to install. For your first Exchange Server, select at least the Microsoft Exchange Event Service (MEES) and the Key Management Server (KMS). The MEES lets you write scripts that help you create groupware applications in public folders. The KMS supports digital signatures and encryption in Exchange Server messages. I'll get into both of these in Chapter 17. Select the other options if you expect to use them. Click OK when you're done.

When you specify installation of the KMS, you'll be given two options for entering a password to start the KMS service: manual entry or entry from a diskette. The password is long and unless you have a very good reason for manual entry, choose the diskette option. Be sure you've got two formatted diskettes on hand.

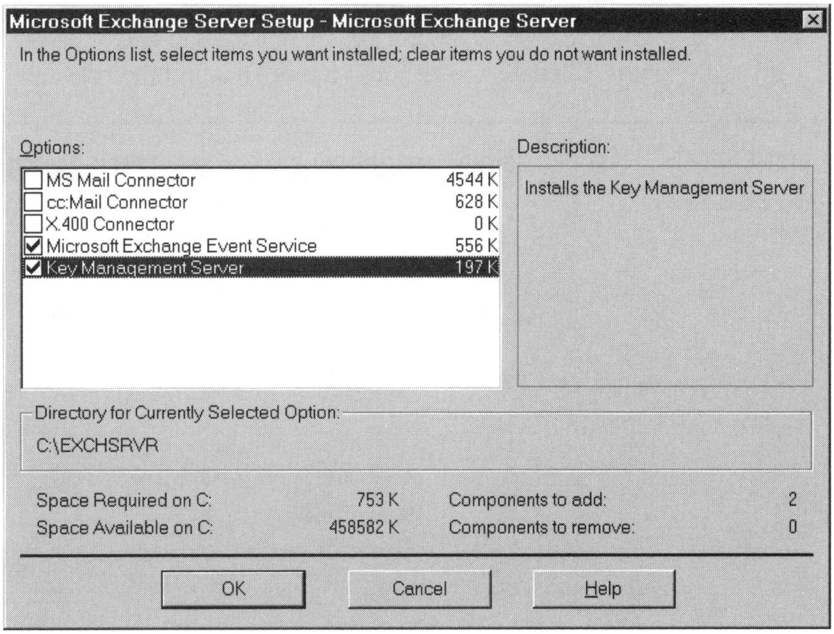

**FIGURE 7.6:**

Selecting Additional Exchange Server components for installation

Microsoft Exchange Server Setup - Microsoft Exchange Server

In the Options list, select items you want installed; clear items you do not want installed.

Options:

| | |
|---|---|
| ☐ MS Mail Connector | 4544 K |
| ☐ cc:Mail Connector | 628 K |
| ☐ X.400 Connector | 0 K |
| ☑ Microsoft Exchange Event Service | 556 K |
| ☑ Key Management Server | 197 K |

Description:

Installs the Key Management Server

Directory for Currently Selected Option:

C:\EXCHSRVR

| | | | |
|---|---|---|---|
| Space Required on C: | 753 K | Components to add: | 2 |
| Space Available on C: | 458582 K | Components to remove: | 0 |

OK        Cancel        Help

For the first Exchange Server installation in a site, it usually makes sense to install all components. So be sure that all boxes are checked and click Continue to move on. If you've already installed Microsoft Internet Information Server, Setup will tell you at this point that it's temporarily stopping the Internet Information Server services. Click OK and you're on to licensing.

---

**WARNING**   You can install Outlook Web Access components on your Exchange server or on another machine. At least to begin with, I suggest you install them on your Exchange server. Outlook Web Access components do their thing in consort with Microsoft's Internet Information Server (IIS). To install Outlook Web Access components on any machine, the machine must be running NT Server 4 with Service Pack 3 or greater. Additionally, it must be running Internet Information Server 3 or greater. Finally, IIS's Active Server Pages must be installed. Whew! See Chapter 6 for more on all of this. If the prerequisite software isn't installed and running, Exchange Server Setup won't even let you think about installing Outlook Web Access components.

---

## Licensing

As you can see in Figure 7.7, client access to Exchange Server is on a per seat basis. Click the box next to I Agree That and then click OK.

---

**FIGURE 7.7:**

Inputting client licensing information

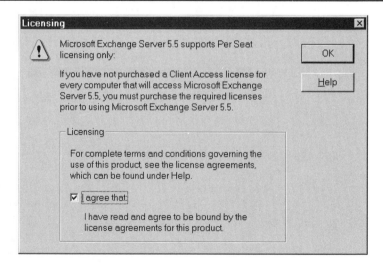

## Entering Organization and Site Names

Here's another point at which to shout, "At last!" You can finally use that organization and site-name information you put together back in Chapter 5. (In Figure 7.8 I've entered the info for my fake company, GerCom.) When you're finished, click OK. When prompted, click OK a second time to confirm that you want to create a new site.

**FIGURE 7.8:**

Inputting Exchange Server organization and site names

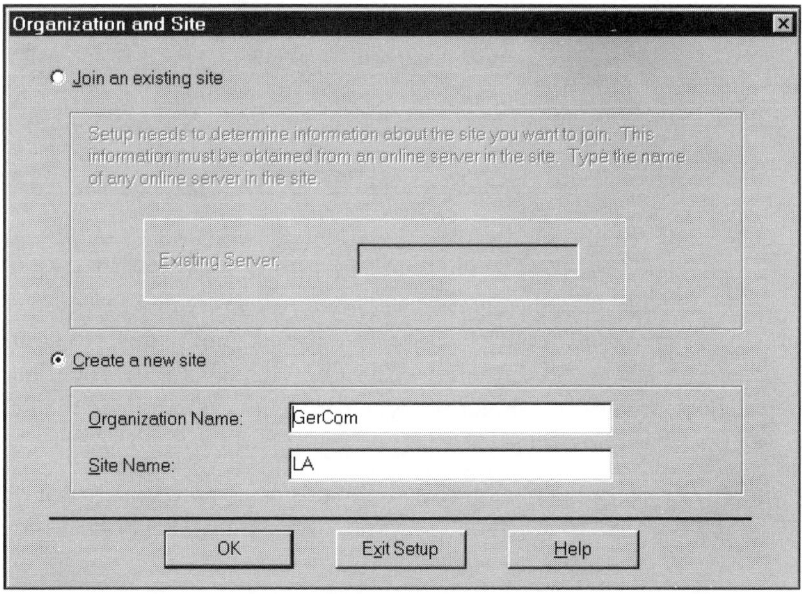

## Specifying a Site Services Account

Now give Setup the name and password for the Site Services account you created a while back. (Figure 7.9 shows the dialog box for doing this.) Be careful here; you want to use the Site Services account you created, *not* the Administrator account you're logged in to right now.

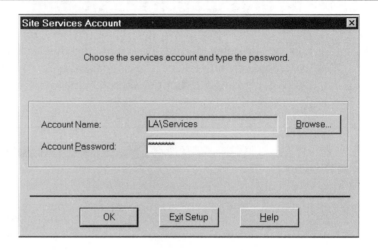

Find the account by clicking Browse. The Add User or Group dialog box pops up. Find the Site Services account you created earlier in this chapter—it'll be called "Services" if you used the account name I suggested. Click the name, then click Add, and finally click OK. This will return you to the Site Services Account dialog box. Enter the password, click OK, and you're done entering installation information.

Setup next informs you that it has granted a series of rights to the Site Services account. Click OK to acknowledge the dialog box message.

## File Installation and System Setup

Setup now begins copying files to your server. Setup then adds objects such as organization and site to the Exchange Server directory. Finally, it installs Exchange services such as the Message Transfer Agent (MTA), information store, and directory service and modifies the registry on your NT server.

After installation is finished, you're offered an opportunity to run the Exchange Server Performance Optimizer, which is a Microsoft Wizard. The Optimizer can improve the performance of your Exchange server by moving Exchange Server database files to other hard drives on the server, setting some memory tuning parameters in the NT server's registry, etc. You can run the Optimizer now or as often as you want later. Its first page is shown in Figure 7.10.

The first page of the
Exchange Performance
Optimizer

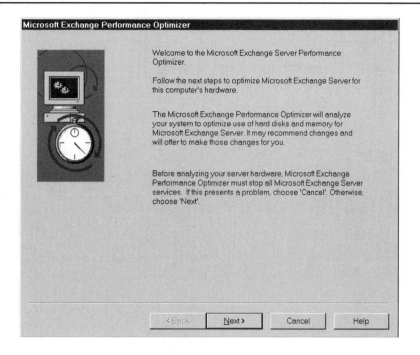

Click the Next button on the first page, and the Optimizer stops all currently running Exchange Server services. You're then taken to the second Optimizer page (see Figure 7.11). Type in the appropriate information for your Exchange server. The only item that might give you some trouble is the one labeled Limit Memory Usage To. If you select this item, Exchange Server will use no more than the amount of RAM memory indicated in the MB field when it runs. This is useful if you're using the server to run other programs such as Microsoft SQL Server or if the server is acting as a primary or backup NT domain controller. If you choose to use this option, allow at least 32MB for Exchange Server. The default value gives Exchange Server access to all server memory.

When you're done filling in the fields on the second Optimizer page, click Next. The Optimizer now begins analyzing and, if appropriate, modifying your NT/Exchange server (see Figure 7.12).

**FIGURE 7.11:**

Entering information to be used by Exchange Performance Optimizer

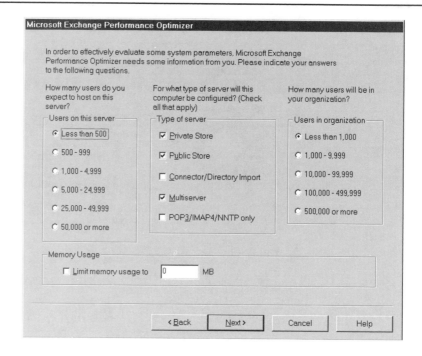

**FIGURE 7.12:**

The Exchange Performance Optimizer analyzes server hard disks to determine where to put Exchange Server database files.

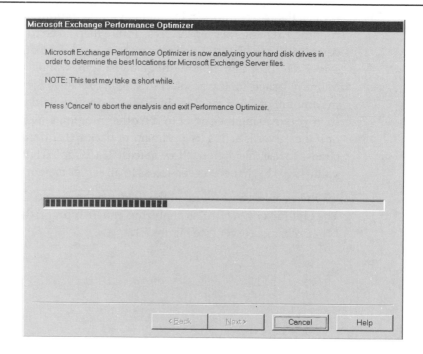

After the Optimizer has finished its analysis and modification of your server, it asks you to click Next to continue. Do so and you're presented with suggested locations for the various Exchange Server databases. If you don't like any of the suggestions, change them and then click Next.

Figure 7.13 shows the suggestions that the Optimizer came up with for my Exchange server. The Optimizer suggests putting the Exchange transaction logs on drive C and the database files on drive D. Remember in the last chapter I created a FAT partition for the transaction logs (D:) and an NTFS partition for the databases (E:)? So, before accepting the Optimizer's suggestions, I'll replace C: with D: for the two transaction logs, and D: with E: for the four databases. The Optimizer next asks if you want it to automatically move the database files it suggested should be moved (see Figure 7.14). Though there is a way to move these files yourself, it's best to let the Optimizer do the moving. So leave the Move Files Automatically option selected and click Next. Since you're running the Optimizer right after installing Exchange Server, don't worry about the warning to back up your database files. If you run the program after you've created Exchange recipients and such, then for added safety be sure to back up those files before letting the Optimizer move them.

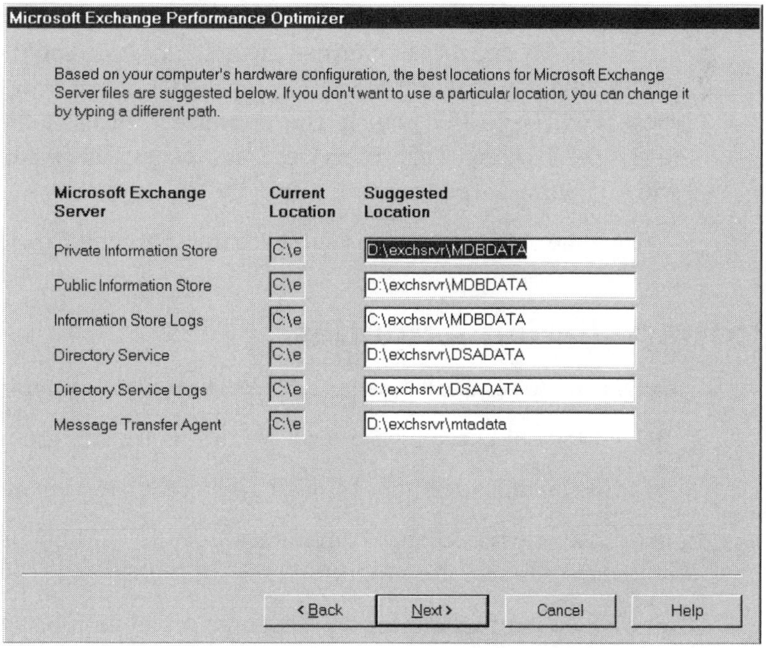

**FIGURE 7.13:**

The Exchange Performance Optimizer suggests new locations for some Exchange databases.

Microsoft Exchange Performance Optimizer

Based on your computer's hardware configuration, the best locations for Microsoft Exchange Server files are suggested below. If you don't want to use a particular location, you can change it by typing a different path.

| Microsoft Exchange Server | Current Location | Suggested Location |
|---|---|---|
| Private Information Store | C:\e | D:\exchsrvr\MDBDATA |
| Public Information Store | C:\e | D:\exchsrvr\MDBDATA |
| Information Store Logs | C:\e | C:\exchsrvr\MDBDATA |
| Directory Service | C:\e | D:\exchsrvr\DSADATA |
| Directory Service Logs | C:\e | C:\exchsrvr\DSADATA |
| Message Transfer Agent | C:\e | D:\exchsrvr\mtadata |

< Back     Next >     Cancel     Help

**FIGURE 7.14:**

The Exchange Performance Optimizer is ready to move certain Exchange Server database files.

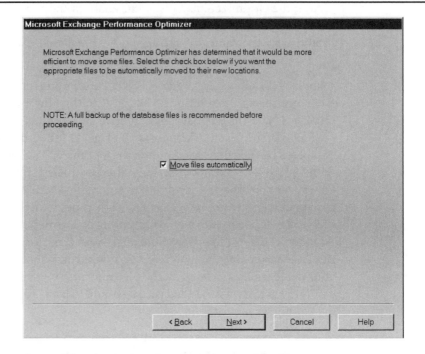

After the Optimizer has churned away for a while, you'll see the last Wizard page telling you that optimization is finished and that a log of the optimization process will be written to disk. The Optimizer will also tell you that it's ready to restart the Exchange Server services it stopped. Click Finish, and the program will save some parameters and restart the services.

When the Optimizer is finished, Exchange Server will be up and running.

## Postinstallation Activities

You'll need to complete a series of tasks immediately after installation:

- Check out Exchange Server's Windows program group
- Ensure that all required Exchange Server processes are up and running
- Ensure that Exchange communications are working properly (by starting up the Administrator program)
- Set up permissions for the Exchange Server administration group

You do these tasks while logged in to your Exchange server as the domain administrator. Since you installed your Exchange server under that login, you should be ready to go.

## Exchange Server's Windows Program Group

The first thing you'll see after successfully installing Exchange Server is a new Windows program group called Microsoft Exchange. Figure 7.15 shows the group as it appears just after completion of Exchange Server installation. To get to this program group under normal circumstances, click the Start button on NT Server's Task Bar, select Programs, and then select Microsoft Exchange. (See Figure 7.16.)

**FIGURE 7.15:**

The Microsoft Exchange program group just after Exchange Server is installed

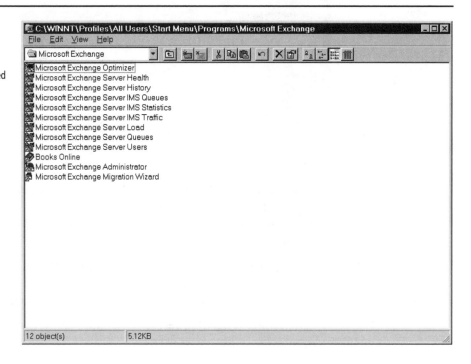

**FIGURE 7.16:**

Getting to the Microsoft
Exchange program group
from the Windows NT
Start Menu

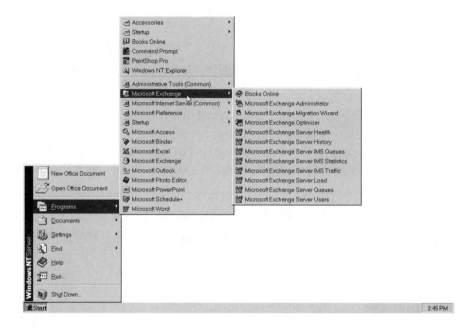

**FIGURE 7.16:**

Getting to the Microsoft
Exchange program group
from the Windows NT
Start Menu

The Microsoft Exchange program group initially contains three key applications:

**Exchange Administrator**   This application is used to do just about everything, from adding users to setting up links with other Exchange servers and foreign messaging systems. You'll use it extensively from here on.

**Exchange Migration Wizard**   The Migration Wizard moves users from various mail systems (for example, Microsoft Mail for PC Networks, cc:Mail, and Novell GroupWise) to Exchange; I'll go over it in Chapter 17.

**Microsoft Exchange Optimizer**   Use this icon to run the Performance Optimizer anytime you want.

Microsoft has also included icons in the Microsoft Exchange program group for a set of preconfigured, Exchange Server–oriented NT Performance Monitor runs. (I talked about the Performance Monitor back in Chapter 4.) These icons let you keep an eye on some key Exchange Server components and can warn you about problems before they get to the trash-your-system stage.

# Verifying That Exchange Server Processes Are Running

Now you need to make sure all Exchange Server processes are running. If they're not, you'll have to do some troubleshooting.

## Are the Services Running?

Open the Start menu by clicking the Start button on NT Server's Task Bar. Select Settings and then select Control Panel. In the Control Panel, double-click the Services icon. This brings up the NT Services monitoring and control dialog box that I first discussed in Chapter 4. A typical NT server has a number of services, so you'll probably have to scroll down to see the services that are specific to Microsoft Exchange. Your Services dialog box should look pretty much like the one shown in Figure 7.17.

**FIGURE 7.17:**

The Services dialog box with Exchange Server processes displayed

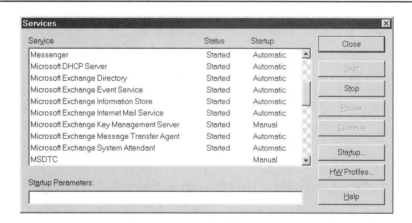

Make sure that the Exchange Directory, Information Store, MTA, and System Attendant are up and running. Remember: Exchange Server doesn't even exist if these four core components aren't running.

Don't try to start any Exchange Server services that aren't running, even if the Services applet says they are to start up automatically. If a service other than one of the four core components isn't running at this time, it shouldn't be running at all. For example, notice in Figure 7.17 that the service MS Mail Connector Interchange isn't running on my server. That's because I haven't yet entered the parameters required to run it.

If all is well, click Close and move on to the next section, which deals with the Exchange Administrator.

### Troubleshooting Problems with Services

If some or all of the Exchange Server processes that should be running aren't, first take a look at the NT Event Log using the Event Viewer, which I discussed back in Chapter 4. The Event Viewer is in the Administrative Tools program group. The Event Viewer can display three logs: System, Security, and Application. If the Application Log isn't being displayed, select Application from the Event Viewer's Log menu. Look for events related to Exchange Server that are marked with a red stop-sign icon—these indicate serious problems such as failure to start a service. If you find a problem that you think you can handle, try to fix it; otherwise, check with Microsoft regarding the event.

In the meantime, you can try shutting down the server and rebooting it. If that doesn't fix things, you can try to start the processes manually. To do this, highlight a service in the Services dialog box (see Figure 7.17) by clicking it, then click the Start button. Your NT server will chug away for a bit, and then the service should start up—along with any other services that this service depends on. Try starting the four core Exchange Server processes in this manner.

## Starting the Exchange Administrator

To set permissions for the Exchange Server administration group you created a while back, you'll use the Exchange Administrator application. The Administrator is in the Microsoft Exchange program group. The first time you run the program, a dialog box like the one in Figure 7.18 pops up. The Administrator is a client to Exchange Server, so you have to tell it which server to connect to. Type in the name of your server (or click Browse to bring up a tree with the Exchange hierarchy on it, then find your server on the tree and double-click it). Select the Set as Default checkbox so that the Administrator will always go to this server on start-up, then click OK.

After a bit of churning, the Administrator window should open—proof that Exchange client/server communications are working. The Administrator (the client) was able to talk to your Exchange server (the server). Note that in this case both the client and server parts of the application are running on the same computer, your NT/Exchange server. Figure 7.19 shows my Exchange Administrator window.

**FIGURE 7.18:**

Selecting a default Exchange server for the Administrator program

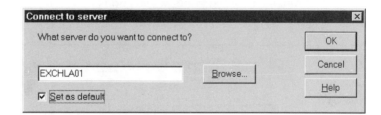

**FIGURE 7.19:**

The Exchange Administrator window

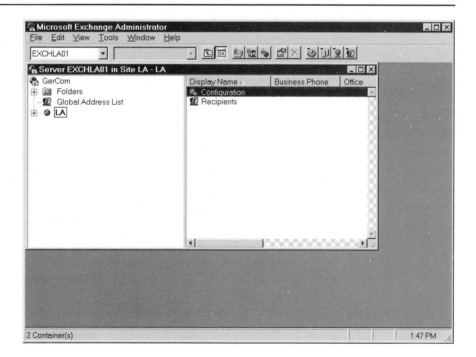

You've seen the Administrator in earlier chapters; now you'll actually start using it. Just to get a feel for how it works, double-click the name of your site in the Administrator window; mine's called "LA." Your window should look similar to the one in Figure 7.20. By double-clicking the LA site object, I opened it and displayed the other objects it contains. There's another way to display the objects an object contains. If there's a little plus sign to the left of an object, it contains other objects. Click the plus sign to display the objects. (All of this probably reminds you of the Windows 95 and NT Explorer displays.) Incidentally, this same tree interface is used in the Exchange client.

**FIGURE 7.20:**

Displaying objects contained in the site object

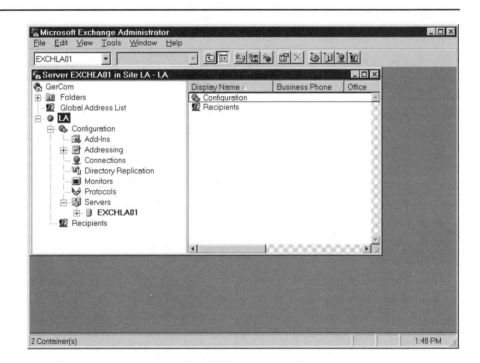

Go ahead and play around with the Administrator's objects; you've earned some rest and relaxation time. Just don't try to delete anything. When you're done, leave the Administrator window open and join me in setting up some key access rights for your Exchange server.

## Running Administrator Remotely

As long as you have the right security permissions, you can run the Exchange Administrator program from any networked NT workstation or server. This is convenient, since you won't have to keep running to an Exchange server to administer it.

To install the Administrator on any other NT computer, just run the Exchange Server Setup program from that machine, select the Complete/Custom installation option, and select only the Microsoft Exchange Administrator for installation. Once the Administrator is installed, start it up and run it just as you did on the Exchange server.

You can't install the Exchange Administrator on an NT server or workstation that is not part of a Microsoft networking domain. The server or workstation doesn't have to be part of the same domain as the Exchange server is located in, but it must be part of some domain. If the server or workstation isn't part of the Exchange server's domain, then the domain it does belong to must have cross-domain access rights to the Exchange server's domain. More on cross-domain access in Chapter 14.

## Setting Permissions for the Exchange Server Administration Group

By setting the appropriate permissions, you'll fix it so that users who are put into the Exchange Server administration group can access your Exchange server. Assuming you're still in the Exchange Administrator, click the site name in the hierarchy tree, then from the Administrator's File menu select Properties. A dialog box like the one in Figure 7.21 pops up.

Select the Permissions property page tab to bring up a dialog box like the one shown in Figure 7.22. Notice that the Administrator account you created when you installed NT Server and the Services account you set up earlier are the only ones with rights to administer in your Exchange site.

Next, click the Add button in the Permissions property page to open up the Add Users and Groups dialog box (see Figure 7.23). Select the Exchange Server administration group you created earlier, then click the Add button in the dialog box.

Before you click OK, take a look at the top of the Add Users and Groups dialog box. The little List Names From drop-down menu at the top lets you give users or groups in trusted domains permission to administer your Exchange server. It's a pretty powerful menu, because it makes possible remote administration from anywhere you've got a network connection to any available domain. We'll use it quite a bit in later chapters.

**FIGURE 7.21:**

The General property page of the site properties dialog box

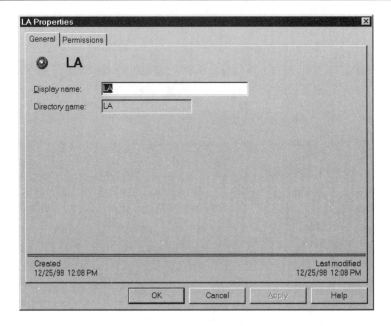

**FIGURE 7.22:**

The Permissions property page of the site properties dialog box

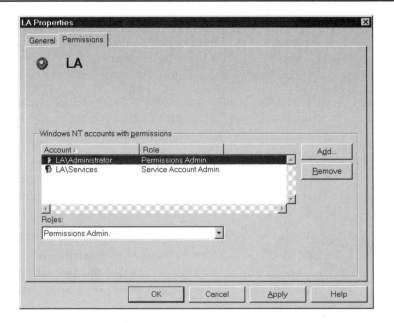

**FIGURE 7.23:**

Granting administrative permissions to an Exchange Server administration group

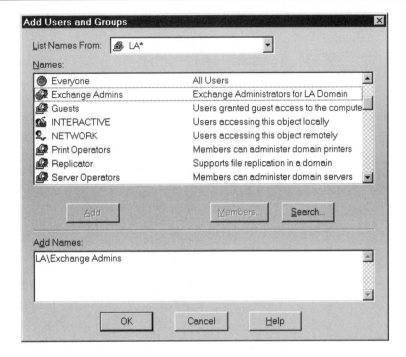

After you click OK in the Add Users and Groups dialog box, you'll see that anyone who belongs to the Exchange administration group now has basic administrative rights for the site (Role = Admin.). (See Figure 7.24.) If you want the group to have full control over the site, assign it the role Permissions Admin. I strongly suggest that you give Permissions Admin. rights to the administration group, unless you and others plan to administer your Exchange server while logged in as NT administrator. The NT administrator account has full control over the site because when you installed Exchange Server it was assigned Permissions Admin. rights for the site by default.

To assign the role Permissions Admin. to your Exchange administration group, open the Roles drop-down list in the Permissions property page by clicking the down arrow on the right-hand side of the list. This opens the list (see Figure 7.25). Click Permissions Admin. in the drop-down list.

Your Exchange administration group now has the rights associated with the role Permissions Admin. (see Figure 7.26). Click OK on the site Properties dialog box and you're done.

The Exchange administration group now has basic administration rights for the site.

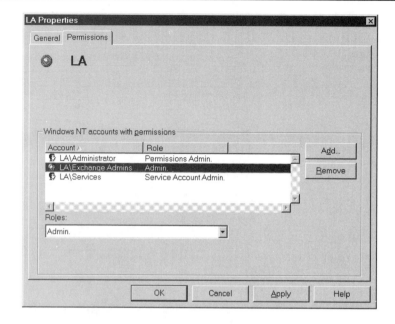

**FIGURE 7.25:**

Granting Permissions Admin. rights to the Exchange administration group

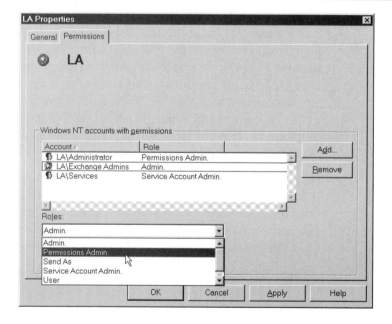

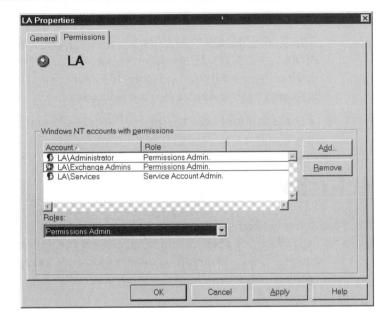

FIGURE 7.26:

The Exchange administration group now has Permissions Admin. rights for the site.

---

**WARNING**    In order to complete the exercises in the rest of this book and to effectively administer your Exchange server, you'll need to give Permissions Admin. rights to the Exchange administration group at the organization, site, and Configuration container levels.

---

Accounts and groups with permissions at the site level inherit rights to the site recipients container, but they do not inherit rights to the Configuration container. So you also need to give the Exchange administration group the rights to the site's Configuration container. To do so, just click the container name (see Figure 7.20 for the location of the Configuration container). Then select Properties from the Administrator's File menu and click the Permissions property page on the resultant Configuration properties dialog box. Finally, repeat the steps you just completed for the site, and you're done.

If your account is included in the Exchange Admins group, you no longer have to log into NT as Administrator to administer any Exchange server in the site. Just to test things out, log out of your NT server. To log out, click the Start button, select Shut Down, click Close All Programs and Log On as a Different User, and then click Yes. When asked, simultaneously press the Ctrl, Alt, and Delete keys to log back in using your own NT account.

To be sure that the Exchange Server administration group is set up properly, double-click the Exchange Administrator icon. If the Administrator runs and you're able to fiddle around in the hierarchy tree, your membership in the group is working as it should. Close the Administrator.

That's it. Your Exchange server is installed, optimized, and ready to use.

# Conclusion

In this chapter you learned how to prepare for an Exchange Server installation, install Exchange Server, and take care of some postinstallation housekeeping chores. In the next couple of chapters, I'll introduce you to basic Exchange Server administration.

# PART III

# Basic Exchange Server Administration and Management

So you've got Exchange Server up and running; now you need to get comfortable with its Administrator program. The next three chapters deal with the basics of Exchange Server administration and management. In Chapter 8, we'll focus on the Exchange Administrator and how you use its menus to do a wide range of useful system administration and management tasks. You'll learn everything from creating new Exchange mailboxes for users to setting up monitors that help keep Exchange servers up and running. In Chapter 9, we get into administering and managing Exchange Server's hierarchy and core components. You'll use the skills you gain to configure and maintain such things as Exchange information stores, message transfer agents, and public folders. And in Chapter 10, we tackle backing up and restoring Exchange servers. This process is as important for a stable and reliable Exchange system as carefully planned, well-administered, and efficiently managed Exchange servers.

# CHAPTER
## EIGHT

# The Administrator and Its Menus

- Administration and management defined

- Exchange Administrator basics

- Exchange Administrator File menu

- Exchange Administrator Edit menu

- Exchange Administrator View menu

- Exchange Administrator Tools menu

This chapter and the next walk you through lots of menus and pages for setting properties of one kind or another. I think you'll find it useful to track through everything once and set some specific Exchange Server parameters when appropriate. When you need to come back to a particular section, it should be relatively easy to find. Just remember that Chapter 8 deals with basic Exchange Administrator program menus, while Chapter 9 covers objects in the Exchange hierarchy, including the four core Exchange components.

# Administration and Management

Notice that this section of the book deals with Exchange Server administration *and* management. There's a real and sharp difference between the two terms. In a nutshell, *administration* is everything you do to set up Exchange Server, while *management* is what you do to keep the server running and its users happy.

Administration includes tasks like creating Exchange Recipients such as mailboxes and distribution lists; setting up Exchange server backups; and configuring Exchange components such as sites, servers, Message Transfer Agents (MTAs), and connectors. Management covers tasks like monitoring Exchange servers and ensuring that they keep running, backing up and restoring a server, tracking mail messages to find out why they weren't delivered, and keeping address book information current as people change offices and phone numbers.

You use the Exchange Administrator program to do both administration and management, so "Administrator" might seem like a less-than-comprehensive name for the program. But when I consider the alternatives—the sexist "Admin-Man," for example—the name seems just fine.

# Administrator Windows

The Exchange Administrator takes advantage of several Microsoft Windows capabilities. For example, it lets you use multiple windows for views of one or more Exchange servers, and each window has two variable-size panes.

## Multiple Windows

Figure 8.1 shows the Administrator window. Inside the window are two additional windows, both labeled in part Server EXCHLA01 in Site LA. This tells you that you're looking at two views of the server EXCHLA01, which resides in the Exchange Server organization GerCom and the site LA.

You may recall from earlier chapters that Exchange Server is object oriented and that the Administrator is the tool you use to manipulate its objects. Also, remember that some Exchange Server objects are containers—that is, they hold other objects. Not all objects are containers, but all containers are objects.

The lower window in Figure 8.1 shows the Recipients container for the LA site, hence the name Server EXCHLA01 in Site LA—Recipients. Notice that the word "Recipients" in the left-hand pane is highlighted, telling you that the container is selected. The objects in the Recipients container—Exchange Recipients—are shown in the right-hand pane.

**FIGURE 8.1:**

Two views of the same Exchange server

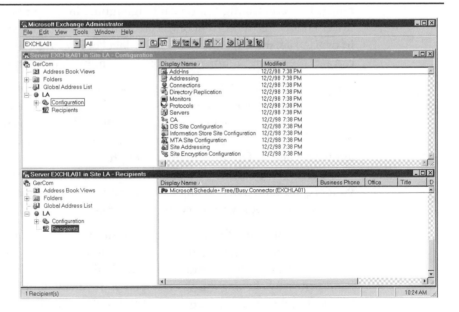

Because I just finished setting up EXCHLA01 and have created no Recipients yet, the only recipient is the Schedule+ Free/Busy Connector. This connector is used to exchange Schedule+ information between Exchange sites and MS Mail post offices.

This allows users in both systems to set up meetings using Microsoft Schedule+ while taking into account the schedules of potential meeting participants.

Notice the scroll bar at the bottom of the lower window. It's showing because there are more columns for the list of Recipients than can be displayed given the window's current width. Two columns aren't displayed in the lower window; these are labeled Department and Modified. Respectively, they show the recipient's department and the date and time when a recipient was last modified. To see columns that aren't displayed in a window, you can either resize the window or scroll over until the columns are visible.

While I'm talking about columns, note that you can re-sort the rows in certain lists. If a list has column title bars like the ones in the two windows in Figure 8.1, you can click some of the bars to re-sort the list by the column. Not all column title bars can be used to sort lists; for example, you can sort Recipients' lists only by display name and the date an object was last modified.

The upper window shows the Configuration container within the LA site container. The term Configuration isn't highlighted in the left-hand pane because the lower window is the current one. The Configuration and Recipients objects show in the LA site; these are the two second-level objects in the LA container. As you can see, the Configuration object contains a number of other objects.

If you want to see all the Exchange Server containers available in your organization, just double-click all the objects in the left pane until there are no objects with plus (+) signs in front of them. Or you can click all plus signs until they become minus (–) signs. At this point all available containers will be open and visible in the left-hand pane. In Figure 8.2 there's enough screen real estate to open most of the containers. There may come a time when you'll have so many sites and servers in your organization that opening all containers gives you repetitive-strain injury, so do it now, while you've got just one site and server.

Now it's your turn. Open the Exchange Administrator. If you completed the exercises in the last chapter, one Exchange server view window opens automatically. You can see what's inside any object in the Exchange hierarchy—in the left-hand pane—by clicking the object. Open your site by double-clicking its name or by clicking the plus sign to the left of the site's name. Then open another window by selecting New Window from the Window menu. Now play with the two windows, getting each to display whatever you'd like. You can open more windows or close any of them at any time.

**FIGURE 8.2:**

Almost all the containers in a new Exchange organization are displayed in the left-hand pane.

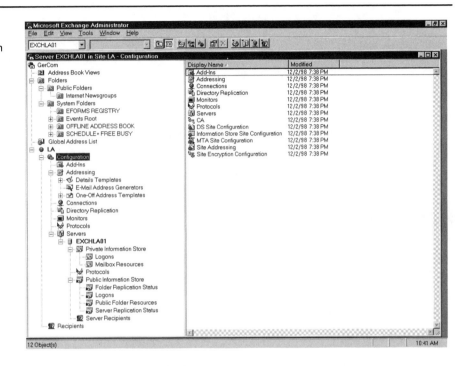

The neat thing about these multiple windows is that you can easily have different servers or sites open in different windows. This lets you manage multiple servers in multiple sites simultaneously (if, of course, you've got the necessary rights to those servers).

---

**NOTE**    Try to start thinking of the collection of objects you see in the Administrator as the *Exchange Directory*. A copy of the directory for an entire Exchange organization is stored on each Exchange server in the organization. As you'll see later, the directory is automatically updated and replicated across the organization. This is what makes centralized management of Exchange servers possible and extremely easy.

---

## Manipulating the Splitbar

The left and right panes of the two windows in Figure 8.1 are divided by a *splitbar*—a bar that lets you adjust for the amount of screen real estate used by the two panes in a window.

To move the splitbar, just move your Windows pointer so that it's touching any part of the splitbar, and the pointer will turn into a crosshair. Then press and hold down the left mouse button. While still holding down the left mouse button, move the splitbar until you're happy with the size of the right and left panes.

# Preliminary Settings

We're going to cover the Administrator's menus pretty much sequentially. Before we start, however, you'll need to set a few parameters in a dialog box that you access from a menu appearing later in the sequence.

## Setting Auto Naming Options

Open the Administrator's Tools menu and click Options to bring up the Options dialog box (see Figure 8.3). Remember when I talked about the near-religious issues surrounding Exchange Server display names and aliases earlier in this book? Well, here's where you get to choose your religion and set the default for the way display names and aliases are created. You use the Auto Naming property page to do this.

Pick your poison. Custom options let you use the variables %First, %Initials, and %Last to construct a name. You can display selected characters from one of the variables by placing a number after the percent sign in the variable name. (For example, %1First displays the initial character in each first name—so the first name *Barry* displays as B.) Click Apply, but don't close the Options dialog box.

**FIGURE 8.3:**

The Options dialog box shown with its Auto Naming property page

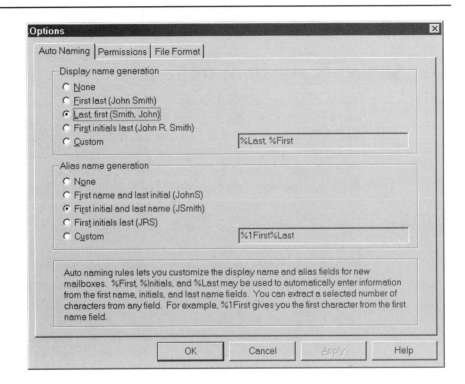

## Setting the Domain for NT Account Selection

Keep an eye on Figure 8.4 as we move along. As I noted earlier, Exchange mailboxes are usually linked to an NT account. When you're creating a new Exchange mailbox, you can select the account you want to link the mailbox to. When you choose to do this, NT presents you with a list of accounts in a specific domain. You can use the Permissions property page on the Options dialog box to tell this copy of Exchange Administrator whether to present the user with a list of NT accounts either from the domain where the Exchange server is installed or from the default domain, which is the domain selected in the drop-down list. In our case, since there's only one domain, LA, we'd get the same domain whichever of the two options we selected. However, if you begin to build multidomain networks, it's very likely that you may want to choose NT accounts from a domain other than the one in which you've installed Exchange Server. You can use these options to ensure that Exchange Administrator presents the most appropriate list of domain users as you create new mailboxes.

## Setting Permissions Options

As you'll remember, Exchange Server security is based on NT Server security. You can give an NT account or group the permissions (rights) to administer and manage all Exchange servers in a site, as you did with your Exchange administration group in the last chapter. You can also permit different users or groups to administer different pieces of Exchange Server—even different Exchange servers. For example, you might give one group permissions to administer a specific site's Recipients, while permitting a different user to administer each of the Exchange servers in a site.

With a few exceptions, if an NT account or group has permissions to an Exchange Server container, these permissions automatically extend to all objects in the container, including nested containers. Objects within the container automatically inherit the permissions that were granted to the account or group at the master container level. For example, when we gave the Exchange administration group (Exchange Admins) permissions in the site container, those permissions were inherited by objects in the site's Recipients container. As you'll discover in Chapter 9, permissions granted at the site level are not inherited by objects in the Configuration container, which is also a subcontainer of the site container. I'll explain this apparently incongruous state of affairs in Chapter 9.

As we go through the Administrator's menus, it will be most helpful if you see all the permissions options for all objects, so you need to ensure that some general Administrator parameters are properly set. Click the Permissions tab in the Options dialog box. Make sure your computer account's domain is showing and that Show Permissions Page for All Objects and Display Rights for Roles on Permissions Page are selected (see Figure 8.4).

Don't worry about the whys and wherefores of these options right now; I promise that by the end of this chapter you'll be on intimate terms with both. If you've changed either of the two options, click Apply, but don't close the Options dialog box yet.

> **NOTE**
>
> You might not want to set separate access permissions for every little piece of Exchange Server. If not, you can go back and deselect Show Permissions Page for All Objects after we've gone through this chapter.

**FIGURE 8.4:**

The Options dialog box shown with its Permissions property page

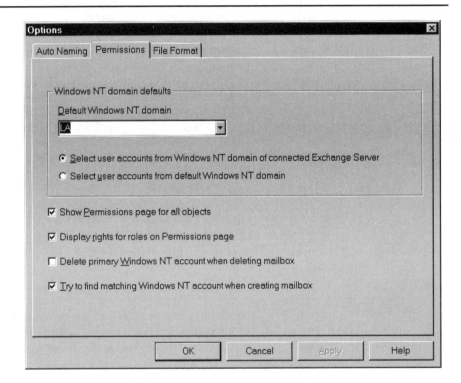

### Setting the NT Account Deletion Option

Recall that you can create NT accounts while creating Exchange mailboxes, and vice versa. When you delete an NT account in the User Manager for Domains, you're asked if you want to delete the mailbox associated with the account as well. When you delete a mailbox in the Exchange Administrator, the NT account associated with it is deleted only if you select the option Delete Primary Windows NT Account When Deleting Mailbox. If you select this option, you are alerted before the deletion and offered the opportunity to not delete the mailbox.

# Setting the Option to Find a Matching Windows NT Account

As you'll soon see, when you create a mailbox you will usually assign an NT account to it. If the account doesn't exist, you can create a new one on the spot. If you want to assign the mailbox to an existing NT account, you can either search for it manually while creating the mailbox or select Try to Find Matching Windows NT Account When Creating Mailbox. If you check this option and, while you're creating a new mailbox, the Exchange Administrator finds an NT account with a username that matches the alias you've given the mailbox, you'll be offered the option of assigning the account to the NT account.

This can save a bit of manual searching time on already established NT systems, so I suggest you accept the default check for the option. When you're finished, click OK.

# Setting File Format Options

The last tab on the Options dialog box is used to set the format for data that is exported from or imported into Exchange Server. The default setting is for standard comma-delimited files. Unless you have a pressing need to alter this option, leave it as is.

**WARNING** The settings you established above apply to the copy of the Administrator program you're running now and to the account you are logged into now. If you install and run the program on another computer or log into the same computer under a different account, you'll need to modify these settings for that computer or account. Be careful here. If your naming conventions aren't the same as Administrator's default, the Recipients you create will be misnamed until you properly set auto naming properties in the Options dialog box.

**WARNING** The setting we're about to make applies to your Exchange site. Once set, it stays in effect for the site until changed—no matter which copy of the Administrator you use to view the setting.

## Changing Site Addresses

When you installed your Exchange server, at least four special site addresses were created for your site: cc:Mail, Microsoft Mail, SMTP (Internet), and X.400. These addresses are appended to Exchange Server recipient alias names to create full MS Mail and SMTP addresses. Exchange Server uses First and Last Names along with the site addresses to create full cc:Mail and X.400 addresses. For example, as you can see in Figure 8.5, the SMTP site address for the GerCom LA site is @LA.GerCom.com. My alias name is BGerber, and my SMTP address is BGerber@LA.GerCom.com.

You can change any of the four site addresses. Use caution here, however, because any changes you make should be based on addresses you have or expect to get in the real world. For example, if you've already got an Internet domain name, you'll want to change the site's SMTP address to reflect that name.

SMTP, cc:Mail, and X.400 addresses are modified in one way (which I'll talk about in a minute). Microsoft Mail addresses are modified using the Microsoft Mail Connector dialog box, which we'll cover in a later chapter. To change a cc:Mail, an SMTP, or an X.400 address, click the Configuration container for your site in the left-hand pane of an Administrator window. Then double-click the Site Addressing object, which is in the right-hand pane of the window, and click the Site Addressing tab. (See Figure 8.2 for help in locating these objects.)

In the resultant Site Addressing dialog box, click the address you want to change, then click Edit (see Figure 8.5). Edit the address using the cc:Mail, SMTP, or X.400 dialog box that pops up, then click OK to close each dialog box.

We're done with the preliminaries. Now we're ready to move on to the first menu of the Administrator: the File menu.

FIGURE 8.5:

The Site Addressing dialog box is used to change the base e-messaging address for a site.

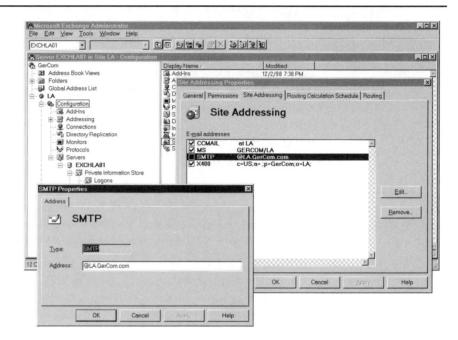

# The File Menu

As you can see from Figure 8.6, the File menu is pretty important. You use it to connect to new servers and create new Recipients and other objects, to quickly export data on your Exchange server, and to view and set object properties and duplicate certain objects, such as mailboxes.

FIGURE 8.6:

The Exchange Administrator's File menu

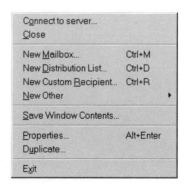

## Connecting to a Server

You use the File menu's Connect to Server option to link to a server and open a new window on it. Since all servers in a site contain copies of all information for the site, you'll generally need to connect to only one server in a site.

As we'll see later, the Connect to Server option is most useful when you have multiple sites; you'll then establish a connection to a server in each site that you need to administer and manage. Remember from our little exercise above that you can open multiple windows in any site by using the New Window option in the Administrator's Window menu.

## Closing a Window

The File menu's Close option is used to close any selected Administrator window.

## Creating a New Mailbox

This is another exciting milestone: You're going to create your first Exchange recipient, a mailbox.

From here on, I'll assume you've already opened the Administrator. Click your site (mine is LA); your Administrator screen should look like the one in Figure 8.7. Next, from the File menu choose New Mailbox. A dialog box like the one shown in Figure 8.8 pops up to tell you that you must create new Recipients in a *site-based Recipients container*—in my case, the LA site Recipients container, since I have no other sites. I've played a nasty trick on you by having you first click your site. There is a method to my madness, however. The first time I saw the dialog box shown in Figure 8.8, I thought that something had broken. Now you know it's just a friendly reminder and the Administrator will take you to the right container. To avoid the dialog box, just click the site-based Recipients container you want to use before selecting New Mailbox. Go ahead and click OK in the warning box.

The next thing you'll see is the mailbox's Properties dialog box, shown in Figure 8.9. Note the twelve tabs on the dialog box; each lets you set a different group of attributes for a mailbox. Let's take a look at each of the eleven property pages used to administer and manage mailboxes.

**FIGURE 8.7:**

The Administrator with a site selected

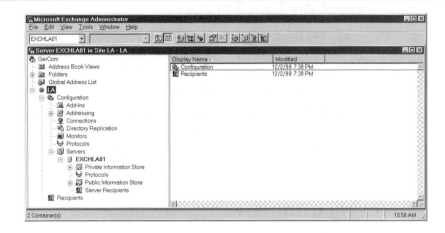

**FIGURE 8.8:**

The Administrator's wrong container warning

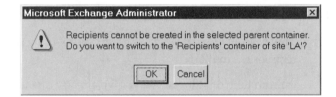

## General Properties

As you can see in Figure 8.9, you use the General property page to fill in all the information about a mailbox and its user. This is also where you grant the right to use the mailbox to a specific NT account.

**Filling in General Information**   In Figure 8.10, I've already filled in information to create a mailbox for myself on the General property page. As I noted in an earlier chapter, the Display and Alias names are created automatically; the ones for your site may look different, depending on how you set your options earlier in this chapter. Now fill in the information for your first mailbox (you'll probably want to make it your own). *Don't* click OK or Apply yet.

NOTEWhen creating a new mailbox, you don't have to fill in every last lovin' field on every property page—only the display and alias fields on the General property page must be filled in.

**FIGURE 8.9:**

The mailbox's Properties dialog box

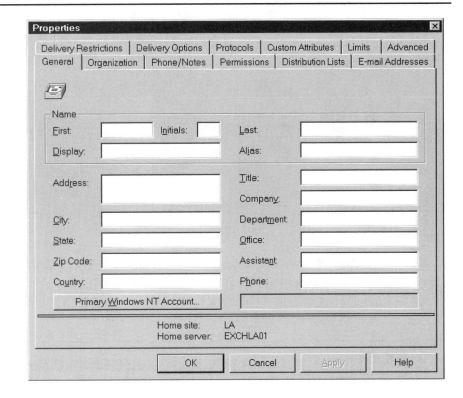

**FIGURE 8.10:**

Filling in the General property page of the mailbox's Properties dialog box

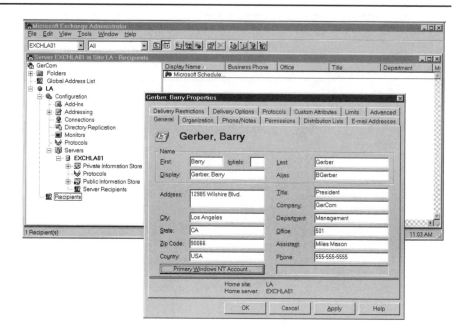

### Granting an NT Account the Rights to a Mailbox

To grant an NT account the rights to a mailbox, click Primary Windows NT Account on the General property page to bring up the dialog box shown in Figure 8.11. You can grant rights to an existing NT account or create a new account.

**FIGURE 8.11:**

Granting mailbox access rights to an existing or new NT account

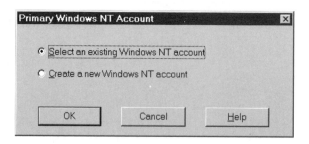

If access rights are to be granted to an existing NT account, click Select an Existing Windows NT Account and then click OK. This brings up the Add User or Group dialog box shown in Figure 8.12. Making sure you're in the right domain, find and click the account you want to give rights to, click Add, and then click OK.

**FIGURE 8.12:**

The Add User or Group dialog box lets you assign rights to a mailbox to an existing NT account.

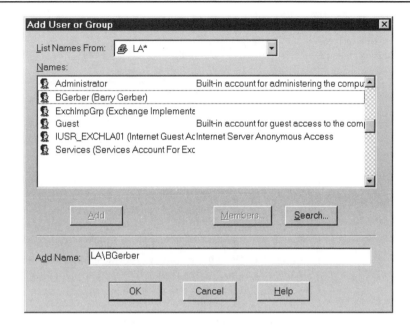

If you selected Try to Find Matching Windows NT Account When Creating Mailbox when you set the Tools/Options/Permissions options discussed above, the Administrator will look for an NT account with the same name as the alias. If one is found, you'll be given the option of using that account here. If you accept the option, you're done. If you don't, you can either locate an account with the Add User or Group dialog box or create a new account.

If you need to create a new NT account and give it rights to the mailbox you're creating, select the Create a New Windows NT Account option from the Primary Windows NT Account dialog box (see Figure 8.11) and then click OK. The Create Windows NT Account dialog box pops up (see Figure 8.13). Be sure the domain is correct, then either accept the default NT account name offered or type in a name of your choice and click OK.

**FIGURE 8.13:**

Creating an NT account to
be assigned rights to a new
mailbox

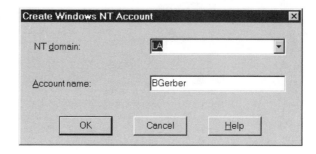

**NOTE**    As you can imagine, based on the limited information Exchange Administrator has
when it creates a new NT account, many of the attributes you might enter for an
NT account are blank. Still, Exchange Administrator does a pretty good job. The NT
account's username defaults to the Exchange mailbox's alias. The account's full
name is set equal to the mailbox's display name and the password is set to blank
so the user will have to change it the first time she or he logs in. If the account will
be used only to access the Exchange mailbox, don't worry; this automatically set
information is sufficient. If, on the other hand, you need to further configure the
account for NT access, you can do that in NT's User Manager for Domains.

## Organization

Use the Organization property page to record information about the mailbox user's
status in your organization's hierarchy (assuming, of course, that the mailbox will be
used by one person and not by a group of people or a custom-programmed application). Here you can set the name of the mailbox user's manager and the names of
those who report directly to the user. You can view this information in other places
in Exchange; for example, the user of an Exchange client can open and view an
Organization property page for any unhidden mailbox in the Exchange Global
Address List.

**The Mailbox User's Manager**    To add information to the Organization property page, first click the Organization tab. Then, to add information about the mailbox user's manager, click Modify in the Manager box. A dialog box showing a list of
valid Exchange Recipients pops up (see Figure 8.14). This dialog box is called the
*address book*. It lists all unhidden Exchange Recipients: mailboxes, distribution lists,
custom Recipients, and public folders. Find the manager's name in the address

book, click the name, and then click OK in the address book. (In the figure, I've selected myself as the manager of my Administrative Assistant, Miles Mason. I created a mailbox for Miles while you weren't looking.)

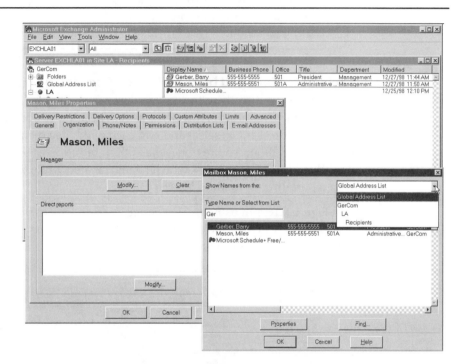

## The Address Book Dialog Box

You'll be seeing the address book dialog box shown in Figure 8.14 a lot throughout the rest of the book, so I want to talk a bit more about how to use it.

Notice in Figure 8.14 that I found myself in the address book by typing in the first three letters of my last name. As the number of Recipients in your organization grows, this is a way to quickly find the one you're looking for.

Another way to narrow down a search is to use the drop-down menu for the Show Names from The option. The menu is open in Figure 8.14; as you can see, it lets you walk down your Exchange hierarchy and pick the specific site and Recipients container to search in.

Finally, you can use the Find button. It brings up a template with fill-in-the-blank fields for things like first and last name, title, and department.

**NOTE**

When you're working in the Exchange client, you'll tend to think of entries in the address book as individuals, groups of individuals, or public folders. When you use the address book in the Exchange Administrator program, try to think of these real-world entities as recipient objects. Doing so will make your life as an Exchange administrator/manager easier—I guarantee.

**Recipients Managed by the Mailbox User**  To add information on Recipients who report directly to the mailbox user, click Modify in the Direct Reports section of the Organization property page. The address book dialog box pops up. From the address book, select and add each of the Recipients reporting to the mailbox user. When you're done, click OK in the address book. (In Figure 8.15, I've added three Recipients—which I again created while you weren't looking—who report directly to Miles Mason.)

In Figure 8.16, I'm using my Exchange client to look at the Organization property page for Miles Mason. As you can see, all the organizational information I entered above is visible to the client.

**FIGURE 8.15:**

Setting the Recipients who report directly to a mailbox user

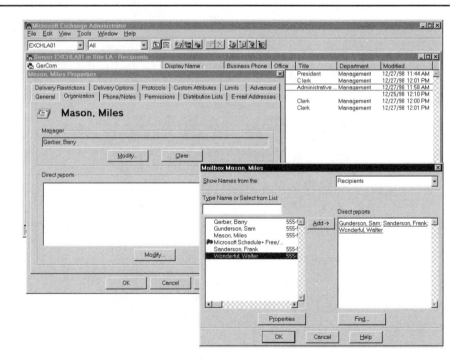

**FIGURE 8.16:**

An Outlook client user views a mailbox's Organization property page.

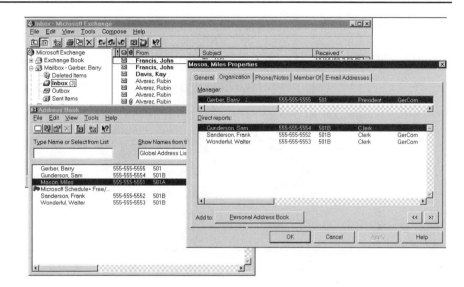

**NOTE**

Before viewing Miles Mason's Organization property page with an Exchange client, I had to use the Exchange Administrator program to apply the changes I made to his mailbox. If I hadn't done this, the changes would not have been available for viewing by an Exchange client. Remember this when you change mailbox attributes on any property page: Until you apply changes you've made to a mailbox (by clicking Apply or OK in the mailbox's Properties dialog box), any changes you make will not be available to the Administrator program or to Exchange client users. This rule applies to modifications you make to any Exchange Server object. When you apply a change, you are saving it to the Exchange directory, where the Administrator program or any Exchange client can access it.

## Phone/Notes

The Phone/Notes property page is pretty basic (see Figure 8.17). The phone number you enter for the mailbox user on the General property page is automatically carried over to this page. You can add a range of other telecommunications-oriented information for the user, and you can also add notes about the user. All this information will be visible to Exchange clients. Go ahead and fill in the page for the mailbox you're creating.

**FIGURE 8.17:**

Entering telecommunications and other information for a mailbox user

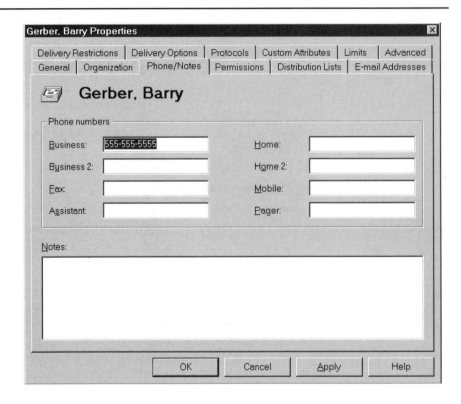

## Permissions

You use the Permissions property page to establish or change rights for the mailbox.

> **NOTE**
>
> If you don't see the Permissions property page, or you don't see the Roles and Rights boxes at the bottom of the page, you've been messing with those options we set back at the beginning of the chapter. To make things right, close the mailbox's Properties dialog box by clicking OK; then open the Tools menu, select Options, tab to the Permissions property page, and be sure that Show Permissions Page for All Objects and Display Rights for Roles on Permissions Page are selected. Click OK in the Options dialog box, then reopen the Properties dialog box for the mailbox you were creating by double-clicking it in the Recipients container. Whew!

**Accounts with Inherited Permissions**   Notice in Figure 8.18 that the permissions of two Windows NT accounts (LA\Administrator and LA\Services) and one NT group (LA\Exchange Admins) have been inherited by mailbox objects. The accounts and the group have permissions at the site level. These permissions are inherited by the Recipients container and all objects in it—individual mailboxes, in this case.

**FIGURE 8.18:**

Controlling access to a mailbox

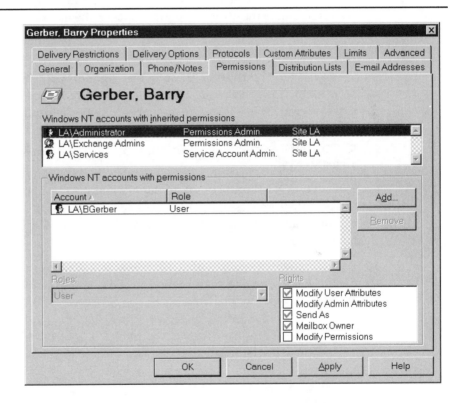

LA\Administrators is the account I used when I installed Exchange Server, so it was granted organization-wide rights by default. I gave permissions to run Exchange services in the LA site to the LA\Services account. Like LA\Administrators, it got organization-wide permissions when I installed Exchange Server. LA\Exchange Admins is the group I granted site-management rights to in Chapter 7. If you followed the instructions in Chapter 7, your Windows NT Accounts with Inherited Permissions box should look similar to mine, except for the site name.

You can't remove permissions on a mailbox from accounts and groups listed in the Windows NT Accounts with Inherited Permissions box; you have to remove the permissions for these accounts or groups at the appropriate container level. (All of this container-level stuff will become clearer as we move along.)

**Granting Permissions to Other Accounts or Groups**     When an NT account is made the Primary Windows NT account for a mailbox on the General page, it is automatically given permissions on the mailbox. As you can see in the Windows NT Accounts with Permissions box in Figure 8.18, BGerber was given permissions for the mailbox.

You can add to this list of NT accounts or groups with permissions on a particular mailbox. You can also limit the role that any account or group with permissions can play. This lets you do a number of things, including creating multiuser mailboxes or assigning a group to perform certain administrative tasks on one or more mailboxes without giving the group full administrative rights or access to all mailboxes.

To give an NT account or group permissions on a mailbox, click Add in the Permissions page and use the Add Users and Groups dialog box that pops up to choose an account or a group. You've used this dialog box before, so I'll let you take it from here.

Each account or group with permissions on a mailbox must have a *role*. Essentially, roles expand or limit what an account or group can do to a mailbox. There are five role types for mailboxes:

- Admin
- Permissions Admin
- Send As
- User
- Custom

Notice that BGerber's role is that of User. You use the Roles drop-down menu to pick a role for an account or group (see Figure 8.18). You won't see the Custom role here, and I'll explain why in just a bit.

Each role type is defined by the rights it has. These rights are listed in the lower right-hand section of the Permissions property page (see Figure 8.18). There are five mailbox rights:

- *Modify User Attributes* permits changes to the mailbox's user-modifiable attributes ("attributes" is another name for properties). For example, in an Exchange client a user can delegate to other NT accounts or groups certain access rights to his or her mailbox.

- *Modify Admin Attributes* permits changes to any mailbox attribute that is modifiable in the Exchange Administrator. For example, those manager and direct-reports attributes you set on the Organization property page can be modified by those with Modify Admin Attributes rights. You certainly wouldn't want users to change their place in the organizational hierarchy, even if it's only in Exchange, would you?

- *Send As* allows the NT account or group granted the right for a mailbox to send messages from other mailboxes to which they have rights such that it appears that the messages came from the Send As mailbox. This right can be useful when, for example, you want an administrative aide to send messages from their own mailbox that appear to have come from a corporate mailbox (e.g., President at GerCom). Send As rights should be granted with care, because they can be dangerous in the wrong hands, like when a disgruntled employee sends out a nasty message that appears to have come from some innocent person's mailbox.

- *Mailbox Owner* can log into the mailbox and send, receive, read, and manipulate messages.

- *Modify Permissions* can change permissions for the mailbox—that is, the entries on the mailbox's Permissions property page.

If the box in front of a particular right is checked in the Rights area of the Permissions property page, the role includes that right. Take a look at the rights for the different roles by selecting each role from the drop-down Roles menu.

There is no preset Custom role. To set up a Custom role, just check off the boxes for the rights you want an account or group to have. If the rights you choose don't match those for a particular role, Custom shows in the drop-down menu as the role type for that account or group.

## Distribution Lists

You can add mailboxes to distribution lists using the Distribution Lists property page (see Figure 8.19). You don't have any distribution lists yet, so you can't do it now, but I'll add my mailbox to a distribution list I sneakily created while you were otherwise occupied.

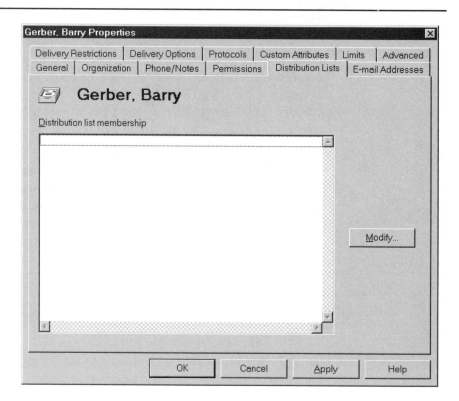

To do this, I click Modify in the Distribution Lists property page to bring up the dialog box shown in Figure 8.20. Then I click the distribution list to which I want to add my mailbox (LA Sales, the only list I have) and click Add. Finally, I click OK in the dialog box. My mailbox has now been added to the LA Sales distribution list.

You can also add a mailbox to a distribution list by using the configuration dialog box for a particular distribution list. This method is easier, since you don't have to open every mailbox you want to add to the list. I'll show you how to do this when we get to distribution lists.

FIGURE 8.20:

Adding a mailbox to a distribution list

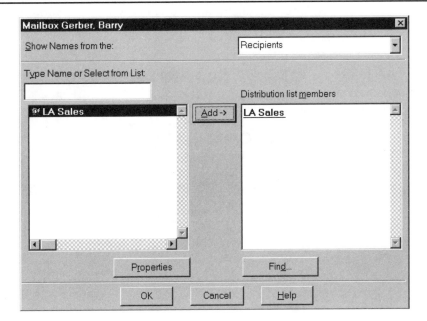

## E-Mail Addresses

You've seen the E-Mail Addresses property page in earlier chapters. It shows a mailbox's addresses for different types of e-messaging systems. Four addresses are created by default: cc:Mail, MS Mail, SMTP, and X.400 (see Figure 8.21). Addresses for cc:Mail and MS Mail are created only if you've installed the cc:Mail Connector and MS Mail Connector, respectively.

Using this property page, you can manually change a specific user's address or add a new address for a user. For example, I sometimes give certain users a second SMTP address that includes their specific department. Adding or changing addresses manually is fun, but not for those new to Exchange Administrator, because it's usually not enough to just change the address. You'll also have to do some things in other areas in Exchange Administrator and maybe even in external systems. I'll talk about all this stuff in a later chapter.

If you wish, Exchange Administrator can regenerate addressing entries on this and all other recipient property pages when you change an e-mail addressing default for an entire site. If you add a gateway for another e-messaging system (fax, for example), the appropriate new gateway address can be added automatically to each recipient's E-Mail Addresses property page.

**FIGURE 8.21:**

Use the E-Mail Addresses property page to display, create, and modify addresses for a mailbox.

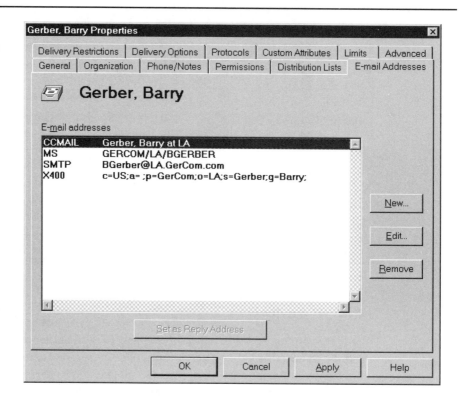

## Delivery Restrictions

If, for whatever reason, you want to let only certain Recipients send messages to a particular mailbox, you use the Delivery Restrictions property page. As you can see in Figure 8.22, you can specify who can and who can't send messages to the mailbox.

You add Recipients to the Accept Messages From or Reject Messages From lists by clicking the appropriate Modify button; you'll see the address book dialog box shown back in Figure 8.14. Select the Recipients you want to add or exclude and then click OK in the Recipients list dialog box. To record your restrictions, click either OK or Apply on the Delivery Restrictions property page.

When a restricted recipient tries to send a message to an off-limits mailbox, the system will return the message (see Figure 8.23).

(I love the Send Again button; you can send the message again until you're blue in the face and you'll keep getting these rejection notices.)

**FIGURE 8.22:**

Use the Delivery Restrictions property page to specify which Recipients can send messages to a mailbox.

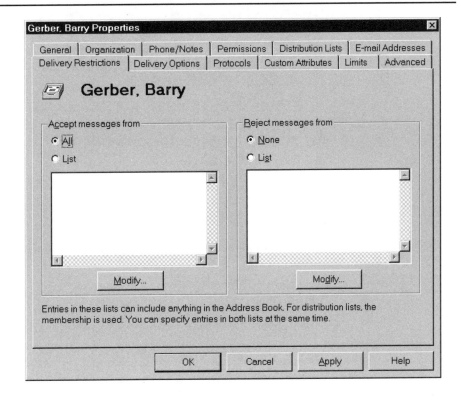

**FIGURE 8.23:**

A system message tells restricted Recipients when they've tried to send a message to an off-limits mailbox.

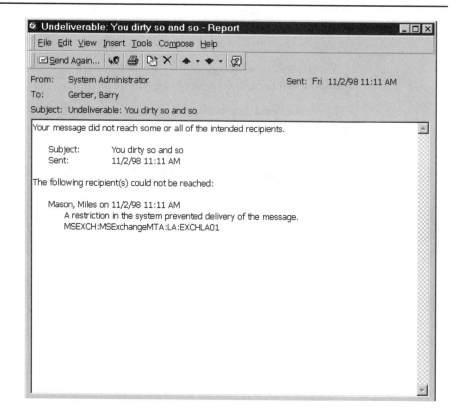

## Delivery Options

You use the Delivery Options property page to give other Recipients rights to the mailbox. You do this when a mailbox owner wants another mailbox owner or group to manage his or her mailbox—for example, when a secretary is assigned to watch a boss's mail, or when people go on vacation and need their mailboxes monitored.

In Figure 8.24, I've given Send on Behalf Of permissions to my mailbox to Miles Mason, my Administrative Assistant. This lets Mason send new messages and reply to messages for me using my mailbox as the return address. The From field in Send on Behalf Of messages identifies both the person sending the message and the individual on whose behalf the message was sent.

**FIGURE 8.24:**

Use the Delivery Options property page to give other Recipients special rights to a mailbox.

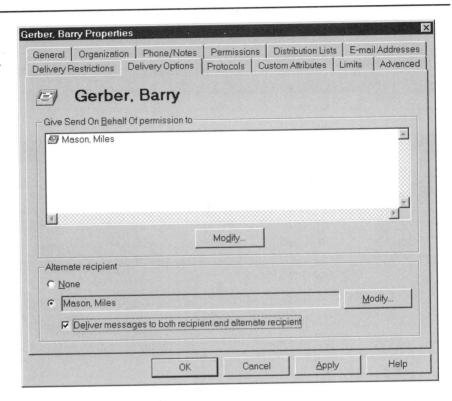

Can you imagine going through and setting Send on Behalf Of options for each user? Whew! But not to worry: Users can do it for themselves using their Exchange clients.

**NOTE**    The Send on Behalf Of permission is different from the role right Send As, which you set on the Permissions property page for a mailbox. Remember, Send As lets the user of one mailbox send a message as though it came from another mailbox, without any hint that the other mailbox didn't send the message itself. If you worry about users sending embarrassing messages that look like they came from another user, then Send on Behalf Of is a far safer option than Send As. If both options are granted to a user, Send As will override Send on Behalf Of.

At the bottom of the Delivery Options property page, I've indicated that messages to me should be delivered to an alternate recipient, Miles Mason. If I hadn't selected the Deliver Messages to Both Recipient and Alternate Recipient option, messages would have been redirected to Mason without a copy being sent to me.

The Alternate recipient option can be used in league with Send on Behalf Of to keep up with incoming mail when an employee is out of the office for one reason or another, or when she or he stops working for the organization. It can also be used to monitor an employee's use of Exchange messaging, since mailbox owners have no idea that messages for their own mailbox are also being sent to another mailbox.

## Protocols

As I noted in earlier chapters, Exchange 5.5 comes with a bunch of new Internet-oriented features. You use the Protocols property page to enable five of these features for a mailbox. I've devoted a whole chapter to these new features. So here I'll give you the most basic of introductions. Follow along, referring to Figure 8.25 as I discuss the Protocols page.

Following are the five new protocols supported by Exchange Server:

- *HTTP (Web)* lets mailbox users access their Exchange server with an Internet browser, for example, to read their e-mail. *HTTP* is an acronym for Hypertext Transfer Protocol.

- *IMAP4 (Mail)* provides access to Exchange server messages and folders through the Internet Message Access Protocol v4.

- *LDAP (Directory)* allows a mailbox user, or even a non-Exchange user, to access the Exchange directory (e-mail addresses, phone numbers, etc.) using a Lightweight Directory Access Protocol (LDAP)–compliant client. This is a neat way to get e-mail addresses when using a non-Exchange client such as a POP3 or IMAP4 client, or to find information about an Exchange user with an LDAP client.

- *NNTP (News)* gives a mailbox user access to Usenet newsgroups stored in Exchange Server's public folders. *NNTP* stands for Network News Transfer Protocol.

- *POP3 (Mail)* support lets a mailbox user read and, with the help of the SMTP e-mail protocol, send mail through her or his Exchange server using a Post Office Protocol version 3 (POP3)–compliant client like Microsoft's Outlook or Outlook Express or Qualcomm's Eudora.

FIGURE 8.25:

Using the Protocols property page to enable and modify the Internet-oriented features available to an Exchange mailbox user

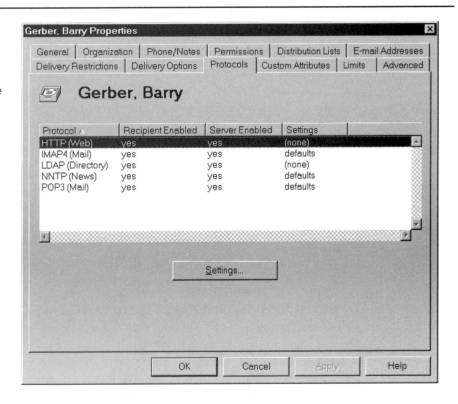

Each of the five protocols can have up to three sets of attributes. These are represented by the columns in the table in Figure 8.25: Recipient Enabled, Server Enabled, and Settings. If "yes" appears in the Recipient Enabled column for a particular protocol, the protocol service is available to the user of the mailbox you're working on. If the Server Enabled column is marked yes, then you know that support for the protocol has been enabled on your Exchange server. The Settings column tells you if there are parameters you can set for a protocol and, if there are parameters, whether the current settings are defaults or custom.

We will cover this much more thoroughly later on.

## Custom Attributes

In the next chapter you'll learn how to create up to ten custom fields to hold information about Recipients. For example, you could create a custom field to hold an employee ID number for each recipient. Custom fields are created at the site level and apply to all Recipients in the site.

Use the Custom Attributes property page to fill in custom fields for a mailbox. For example, imagine that you've created a custom attribute called Employee ID for all Recipients. You enter the specific Employee ID for the user of a specific mailbox on that mailbox's Custom Attributes property page. Since we haven't yet created any custom attributes, there's nothing much we can do here. (If you find all of this still a bit murky, don't worry. Things will clear up in the next chapter.)

## Limits

You use limits to save disk space on your Exchange server. In a world where giga-bytes of storage are never enough, limits judiciously used are most welcome. However, be careful not to overly limit user storage or you're likely to find the cost of fixing problems related to too little storage more expensive than adding more disk storage.

**Deleted Item Retention Time**    Exchange 5.5 includes a nifty new feature. You can tell Exchange Server to hold on to items that are deleted from users' Deleted Items folders. Prior to Exchange 5.5, once a user or automatic process deleted items from the Deleted Items folder, they were gone forever. As you'll see in Chapter 9, you can set a default number of days that messages are retained in the information store before real, final, that's it deletion. You can use the mailbox Limits property page to override the information store default.

**Information Store Storage Limits**    Use the Information Store Storage Lim-its options to either accept the mailbox's default maximum size limits that were set elsewhere—you'll learn how to do this in the next chapter—or set your own maximum limits for the mailbox. As shown in Figure 8.26, you can use any or all of three options when setting your own limits. The mailbox user gets a warning when the first limit is reached and then on a specific schedule thereafter until storage drops below the limit. The warning message schedule is set on the Site Warnings schedule page on the Information Store Site Configuration object (in the Configuration container). When the second limit is reached, the mailbox can no longer send mail. It still can receive mail, however, since you might not want those who send messages getting a bunch of bounced message notifications just because a mailbox user is a resource hog. The third limit prevents reception as well as sending of messages. This option is useful when a user will be out of the office for an extended period and you don't want their mailbox to fill with gobs of unanswered messages.

The Limits Property page helps control Exchange Server storage.

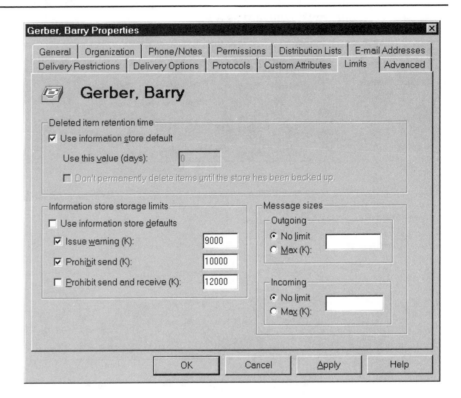

**Message Sizes**    The Message Size Limits field lets you set maximum sizes for outgoing and incoming messages from and to a mailbox. In the next chapter you'll learn how to set site-based default sizes for outgoing and incoming messages; with Message Size Limits, you can refine that setting for an individual mailbox. Use the Max (K) field for either incoming or outgoing messages, and type in the message size limit in kilobytes.

## Advanced Properties

The Advanced property page is fun (see Figure 8.27). It's where you can do a lot of interesting but often esoteric things.

Figure 8.27 shows the Advanced property page for my mailbox. I've filled in a few fields, but your page should look pretty similar. Starting at the top left-hand corner of the property page, we'll move more or less from left to right, inching our way downward as we go.

**FIGURE 8.27:**

The Advanced property page for a mailbox

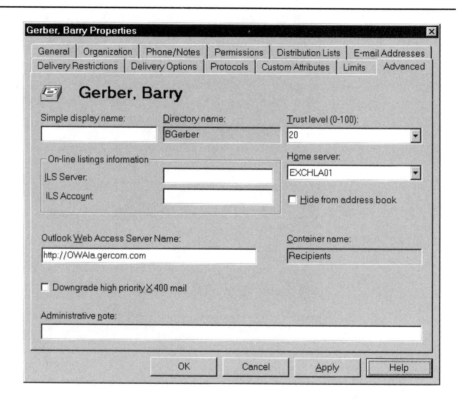

**The Simple Display Name**    The Simple Display Name field is especially useful in certain multilingual Exchange environments. Exchange clients and the server's copy of the Administrator program show the simple display name when the full display name can't be properly displayed. For example, if a full display name is stored in a double-byte character set like Kanji, and a particular copy of the client or the Administrator program isn't set to display the character set, the simple display name is shown in place of the full display name.

**The Directory Name**    Directory names are unique identifiers for objects stored in the Exchange directory. Generally, you're offered a default directory name for any kind of object, and although you can change the name while creating the object, you can't change it afterward.

For a mailbox, the default directory name is the alias constructed by Exchange Server when you filled in the new mailbox's General property page. In Figure 8.26, the alias for my mailbox, BGerber, is offered as the default directory name. You can change the directory name while creating a mailbox, but you can't change it after you've clicked either OK or Apply in the mailbox's Properties dialog box. The only way to change a directory name after you've gone this far is to delete the object and re-create it, so name with care.

**Trust Level**    Use the Trust Level field to tell Exchange Server whether it should include the mailbox when it does directory synchronization with cc:Mail, Microsoft Mail 3.2, or compatible systems. We'll talk about this in a later chapter.

**Online Listings Information**    Microsoft's Internet Locator Service (ILS) server can be used to locate an Exchange Server mailbox owner and set up online meetings, using, for example, Microsoft's NetMeeting software. If an ILS server is available, you can enter the server's name and account names here.

**Home Server**    The Home Server field is where you specify which server the mailbox is to be created on; it's the place where messages for the mailbox are stored. If you change the home server on the Advanced property page, Exchange Administrator asks if you want to move the mailbox to the server you've just chosen. Answer yes, and the mailbox is moved. (There's another way to move a mailbox to another server. We'll get into that method in a later chapter.)

**Hide from Address Book**    Select Hide from Address Book to prevent a mailbox from showing up in the various address lists in the Exchange address book (not just Global Address List). Generally, you'll want to hide a mailbox from the address book to protect a particular mailbox's privacy or when it is used by custom-programmed applications rather than by human users.

**X.400 Priority**    Check the box next to Downgrade High Priority X.400 Mail to prevent the mailbox from sending X.400 mail at high priority. If the mailbox user attempts to send a message destined for an X.400 system at high priority, the Exchange Server downgrades the priority to Normal.

**Container Name**   Use the Container Name option to set the name of the Recipients container that will hold the mailbox. As you'll see soon, you can have multiple Recipients containers in a site. To change the name of the Recipients container, click Modify; this brings up a little tree that shows you the Recipients containers available in the site where you're creating the mailbox. You can't pick a container outside this site, and once you've clicked Apply or OK for the mailbox you're creating, you can't change the Recipients container assigned to it. After that point, you won't even see the Modify button. That's why the Modify button isn't displayed in Figure 8.27. My mailbox had already been created by the time I captured the screen for the figure.

**Outlook Web Access Server Name**   As you'll see in Chapter 18, Outlook Web Access lets you get to your Exchange Server messages and calendar as well as Web-based forms with an Internet Web browser, such as Netscape's browser products or Microsoft's Internet Explorer. If you choose to use a POP3 or IMAP4 Internet mail client to access your messages, how do you get to your calendar and the Web forms? If you set the name of an Outlook Web Access Server on the Advanced property page of your mailbox, you can use your Internet mail client to access messages and access your calendar and the Web forms with a Web browser through Outlook Web Access. You can set this value for all mailboxes on a server on the General properties page of the Private Information Store for the server. We'll look at this page in the next chapter.

**Downgrade High Priority X.400 Mail**   Select this option to prohibit this mailbox from sending high priority messages through X.400 connectors. Messages bound for X.400 sites are automatically downgraded to a priority status of normal.

**Administrative Note**   The Administrative Note field is a place where you can type in up to 1,024 characters of descriptive text about the mailbox or its user. This information is visible only in the Administrator program.

That covers as much about mailboxes as we need to cover for now. Let's continue with the next option on the Administrator's File menu, New Distribution List.

## Reconfiguring an Existing Mailbox

To reconfigure an existing mailbox, just locate it in the Recipients container and double-click it. You'll get the same Properties dialog box you've been using to create new mailboxes. Now just edit as you wish and click OK or Apply to save your changes.

Follow these same directions to modify any existing recipient, whether mailbox, distribution list, custom recipient, or public folder.

## Creating a New Distribution List

As you'll remember, distribution lists are another form of Exchange recipient. To create a new distribution list, click New Distribution List in the Exchange Administrator's File menu. This pops up the Distribution List Properties dialog box shown in Figure 8.28.

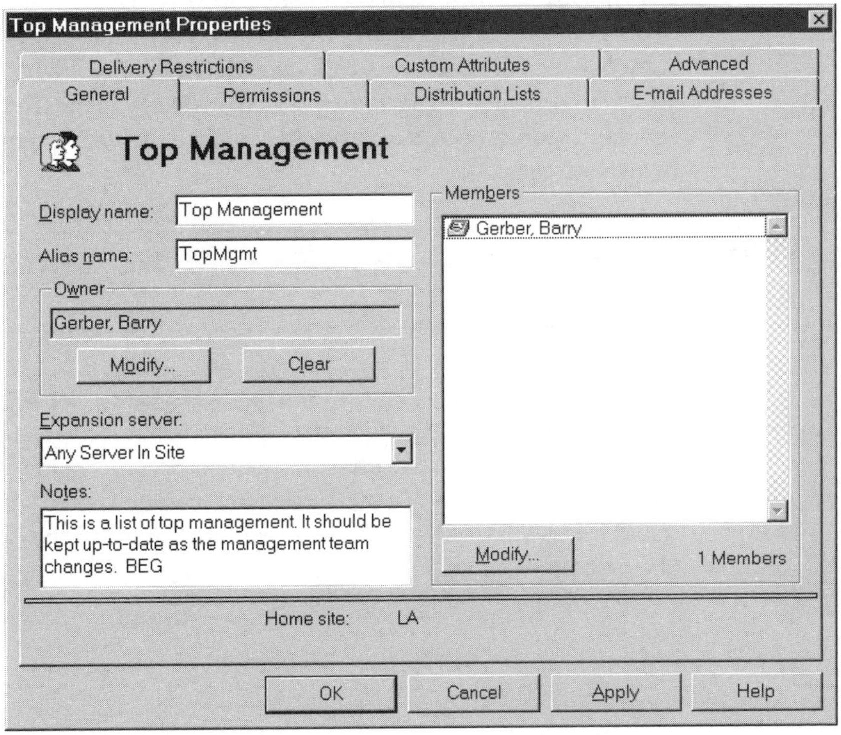

**FIGURE 8.28:**

The General property page of the Distribution List properties dialog box

An Exchange Server distribution list has most of the properties of a mailbox, except that five property pages are missing—Organization, Phone/Notes, Limits, Delivery Options, and Protocols—none of which make much sense for a distribution list. The other seven pages are either exactly like or very similar to their mailbox-based cousins. I'll emphasize the differences here and refer you back to the mailbox property pages for the similarities.

## General Properties

Let's look first at the items on the left-hand side of the General property page, then at the items on the right.

**Display and Alias Names**   You need to fill in a Display name and an Alias name. The Display name will show in the address book; the Alias will be used in creating e-mail addresses for the address list.

**Owner**   The name in the Owner field is the person to whom users should forward requests to be added to or removed from a distribution list. By default the list owner is given rights to add and delete users from within an Exchange client. Since my GerCom list will include the company's top management, and since I'm the president of this mythical company, I've assumed ownership responsibilities. (I don't want anyone but a top exec involved in decisions about whom to admit to this list.) To set an owner for a distribution list, click Modify in the Owner box to bring up a standard address book dialog box like the one shown back in Figure 8.14. Select the owner and click OK.

> **NOTE**   Only one Exchange recipient can own a distribution list. A distribution list cannot own another distribution list.

**Expansion Server**   Distribution lists must be *expanded*—that is, the members of the list must be identified and an efficient route to each member must be determined. Expansion is done on an Exchange server in a site; if a distribution list is large (with thousands of users), you may want to specify an expansion server for it that is less busy. For smaller lists, you don't have to change the Any Server in Site default.

**Notes**   Put anything you like in the Notes field of the distribution list. This information will be displayed for users when they look at the properties of the list using an Exchange client.

**Members**   Finally, add list members. Click Modify in the Members area and select members from the address book dialog box that pops up. Click OK when you're done.

Click Apply if you want to record your work so far, but don't close the distribution list's properties dialog box yet.

## Permissions

The distribution list's Permissions property page looks and behaves almost exactly like the one for a mailbox—the only thing missing is the Mailbox Owner right, which is irrelevant for a distribution list. So, refer to mailbox permissions if you have any questions about the Permissions page for the distribution list.

### Those No Account Distribution Lists

Unlike mailboxes, distribution lists don't have Primary NT accounts. You can see this by comparing Figure 8.10 (for a mailbox) with Figure 8.28 (for a distribution list). Figure 8.10 includes the Primary Windows NT Account button, while Figure 8.28 doesn't.

**NOTE**   If you want to take away a distribution list owner's right to add and remove the list's members while using an Exchange client, remove the Modify User Attributes right from the owner's role. Similarly, if you want to give other users the right to modify a distribution list, add their NT accounts to the Permissions page for the list and assign their accounts the Modify User Attributes right.

### Included Distribution Lists

Distribution lists can include other distribution lists. You use the Distribution Lists property page to optionally add your new list to selected existing distribution lists. Click Modify in the Distribution Lists property page to bring up a dialog box showing existing distribution lists (see Figure 8.29). Use the dialog box to add your new list to existing lists and click OK when you're done.

**FIGURE 8.29:**

Adding a new distribution
list to existing
distribution lists

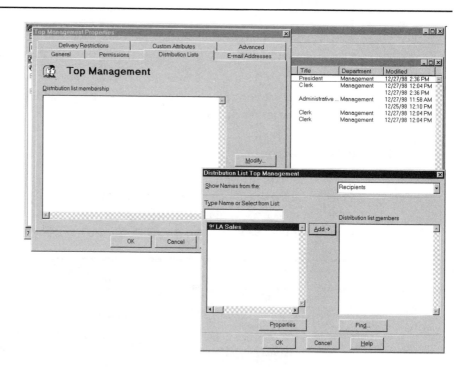

## E-Mail Addresses

Exchange Server distribution lists have their own e-mail addresses. Among other benefits, this allows users of foreign e-messaging systems to send messages to the distribution lists. Except for different addresses, the distribution list's E-Mail Addresses property page looks exactly the same as the one for mailboxes.

## Delivery Restrictions

The Delivery Restrictions property page for distribution lists is a carbon copy of the one for mailboxes, pure and simple. You'll probably use this page more often than the one for mailboxes because it lets you specify which mailboxes, additional distribution lists, and custom Recipients can easily send one message to large groups of users. For example, you can prevent a slew of mass mailings—those advertising everything from cars for sale to apartments for sublet—by giving only a narrow set of mailboxes the rights to send messages to large distribution lists such as those containing all Recipients in a department, a site, or an entire Exchange organization.

## Custom Attributes

The distribution list's Custom Attributes property page is identical to the one for mailboxes. As I noted above, I'll cover custom attributes in more detail in the next chapter.

## Advanced Properties

The Advanced property page for distribution lists differs enough from the one for mailboxes that it's worth taking a quick look at the differences. Figure 8.30 shows the Advanced property page. First note that there is no Home Server field as there is for a mailbox (see Figure 8.27). Distribution lists live only in sites and their attributes (names, members, etc.) are stored in the site directory. While mailbox attributes are stored in the site directory, mail itself is stored on a specific home server, so it's reasonable to say that mailboxes live both in sites and on servers.

**Message Size Limit**     You'll notice that, unlike the Limits property page for mailboxes, distribution lists don't have size-limit options for both incoming and outgoing messages; instead they have a Message Size Limit setting. Distribution lists receive messages; they usually don't send them, though by giving a list Send As rights, you can use it to send messages. The limits you set on the Advanced property page are for incoming messages only.

FIGURE 8.30:

The Advanced property
page for distribution lists

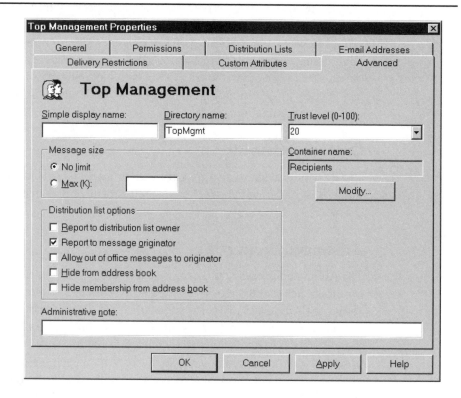

**Distribution List Options**    Let's look at Distribution List Options in the
Advanced property page one at a time. I've already talked about the Hide from
Address Book option, so I won't cover it again.

- *Report to Distribution List Owner* sends notification to the owner of the distribution list when a message sent to the list has requested a delivery notification message or when the message is undeliverable.

- *Report to Message Originator* sends delivery notification or undeliverable
  message information to the message originator for each member of the list.
  If this option is not selected, delivery notifications and non-delivery messages are sent to the message originator for the list as a whole. If a list member is hidden from the Address Book, to protect the secrecy of hidden
  members, delivery notification and undeliverable information messages are
  sent for the list, not its individual members.

- *Allow Out of Office Messages to Originator* sends to the originator of the message individual out-of-office messages from all list members who have active out-of-office messages.

- *Hide Membership from Address Book* protects the privacy of the members of a distribution list. Even if the list itself isn't hidden, users can't tell whose names are on it.

   Now that you are familiar with distribution lists, you're ready to move on to the next option on the Administrator's File menu, New Custom Recipient. Refer back to Figure 8.6 for a view of the File menu.

# Creating Custom Recipients

You'll remember that custom Recipients are essentially aliases for Recipients in foreign e-messaging systems. They're helpful when a lot of people in your organization need to communicate with users of non-Exchange systems.

## Setting Type of Address

To create a custom recipient, click New Custom Recipient in the Exchange Administrator's File menu. This brings up the dialog box shown in Figure 8.31. Select the type of address for the custom recipient and then click OK. (In the figure, I've chosen to create a custom recipient with an Internet address.)

**FIGURE 8.31:**

Selecting the type of address for a new custom recipient

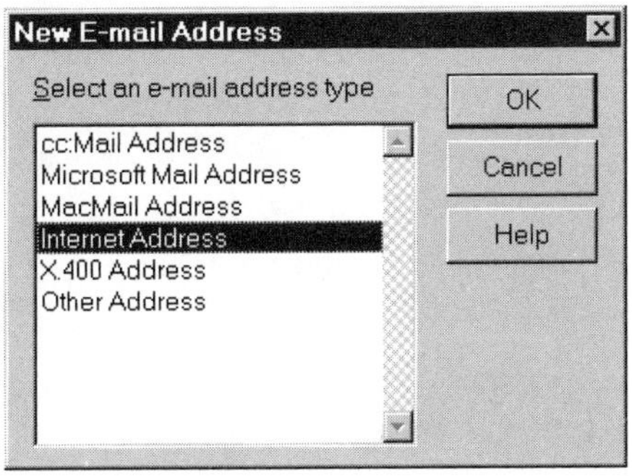

## The E-Mail Address Type Properties Dialog Box

The next thing you'll see is a dialog box for entering the custom recipient's e-messaging address. Figure 8.32 shows the dialog box for the new Internet-based custom recipient I want to create. If you're creating a custom recipient for a different type of messaging system, you'll see a dialog box with fields appropriate to that system. When you're done entering the address, click OK.

The Internet Address Properties dialog box contains a second tab. See Figure 8.32. It's used to modify the way messages are coded before being sent out across the Internet. I'll discuss Internet message coding in some detail in Chapters 15 and 18.

**FIGURE 8.32:**

The Internet Properties dialog box

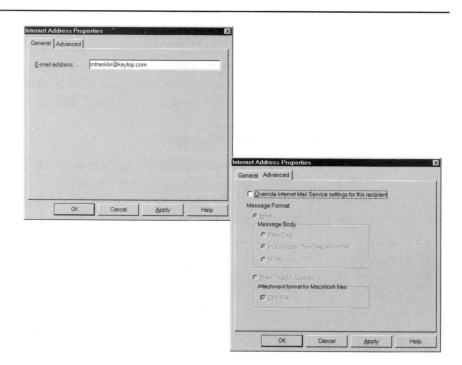

## Standard Property Pages

Next you'll see the Properties dialog box for custom Recipients. It looks very much like the one for a mailbox configuration, except that it's missing the Delivery Options and Limits property pages, which are not of much use here anyway (see Figure 8.33). If you think of a custom recipient as a sort of mailbox–distribution list hybrid, nothing in these property pages should surprise you. That said, I'll leave the rest of custom recipient configuration to you.

**FIGURE 8.33:**

The Properties dialog box for custom Recipients

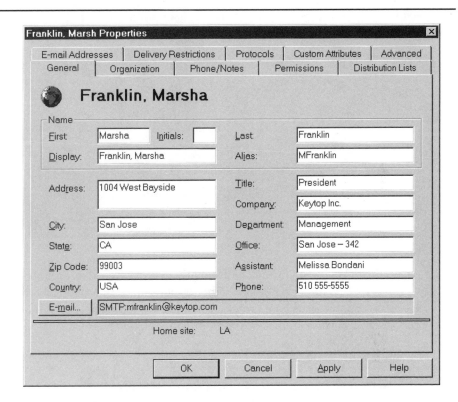

## New Other Options

Figure 8.34 shows the menu that pops up when you select New Other from the Exchange Administrator's File menu. You can use this submenu to create a variety of objects and services. For instance, this is where you create new monitors that watch the health of Exchange servers and links to other sites and systems. This is also where you establish new Recipients containers for a site and new information stores, as well as where you create Exchange Server connectors and set up directory synchronization with other systems.

FIGURE 8.34:

The New Other
options menu

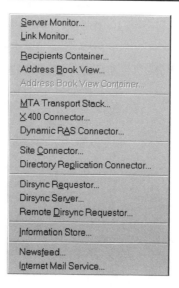

You won't be able to use many of the New Other options until you've got more than one server or site. Other options are a bit advanced for our needs right now. So, I'll focus here on server monitors and Recipients containers. I'll cover everything else on the New Other menu in later chapters.

## Public Folders Are Recipients, Too

As you'll remember from earlier chapters, public folders are the fourth type of recipient. However, they're created by users, not by Exchange Server administrators; that's why there's no New Public Folder option on the Exchange Administrator program's File menu. We'll discuss the administration and management of public folders in the next chapter.

### Configuring a Server Monitor

Server monitors are really impressive. They watch over Exchange servers, their clocks, and the services running on them. One server monitor can operate on one or more of the servers in a site. You can set up multiple monitors in a site or even in an organization. You can also set up a monitor so that it notifies you if a service shuts down or never starts, if clients can't connect to the server, or if the server disappears from the network. Server monitors are also able to restart computers or services and synchronize server clocks.

Server monitors are important; you should get comfortable with them right away. Let's create one for your server. From the Administrator's File menu, select New Other, then select Server Monitor. Since monitors are created in the Monitors container for a site, Exchange will warn you if you're not in one of these and will offer to take you there, just as it does if you're not in a site Recipients container when you create a mailbox.

**General Properties**   When you see the server monitor's Properties dialog box shown in Figure 8.35, you're ready to go. I've already filled in the General property page for my server EXCHLA01.

**FIGURE 8.35:**

Configuring the General property page for a Server monitor

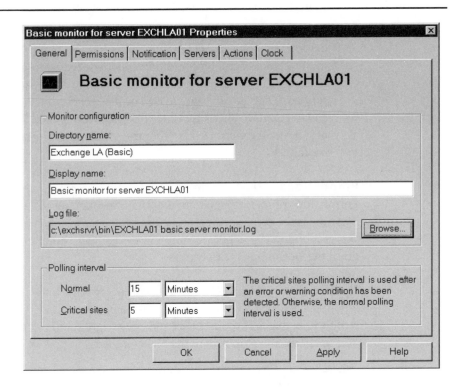

You can set several options on the General property page:

- *The Directory Name,* as with all standard directory names, cannot be changed after you create the server monitor.

- *The Display Name* is what you see when you look into the Monitors container. It can be up to 256 characters long.

- *The Log File* specifies the file in which the server monitor puts information about its activities. Even if a monitor can watch over many servers, I generally store its log file on the server that the monitor will run on. That way, if the network goes down, the monitor will still be able to write to its log file. Click Browse to set the directory and filename.

- *The Normal Polling Interval* is the time period the monitor waits before checking to see that all is running properly on the server. The default is fifteen minutes, which is just about right in most situations.

- *The Critical Sites Polling Interval* is the time period the server monitor waits before checking servers that are in trouble and that it is trying to fix. ("Sites" in this context actually refer to Exchange servers, not Exchange sites.) The default polling interval is five minutes. As you'll see in a bit, reviving a dead service or server can involve two or three cycles, each of which will require a wait equal to one critical sites polling interval. You'll have to decide on the best interval for each server monitor you create. For now, accept the default setting.

**Permissions**    The list of role rights is a bit different on the server monitor's Permissions property page than on other permissions pages you've worked with. The only right you haven't seen before is Delete, which is the right to delete the server monitor. If you give monitor access rights to other accounts or groups, grant the Delete right with caution.

**Notification**    Use the Notification property page to tell the server monitor whom to contact (and how to do it) when a problem arises. Click New and the New Notification dialog box opens (see the lower right-hand corner in Figure 8.36). You're offered three options in the New Notification dialog box:

- *Launch a Process* starts a program. For example, it can start a program that sends information about the problem to an alphanumeric pager.

- *Mail Message* sends a mail message about the problem to a specific recipient.

- *Windows NT Alert* sends a standard network message about the problem to a specific computer.

Click the Notification option you want and then click OK in the New Notification dialog box. The Escalation Editor dialog box for the option you've chosen pops up. This dialog box looks pretty much the same for all three options; Figure 8.37 shows how it looks when the Mail Message option is chosen. For the other two options, the Mailbox to Notify field is replaced by other fields appropriate to the particular notification action you're setting up.

To fill in the Escalation Editor dialog box for mail message notification, enter the time interval that the monitor should wait before issuing notification when it detects a problem. (The default is fifteen minutes, but in many cases you'll want more immediate notification.) As you can see in Figure 8.37, you can set the time unit to minutes or hours.

**FIGURE 8.36:**

The New Notification dialog box

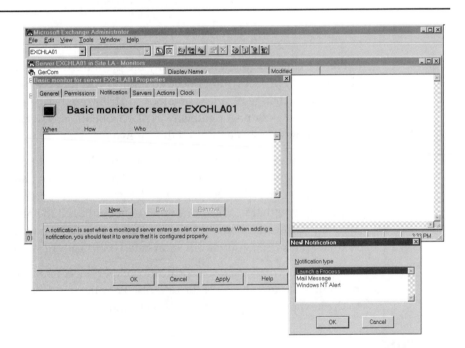

If you select Alert Only in the Escalation Editor dialog box, the monitor sends notification to this recipient only when actual problems exist. If you *don't* select Alert Only, then the monitor notifies the recipient about warnings and potential problems, as well as actual problems. This is a nice option: You can tell the monitor to notify certain people both when a problem starts brewing and when it reaches a critical level, while notifying others only when things actually go wrong.

FIGURE 8.37:

Using the Escalation Editor
(Mail Message) box to
configure notifications

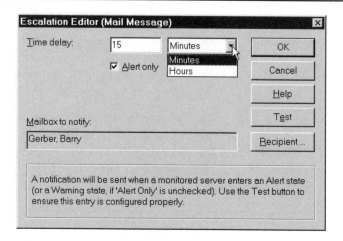

Finally, click Recipient to select any recipient from the resultant address book dialog box. (I probably don't need to remind you that the recipient here can be any valid Exchange recipient, mailbox, distribution list, or custom recipient.) If you've got a fax or pager gateway in place, of course, you can send the message to Recipients accessible through the gateway as well.

When you've finished selecting a recipient, click Test. Exchange will run a check to ensure that you've picked a valid and reachable mailbox. If you don't get an error message, click OK in the Escalation Editor dialog box. You'll get a warning telling you that notifications will not be sent until the next polling interval after the notification time (the delay you just entered) has passed. Click OK again and you'll now see your notification listed on the Notification property page.

With all this mail message notification experience behind you, you should have no trouble setting up one of the other two notification processes. So let's move on to the next property page for the server monitor.

**NOTE**
You can set up as many kinds of notifications as you want. Just click New in the Notification dialog box and fill in the New Notification and Escalation Editor dialog boxes with your information.

**Servers**    You use the Servers property page to choose the servers and services you want monitored (see Figure 8.38).

Click the name of your server and then click Add to put it into the Monitored Servers scroll box. If you want to include more than one server in this monitoring operation, add it here. If you have access to other sites, you can add servers from them by choosing another site from the Site drop-down menu in the lower left-hand corner of the Servers property page.

Now select your server in the Monitored Servers scroll box and then click Services, just below the right-hand scroll box, to bring up the dialog box shown in Figure 8.39. By default, three of the four core Exchange services are listed in the Monitored Services scroll box: the directory, the information store, and the MTA. (The System Attendant isn't automatically included because it's largely responsible for all monitors; if it dies, active monitors die with it.)

**FIGURE 8.38:**

Selecting a server to monitor

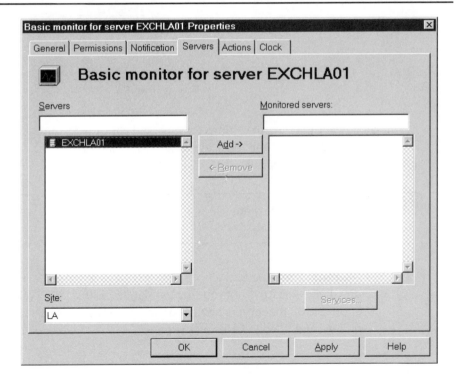

**FIGURE 8.39:**

Selecting services to be monitored on a server

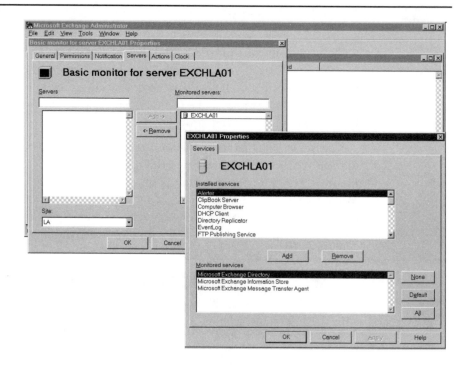

Leave the default settings for now and click OK in the Services dialog box. You can come back later and add any service you'd like, whether it's an Exchange Server service or not.

---

**NOTE**    As should be pretty obvious from what we've just done, a server monitor can watch different services on each of the servers it monitors.

---

**Actions**    You use the Actions property page to tell your server monitor what to do when a service is not running (see Figure 8.40). What you put on this page applies to all the servers being monitored. In the figure, I've already selected options and filled in fields on the page.

FIGURE 8.40:

Setting options for actions
to be taken when a service
is not running

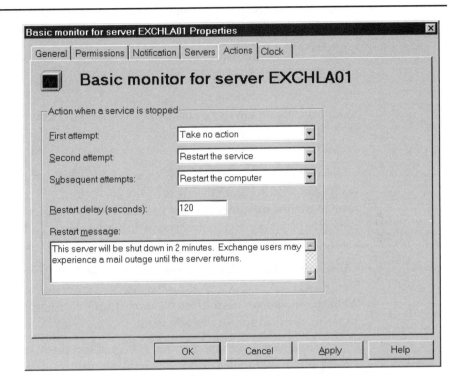

You have three options when a service is not running: Take No Action, Restart the Service, or Restart the Computer. As you can see, I've instructed the monitor to do nothing on the first attempt, to restart the service on the second attempt, and to restart the computer on subsequent attempts. Timing for these actions is based on the polling intervals that were set on the General property page. When you request a computer restart, you can set a delay time before it restarts and include a message that will be sent to users logged in to the computer. I've selected a 120-second delay. The default is 60 seconds.

**NOTE**   An Exchange Server client is almost always able to survive the disappearance of its Exchange server or servers without your having to restart it or reboot your workstation. This is true whether the disappearance is due to a server outage or a network problem. If you're responsible for administering an MS Mail installation or any of the other file-based e-messaging systems out there, I bet you'll consider this little feature of client-server messaging alone to be worth the price of an Exchange system.

**Clocks**   The Clock property page deals with keeping Exchange server clocks synchronized. We'll come back to it later when we have more than one installed Exchange server.

**Starting a Server Monitor**   When you're through setting parameters, click OK in the server monitor's Properties dialog box. You'll see your monitor in the Monitors container for your site. Double-clicking the server monitor reopens the Properties dialog box, which you can use at any time to change the monitor's properties.

Now you have to start the server monitor. Click the monitor name and then select Start Monitor from the Tools menu. Next, you're asked what server you want to run the monitor on. After you answer, the monitor's window opens, indicating that your server monitor is now up and running and ready to act as you instructed should anything go wrong (see Figure 8.41).

If you double-click the line in the monitor that displays the monitor's name (see Figure 8.41), a dialog box pops up that lets you see how things are going. Try it. When you no longer need to see the monitor, minimize its window for better access to other Administrator windows.

Server monitors continue running when you exit the Administrator and resume when a server is rebooted. To stop a server monitor, close its window.

To test your server monitor, double-click the Services applet in your Exchange server's Control Panel, then halt a core Exchange Server service, such as the MTA. The monitor should restart the service just fine.

For a really serious test, disable the service by clicking Startup in the Services dialog box and selecting Disabled. The monitor will now be unable to restart the service—so if you've specified a computer restart, your Exchange server will be rebooted after any polling and service restart intervals have passed. Since you've disabled it, of course, the service won't start on reboot, either, so change the service's startup status back to Automatic after the reboot. The monitor will now be able to restart the service. (Remember to give the monitor enough time to go through the polling and restart delays you've set.)

**FIGURE 8.41:**

A server monitor up and running

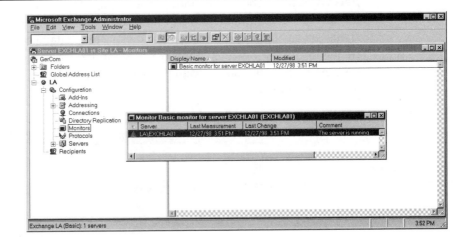

## Creating a New Recipients Container

You can put all the Recipients in a site into one container—the default container named Recipients—or you can create separate containers to hold specific kinds of Recipients. You can use multiple Recipients containers to more easily manage different types of Recipients. For example, you could set up separate containers to hold the Recipients used by specially programmed messaging-enabled applications or put all distribution lists in a single container.

You can't move existing Recipients once they've been created in a specific Recipients container, so plan additional Recipients containers carefully before you start adding Recipients to one container or another.

You can create a new Recipients container in a site or in an existing Recipients container. First highlight either the site or an existing Recipients container, then select Recipients Container from the New Other options menu under the Exchange Administrator's File menu. A Properties dialog box like the one in Figure 8.42 pops up.

**General Properties**    On the General property page for the Recipients container, fill in the display and directory names and add an administrative note if you want, as shown in Figure 8.42.

**Permissions**    The Permissions property page for the new Recipients container has one new role right on it: Add Child. An NT account or group with Add Child rights can create subcontainers under the master container. You'll see this right frequently on Permissions property pages for the various containers I'll discuss in the next chapter. For now, accept the defaults and click OK in the Properties dialog box for the container.

**FIGURE 8.42:**

The Properties dialog box for a new Recipients container

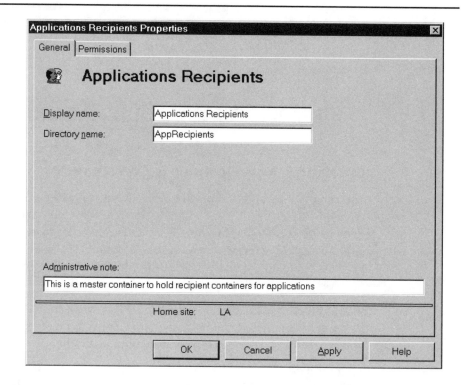

**The New Container**    In Figure 8.43 you can see the new Recipients container I created to hold Recipients containers for different custom-programmed messaging applications. Because I created it while the Recipients container was selected, the new container is a subcontainer of the Recipients container.

That's it for the New Other menu for now. Let's move on to the remaining options on the Administrator's File menu. Refer back to Figure 8.6 for a reminder of the File menu.

**FIGURE 8.43:**

A container to hold other Recipients containers for custom-programmed messaging-enabled applications

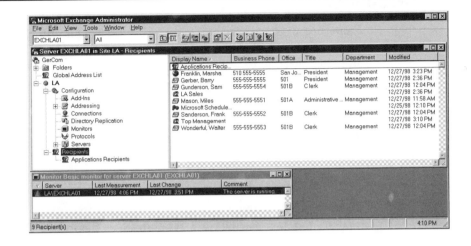

## Save Window Contents

Exchange 5.5 adds a neat and useful item to the File menu, Save Window Contents. When you choose this item, a select set of attributes for the Recipients in the Window (container) you're currently viewing (for example, the Recipients container) is exported to a file. For each recipient, Save Window Contents exports all of the attributes represented by the columns shown in the Window. In Figure 8.43, for example, Display Name, Business Phone, Office, Title, Department, and [Date] Modified would be exported.

After you select Save Window Contents, you're offered a chance to name the file to hold the export. The file is saved in the default format for your specific copy of Exchange Administrator. Unless you change it, the default file format is comma delimited.

In Chapter 17, I'll show you how to do much more complex exports and imports of recipient attributes. For now, consider this a quick and easy way to export a limited number of key attributes. You can use files created with Save Window Contents in a number of ways. For example, they can be used to create import files that modify all or selected Recipients (more in Chapter 17), or even as a kind of container backup that lets you restore lost Recipients by importing all or part of a file created by Save Window Contents. In the latter situation, however, exercise caution. Recipient objects usually have far more attributes than those showing in the display window. If you want to export any of the attributes not showing in the display window, see Chapter 17.

## Properties

Properties, of course, are what you've been setting on all those property pages. You can view the properties of any Exchange object either by clicking the object and then selecting Properties from the Exchange Administrator's File menu or by holding down the Alt key while pressing the Enter key. For objects other than containers, you can also see properties by double-clicking the object in the right pane. However, this won't work with containers since clicking once, twice, or a million times on a container only shows you what's inside.

## Duplicating Objects

You can duplicate any non-container object. For example, you can duplicate a mailbox and then use the copy to set up a new mailbox with similar properties.

To duplicate an object, click it and select Duplicate from the Administrator's File menu. This brings up a standard Properties dialog box for the object with all the properties of the original intact, except that blanks replace the information that makes the original object unique. For example, all four fields are blank in the Name area on the General property page for a duplicate mailbox. (Look back at Figure 8.10 for the location of the Name area.)

# The Edit Menu

The Exchange Administrator's Edit menu is pretty plain-vanilla. It includes all the usual items: Undo, Cut, Copy, Paste, Delete, and Select All. 'Nuff said.

# The View Menu

Figure 8.44 shows the Exchange Administrator's View menu. Use this menu to indicate which Exchange objects are to be shown and how the views of Exchange's hierarchy are to be formatted. You can also use it to move the splitbar and to toggle on and off both the toolbar (below the menu bar on the Administrator window) and the status bar (at the bottom of the Administrator window).

**FIGURE 8.44:**

The Exchange Administrator's View menu

## What to View

Most of the time, I like to see all Recipients in the Administrator, so I select All on the Administrator's View menu. To view only certain Recipients, select the ones you want using the View menu; to view Recipients you've hidden, select Hidden Recipients.

You can also select the recipient types you want to view from the drop-down menu in the toolbar, as shown in Figure 8.45. Notice that hidden Recipients aren't listed in the drop-down menu; the only way to view hidden Recipients is by using the View menu.

**FIGURE 8.45:**

Selecting Recipients to view using the Exchange Administrator's toolbar drop-down menu

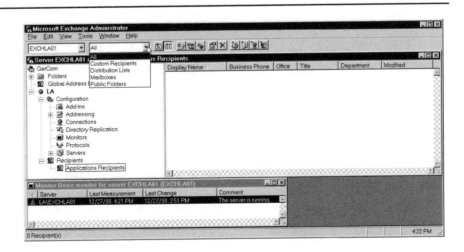

# Recipient Attributes and Views

Exchange Recipients can have a plethora of attributes or properties; Figure 8.46 shows some of these. A number of recipient attributes are used for column heads when you view a list of Recipients in a Recipients container. Note that the attributes shown in the right-hand scroll box in Figure 8.46 are the titles of the column bars for the Recipients listing in Figure 8.47.

**FIGURE 8.46:**

Some of the attributes of Exchange Recipients

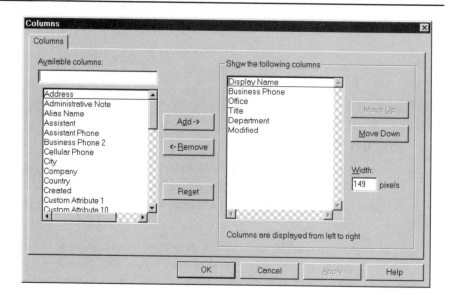

**FIGURE 8.47:**

Recipient attributes are displayed as column heads in a recipient listing.

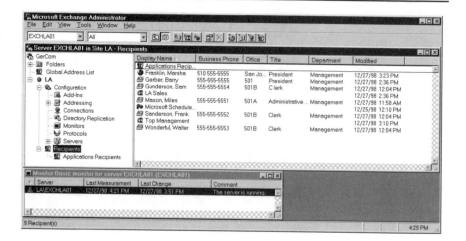

To change the attributes (columns) used in a display of Recipients, select Columns from the Administrator's View menu. This brings up the Columns dialog box shown in Figure 8.46. Use the dialog box to add and remove attributes to be displayed. The topmost attribute in the right-hand box in Figure 8.46—Display Name—is the leftmost column in the Recipients list in Figure 8.47. The second attribute, Business Phone, is the second column in the Recipients listing, and so on.

To change the column display order, highlight a column title and use the Move Up and Move Down buttons to position the title as you wish (see Figure 8.46). To set the column width for an attribute, click the attribute and enter the measurement (in pixels) in the Width box. Each column has its own width setting.

To resize the Recipients display columns, place your Windows pointer on the little line between any two column title bars (see Figure 8.47). The pointer turns into a crosshair. Hold down the left mouse button and move the crosshair until you're happy with the real estate that each column occupies.

## Sorting Lists

You can sort certain Exchange Server lists—Recipients lists, for example—by column headings. The Sort By option on the View menu lets you select a default sort column. There are two options: Display Name (the default) and Last Modified Date.

Remember, you can change the sort order for any list by clicking the column title bar you want to sort by. If you're permitted to sort by that column, the list will be resorted.

## Fonts

Use the Font option on the View menu to change the display font used by the Exchange Administrator.

## Move Splitbar

The Move Splitbar option on the View menu is another way to set the splitbar on an Administrator window. Select it and your Windows pointer is automatically placed on the splitbar of the current Administrator window. At that point, you can move the splitbar as you wish, changing the real estate occupied by the two panes in the window.

# The Toolbar

As you already know, you can use the toolbar, which is located below the menu bar, to set the type of Recipients you want to view. The toolbar also lets you select the Exchange server you want to focus your attention on. More about this capability later.

Finally, the toolbar contains buttons for performing various Administrator functions. You can see these in Figure 8.47. Here's what the buttons do in the order they appear from left to right:

- Move up one level in the Exchange hierarchy

- Show or hide the container tree view in the left-hand pane of an Administrator window

- Create a new mailbox

- Create a new distribution list

- Create a new custom recipient

- Show the properties of an object

- Delete an object

- Move to Configuration container

- Move to Servers container

- Move to Connections container

- Move to Recipients container

You don't have to worry about memorizing these functions. Just hover over the button you're interested in with your mouse pointer and in a second a standard Windows tooltip will pop up telling you the button's function.

# The Status Bar

The status bar is in the bottom area of the Administrator screen. In Figure 8.47, the status bar displays "9 Recipient(s)" to tell you that there are nine objects (Recipients) in the currently selected container. Keep the status bar turned on—it doesn't cost you anything.

# The Tools Menu

The Exchange Administrator program's Tools menu is chock-full of interesting functionality (see Figure 8.48). The first four items on the menu make it easier to create mailboxes en masse. The items fit nicely into the category of advanced Exchange Server administration, so I'll cover them in later chapters.

**FIGURE 8.48:**

The Exchange Administrator's Tools menu

Directory Import...
Directory Export...
Extract Windows NT Account List...
Extract NetWare Account List...

Find Recipients...
Move Mailbox...
Add to Address Book View...
Clean Mailbox...

Start Monitor...
Track Message...

Forms Administrator...
Newsgroup Hierarchies...

✓ Save Connections on Exit
Save Connections Now

Customize Toolbar...
Options...

## Finding Recipients

The Find Recipients option gets more and more valuable as the number of Recipients and servers in your Exchange organization grows. To search for a recipient, select Find Recipients from the Tools menu. If you're asked which server you want to connect to, click Browse, find your server, and click OK in the Connect to Server dialog box. The Find Recipients dialog box will pop up (see Figure 8.49).

**FIGURE 8.49:**

Finding specific Exchange
Recipients

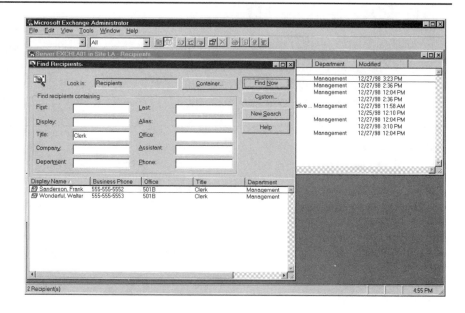

You can search on attributes such as first name and last name, as shown in Figure 8.49. And by clicking the Custom button, you can search on those custom attributes I'll talk about in the next chapter. Clicking Container brings up a dialog box that lets you select the site and Recipients container to search in.

When you've filled in the appropriate fields in the Find Recipients dialog box, click the Find Now button. When the searching is finished, you'll see a list of all Recipients that meet the criteria you entered. (In Figure 8.49, I searched for all the Recipients in GerCom's LA site with a title of Clerk.)

Recipients are listed by the columns set under the Columns option of the Administrator's View menu (see Figure 8.46). You can use the list of found Recipients pretty much as if it were a Recipients container. For example, you can double-click any found recipient to edit its Properties dialog box.

## Moving a Mailbox

When users move to new locations, or when you need to move a mailbox for administrative reasons, it's nice to be able to move mailboxes from one Exchange server to another. The Tools menu's Move Mailbox option makes this easy. You can move mailboxes only within a site, however. Since we'll need at least one additional Exchange server to move a mailbox, I'll talk about mailbox moves in a later chapter.

## Adding to an Address Book View

You might have noticed that the New Other menu includes an option that lets you create different views of the Exchange address book. (Refer back to Figure 8.34.) The address book is used to find e-mail and other information stored in the Exchange directory. Having various views of the address book can make it easier for users to find specific addresses or other information. I'll talk about address book views and the various options associated with them in Chapter 17.

## Cleaning Mailboxes

Users tend to fill up their mailboxes at breakneck speed, so Exchange Server provides a number of ways to deal with this problem. One way is to set limits on the amount of storage available to mailboxes; another is to remove messages from any or all recipient mailboxes based on specific criteria.

To set up criteria for cleaning mailboxes, select the Recipients whose mailboxes you want to clean. You can select any or all Recipients in the following:

- The Global Address List

- Any site's or server's recipient containers, including those you've created yourself

- A found Recipients list created using the Find Recipients option on the Tools menu

Use Windows's standard list-selection keys to select the Recipients. For example, to select a noncontiguous group of mailboxes, hold down the Ctrl key while clicking each mailbox you want to clean. Once you've selected the Recipients, click Clean Mailbox on the Tools menu; this brings up the dialog box shown in Figure 8.50.

Everything in the dialog box should be pretty easy to figure out except for Sensitivity, which is a privacy-based attribute that's set by the person sending a message. Select all of the criteria you want and click OK to start the mailbox-cleaning process immediately. This is a powerful little tool; use it with care.

**FIGURE 8.50:**

Specifying criteria for
cleaning mailboxes

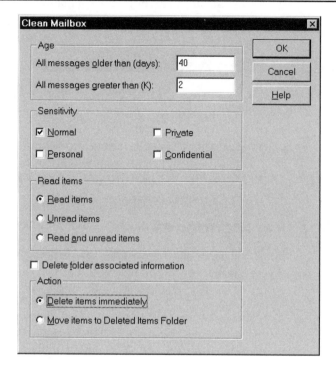

## Starting a Monitor

You've already used the Start Monitor option to start the server monitor you created earlier in this chapter, so you already know what this option is for and how it works.

## Tracking a Message, Administering Forms, and Working with Newsgroup Hierarchies

You'll learn how to track a message, administer forms, and deal with newsgroup hierarchies in later chapters. Tracking messages is much more fun when you have more than one server. The last chapter of this book deals exclusively with Microsoft Exchange and Outlook Forms Designers. We'll cover newsgroups and their hierarchies in the chapters on the new Internet-oriented services that come with Exchange 5.5.

## Saving Connections

You can save the Administrator's connections to Exchange servers upon exiting from the Administrator or at some other time. When you come back into the Administrator, the connections are automatically reestablished. To save connections upon exit, select that option. To save connections at any time, select Save Connections Now.

## Customizing the Toolbar

You can add to or subtract from the Administrator's toolbar. Just select the Customize Toolbar option from the Tools menu and use the friendly interface to tailor the toolbar to your own special needs.

## Options

You already used the Options option way back at the beginning of this chapter, so we've now covered everything in the Tools menu.

## Raw Properties

I can't resist showing you a well-hidden little capability of the Exchange Administrator. It lets you start up Administrator in such a way that you can examine and modify every last bloody property available for any object. When you start the Administrator this way, you're in what Microsoft calls "raw mode." Even if you never use raw mode, you should check it out to see how absolutely detailed the object properties can get.

To start the Administrator in raw mode, open a DOS Command Prompt window. At the command prompt, go to the disk drive where you installed Exchange Server. Then change to the directory C:\exchsrvr\bin and type **admin/raw**. Or you can click the NT Start menu, select Run, type **<drive>\exchsrvr\bin\admin –r** and click OK. <drive> is the hard disk drive where you installed Exchange Server, usually your C drive.

That's it. When the Administrator starts, highlight any object and open the File menu. You'll find a new option on the menu, Raw Properties, located just below Properties. Click it and play to your heart's content. One warning: Use your mouse, and keep your hands off your keyboard so there's no chance you'll change anything. You're not ready for that kind of stuff yet.

*continued on next page*

The graphic included in this sidebar shows some of the raw properties or attributes for the mailbox I created earlier in this chapter.

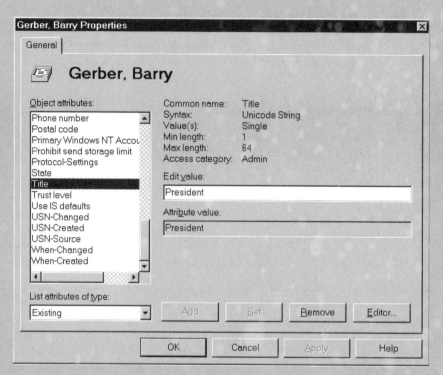

The Title attribute is selected, and my title—President—is listed and can be edited in the Edit Value box. Notice that the Access category for Title is Admin. This means that only NT accounts or groups with Admin role permissions for the mailbox can change this property.

# Conclusion

In this chapter, you learned about the Exchange Administrator program and how to use it and its menus to do a number of administrative and management tasks. In the next chapter, we'll continue using the Administrator to configure Exchange Server's hierarchy and core components.

# The Exchange Server Hierarchy and Core Components

**Basic administration and management of the following:**

■ The Exchange Server hierarchy

■ The directory service

■ The information store (both private and public)

■ The System Attendant

**A**fter plowing through the last chapter, you're probably beginning to appreciate at least some of the effort that Microsoft put into developing Exchange Server to achieve such a high level of flexible, easy-to-implement functionality. This and coming chapters will add to that appreciation—I guarantee it.

Now that you're comfortable with Exchange Server's Administrator program, its menus, and a number of its functions, I want to show you how to use it to administer and manage the Exchange Server hierarchy and core components. As in the last chapter, I'll focus mainly on the basics here, saving advanced administration and management for later chapters.

> **NOTE**    As you've probably already discovered, some types of property pages are very similar, no matter where you encounter them. The Permissions page is a good example. So, from this point on, if we've already covered the subject matter of a particular property page, I'll skip over it without comment. I'll still let you know when we're bypassing material we'll cover in later chapters. Therefore, if I don't say anything at all about a specific property page or property, I'm assuming that you already know how to deal with it. Check back to earlier discussions for specifics.

# The Exchange Server Hierarchy

You'll remember from Chapter 2 that the Exchange Server hierarchy includes the organization as well as its sites, servers, and recipients. In the last chapter, we talked a good deal about three kinds of recipients: mailbox, distribution list, and custom. Here we'll focus on the organization, sites, and servers. We'll also cover the last of the four recipient types: public folders.

Let's see what tools are available for administering and managing the hierarchy. Open the Administrator program and make the left-hand pane look like the one shown in Figure 9.1. As we move along, refer back to this figure if you need help in finding a particular object in the Exchange hierarchy.

**FIGURE 9.1:**

The Exchange Administrator, ready to administer and manage the Exchange hierarchy

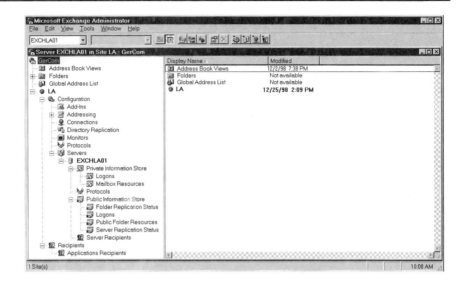

## The Organization

Click the name of your organization in the left-hand pane of the Administrator window, and then open the File menu and click Properties. This brings up the Properties dialog box for the organization (see Figure 9.2).

### General Properties

Talk about starting off easy! There's only one thing you can change on the General property page—the display name for your organization.

The *display name* is what you see when you look at the Exchange Server hierarchy in the Administrator; it's also the organization name that Exchange client users see in their address books. The default display name, which can be up to 256 characters long, is the organization name you entered when you installed the first server in your Exchange organization. You can change the display name to make the organization's name more meaningful to those who administer and use your Exchange system. For example, I could change "GerCom" to "Barry Gerber's Wonderful Enter Key Company" (but I won't).

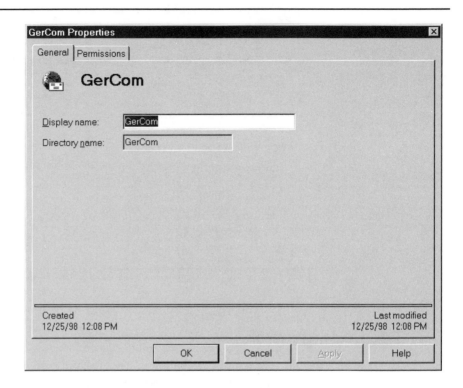

Changing the display name doesn't change the *directory name* (shown below the
display name in Figure 9.2). Like the display name, the directory name defaults to
the organization name you entered when you installed the first server in your
Exchange organization. Unlike the display name, however, the directory name
can't be changed with the Administrator program; that's why it's grayed out. The
only way you can change the directory name is by reinstalling Exchange Server
on every server in the organization!

**NOTE**     Remember that an object's directory name is used to identify the object within
your organization's Exchange Server directory, so the directory name for each
object must be unique. Also, remember that once a directory name has been created, it can't be changed.

## Permissions

The Permissions property page (shown in Figure 9.3) is pretty similar to the ones you saw in Chapters 7 and 8, but it includes one role and two rights you've never seen. The new role is Search, and the two new rights are Replication and Search. The Search role consists solely of the Search right. The Search role/right allows the account or group given the role to search the container and subcontainers via the Internet-based Lightweight Directory Access Protocol (LDAP). I'll talk more about LDAP in Chapter 18. By default, when no account has search rights within an Exchange Organization or Site or Configuration container, everyone can search those containers and the ones below them via LDAP. As soon as one account is given the search right, then only accounts with the search right can search via LDAP. Also, in order to give out the search right to anyone, the Anonymous account for the site must first be defined on the General property page of the DS Site Configuration object in the Configuration container for a site. An NT account with Replication rights can administer and manage Exchange Server directory replication.

**FIGURE 9.3:**

The Permissions property page for an organization

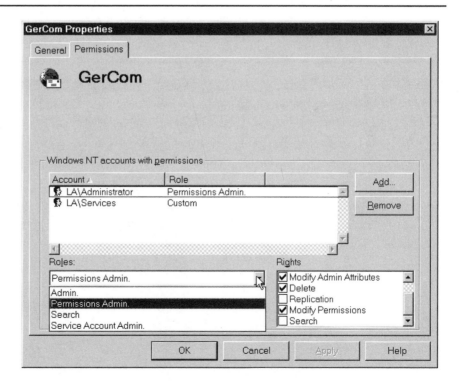

Notice that only the NT domain Administrator account (LA\Administrator) and the account we designated to run our Exchange server's services (LA\Services) have permissions at the org level. The two accounts received these permissions by default when we installed Exchange Server. The Exchange Admins group we created back in Chapter 7 isn't here, because we gave the group permissions at the site level. You'll see the Exchange Admins group in a bit when we look at site-level permissions.

## Sites

To bring up the Properties dialog box for your site, click the site name and select Properties from the Exchange Administrator's File menu (see Figure 9.4).

### General Properties

As with the organization's General properties page, you can change a site's display name. And as with an organization, changing a site display name affects only what you see on the hierarchy tree in the Administrator and what users see in an Exchange client's address book.

**FIGURE 9.4:**

The Properties dialog box for a site

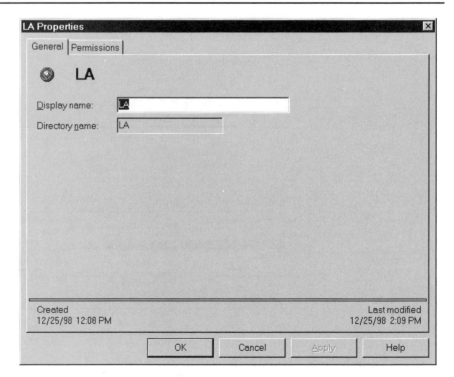

## Permissions

As you can see in Figure 9.5, the Exchange Admins group we gave site permissions to back in Chapter 7 does indeed have those permissions. Also, notice that the Services account has permissions at the site level. As with organization-level permissions, these were granted by default upon installation of our Exchange server.

**FIGURE 9.5:**

The Permissions property page for a site

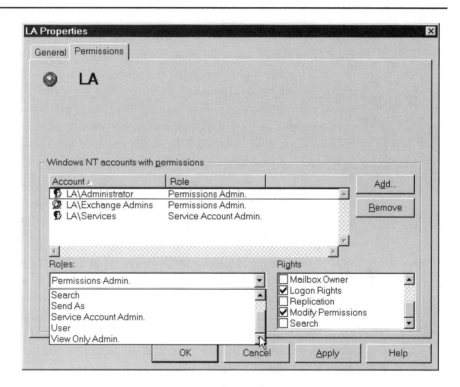

The Sites Permissions page has one new right, Logon Rights, as well as one new role, View Only Admin. Logon Rights allow an NT account or group to log on to any server in the site with the Administrator program. Logon Rights let a user view objects but not change them. Beyond that, once they are logged on to a server, what an account or group can do is controlled by other rights granted at the site level and lower levels in the Exchange hierarchy. View Only Admin gives an NT account Logon Rights to the site and nothing more. Go ahead and browse through the roles and rights on the site's Permissions page to see how things hang together.

## Servers

The Servers' General and Permissions property pages are very much like those for the organization and site. We'll talk a bit more about permissions at the Servers-container level in a bit. For now, let's move on.

## Specific Servers

The Organization, Site, and Servers Properties dialog boxes sport only two property pages. Individual servers, on the other hand, have Properties dialog boxes with a number of pages, so there are lots of things you can do in their administration and management. Locations are clusters of Exchange servers that are linked by higher bandwidth networks. When an Exchange client or server needs to access information or services that reside on multiple servers, it will go to servers in other locations only if it can't get the information or service from a server in its own location. In Exchange 5.5, locations are used to control public folder access and which address spaces Exchange clients can use to send messages.

Let's look at the Properties dialog box for a specific server right now. Click the name of your server in the left-hand pane of the Administrator window (mine is named EXCHLA01). Then select Properties from the File menu. This brings up that server's Properties dialog box, as shown in Figure 9.6.

We'll talk about address spaces in more detail later. For now, think of them as little doors where mail comes in and goes out of the Exchange system. Address spaces are associated with various message types, for example, Internet messages. You can limit a mail client to sending messages only to the address spaces associated with a specific server location. In this way you can assure that users send their messages to servers with the computing and networking power required to handle the task.

FIGURE 9.6:

The Properties dialog box
for a server

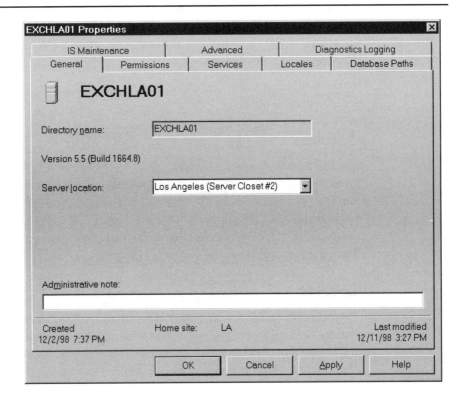

## General Properties

You can enter information about the server's physical location in the Server location field. You can create as many different locations as you'd like. Think of locations as subsites that you can use to improve Exchange client-server performance and control network traffic. Locations are clusters of Exchange servers that are linked by higher bandwidth networks. When an Exchange client or server needs to access information or services that reside on multiple servers, it will go to servers in other locations only if it can't get the information or service from a server in its own location. In Exchange 5.5, locations are used to control public folder access and which address spaces Exchange clients can use to send messages.

If a public folder is replicated across two or more locations and the location contains a replica of the folder, any access to it will be within the accessing client's or server's location. If the location doesn't contain the replica, then a replica will be accessed in another location.

The only other thing you can do on the General property page is to add an administrative note.

## Services

Back in the last chapter, you set up a server monitor, which among other things involved selecting the specific services to be monitored on each server. The Services property page is just another place to select those services. The page looks and acts just like the one shown back in Figure 8.39; refer to the figure and its related text if you need to modify the services being monitored for a specific Exchange server.

## Locales

If you need support for languages other than English on an Exchange server, you use the Locales property page to select the languages. As you can see in Figure 9.7, a wide variety of languages is available. To select one, highlight it and click Add. You can add as many languages as you like.

Language support is more important than you might expect. Even if your users only work in English, there are times when you may need language support just to allow an Exchange server to receive certain messages. For example, one Exchange site I set up had difficulty receiving mail from someone in Northern California. It turned out that the person was using a recent flavor of Netscape Navigator with support for Korean. After we installed support for Korean on the servers in the site, the messages came through just fine.

---

**NOTE**     Exchange Server's support for locales requires support by NT Server for each selected language. Check with Microsoft for more information on availability and licensing issues.

---

FIGURE 9.7:

Use the Locales property
page to select language
support for an Exchange
server.

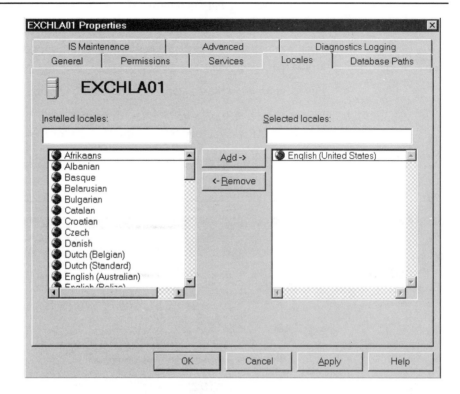

## Database Paths

You'll remember that I advised you to put multiple disk drives in your Exchange
server. If you did, you can improve the performance of your server by moving
key files to other drives. Here's a quick look at the path-change options on the
Database Paths property page, which is shown in Figure 9.8.

- *Directory Database* holds the copy of the Exchange Server directory stored on
  this server.

- *Directory Transaction Logs* are used by Exchange to improve database fault
  tolerance and performance.

- *Directory Working Path* is where temporary files related to the Exchange directory are stored.

- *Private Information Store Database* holds user mailboxes (the ones stored on an Exchange server).

- *Public Information Store Database* holds public folders.

- *Information Store Transaction Logs* perform the same function for the information store as the directory transaction logs do for the directory.

- *Information Store Working Path* performs the same function as the directory working path does for the directory.

**FIGURE 9.8:**

Use the Database Paths property page to change NT directories for key Exchange files.

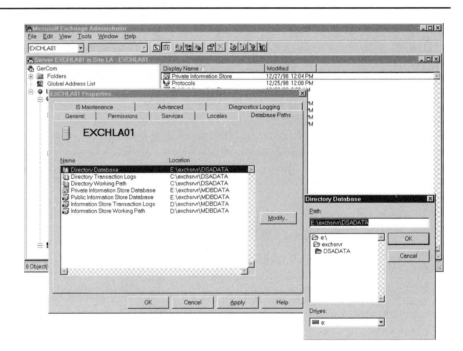

**NOTE**   You can (and usually should) let Exchange Server's Performance Optimizer program, discussed in Chapter 7, take care of modifying database paths. The Performance Optimizer runs a set of built-in tests to determine whether changing the path of a particular database is likely to have a positive effect on performance. If the tests indicate that a database path change makes sense, the Performance Optimizer then moves the database and makes the required system changes automatically.

To change a database path, first create the directory on any drive you wish. Next, click the existing path in the list of database paths and then click Modify. You'll get a standard Windows NT directory walker, as shown in the lower right-hand corner of Figure 9.8. Find the drive and directory you want and click OK. Moving a database using the Database Paths property page not only moves files but also changes system parameters. That's why you should never move databases without using the Database Paths page.

## IS Maintenance

The IS Maintenance property page is used to set up a schedule for all maintenance functions—such as how frequently Exchange Server is to check for and delete messages in public folders that are past their age limits—on an Exchange server's private and public information stores (ISs).

As you can see in Figure 9.9, you have two general options for scheduling: Always and Selected Times. If you pick Always, the IS maintenance is done every 15 minutes. That's much too frequent, especially for a new Exchange server, so I don't recommend selecting Always.

**FIGURE 9.9:**

The IS Maintenance property page and its default schedule

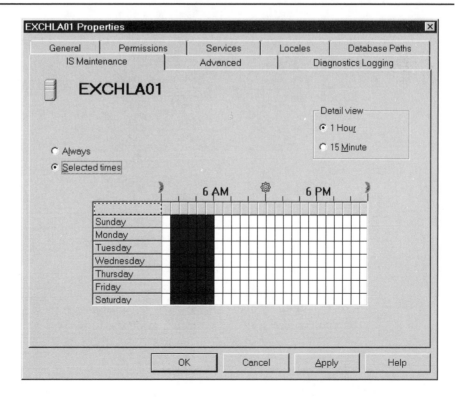

If you choose Selected Times, you can set up a custom maintenance schedule using the little day/time table on the IS Maintenance property page. You can look at the Selected Times schedule table in one-hour increments—the default shown in Figure 9.9—or in 15-minute intervals. Pick your poison in the Detail View box. For now, you can't go wrong if you accept the daily 1 A.M. to 6 A.M. default.

## Advanced Properties

Check out Figure 9.10 as we look at the Advanced property page for a server. Those directory and information-store transaction logs I talked about earlier can get pretty humongous. As you'll see in the next chapter, they're deleted when you back up the Exchange directory or information store. If you don't do a backup—and for the life of me I can't figure out why you wouldn't—the logs just accumulate.

**FIGURE 9.10:**

Setting Advanced
properties for a server

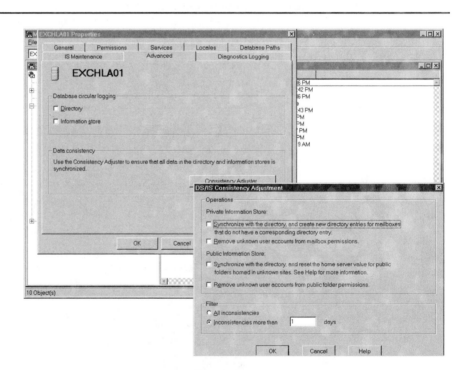

If circular logging is turned on for the directory and information store, Exchange Server continually overwrites earlier transaction logs. By default, circular logging for both the directory and information store is turned on. However, since I'm such a backup nut, I strongly suggest you turn these options off and instead rely on NT's Backup program to prune your server's transaction logs.

In certain situations, the information store and directory on an Exchange server can get out of sync. For example, when you restore an Exchange server from a backup tape, you may wind up with mailboxes in the private information store that aren't represented in the directory, or vice versa.

You can adjust for these inconsistencies on the Advanced properties page. As you can see in Figure 9.10 (the DS/IS Consistency dialog box), you can adjust for inconsistencies relating to mailboxes and public folders. You have two options for each of these.

**Mailboxes**    If a mailbox is found in the private information store without a directory entry, Exchange creates the directory entry. In such a case, you'll have to reenter any information for the mailbox using the Properties dialog box for mail-boxes you worked with in the last chapter.

If a directory entry is found without a corresponding mailbox in the private information store, the entry is left untouched. This is done because a new mailbox gets a directory entry immediately upon creation in Exchange Administrator, but the mailbox isn't created in the private information store until its user logs into it for the first time or the mailbox is sent its first message.

If an NT account is no longer available, any permissions it had to a mailbox or mailboxes are removed.

**Public Folders**    If a public folder is found that is homed (supposed to exist) on a server in a site that is no longer in the directory, the consistency checker looks in the directory for new folder homing information. If the information exists, the home server is reset. If the information is unavailable, the home site and server of the folder is set to the server the consistency tool is being run on. The tool also places an entry in the NT event log noting that this has been done.

When an NT account is no longer available, its permissions on all public folders are removed.

As Figure 9.10 shows, the Advanced properties page lets you adjust for all inconsistencies or for only those of a certain age. If you're adjusting for a certain age, run the check once to mark inconsistencies, and then run it again $n$ days later, where $n$ is greater than the number you enter in the dialog. Then only the inconsistencies older than the number of days you entered will be reconciled.

This way adjustments will not be made for inconsistencies that may be fixed in the normal course of directory replication. Click the Adjust button to start an inconsistencies reconciliation.

## Diagnostics Logging

Exchange Server can write diagnostic information to NT Server's Event log. As I noted in Chapter 4, some of this logging happens automatically. You use the Diagnostics Logging property page to specify additional items to log and the depth of logging to be done for each.

Most of the time, you'll do diagnostics logging when you've got a problem. In many cases, knowledgeable technical support folks at Microsoft or another group will tell you what they want logged and then ask you to turn it on. However, it's still worth knowing how to use the Diagnostics Logging page, so let's try it.

When you first tab over to the Diagnostics Logging property page, it looks pretty sparse. All you see are the name of the server, a tree listing several cryptic names that you might correctly assume represent Exchange Server objects, and at the bottom, some unselected logging-level options.

You can set diagnostic logging options for most services at the root level, except for the information store, MSExchangeIS. Double-clicking MSExchangeIS opens a list of public and private information store subservices as well as system and Internet protocol services (see Figure 9.11).

When you click a service in the left-hand Services pane, the right-hand pane shows the specific items within the service that can be logged. Figure 9.11 shows some of the diagnostic items for MSExchangeDS, the directory service.

You can set a logging option for any item in the right-hand box by clicking the item and then selecting an option in the Logging Level area at the bottom of the property page. (In Figure 9.11, I've chosen a medium level of logging for directory service security.)

To set the same logging level for a group of items, just use the standard Microsoft Windows selection options: Ctrl+mouse-clicks for noncontiguous items and Shift+mouse-clicks for contiguous items.

FIGURE 9.11:

The Diagnostics Logging
property page

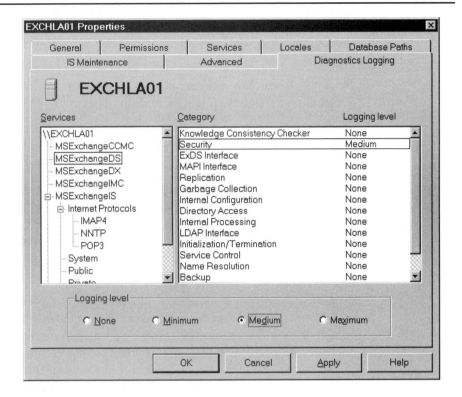

Use diagnostics logging with care and as a short-term debugging tool. It can eat disk space faster than you can say *Exchange Server,* especially when you set logging levels to Maximum. If the disk that happens to be the one where your Exchange server's databases or logs reside, Exchange Server might not have enough disk space to run and will shut itself down.

## Recipients: A General Overview

There are five types of recipients containers in the Exchange 5.*x* hierarchy: site recipients containers, server recipients containers, Address Book view containers, the Global Address List (GAL), and the Public Folders container. Exchange Server uses recipients containers to construct address books, and the Exchange Administrator program uses them to organize access to recipient objects when they are administered and managed. Each recipient has a home in (is "homed" in) a particular site-based recipients container. Through the use of pointers, a recipient may also have a virtual home in other containers like an Address Book view or the GAL.

From our discussion of them in Chapter 8, you already know a little about site recipients containers. We'll talk more about them in just a bit.

The GAL is the master recipients container for an organization. It contains all of the recipients in all sites in the organization, except for hidden recipients. The GAL is near the top of the Exchange hierarchy (see Figure 9.1).

The recipients container for each server holds the mailboxes that have their homes on the server (see Figure 9.1, lower left-hand corner). You'll remember from the last chapter that you set a mailbox's home server while creating it, but this can easily be changed to another server in the site by using Move Mailbox. Remember too that you set a mailbox in motion by changing the mailbox's home server on its Advanced property page.

The other three types of recipients—distribution lists, custom recipients, and public folders—are not represented in server recipients containers. As noted in the last chapter, distribution lists and custom recipients are represented in site recipients containers. As you'll soon see, public folders are represented in both site recipients containers and in the Public Folders container near the top of the Exchange hierarchy and in the Global Address List if they're not hidden (see Figure 9.1).

Of the five types of recipients containers, only site recipients containers have revisable properties. So let's spend a bit of time exploring these properties.

## Site Recipients Container Properties

As you know, each site starts with one default recipients container called *Recipients,* and you can create more containers as needed. What I say here about the default Recipients container applies to any other recipients containers you create.

To display the Properties dialog box for Recipients, select the container by clicking it. Then select Properties from the Exchange Administrator's File menu. As you can see from Figure 9.12, the Properties dialog box for Recipients looks similar to the ones for the organization and sites.

FIGURE 9.12:

The Properties dialog box
for the default Recipients
container

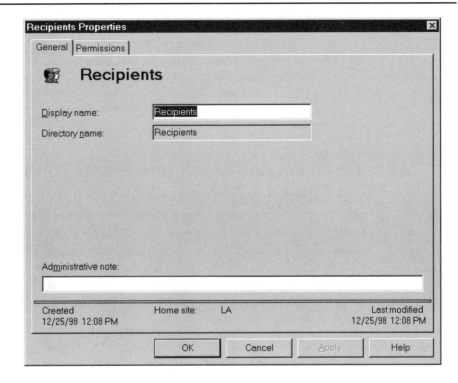

## General Properties

The only addition to the General property page for Recipients is an Administrative Note field. Like all such notes, this one is visible only to NT accounts and groups with Exchange administrative rights for the recipients container.

## Permissions

The rights and roles on the Permissions property page for Recipients are mainly a combination of what makes sense from the property pages for the mailbox (see the last chapter) and the site (see above). There are no rights here that you haven't seen before.

**NOTE**

If an NT account or group has permissions at the site level, these permissions are inherited by all recipients containers in the site. So, for example, if an account has Mailbox Owner rights at the site level, it also has those rights for any recipients containers in the site. Take a look at the permissions for your Recipients container. You'll see that the permissions of your Administrator and Services accounts and your Exchange Admin group have been inherited by the container.

## Administering and Managing Public Folders

In the last chapter on Administrator menus, we covered most of the basics of recipient administration and management. However, one type of recipient isn't created using Administrator menus: public folders. Users—or more correctly, *Exchange mailbox users*—create public folders while in their Exchange clients. Folder creators and their designees and Exchange Server administrators share the role of administering and managing public folders. In this section, we'll cover the role of administrators; we'll deal with the administrative and management role of public folder creators and their designees in a later chapter.

As you probably haven't installed an Exchange client yet and thus don't have any public folders, I'll walk you through this section using one of mine. To administer and manage a public folder, locate it in the Public Folders container under your organization, highlight it, and select Properties from Exchange Administrator's File menu. This brings up a Properties dialog box for the folder; see Figure 9.13 for the location of the Public Folders container and a view of the dialog box.

**NOTE**

The organization-level Public Folders container isn't the only place you can access public folders. In each site, you designate a recipients container to hold your public folders. (We'll talk later about how you do this.) This can be the default Recipients container or any other recipients container you create. Public folders created by mailbox owners in a site reside in this recipients container.

**FIGURE 9.13:**

The Properties dialog box for a public folder

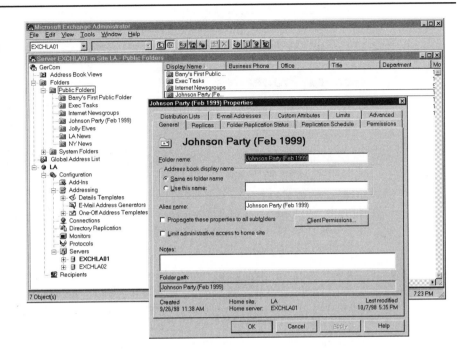

By default, public folders are marked as hidden when they're created. A hidden public folder can't be seen in its site recipients container, and—because Exchange address books are constructed using the unhidden recipients in recipients containers—a hidden recipient does not show up in the address book. Public folders are hidden by default because, except for very specific applications, there's no reason for users to mail messages to public folders instead of directly posting to them. It's better not to clutter the address book with addresses that won't be used—or, worse, might be used by accident.

If you want to see hidden public folders, select Hidden Recipients from the Administrator's View menu. You don't need to worry about all of this too much, though. Just work on public folders in the organization's Public Folders container, which shows all such folders, hidden or not.

A number of the properties for public folders have to do with cross-server public folder replication. We'll cover those properties in a later chapter that deals specifically with public folder replication.

## General Properties

Among other things, the General property page is used to set some names, give Exchange client users rights to the folder, and enter notes.

**Folder and Address Book Display Names**    The folder name is displayed in Exchange client folder hierarchy trees; the address book display name is what an Exchange client sees in the address book when a public folder isn't hidden. By default, the folder name and address book display name are the same. You can override the default by entering a different address book display name in the Use This Name field.

You'll want to use the different address book display name option when you have subfolders with the same name. In the Exchange client folder hierarchy, these will make perfect sense. For example, say you have master folders with the names *Windows NT* and *Exchange Server,* and under each master folder you have a *Specs* subfolder to hold specification information for each product. In the Exchange client folder hierarchy, it will be clear which Specs folder is for each product, since it will be shown as a subfolder of the product.

However, in the address book—which is a flat alphabetical listing—you'll just see two folders named *Specs* next to each other and far removed from the names of their parent folders. Giving address book display names like *Windows NT Specs* and *Exchange Server Specs* to the Specs folders helps alleviate this confusion.

**Alias Name**    The alias name can be up to 64 characters long and is used to construct e-mail addresses for the folder. In addition, as with other recipient aliases, an Exchange client user can type in all or part of a public folder's alias when addressing a message to the folder. When the user sends the message, the user's client finds the alias's real e-mail address and sends the mail.

If you change the name, keep it simple; otherwise, people outside your organization who address messages to the folder will have to type in a long name—and that can lead to addressing errors, not to mention outright anger for those with short tempers.

**Propagate These Properties to All Subfolders**   If a public folder has sub-folders, you'll see this option on the General property page. If you select it, the properties of this folder on the General and other property pages are passed on to all folders under the folder.

**Limit Administrative Access to Home Site**   If this option is selected, only users of NT accounts with Administrative permissions in the public folder's home site and who are connected to the folder's home site can change the folder's home server (see the Advanced property page) and replicate the folder.

This setting is important. Public folders have a home server the same way a mailbox does. If the public folder is replicated to another server and the home server goes down, Exchange will automatically "rehome" the public folder to another folder. To keep a public folder from rehoming, ensure the Limit Administrative Access to Home Site option is selected.

**Client Permissions**   Clicking the Client Permissions button lets you assign specific folder rights to recipients who can then work with a public folder using their Exchange clients (hence the term *Client Permissions*). Figure 9.14 shows the Client Permissions dialog box. As the folder's creator, I'm given the role of Owner. As you can see, the Owner has complete control over the folder.

**NOTE**   In Figure 9.14, the mailbox used by Barry Gerber—*not* the NT account used by Barry Gerber—is given Owner permissions for the folder. This is an important distinction. As you'll see in a later chapter, the creator of a public folder can also give out client permissions to other recipients. All of this is also done at the Exchange recipient level rather than the NT account level. Users don't have to worry about NT accounts; Exchange server makes the links between recipient mailboxes and the Exchange accounts that are granted permissions to them.

FIGURE 9.14:

The Client Permissions
dialog box

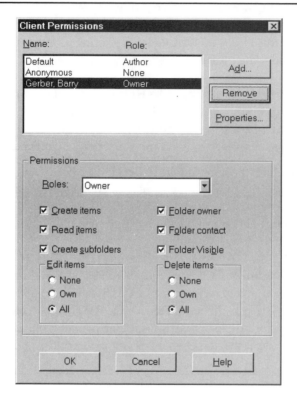

**FIGURE 9.14:**

The Client Permissions
dialog box

There is a default group that includes all Exchange recipients not separately
added to the Name list box. When the folder is created, this group is automatically
given the default role of Author (see Figure 9.14). Authors don't own the folder and
can't create subfolders. Users falling into the default group (because they aren't
listed separately) cannot serve as folder contacts. A folder contact receives notifications about the folder (for example, a warning that the folder's storage limits have
been exceeded or that a conflict has occurred in folder replication). A folder contact
is also the person whom users should ask for access to the folder. The contact may
or may not have permission to change permissions on the folder. Only a folder
owner can change permissions. A contact without owner permissions can receive
requests for access but has to ask someone with owner permissions to actually set
up the access. Authors can edit and delete only their own folder items, while owners can edit and delete anything in the folder.

Microsoft has come up with several interesting roles—including Owner, Publishing Editor, Editor, Publishing Author, Author, Nonediting Author, Reviewer, and Contributor—each with a different combination of client permissions. I'll leave it to you to check out the specific permissions assigned to each of these roles when you've got some public folders to work with.

One way to control access to a public folder is to edit the default group's permissions. You can also control access to a public folder by adding recipients with permissions on it. To do so, click the Add button in the Client Permissions dialog box and select the recipient you want from the standard recipients list dialog box that pops up. You can then assign a role to the added recipient. Click OK in the Client Permissions dialog box when you're done.

**NOTE**    Wondering about that Anonymous user in Figure 9.14? You set access rights to a public folder for users who don't have Exchange mailboxes through the Anonymous user. When such users access a public folder, for example, with an Internet browser, the rights granted to the Anonymous user control what they can do with the folder. More about this neat little feature in Chapter 18.

**Notes**    Let's go back to Figure 9.13. The notes you enter in the Notes field of a folder's Properties dialog box can be used for administrative purposes. They also show up as a property of the folder in the address book used by Exchange clients. So be careful what you put in this field.

**Folder Path**    The folder path is the location of the folder in the public folder hierarchy. This path will change if a user moves a public folder—say, into another public folder.

## Skipped Property Pages

One item on the Limits property page and all of the Replicas, Folder Replication Status, and Replication Schedule property pages deal with public folder replication. I'll talk about these in Chapter 14.

The Permissions, Distribution Lists, E-Mail Addresses, Custom Attributes, and Advanced property pages and most of the Limits page are pretty much like the ones you've seen for other recipients. So we'll skip them here; you can check Chapter 8 for information on these property pages.

---

**NOTE**   As I mentioned above, public folders are by default hidden from the Exchange address book when they're created by Exchange clients. Only an Exchange Server administrator can "unhide" a public folder from the address book. To do this, deselect Hide from Address Book on the Advanced property page for the folder.

---

# Exchange Server Core Components

That's it for the Exchange hierarchy. Now let's move on to the core components. As you'll remember from Chapter 3, there are four core components: the directory service (DS), the Message Transfer Agent (MTA), the information store (IS, both private and public), and the System Attendant (SA).

Let's discuss how to administer and manage the four core components. You deal with core components at two different levels: the site and the server.

At the site level, you work in the Configuration container. Before we actually deal with the core components, I need to tell you a bit about permissions at the Configuration-container level and below.

Notice in Figure 9.1 that the Configuration and Recipients containers are at the same level in the Exchange hierarchy: They're both second-level objects in the site. You'll remember from our discussion earlier in this chapter that site-level permissions for NT accounts or groups are inherited by recipients containers in the site.

The same rule doesn't apply to the site Configuration container, even though it's at the same level in the Exchange hierarchy as recipients containers. Except for the Administrator and Services accounts, which get their usual default permissions for the Configuration container when your Exchange server is installed, you have to specifically grant accounts or groups permissions for a site's Configuration container. So, for example, the permissions of the Exchange Admins group aren't inherited by the Configuration container, even though you gave the group permissions at the site-container level.

You have to add permissions at the Configuration-container level for the Exchange Admins group or any other NT accounts or groups that should have access to the Configuration container. To do this, click the Configuration container and select Properties from the Administrator's File menu. Then use the Permissions property page in the resultant Configuration Properties dialog box to add NT accounts or groups and to set appropriate permissions, which in most cases means assigning the permissions role Permissions Admin to the account or group.

There's a good reason for the different inheritance rules that apply to the Configuration container and recipients containers. Site configuration is a complex task that requires a clear understanding of the complexities of Exchange Server. On the other hand, while recipient administration and management is not for the technically unaware, it doesn't take the same level of Exchange Server mastery as site configuration does. By limiting site-based inheritance only to recipients containers, Microsoft has ensured that you will never accidentally assign site-configuration permissions to people who aren't trained to do it.

The buck *does* stop at the Configuration-container level. Once you've granted an NT account or group rights at the Configuration container level, all objects in the Configuration container (including subcontainers) inherit those rights. For example, once you've granted site Configuration-container level permissions to your Exchange Admins group, individual servers in the site inherit those permissions.

Okay, let's get going. If it's not already open, start up the Exchange Administrator and make it look like the window shown in Figure 9.15. Be sure you've clicked the site's Configuration container in the left-hand window pane. Notice the three core component configuration options in the right pane: DS Site Configuration, Information Store Site Configuration, and MTA Site Configuration. Let's walk through each of these options.

---

**NOTE**    You can manage the System Attendant only at the server level. That's why it doesn't show up in the site's Configuration container.

---

**FIGURE 9.15:**

Finding the site configuration options for Exchange Server's core components

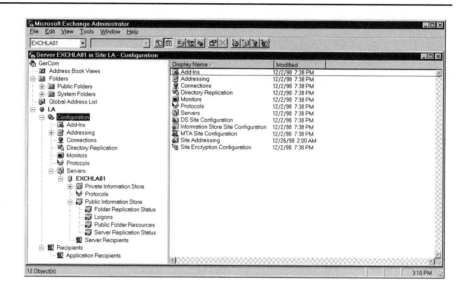

# Administering and Managing the Directory Service

As you'll remember, the directory contains all of the objects for a site. Much of directory service (DS) administration and management is for multi-server sites, which we'll cover in Chapter 13. For now, we'll look at those directory service properties that are useful in sites with only one server.

## Administering and Managing the DS at the Site Level

You use the DS Site Configuration Properties dialog box to set some of the system maintenance and offline address book parameters. This is also the place to create those custom attributes for recipients that I wrote about in the last chapter.

To open the dialog box, click the Configuration container for your site. Then either double-click DS Site Configuration or click DS Site Configuration and select Properties from the Administrator's File menu. This pops up a dialog box like the one in Figure 9.16.

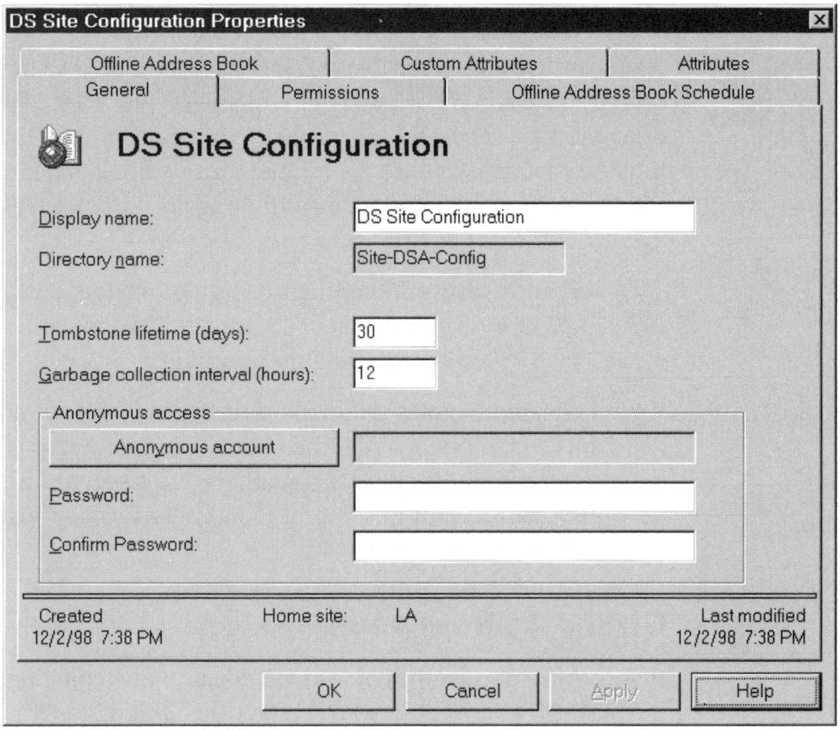

**FIGURE 9.16:**

The DS Site Configuration Properties dialog box

## General Properties

We'll cover General properties, such as *tombstones* and *garbage collection*, when we talk about public folder replication in a later chapter.

The anonymous account allows the directory to access Exchange containers (e.g., the Recipients container) when anonymous users connect to Exchange Server. It supports such things as Web-based anonymous access to public folders or recipients containers. Click Anonymous account to select an existing NT account or to create a new one. Users who connect anonymously get whatever permissions you've given to the anonymous NT account.

## Offline Address Book Schedule

You use the offline address book when you're not connected to your Exchange server—for example, when users are away from the office and connecting to the server only to send and receive new messages. When users compose messages offline, the offline address book lets them address the messages.

Generally, before users leave the office they'll download an updated copy of the offline address book or they'll download it when remotely connected. Exchange Server constructs the address book from the recipients containers you specify (see the next section). You use the offline Address Book Schedule property page to set the schedule used to update the offline address book to reflect new and recently deleted recipients in your site or organization.

The offline Address Book Schedule property page looks almost exactly like the IS Maintenance property page in Figure 9.9. Take a look at Figure 9.9 and its associated text for details on setting the schedule.

How frequently you should schedule updates to your offline address book depends on how often you add and delete recipients for your site, how many addresses are in the recipients container used to generate the address book, and how busy your Exchange server is. You might want to start with a single daily update at around midnight.

## Offline Address Book

A site's offline address book can include as many containers with recipients in them as you like. In Figure 9.17, I have the option of including any address book view I might have created (more about these in Chapter 17), the Global Address List, or any recipients container. The site Recipients container is included in the offline address book by default. In most cases, you'll want to include the Global Address List (GAL). That way, all of the addresses in your Exchange organization will be available to offline users. If you include the GAL in your offline address book, be sure that your users have sufficient local disk space to download what can be a pretty large file.

Use the Offline Address Book server drop-down list to select the Exchange server where the offline address book will be generated and stored. When users download the offline address book, they connect to the offline address book server and download the address book from a hidden public folder. If you expect heavy offline address book download traffic, select a less busy server.

To add a new container to the offline address book, click Add on the Offline Address Book property page. Then select the container you want from the Offline Address Book Container dialog box (see Figure 9.17) and click OK. To remove a container, select it and click Remove.

**FIGURE 9.17:**

Selecting the recipients
containers used to
generate the offline
address book

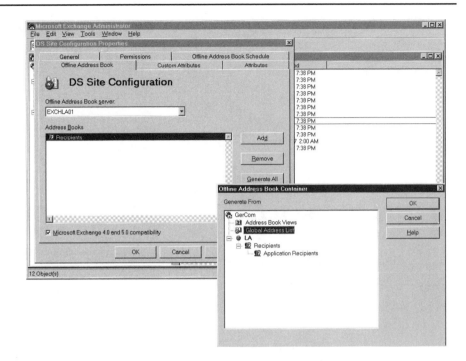

You can regenerate the offline address book any time you need to. Just click the Generate All button on the Offline Address Book property page. This way, you can immediately update the address book after making changes to one or more included containers and you don't have to wait for the scheduled update.

If your users still work with Exchange 4 or 5 clients, be sure to leave the Microsoft Exchange 4 and 5 Compatibility box checked. This way the offline address list will be generated in a format that is usable by Exchange 5.5's Outlook client as well as older Exchange 4 and 5 clients.

## Custom Attributes

You use the Custom Attributes property page to create up to ten of those custom fields I talked about in the last chapter. In Figure 9.18, I'm creating a new custom field called Employee ID. As soon as I click Apply, that field will show up on the Custom Attributes property page of *every* old and new recipient in the site; in fact, even public folders will get the field.

**FIGURE 9.18:**

Creating a new custom attribute field, Employee ID, for all recipients in a site

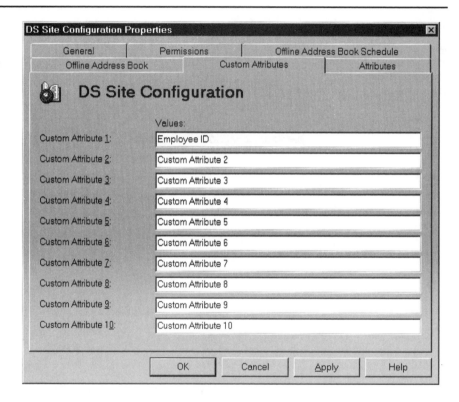

Figure 9.19 shows the Custom Attributes property page for my mailbox. The newly created field is right up at the top; someone is typing in my employee ID right now.

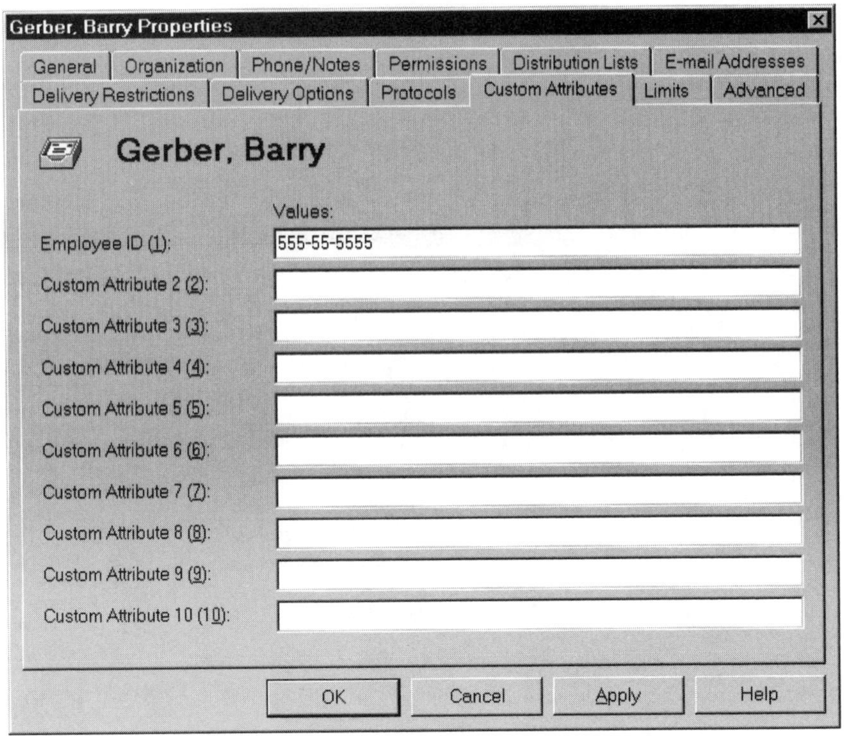

**FIGURE 9.19:**

The new Employee ID field appears on the Custom Attributes property page of all recipient objects, including this mailbox.

## Attributes

The Attributes property page lets you restrict access to specific recipient attributes for Lightweight Directory Access Protocol (LDAP) client access and controls what gets replicated between sites. For example, you may want fully authenticated Exchange mailbox users—those who log in using NT account security—to see the phone numbers connected with a mailbox or custom recipient. However, you may not want anonymous users, who you permit to browse your Exchange directory using a Lightweight Directory Access Protocol client, to be able to see phone number attributes.

As Figure 9.20 shows, you can set attribute access parameters at three levels: anonymous requests, authenticated requests, and intersite replication. You already know what the first two of these are from the paragraph above.

FIGURE 9.20:

Restricting access to specific directory attributes

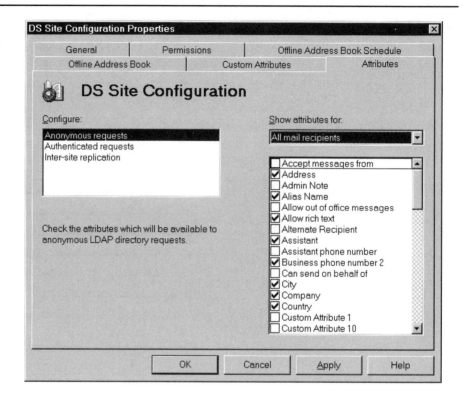

Intersite replication is the process by which the directories in one Exchange site are replicated to another site. If you don't want some directory attributes to be replicated to other sites, here is where you specify which attributes aren't to be replicated. This option has no effect on directory replication between the servers in a site. All attributes are replicated within a site.

The drop-down menu in Figure 9.20 lets you select the recipient type you wish to change access parameters for. The default is All Mail Recipients. The drop-down menu lets you select a specific recipient type: mailbox, distribution list, public folder, or "remote address" (another name for custom recipient).

### Administering and Managing the DS at the Server Level

All server-level directory service administration and management focuses on multi-server, multi-site Exchange systems. We'll get into this whole can of spaghetti in later chapters.

# Administering and Managing the MTA

Because the Message Transfer Agent moves messages in and out of an Exchange server, it's too early to discuss it at this time, since we've got only one server up and running. We'll devote lots of time to MTA administration and management in later chapters.

# Administering and Managing the Information Store

As you'll remember from earlier chapters, the Exchange Server information store includes both a private and public segment. At the site level, you administer and manage the information store, not its two component parts. At the server level, however, administration and management of the private and public information store are done separately.

### Administering and Managing the Information Store at the Site Level

You use the Information Store Site Configuration Properties dialog box to set a variety of properties for mailboxes and public folders. To open the dialog box for site-level administration and management of the information store, double-click the Information Store Site Configuration object in the Administrator's right-hand pane. (Take a look back at Figure 9.15 if you need help finding the object.) When you've found and double-clicked the appropriate object, you'll see a Properties dialog box like the one in Figure 9.21.

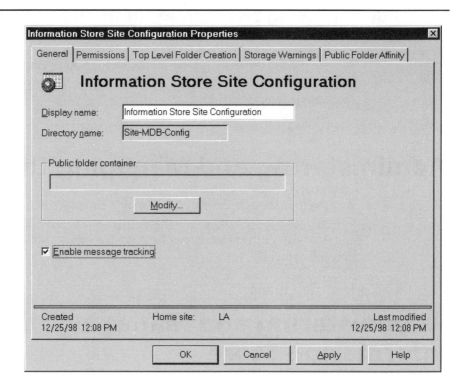

## General Properties

Like all recipients, every public folder is represented in multiple containers. At the site level, public folders are represented by default in the site container named Recipients. The Public Folder Container field is blank if the default is selected. You can change the default public folder container on the General property page; however, I suggest you leave it as is, unless you have strong reasons for using another container. To change the container, click Modify and pick a container from the Public Folder Container dialog box that pops up.

---

**NOTE**    As I advised earlier, even though public folders are represented in the site's Recipients container (or whatever alternative you choose), you should view and work with them in the organization-level container called Public Folders. This will help keep your attention focused on the fact that, due to replication, public folders often live in an organization, not just a site.

---

If the Enable Message Tracking check box is selected, a daily log file is kept on all messages that the information store handles. Exchange Server's Message Tracking Center (which I'll talk about in Chapter 17) uses these log files to help you figure out what might have happened to wayward messages. I suggest you enable message tracking right now and start building the log files. If you want to play with the Message Tracking Center once something is in the log files, select Track Message from the Administrator's Tools menu.

## Top-Level Folder Creation

As I noted above, almost too many times, public folders are created by Exchange users working in their Exchange clients. You use the Top Level Folder Creation property page to specify which recipients can create public folders at the top (or root) level of the public folder hierarchy. Until a top-level folder is created, it's not possible to create subfolders within it.

By limiting top-level public folder creation to specific recipients, you ensure that public folders won't multiply out of control—at least at the root level. Recipients with top-level folder creation rights can give other recipients the rights to create subfolders. This lets you distribute responsibility for public folder administration and management.

As you can see in Figure 9.22, the default is to allow all recipients to create top-level public folders. You should change this default quickly. Use your imagination, but get some kind of controls in place right away.

To specify which recipients are allowed to create top-level public folders, click the Modify button on the *left-hand* side of the Top Level Folder Creation property page. A standard address book dialog box opens; use it to select which recipients can create top-level public folders. To specify which recipients aren't allowed to create top-level public folders, click Modify on the *right-hand* side of the property page and select from the address book dialog box that pops up.

---

**NOTE**    If you grant top-level public folder creation rights to one or more recipients and leave the None option selected on the right-hand side of the property page, only those recipients who have been granted the rights will be able to create top-level public folders. In other words, you don't have to create a specific list of *excluded* recipients. You can give a subset of a distribution list rights by including the distribution list in the allow list and including the users in the distribution list that you don't want to give rights to in the not allowed list.

---

Top Level Folder Creation property page settings determine which recipients can create top-level public folders.

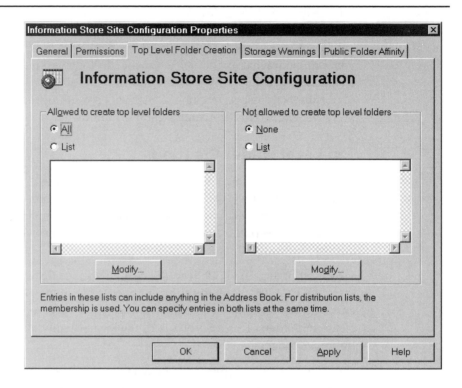

## Storage Warnings

You can set maximum size limits for mailboxes and public folders. When these size limits have been exceeded, Exchange can send warning messages to users responsible for the offending mailboxes or public folders. You use the Storage Warnings property page to set the schedule for issuing these warnings.

This page looks and behaves almost exactly like the IS Maintenance schedule page shown back in Figure 9.9. The only addition is a Never option to accompany the Always and Selected Times options. Select Never if you don't ever want to warn users when they've exceeded message size limits. If you want to issue warnings, the default Selected Times schedule should be fine.

## Public Folder Affinity

You use the Public Folder Affinity property page when you have multiple sites, and users in one site need to access public folders in another. We'll cover this page in Chapter 14.

# Administering and Managing the Private Information Store at the Server Level

Because this is the first time we'll actually do some administering and managing at the server level, here's how you get to and open the Private Information Store properties page. First, be sure your server is visible in the left-hand pane of the Administrator window; then click it. Your Administrator window should look something like the one in Figure 9.23.

**FIGURE 9.23:**

Selecting server-level core component administration and management options

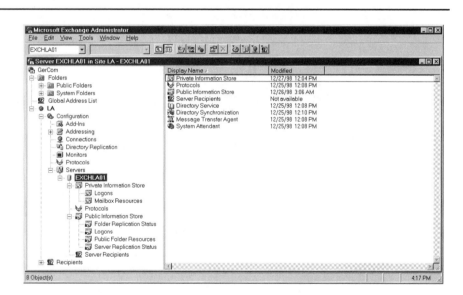

As you can see in the figure, your server contains a number of objects. Focus on the five objects for administering and managing core components that are listed in the right-hand pane of the window: Private Information Store, Public Information Store, Directory Service, Message Transfer Agent, and System Attendant. As I noted earlier, we'll deal with directory service and MTA administration and management in later chapters.

Let's get started with the private information store. Click Private Information Store once and select Properties from the Administrator's File menu to bring up the Properties dialog box shown in Figure 9.24.

**FIGURE 9.24:**

Setting server-specific parameters for the private information store

An Exchange server's private information store holds the contents of mailboxes. Because it contains user and application folders and messages, it can grow to immense proportions in the twinkling of an eye. So managing and administering the private information store often focuses on controlling mailbox storage.

**WARNING**  If you double-click Private Information Store, you'll be taken to the Private Information Store container just below your server's name. (See Figure 9.23 where the Private Information Store container is shown right under my server's name, "EXCHLA01.") More about this in a bit.

## General Properties

Keep an eye on Figure 9.24 as I discuss the General property page. I like to set the time for holding onto deleted items to seven days and to ensure the held items aren't permanently deleted until they're backed up. That way you can recover accidentally deleted items from the server for seven days after deletion and from tape for as long as you keep appropriate tape backups. In the last chapter you learned how to set specific storage limits for a mailbox; here you set the default limits for *all* mailboxes stored on the server. You can set three parameters. With the first, a mailbox user is warned per the Storage Warnings schedule until the storage space consumed falls below the total kilobyte value set. With the second parameter, the mailbox can no longer send messages when storage reaches this limit. Messages are still received, but none can be sent. When the third limit is reached a user can no longer send or receive messages.

Public folders created by users of mailboxes on a specific server don't have to be stored on the same server as the mailboxes—they can be stored on any server in a site. You can use the Public Folder Server drop-down list on the General property page to change the default (which is to use the same server, if it has a public information store; if not, the first server in alphabetical order with a public information store is used). Because we have only one server right now, this option isn't of much use. It can, however, be a nice way to balance loads when you've got multiple servers.

## Logons

The Logons property page shows you which mailboxes are linked to the server as clients. Both user and system client connections are displayed. Figure 9.25 shows logon information for a range of mailboxes on my server. A single mailbox usually has many logons because the mailbox connects to a variety of Exchange Server services. Each logon is a connection to a different service. Sometimes the same username will appear as having multiple mailboxes open. This happens when a person has rights to open multiple mailboxes as, for example, when a secretary has rights to open a boss's mailbox to read and print out the boss's mail. Yes, there are still such bosses in the world.

**FIGURE 9.25:**

The Logons property page shows client connections to a server.

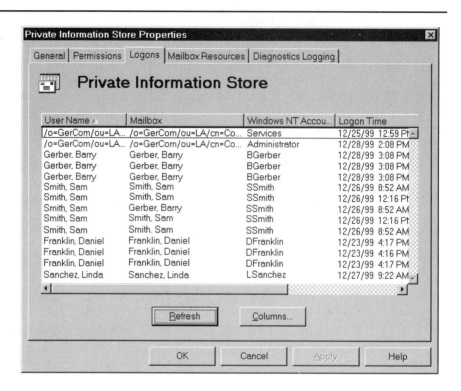

**FIGURE 9.25:**

The Logons property page shows client connections to a server.

You can use the Columns button to change the columns included in the Logons list. In the last chapter, when I talked about the Administrator's View menu and recipient attributes, I showed you how to change display columns. (Refer back to Figure 8.46 and its related text for more information.) You can sort the rows in the Logons list by any column simply by clicking the title bar at the top of the column.

**NOTE**    A page or so back, I noted that double-clicking Private Information Store in the container for your server takes you to the Private Information Store container just below your server's name. You'll notice in Figure 9.23 that the Private Information Store container has a couple of subcontainers: Logons and Mailbox Resources. Instead of opening the Private Information Store properties dialog box shown in Figure 9.24 to see the logon information shown in Figure 9.25, you can just click the Logons container and see the same info. This is a pretty neat time-saver that also applies to Mailbox Resources, discussed immediately below and, as you can see in Figure 9.23, to a number of the properties of the public information store.

## Mailbox Resources

The Mailbox Resources property page provides another tool for controlling mailbox storage. As you can see in Figure 9.26, when you sort the mailbox resources list by Total K, you can quickly spot the disk-resource hogs on a server. The list shows only the names of mailboxes that have been logged into at least once or that have received at least one message.

**FIGURE 9.26:**

Use the Mailbox Resources property page to determine which mailboxes use a lot of disk storage.

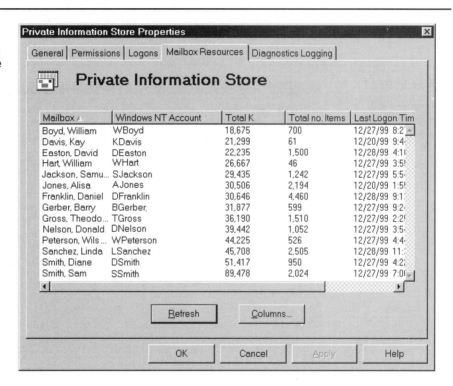

Private Information Store Properties

General | Permissions | Logons | Mailbox Resources | Diagnostics Logging

### Private Information Store

| Mailbox | Windows NT Account | Total K | Total no. Items | Last Logon Tim |
|---|---|---|---|---|
| Boyd, William | WBoyd | 18,675 | 700 | 12/27/99 8:2 |
| Davis, Kay | KDavis | 21,299 | 61 | 12/20/99 9:4 |
| Easton, David | DEaston | 22,235 | 1,500 | 12/28/99 4:1 |
| Hart, William | WHart | 26,667 | 46 | 12/27/99 3:5 |
| Jackson, Samu... | SJackson | 29,435 | 1,242 | 12/27/99 5:5 |
| Jones, Alisa | AJones | 30,506 | 2,194 | 12/20/99 1:5 |
| Franklin, Daniel | DFranklin | 30,646 | 4,460 | 12/28/99 9:1 |
| Gerber, Barry | BGerber | 31,877 | 599 | 12/27/99 9:2 |
| Gross, Theodo... | TGross | 36,190 | 1,510 | 12/27/99 2:2 |
| Nelson, Donald | DNelson | 39,442 | 1,052 | 12/27/99 3:5 |
| Peterson, Wils... | WPeterson | 44,225 | 526 | 12/27/99 4:4 |
| Sanchez, Linda | LSanchez | 45,708 | 2,505 | 12/28/99 11: |
| Smith, Diane | DSmith | 51,417 | 950 | 12/27/99 4:2 |
| Smith, Sam | SSmith | 89,478 | 2,024 | 12/27/99 7:0 |

Refresh          Columns...

OK          Cancel          Apply          Help

**NOTE**    Wouldn't it be lovely to have a printout of this report, which you could use to clean out the worst storage hogs? Well, you can have just that and a number of other useful stats on your Exchange Servers. Check with Seagate Software and Microsoft for various Exchange Server–oriented tools available for Seagate's Crystal Reports report generation software.

## Administering and Managing the Public Information Store at the Server Level

To open the Public Information Store Properties dialog box, click your server in the Administrator window, and click Public Information Store in the right-hand pane, then choose File ➢ Properties. This opens the dialog box shown in Figure 9.27. Many of the property pages for this dialog box—including Instances, Replication Schedule, Age Limits, Folder Replication Status, and Server Replication Status—are used for public folder replication. I'll talk about them in a later chapter. For now, we just need to look at the General property page.

**FIGURE 9.27:**

Setting server-specific parameters for the public information store

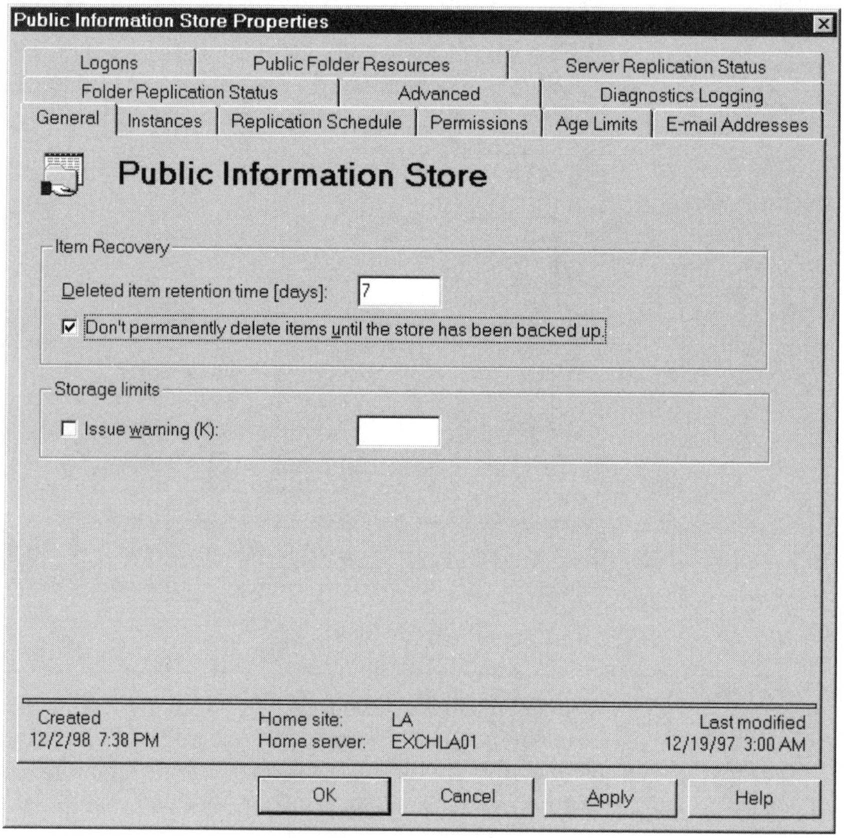

The General property page lets you set deletion recovery parameters and storage limits for all public folders created on the server. You can override these settings from the Limits property page of any public folder.

# Administering and Managing the System Attendant

The System Attendant performs lots of functions on an Exchange server—from watching for and fixing inconsistencies in server-based copies of site directories to enabling and disabling certain aspects of Exchange security. You can manage the System Attendant only at the server level. As you'll see, there's not much you need to do there.

Click your server name in the left-hand pane of the Administrator window, then double-click System Attendant in the right-hand pane. This brings up the System Attendant Properties dialog box shown in Figure 9.28. We need to look only at the General property page.

**FIGURE 9.28:**

Setting parameters for a server's System Attendant

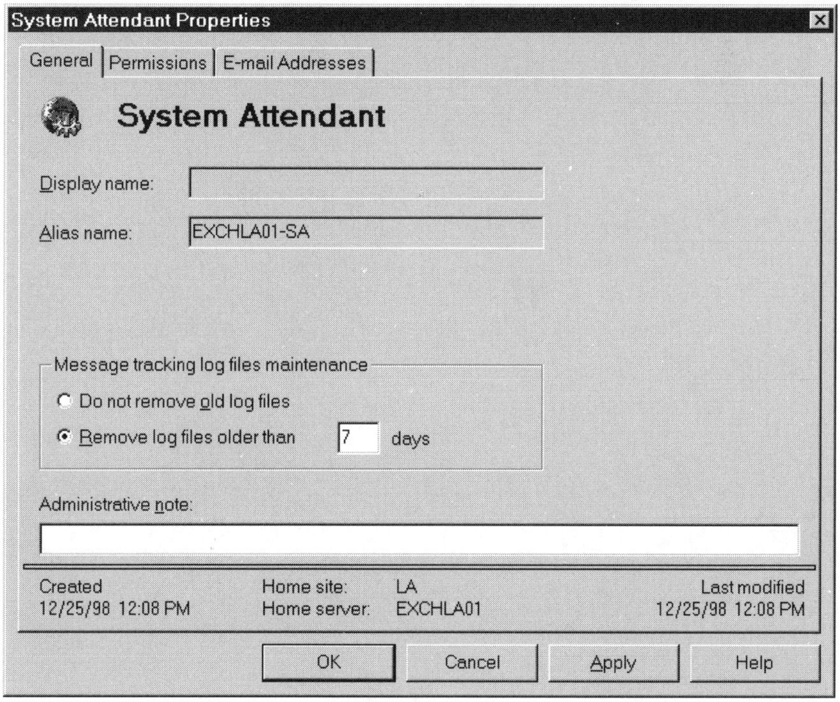

Right now, it's pretty safe to accept the default and let the System Attendant delete message-tracking log files more than seven days old. Later, when you've got multiple servers and sites, you might want to extend the number of days. However, if you back up your server regularly using the backup cycle I suggest in the next chapter, seven days should be fine. You'll always be able to restore recent log files from your backup if you need them.

# Conclusion

In this chapter you learned how to do a range of basic administrative and management tasks for objects in Exchange Server's hierarchy and for its core components. At this point, you've got a lot of practical knowledge under your belt. The coming chapters will add significantly to that knowledge.

# CHAPTER

## TEN

# Backing Up an Exchange Server

- Backup basics

- The role of Exchange Server transaction logs in backup

- How to set up an Exchange Server backup

- How to restore from an Exchange Server backup

- How to automate an Exchange Server backup

- Third-party backup solutions

In Chapter 6 you learned how to use NT Server's Backup utility to back up an NT Server. Backup includes special features for protecting the two key Exchange Server databases—the information store and the directory. When you use these features, you can back up the databases without shutting down your Exchange Server and without denying Exchange clients access to the server. In this chapter you'll learn how to use these features.

We'll cover six topics here:

- Some backup basics

- Exchange Server transaction logs and backup

- Setting up an Exchange Server backup

- Restoring from an Exchange Server backup

- Automating a backup

- Using third-party products to back up an Exchange server

# Some Backup Basics

Before we get into Exchange Server backups, let's make sure you're comfortable with some backup basics. First, we'll go through a brief tutorial on the archive bit. Then we'll do a quick overview of the types of backups supported by NT's Backup program. Finally, I'll talk briefly about basic backup strategies.

## The Archive Bit

Every NT file has a bit called the *archive bit*, which is set to "on" by the operating system when a file is created and when anything is written to the file. As you'll soon see, certain types of backups turn the bit to "off" to indicate that a file has been backed up. This makes the archive bit a great tool for determining when a file needs to be backed up. If the bit is on, a backup is required. If it's off, the file has already been backed up.

# Backup Types

NT's Backup program lets you do five types of backups:

**Normal**    All selected files are backed up irrespective of their archive bit settings. After backup, the archive bit for each file that has been backed up is turned off.

**Copy**    All selected files are backed up irrespective of their archive bit settings. After backup, the archive bit for each file that has been backed up is *not* changed.

**Incremental**    All files with their archive bit turned on are backed up. As with a normal backup, the archive bit for each file that has been backed up is turned off.

**Differential**    All files with their archive bit turned on are backed up. The archive bit for each file that is backed up is *not* changed.

**Daily**    All files that have changed on the day of the backup are backed up. The archive bit for each file that is backed up is *not* changed.

# General Backup Strategies

Standard backup practice is to do a normal backup once a week and incremental or differential backups every other day. Because a differential backup doesn't change the archive bit, every differential backup covers all new files, as well as files that were changed since the last normal backup. To recover a failed server when you do differential backups, all you have to do is recover the last normal backup and the last differential backup. For this reason I prefer differential backups over incremental ones.

If you perform incremental instead of differential backups, to restore a failed server you have to recover the last normal backup and then, in order, all of the incremental backups since the last normal backup. That's not only more work, it also leaves more room for error: Imagine what a mess you could have if you were to restore those incremental backups even slightly out of order. Though this ordering stuff applies to incremental backups of regular files, it doesn't apply to a restoration involving an Exchange incremental backup. Exchange itself sees to it that restored incrementally backed up files are properly restored to its databases, whatever the order in which you restore the files to the Exchange server.

Differential backups use more tape, since they tend to back up more stuff every day. But tape is cheap compared to the lost time—not to mention the potential for error—that comes with incremental backups.

Whatever basic backup strategy you choose, be sure to protect your backup tapes in some way. Store them in a fireproof safe and/or off-site. If your company has a disaster-recovery plan, Exchange Server and its backups should be included in it.

## Exchange Server Component Backup Strategies

You need to come up with a plan for backing up Exchange Server components. Here are some thoughts and ideas that might prove helpful.

I considered presenting some of this section's material later in the book, when you'll have more than one server up and running in your site. However, I've decided to include it here, both because it's useful and interesting and because I think you're ready for it.

You'll remember that Exchange Server automatically maintains a copy of its directory on each server in a site. This is done through a process called *directory replication*. In directory replication, Exchange Servers in a site check with each other to ensure that their directories are up-to-date. If a server determines that its directory is out of sync with the others, it gets updates from one or more servers in the site.

Because of directory replication, if you have to restore a server's directory it doesn't matter whether the backup contains the absolutely most-current copy of the directory. Once the restore is complete, the other servers in the site will quickly update the newly restored directory through the replication process.

I prefer to do a normal backup of the directories on all servers every Sunday at midnight, followed by a differential backup of each server's directory at midnight on each of the other six days of the week. I use a four-week cycle, holding the fourth week's tape as an archive for a year.

I suggest using the same backup strategy for the private and public information stores on a server. Keep the directory and information store backups as closely synchronized as you can to ensure the least amount of difference between the two.

**WARNING**    If e-messaging is particularly critical to your organization, you might want to do more than one differential backup of Exchange Server directories and information stores per day. Certain situations might even require you to do a backup every two hours.

# Exchange Server Transaction Logs and Backup

Like all good client-server database systems, Exchange Server uses *transaction logs* to improve server fault tolerance. All changes to a server's directory and private and public information stores are written first to files called *transaction log files*. Different sets of log files are used for the directory and information store.

Once the directory or information store service has written data in RAM to a transaction log file, it then writes the data to the database itself. Writing to a database entails lots of overhead, including indexing and other tasks. Writing to a transaction log file requires no such overhead, so data moves quickly from RAM to the log files, reducing the likelihood that a specific transaction will be lost if a server crashes. In the event of a crash, the database can be recovered back to currency using the transaction log files.

When you use the Backup utility to back up Exchange Server's directory or information store, you can use all of the backup types except Daily. A normal backup backs up the databases and associated transaction logs; when it's finished, Backup then deletes the transaction log files that have been backed up.

When you do an incremental directory or information store backup, only the transaction log files are backed up. Nothing in the actual directory or information store databases is, or needs to be, backed up, because all changes since the last backup are contained in the transaction log files. Once the transaction log files are incrementally backed up, the Backup program deletes them, leaving you ready for the next full or incremental backup.

When you do a differential or copy backup, transaction log files are not deleted.

---

**WARNING**   If you don't routinely do normal or incremental backups of a server's directory and information store, the transaction log files—which can consume a large amount of disk space at 5MB a pop—will accumulate quickly. You can use circular logging, which you'll remember we discussed in the last chapter. But for my money, you're better off backing up and letting the Backup program delete those transaction log files.

---

# Setting Up an Exchange Server Backup

I'll assume that, following the instructions back in Chapter 6, you've installed a tape drive on your Exchange Server and are backing up from that server.

The Backup utility interacts with the Exchange Server directory and information store services to back up the directory and information store as objects. Before you can back these up, the directory and information store processes must be up and running on your Exchange Server.

Also, to back up any server you must be a member of the NT Backup Operators group on the server. This group is automatically created when NT is installed. As NT administrator, you can use the User Manager for Domains to add yourself to this group. If you're logged in as NT administrator, you've already got these rights.

## Selecting Exchange Servers and Components

To start, you need to open Backup. You'll find the utility in the Administrative Tools program group on your NT server. Find the Backup icon and click it to bring up the program (see Figure 10.1). If it's not open already, you'll need to open the Microsoft Exchange backup window. Open the Operations menu and click Microsoft Exchange. Then tell Backup which Exchange server you want to work with using the little Microsoft Exchange dialog box that pops up.

Next, you need to select the server or servers that you want to back up from the left-hand pane in the Microsoft Exchange window. As you can see in Figure 10.1, you can choose to back up anything—whether it's all the servers in an organization or a single server—just by clicking the box next to the organization, site, or server name.

If you want to refine your backup, move to the right-hand pane of the Microsoft Exchange window. There you can select the Exchange Server components you want to back up. When you first open the Microsoft Exchange Window, you'll see your Exchange site or sites in the right-hand pane. To open a site, double-click the site name. Now the server or servers in the site become visible. Next, double-click the server you want to focus on and you'll see two icons representing the server's directory and information store. (Refer to Figure 10.1.) You can select the Directory, the Information Store, or both for backup. You must back up both the private and public segments of the Information Store. As you'll see later in this chapter, you can restore either or both of the information stores.

For now, just click your server name in the left-hand pane. Your Backup window should now look like the one in Figure 10.1.

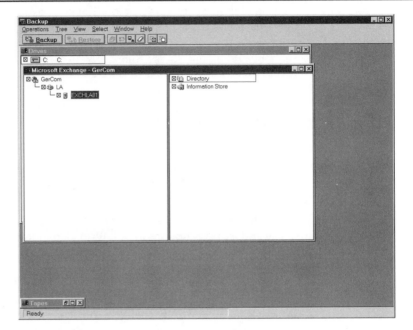

## Backing Up NT Server Drives

If you prefer, you can use Backup to simultaneously back up Exchange Server components and other files on your NT server. Here's how to add one or more drives to your backup.

Select the drives you want to back up from the left-hand pane of the Drives window. In Figure 10.1, the Drives window is just peeking out over the top of the Microsoft Exchange window. As you can see, I've selected my C drive for backup, along with the directory and information store on my Exchange Server.

I won't go into details here, but you can also back up selected files on any drive. Just double-click the drive letter in the Drives window; this pops up a window with a directory tree for the drive you selected. Then simply click the directories and files you want to include in your backup.

> **NOTE**
>
> If you're already using another program for general NT Server backup, you can continue to use it. If the program has a module specifically designed to back up Exchange Server, you can use that too. But, don't try to back up your Exchange Server databases and logs with a standard backup utility while they're online. It won't work. You can use a standard backup program if you shut down Exchange Server before beginning the backup.

## Selecting Backup Options

Now click the Backup button right under the Operations menu. This brings up the Backup Information dialog box, shown in Figure 10.2. The figure shows that I accepted the default Tape Name and Operation parameters. (*Append* means that the backup you're setting up will be added to the tape after the last backup. *Replace* means that this backup will overwrite everything already recorded on the tape. Use the Replace and Append options as you wish, depending on how many normal, incremental, or differential backups you prefer to put on a single tape.)

You should always verify a backup. If a backup doesn't run properly, your data isn't protected. Backup verifies ordinary NT files based on a file-by-file comparison. This is not possible with Exchange Server components, since they can change from moment to moment. So verification for these components is based on a simple checksum test to ensure that the data written to tape is readable.

Since I'm backing up the drive that contains the NT Registry for EXCHLA01, I've selected the Backup Local Registry option. Remember that the Registry is a storage place for all the key information about the NT server itself as well as the NT/Windows 95–compatible applications installed on the server. The Registry is the equivalent of Windows 3.*x*'s WIN.INI and SYSTEM.INI files and much, much more. You should therefore back up the Registry with great regularity.

I haven't marked the Restrict Access to Owner or Administrator option, though this is a good way to increase security. To access a backup set with this option selected, you must be logged on as the owner (the person who created the backup) or a user who's a member of the administrators or backup operators groups.

**FIGURE 10.2:**

Providing information
about the backup

I also haven't selected Hardware Compression. As I mentioned in Chapter 6, hardware compression saves tape, but tapes created with it are readable only in drives that use the same hardware compression algorithm. Different manufacturers tend to use different compression algorithms—so you're up a creek if your current drive breaks and can't be repaired, and the manufacturer no longer makes a drive using the same algorithm. Uncompressed tapes, on the other hand, are pretty much readable in drives of the same type regardless of manufacturer. I want the freedom to use anyone's tape drive, hence my choice of options.

Right below the Hardware Compression option is a box named Backup Set Information (1 of 3 Sets). Notice that the box has a scroll bar on it. You enter specific information for each of the backup sets you're creating in this box, using the scroll bar to move through the different backup sets. As Figure 10.2 shows, my first backup is of my C drive. I've described this backup set as "All of Drive C:," and I've told Backup to do a normal backup.

Once you've finished with the first backup set, use the scroll bar to move to the next backup set information box. Figure 10.3 shows my second backup set, which is for the Exchange directory. Again, I've chosen a normal backup, though I could have chosen a different backup type for this set if I had wished. Notice that the Backup Local Registry option is now grayed out: I can back up my NT server's Registry only when I'm backing up files on the disk that contains the Registry. Backing up Exchange Server components, even if they're on the disk with the Registry, doesn't count.

**FIGURE 10.3:**

Entering information for an Exchange Server directory backup

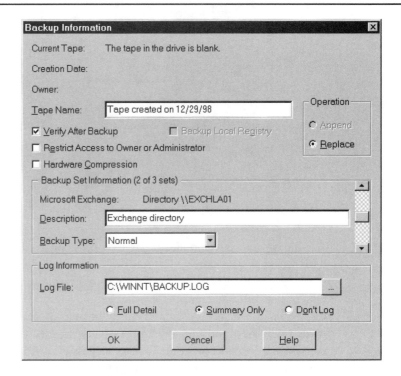

In Figure 10.4, I've entered information for my third and final backup set; it's for the information store.

---

**NOTE**   Only the Description and Backup Type fields can be unique for each Backup Set Information box. When you set anything else in the Backup Information dialog box, it applies to all the backup sets you're creating. So, for example, if you change the Operation mode from Replace to Append, all your backup sets will use the Append option.

---

| NOTE | Seeing Replace as the Operation option for all three of my backups gave me a bit of a scare the first time. Was Backup going to back up my C drive in its entirety, write the directory backup over the first backup set, and then write the information store backup over the directory backup set? Not to worry. The first backup set overwrites whatever is on the tape. The remaining backup sets in the group are appended to the ones that come before. |
|---|---|

**FIGURE 10.4:**

Entering information for an Exchange Server information store backup

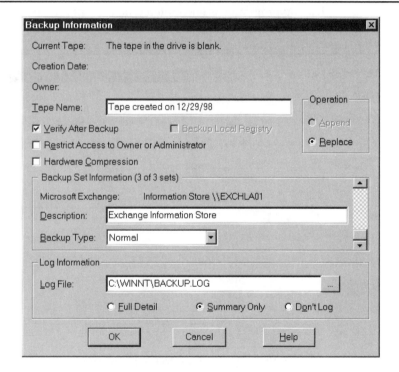

When you've finished entering information about your backup sets, the only thing left to fill out before you start the backup is the Log Information box just below the Backup Set Information box. For now, leave the settings at their default values. The default log file directory and filename are fine, and most of the time you don't need to gather more than summary information in your tape log files. Click OK to begin your backup.

## Monitoring Backup Progress

Once your backup starts, you'll see a Backup Status dialog box like the one in Figure 10.5. You can use this dialog box to monitor backup progress. As the Summary box shows, Backup is creating backup set #1, the backup of my whole C drive. The Summary box shows that drive C is being backed up and that this is the first backup set on the tape; in the figure, the file \EXCHSRVR\BIN\EMSMTA.EXE is currently being backed up. So far, the backup has been under way for 37 seconds, during which 3 directories, 49 files, and 12,346,253 bytes have been backed up. The Backup program has encountered no corrupt files, nor have any files been skipped up to this time.

**FIGURE 10.5:**

Backup status for the C drive

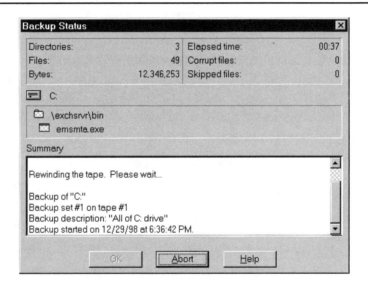

When Backup moves on to the Exchange Server directory database, the Backup Status dialog box will look like the one shown in Figure 10.6. Notice that this figure shows backup set #2. After backing up the directory, Backup turns to the information store and backs it up to backup set #3 (see Figure 10.7).

When it's finished backing up the information store, Backup begins its verification of each of the three backup sets. You'll see a dialog box much like the Backup Status dialog box, except that it's named Verify Status.

When Backup is done verifying all the backup sets—assuming everything went well (and it usually does)—it tells you that it has successfully finished its work. Click OK in the Verify Status dialog box, and you're done with the backup.

**FIGURE 10.6:**

Backup status for the Exchange Server directory

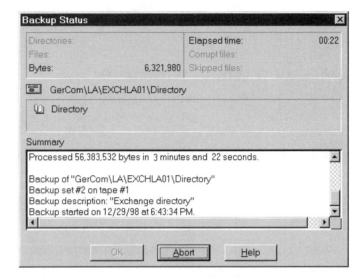

**FIGURE 10.7:**

Backup status for the Exchange Server information store

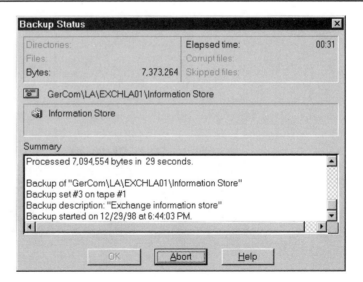

# Restoring from an Exchange Server Backup

To restore from an Exchange Server backup, you first need to tell Backup what you want to restore. Then you need to tell it how to do the restore.

## Specifying What to Restore

To restore from a backup set, start the Backup program. Maximize the Tapes window, which you'll find down in the lower left-hand corner of the Backup window. In Figure 10.8, I've told Backup to restore both the Exchange Server directory and information store databases (see the right-hand pane of the window). If you don't see the detailed information on your backup sets, double-click the drive letter in the right-hand pane of the Tapes window. This will cause Backup to read backup set information from the tape and display it.

**FIGURE 10.8:**

Specifying Exchange Server components to be restored

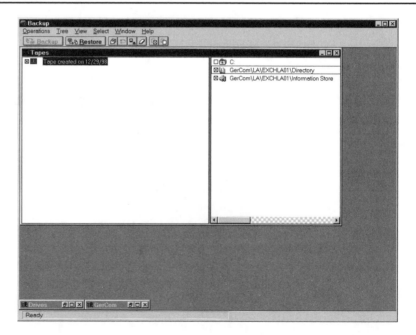

You can also use the Tapes window to restore other files that were backed up. Just double-click the drive letter in the right-hand pane of the Tapes window. This opens up a window with a directory tree for the drive. Use this directory tree to choose files for restoration.

**WARNING**     If you need to restore these other files as well as the Exchange Server directory and information store, always restore the other files first. Otherwise, you could over-write directory or information store data when restoring the other files.

## Specifying How to Restore

After you've told Backup what to restore, click the Restore button in the upper left-hand corner of the Backup window. This brings up a Restore Information dialog box. Figure 10.9 shows the dialog box for restoring the Exchange Server directory. Figure 10.10 shows the dialog box for restoring the information store.

**FIGURE 10.9:**

The dialog box for restoring the Exchange Server directory

Restore Information

Backup Set Information (1 of 2 sets)

Tape Name:          Tape created on 12/29/98

Backup Set:         Exchange directory

Creation Date:      12/29/98  6:43:17 PM

Owner:              LA\Administrator

Restore

Original Server:    EXCHLA01

Destination Server:  EXCHLA01

☐ Erase all existing data

☑ Verify After Restore             ☑ Start Service After Restore

Log Information

Log File:    C:\WINNT\BACKUP.LOG

○ Full Detail    ● Summary Only    ○ Don't Log

OK          Cancel          Help

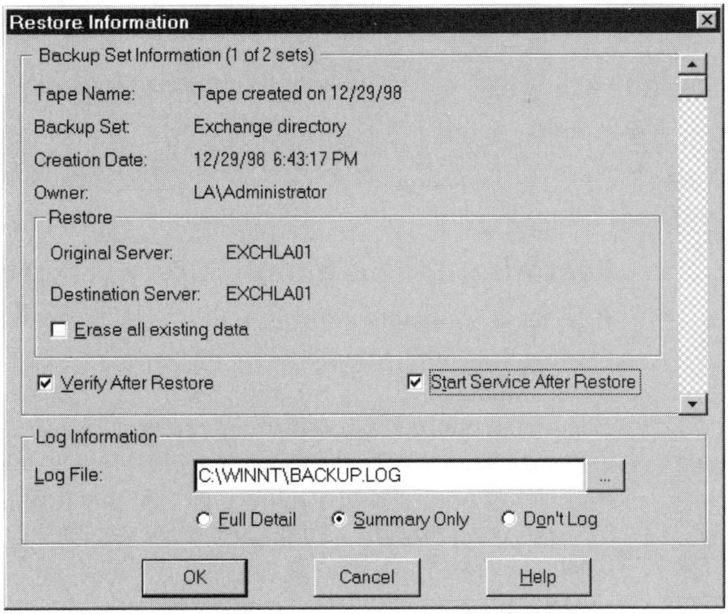

You use the scroll bar on the Restore Information dialog box to move between dialog boxes for each of the backup sets from which you've chosen to restore. You set restore parameters for a specific backup set after scrolling to the dialog box for that backup set.

**FIGURE 10.10:**

The dialog box for restoring the Exchange Server information store

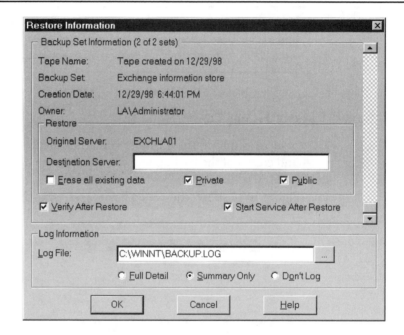

## Restoring the Exchange Server Directory Database

Keep your eye on Figure 10.9 as you move through this section. The Erase All Existing Data option is important: If you *don't* check it, Backup tries to restore the directory database using the directory database already on the server and whatever directory information is stored on tape. This is the first thing to try if your Exchange Server's directory database is in trouble. It's faster and less messy, because it doesn't delete the directory database (as does the Erase All Existing Data option). If this method doesn't work, repeat the restore with the Erase All Existing Data box checked.

Of course, you'll want to verify after restoring, and you'll generally want to start the directory service after restoring the directory. Leave the Log File information as is, unless you have a problem restoring; if you do have trouble, select

Full Detail from the three options just below the Log File name field. Those details might help you figure out why you're having trouble.

## Restoring the Exchange Server Information Store Database

As you can see in Figure 10.10, the Restore Information dialog box for the information store looks pretty much like the one for the directory. There are two differences, though: You can modify Destination Server, and you can choose to restore the private information store, the public information store, or both.

Depending on where your problem lies, decide whether to restore one or both of the information stores. If you're having trouble with mailboxes, restore the private information store. If the problem is with public folders, restore the public information store.

You can restore one or both of the information stores either to the original server you backed up or to another destination server. Most of the time you'll do the former. The only time you'd restore to another server would be to recover information for a user or a set of users without changing the contents of the original information store. You'd need a spare offline Exchange server with the same organization and site names as the original for this sort of restore. Microsoft has said it will, at some unnamed date, modify Exchange Server to allow for selective restoration of data directly to Exchange's databases. Until that happens, you'll have to restore to a spare offline server and then manually move restored data to the in-service Exchange server.

Make your selections, then click OK in the Restore Information dialog box. When the restore starts, you'll see a Restore Status dialog box that looks pretty much like the Backup Status dialog boxes in Figures 10.6 and 10.7. From here on, it's just a matter of waiting for the restore to finish.

---

**WARNING**    Good backup practice requires that you test your backups regularly. That spare off-line server I talk about in this section is a great place to test. Test at least once a month; more frequently if you consider e-messaging mission critical.

---

# Automating a Backup

You can create batch files to automate backups of your NT/Exchange Server, including its directory and information store databases. Then you can use NT Server's built-in task scheduler to automatically run these batch files when you want.

## Creating a Batch File for Backup

In addition to running Backup by clicking its icon in the Administrative Tools program group, you can start it in a DOS command prompt session; the program is called NTBACKUP.EXE. It has a number of command-line switches that you can use to specify just what you want backed up and how the program is to proceed. The syntax of an NTBACKUP.EXE command is as follows:

```
ntbackup operation path [/DS server /IS server][/a][/v][restricts
access to Owner or Administrator][/d "text"][/b][/hc:{on / off } ]
[/t {option}][/l "filename"][/e][/tape:{n}]
```

> **operation**   Specifies the operation: backup or eject.

> **path**   When backing up a drive, specify one or more directory paths to be backed up. When backing up Exchange Server components, specify the component and the server as follows:

> > **DS** *server*

> > **IS** *server*

> where *server* is the name of the server you're backing up in Uniform Naming Convention format. (For us mere mortals, that means the server name with two backslashes in front of it; for example, \\EXCHLA01. DS requests a directory backup. IS requests an information store backup.)

Each path specified creates a separate backup set.

> **/a**   Adds the backup set or sets following the last backup set already on the tape. Without /a, this backup overwrites whatever is on the tape.

> **/v**   Verifies the backup.

> **/r**   Restricts access to the Owner or Administrator.

> **/d "text"**   Is a description of the backup contents.

**/b**   Requests a backup of the Registry.

**/hc:on or /hc:off**   Turns hardware compression on or off.

**/t {option}**   Selects the backup type; options are Normal, Copy, Incremental, Differential, and Daily. (Daily doesn't apply to Exchange Server component backup.)

**/l "filename"**   Requests logging to *filename*, including any path you specify. If you don't include the /l option, no log will be created.

**/e**   Requests that only exceptions be written to the log. This is equivalent to selecting Summary Only in the Log Information area of the Backup Information dialog box. If you leave out /e, your log will include full details.

**/tape:{n}**   Specifies which tape drive to use for the backup when you have multiple tape drives, where *n* is a number from zero to nine. Tape drive numbers are listed in the Registry. See *Mastering Windows NT Server 4*, by Mark Minasi, Christa Anderson, and Elizabeth Creegan (Sybex, 1998), for help on accessing the Registry.

Here's the NTBACKUP command that does pretty much what we did in the non-automated backup a few sections back. The only thing we can't do is specify different descriptions and backup types for each backup set.

```
ntbackup backup E:\ DS \\EXCHLA01 IS \\EXCHLA01 /v /d "Backup of
EXCHLA01-Exch. Srvr. Components + dirs" /b /hc:off /t Normal /l
"C:\WINNT\BACKUP.LOG" /e
```

To do a differential backup, the only thing you'd change is the option for /t from Normal to Differential.

Next, save the normal backup command to a batch file called NORMAL.BAT and the differential backup command to a batch file called DIFFERNT.BAT. To run either backup, just type the batch filename at the DOS command prompt. Or you can create a new Windows desktop shortcut that links the batch file to an icon. You can then run the backup just by double-clicking the appropriate icon.

## Using NT's Task Scheduler to Automate Backups

In the old days (a few months ago at this writing), you could schedule tasks at an NT command prompt or use a little graphical app that came with the NT Resource

Kit called *WINAT.EXE*. Today, you can still schedule at the command prompt or you can use a new and much improved GUI-based scheduler that comes with Microsoft Internet Explorer 5. When IE 5 is installed, a folder named *Scheduled Tasks* is installed within My Computer on your desktop. Assuming you've installed IE 5, double-click My Computer to open it. Then double-click Scheduled Tasks, and you're off and running.

You use the Scheduled Tasks app to schedule tasks to be run by an NT service called the Task Scheduler. If that service isn't running, Scheduled Tasks starts it and sets it to start automatically every time your computer is rebooted.

The Scheduled Tasks window looks pretty much like NT's file Explorer, thought it has some unique menus (see Figure 10.11). To schedule a command, double-click Add Scheduled Task in the Scheduled Tasks window. This brings up the Scheduled Task Wizard. Click Next and you'll see the panel where you tell the Wizard which executable to run. Click Browse and either type in or search for the file NORMAL.BAT. Be sure to include the path to the file. Click Next for the next Wizard panel. Figure 10.12 shows this panel. I'm scheduling my normal backup to take place once a week, and in Figure 10.13, after clicking Next, I'm scheduling the backup for Sunday starting at midnight.

**FIGURE 10.11:**

The Scheduled Tasks application's window

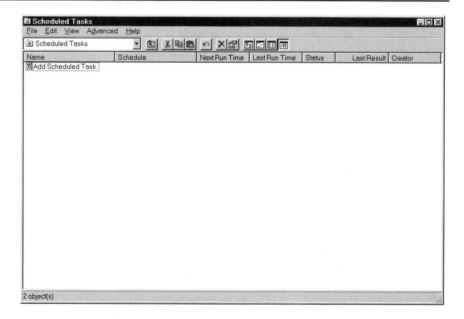

**FIGURE 10.12:**

Using the Scheduled Task Wizard to schedule a weekly backup

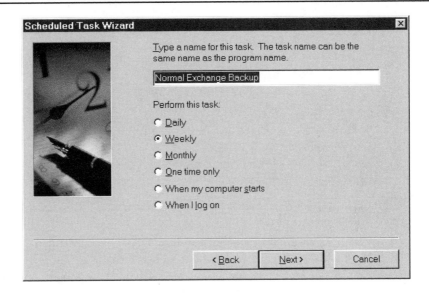

**FIGURE 10.13:**

Using the Scheduled Task Wizard to schedule a weekly backup for every Sunday at midnight

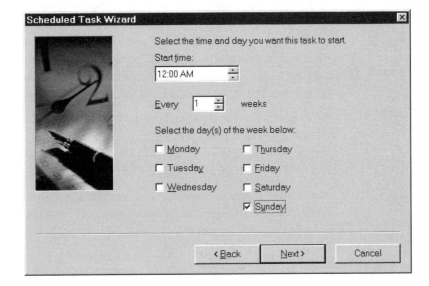

## Don't Use Task Scheduler with Scheduled Tasks

If your backup will require more than one tape, don't use the Scheduled Tasks application to run your backups. If you do, your backups will fail, because scheduled tasks run without displaying user interfaces. So, you'll never see NTBACKUP's request for another tape, let alone be able to tell it you've inserted the new tape in your backup unit.

If you've had to back up so much stuff that you need more than one tape, use one of the third-party backup solutions discussed in the next section of this chapter. They automate backups far beyond what's possible with the Scheduled Tasks application and they work great with auto-changer tape hardware to make those multi-tape backups really easy.

Click Next to see the best thing about the Scheduled Tasks application. Like all NT services, the Task Scheduler service runs under one and only one NT account. If you try to execute a program with the Task Scheduler that does something the Task Scheduler account isn't permitted to do, your scheduled task or tasks will fail. Before the Scheduled Tasks app, you had to jump through hoops to assure that the Task Scheduler account could execute the programs you scheduled. Now, as you can see in Figure 10.14, you can set the NT account rights and permissions that will apply when each specific scheduled task is run. The Task Scheduler still runs under its one and only NT account, but when it comes time to determine if an account can do a specific scheduled task, the rights and permissions of the account you specify on this panel of the Task Scheduler Wizard rule.

After you enter the appropriate account information, click Next and you'll see the final Scheduled Tasks panel (Figure 10.15). If you want to see all the task scheduling options available, before you click Finish, click Open Advanced Properties for This Task When I Click Finish. Try it. There are tons of options.

When you're all done with the Wizard, the Scheduled Tasks window should look like the one in Figure 10.16. You can modify the task and see all the options you have available by double-clicking the task.

To schedule your differential backups, repeat the process above using the file DIFFERENTIAL.BAT. Schedule your differential backups for midnight on every day of the week but Sunday.

**FIGURE 10.14:**

Setting the NT account rights and privileges that are to be used when a task executes

**FIGURE 10.15:**

The last panel of the Scheduled Task Wizard

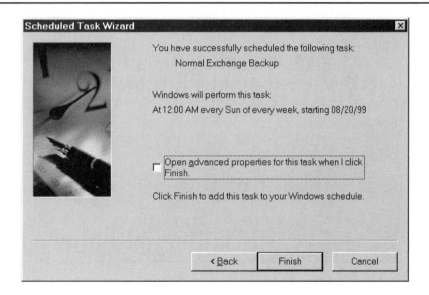

**FIGURE 10.16:**

The Scheduled Tasks window and a newly scheduled task

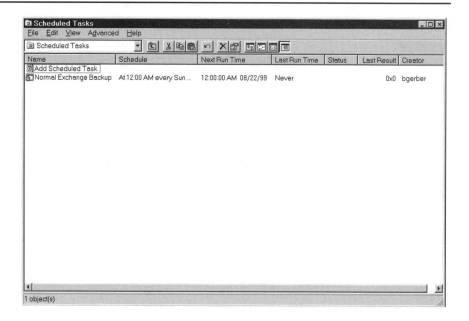

# Exchange Server Backups Using NT Backup on a Computer without Microsoft Exchange Server or Administrator

When you install Exchange Server or just the Exchange Administrator, the installation program copies the files that customize NT's Backup program for Exchange Server. If you need to do an Exchange backup from an NT Workstation or Server computer without either Exchange Server or Administrator installed, you can manually copy the files from the Exchange Server CD-ROM. Just copy EDBBCLI.DLL, BACKUP.CNT, and BACKUP.HLP from the appropriate directory on the CD-ROM to the NT System32 directory on the computer you want to use for backups.

## Did That Backup Work?

You should always monitor backup logs to be sure that a backup has been completed successfully. One easy way to do this is by using a little utility that comes with the Exchange Server Resource Kit. (Contact Microsoft for details on obtaining this free collection of useful programs.) There is a utility called mapisend.exe. The Resource Kit's mapisend.exe utility lets you send a message to any Exchange mailbox and even attach a file. Using mapisend and Command Scheduler, I've set up a little batch file that sends me Backup's log file after my nightly backups have completed. My backups start at midnight, and I have mapisend send the log file to me at 6 A.M.

I've included my batch file below. It's the second listing. Before that, there's a generic version of the batch file with explanatory information. I've also included a second version of the batch file where explanatory information in square brackets replaces the actual parameters shown in the first version of the file. Armed with the two files and what you already know about the Scheduled Tasks app, you should have no trouble setting up an automated mailing of the backup log each day.

```
c:\exchsrvr\mapisend -u [name of the Exchange client MAPI profile
    you want to use (See Chapter 12 for more on profiles and how to
    use them.)] -p [password for the MAPI profile] -r [Exchange mail-
    box to receive the message] -m [text to include in the message] -s
    [subject of the message] -f [file to attach to the message]

c:\exchsrvr\mapisend -u BarryGerber -p secret -r bgerber -m
    "EXCHWW01 Backup Log" -s "Backup Log" -f c:\winnt\backup.log
```

It's wonderful to be able to check the backup log each day, right from my Exchange Inbox. Most of the time everything is just fine. However, I have discovered a few backups gone wrong and fixed them quickly. I can even check things out when I'm away from the office, using one of the many clients available for my Exchange mailbox. Yep, it's wonderful!

# Third-Party Backup Solutions

Any vendor can splice into the application-programming interface that NT Backup uses when it does an online backup of the Exchange directory and information store. A number of vendors have done just that, including Computer

Associates (ArcServeIT; `http://www.cai.com`), Legato Systems (Legato Networker for Windows NT; `http://www.legato.com`), and Veritas (Backup Exec; `http://www.veritas.com`).

Third-party backup solutions add value beyond NT's own built-in backup program. For example,

- They let you back up multiple servers and even other workstations on the network.

- They support online Exchange Server backup as well as online backup of other application services such as Oracle or Microsoft SQL Server.

- And, they make scheduling and monitoring the whole backup process very easy.

Because I like it best of all the products on the market at this writing, I'm going to focus here on Veritas Backup Exec, formerly Seagate Backup Exec. Seagate decided to get out of the backup software business a while ago, and Veritas is now the proud owner of Backup Exec. That's all to the good, because the product is now getting the kind of attention it deserves and that Seagate stopped giving it a while ago.

My goal here is not to provide exhaustive instructions on the use of Backup Exec. As with any modern piece of computer software, Backup Exec is fodder for a book all its own. What I want to do in a few pages is to introduce you to a particular third-party backup solution and some of the super bells and whistles that make it especially attractive.

Backup Exec comes in a variety of flavors. You can buy versions that back up Windows 95/98, NT Workstations, single NT Servers, and whole networks of servers and workstations. In my own environment, I use Backup Exec Multi-Server Edition. This lets me back up any number of NT servers and workstations as well as Windows 95/98, NT, Apple Macintosh, and UNIX workstations. I run the software on one server to back up all the above. I need to run special Backup Exec agents on Win 95/98, Mac, and UNIX workstations in order to back them up. NT servers and workstations require no workstation agents, though I do use the Backup Exec agent accelerators for NT to speed up the backup process.

In Figure 10.17, I'm selecting the Exchange components for Backup Exec to back up. You can't see it, but the tree that includes the Exchange components also includes the drives on the server running Backup Exec and all the other servers and workstations that are available for backup by Backup Exec. And, before you ask, no, Backup Exec doesn't have to be installed on an Exchange server in order to back up the server's Exchange components.

Notice in Figure 10.17 that I can back up not only the Exchange directory and information store but also all or part of each Exchange mailbox. Individual mailbox backup is a neat idea. Without it, to restore a single mailbox from an information store backup, you have to restore the entire information store to an offline server, then export the contents of the mailbox from the restored information store, and finally import those contents into the mailbox in your production information store.

**FIGURE 10.17:**

Setting up an Exchange information store backup using Veritas Backup Exec

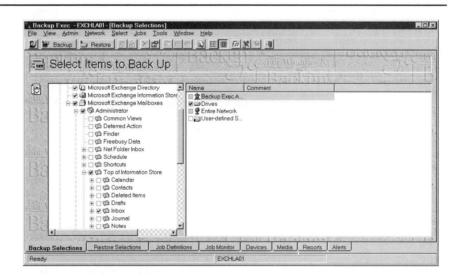

I must offer one caution. Individual mailbox backup is slow. The first time I tried it, I just clicked each mailbox and let 'er rip. Well, *rip* isn't exactly the right word. How about *crawl*. It took hours to back up all those mailboxes in my Exchange server's large information store. If you need to back up mailboxes, be selective. Pick the mailboxes and/or folders within them that really need protection. Fact is, you'll rarely need to restore a mailbox these days, now that Exchange Server 5.5 lets a user recover items they've deleted from their Deleted Items folder.

Figure 10.18 shows Backup Exec's job monitor window. This is where you manage backup, restore, and other Backup Exec jobs. The window in Figure 10.18 includes backups and restores. Just to show you that nothing is perfect, some failed backups are included. Actually, these aren't critical failures. They happened when I went off on a couple of business trips and took my laptop, which is part of the backup process, with me. No laptop, Backup Exec reports an error.

By double-clicking any job in the job monitor window, I can see the status of the job and even look at a log of the whole backup session. You can set it so that this log is as detailed or brief as you like.

Backup Exec can also send messages using the same application-programming interface used by the program MAPISEND.EXE, which is discussed in the above sidebar "Did That Backup Work?" It e-mails the backup log to you and it tells you if the backup was successful. It even tells you when it needs a new tape.

**FIGURE 10.18:**

Monitoring and managing Backup Exec jobs

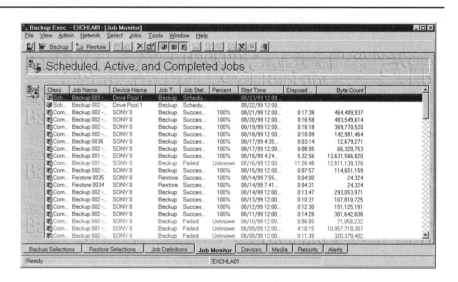

Finally, since no backup system is worth much if you can't restore, in Figure 10.19 I'm asking Backup Exec to restore its August 8, 1999 backup of the Exchange Server information store on the server EXCHLA01. Could anything be easier? Of course, you need to be most careful when you choose to restore anything. Before doing so, you should exhaust all your pre-restore options, like repairing an Exchange database. In Chapter 17, I'll discuss some of the things you can do to repair Exchange directories and information stores.

FIGURE 10.19:

Restoring an Exchange
information store backed
up on a specific date

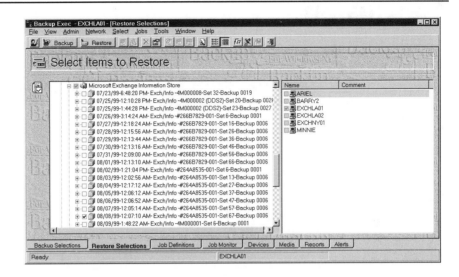

Let me close this brief tour of Backup Exec by mentioning a few of the other
neat features of the product.

As with the Exchange Server Administrator, you can run the Backup Exec Manager, the one in the figures above, on any NT server or workstation on your network. This gives you complete client-server control over the backup process on
all protected servers and workstations. You can back up, restore, and run other
jobs from anywhere in your organization's building, from home, or even from a
distant location. All you need is a network connection.

Backup Exec includes a nice virus scan and fix capability. Files are scanned and
repaired before the actual backup is run, so you don't wind up with a backup full
of virus-infected files. It doesn't take care of those viruses in Exchange Server
mailboxes, but we'll get to that in Chapter 17.

Intelligent Disaster Recovery, a Backup Exec option, helps you get any server
back up and running with minimal effort. After you install Intelligent Disaster
Recovery, you use it to create a set of three special NT Server setup diskettes or
you can generate a bootable image that you burn onto a CD-ROM. After a hardware crash, either of these boots up a repaired or new computer and installs just
enough NT Server software to run a Backup Exec restore of your most recent
backup. These folks at Veritas have thought of just about everything.

# Conclusion

In this chapter you learned a bit about backups in general, and NT and Exchange Server backups in particular. You also learned how to manually and automatically back up an Exchange Server using NT Server's Backup program. And, for good measure, you learned a little about third-party backup options.

# PART IV

# Exchange Server Clients for Windows

Exchange Server is a pretty nifty little gadget. But without clients, it's nothing more than fancy technology. Though this is a book on Exchange Server, we need to spend a little time talking about Exchange Server clients. This section is devoted to that discussion.

In Chapter 11, we'll take an administrative perspective as we focus on the Outlook 2000 client for Windows that is part of the Office 2000 Suite. We'll cover installation of the clients both on a server and, from the server, onto user workstations. In Chapter 12 we'll take a look at the Outlook 2000 client for Windows from the user's perspective. We'll take a quick tour of Outlook's menus to get comfortable with the impressive functionality that Microsoft has built into the client.

# Installing the Outlook 2000 Client for Windows

- Customizing Outlook 2000 for installation on user workstations

- Installing Outlook 2000 on a workstation

**E**xchange Server has been around for about five years. In that time, Microsoft has generated a slew of new and increasingly improved Exchange clients. These include the

- Original DOS, Windows 3.*x*, Windows 95, and Windows NT clients that came with Exchange Server 4 and 5

- Exchange client for the Macintosh

- Windows 95 and Windows NT Outlook client that comes with Office 97

- Windows 95 and Windows NT Outlook client that comes with Exchange Server 5.5

- Outlook 98 client

- Outlook 2000 client

In addition to these Exchange clients, which provide access to the full range of Exchange Server capabilities, Exchange Server also supports POP3 and IMAP4 clients from Microsoft and other vendors. I'll focus here on the native Exchange Server clients and reserve discussion of the POP3 and IMAP4 clients for Chapter 18.

Exchange Server 5.5 comes with a DOS client and Outlook clients for Windows 3.*x*, Windows 95, and Windows NT. However, unless you need a DOS or Windows 3.*x* Exchange client, I strongly recommend that you stay away from the original Exchange 5.5 clients. Instead, turn to the latest incarnation of the Outlook client. At this writing, that means the Outlook 2000 client.

In this chapter we'll cover installation of Outlook 2000. First we'll tackle customizing Outlook 2000 for installation from a network server onto user workstations. Then we'll install Outlook 2000 on an individual workstation using our custom server–based setup. If you need to install any of the older Exchange Server clients, get your hands on the third edition of this book or check out the docs that come with the client you need to install.

---

**NOTE**   "Wait," you say, "setting up server-based installations isn't my thing. I want to get started using Outlook 2000 right away." If that's you, go ahead and install Office 2000 or just Outlook 2000 directly on your workstation. Pop in the Office 2000 CD-ROM and follow the online installation instructions. When you're done, flip over to Chapter 12 for a look at Outlook 2000 in action.

---

We'll save some topics for later chapters. These include a more detailed discussion of Outlook profiles and support for remote (dial-up) client access.

# Customizing Outlook 2000 for Installation on User Workstations

If you've ever attempted to customize the installation of older Office products for Windows and you're still certifiably *sane*, you'll really appreciate the new Windows installer for Office 2000 products like Outlook 2000. Installations of past Office components used the infamous Acme Setup program. Bad old Acme required endless lines of text instructions to copy program files, set Windows registry entries, and do whatever else was required to get Office programs on a user's computer.

Office 2000 Windows installer technology replaces Acme Setup. All the default data required to install each Office 2000 product resides in a relational database with the extension MSI for *Microsoft Installer*. Data to uniquely customize an Office 2000 installation—data you create that overrides or adds to default settings—is also stored in relational databases with the extension MST for *Microsoft Transform*. Not only is data in these files used to set up basic and custom installations, it's also used to update and repair existing installations. You can even install apps or parts of apps so that they aren't actually placed on a user's hard disk until they are used for the first time.

All things considered, we IS types are the winners here. Customizing installations is easier, and to a fair extent, Office 2000 reduces day-to-day maintenance because it is self-healing in a variety of ways.

---

**TIP**  For more on Windows installer technology, take a look at the *Microsoft Office 2000 Resource Kit* from Microsoft Press (1999).

---

In this chapter, we're going to focus on building the MST databases required to deliver customized versions of Outlook 2000 to a user's desktop. Then we'll manually run a customized installation of Office 2000 on a workstation. I'll leave it to you to deal with automatic delivery of the software to the user hard disks. There are several ways to accomplish this end, including

- Automating the execution of the customized installation program through a batch file or an NT login script

- Automating the customized installation using Microsoft's Systems Management Server (SMS) or other systems management tools such as Intel LAN-Desk (http://www.intel.com) or HP OpenView Desktop Administrator (http://www.hp.com)

- Burning and running a CD-ROM or DVD that executes the customized installation program

- Creating a hard disk image of a model end-user drive with everything from the operating system to applications pre-installed and then automatically writing the image to each new or repaired hard disk using a product like Norton Ghost (http://www.symantec.com)

- Creating an image of Office 2000 or Outlook 2000 and installing it on user workstations using a product like wINSTALL (http://www.install.com)

Check the Office 2000 Resource Kit for more on these options.

# Installing Office 2000 on an Administrative Installation Point

Before you can customize an Office 2000 installation, you first must install a copy of 2000 on a server. This copy of Office 2000 is installed on what is officially called an *administrative installation point*.

## Creating an Administrative Installation Point

An administrative installation point is a shared folder on a Windows 95, 98, or NT computer. You can put an administrative installation point on your Exchange server for testing, but I suggest you use another server in production mode. Office 2000 installations can eat up a lot of server resources, resources better dedicated to running Exchange Server.

You'll need about 550MB of free disk space to install Office 2000 on an installation point. So, don't move on to the next paragraph until you've located a disk drive with sufficient space.

To create a folder, in Windows Explorer, find the place where you want to create the share in Explorer's left-hand pane and click it. Then with your mouse pointer in Explorer's right-hand pane, right-click and select New ➢ Folder. Name the folder something like *Off2000*. Since the Office 2000 setup program runs under MS-DOS on Windows 95/98 machines, keep the name of the directory at or under eight characters. If you don't, the setup program will fail with a command line error.

To share your new folder, right-click it and select Sharing from the menu that pops up. Next click the Permissions button on the properties dialog box for your folder. In the Access through Share Permissions dialog box, change the Everyone group's permissions to Read; add the NT group Administrators, and give it Full Control permissions. If any of this is even a bit vague, see Figure 11.1.

That's it! Now you can install Office 2000 on the administrative installation point.

**FIGURE 11.1:**

Setting up a share for an administrative installation point

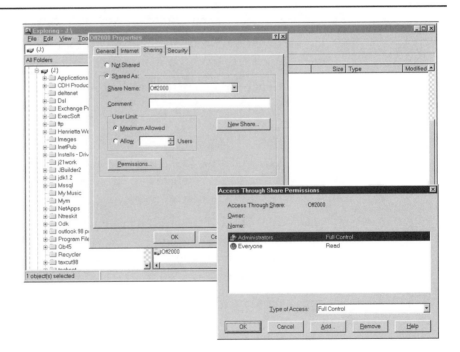

## Installing Office 2000 on an Administrative Installation Point

Before we begin our installation, I need to make three points:

1. I want to be sure you understand that we are not installing Office 2000 on this computer so we can use it for word processing, e-mail, spreadsheets, etc. We're installing it so we can customize it and make it available for installation on the workstations of others.

2. Though we are going to install all of Office 2000, if you purchase a separate copy of Outlook 2000, you can install it just as we are here.

3. You must purchase a workstation license for each workstation where one or more Office 2000 components is installed. Check with Microsoft or a reseller for info on licensing plans and prices.

To install Office 2000 on an administrative installation point

- Put the CD-ROM disk labeled "Office 2000 Disc 1" into the CD-ROM drive on the server where you want to do the installation.

- Open a Command Prompt (Start Menu ➤ Programs ➤ Command Prompt).

- Change over to your CD-ROM's root directory and type **setup.exe /a data1.msi**.

The file DATA1.MSI is the MSI database that comes with Office 2000. When you type the above command, you're telling SETUP.EXE to use this file for all the default Office 2000 application settings.

The installer for Office 2000 starts up in administrative mode (see Figure 11.2). Enter the default organization name for all installations from this administrative installation point. This can be the same as or different from your Exchange Server organization name. Click Next and read and agree to the license terms. Then click Next and specify the share you just created as the location where Office 2000 should be installed (as I'm doing in Figure 11.3).

**FIGURE 11.2:**

Windows installer for
Office 2000 in
administrative mode

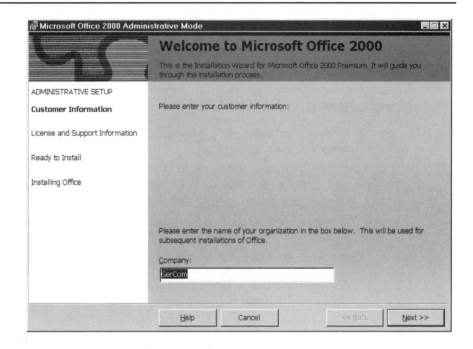

**FIGURE 11.3:**

Specifying where
Office 2000 should
be installed

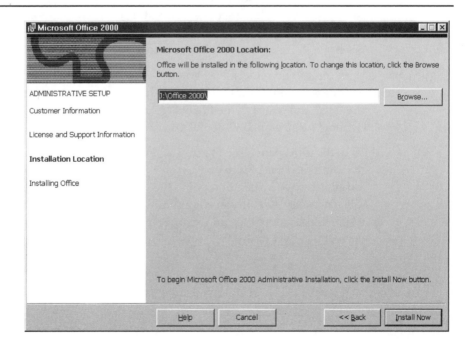

Finally, click Install Now and Windows installer takes off. Well, *takes off* may be a bit of an exaggeration. Let's say runs…and runs…and runs…and… Fear not, though. You'll only have to do this once for each custom installation you need to set up. For small to middle-sized organizations, that usually means once.

# Customizing Outlook 2000

Before you can customize the installation of Office 2000 you just placed on your new administrative installation point, you have to install Office 2000 Custom Installation Wizard. The Wizard comes with the Office 2000 Resource Kit I mentioned earlier in this chapter. To install the Wizard and a whole bunch of other neat tools and docs, put the Office 2000 Resource Kit CD-ROM into your CD-ROM drive and track through the auto-run Resource Kit installation program.

## Getting Started with the Custom Installation Wizard

When installation is finished, run the Custom Installation Wizard: Start Menu ➢ Programs ➢ Microsoft Office Tools ➢ Microsoft Office 2000 Resource Kit Tools ➢ Custom Installation Wizard. Whew!

The Wizard has lots of panels to guide you through customization of Office 2000. Let's take a look at key panels, especially as they relate to Outlook 2000. I'll assume that you can any handle panels I don't discuss here without any input from me. If you have any questions, check out the Office 2000 Resource Kit or Microsoft's Web site (http://www.microsoft.com).

In the second panel of the Wizard, you select the MSI file that holds the default settings for your Office 2000 installations. In Figure 11.4, I'm pointing the Custom Installation Wizard to the file DATA1.MSI on the administrative installation point where I just installed Office 2000.

In the third panel (see Figure 11.5), accept the default option Do Not Open an Existing MST File. Since you haven't yet customized the configuration for this administrative installation point, there are no MST files to open. You want to create a new MST file. If you were coming back to modify a custom configuration, you would select Open an Existing MST File and do your modifications using it as your starting point.

**FIGURE 11.4:**

Setting the default configuration file to be used during Office 2000 customization

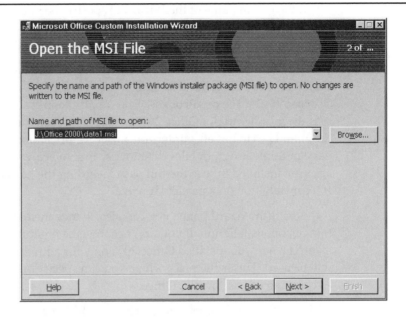

**FIGURE 11.5:**

Telling the Custom Installation Wizard to use a new file for the current customization session

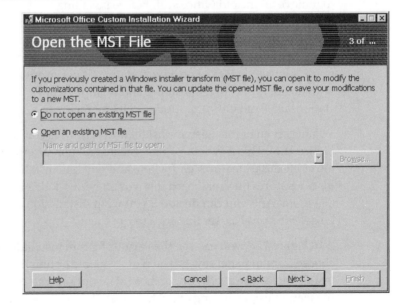

Use the fourth panel of the Wizard to specify the name of the new MST file you'll use for this customization session. Keep the name under eight characters so it's available to Win 95/98 workstations. Try CUSTOM01.MST.

On the fifth Wizard panel, you set the default directory to be used when Office 2000 applications are installed, for example, `D:\Program Files\ Microsoft Office` or `<Program Files>\Microsoft Office`. <Program Files> tells the installer to put Office 2000 components into the first directory named Program Files that it encounters on a user's workstation. If users are likely to have multiple Program Files directories, and you care which one Office 2000 apps are installed in, use the full path including the hard disk drive letter to force installation on a particular drive.

On the fifth Wizard panel, you can also change the name of the organization for this custom installation. If you don't change the organization name, the one you entered when you installed Office 2000 on your administrative installation point will be used. This is the place where you can specify organization names like Accounting or Los Angeles Office.

The sixth Wizard panel lets you choose which legacy Office applications should be removed when the new Office 2000 components are installed. It's good policy to remove all the old Office stuff before installing the latest and greatest Office apps. To do so, select Remove the Following Versions of Microsoft Office Applications and uncheck any you want to keep. If you accept the default option Default Setup Behavior, the Office 2000 installer will ask if it should remove old Office applications if they exist on a workstation. If you want to do a silent installation with no queries from the installer and no input from a human, and if your workstations have old Office products on them, then you don't want the default here.

Panel seven of the Custom Installation Wizard is chock-full of neat options (see Figure 11.6). This is where you tell the installation program whether to install various Office 2000 features and where and when to install them. You can choose to install features on users' hard disks or on network drives or to run them from CD-ROM. And you can decide if you want installation of all or some features to be deferred until a user first tries to run them.

In Figure 11.7, you can see the various feature installation state options you can choose from in panel seven. The Not Available option tells the installer not to install the feature at all. Any of these state options can be applied at any level in the feature list, including at the top level. If you choose the Not Available option for an entire Office 2000 application, that application won't be installed.

FIGURE 11.6:

Setting feature
installation states

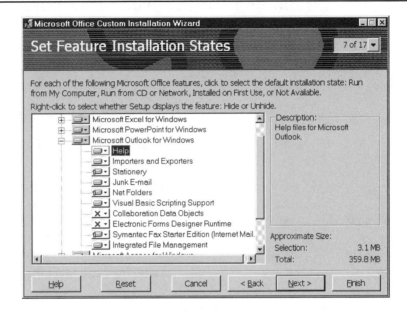

FIGURE 11.7:

Feature installation
state options

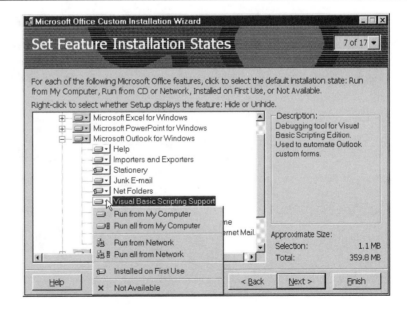

## Customizing Outlook 2000 with an OPS File

The eighth Wizard panel shown in Figure 11.8 is an important one. To understand this panel's function, you need to understand how Office 2000 application installations are customized.

As you'll see in a bit, many Outlook settings of import can be modified right in the Custom Installation Wizard. But there are other options you can only customize using what is called a *profile*. Just to prevent a little confusion, these profiles have nothing to do with either Microsoft operating system profiles or the Outlook profiles I'll discuss in the next chapter.

You customize all the major Office 2000 applications with a single profile file. To create a profile, you first install and run each Office 2000 application you want to customize, changing its custom configuration settings to suit your needs. Then you run the Office 2000 Resource Kit's Office Profile Wizard on the same computer. The profile Wizard processes your custom settings and creates an Office application settings profile file with the extension OPS. This file is then used by the installer to customize the settings for Office 2000 applications when they are installed on a user's workstation.

**FIGURE 11.8:**

Selecting an Office application settings profile, which will be used to customize an Outlook installation

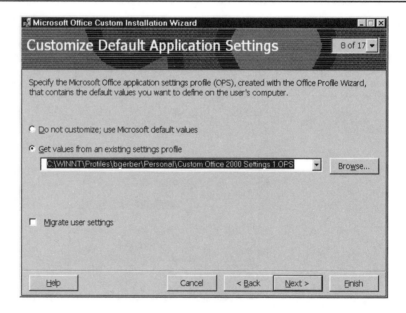

Let's walk quickly through this process, as it might be implemented for Outlook 2000. Say, to reduce network traffic, you want to change the frequency with which Outlook checks the Exchange Server for new e-mail. You'd run Outlook on a workstation, bring up the Options menu, and change the mail check frequency. Then you'd close Outlook and run the Profile Wizard to convert the custom configuration for that instance of Outlook 2000 into the OPS file format. Finally, you'd use the Profile Wizard to save the converted configuration into an OPS file, which then can be used to customize all installations of Outlook 2000.

The only pain in all this is that you have to install Outlook or any other Office 2000 application to generate a custom OPS profile. On the other hand, this is heaven compared to the hoops you had to jump through to create and edit profiles for earlier Office products.

---

**TIP**    The first time I ran the Profile Wizard, I forgot to note where the Wizard stored the OPS file it created. I spent a fair amount of time looking for the file and quietly cursing. The Profile Wizard shows the path where it saves each OPS file. Be sure to write down the path. Generally, the Wizard saves OPS files in your personal folder. For me, that's \WINNT\PROFILES\<NT_USERNAME>\PERSONAL, where **NT_LOGIN_ID** is my NT username when I ran the Profile Wizard.

---

Now back to the eighth Custom Installation Wizard panel. You use this panel, shown in Figure 11.8, to specify whether you want to use default configuration profiles for the various Office 2000 applications or if you want to use a custom OPS file that you've created.

In Figure 11.8, I've chosen to use a custom OPS file I created. Note that there is room here for only one OPS file. As I pointed out earlier, for a given installation, all the custom profile settings for OPS-file–customizable Office 2000 applications must reside in one and only one OPS file. This file is incorporated right into the MST database file. This means that, unlike older Office customization processes, you don't need to keep track of the location of separate profile files.

If you check Migrate User Settings, the installer will retain each user's Office 97 settings where they exist. This option is automatically disabled when you select Get Values from an Existing Settings Profile. That's because you're likely to want to leave the settings in your new OPS file in place and not replace them with older settings.

## Continuing On with the Custom Installation Wizard

Wizard panel nine lets you request that non–Office 2000 files be installed along with the regular Office 2000 application files. You could use this to install special templates or sample data files used in your organization, Word or Excel files, for example. You use panel 10 to add registry entries during the Office 2000 installation. You might use this to modify a standard Office 2000 registry entry.

The eleventh of the Custom Installation Wizard's panels lets you specify which Office 2000 program icons are displayed. In panel 12 you can create a list of all servers that have a copy of the administrative installation point and its contents. Users can then install from any of these installation points. One of these alternative servers is used when the original installation server is not available and a workstation needs to repair itself, access Office 2000 files set to run from a server, or install new software set for installation on first use.

Use Wizard panel 13 to specify other programs to run after Office 2000 installation is completed. This might include a setup program to install other applications or modify applications you've already installed. See the Office 2000 Resource Kit for some interesting options, including one where you modify Outlook settings using an application called *NEWPROF.EXE*.

## More Outlook Customization Options

Panel 14 is just for Outlook. You can set a range of Outlook options in this panel. See Figure 11.9. As you set these options, you are building what is called an *Outlook profile*. As I noted earlier, this is something very different from an OPS profile or a Windows system profile.

You use Outlook profiles to set the type of e-mail systems a user is able to access and many of the parameters associated with those systems. As you'll see at the end of this chapter, one user can have multiple profiles, each of which allows for access to different mail systems or parts of a single mail system.

Let's take a brief tour of panel 14. You use the drop-down menu that's open in Figure 11.9 to select the master configuration for the Outlook profile you'll create. Your options are Exchange Server–oriented-with-Internet (Corporate or Workgroup Settings) or Internet-oriented (Internet Only Settings). Since we're focusing on Exchange Server here, select the Corporate or Workgroup option.

Figure 11.9 shows the General property settings for an Outlook profile. The profile name is used to identify this particular profile. If a user has multiple Outlook profiles, this is the name that the user picks when selecting which profile to use when starting Outlook.

**FIGURE 11.9:**

Setting Outlook profile configuration parameters

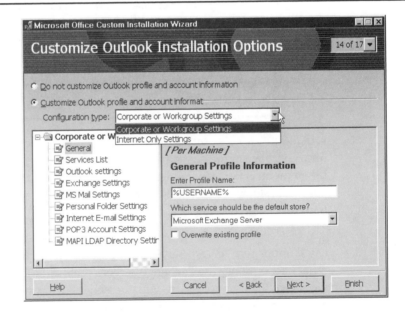

I've entered %USERNAME% in the Enter Profile Name field in Figure 11.9. USERNAME is an operating system environment variable. In the NT operating system, USERNAME is a system environment variable that contains a user's NT username, which is what you type in before your password to log into your NT account. In Windows 95/98, you can set USERNAME or any other environment variable to whatever you want in a login script or in the AUTOEXEC.BAT file. The command to create the environment variable USERNAME and set it to BGERBER is set USERNAME = BGERBER.

Why the percent signs in *%USERNAME%*? When an environment variable is used in setting Outlook 2000 profile parameters, it is prefixed and suffixed with a percent sign.

This is a wonderful new feature of Outlook 2000 profile configuration. In the past you had to enter a constant in the Profile Name field or leave it blank, which then required that the user enter a profile name on initially running Outlook. Now you can enter a variable from which the installer takes the name of the profile.

**WARNING**    If you need to set USERNAME as an environment variable for Windows 95/98 workstations, use AUTOEXEC.BAT if only one user will log into the workstation. If the workstation will have more than one user, use a unique login script for each user. There is one and only one AUTOEXEC.BAT on a workstation. It runs when the workstation first boots up. Anyone logging into the workstation will have the same USERNAME if you use AUTOEXEC.BAT to set USERNAME. If you use a unique login script for each workstation user, then each user will get her or his own USERNAME.

In Figure 11.9, I've selected Microsoft Exchange Server as the default location for the storage of messages and other items. The other alternative on the drop-down menu is Personal Folders. You'll remember from an earlier chapter that personal folders are generally stored outside of Exchange Server on a user's own hard disk or on the network.

You select the services to be installed with Outlook from among the properties listed under *Services List*. Services support different kinds of mail systems and other neat options. The Exchange Server, Microsoft Mail, and Internet e-mail services give the user access to—you guessed it—Exchange Server, Microsoft Mail, and Internet e-mail systems. As you can see in Figure 11.10, I've selected Exchange Server, Personal Folders, and the Microsoft LDAP Directory.

**WARNING**    If you select a mail service, be sure to configure it in the appropriate place in panel 14. If you don't, your users will be asked all kinds of confusing questions about parameters for any unconfigured mail services when they start up Outlook 2000 for the first time. Of course, if you have knowledgeable users or plan to provide training or cheat-sheets, you can ignore this note.

FIGURE 11.10:

Selecting Outlook services
to be installed

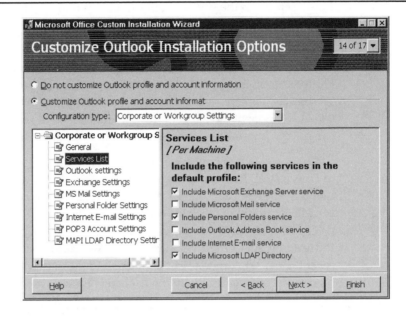

FIGURE 11.10:

Selecting Outlook services
to be installed

The Personal Folders service provides the user with the ability to store messages and other items locally. However, because of previous selections, these personal folders are just for drag-and-drop storage. Messages will be delivered to the Exchange Server mailbox, not to personal folders. Other Outlook features like scheduling or contact management will be in the user's Exchange Server mailbox, not in personal folders. To get all of that stuff in personal folders, I would have had to select the Personal Folders as the default store.

The Outlook Address Book service is pretty much a holdover from past versions of Outlook. Outlook's contact management feature is a far better place to store personal e-mail addresses. So, select this option only if you've got a good reason or if you're upgrading from a previous version of Outlook.

The Microsoft LDAP Directory service is neat. As you'll learn in Chapter 18, the Lightweight Directory Access Protocol (LDAP) is a way to access information about e-mail addresses and such from servers anywhere on the Internet. Exchange Server supports LDAP, but this service is more about LDAP on other Internet-based servers. A bunch of these servers just sit out there collecting names, e-mail addresses, etc. When you search for an e-mail address by a person's name, your Outlook client firsts looks locally at your contacts and at addresses on your Exchange servers. If it doesn't find the name there, it goes out to one of the big

LDAP servers in the sky. Amazingly, it often finds the name you're looking for. Unless your corporate policy runs contrary to this sort of stuff, do include the LDAP service in your Outlook installations.

Continuing our climb down the tree of Outlook custom installation options, the Outlook Settings properties relate to providing access to Outlook forms through a Web server. For a refresher on forms, see the section in Chapter 3 on Exchange Client components. We'll get into all of this later. For now, just remember that you can control Internet-based access to Outlook forms right here.

Move on down to Exchange Settings. This is an important one. As you can see in Figure 11.11, I've entered our friend %USERNAME% as the name for user mailboxes. Again, each user's mailbox will get the name stored in the USER-NAME environment variable on his or her computer. I've specified my server EXCHLA01 as the server the user should connect to when Outlook first runs. As the text in Figure 11.11 indicates, if you have multiple Exchange servers, you can enter the name of any one of them here and the user will be directed to his or her own server automatically by the Exchange Server system.

**FIGURE 11.11:**

Setting Exchange
Server–based configuration
parameters

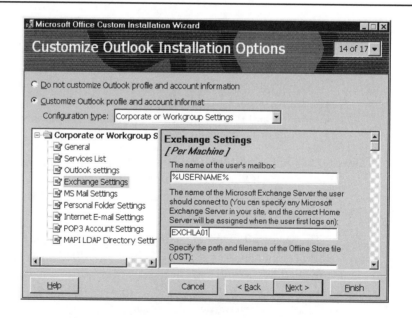

Figure 11.12 shows your other Exchange Server options. Users can make a local copy of their Exchange mailbox and the Exchange address book. This is most useful

if the installation is on a laptop, but it's also comforting to have these files on a fixed workstation's hard disk in case network connectivity is lost. You can specify the path where the offline mailbox and address book files are stored, or you can leave these options blank and these two files will be stored in the user's personal folder.

**FIGURE 11.12:**

Setting Exchange Server–based configuration parameters continued

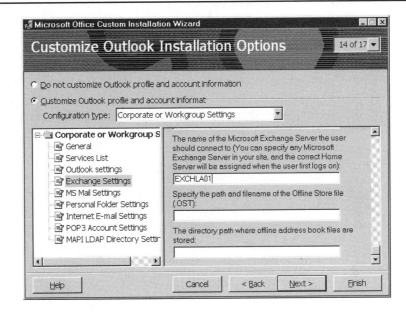

We can cover the other options on panel 14 quickly. Use the MS Mail Settings properties to preset a passel of parameters such as the path to the MS Mail server, the name of the user's mailbox, and the connection type. If you're an MS Mail aficionado, all this will make sense to you.

The Personal Folders Settings options let you specify the name of the file that contains personal folders and the type of encryption to be used on personal folders. The last three options on panel 14—Internet E-Mail Settings, POP3 Account Settings, and MAPI LDAP Directory Settings—are used to specify parameters for these Internet-oriented services. If you know what's what in regard to Internet services, you should be able to use what you've learned here to modify these settings. If Internet services are still a bit of a mystery to you, you'll be better able to tackle these settings after you read Chapters 15 and 18.

## Finishing Up with the Custom Installation Wizard

Wizard panel 15 is used to customize Internet Explorer. To install Outlook 2000, Internet Explorer 4.01 or greater must be installed on the user's workstation. IE is used to support such things as Outlook 2000's extended encryption options. The Office 2000 Resource Kit comes with a copy of the Internet Explorer Administration Kit. Click Customize on panel 15 and the Kit runs. Then you can customize the version of IE 5 that's installed with Office 2000 to your heart's content.

You can modify existing Setup properties or add and remove new ones with panel 16. For example, you can change the default language used during the installation process (see Figure 11.13). Two options on this panel relate directly to Outlook 2000: *OUTLOOKASDEFAULTAPP* and *OutlookConfiguration*. As you can see in Figure 11.13, by double clicking OUTLOOKASDEFAULTAPP, you can choose how the installer handles making Outlook 2000 components the default application on a user's workstation.

OutlookConfiguration does the same for the Outlook master configuration. You can choose Corporate or Workgroup, Internet Only, or Ask User When Outlook First Runs. You'll remember that we set this option back on the Custom Installation Wizard's eighth panel. What you do on the sixteenth panel overrides any other settings you've made. So, if you select another option here, it, not the option you set in panel eight, becomes the default.

Wizard Panel 15 contains a lot of interesting options. For example, if you want to force the user's workstation to reboot after setup is complete, which you might if this were to be a totally non-interactive installation of Office 2000, just set *REBOOT* to *Force*.

That's it! Click Finish on the final panel of the Custom Installation Wizard and you're done customizing your Office 2000 installation. The Wizard will save your MST file to your administrative installation point.

There is one more thing you have to do before running a test installation. You need to specify at least one command line argument for Office 2000's SETUP.EXE program. This argument specifies which custom MST file or files should be used by SETUP.EXE. These arguments are set in the Office 2000 SETUP.INI file in the root of your administrative installation point. Then when a user double-clicks SETUP.EXE in your OFFICE 2000 share or SETUP.EXE is run in a batch file or login script, the program includes your custom settings and any other options you've specified on the command line.

**FIGURE 11.13:**

Modifying Setup properties

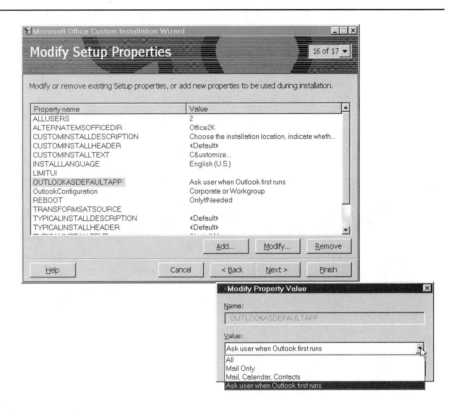

When you edit the Office 2000 SETUP.INI file to add the name of your MST file, be very, very sure to uncomment (remove the semicolon before) the MST section header *[MST]*. If you don't, your MST file won't be applied during installation.

Using Windows Explorer, find the file SETUP.INI in the root of your administrative installation point. As you'll remember, mine is the shared folder OFF2000. Double-click SETUP.INI to open it in Window's Notepad app. Add a line like the one below to the [MST] section of the file.

```
MST1=\\EXCHLA01\Off2000\custom01.mst
```

This tells the SETUP.EXE program to use the database CUSTOM01.MST located on my Exchange server EXCHLA01 in the share OFF2000 when it installs Office 2000 from this administrative installation point. Also, as I warned earlier, be sure to remove the semicolon in front of [MST] or your MST file won't be included in the installation and all your work will be for naught.

You can do lots more to enhance the installation of Office 2000. For example, you can add command line parameters directly to the SETUP.EXE command that cause the installation to proceed without requiring any user input and without displaying any output. For example, you could run setup like this: `setup.exe /qn+`, where */qn+* tells SETUP.EXE to run silently, requiring no input and providing no output except for a notice that the installation has completed. You'd especially want to do this if you were going to install Office 2000 components using one of the automatic methods I discussed early in this chapter, such as running it from an NT login script. Check out the Office 2000 Resource Kit for more on all this.

## Watch Those SETUP.EXE Command Line Arguments

Be careful about using direct command line parameters with SETUP.EXE. Just before the Custom Installation Wizard terminates, it offers a sample command line that looks something like this: setup.exe TRANSFORMS=J:\Off2000\custom01.MST /qn+. /qn+. You already know what /qn+ does. The TRANSFORMS parameter points the Office 2000 installer to the MST file to be used to customize the installation.

You might be tempted to create a batch file with this command on the administrative installation point and have users run it to install Office 2000. If this command is run on the workstation where you installed Office 2000 on the administrative installation point, all will be fine. J: directs the workstation to the correct path for the installation point. However, if this command is run on any other workstation, it won't work, unless the net use command is run before SETUP.EXE in the same batch file to map the drive letter J to the share containing the installation point, \\EXCHLA01\Off2000 in my case.

The next command in the batch file after the net use command should be J: to assure that the workstation is on the right drive to run SETUP.EXE. If you do map the drive before running SETUP.EXE, remember to unmap the drive letter after SETUP.EXE runs using the net use /delete option. Here's an example:

    net use J: \\EXCHLA01\OFF2000

    J:

    setup.exe TRANSFORMS=J:\Off2000\custom01.MST /qn+. /qn+

    net use J: /delete

If you're not sure about the syntax for the net use command, just type **net use /?** at the command prompt.

# Installing the Outlook 2000 Client on a Workstation

At last! Let's get right to installing a client.

From a workstation that doesn't have Office 2000 installed on it, open NT or Windows 95/98 Explorer. Find and open Network Neighborhood inside Explorer. Then find the server with your Office 2000 administrative installation point and click it in the installation point, \\EXCHLA01\OFF2000 in my case. Find SETUP.EXE and double-click it.

After a bit, the setup wizard starts, gives you a few installation options, and begins installation. When the installation is done, your computer will reboot, your system settings will be updated, and Office 2000 installation will run to completion.

At this point, Office 2000 is in place and Outlook 2000 and any of the other Office 2000 components you installed should run like a charm with little or no intervention on your part. We'll actually run Outlook 2000 for the first time in the next chapter.

That's it for installation. Not much, huh? That's because of all the work you did preparing everything with the Custom Installation Wizard.

# Conclusion

In this chapter you learned how to set up Outlook 2000 software so it can be installed from a network server onto user workstations. You also installed the Outlook 2000 client from your network server. Now we're ready to explore Outlook 2000. If you will, please flip a couple of pages and join me in the next chapter.

# CHAPTER

## TWELVE

12

# Using the Outlook 2000 Client with Exchange Server

- Starting up a newly installed Outlook 2000 client

- Sending and receiving messages with an Outlook 2000 client

- Outlook profiles continued

- Creating a public folder

- Working with shared mailboxes

- Using Outlook 2000's e-mail menus

**B**ecause the focus of this book is on Exchange Server, I really don't have a lot of time for the client side of things. So my goal here is to provide you with enough information to use Outlook 2000 in your explorations of Exchange Server from this point forward.

In spite of the limited time we can devote to Outlook 2000, we're still going to cover quite a bit of territory in this chapter. We'll set up a new Outlook 2000 client, send and receive a message, continue the exploration of Outlook profiles we began in the last chapter, create a new public folder, create and access a shared mailbox, and take a quick tour of some Outlook 2000 menus. That's quite a handful, so let's get started.

## Before We Begin...

As you go along, remember that this is exactly the experience an end user will have when starting and using Outlook 2000 for the first time. Try to think like a non-technical user throughout this chapter. This will help you come up with ideas for special instructions or other help you might want to give your users. As will become more and more obvious as you move through the rest of this chapter, it's much easier on your users if you do some of the preliminary setup work that I discussed in the last chapter.

I'm assuming that you've been using the NT account you created for yourself. If you expect to have new users who will be logging into their NT accounts for the first time to set up and use their Outlook clients, remember to tell them their password. If you created a user's NT account while creating her or his mailbox with the Exchange Administrator program, the default password is blank and the user will be prompted to change it the first time he or she logs in. If you created the NT account using User Manager for Domains, then depending on the options you select when creating accounts, you'll need to provide the user with whatever password information will be needed to log in.

I'm also assuming that you've added your personal NT account to the Exchange Admins group you created back in Chapter 7. If you didn't, you should now, since you won't be able to do some of the tasks discussed here unless you are a member of that group.

# Starting Up a Newly Installed Client

In the last chapter, you installed Outlook 2000 on an administrative installation point and then installed a customized copy of Outlook 2000 onto a workstation from the installation point. To start Outlook 2000, find the desktop icon labeled Microsoft Outlook and double-click it.

The Outlook 2000 client should open right up in your Exchange mailbox if you

- Created an Exchange Server mailbox for yourself back in Chapter 8

- Installed the Outlook client while logged in as yourself

- Are now logged into your NT domain as yourself

- Modified your NT Outlook client as I suggested in the last chapter

If things didn't turn out that way, welcome to the club. It took me several iterations of the installation customization steps in Chapter 11 to get everything to work as advertised.

**SQUARE ONE** (SQUARE ONE? Don't ask; you'll understand in a bit.): Check to make sure your custom MST file is indeed in the shared directory that is your administrative installation point. If it's not there, then either you saved it somewhere else while running the Custom Installation Wizard or the Wizard never saved it. If the file is missing, you can look for it with Explorer or just rerun the Wizard and create a new MST file. Be sure to save the file in your administrative installation point.

If your MST file is there, rerun the Wizard, open the MST file, and check to make sure all the custom settings you set up are there. If anything is missing, add it back and save the changed MST file.

When you're sure about your MST file, run SETUP.EXE from your administrative installation point and choose to remove Office 2000 from your workstation. After everything is removed, run SETUP.EXE again and reinstall Office 2000. If all is well, Outlook 2000 should act as indicated above. If not—you guessed it—back to **SQUARE ONE**.

All I can say is, given the time it takes to uninstall, reboot, and reinstall Office 2000, you'll find that patience is a real virtue as you work the kinks out of your custom installation.

Okay, your Outlook 2000 client is finally up and running as expected. Figure 12.1 shows what the client looks like when starting up for the first time. Of course, depending on a variety of things, your client might look somewhat different. We'll fix that in the next section.

**FIGURE 12.1:**

The Outlook 2000 client immediately after installation

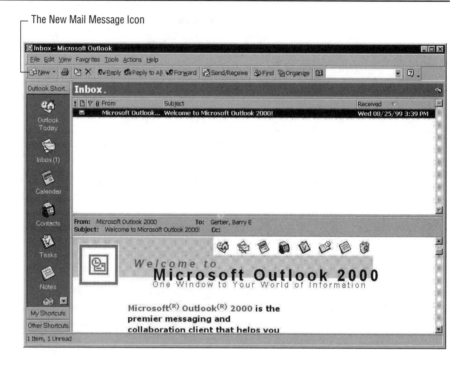

── The New Mail Message Icon

# Sending and Receiving a Message with an Outlook 2000 Client

Your client window is probably kind of small and scrunchy, so go ahead and enlarge it until it looks like the one in Figure 12.1. Now let's do some quick reconfiguring to make the client really useful.

If you can't see the toolbar just under the Outlook 2000 menu bar, select Standard, then Advanced, from the View menu's Toolbar submenu. If you're used to the left-hand pane from the older Exchange clients that shows your folders, select Folder List from the View menu or click the Folder List button on the Advanced toolbar. Then turn off the Outlook bar by deselecting it on the View menu. Finally, turn off the pane by deselecting it on the View menu or by clicking the Preview Pane button on the Advanced toolbar. When you're done, your Outlook 2000 client should look like the one in Figure 12.2.

If some of the configuration options I've asked you to make clash horribly with your own aesthetic or practical values, please feel free to change them when you're done with this chapter. But, do wait until then or you'll have a devil of a time tracking through what is to come.

**FIGURE 12.2:**

Outlook 2000 configured according to Gerber's aesthetic and practical view of e-messaging GUIs

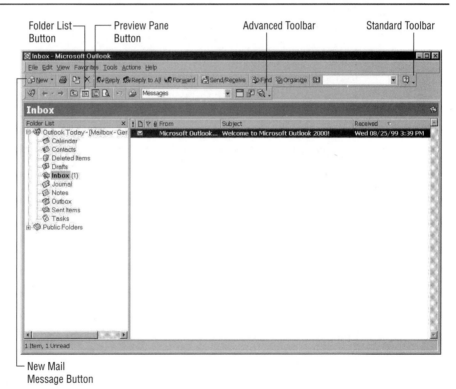

Now you should be able to see all seven of the client's default column titles. These include the following:

- Exclamation mark: message importance

- Sheet of paper: type of message

- Flag: status of messages marked for follow-up

- Paperclip: message attachments

- From: who sent the message

- Subject: what the sender says the message is about

- Received: the date and time the message was received by the Exchange Server

Like the Exchange Administrator, Exchange remembers the window size you've set when you exit. Every time you run the client, the window will be set to that size. Also, like the Exchange Administrator, the client is divided into two resizable panes (three, if you activate the folder list). The left-hand pane, called the *Outlook bar*, contains the major Outlook folders plus any folders you add. The middle pane, the folder list, shows mailboxes and public and personal folders in a hierarchical arrangement. The right-hand pane, the message items pane, displays the messages contained in the folder that has been selected in the Outlook bar or folder list. And, if you've turned on the preview pane, you'll see a pane below the message items pane that automatically displays the contents of whatever message is selected in the message items pane.

## Sending a Message

Before we start, double-click the message from Microsoft Outlook 2000 in the message items pane. Read it, enjoy it, close it, and then delete it by clicking the big **X** on the Standard toolbar. Good, now we have a totally empty message items pane to work with—more of Gerber's aesthetic and practical values.

Let's start by sending ourselves a message. Click the New Mail Message button on the Standard toolbar (see Figure 12.2 for the icon's location). This opens a New Message window like the one in Figure 12.3. If you don't see the standard toolbar for managing messages in the New Message window, select Standard from the Toolbar submenu on the message's View menu. If the text-formatting toolbar isn't visible in the New Message window, select Formatting from the Toolbar submenu on the message's View menu. Your client will remember that you've turned on these toolbars and present them on every new message window.

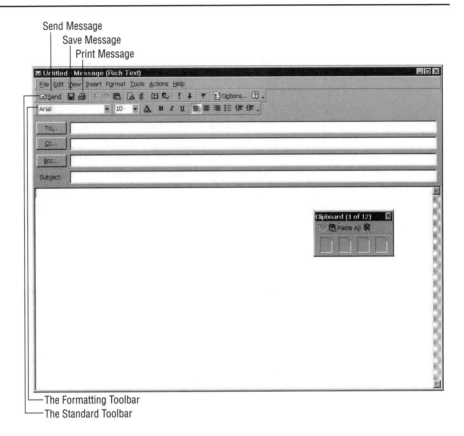

Send Message
Save Message
Print Message

The Formatting Toolbar
The Standard Toolbar

If you really want a thrill, select Clipboard from the View menu's Toolbar sub-menu. This is new to Office 2000. The Office 2000 clipboard is really multiple clip-boards: up to 12. So, you can copy different stuff to each clipboard and then paste whatever you need from whichever clipboard. If you don't like the floating ver-sion of the clipboard, just drag it up to the toolbars section above the message and it'll turn into a toolbar.

If you didn't know you were in an Outlook client, you just might think you were running a word processing application. The top of the screen includes drop-down menus and a number of icons that you've probably seen in your Windows-based word processor. These allow you to produce very rich messages that can include text in different fonts, sizes, formats, and colors, as well as variously for-matted paragraphs and lists.

The New Message window starts to look more e-messagy just below the for-matting toolbar. This is where you enter the address of the recipient(s) of your message. Click To; this brings up our old friend the Address Book dialog box (see Figure 12.4), called Select Names in the Outlook 2000 client.

Notice in Figure 12.4 that I've clicked open the drop-down list of address lists and have selected the Global Address List—which, of course, is the same Global Address List you encountered in the Exchange Administrator. It holds addresses for all unhidden recipients in your Exchange organization. The Recipients list is the address list only for GerCom's LA site. You'll remember that we created the recipients container Application Recipients back in Chapter 8 when we were experimenting with the Exchange Administrator. You store your own Exchange and other addresses in the Outlook Contacts List or the Outlook Address Book. You can change the address book that is shown by default when you click the To or Cc buttons. We'll talk about that later.

**FIGURE 12.4:**

The Exchange address book as viewed from an Outlook client

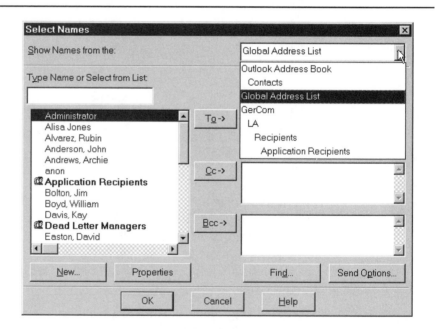

Because you'll be sending this message to yourself, click your name in the Global Address List, then click To and OK in the Select Names dialog box. This returns you to your message (see Figure 12.5).

**FIGURE 12.5:**

Composing a new Outlook message

The Send Icon

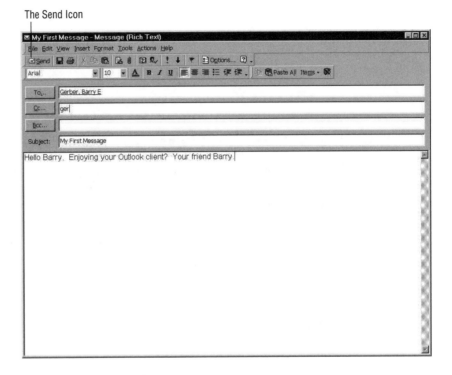

Now move to the Subject field, using either your mouse or the Tab key. Type in some text for a subject title.

Next, move to the message field and type in a message. Now place the text cursor in the Cc (carbon copy) field of your message. Type in the first few letters of your first or last name, depending on how you chose to show display names back in Chapters 5 and 8. If you chose the First Last option, type in the first few letters of your first name. If you selected Last, First, type in the first few letters of your last name. Don't do anything else in the Cc field. You'll see why we did all this in just a bit.

Now, click the Send button on the Standard toolbar. In a second or two, the message should show up in your Inbox.

> **NOTE**
>
> A few of the icons on the main Outlook client window in Figures 12.6 and 12.7 are labeled for your information. The rest of the icons are not terribly important right now. Anyway, as with most Windows apps, you can always find out what an Outlook client icon is for just by putting your mouse pointer on it and waiting a second for a tiny information box to show up.

## Reading a Received Message

Let's take a look at your newly received message. Double-click anywhere on the message line in the Inbox window (see Figure 12.6) to open it. Figure 12.7 shows the open message. Take a look at the Cc field—notice how your Outlook client figured out your name from the few letters you typed in while composing the message? Entering partial names into message address fields can save time compared with clicking the To button and finding names in the Address Book. Separate partial names in address fields with semicolons. If you enter a partial name that's not in the Address Book, or one that appears in more than one display name or alias name, the client will offer you a chance to change what you've entered or to pick from a list of all recipients containing the partial name.

**FIGURE 12.6:**

The new message shows up in the Outlook 2000 client's Inbox.

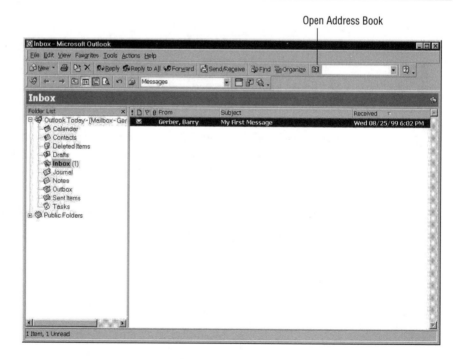

Open Address Book

**FIGURE 12.7:**

A received Exchange message

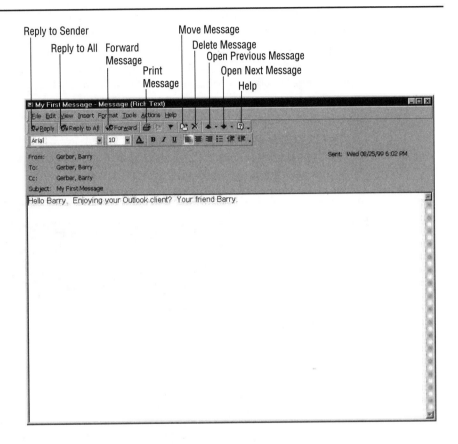

I won't go into detail about the message's Standard toolbar icons here; check out Figure 12.7 for specifics. If you don't see the toolbar in your message, select Standard from the Toolbar submenu on the message's View menu.

# Outlook Profiles Continued

Back in Chapter 11 we customized an Outlook profile using the Office 2000 Custom Installation Wizard. I promised then that we'd pick up on the topic in this chapter. This time, instead of dealing with Outlook profiles in the abstract, we'll take a hands-on look at them using our Outlook 2000 client.

You'll remember that profiles determine what e-mail system you can access and provide you with special features such as personal folders and special address books. Each Outlook 2000 user can have one or many personal Outlook profiles. You can set up different Outlook profiles so that each allows access to a different Exchange mailbox or to one or more Internet mail services or to a combination of an Exchange mailbox and Internet mail services or...you name it.

Be sure that Outlook 2000 is closed. Then right-click the Microsoft Outlook icon on your desktop and select properties from the menu that pops up. This opens your Outlook properties dialog box (see Figure 12.8). Your default profile is displayed. We'll talk about default profiles in a bit.

**FIGURE 12.8:**

The Outlook properties dialog box

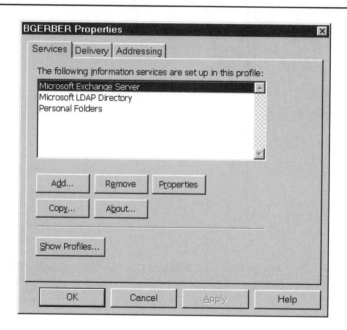

Click Show Profiles to open a dialog box for managing your profiles. Figure 12.9 shows this dialog box. To add a profile, click Add. This opens up the Microsoft Outlook Setup Wizard (see Figure 12.10). Let's step through the Wizard.

**FIGURE 12.9:**

The Outlook profiles properties dialog box

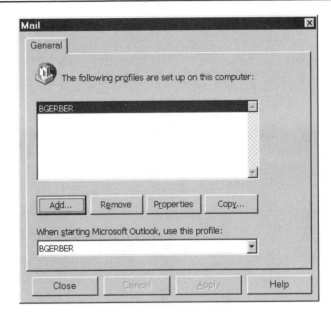

**FIGURE 12.10:**

The Microsoft Outlook Setup Wizard

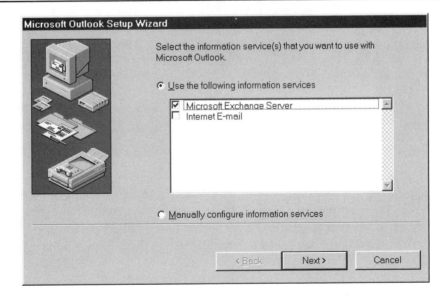

You use the first panel of the Outlook Setup Wizard to select the e-mail system or systems you want to access through your new profile. Select Microsoft Exchange Server. When you're an Outlook profile wizard in your own right, you can bypass the Wizard by selecting Manually Configure Information Services at the bottom of the first panel.

In the second Wizard panel, you name your profile (refer to Figure 12.11). I'm naming my new profile BarryGerber. You'll see why in just a bit. In the next panel of the Outlook Setup Wizard, you indicate the Exchange server and mailbox you want to use (see Figure 12.12). I've created a new mailbox called BGerber2 for this profile. You can enter either the mailbox name or the display name for the mailbox in the Mailbox field.

**FIGURE 12.11:**

Naming a new Outlook profile

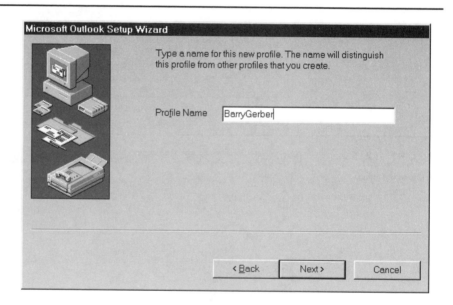

The next Wizard panel lets you configure your profile to support mobile computers (see Figure 12.13). If you answer yes here, the profile will support synchronizing your Exchange Server–based folders for e-mail, contacts, to-do lists, etc. to local files on your computer's hard disk. Then, when you're at home or in an airplane and not connected to the network, you'll still be able to access your Outlook messages, contacts, etc. A yes answer also allows you to compose e-mail messages while you're not connected to the network. When you reconnect, the messages you've composed are sent. I love this capability. In fact, I'm going to use it this very day, as I travel up to Silicon Valley to visit some of GerCom's customers.

FIGURE 12.12:

Specifying the Exchange server and mailbox for the new profile

FIGURE 12.13:

Setting the new profile to support folder synchronization

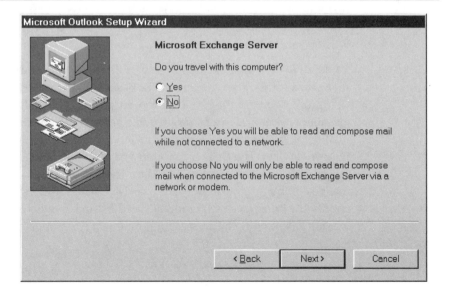

If you're concerned about how your users will access their e-mail, contacts, etc. if your network should go down, consider enabling folder synchronization on their fixed workstations. That way, should the network crash, users can still open Outlook and use whatever folders they've synchronized. More on picking folders to be synchronized later in this chapter.

The last Wizard panel tells you what services have been installed. Click Finish to save your profile and leave the Wizard.

Now let's take a look at your new profile. After you click Finish on the Outlook Setup Wizard, you should see the Outlook profiles manager (refer back to Figure 12.9).

Before you do anything else, notice the drop-down menu at the bottom of the Outlook profiles manager (see Figure 12.9). You use it to select which profile you want to be active (in this case, the default profile) when you start up Outlook. If you need to change the default profile, then before starting Outlook, right-click the Microsoft Outlook icon on your desktop, bring up the Outlook profiles manager, and select the default profile you want from the drop-down. When you start up Outlook, the profile you choose will control your Outlook session. Later in this chapter, I'll show you how to force Outlook to ask you which profile to use when it starts up.

Okay. Now, double-click your new profile and you should see the properties dialog box for your profile. Figure 12.14 shows the properties dialog box for my new profile. You use the Services property page of this dialog box to view and alter existing services and to add services like personal folders or support for Internet mail or for the Internet's Lightweight Directory Access Protocol. You can also remove services. The Delivery property page on the dialog box lets you specify where messages should be delivered for this profile, for example, into an Exchange mailbox or into private folders if they exist. Use the Addressing property page to specify the order in which Outlook should search contact lists and address books when it's looking up addresses for e-mail you're composing.

FIGURE 12.14:

The dialog box for a
specific profile

FIGURE 12.14:

The dialog box for a
specific profile

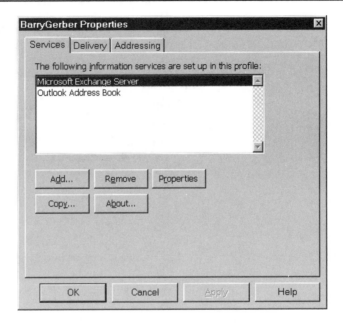

I'll leave it to you to explore most of these profile configuration options. Let's focus here on Exchange Server properties. Double-click the Exchange Server service. Figure 12.15 shows the General property page of the Exchange Server properties dialog box. Here you can indicate whether you want your Outlook 2000 client to automatically detect whether it can connect to your Exchange server or default to an offline or network-based connectivity mode. And you can set the timeout period after which Outlook will assume it can't connect to your Exchange server and open in offline mode.

You can also use the General property page of the Exchange Server properties dialog box to check to see if your Exchange server and mailbox are available. Just delete and retype all or part of what's in the Microsoft Exchange server or Mailbox field. At this point, your mailbox name will no longer be underlined. Then click Check Name. If all is well and Outlook can connect to your Exchange server and your mailbox, your mailbox name will again be underlined. This is a very useful way to check connectivity when you're setting up a new Exchange Server/Outlook 2000 user.

**FIGURE 12.15:**

The Exchange Server
properties dialog box

On the Advanced property page you can open additional mailboxes so that you can access them in Outlook at the same time as your own mailbox. We'll use this capability later in this chapter. You can also use the Advanced property page to set encryption options for different kinds of connectivity, choose the kind of network security you'll use, and set up offline access to synchronized folders. We'll look at the latter capability later in this chapter. I'll let you work through the other options on your own.

The Dial-Up Networking property page is used to specify parameters for direct dial-up connectivity between your Outlook client and your Exchange server. This is different from dialing up to your network or to an Internet Service Provider and using a generic NetBEUI or TCP/IP link to connect to your Exchange server and other applications like a Web server.

You can use the Remote Mail property page to designate how Outlook will act when it contacts your Exchange server through a direct dial-up connection you've set up on the Dial-Up Networking property page. For example, you can download only message headers (sender, subject, date, time, etc.) and then choose which messages to download in their entirety. I'll leave it to you to follow through on direct dial-up networking and remote mail settings.

Well, that's about it for Outlook profiles. Let me close with one follow up thought. Back in Chapter 10, I showed you how to automatically send the NT Backup log to yourself or others using the program MAPISEND.EXE. In the sidebar that discussed all this stuff at the end of the chapter, I promised that you'd learn more about Outlook profiles in Chapter 12. You have and you should now know all you need to create a profile to implement the little project in the sidebar in Chapter 10.

# Creating a New Public Folder

Remember that Exchange public folders are created by mailbox users in their clients. For coming chapters we're going to need a public folder or two, so I want to show you how to create one now.

Open your Outlook client and make sure that the folder list is displayed. Next, double-click Public Folders in the folder list, or click the plus-sign icon just in front of Public Folders. Do the same for the All Public Folders subfolder. Your client window should look something like the one in Figure 12.16. (Notice that the little plus sign becomes a minus sign when a folder is expanded to show the folders within it.)

**FIGURE 12.16:**

The top level folder for public folders and two default subfolders

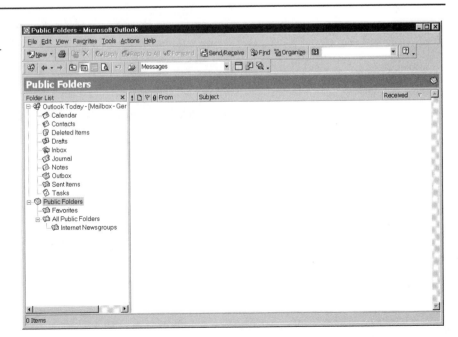

You've opened the top level folder for public folders, which contains two subfolders: Favorites and All Public Folders. The All Public Folders folder has one subfolder, Internet Newsgroups. If your Exchange organization has a large number of public folders, you can drag the ones you use a lot to your Favorites subfolder. This makes them easier to find. Folders in the Favorites folder are also the only ones that are available when you work offline without a connection to your Exchange server.

You create new public folders in the folder All Public Folders. So click All Public Folders and then select New ➢ Folder from your Outlook client's File menu. This brings up the Create New Folder dialog box (see Figure 12.17). Enter a name for the folder; I've given mine the somewhat unimaginative name Barry's First Public Folder. When you're done, click OK.

If you're told you don't have sufficient permissions to create the folder, you'll need to give yourself those permissions in the Exchange Administrator. See the section in Chapter 9 about top-level folder creation (it's near Figure 9.21).

**FIGURE 12.17:**

Naming a new folder

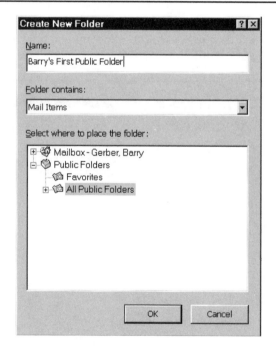

Have you noticed that public folder Internet Newsgroups? It was created when I
installed Exchange Server back in Chapter 7. It'll hold USENET newsgroups and
their messages when I begin using newsgroup services in Chapter 18.

The new public folder now shows up under the All Public Folders hierarchy
(see Figure 12.18). If you can't see the full name of your new folder, use the splitbar (which I discussed in Chapter 8) to make the folder list a little larger.

Now right-click your new folder and select Properties from the pop-up menu.
This brings up the Properties dialog box for the folder, shown in Figure 12.19.

**FIGURE 12.18:**

The new folder in the All
Public Folders hierarchy

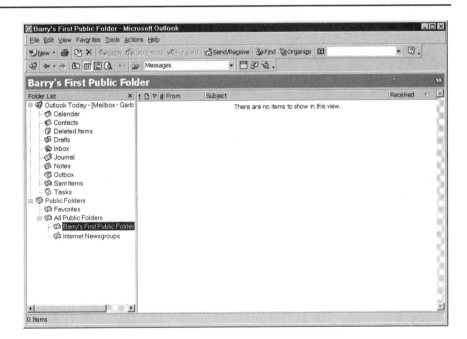

**FIGURE 12.19:**

The Outlook client's Properties dialog box for a public folder

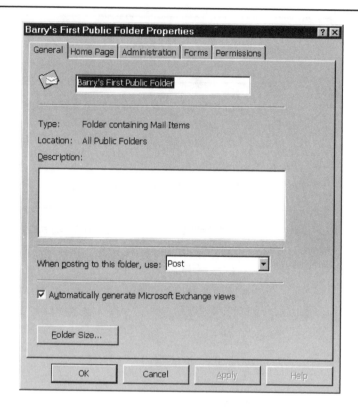

We're not going to spend a lot of time with this dialog box. Among other things, mailbox owners use public folder Properties dialog boxes to do the following:

- Add a description for other mailbox owners who access the folder
- Make the folder available on the Internet
- Set up views of the folder based on specific column title bars
- Set up some administrative rules on folder characteristics, access, and such
- Manage those neat electronic forms I talked about earlier
- Set permissions for using the folder

Go ahead and look around in the Properties dialog box. When you're done, click Cancel, unless you've made some changes. If you have, then click OK to save your changes.

You create and manage private folders inside of mailboxes in the same way you create and manage public folders. 'Nuff said.

Now let's take a look at our new public folder from an Exchange administrator's point of view. Open the Exchange Administrator, then open the Folders container just under the organization container, and finally open the Public Folders container. Your Administrator screen should look pretty much like the one in Figure 12.20, and you should see the folder you just created in the Public Folders hierarchy.

Next, click your new public folder and select Properties from the Administrator's File menu. This brings up a dialog box you've seen before: the Administrator's Properties dialog box for a public folder—in this case, your new public folder (see Figure 12.21). The last time you saw this dialog box, back in Chapter 9, we were working with one of my public folders, since you didn't have any at the time. Now that you've got your own folder, you might want to go back over Chapter 9's section on public folder management. Go ahead. I'll wait. I promise.

**FIGURE 12.20:**

Finding a public folder in the Exchange Administrator

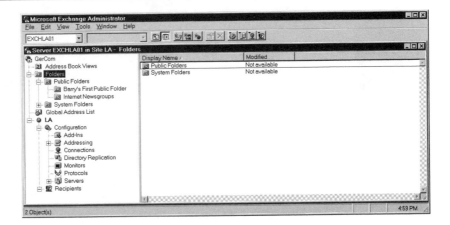

**FIGURE 12.21:**

The Exchange Administrator's Properties dialog box for a public folder

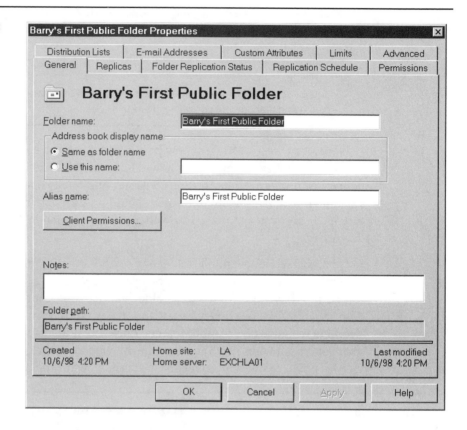

## Public Folders: Now You See 'Em, Now You Don't

Remember how public folders are hidden from the Address Book when they're created? That means they're also hidden from the container that holds them. Check it out. Look in the recipients container your public folders are stored in. (Unless you've changed the default, it's the Recipients container for your site.) The folder is nowhere to be seen. And because your public folder isn't visible in the Recipients container, it's also not visible in your site address list or in the Global Address List, which is based on the contents of site-level recipients containers.

To make your public folder visible, tab over to the Advanced property page on the Properties dialog box for your folder and deselect Hide from Address Book. Now you'll see it in the Global Address List and the Recipients container.

*continuued on next page*

Though it's hidden from the Address Book, the folder is still visible to all in the Outlook client Public Folder hierarchy. While in an Outlook client, the folder owner can use the Permissions property page (on the folder's Properties dialog box discussed above) to limit access to the folder. Those who don't have access to the folder can still see it, but they can't access items in the folder or put new items into it. Those with no access to a folder's contents also can't see subfolders within the folder. You can hide the folder from the public folders list by deselecting the Folder Visible property on the folder's permissions tab. Then only users you've specifically given access can see the folder from their Outlook clients.

# Creating, Accessing, and Using a Shared Mailbox

As I mentioned in Chapter 2, you can create special mailboxes to support the activities of small groups of people who work together.

Say a small local committee is set up to recruit a new plant manager to replace the old manager. By setting up a mailbox that all members of the committee can access and then hiding that mailbox from Exchange address books, the group can work together assured of a fair amount of privacy.

Shared but unhidden mailboxes can work well for other applications. For example, users could send questions to a mailbox shared by help-desk personnel. To organize the help-desk function, subfolders could be created in the mailbox to hold each person's active and inactive items. A help-desk coordinator could even be made responsible for assigning questions to different personnel. An assignment would be as easy as dragging a new message into a specific user's subfolders. Public folders also can be used to implement these sorts of applications, especially if you make use of the Folder Visible property, which lets only specified mailbox owners see the folder.

## Creating a Shared Mailbox

You create a shared mailbox in Exchange Server's Administrator program and access it through your Outlook client. Open the Administrator and select New

Mailbox from the File menu. (By now you should be quite familiar with the Properties box for mailboxes.) Fill in a name for the mailbox. As you can see in Figure 12.22, I'm calling mine HR Committee #1.

Just let the Exchange Administrator create a new NT account for the mailbox. No one is going to log directly into the mailbox. Several people will open it in addition to their existing mailbox. You just have to give those people User permissions for the new mailbox. You do this on the new mailbox's Permissions property page (see Figure 12.23). When you click either Apply or OK to record your new mailbox entry in the Exchange directory, the Administrator program gives you the opportunity to associate an NT account with a mailbox. Just click Cancel in the Primary Windows NT Account dialog box to skip this option and create the mailbox without associating it with a primary NT account.

---

**NOTE**

Depending on the option you've chosen for creating display names and aliases, you may have to alter the default names that the Administrator suggests to get the display name or alias you want. That's quite easy to do: Just delete the suggested name you don't like and then type in the name you want.

---

**FIGURE 12.22:**

Creating a shared mailbox

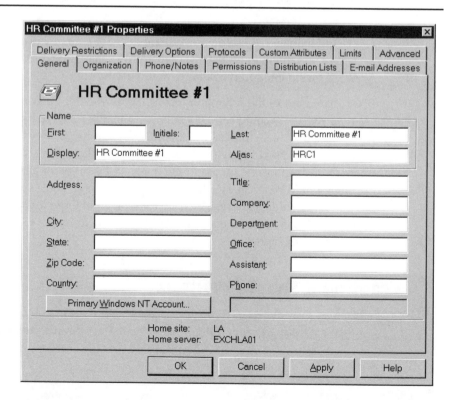

**FIGURE 12.23:**

Giving NT users and groups access to a shared mailbox

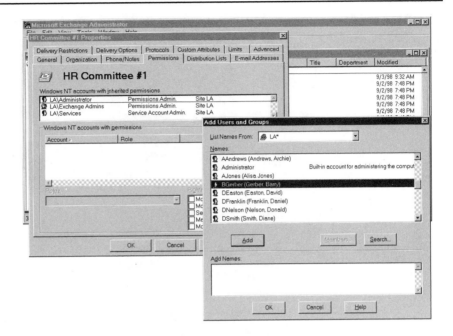

<table>
<tr><td>**WARNING**</td><td>Don't take on the management role for every shared mailbox you create; let the mailbox users do this collectively or by assigning the responsibility to one of them. Users can grant various levels of access permission for the mailbox, and they can remove these permissions as well. I'll show you how this is done a little later in this chapter.</td></tr>
</table>

That's it. You've created a mailbox that can be shared by a group of users. Now you need to tell your Outlook client to open the mailbox when it starts up and add its address to your Personal Address Book. After we do that, I'll show you how to hide the mailbox from the address book for privacy.

## Accessing a Shared Mailbox

Now go to your Outlook client. As you go along, keep an eye on Figure 12.24.

**FIGURE 12.24:**

Telling an Outlook client to open additional mailboxes when starting up

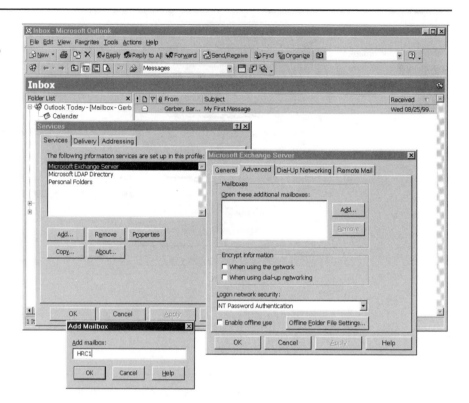

From the Tools menu in the Outlook client's main window, select Services. Be sure that Microsoft Exchange Server is selected in the Services dialog box, then click the Properties button in the Services dialog box.

Select the Advanced property page tab on the dialog box labeled Microsoft Exchange Server. In the Mailboxes area, click Add to add another mailbox to be opened. Enter the mailbox's name in the Add Mailbox field in the Add Mailbox dialog box. Click OK when you're done, and the mailbox's display name will be added to the Open These Additional Mailboxes field (see Figure 12.25). If you try to open the mailbox in an Outlook client but don't have the correct permissions, you'll get an error.

FIGURE 12.25:

A shared mailbox will now be opened when an Outlook client starts up.

To get back to the Services dialog box, click OK in the Microsoft Exchange Server dialog box and then click OK in the Services dialog box to complete your work. The new mailbox now shows up in the folder list in the middle pane of your Outlook client's main window. Click the plus-sign icon to the left of the mailbox's name to open the mailbox and see the standard folders included in it (see Figure 12.26).

Now let's add the mailbox to your Personal Address Book. Click the Address Book icon in your Outlook client's main window (the icon looks like a little book, as shown in Figure 12.26). This brings up the address book. Find the mailbox, click it, and then click the Add to Personal Address Book icon (see Figure 12.27). That's it. The mailbox is now in your Personal Address Book.

**FIGURE 12.26:**

A new shared mailbox shows up in an Outlook client's folder list

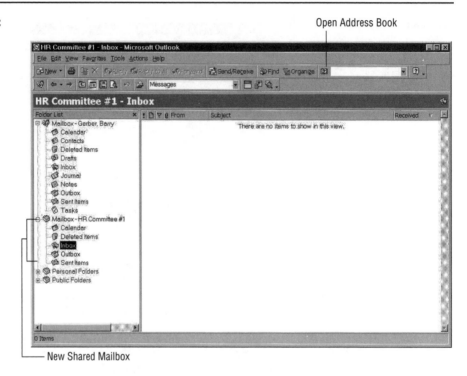

New Shared Mailbox

**FIGURE 12.27:**

Adding a shared mailbox to your Personal Address Book

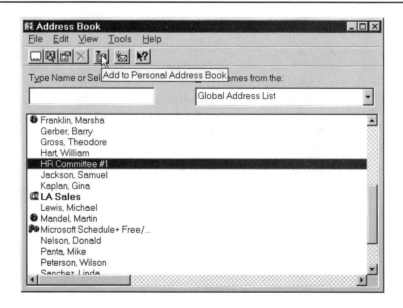

**NOTE**    To grant other recipients access to your shared mailbox, right-click the shared mailbox when you're in your Outlook client and then select Properties. This brings up a Properties dialog box for the mailbox. Tab over to the Permissions property page and click Add. You'll get a standard Address Book dialog box. Pick the recipients you want to add from the dialog box, such as a mailbox, distribution list, custom recipient, or a public folder, then click OK. Once you've added a recipient to the Permissions property page, you can grant it many different roles—ranging from None, which allows no access to the folder at all; to Reviewer, which allows read access to the folder but not write access; to Owner, which gives full read, write, and change permissions control over the mailbox.

## Hiding a Shared Mailbox from the Address Book

You don't have to hide a shared mailbox from the Address Book. You certainly wouldn't want to hide the help-desk mailbox I talked about above, for example. However, if you've created the mailbox for a sensitive purpose like that of our human resources mailbox—and there's no reason for others to see it—you're better off hiding it. That way others won't even know it exists, and they won't be able to send messages to it either purposely or unintentionally.

Once you and any other users have added the shared mailbox to your Personal Address Books, you can go ahead and hide the mailbox from the address list.

**WARNING**    If you hide the mailbox before trying to add it to Personal Address Books, you won't be able to select it from the Global Address List or the site's Address Book. You'll have to add the address manually using the little Rolodex-card icon on the Address Book toolbar.

Here's how to hide the mailbox. In the Exchange Administrator, find the mailbox in the Recipients container and double-click it to bring up its Properties dialog box. Tab over to the Advanced property page and select Hide from Address Book (see Figure 12.28). When you're done, click OK. Now, in your Outlook client, open the Global Address List or the site's Address Book. The mailbox is no longer there.

**FIGURE 12.28:**

Hiding a shared mailbox from the Address Book

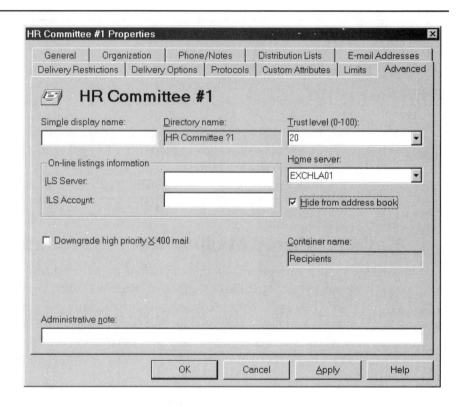

## Sending a Message to a Shared Mailbox

Okay, let's send a message to the shared mailbox. Click the New Mail Message icon. This brings up a New Message window. Click the To button, then click the Show Names from the drop-down box and select Personal Address Book. Double-click the shared mailbox's name and click OK. Add a subject and some text for the body of the message, then click the Send icon on the New Message window to send the message.

Within a second or two, the message is delivered to the shared mailbox. Click the mailbox's Inbox and you should see the message. Double-click the message to read it. That's it. Pretty neat, huh?

# Using Outlook 2000's E-Mail Menus

To conclude this chapter, we'll take a quick tour of the e-mail menus for the main window of an Outlook 2000 client. These menus apply to Outlook's Deleted Items, Drafts, Inbox, and Outbox folders.

My goal here is merely to highlight the capabilities of Outlook as an e-mail client, not to teach you how to use all the options on the Outlook e-mail menus. To save time, I'll skip over obvious items you should know about from using other Windows applications, such as the File menu's Page Setup, Print Preview, and Print options or the Edit menu's Cut, Copy, and Paste options. And I won't be discussing the menus for new and received messages here—partly because some of what's in them was covered as we looked at message menus earlier in this chapter, and partly because I don't want to turn this into a full-blown tutorial on Outlook clients.

---

**NOTE**      Menus for non–e-mail Outlook-created folders in a mailbox have a lot in common with their e-mail brethren. However, they also have their own special options. For example, the Calendar folder's File menu includes an option to save your calendar as a Web page for viewing by others. I'll leave to you the joy of discovering all the neat non–e-mail folder options.

---

## The File Menu

The Outlook 2000 File menu is shown in Figure 12.29. If you see a little downward-pointing double arrow at the bottom of the menu, it means that all of the selections on the menu aren't being displayed. To display all selections, wait a second or two or move your mouse pointer over the double arrow and leave it there for a second. The menu will bloom open and you'll see all of the menu's options.

**FIGURE 12.29:**

The File menu of an Outlook client's main window

### New

The New submenu on the Outlook 2000 File menu holds a whole bunch of exciting options. Here you can start a new message or enter a new item for Outlook's calendar, contact manager, task list, journal, or notes folder. You can also select forms or templates to use in messages, or even create a new folder.

A number of functions on the New submenu can also be initiated by clicking a button (for example, the New Mail Message button on the main Toolbar) or by right-clicking an object and selecting an option (for example, to create a new subfolder).

### Open

The File menu Open option in most applications is pretty boring. This is not the case with Outlook 2000. Of course, you can open (display) messages in a folder by highlighting and selecting the Selected Items option on the Open submenu. But, what's really interesting is the option that lets you open select folders in another user's mailbox. Assuming you've been given rights to do so, you can open one or more of the following folders in another's mailbox: Inbox, Calendar, Contacts, Journal, Notes, or Tasks. I often use this option to make calendar folders for scheduling rooms and other resources available to Exchange Server users.

**TIP**
To allow someone to access one of your folders, right-click the folder and select Properties from the pop-up menu. Select the Permissions property page, click Add, and select the user's name from the Exchange address book.

## Close All Items

If you have a number of messages open, click Close All Items to close all of them.

## Save As

This works pretty much like Save As for files. However, it lets you save an item in a folder as a text file, as an Outlook message file, or as an Outlook template. If the item in a folder is an application file, e.g., a Word document, you can save it to disk as an application file.

## Save Attachments

If a message contains attachments such as spreadsheet files, you can use the Save Attachments submenu to select the attachments you want and save them to disk.

## Folder

Use the Folder submenu to create subfolders; to copy, move, delete, rename, or check the properties of the selected folder; or to add a public folder to the Favorites folder. See Figure 12.16 and related text for more on the Favorites folder. The Folders submenu is also the place to go if you want to copy the design of one folder to another folder. Folder designs include such things as the attributes of messages that are displayed in the columns of a folder and specifications for the way messages are sorted in a folder.

## Share

You can share folders that are not in your mailbox, in other words *private folders*, with anyone you can communicate with by e-mail. The person you want to share with must have installed the Net Folders option that comes with Outlook 98 and 2000. To share a folder, locate the folder you want to share and click it. Then select Share ➢ This Folder from the File menu. A wizard guides you through the folder sharing process. When you're done, those you're sharing with are informed by an e-mail message that sharing is enabled for the folder and they're told how to share the folder. It's all done through e-mail and is pretty nifty.

## Import and Export

Use the Import and Export options to input data into Outlook 2000 from a range of applications such as cc:Mail, Eudora or Netscape mail, ACT!, ECCO, Schedule+, or Sidekick. You can also import data in standard VCARD format (for Outlook 2000 Contacts) or standard iCalendar or vCalendar format (for Outlook 2000 Calendar). Items in a folder can be exported in a variety of file formats including comma delimited and Access and Excel format. Import and Export operates on the currently selected folder.

## Archive

You can save Exchange server storage space by moving Outlook folder contents to an archive Personal Folders file. Use the Archive option to customize the archiving process to your heart's content.

## Properties

Mailboxes, folders, and messages all have properties. Select the message or folder whose properties you want to see and then click Properties. You can also see the properties of most Outlook objects by right-clicking the object and selecting the properties option on the menu that pops up.

## Exit, and Exit and Log Off

Select Exit to leave Exchange while remaining logged in to all information services. You'll use this option when you want to close Outlook 2000 but still want to run other applications that use your information services. Choose Exit and Log Off to leave Outlook and log off of all information services.

# The Edit Menu

The Outlook client's Edit menu is shown in Figure 12.30.

## Move to Folder and Copy to Folder

You can use these menu options to copy or move an item or set of items from the currently selected folder to another folder. You can also move items by highlighting them, right-clicking them, and selecting Move to Folder from the menu that pops up. In addition, you can simply drag highlighted items from one folder to another to move them. If you hold down the Ctrl key while dragging, the items are copied to the second folder instead of being moved to it.

## Mark as Read, Mark as Unread, and Mark All as Read

When a message has not been read, its subject line as seen in a folder appears in bold type. When a message has been read, its subject line is in plain type. Select the messages for which you want to change the read status, then click either of the first two options on the menu as appropriate. Choosing Mark All as Read will mark all messages in the open folder as having been read, regardless of which lines are selected.

## Categories

You can place messages in one or more categories. Categories are used like key words when you search for messages. To categorize one or more messages, select the messages you want to categorize in the message items pane and click Categories on the Edit menu. Then check off the categories you want to use for the message on the Categories dialog box that pops up. You can add new categories by clicking Master Category List on the Categories dialog box.

## The View Menu

The Outlook client's View menu is shown in Figure 12.31.

**FIGURE 12.31:**

The View menu of the Outlook client's main window

### Current View

The Current View submenu lets you view the messages in a folder in a range of interesting ways. For example, with the AutoPreview option selected, the first several lines of each unread message are displayed just below each message's standard message header. AutoPreview saves you time, because you don't have to open each unread message to view its contents and decide whether you need to give it your immediate attention. Among other things, Current View submenu options let you see only the last seven days of messages or sort messages by conversation topic or sender. As you'll see in a bit, you can create your own views that are then available under the Current View submenu.

The Current View submenu also lets you customize your view of the currently selected folder by adding columns (message size, for example) to the view or sorting and grouping by one or more columns (sender or message importance, for example). And, if that weren't enough, you can format the columns that are displayed in a folder and design your own custom views.

## Outlook Bar and Folder List

You'll remember the Outlook Bar and Folder List from earlier discussions in this chapter (see Figures 12.1 and 12.2 and related text). You turn the bars on and off here.

## Preview Pane

The preview pane is a window just below the pane containing messages. The currently highlighted message is displayed in the preview pane window so you don't have to open the message to see what's in it. Click the preview pane button on the View menu to turn the preview pane on or off.

## AutoPreview

The View menu's AutoPreview option shows you each message and the first several lines of each message. AutoPreview differs from the preview pane in that the former shows you all messages in a single pane (message header followed by content), while the latter shows you the message header in the standard message pane and the content in the preview pane.

## Expand/Collapse Groups

If you've set up group by options for columns in a folder, you can use this menu item to expand or collapse the grouped views. As with hierarchies in Outlook 2000's Folder List, groupings that can be expanded are shown with a little plus sign to their left. Expanded groupings have a minus sign in front of them. You can click the pluses and minuses to open and close groupings instead of using the Expand/Collapse Groups option.

## Toolbars

Use the Toolbars submenu to turn Outlook's Standard, Advanced, Remote, and Web Toolbars on or off. The Standard Toolbar is just below the Menu bar on the Outlook client. The Remote Toolbar is used when you connect to your Exchange server with a modem without a direct LAN connection. You can also customize toolbars by adding or removing commands from them and setting a variety of formatting options for them.

### Status Bar

The status bar is at the bottom of the Outlook client's main window. It provides information about the contents of whatever folder is displayed in the window. Back in Figure 12.6, the status bar reads "1 Item, 1 Unread."

## The Favorites Menu

This one's a little weird from my perspective. It's the same view menu you see on Microsoft's Internet Explorer. It shows your favorite Internet sites. When you select a site from the Favorites menu, the message pane (your Inbox, for example) turns into a Web browser.

At first, I thought this was the neatest thing. After the novelty wore off, however, I stopped using the Favorites menu. The Web browser in Outlook doesn't have the same functionality as Internet Explorer. For example, you can't open multiple browser windows simultaneously and once you click any folder in the folder list, your ability to return to the Web page you were looking at in Outlook's Web browser is severely limited.

## The Tools Menu

The Outlook client's Tools menu is shown in Figure 12.32.

### Send, Send/Receive

Send does just what it says—it sends any messages in your Outbox. Send/Receive lets you send to and receive mail from all of your currently defined mail services or pick a service to send to and receive from.

### Synchronize

When you work offline with your Outlook client, you can have an image of your online Exchange Server/Outlook client environment, including items stored in folders, in your mailbox and in public folders. That image is stored in a file outside of your Exchange server. What's included in that file is determined by your folder synchronization setup. You keep this image up to date by synchronizing it with your online environment. You can use this file and its contents whenever you're not connected to the network, whether on a laptop or your stationary workstation.

**FIGURE 12.32:**

The Tools menu of the Outlook client's main window

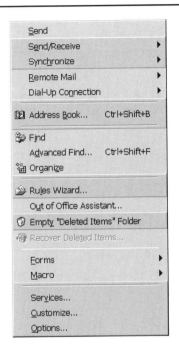

You can synchronize when connected remotely or when connected directly to the network, as you might do with a laptop. If connected remotely by modem and your connection isn't too expensive, you can fire off a synchronization nightly or even set synchronization to happen every few minutes. If you're using a laptop on the road, when you return to the office with your folders full of new items, you can update your online environment by synchronizing it with your offline file. If there are any messages waiting to be sent in your Outbox, they're sent out through your server and any messages waiting for you on the server are copied to your offline folders.

Here's how to set up offline folder synchronization. If you didn't select this option during installation of Outlook 2000 or when setting up a new profile, you must set it up now. Select Services on the Tools menu. Double-click Microsoft Exchange Server on the Services dialog box. This brings up the Microsoft Exchange Server dialog box shown in Figure 12.33. Tab over to the Advanced property page. Click *Enable Offline Use*. Then set the directory where your offline folder file will be stored. If you're not automatically asked for the name and location of the file, click the *Offline Folder File Settings* button right next to Enable Offline Use. Finally, click OK until you've closed the Services dialog box.

**FIGURE 12.33:**

Turning on offline folder synchronization and setting the location of the file to hold offline folders

Next you have to specify which of your Outlook/Exchange private and public folders should be synchronized. You can do this in two different ways.

1.   Right-click any folder and select properties. Tab over to the Synchronization property page in the resultant Properties dialog box, then select When Offline or Online from the page.

2.   Select Tools ➢ Synchronize ➢ Offline Folder Settings. Then select the folders you want to synchronize from the tree on the Offline Folder Settings dialog box (see Figure 12.34).

The second option is new to Outlook 2000. It alone is worth the price of admission if you're a heavy offline folder synchronizer. You have to go through the first option for every folder you want to synchronize. It's a pain, trust me. With the second option, you just check off the folders you want to synchronize from the tree and that's it. Thanks, Microsoft.

**FIGURE 12.34:**

Selecting Outlook folders
for offline synchronization

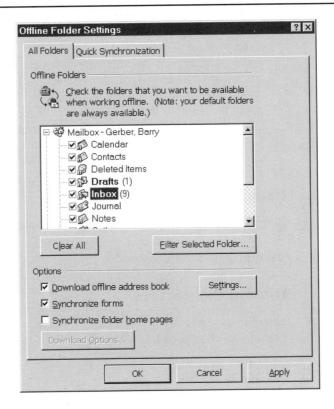

**WARNING**   The *Offline Folder File Settings* option on the Advanced property page of the Microsoft Exchange Server dialog box (Figure 12.33) is quite different from the Offline Folder Settings option (Figure 12.34). The former lets you select the directory where the file that holds your offline folders will be stored. The latter lets you select which folders will be synchronized for offline use. What a difference a word makes.

Next use the Synchronize option on the Tools menu to ensure that your online and offline Outlook client environments are the same. The menu includes a small submenu that lets you synchronize all folders or only the currently selected folder. This submenu also allows you to download the current copy of the offline address book, which we discussed in Chapter 9.

TIP

When setting people up to use an Outlook client at home, I often ask them to bring their workstation to the office. I connect the workstation to the network and set up and perform a synchronization of all folders. For users with big mailboxes, this method is especially nice, because they don't have to run the first and most time-consuming synchronization when connected at home at 56.6Kbps. And don't forget those public folders. Any public folder you drag into the Favorites folder under Public Folders will be copied during synchronization if you've selected the folder for synchronization.

## Remote Mail

Remote mail lets you set your client to do such things as periodically dial up your Exchange server to pick up message headers or messages. The interface is pretty self-explanatory. So have fun.

## Dial-Up Connection

You manage and activate NT Remote Access Service links to Internet Service Providers and to your Exchange server here.

## Address Book

Select the Address Book menu item to see and work with the Address Book. Because you can easily access the Address Book when composing a message, you're most likely to select it from here when you want to add an item to your Personal Address Book. (You can also bring up the Address Book by pressing Ctrl+Shift+B or by clicking the Address Book icon in your Outlook client's main window.)

## Find and Advanced Find

The Find option on the Tools menu opens a quick search pane on Outlook 2000. The pane applies to messages and other items in the currently selected folder. Type in what you want to find, click Find Now, and Outlook shows you messages with the text in the From, Subject, and message body fields.

Advanced Find opens an impressive GUI that lets you specify multiple find criteria including those in the Find command. Advanced Find adds such filters as who the message was sent to, times such as sent time or received time, items with or without attachments; you name it, Outlook 2000's got it.

## Organize

You can organize any folder in a variety of ways by selecting the Organize option on the Tools menu while the folder is selected. Like Find, Organize uses a pane on the Outlook 2000 GUI. You can move messages from the currently selected folder to other folders, set Outlook to display messages in the folder from different senders in different colors, and change the current view that is used with the folder.

## Rules Wizard

The Rules Wizard is a very nice rules-based agent with a helpful graphical user interface. When installed, Exchange Server and Outlook 2000 can perform a wide range of functions with mail that comes into your Inbox—for example, putting the mail into another folder, forwarding a message to another address, or performing a custom action that deals with the message. All these tasks can be based on various properties of the messages, from the sender to the occurrence of specific text in the subject line or body of the message.

## Out of Office Assistant

The Out of Office Assistant is another neat GUI agent that you can use to send an auto-reply message telling people you're out of the office—and letting them know what the consequences might be (for example, that you won't be getting to your mail until a specific date). The Out of Office Assistant generates only one message to a specific message originator during the time you're away from the office. If the original message is sent to an Exchange Server distribution list, the Out of Office Assistant generates out-of-office messages for the list's members, provided the option has been selected in Exchange Administrator on the Advanced property page of the list. The services of the Inbox Assistant are also available as you set up out-of-office message scenarios.

## Empty "Deleted Items" Folder

This one's obvious. The key here is that nothing is deleted until the Outlook 2000 Deleted Items folder is emptied. With Exchange Server 5.5, even that may not be the end of "deleted" items, because you can set up Exchange server so items that are deleted from an Outlook user's Deleted Items folder remain on the Exchange server for a set period of time.

To recover deleted items, click the Deleted Items folder and select *Recover Deleted Items* from the Tools menu. You'll be offered a list of items that can be recovered. Highlight the ones you want and click the little Envelope on the Recover Deleted Items window. Be sure to note the date of the item you're recovering, because the item is silently recovered to your Deleted Items folder. If that folder is full of yet-to-be-deleted items, you might have a difficult time finding the recovered item if you don't know its date. This works best, of course, if your Deleted Items folder is sorted by the default received date.

## Forms

I talked a bit about electronic forms back in Chapter 1 (see Figure 1.10 and surrounding text). I'll go into much more detail about them in Chapter 19. You use the Forms submenu to select existing forms and to create new ones.

## Macro

Using Visual Basic for Applications, you can create macros to do various tasks in your Outlook 2000 client. You create and execute macros from the Macro submenu.

## Services

You use the Services option to add, modify, or delete information services. (You've already used Services to set up access on that shared mailbox you created earlier.)

## Customize

This option lets you customize toolbars and menus.

## Options

The Options item is where users can override many of the default settings. It's also the place to give permission to other recipients to send messages on behalf of yourself, as well as a myriad of other neat functions.

While we're on Options, I'll keep a promise. Remember earlier in this chapter, I promised to show you how to get Outlook 2000 to prompt you for the Outlook profile to use when it starts up. Here's how.

Select Options from the Tools menu and tab over to the Mail Services properties page (see Figure 12.35). Click Prompt for a Profile to Be Used. That's it.

**FIGURE 12.35:**

Setting Outlook 2000 to
prompt on start up for the
Outlook profile to be used

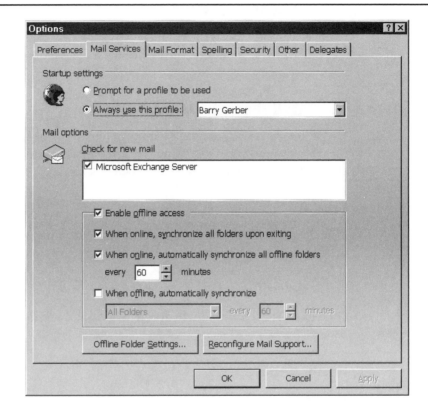

## The Actions Menu

The Outlook client's Actions menu is shown in Figure 12.36.

**FIGURE 12.36:**

The Actions menu of
the Outlook client's main
window

## New Mail Message

Select New Mail Message to compose a message in a new message window. Clicking the New Mail Message icon in the main window or pressing Ctrl+N has the same effect.

## New Mail Message Using

You can create messages with a variety of look and feel options. These range from plain old text messages to messages that use one of the cool-looking pieces of electronic stationery that comes with Outlook 2000.

## Find All

Need to quickly find messages similar to the one you're reading? Highlight a message and select *Related Messages* or *Messages from Sender* on the Find All menu.

## Junk E-Mail

Outlook 2000 has the ability to deal with junk and pornographic messages. You manage this feature here.

## Reply and Reply to All

Use the Reply or Reply to All options to answer a selected or open received message. You can reply either just to the person who sent the message (Reply) or to all its recipients (Reply to All). When working with an open received message, you'll find it far easier to use the message's own Reply and Reply to All icons, which appear on the message's toolbar (see Figure 12.7). You can also use keyboard alternatives: Ctrl+R for Reply to Sender, or Ctrl+Shift+R for Reply to All.

## Forward

The Forward option sends a copy of a received message to one or more other recipients; Ctrl+F is the keyboard alternative. As with replies, it's easier to use the Forward icon on the toolbar of an open received message (see Figure 12.7).

# Conclusion

In this chapter you started up an Outlook 2000 client for the first time. You also learned how to compose, send, and read a message; create and manage Outlook profiles; create a new public folder; and create and access a shared mailbox. Finally, you took a quick tour of your Outlook client's main window.

This concludes the part of this book dedicated to the Outlook 2000 client. Now we're ready to expand our Exchange environment to include additional servers and to administer and manage those servers using the Exchange Administrator program. See you in the next section.

# PART V

# Expanding an Exchange Organization

In Chapter 13 we'll install a second Exchange server in our site. Then we'll look at the tools the Exchange Administrator program provides for administering and managing sites with multiple servers. In Chapter 14 we'll add a third Exchange server. This time, however, we'll install it in a new site in our organization. Then we'll focus on administering and managing a multisite Exchange organization.

# CHAPTER

## THIRTEEN

13

# Administering and Managing Multiserver Exchange Sites

- ■ Adding an Exchange server to a site

- ■ Using the Exchange Administrator in multiserver sites

- ■ Administering and managing multiserver sites

- ■ Exchange Administrator menu items useful in multiserver sites

- ■ Administering and managing the directory service in multiserver sites

- ■ Administering and managing the Message Transfer Agent in multiserver sites

**O**kay, we're finally ready to add a second Exchange server to our site and to start administering and managing it and its older sibling. Generally, you add new servers in a site to handle the load created by additional users or to provide local area network connectivity for a group of users with slower wide-area links to other Exchange servers in the site. We'll be moving pretty fast in this and the following chapter, so fasten your seat belts.

# Installing an Additional Exchange Server in a Site

You've already installed one Exchange server in your site, and installing another is a pretty basic task since it will be almost a carbon copy of the first installation. (You will need a second NT server on which to install Exchange Server.) Instead of going through the second installation in detail, I'll just call your attention to any differences you'll encounter when installing another server in your site. You'll find full details on installing NT Server in Chapter 6 and Exchange Server in Chapter 7.

## Installing an Additional NT Server

For our purposes here, you should install your second server in your existing domain—the one you used for your first installation. (For me, that's my LA domain.)

Before you install your second server, open the program Server Manager in the Administrative Tools program group on your first server or NT domain controller. Select the computer menu and then select the Add to Domain item on the menu. Add the name of your server-to-be. This is a security measure that gives your second server the right to enter the domain. As you'll see, you can also add the new server to the domain while installing it, but going through this little exercise helps you get comfortable with a key level of NT security. Also the directions below depend on your having preadmitted your server-to-be in the domain.

Unless you have a good reason not to, let the second NT server act as a backup domain controller. And don't forget to name the server according to the naming conventions you've set up. (Mine will be called EXCHLA02.) When you're done and your new NT server is up and running, be sure you can see it from your first server. Try connecting to one of the second server's drives from your first using NT server's Network Neighborhood.

---

**WARNING**    It can take a while before your two servers see each other, so wait 15 minutes or so before trying this. At a more basic and immediate level, if you've installed support for TCP/IP, try pinging your new server from your first. (You can run ping from a command prompt. Just type **ping ip_address**, where ip_address is the IP address you assigned to the new server when configuring it for networking.) A successful ping means that at least your adapter and TCP/IP services are working.

---

## Installing an Additional Exchange Server

Run SETUP.EXE from the Exchange Server CD-ROM. When you get to the Organization and Site dialog box, select Join an Existing Site and enter the name of your existing Exchange server. The Setup program will use this information to contact the server and gather information on the site you want to join (see Figure 13.1).

**FIGURE 13.1:**

Exchange Setup's Organization and Site dialog box

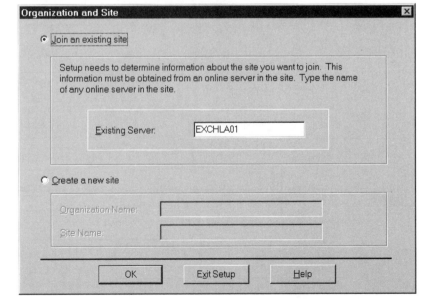

After a short wait, Setup shows you the organization and site information it has found (see Figure 13.2). If the information is correct—and it should be in this case—click Yes to continue.

Next, Setup presents you with the name of Exchange's Site Services account—whichever account you gave as the Services account when you installed your first Exchange server—and asks you to enter its password (see Figure 13.3). Do so and click OK to continue.

Installation will now begin, and it will take a bit longer than your first Exchange server installation. Among other things, once your new Exchange server is up and running, Setup automatically configures directory replication between your two servers and then starts it up. From this point on, the two servers will cross-replicate directory changes automatically. Ain't computers wonderful?

**FIGURE 13.2:**

Confirming Exchange organization and site information

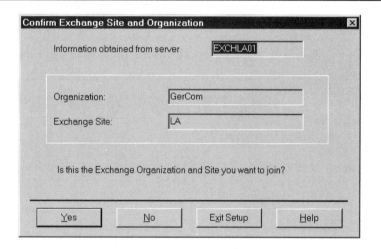

**NOTE**  You don't need to reinstall the Exchange client files. Users of the new Exchange server can install them from your first server.

**FIGURE 13.3:**

Entering a password for the Exchange Site Services account

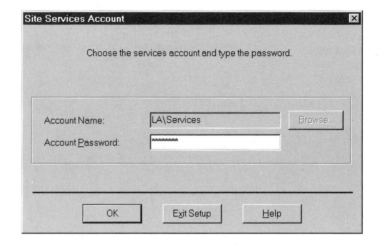

To prove that the installation is working, open the Exchange Administrator program on your first server. You should now see two servers under your site (see Figure 13.4). Now go over to your new server and open its copy of the Administrator. You should see the same two servers, although things will look a little different from how they appear on the first server (see Figure 13.5). I'll talk about the differences shortly.

**FIGURE 13.4:**

The newly installed Exchange server, viewed through the Administrator program running on an already-installed Exchange server

**FIGURE 13.5:**

The newly installed Exchange server, viewed through the Administrator program running on the new server

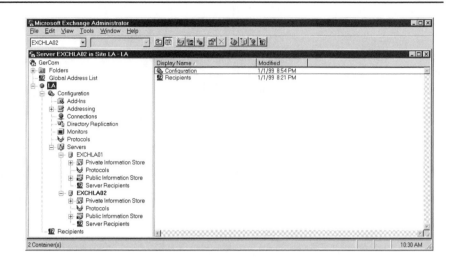

---

**WARNING**   Whichever server you run the Administrator from, you won't see all the details about the other server until directory replication has finished. The replication can take up to an hour—and sometimes even longer—to complete, depending on the size of your first server's directory, the computing power available in each server, and network load. So if you can't see everything, don't assume that something is wrong right off the bat. As long as your two Exchange servers are talking over the network, the core component services are running, and your servers are installed in the same site, in time everything should work fine.

---

# Using the Exchange Administrator in Multiserver Sites

The Exchange Administrator was designed to let you manage a whole Exchange organization from one workstation or server. In this section we'll focus on understanding the concept of the default server, connecting to multiple Exchange servers, and navigating a multiserver site hierarchy.

## The Default Server

In any Exchange server window, one server is the default server. The Administrator program lets you know which one is the default in three ways: The name of the server is displayed in the drop-down list at the top of the Administrator window; the title of the server window shows the server's name; and it's also displayed in bold in the hierarchy tree of the window's left-hand pane.

In Figure 13.4 the server name EXCHLA01 appears in the drop-down list on the Administrator's main window, which means EXCHLA01 is the default server. Also indicating the name of the default server are the server window title Server EXCHLA01 in Site LA—LA and EXCHLA01 in boldface type on the Exchange hierarchy tree.

Figure 13.5 shows the Administrator running on my new server, EXCHLA02. Here the default server is EXCHLA02, as you can see from the drop-down list, the server window title, and the boldface name in the left-hand pane.

Using just the window shown in Figure 13.4 or Figure 13.5, you can administer and manage either of your Exchange servers. Just remember that during some Administrator operations, you'll have to specify an alternative server if you don't want to work with the default. For example, if I'm running the Administrator on my first server (EXCHLA01) and want to add a new mailbox to my second server (EXCHLA02), I would have to override the default home server setting, EXCHLA01, by selecting the new server's name, EXCHLA02, from the Home Server drop-down list on the Advanced property page of the new mailbox's properties dialog box. In Figure 13.6, I've popped down the Home Server list so I can make EXCHLA02 the home server for the new mailbox I'm creating for John Lewis.

**FIGURE 13.6:**

Setting the home server for a new mailbox when the home server is to be different from the default server

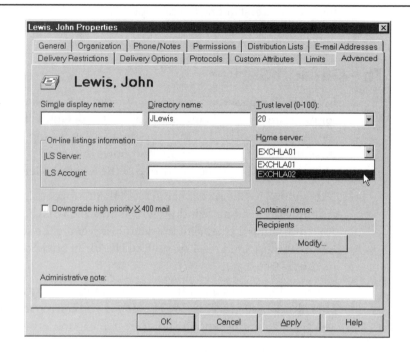

## Connecting to Multiple Exchange Servers

If you need to create a lot of mailboxes, you might find it easier to physically go to your other server (EXCHLA02 in my case), rather than changing the home server while you create each new mailbox. That's no problem if the other server is nearby. But if it's not, there's a much easier solution: By opening a window connected to your second server, you can administer and manage your Exchange system with the second server as the default server.

To open additional server windows, select the Connect to Server item from the Administrator's File menu. This brings up the Connect to Server dialog box. Type in the name of the Exchange server you want to connect to, or click Browse to open the Server Browser dialog box and find the server in your Exchange hierarchy (see Figure 13.7). If you use the Server Browser, click OK when you're done and then click OK again in the Connect to Server dialog box. (In my case, I'm on EXCHLA01 and I'm opening a connection to EXCHLA02.)

**FIGURE 13.7:**

Opening a new window on an Exchange server

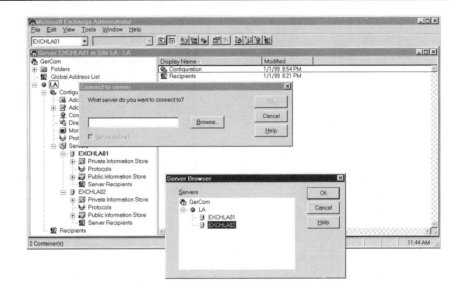

A new window now opens on the server you choose; in Figure 13.8, it's the lower window. Notice that the Administrator's server name drop-down list, the server window's title for EXCHLA02, and the boldface name in the hierarchy tree tell me that my default server is EXCHLA02.

If I now attempt to create a mailbox in the new window, all is well. The default home server is my second server, EXCHLA02 (see Figure 13.9).

This game of "musical windows" may be interesting, but what you should take away from this section—above all else—is the sense that you can administer and manage your Exchange servers from anywhere within your site. "Anywhere" means from any Exchange server or even from an NT workstation that has network connectivity to your Exchange servers, because, remember, you can install the Administrator on your NT workstation and access all the servers in your site from there.

**FIGURE 13.8:**

The Exchange Administrator with a new server window opened

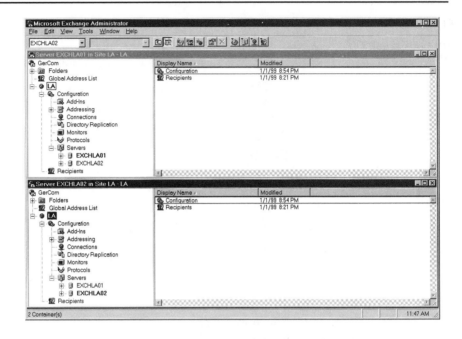

**FIGURE 13.9:**

When a mailbox is created in the second Exchange server's window, that server is offered as the default home server.

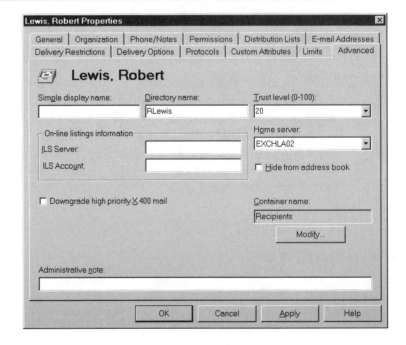

**NOTE**  I hope you've noticed that you didn't have to grant any special rights to your new server before you could access it with the Administrator and that your two servers were able to talk to each other and replicate their directories without receiving such rights. That's because of three things: Both servers are in the same NT domain; the Exchange Admins group (which you created back in Chapter 7) has permissions to administer and manage all Exchange servers in the site; and the servers share a common Site Services account. It works differently when your servers are in different domains and sites, as we'll see in the next chapter.

## Navigating the Site Configuration Hierarchy

As I'm sure you realized back in Chapter 9, administering and managing Exchange servers is largely a matter of finding the correct configuration tool in the hierarchy of the Administrator window's left-hand pane. Figure 13.10 shows some of the site-relevant configuration options you have with Exchange Server.

**FIGURE 13.10:**

Site-based configuration options displayed by Exchange Server's Administrator program

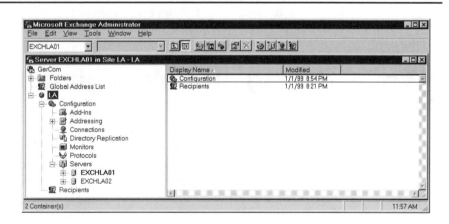

To see some configuration options, you have to select the container that holds them. For example, selecting the Configuration container shows you all the options it contains (see Figure 13.11).

**FIGURE 13.11:**

A closer look at the options
in the Configuration
container

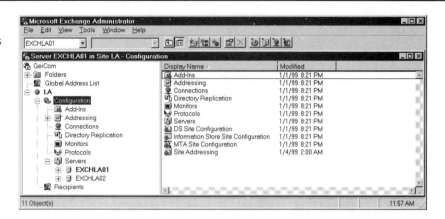

**FIGURE 13.11:**

A closer look at the options
in the Configuration
container

Because some of the options in the Configuration container are suboptions—
Addressing, for example—they are shown in the tree below the Configuration
container (in the left-hand pane) as well as in the Configuration container (right-
hand pane). Other options such as DS Site Configuration have no suboptions, so
they show up only in the Configuration container itself (in the right-hand pane).

# Administering and Managing
# Multiserver Sites

Remember all the times we bypassed an item in the Administrator program's
menus or skipped an opportunity to configure one of Exchange's core components? Well, now we can turn our attention to some of these items—the ones that
are relevant to multiserver sites. We'll also look at some stuff I haven't talked
about yet. When we're done here, you'll at least know what every site-relevant
configuration item is all about.

> **NOTE**
>
> As in earlier chapters, when we've already beaten a particular property page to
> death, I'll generally bypass the page silently.

# Administrator Menu Items in Multiserver Sites

Right now we need to discuss two options in the Administrator's File menu: server monitors and link monitors.

## Server Monitors

When I talked about server monitors in Chapter 8, we passed over the Clock property page. Well, now's the time to get to it, using the server monitor we created back in that chapter. If yours is running, stop it by closing its window.

### Adding a New Server to a Server Monitor

Before you can make use of the Clock property page, you've got to add your new server to your server monitor. So let's open the monitor now; you'll find it in the Monitors container in the left-hand pane of the Administrator window. Click the Monitors container, double-click your monitor to open its Properties dialog box, and then tab over to the Servers property page. Click your new server and then click Add to move the server to the Monitored Servers box (see Figure 13.12).

**FIGURE 13.12:**

Adding an Exchange server to a server monitor

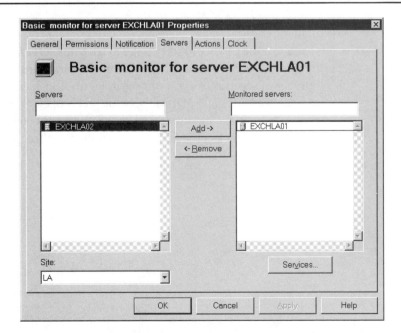

## The Server Monitor's Clock Property Page

The clocks on the Exchange servers in an Exchange organization should be kept as closely synchronized as possible. Among other things, good clock synchronization means that sent and received messages will be stamped with accurate times; it also helps ensure accurate replication of directories and public folders.

A server monitor can watch the clocks of the Exchange servers that it's responsible for and keep their clocks in sync with the clock on its own server. It can even take time-zone differences into account, using NT's time-zone information.

### Synchronizing Lots of Clocks

As your Exchange network grows, think about running secondary or backup server monitors for redundancy. On the other hand, try not to assign clock synchronization responsibilities for the same Exchange server to too many monitors. If you do, you'll wind up with an unmanageable plate of server-monitor spaghetti.

Hey, this is starting to sound pretty complicated. The best way to get a handle on clock synchronization is to lay out a diagram on paper. You can start with the server locations and connectivity diagrams from Chapter 5; they'll give you a good sense of the way your servers cluster and communicate. From there you can select your monitoring and monitored servers and determine which are the best candidates to run primary and backup monitors.

You use the Clock property page to tell your server monitor what to do if a monitored server's clock deviates from the monitoring server's clock by a specific number of seconds. As you can see in Figure 13.13, you can ask a server monitor to issue warnings and alerts at specific levels of clock deviation. You can also choose to have the monitor synchronize the errant clock with its own clock. It's usually best to select the Synchronize option for both warning and alert states.

Setting parameters to keep
Exchange server clocks in
synchronization

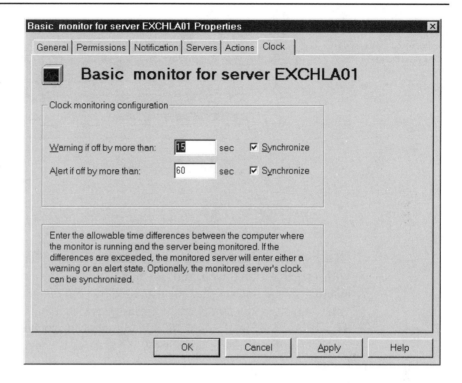

Be sure that your Clock property page looks like the one in Figure 13.13 and
click OK in the monitor's properties dialog box. Then restart your monitor by
selecting Start Monitor from the Administrator's Tools menu. Your server monitor should look something like the one in Figure 13.14. The clocks are synchronized. The Comment column of the Monitor window indicates when things are
OK or not. Right now they're OK as indicated by the message "The server is running" for both servers. When the monitor started for the first time, the clock for
EXCHLA02 was 10 minutes out of sync with the clock on EXCHLA01. After 30
minutes, all is well.

**FIGURE 13.14:**

A server monitor keeps clocks synchronized.

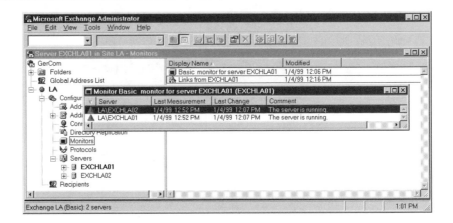

Of course, you should keep the clock on the monitor's host server synchronized with a reliable time source. You can manually keep the clock in sync with an external source, such as the time provided by your telephone company or, if you're a real stickler for accuracy, the atomic clock maintained by the United States Bureau of Standards. Alternatively, you can synchronize the clock with another server monitor whose host server's clock is in sync with an external time source.

## Synchronizing Clocks to a Standard Time Source

To ensure that the clocks are accurate on my clock-monitoring Exchange servers, I use the program TIMESERV.EXE that comes in the NT Resource Kit. Using NT's Task Scheduler (see Chapter 10), I schedule TIMESERV.EXE to run daily on the clock-monitoring servers and, voila, no more time-drift problems across my Exchange system. Check the Resource Kit for more info on TIMESERV.EXE.

## Link Monitors

Link monitors watch connections between multiple Exchange servers as well as between Exchange servers and foreign e-messaging systems. Like server monitors, they can notify you of problems in a variety of ways.

To set up a link monitor, select Link Monitor from the New Other submenu of the Administrator's File menu. This opens the link monitor's properties dialog box (see Figure 13.15).

**FIGURE 13.15:**

The link monitor's properties dialog box

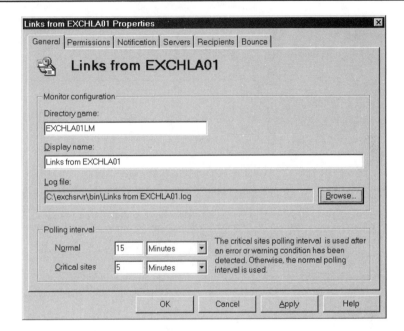

Fill in the Directory Name and Display Name fields. It took me a while to come up with a naming convention for this. Here's my logic for choosing the display name Links from EXCHLA01: I'll be running this monitor from the EXCHLA01 server. The monitor will check all links from EXCHLA01 to other servers and for-eign e-messaging systems. For redundancy, I'll also run monitors on other servers in my LA site. The one I run on EXCHLA02 will be called Links from EXCHLA02. Make sense?

Set a log file name. It's a good idea to give it the same name as the monitor itself. Then set the polling interval—that is, how frequently the monitor will check links. You can leave the default settings for now. (For more on monitor polling intervals, see Chapter 8.)

When you're done with the link monitor's General property page, tab over to the Notification page, which will look something like the one in Figure 13.16. This property page works just like the Notification page for a server monitor. Let's quickly set up a mail notification. Click New, select Mail Message from the New Notification dialog box, and click OK (see Figure 13.17).

FIGURE 13.16:

The link monitor's Notification property page

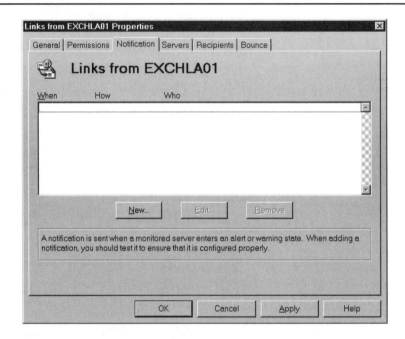

FIGURE 13.16:

The link monitor's Notification property page

FIGURE 13.17:

Selecting a notification type in the New Notification dialog box

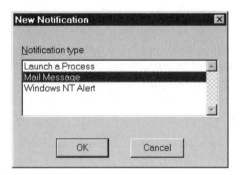

Next you'll see the Escalation Editor dialog box shown in Figure 13.18. Deselect the Alert Only check box if you want messages to be sent when the link monitor enters both warning and alert states.

**FIGURE 13.18:**

Setting rules for escalation upon a link failure

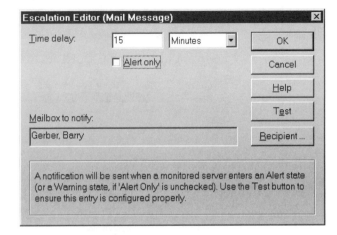

To select a mailbox to notify, click Recipient and choose a mailbox from the Address Book dialog box that pops up. When you're done, click OK in the Escalation Editor dialog box. At this point your Notification property page should look something like the one in Figure 13.19.

Now tab over to the Servers property page (see Figure 13.20). Highlight each server link you want monitored, then click Add to add the server(s) to the Monitored Servers list.

Link monitors are able to automatically check connections to other Exchange servers in an Exchange organization. The Recipients property page, shown in Figure 13.21, is used to check links to foreign e-messaging systems, including other Exchange organizations. Basically, the link monitor sends a message to a valid or invalid address in the foreign system. Then it waits for an automatically generated reply from a valid recipient in the foreign system or, if the message was sent to an invalid address, for a non-delivery message from the foreign system. Either response can be taken as proof that the foreign system is up and running.

**FIGURE 13.19:**

A completed Notification property page

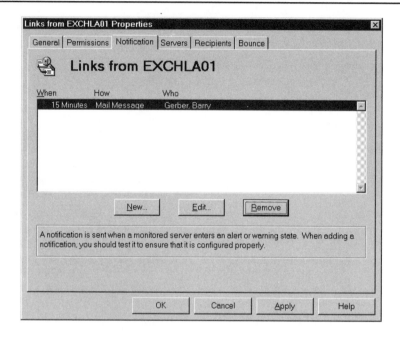

**FIGURE 13.20:**

Selecting server links to be monitored

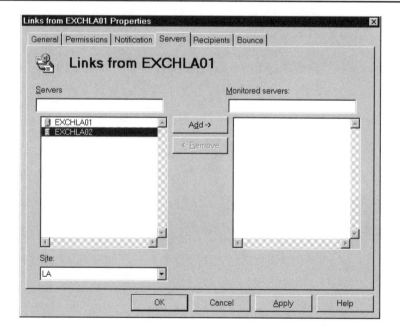

**FIGURE 13.21:**

The Recipients property page is used to check links to foreign e-messaging systems.

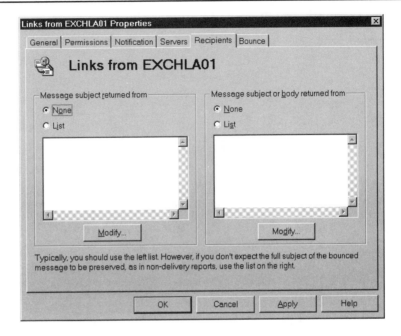

**NOTE**   Although the Recipients property page is intended for foreign e-messaging systems, you can test it out inside your Exchange system. Just set up a link monitor on your first server that sends a periodic link-check message to a mailbox on the new server you just installed. Then, as a client logged into the mailbox, use the Inbox Assistant to generate a blank reply to any messages from the System Attendant.

Finally, tab over to the Bounce property page (see Figure 13.22). Here you set the time interval for how long the monitor should wait before entering warning and alert states when it doesn't receive a reply from a server. You can set a link monitor's time units in seconds, minutes, and hours. Accept the defaults for now. Later, for critical links, you'll want to experiment to determine the shortest bounce-message return times you can set without causing the link monitor to generate false failed-link results.

**FIGURE 13.22:**

The link monitor's Bounce property page

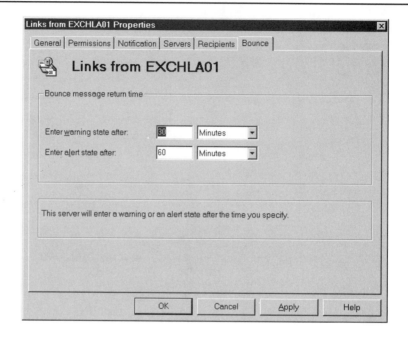

When you're done with the Bounce property page, click OK in the link monitor's properties dialog box. The new link monitor will show up in the Monitors container for your site (see Figure 13.23). To start the new monitor, click it, select Start Monitor from the Administrator's Tools menu, and specify the server on which to run the monitor. Within a few seconds a new window for the link monitor opens, and the monitor is up and running.

**FIGURE 13.23:**

After it is started, a new link monitor appears in the Monitors container and is soon running.

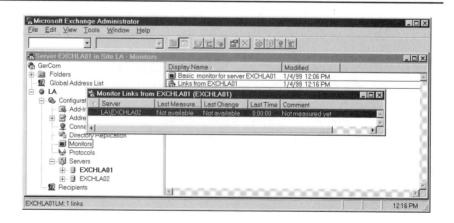

You'll notice, however, that the link monitor in Figure 13.23 shows the link to EXCHLA02 as unavailable. As noted in the Comment column, that's because the monitor hasn't even checked the link. As soon as the monitor takes its first measurement (assuming that the link is up), the monitor changes to show that the link is operational (see Figure 13.24).

**FIGURE 13.24:**

A link monitor indicates that a server link is operating.

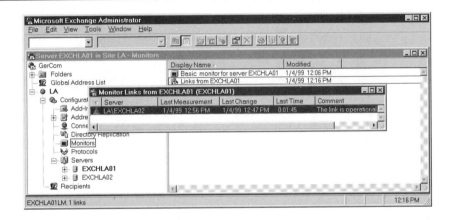

If you're an e-messaging veteran, you've got to be thinking, "Wow! Why did it take so long to come up with these sorts of goodies? The only other thing I could ask for is that the monitor tells me which component is responsible for the failed link." I agree—and I'd bet that Microsoft or third-party companies will do something about this in the not-too-distant future. For now, of course, you can always use third-party monitoring systems to deal with general network failures.

# Exchange Core Components in Multiserver Sites

The Site Configuration container offers you tools for administering and managing three of the four Exchange Server core components: DS Site Configuration, Information Store Site Configuration, and the MTA (Message Transfer Agent) Site Configuration. As you remember from Chapter 9, the fourth core component, the System Attendant, is configured solely at the server level.

We covered DS Site Configuration in its entirety in Chapter 9—remember all that stuff about offline address books and custom attributes? We'll talk a bit more about Information Store Site Configuration in the next chapter. And although we bypassed MTA Site Configuration in Chapter 9, we're ready for most of it now.

As you'll remember from Chapter 9, some site-relevant administration and management of Exchange Server's core components is done at the server level. We finished with the private information store and the System Attendant back in Chapter 9. We'll cover server-level Directory Service and MTA administration and management here.

Because you can replicate public folders across Exchange servers in a site, we could also get into server-level public information store administration and management in this chapter. However, I want to wait until the next chapter, where I'll be able to talk about both intrasite and intersite folder replication.

Whew! Got all that? Let's go.

# Administering and Managing the DS in Multiserver Sites

Because we've already covered site-level directory service (DS) administration and management, we'll focus on the server level here.

## Server-Level DS Administration and Management in Multiserver Sites

As you'll remember, the directory is a site-based database that holds detailed information about all Exchange Server recipients. The directory is automatically replicated between all the servers in a site.

There's very little we need to deal with here. Figure 13.25 shows the properties dialog box for server-level administration and management of the directory service. You use the General property page to force intrasite directory replication and to ensure that the information required to carry off directory replication is in order.

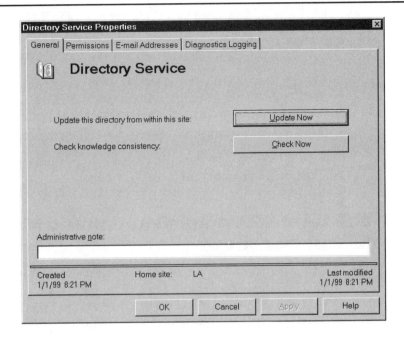

Through automatic directory replication, each server in a site has a copy of the directory for the site—not just for its own directory objects. Generally, automatic directory replication keeps directory copies on all servers in sync. When you add a new server to a site or recover a server from a backup, you can force a replication update for a server by clicking the Update Now button on the directory service's General property page.

Normally, a server checks once a day to see if its knowledge about new servers that have come online is consistent with reality. If new servers are found, automatic replication starts between existing servers and the new servers. You can force this process by clicking the Check Now button on the directory service's General property page. As with the Update Now button, you'll find the Check Now button most useful when a new server is added to a site or when a server is restored from a backup.

We won't get into the details of the other three property pages on the directory service's properties dialog box—Permissions, E-Mail Addresses, and Diagnostics Logging—because they should already be quite familiar to you at this point.

# Administering and Managing the MTA in Multiserver Sites

The MTA is primarily responsible for routing messages to other Exchange servers and—with help from various connectors and gateways—to foreign e-messaging systems. The MTA also converts messages to and from X.400 format. It has little to do with messaging between recipients on a single server.

First, let's focus on site-level tools for MTA administration and management. Then we'll deal with the server-level tools.

## Site-Level MTA Administration and Management in Multiserver Sites

Among other things, you use the MTA Site Configuration properties page to enable message tracking and to set a number of key parameters that govern the behavior of MTAs in the site. Click the Configuration container in the left-hand pane of an Exchange Administrator window, then double-click MTA Site Configuration in the right-hand pane. This opens the MTA Site Configuration properties dialog box (see Figure 13.26).

### General Properties

If the Enable Message Tracking box is checked, a daily log file will be created and the MTA will log all its message transactions to the file. As with log files for the information store (which we covered in an earlier chapter), the MTA's log files are used by Exchange Server's Message Tracking Center to help you ride herd on stray messages. As with the information store, I strongly suggest that you enable MTA message tracking right now.

### Messaging Defaults

Messaging defaults define and control communications for the MTAs on a site's servers. As you can see in Figure 13.27, the Messaging Defaults property page is loaded with options. Generally, you can accept the default values you see when you tab over to the page. As you work with your Exchange servers and their links to each other and to the outside world, you'll come up with your own values for some or all of the parameters.

**FIGURE 13.26:**

Setting sitewide parameters for Message Transfer Agents

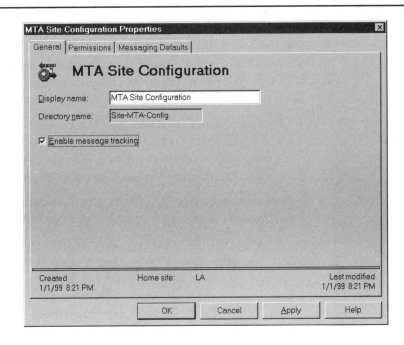

**FIGURE 13.27:**

Setting sitewide default parameters for intra-server MTA message transfers

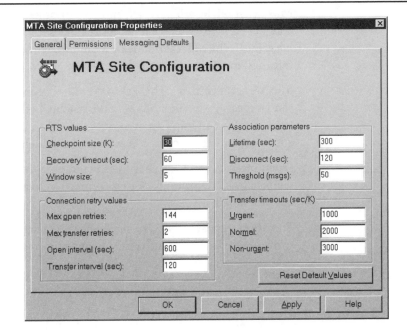

Here's a quick overview of the options on the Messaging Defaults property page.

**RTS Values**    *RTS* stands for "Reliable Transfer Service." It's part of the Open Systems Interface spec for electronic mail, which is based on CCITT X.400 mail recommendations. RTS is responsible for preventing the loss of mail sent between two MTAs, even in the face of repeated connection crashes.

> **Checkpoint size (K)**    Checking if a message has been received correctly at given points in the transmission—say, after the transmission of each 30K—eliminates the need to resend the whole message in case of a crash; upon reconnection, sending can begin just after the last successful checkpoint.

> **Recovery timeout (sec)**    If restarting a connection takes more than this number of seconds, checkpoint information is deleted and the entire message is sent again.

> **Window size**    This is the number of checkpoints (also called *window slides*) that are sent before the server hears from the receiving side. For best performance, the more window slides sent the better; increase or decrease the window size until an optimum is reached.

### Connection Retry Values

> **Max open retries**    This is the number of times an MTA attempts to open a connection to another system before it tries to find another route for the message. If the MTA can't locate an alternate route, the message is returned to the sender.

> **Max transfer retries**    This is the number of times an MTA attempts to send a message when it has actually established a connection to another system before attempting to reroute the message. If the MTA can't locate another route, the message is returned as undeliverable.

> **Open interval (sec)**    This is the time interval in seconds that the MTA waits before attempting another connection to a system when the last attempt failed.

> **Transfer interval (sec)**    This is the time interval in seconds that the MTA waits to resend a message once a connection is open.

**Association Parameters**    An *association* is created when an MTA opens a connection to another system. While the association is open, the MTA can send any number of messages destined for the other system. Once the association is closed, another one must be opened before new messages can be sent.

> **Lifetime (sec)**    This is the time interval in seconds that an association remains open if there is no activity on the association.

> **Disconnect (sec)**    If an MTA sends a disconnect request to a remote system and gets no response, the MTA waits this number of seconds before terminating associations and the connection on its side.

> **Threshold (msgs)**    When the number of messages queued for another system exceeds this threshold, the MTA opens another association and sends multiple streams of messages to the system to speed up message transmission. Whatever the value set for this parameter, the MTA automatically opens additional associations for messages marked by their senders as "high priority."

**Transfer Timeouts (sec/K)**    Each Exchange message has an importance (priority) level of high, normal, or low that is set when the message is composed. The default importance level is Normal. The values assigned to Urgent, Normal, and Non-Urgent determine the total amount of time that can pass before the MTA gives up and returns the message as undeliverable.

That's it for site-level MTA administration and management.

## Server-Level MTA Administration and Management in Multiserver Sites

To get to the MTA properties dialog box for a server, find the server's name in the left-hand pane of an Exchange Administrator window and click it. (You may have to double-click the Servers container in the pane to see the specific servers in it.) Next, double-click Message Transfer Agent in the right-hand pane of the window. The properties dialog box for the MTA pops up (see Figure 13.28).

As we move through the property pages for the MTA, don't change anything. This will be a hands-off sightseeing trip.

FIGURE 13.28:

The Server-Level Message
Transfer Agent Properties
dialog box

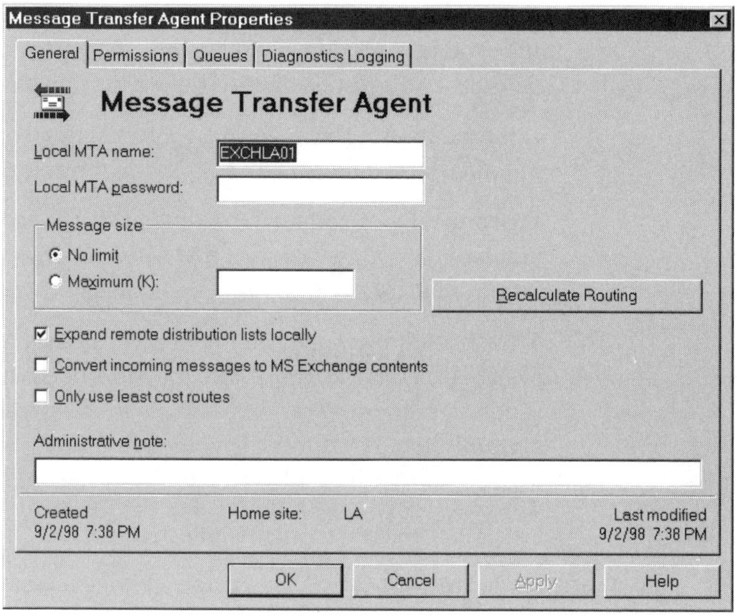

## General Properties

You use the General properties page for the MTA, as shown in Figure 13.28, to set a variety of parameters.

**Local Name and Password**    The local name is used to identify the MTA to foreign e-messaging systems. The password is used by foreign e-messaging systems when they connect to the MTA.

**Maximum Message Size**    If you've set a maximum message size, the MTA returns any messages larger than the maximum to the sender. This maximum applies to both outgoing and incoming messages.

**Recalculate Routing**    Remember that the MTA is responsible for keeping the message routing table up-to-date. Whenever you do something that might change a routing table (such as adding a gateway or reconfiguring a connector), you're asked whether you want to rebuild the table. You can do this immediately or, since rebuilds take at least a few minutes, wait until you're all done reconfiguring and then rebuild it manually. To do this, click Recalculate Routing.

**Expand Remote Distribution Lists Locally**   A remote distribution list is one that is created in one site and made available to other sites by way of directory replication. When a message is sent using any distribution list, the list has to be expanded—that is, the addresses of its individual members must be found—before the message can be sent to list members. Messages using remote distribution lists can be expanded at the local site or sent to the remote site for expansion.

Local expansion is more efficient if you have a lot of distribution lists that include members from different sites. When a list is expanded locally, the message is delivered to local members immediately, and a single copy of the message—along with a list of recipients—is sent to each site with list members.

**Convert Incoming Messages to MS Exchange Contents**   When the Convert Incoming Messages to MS Exchange Contents option is selected, the MTA converts messages in X.400 format to Exchange's MAPI format.

**Only Use Least Cost Routes**   You can set routing costs for different address spaces on an Exchange connector, for example, the Internet Mail Service. Costs can relate directly to real dollar costs, but more often relate to the bandwidth of the connector. If you select Only Use Least Cost Routes, the MTA will route each message only via the lowest cost route it can take to its destination. This allows you to prevent messages from being routed through connectors in remote sites when connectors in the local site are down. If the lowest cost route is unavailable, a non-delivery report is sent to the message's sender.

## Queues

An Exchange server sets up a different queue for each server in a site, as well as queues for connectors and gateways. You can view messages in queues and manage them from the Queues property page. Tab over to the Queues property page (see Figure 13.29) and open up the Queue Name drop-down list to see which queues your server's MTA supports. In addition to the private and public information stores, at the very least you'll see your other Exchange server.

When a queue has messages, you can get detailed information on them (select the message and click Details); change the priority of messages in the queue to reorganize the order in which the MTA will send them (select the message and click Priority); and delete messages (select the message and click Delete).

**FIGURE 13.29:**

Managing MTA queues using the Queues property page

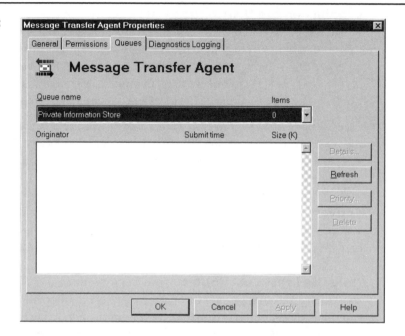

# Conclusion

In this chapter you installed an additional Exchange server in an Exchange site. You then learned how to use the Exchange Administrator program to administer and manage multiserver sites—including building multiserver server and link monitors, as well as administering and managing the directory service (at the server level) and the MTA (at both the site and server levels).

Now let's hurry on to the next chapter, where we'll work with multisite Exchange organizations.

# CHAPTER
## FOURTEEN

**14**

# Administering and Managing Multisite Exchange Organizations

- Installing an Exchange server in a new domain and site

- Connecting domains and sites

- Setting up directory replication between two sites

- Adding servers to server and link monitors

- Giving users access to public folders stored in other sites

- Using tools for administering and managing intersite routing

**N**ow that you know how to install and deal with new Exchange servers in a site, you're ready to tackle something new: the installation, administration, and management of new sites in an Exchange organization. There's a lot to do, and this is a long chapter. Take it in small, easy bites and keep your seat belts fastened.

# Installing an Exchange Server in a New Site

Back in Chapters 6 and 7, you already did almost everything you need to do to establish a new server in a new site. So I'm going to take you through the steps very quickly, adding anything you need to do to make your multisite Exchange system work.

## Installing an NT Server in a New Domain

In this section we'll get a new NT server up and running in a new Windows NT domain. Then we'll set up some trusts that let one domain's resources (such as Exchange servers) interact freely with resources in our other domain. Finally, we'll establish some permissions that let NT administrators in each of our two domains administer and manage users, groups, and so forth, in the other domain.

### Installing the NT Server

You'll install this NT server just as you installed the one in Chapter 6. Remember to create a new domain for the server (mine will be NY, for GerCom's New York City offices). Go to it! I'll see you in the next section, after you've finished installing your new NT server.

### Setting Up Cross-Domain Trusts

Since your new NT server is in a different domain from your old server, you must set up trust relationships between your two domains for Exchange to work properly. Cross-domain trusts also let users in your two domains share resources. And, with the addition of some cross-domain permissions, you'll be able to administer and manage your first domain from your second domain, and vice versa.

In the following two subsections, I'll show you how to set up cross-domain trusts. Then, in the next section, I'll help you establish cross-domain administrative permissions.

You'll be physically switching back and forth between your two domains a couple of times in this section, so work with care here. Of course, if your domains are separated by miles, rather than steps, you'll have to work cooperatively with someone in the other domain.

**Setting Up Trust Permissions in Each Domain**    Let's start in the first domain you created (mine is LA, remember?). Log in to the domain as Administrator. Then, from an NT server or workstation in the domain, open User Manager for Domains, which is in the Administrative Tools program group. From the program's Policies menu, select Trust Relationships. The Trust Relationships dialog box pops open (see Figure 14.1).

**FIGURE 14.1:**

The NT Server Trust Relationships dialog box

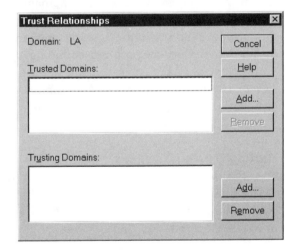

First we need to let your new domain trust your first domain. So click Add for the Trusting Domains box. This pops up the Add Trusting Domain dialog box shown in Figure 14.2.

**FIGURE 14.2:**

Allowing one domain to
trust another

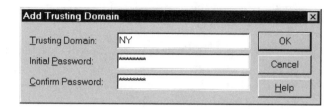

Enter the name of your new domain (mine is NY). Then type in the password that the new domain must give when setting up a trust relationship with your first domain. Type in the password again to confirm, then click OK. Be sure to write down the password, unless it's one you can easily remember. Leave the User Manager's Trust Relationships dialog box open.

Now you need to work in your new domain. So, while logged in to your new domain as Administrator, open User Manager for Domains. At this point, it's probably easiest to run User Manager for Domains from your new NT server, though you could run it from a workstation in your new domain (if you've installed one). Once the program is running, do exactly what you just did for your first domain, but enter the name of the first domain here, to give it permission to trust your new domain. (For example, I'd enter "LA".) You can enter the same or a different password. Click OK when you're done, and leave the Trust Relationships dialog box open.

**Adding Trusted Domains**   At this point we need to add the trusted domains on each side. So go back to the User Manager for your first domain. In the Trust Relationships dialog box (as shown earlier in Figure 14.1), click the uppermost Add button, the one for Trusted Domains. The Add Trusted Domain dialog box opens (see Figure 14.3).

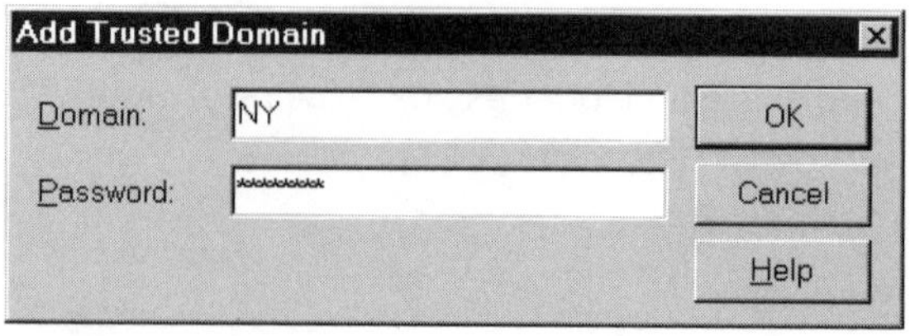

**FIGURE 14.3:**

Adding a trusted domain

Enter the name of your new domain and the password that you set for it in the last step, then click OK. After a bit, you should see a message telling you that the trust relationship has been established, and the Trust Relationships dialog box should look something like the one shown in Figure 14.4.

> **NOTE**  The domain name is the same in both boxes. This makes sense since you've given your new domain the rights to trust your first domain, and you want your first domain to trust the new domain. (I won't hold it against you if you go back and reread the last two sentences.)

**FIGURE 14.4:**

One side of a cross-domain trust relationship is established.

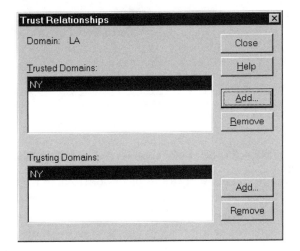

If you have any problems, repeat the process outlined above. Be sure you're logged in to both domains as Administrator and that you enter the correct domain name and password. If that doesn't work, make sure that your network is running properly and that your NT servers are communicating with each other. When everything is the way it should be, click Close in the Trust Relationships dialog box for your first domain.

Now you've got to set the trusted domain for your new domain. Go back to the User Manager for your new domain and do the same thing you just did in your first domain, substituting the name of your first domain. When you're all done, the Trust Relationships dialog box should look like the one in Figure 14.5, except that the name of your first domain should appear in both boxes. When everything is okay, click Close in the Trust Relationships dialog box and you're done.

The other side of a cross-domain trust relationship is established.

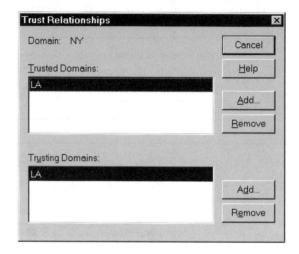

## Setting Cross-Domain Administrative Permissions

You can remotely administer one domain from another. This lets you create new users, groups, and so on, for the second domain from the comfort of your first-domain easy chair. You don't *have* to do this, and in some cases for security reasons you won't want to enable cross-domain NT administrative rights. However, in most cases such permissions are welcome, because they not only make administration easier, they also let administrators at different locations help each other out remotely.

Here's how to set up cross-domain NT administrative permissions. If it's not already open, open User Manager for Domains on a workstation or server in your first domain (again, mine is LA). In the Groups pane of the window, find the Administrators group; in Figure 14.6, it's the second group.

FIGURE 14.6:

Locating the Administrators group in User Manager for Domains

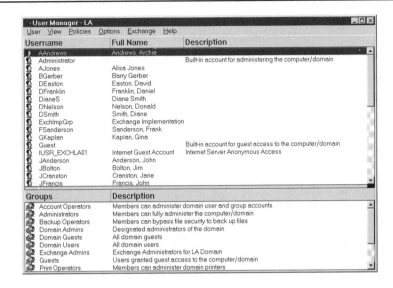

The Administrators group is created by default when NT is installed. It has full rights to administer and manage users, groups, and the like in a domain. Any user or group added to this group gets full administrative rights for the domain. The user Administrator becomes a member of this group when NT is installed.

## Administering NT Using Your Own Account

If you had added your NT account to the Administrators group, you could be doing all the cross-domain trust setup while logged in to that account instead of the Administrator account. But be careful here: you may not want to do this, because when you do, anyone who gains access to your account has full administrative rights.

If you do add your account to the Administrators group, be sure to take precautions to keep others out of your account. For example, when logged in with your own account, always lock your NT workstation when you go away from your computer. To do that, simultaneously press the Ctrl, Alt, and Delete keys and then select Lock Workstation from the resultant Windows NT Security dialog box. To unlock your workstation, enter your password. Heck, it's okay with me if you lock your workstation even if your account isn't in the Administrators group.

We need to add the Administrator account from our new domain to the Administrators group for our first domain, and vice versa. As we proceed, follow along using the figures as a guide. Double-click the Administrators group, or select it and then click Properties from the User Manager's User menu. This opens the Local Group Properties dialog box (see Figure 14.7). (For more on NT's local and global groups, see *Mastering Windows NT Server 4*, by Mark Minasi, Christa Anderson, and Elizabeth Creegan (Sybex, 1996).) Click Add in the Local Group Properties dialog box to open the Add Users and Groups dialog box shown in Figure 14.7. Then click open the List Names From drop-down list and select the name of your new domain (mine is NY).

After a bit of churning, the Add Users and Groups dialog box will list the users and groups in your second domain (see Figure 14.8). Select the user Administrator and click Add; the Administrator user will appear in the Add Names pane at the bottom of the Add Users and Groups dialog box. Click OK to add the Administrator user from your new domain to the Administrators group in your first domain (see Figure 14.9).

**FIGURE 14.7:**

Selecting the domain whose Administrator account will have cross-domain administrative permissions

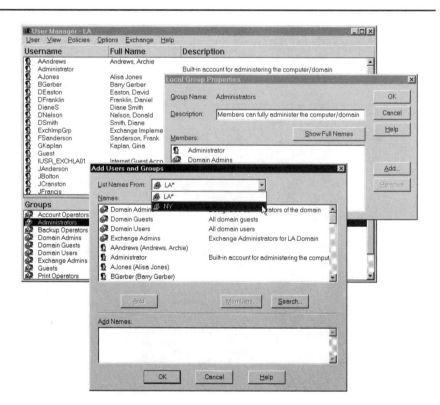

**FIGURE 14.8:**

Giving permission to the
NY domain administrator
to administer and manage
the LA domain

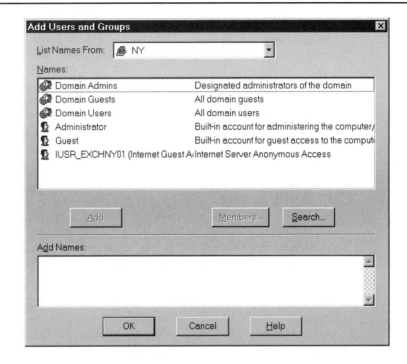

**FIGURE 14.9:**

The NY Administrator has
permission to administer
and manage the LA
domain.

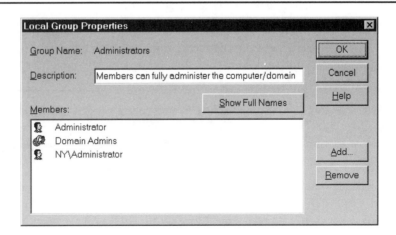

That's it for one side of the cross-domain relationship. Now you need to go to
your new domain, run User Manager for Domains, and repeat the steps above.

When you're done, the Administrator in one domain will be able to remotely administer and manage the other domain, and vice versa. If you want to give any other users cross-domain rights, just add them as we did above.

# Installing an Exchange Server in a New Site

In this section we'll get a new Exchange server up and running and set up cross-site permissions that let you administer each site from the other. After we get these permissions in place, we'll be able to link the servers so that they can replicate directories and public folders.

## Installing the Exchange Server

You can go ahead and do your new Exchange site/server installation just as you did your first one back in Chapter 7. Just be sure your organization and site names are set correctly (mine are GerCom and NY). And be sure to set up an Exchange Server administration group for your site, just as you did the first time in Chapter 7; for ease of administration later on, I suggest that you give your new group the same name as your first Exchange Server administration group. (Remember, I suggested the name Exchange Admins.) And don't forget to assign this group the role Permissions Admin for both the site and Configuration container; check back to Chapter 7 if you need help doing this. When you're done with the installation, we can rendezvous in the next paragraph.

All done? Good. Just to make sure everything worked properly, open the Exchange Administrator program on the new Exchange server in your new site. It should look something like mine, which is shown in Figure 14.10.

**FIGURE 14.10:**

A new Exchange site as viewed from the Administrator program

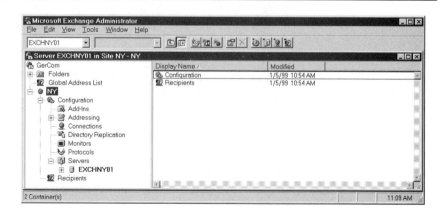

# Setting Up Required Cross-Site Permissions

We're now ready to link our two sites. First, however, we have to set up some cross-site permissions. These are the basic permissions you need for cross-site administration and management.

To begin, open the Exchange Administrator in your first site; select your site name—LA in my case—by clicking it (see Figure 14.11). Next, select Properties from the Administrator's File menu to bring up a properties dialog box for the site. Tab over to the Permissions property page (see Figure 14.12).

**FIGURE 14.11:**

Selecting the site name

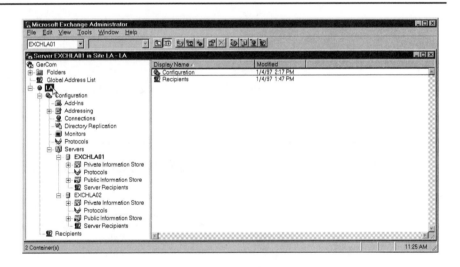

Next, click Add in the site's properties dialog box to open the Add Users and Groups dialog box (see Figure 14.13). Select your other domain—mine is NY—from the List Names From drop-down list.

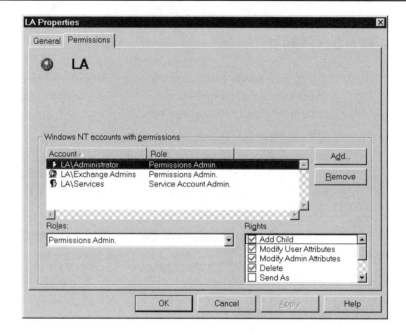

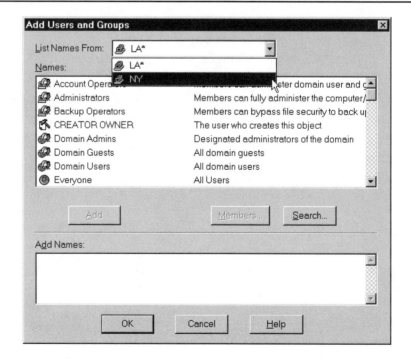

Now you should see the users and groups in your other domain (see Figure 14.14). Select Exchange Admins (or whatever you named your Exchange Server administration group when you installed your new NT and Exchange servers just a bit ago) and click Add in the Add Users and Groups dialog box. The name of the Exchange Server administration group in your other site (NY\Exchange Admins in my case) now shows up in the Add Names pane at the bottom of the Add Users and Groups dialog box (see Figure 14.15).

Click OK in the Add Users and Groups dialog box. The Exchange Server administration group from your other site now appears in the Windows NT accounts with the Permissions box. Change the group's role from the default Admin. to Permissions Admin. so that it can fully administer this site (see Figure 14.16). Finally, click OK in the properties dialog box for your site.

**FIGURE 14.14:**

Finding the Exchange Server administration group from another site that will have administrative permissions in this site

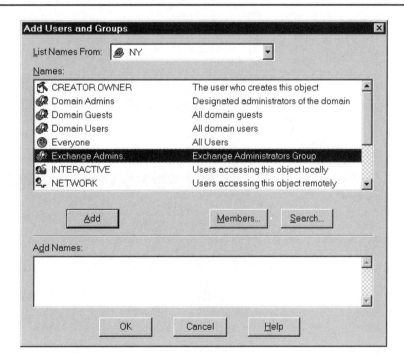

**FIGURE 14.15:**

Giving administrative permission in this site to the Exchange Server administration from another site

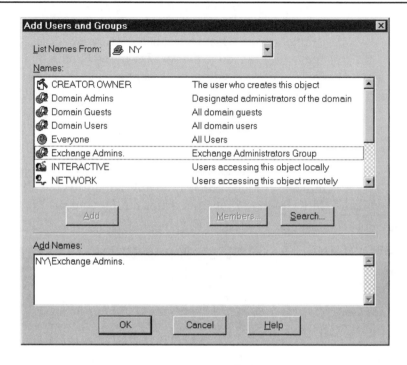

**FIGURE 14.16:**

The Exchange Server administration group from another site is given administrative permissions in this site.

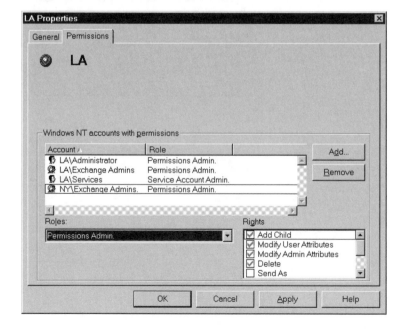

**NOTE**    There's nothing magic about your Exchange Server administration group. You can create other groups or assign permissions to any existing NT account or group. I'm using the Exchange Admins group because it contains the users whom I trust to administer across these two sites.

**WARNING**    You're not finished yet. Now you need to go to your new Exchange site and give the same site-level permissions to the Exchange Server administration group in your first site. This is exactly what you just did—only this time you'll do it from your new site, and you'll give permissions to the first site's administration group.

You're still not finished. Now you need to add some permissions at the Configuration container level. Because you're fresh from adding permissions, I'll just give you general directions for completing this task.

Select the Configuration container in your first site by clicking it, and then select Properties from the Administrator's File menu. Next, tab over to the Permissions property page in the resultant Configuration Properties dialog box. Add the Exchange administration group (probably called Exchange Admins) from your other site and assign it the role Permissions Admin. Then add the Site Services account (probably called Services) from your other site and assign it the role Service Account Admin.

When you're done, your Configuration dialog box's Permissions property page should look something like the one in Figure 14.17.

You're almost done—but not quite. Now you've got to repeat the tasks outlined above for your other site. Go to it!

The Configuration dialog box's Permissions property page with cross-site permissions properly set

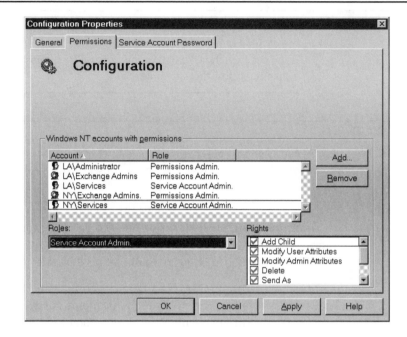

# Setting Up a Site-to-Site Link

Exchange sites, as you'll recall from Chapter 3, are linked by connectors; they're also linked in pairs. You set up a connector in each of two sites and configure them to talk to each other. If you have multiple sites, you need one pair of communicating connectors for every pair of sites you want to link. Connectors carry information about user communications, directory replication, and public folder replication between sites in the form of messages.

Now we're ready to set up our first site connection. We'll use the Exchange Site Connector. It's going to be quite easy for two reasons: the Site Connector is the simplest of the Exchange site connectors to implement, and we've set up the proper cross-site permissions.

**NOTE**    From here on, I'll use the term *site connector* to refer to site connectors in general and *Site Connector* to refer to the specific connector we're about to install. It would have been better if Microsoft had given the Site Connector a different name to distinguish it from the collective group of site connectors. That didn't happen, hence my naming conventions.

## Setting Up the First Site

You can begin setting up a Site Connector from either of the two sites you're going to connect. Let's start in your first site. Open the Exchange Administrator, then select the Connections container (see Figure 14.18). Depending on the options you chose when installing the two Exchange servers in your first site, you may not see all the connectors shown in the right-hand pane of the Administrator window in Figure 14.18.

Now select New Other from the Administrator's File menu, then select Site Connector from the New Other submenu (see Figure 14.19). This brings up the New Site Connector dialog box.

In the New Site Connector dialog box, type in the name of the new server you just installed and click OK (see Figure 14.20). The Exchange Administrator now looks for this site. When it finds the site, the Administrator checks to see if you have the proper cross-site permissions. The cross-site rights you just granted to the Exchange Admins group and the Services account in each of your two NT domains are what's key here. If all the rights are in order, Administrator opens the Site Connector Properties dialog box shown in Figure 14.21. This is a Site Connector from your first site to your second site. The Site Connector is for the second site—hence its default name (Site Connector (NY) in my case).

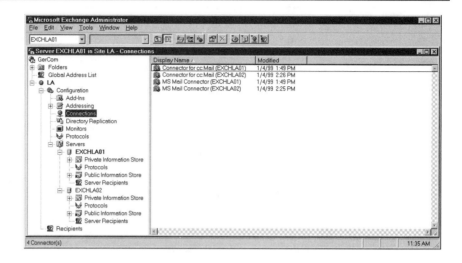

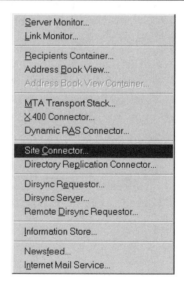

**FIGURE 14.20:**

Specifying a server in the site to which to connect

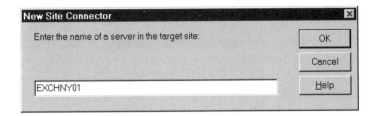

**FIGURE 14.21:**

The Site Connector Properties dialog box

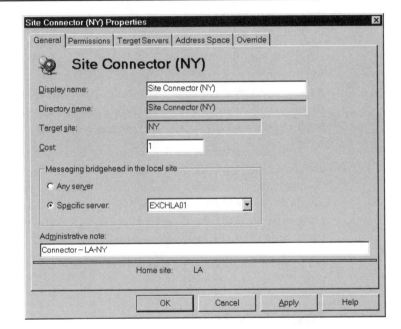

> **NOTE**    If you're told that you don't have permission to contact the other site, be sure that the NT user account you're working from in your first site is a member of the Exchange Server administration group (probably Exchange Admins) for your first site.

# General Properties

Accept the default display and directory names in the Site Connector Properties dialog box. (The target site will be automatically chosen for you; it's NY in Figure 14.21.) Cost is a number from 1 to 100 that's used when you're running more than one connector to a site. When messages need to be sent between sites, the available site connector with the lowest cost is used. This is very useful if, for example, you have a fast link like the Site Connector running as your primary connection and a slower link such as the Dynamic Remote Access Service Connector (DRASC) running as a backup. When setting up the DRASC, give it a higher cost number than the Site Connector's; that way, messages will always be sent between your sites using the Site Connector except when it is down.

The Messaging Bridgehead in the Local Site option defaults to any server, meaning that any server in the local site can send messages to the other site. If you choose a specific server, as I have in Figure 14.21, then only that server can send messages to the other site. All other servers in the site must send messages to the bridgehead server, which then sends out all messages over its Site Connector.

A bridgehead server can help reduce network traffic a bit when your two sites are connected by a wide area network. This is so because with a bridgehead server only one Exchange server needs to open and maintain communications sessions across the WAN. And because the Message Transfer Agents (MTAs) on servers other than the bridgehead server don't have to transfer messages between sites, you'll save a little processing power on those servers.

The administrative note I entered in Figure 14.21 helps me remember the direction of the connection—from LA to NY.

## Target Servers

The Target Servers property page is shown in Figure 14.22. *Target servers* are the servers in the remote site that will handle messages sent from this site to the remote site. By default the name of the server you typed in the New Site Connector dialog box (shown in Figure 14.20) is selected as a target server. If other servers are listed in the Site Servers box on the left-hand side of the Target Servers property page, you can add one of these to the Target Servers box (on the right-hand side of the property page) by selecting it and clicking Add. To delete a server from the right-hand Target Servers box, select it and click Remove.

*Target server costs* are used by servers in the local site to determine which target server to communicate with. As with the Site Connector cost parameter on the General property page, target server costs can range from 1 to 100, and you can set a different cost for each target server. You use target server costs to control message transfer loads—giving higher costs to target servers that you want to receive messages less frequently. To set a cost parameter for a specific target server, select the server by clicking it, enter a value in the Target Server Cost field, and click the Set Value button. When messages are transmitted, target servers with higher costs will have messages sent to them only when servers that have lower costs associated with them are unavailable.

**FIGURE 14.22:**

Selecting target servers for a Site Connector

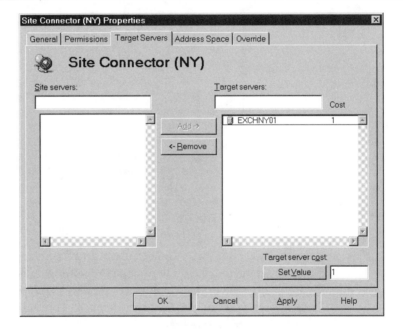

## Address Space

You use *address spaces* to direct messages with specific addresses to and through Exchange connectors, for connections between Exchange servers, and for connections between Exchange servers and foreign e-messaging systems. For now, you don't have to worry about address spaces. The Exchange Administrator creates one default X.400 address space that is sufficient to move all messages in and out of the site you're working in (see Figure 14.23). Notice that the X.400 address covers my entire NY site, GerCom NY.

**FIGURE 14.23:**

The Address Space property page with its default X.400 address

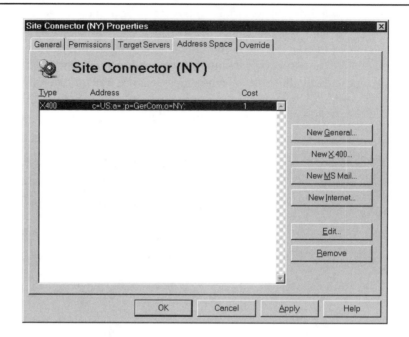

## Override

If you can establish cross-domain trusts and the specific Exchange Server permissions we set up above, you won't need to use the Override property page (see Figure 14.24). However, for political or other reasons, this sometimes isn't possible. In such cases, you can use the Override page to provide the security information required to create and operate a Site Connector.

On the Override page, you enter an account in the other site, along with its password and the name of the domain where the other site resides. To avoid permissions problems, use the Exchange Site Services account for the other site (named Services, if you used the naming conventions I suggested). Of course, your counterpart in the other site has to do the same thing using your Site Services account name, password, and domain name.

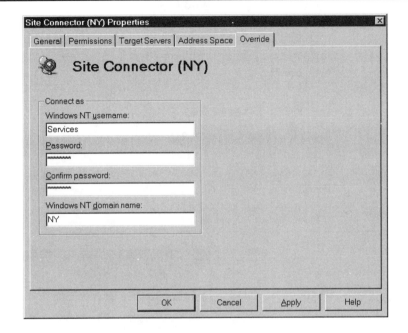

I typed in the Services account username and password as well as the name of
my NY domain just to show you what would go in this space, if I didn't have the
required permissions set up. Unless you can't set up these permissions, you can
leave the Override property page blank.

## Setting Up the Second Site

Setting up the Site Connector in your second site is really easy. After you click OK
on the Site Connector Properties dialog box, a little box pops up and asks you if
the Administrator should create the Site Connector in your remote (second) site
(see Figure 14.25). If you click Yes—which you should—the Site Connector for the
second site is created automatically, and you're presented with a Site Connector
Properties dialog box for that site (mine is NY). Figure 14.26 shows the dialog box.

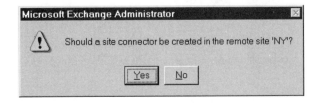

Now, make sure you understand what is happening here. You're still using the Exchange Administrator in your first site. Because of the permissions you set up earlier in this chapter, you can configure the remote site connector without changing servers or doing anything other than answering Yes when presented with that little box in Figure 14.25.

## General Properties

Look closely at Figure 14.26, which shows a site connector to your first site from your second site. The name of my connector is Site Connector (LA), and it has been created in my NY site. That's why when I pick a specific bridgehead server, I'm offered EXCHNY01. You'll also notice that the administrative note I entered recognizes that this is the NY-to-LA connector.

**FIGURE 14.26:**

The Site Connector Properties dialog box for the second or remote site

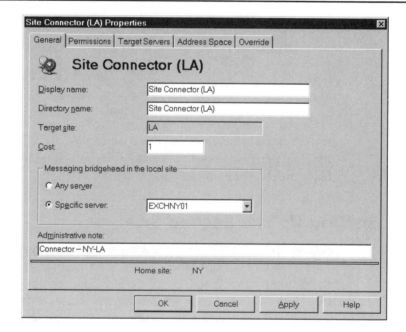

## Target Servers

Because we have two servers in our first site and because we want only one (EXCHLA01 in my case) to be the bridgehead server, we need to be sure that the other server is not in the Target Servers box on the right, since we don't want our

NY bridgehead to contact it. If it does appear in the Target Servers box, select it and click Remove. In Figure 14.27, I'm about to remove my second LA server, EXCHLA02, from the Target Servers list.

When you're finished, click OK in the Site Connector Properties dialog box, and you're done. Your sites are now connected and talking to each other at a basic level.

**FIGURE 14.27:**

Removing a server from the Target Servers list

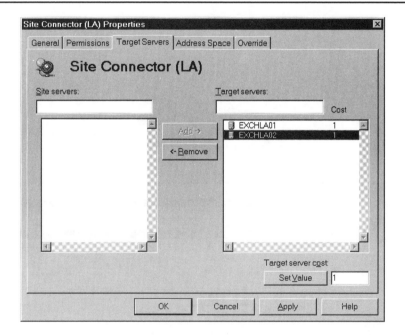

## Did It Work?

You should now see the Site Connector to your second site in the Connections container for your first site (see Figure 14.28). And you—or whoever is stationed at your second site—should see the Site Connector to your first site in the Connections container for your second site (see Figure 14.29).

**FIGURE 14.28:**

The Site Connector from the first site to the second site

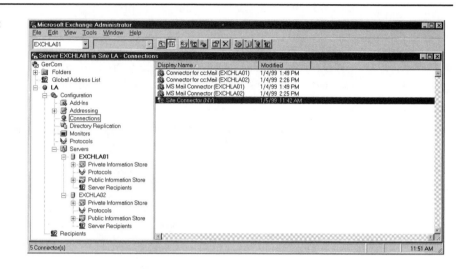

**FIGURE 14.29:**

The Site Connector from the second site to the first site

# Setting Up Directory Replication between Sites

Okay, our two sites are connected for messaging. Now we need to set up directory replication between them.

## Setting Up Directory Replication in the First Site

From the Exchange Administrator, select the Directory Replication container for your first site. Then select the Directory Replication Connector item from the New Other submenu in the Administrator's File menu (see Figure 14.19). This brings up the New Directory Replication Connector dialog box shown in Figure 14.30. We're setting a Directory Replication Connector from our first site (mine's LA) to our second site (mine's NY).

Make sure the name in the Remote Site Name field is correct, and enter the name of a server in the site. Because the site is available on the same network, be sure to select the Yes, the Remote Site Is Available on This Network option. And, of course, let the Administrator configure replication on both sides. When you're done, click OK.

Next you'll see the Directory Replication Connector Properties dialog box shown in Figure 14.31. We need to look only at the General and Schedule property pages right now.

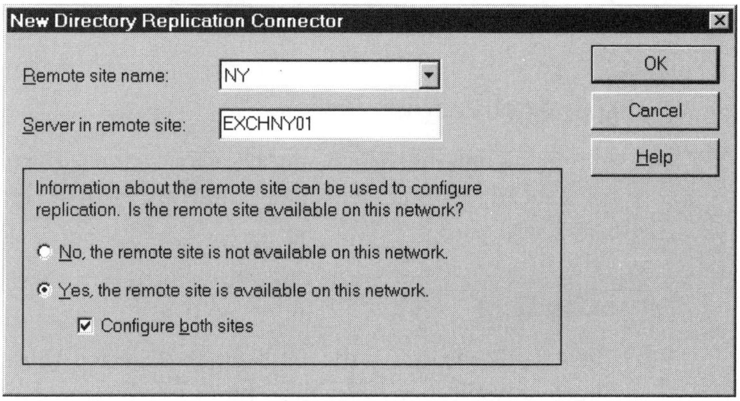

**FIGURE 14.30:**

The New Directory Replication Connector dialog box

**FIGURE 14.31:**

The Directory Replication Connector Properties dialog box

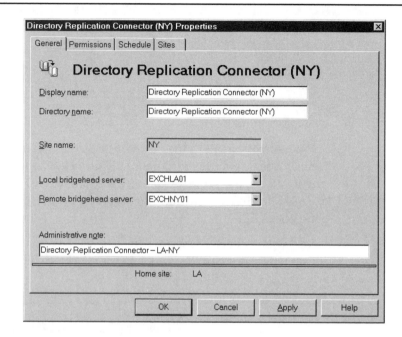

## General Properties

Accept the default Display and Directory names. Be sure that local and remote bridgehead server choices are as you want them to be, and add an administrative note if you wish.

## Schedule

The default schedule is the one set in the Selected Times calendar; it allows for directory replication every three hours (see Figure 14.32). Using the default should be fine in most cases; if the two sites are connected by a low-bandwidth network or one with very high traffic, you may want to do replication even less frequently. If you add and delete recipients at a breakneck pace throughout the day, every day, then more frequent directory replication might be necessary. (The Always option means replication every 15 minutes.)

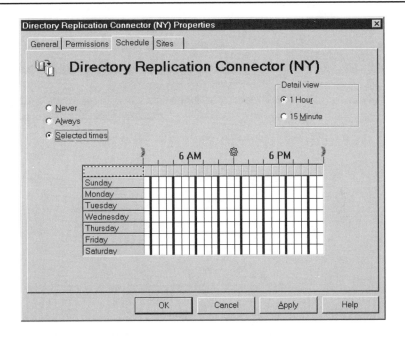

## Setting Up Directory Replication in the Second Site

Things just don't get any easier than this. When you're done with the Schedule
property page, click OK in the Directory Replication Connector Properties page.
Remember how, back on the New Directory Replication Connector dialog box
(Figure 14.30), you asked to have the other side of the Directory Replication Connector automatically configured? Well, that's what happens. The Connector in
your other site is configured without any action on your part, and directory replication begins.

## Did It Work?

First, use the Exchange Administrator at each of your two sites to see if the directory replication connectors have been created; they'll be in the Directory Replication container for each site. Figures 14.33 and 14.34 show my two sites with the
directory replication connectors created in each.

While you're in your second site, create an Exchange mailbox or two. If you need to refresh your memory about this, go back to Chapter 8.

**FIGURE 14.33:**

The directory replication connector for the first site

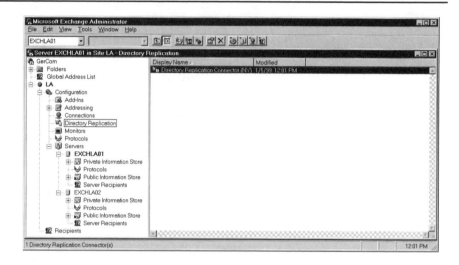

**FIGURE 14.34:**

The directory replication connector for the second site

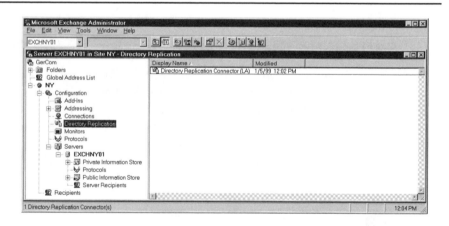

Next, after 10 or 20 minutes, depending on server and network performance, take a look at the Exchange Administrator in each site. You'll find that you can now see all the objects for both sites from either site. Your directories have been fully replicated across your two sites (see Figures 14.35 and 14.36).

**FIGURE 14.35:**

An Exchange Administrator view from one site (LA) shows the objects in both sites (LA and NY)

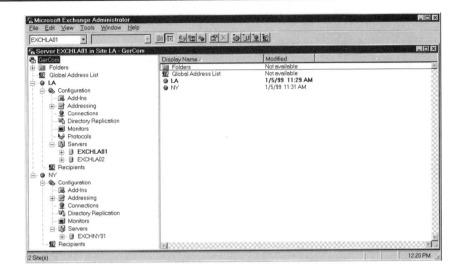

**FIGURE 14.36:**

An Exchange Administrator view from one site (NY) shows the objects in both sites (NY and LA)

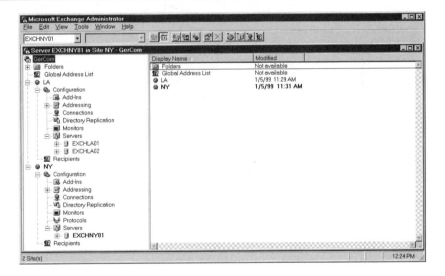

If what you have isn't what the figures show, there are a few things you can do to speed up directory replication. Everything you're going to do here is done automatically by Exchange Server over the course of a day—you're just forcing these actions so you can assure yourself that it's all happening as advertised.

Perform the following steps in each of your two sites. If you need more info about the first two dialog boxes discussed here, see Chapter 13.

- Double-click Directory Service in the container for the default server. Then, on the General property page of the resultant Directory Service dialog box, click Check Now. This forces the server to discover information about new sites in your organization. Close the dialog box.

- Double-click Message Transfer Agent in the container for the default server, then click Recalculate Routing on the General property page of the resultant Message Transfer Agent dialog box. When you do this, the server updates its routing tables and creates an MTA queue for the new site. Tab over to the MTA dialog box's Queues property page to see the queue created for the server in the other site. Close the dialog box.

- Double-click the Directory Replication Connector in the site's Directory Replication container. Next, on the Sites property page of the resultant Directory Replication Connector dialog box (see Figure 14.37), click the name of your inbound site and then click Request Now to force an update of directory replication information for the site. Close the dialog box.

---

**NOTE**    As you create and tear down Exchange connectors in the sections below, follow the above three steps any time you need to force a quick update of the Exchange directory database. This lets you see the fruits of your work more immediately than if you wait for your Exchange servers to do these tasks automatically. When you're running a production Exchange environment, you'll rarely if ever need to track through these steps; Exchange Server's automated processes will take care of everything in more than enough time.

---

To further confirm that all is well, look in the organization-wide Global Address List container in one of your sites. You should see the addresses for both sites in the list (see Figure 14.38).

**FIGURE 14.37:**

The Sites property page allows for selective directory replication updates.

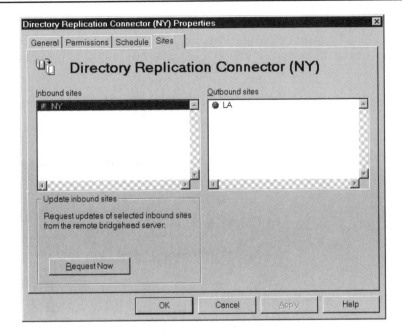

**FIGURE 14.38:**

Addresses for both sites are visible in either site's copy of the Global Address List.

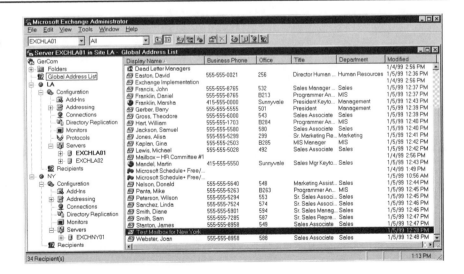

Finally, open an Outlook client and click the Address Book icon on the toolbar (you'll remember that it looks like a little open book). Click open the Show Names from The drop-down list. You should now see your second site along with your first, as shown in Figure 14.39. Take a close look at the Global Address List. You should see addresses from both your first and second sites in the book.

Congratulations! You've managed to get a pretty sophisticated Exchange system up and running.

**FIGURE 14.39:**

Both the first (LA) and second (NY) sites are available in the client Address Book.

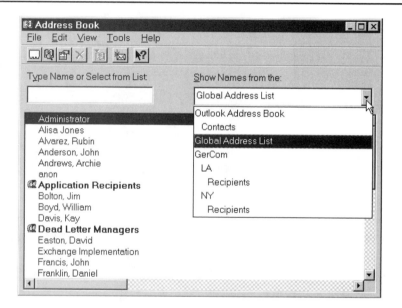

# Using the Exchange Administrator in a Multisite Organization

What you learned in the last chapter about using the Exchange Administrator in multiserver sites should help you here. Using Figure 14.40 as a guide, notice that

- The default server in the currently selected site/server window is visible in the drop-down list near the top of the main Exchange Administrator window (EXCHLA01 in Figure 14.40).

- The title bar for each site/server window includes the site name to help you know which site and server are your defaults (Server EXCHLA01 in Site LA—LA for the first window and Server EXCHNY01 in Site NY—NY for the second window in Figure 14.40).

- The default site and server in each site/server window are bolded (LA and EXCHLA01 in the first window; NY and EXCHNY01 in the second window in Figure 14.40).

**FIGURE 14.40:**

Administering and managing two sites from the same Exchange Administrator program

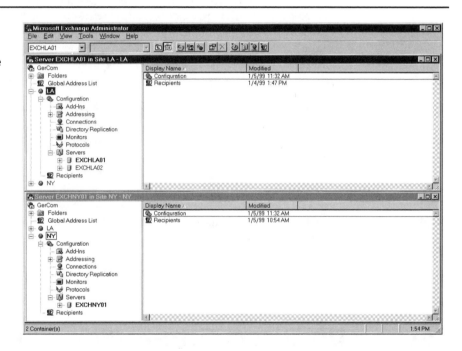

You can open additional windows on either your default site or your other site; just select Connect to Server from the Administrator's File menu, click Browse, and then select the site and server you want to connect to from the Server Browser dialog box that pops up.

Because of the cross-site permissions you gave the Exchange administration group in each of your two sites earlier in this chapter, you have tremendous control over your entire Exchange system. From this point on, you can administer and manage your first site from your second site, and vice versa. Just select the Connect to Server option from the File menu of the Exchange Administrator in one site and use the Server Browser dialog box to connect to a server in the other site. Then use the new Administrator window to administer and manage that site (see Figure 14.40). It's as easy as pie. If you need a refresher on connecting to servers, check out Chapter 13.

---

**WARNING**   You can't fully administer and manage a site if you're not connected to a server in it. For example, from the first site/server window in Figure 14.40, I can view, create, and edit all objects in my LA site. Because I am not directly connected to a server in my NY site in this window, I can only view objects in the NY site from this window; I can't create or modify them. To fully administer and manage NY site objects, I must work in the second site/server window in Figure 14.40, which is directly connected to the server EXCHNY01 in the NY site.

---

**TIP**   If those two windows in Figure 14.40 tend to overload your personal information processing circuits, here's how you can cut the visual stimulation a bit. Just drag one of the windows on top of the other so that the other window is covered. Resize the windows and the main Exchange Administrator window to your aesthetic preferences. Then, when you need to work with the window that's hidden, select its default server from the drop-down default server name list at the top of the Exchange Administrator's main window. The hidden window instantly comes to the top of the window stack, and the other window is hidden until you call it up with the drop-down list. Neat!

---

# Setting Up Direct Site-to-Site Links Using Other Exchange Connectors

You'll remember from Chapter 5 that you can link Exchange sites using a variety of connectors other than the Site Connector: the X.400 Connector, the Dynamic Remote Access Service Connector (DRASC), and the Internet Mail Service (IMS). We'll cover the X.400 and DRAS Connectors here, saving the IMS for later chapters.

Remember that the X.400 Connector can do both direct (point-to-point) and indirect (via foreign e-messaging systems) site links. Here we'll deal only with direct X.400 site connections; I'll talk about indirect links in a later chapter. The DRAS allows only for direct site-to-site links; we'll cover it in this chapter.

As with the Site Connector, you set up like connectors in each site and point them at each other. Each connector supports communications between two Exchange servers.

Before we can install our connectors, we need to set up a network transport stack for each connector. As we go along, remember that transport stacks live on Exchange servers, while connectors live in Exchange sites.

## Setting Up an MTA Transport Stack

Exchange connectors ride atop MTA transport stacks. Site Connectors automatically take care of transport stack issues. You have to install transport stacks for other connectors. A number of MTA transport stack options are available, as shown in the following table.

| Protocol(s) | Prerequisite |
| --- | --- |
| X.25 using Eicon Technology Corporation's X.25 port adapter hardware | Eicon X.25 networking support must be installed (comes with Eicon hardware). |
| Asynchronous, ISDN, and X.25 using NT Server's Remote Access Server | Remote Access Server must be installed (comes with NT Server). |
| TCP/IP | TCP/IP networking support must be installed (comes with NT Server). |
| Open Systems Interface (OSI) TP4 | TP4 networking support must be installed (comes with Exchange Server). |

Except for the Eicon MTA transport stack, you can install only one of each MTA transport stack per Exchange server. You can install multiple Eicon port adapters in an Exchange server and set up one transport stack per adapter. All MTA transport stacks can support multiple Exchange connectors. So, using one MTA transport stack on one server, you can connect to any number of Exchange servers—the only requirement being that those servers are reachable on the same network.

By way of example, we'll set up TCP/IP and Remote Access Server (RAS) MTA transport stacks. (You'll find detailed instructions for setting up the Eicon and OSI stacks in the Exchange documentation.) For the TCP/IP stack, you'll need to have the TCP/IP protocols installed on the server in each site that will house the connector. For the DRASC, NT Server's RAS must be installed on the servers in each site that will house the DRASC. (For help installing and configuring these, see Sybex's *Mastering Windows NT Server 4*.)

## Setting Up a TCP/IP Transport Stack

In your first site, open the Exchange Administrator's File menu. Select New Other and then select MTA Transport Stack from the New Other submenu (look back at Figure 14.19). This pops up the New MTA Transport Stack dialog box (see Figure 14.41). Select TCP/IP MTA Transport Stack, select the server you want to install the stack on (I've chosen EXCHLA01), and click OK.

**FIGURE 14.41:**

Selecting the networking protocol and server for a new MTA transport stack

The next thing you'll see is the TCP Properties dialog box shown in Figure 14.42. Unless you have a strong reason for doing otherwise, accept the default Name; you need to enter OSI address information only if other applications or services that communicate with an X.25 service are installed on the server. The OSI address information ensures that the existing X.25 service and the TCP/IP transport stack you're creating don't clobber each other.

For all intents and purposes, you're now finished. The Connectors property page simply shows the Exchange connectors that are riding atop the MTA transport stack. Since you haven't created your connector yet, you won't find anything on that page right now. After your connector is in place, come back to the Connectors page; the connector you linked to this MTA transport stack will appear.

Click OK in the TCP Properties dialog box, then look in the container for your server. Your MTA transport stack should show up in the right-hand pane (see Figure 14.43).

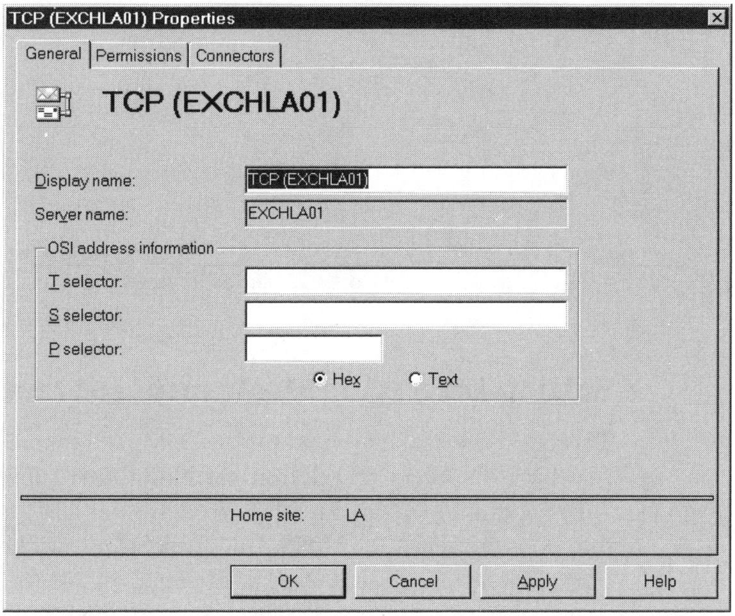

**FIGURE 14.42:**

The TCP Properties dialog box is used to configure a TCP/IP MTA transport stack.

Now you need to set up a TCP/IP MTA transport stack in your other site. To do this, just repeat the process outlined above for a server in your other site. If the Site Connector and directory replication connector we created in the last section are in place (or even if they aren't in place, but the cross-domain, cross-site permissions I discussed earlier are), you don't have to actually visit the other site. Just connect to a server in the other site and use the new Exchange Administrator window for that connection to add the MTA transport stack.

**FIGURE 14.43:**

A new TCP/IP MTA transport stack in its home server container

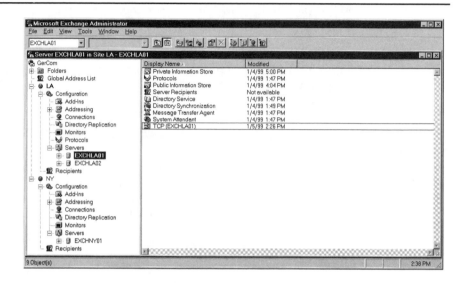

## Setting Up a RAS MTA Transport Stack

This one's even easier than the TCP/IP MTA transport stack. In your first site, select MTA Transport Stack from the New Other submenu in the Exchange Administrator's File menu. Then, from the New MTA Transport Stack dialog box that pops up, select RAS MTA Transport Stack and the server you want the transport stack installed on. (Refer back to Figure 14.41 for a view of the New MTA Transport Stack dialog box.) This brings up the RAS Properties dialog box (see Figure 14.44).

You can optionally enter the telephone number used to make a dial-up connection to the server on which you're installing the RAS MTA transport stack. This security-enhancing feature allows RAS MTA transport stacks in other sites to call back to this server upon being contacted by it. As with the TCP/IP MTA transport stack, the Connectors property page for the RAS Properties dialog box is useful only after you've created at least one Exchange connector and assigned it to this transport stack. So click OK in the RAS Properties dialog box when you're done.

The RAS MTA transport stack now joins the TCP transport stack in the container for the server it was installed on (see Figure 14.45).

FIGURE 14.44:

The RAS Properties dialog box is used to configure a RAS MTA transport stack.

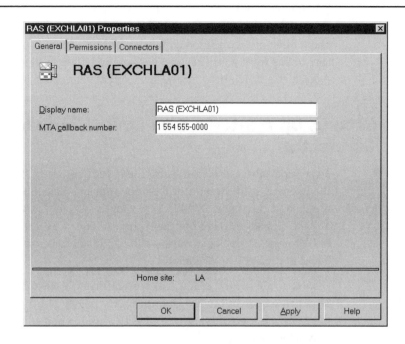

FIGURE 14.45:

A new RAS MTA transport stack appears in its home server container.

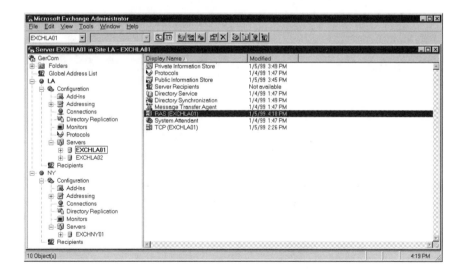

Before you move on, be sure to create a parallel RAS MTA transport stack in your other site. Again, if your sites are already connected by some sort of site connector and a directory replication connector, or if the correct permissions are in place, you can do this from your first site. Just open a server in the other site and use the new Administrator window for the site to create your RAS MTA transport stack.

## Setting Up a Site-to-Site Link Using the X.400 Connector

To set up a site connection using the X.400 Connector, first open the File menu on the Exchange Administrator for your first site. Select New Other from the File menu, and then select X.400 Connector from the New Other submenu. The New X.400 Connector dialog box pops up (see Figure 14.46). Since only your TCP/IP MTA transport stack can support the X.400 Connector, it will be the only one listed in the Type box. Click OK.

Next you'll see the dialog box for your new X.400 Connector (see Figure 14.47). The dialog box contains a lot of property pages, but don't worry. At least when the X.400 Connector is used to directly link Exchange sites, you need to deal with only a few of these.

**FIGURE 14.46:**

Selecting an MTA transport stack with the New X.400 Connector dialog box

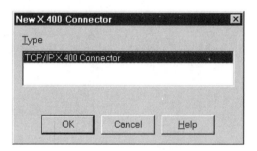

**NOTE**   We won't talk about the Delivery Restrictions property page here, even though you can use it productively for site-to-site connections. We already discussed it back in Chapter 8.

**FIGURE 14.47:**

The dialog box for an X.400
Connector

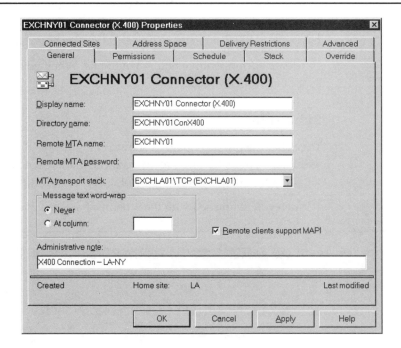

## General Properties

Give the connector a name; *Remote_Server_Name + Connector + (X.400)* is a good model. Because I'm setting up this connector in my LA site and the target site is NY, I've named the connector EXCHNY01 Connector (X.400) to clearly indicate that communications are from LA to NY by way of X.400. As you'll see in a bit, this name makes it easy to find the right connector when you've got more than one in a site.

The Remote MTA Name field contains the name of your remote MTA, which is by default the name of the remote Exchange server (EXCHNY01 in my case). For greater security, you can set passwords for X.400 MTAs. You'd enter the password for the remote MTA here, if it had one. You set the name and password for the local MTA—the Exchange server you're working on right now—from the server's MTA General page or optionally, from the Override property page of the X.400 Connector dialog box you're working on right now.

Leave the Message Text Word-Wrap and Remote Clients Support MAPI options set to their defaults. You may need to change one or more of these defaults when using the X.400 Connector to link to foreign e-messaging systems.

Add an administrative note if you'd like. When you're finished, tab over to the Schedule property page.

## Schedule

The Schedule property page is shown in Figure 14.48. Leave the Always default as is; since your sites are directly connected, there's no reason to change the default, other than a need to control really heavy traffic.

When you're finished with the Schedule page, tab over to the Stack property page.

**FIGURE 14.48:**

Setting a schedule for X.400 connections

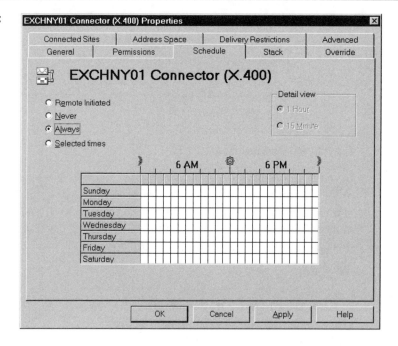

**NOTE** You may have noticed that the X.400 Connector has a Schedule property page, while the Site Connector has none. You can't schedule links with the Site Connector—they're continuous by definition. "But," I can hear you thinking, "didn't I encounter a schedule recently?" You sure did, but it was for the directory replication connector you created. Put simply, directory replication can always be scheduled. Connections between sites using the Site Connector can't be scheduled, but connections between sites using other site connectors can. Eee-aye-eee-aye-oh.

## Stack

See Figure 14.49 for the Stack property page. Since we're running our X.400 Connector on top of a TCP/IP stack, all we need to do here is enter an Internet domain name for the other Exchange server or its IP address. (I entered the IP address of my Exchange server in New York, EXCHNY01.) When you're done, tab over to the Address Space property page.

**FIGURE 14.49:**

Providing stack addressing information

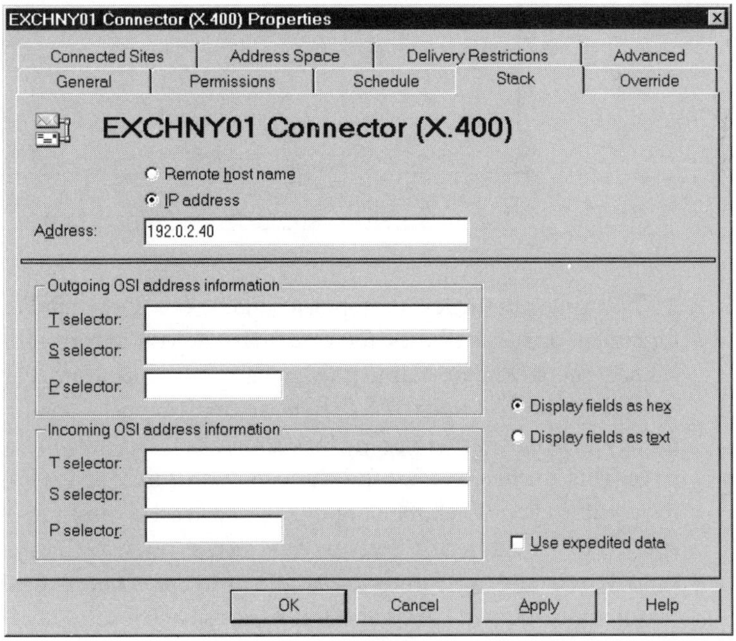

## Address Space

Figure 14.50 shows the Address Space property page as you'll first see it. You need to add an address space for your other server. It should be an X.400 address space, so click the New X.400 button on the right-hand side of the page.

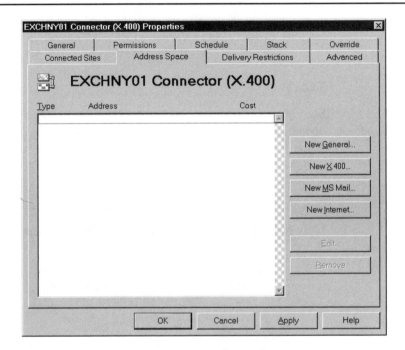

This brings up the X.400 Properties dialog box shown in Figure 14.51. Fill in the Organization name (that is, the Exchange site you're connecting to) and the Private Management Domain Name (the Exchange organization). Hey, we're talking apples (Exchange) and oranges (X.400) here, so don't expect a one-to-one parallel in terminology. Leave the other parameters as they are. Tab over to the Restrictions property page. This is where you set the scope of this address space or, in other words, which recipients in your Exchange organization can send messages through this address space on your connector. You can leave access open to all in your organization or limit it to the site the Connector runs in or to the Location this server resides in. You'll remember we talked about Locations back in Chapter 9. When you're done with the X.400 properties dialog box, click OK.

You're returned to the Address Space property page (see Figure 14.52). The new X.400 address should be in place.

**FIGURE 14.51:**

Entering an X.400 address for the other site

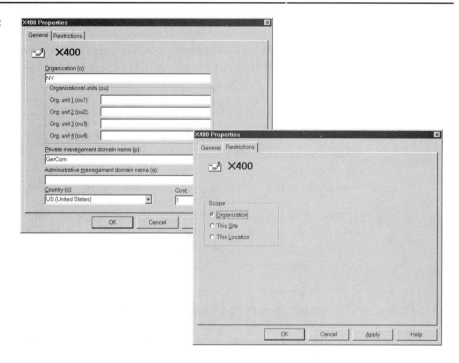

**FIGURE 14.52:**

The Address Space property page with the X.400 address entered in Figure 14.51

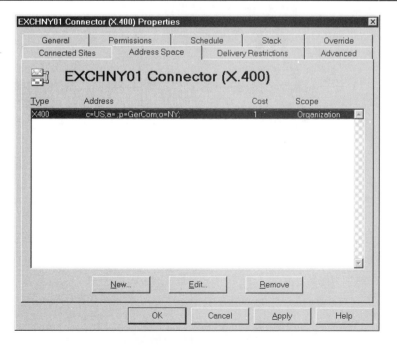

## Override

If you need to, you can use the Override property page to set up an MTA name and a password that are different from your Exchange server's own MTA name and password. You can also use the Override page to set alternate messaging parameters from those of your server's MTA's defaults.

You're now done with this site; click OK on the dialog box to create the connector.

Now you need to create a parallel X.400 Connector on your other server. Just follow the instructions above, adjusting for the fact that you're setting up the connector on that server. When you're done with both sites, you should see the new connectors in the Connections container for each site (see Figure 14.53).

Notice in Figure 14.53 how the names of the connectors—EXCHNY01 Connector X.400, for example—make it very easy to see not only the target Exchange server, but also the type of connection being used. As you'll soon see when we add our next connector, the names can really help.

**FIGURE 14.53:**

The X.400 connectors are in place in each site.

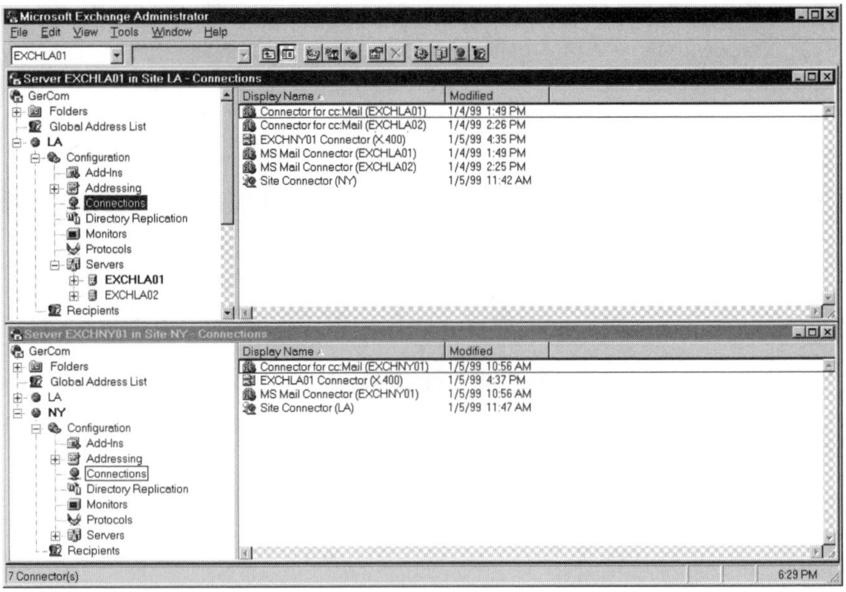

## Connecting Sites

You need to do one last thing before your sites can communicate. For each site, double-click your new X.400 Connector and tab over to the Connected Sites property page in the resultant Connector Properties dialog box (see Figure 14.54).

**FIGURE 14.54:**

The Connected Sites property page

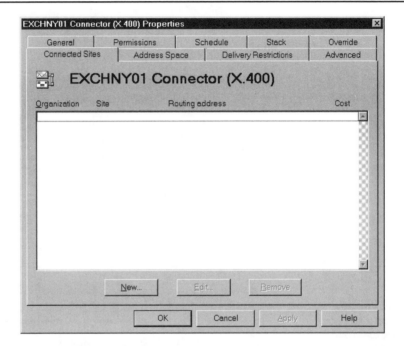

While in your first site, you need to add a connection to your other site. Click New on the Connected Sites Properties dialog box to bring up a site-selection Properties dialog box (see Figure 14.55). Be sure the Exchange organization name is correct, then type in the name of the site you want to connect to. When you're done, click OK.

The Properties dialog box closes and the connection shows in the list box in the Connected Sites property page (see Figure 14.56). You're now done with this page. Click OK.

**FIGURE 14.55:**

Entering site connection information

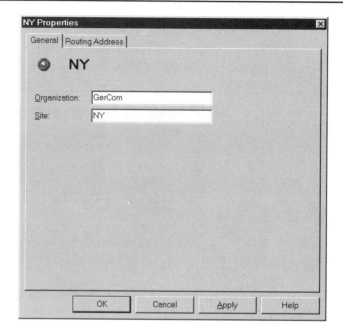

**FIGURE 14.56:**

The Connected Sites property page containing the specified connection information

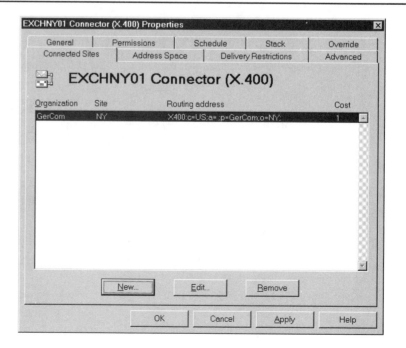

Now do the same thing with your other server. Your sites are now linked by X.400 Connectors.

**NOTE**    If you haven't installed a directory replication connector between your two sites yet—which would be the case if you didn't track through the installation process for the Site Connectors and directory replication connector detailed above—you need to do that now. Refer to the section earlier in this chapter on setting up a directory replication connector.

### Did It Work?

If you've got Site Connectors in place, you might want to delete them from both sites, just to be sure that your X.400 connectors are working. Now that you know how easy it is to re-create your Site Connectors, this shouldn't phase you at all.

For a quick test, create a new mailbox in one of your sites. Then follow the three steps outlined earlier in this chapter for manually forcing directory replication. If everything is working, you should see the new mailbox in the Global Address List from each site. If this isn't the case, go back and retrace your steps in creating your MTA transport stacks and X.400 connectors.

## Setting Up a Site-to-Site Link Using the Dynamic RAS Connector

We'll cover this process more quickly, depending on a lot of things you learned in the last section.

Select the Connections container in your first site, then select Dynamic RAS Connector from the New Other submenu of the Exchange Administrator's File menu. This opens up the Dynamic RAS Connector Properties dialog box (see Figure 14.57).

### General Properties

Name the connector using the conventions I suggested for the X.400 Connector, changing (X.400) to (DRAS). Enter the name of the remote server—EXCHNY01 in my case—which is the Exchange server in your other site—NY in my case. Select the MTA RAS transport stack from the RAS stacks that exist in the site.

**FIGURE 14.57:**

The Properties dialog box
for a Dynamic Remote
Access Service Connector

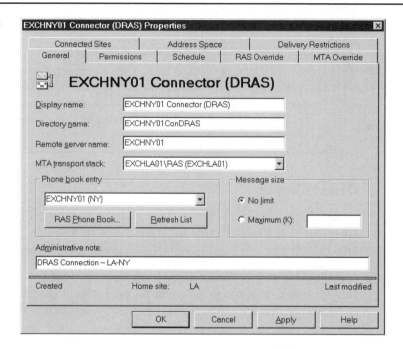

In the Phone Book Entry field, choose the RAS phone book entry that will dial up your other server with a Dynamic Remote Access Service Connector (DRASC).

---

**NOTE**
You can add phone numbers to a RAS phone book only while locally logged in to the server running the RAS—you can't, for instance, add numbers to a phone book on Server B while administering Server B from Server A. You'll have to add the numbers while locally logged in to the server running the RAS (Server B).

---

If you wish, you can set a maximum size for messages transmitted over this connector. Generally, I suggest that you not set a limit. If your DRAS Connector is being used as a backup to another site connector that goes down, you might want to temporarily set a maximum message size limit. This would ensure that your slower DRAS Connector doesn't spend its time delivering one or two large messages while many smaller messages go undelivered.

When you're finished with the General property page, tab over to the Schedule page.

## Schedule

The default schedule is Always, which for some dial-up connections may be too frequent. I like the schedule shown in Figure 14.58: one contact at midnight and subsequent contacts every other hour from 9 A.M. to 11 P.M.

**FIGURE 14.58:**

Scheduling site links for a Dynamic Remote Access Service Connector

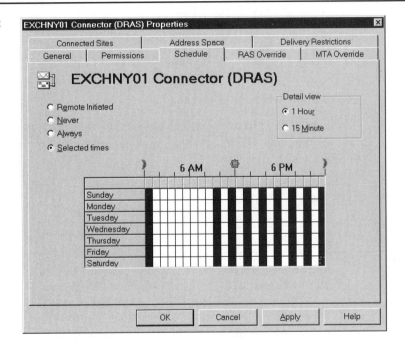

## Other Property Pages

You probably didn't need to enter any account or domain information into the Override page of your Site or X.400 Connector Property dialog boxes. However, you do have to do this on the RAS Override page of the DRAS Connector Property dialog box. Enter the name of the account you want to connect to in the other site (usually the Exchange services account) along with the account's password and the NT domain in which the account is located. Check Figure 14.24 for a specific example. The RAS Override property page includes two items not relevant to the Site Connector Override page: the MTA callback number and the overriding phone number. The remote MTA uses the callback number to contact your Exchange server's MTA after contact by your server. The overriding phone number is used instead of a phone number listed in the RAS phone book.

On the Address Space property page, create an address for your other site as you did for your site and X.400 connectors. Use the following format for the address:

```
c=[Your Country, e.g., US];a= [a space];p=[Your Exchange Organization
Name, e.g., GerCom];o=[Name Of Site You Want To Contact, e.g., NY]
```

Be sure to type everything on one line and to leave a space after a=.

On the Connected Sites property page, set a routing link to your other site. Just click New, enter the name of your other site in the resultant Properties dialog box, and click OK when you're finished.

You know what to do with the Delivery Restrictions property page. When you're done, click OK in the Dynamic RAS Connector Properties dialog box, and your DRASC is all set up.

## The Next Steps

Now create a DRAS Connector in your other site.

> **NOTE**
> If you haven't yet installed a directory replication connector between your two sites—which would be the case if you didn't track through the installation procedures for the Site Connector/directory replication connector and the X.400 Connector as detailed above—you'll need to do that now. Refer to the section on setting up a directory replication connector earlier in this chapter.

When everything is set, you'll see two functioning DRAS Connectors—one in the Connections container for each site (see Figure 14.59).

Now notice how smart we were to have named the connectors as we did. You can immediately tell which is the DRAS Connector, the X.400 Connector, and the Site Connector. Double-click the one you want; the appropriate connector dialog box pops up and you're ready to administer and manage the connector. What could be easier?

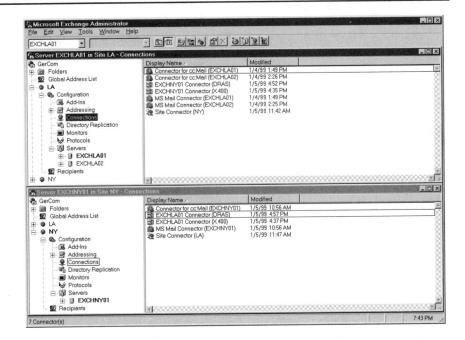

**FIGURE 14.59:**

DRAS Connectors in place
for each site

# Some Clarifying Comments on Site-to-Site Connections

Before we move on to monitors and public folder replication, I want to make sure you understand a couple things. You can set up only *one* directory replication connector for each unique pair of sites. If you tried right now to create another directory replication connector (assuming you have only the two sites you've already connected for directory replication), the Exchange Administrator program wouldn't let you do it. If you have more sites and you create connections between them, then the Administrator would happily let you create another directory replication connector.

It's important to note, however, that for purposes of redundancy your single directory replication connector can run on top of multiple site connectors. That's why you should keep both your DRASC and either your Site Connector or X.400

Connector in place. Keeping both your Site Connector and X.400 Connector in place—assuming that both use the same physical network, as ours do in the previous examples—doesn't make much sense, since there's no redundancy advantage.

# Adding New Servers to Server and Link Monitors

Remember the server and link monitors we created in previous chapters? Well, now we can add the new server we set up in this chapter to those monitors. (If you need more information while doing the next two tasks, refer to the sections on server monitors in Chapters 8 and 13, or to the section on link monitors in Chapter 13.)

If your server monitor is running, close it. Select the Monitors container for your first site, then double-click the server monitor you set up back in Chapter 8. When the Properties dialog box for the server pops up, tab over to the Servers property page and select your new site from the drop-down list and add your new server. Click OK in the Properties dialog box. Open your server monitor and you'll see that the new server is now being monitored.

If your link monitor is running, close it. Select the Monitors container for your first site, then double-click the link monitor you created in Chapter 13. When the Properties dialog box for your link monitor pops up, tab over to the Servers property page and add your new server from your new site. Click OK in the Properties dialog box. Open your link monitor and you'll see that the new server has been added. After several minutes, the monitor tells you that the link to your new server is working correctly.

Figure 14.60 shows my server and link monitors with my new server added to each.

**FIGURE 14.60:**

A new server is added to the existing server and link monitors.

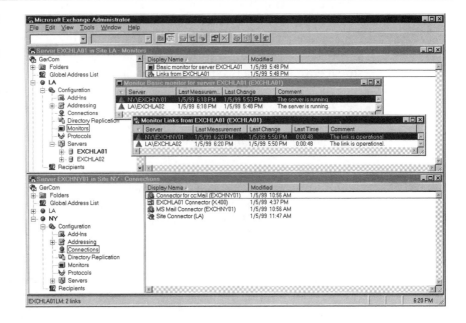

# Setting Up Cross-Site Public Folder Access

The only issue we haven't covered in the area of information store administration and management is cross-site public folder access. This is the perfect time and place for that, so let's get going.

If a site is included in directory replication, users at any site in the Exchange organization can see its top-level public folders and all levels of subfolders from their Outlook clients. However, a user (for example, an Exchange mailbox user) at one site (Site A) can access a specific public folder that lives at another site (Site B) *only* if the user has permission to access the folder *and* if one of the following criteria is met:

*Option 1:* Users from Site A are permitted to connect directly to all the public folders in Site B.

or

*Option 2:* Public folders from Site B are replicated in Site A.

In the following two sections, you'll learn how to set up both cross-site direct access to public folders and public folder replication. Before we start, you should have at least two public folders on each of the servers in each of your sites. If you've been paralleling my examples, you should now have three servers. Be sure there are at least two public folders on each server. Put a couple messages in each folder. (If you need a refresher on public folder creation, refer back to Chapter 12. Remember, Outlook clients create public folders, so you'll need to install clients in your sites if you haven't already done so. Check out Chapters 11 and 12 if you need help installing clients.)

---

**NOTE**    As you may remember from earlier chapters, in the simplest model public folders are stored on the home server of the mailbox used to create them. However, this does not have to be the case. You can designate any Exchange server in a site to hold public folders created by users with mailboxes on any other server in the site.

---

For the following exercises, be sure that any public folders created on the second server in your first site are stored on that server. Use the Private Information Store Properties dialog box for the second server to check this setting. Refer back to Chapter 9 if you need help with this dialog box.

# Allowing Users in One Site to Connect to Folders in Another Site

Let's start with Option 1 in that little list above detailing cross-site connections to public folders by users. This option has one prerequisite: Users must have a direct network link to the site whose public folders they will connect to. An indirect link through a foreign e-messaging system isn't enough.

## Setting Up Public Folder Affinity

In the Exchange Administrator, select the Configuration container for your first site, then double-click Information Store Site Configuration. This brings up the Information Store Site Configuration Properties dialog box. Back in Chapter 9, we covered everything about this dialog box in detail, except the Public Folder Affinity property page. And are we ready for that page now!

You use the Public Folders Affinity property page to give users in one site the ability to connect directly to all public folders in another site (see Figure 14.61).

The page shows the sites for which you can set affinity in the Sites box on the left-hand side. Select your site and click Add to create an affinity in your first site for public folders in your second site. The selected site then appears in the Public Folder Affinity box on the right-hand side of the property page. In Figure 14.61, you can see that I have only one choice from my first (LA) site—and that's my NY site.

**FIGURE 14.61:**

Permitting users in one site to access all public folders in another site

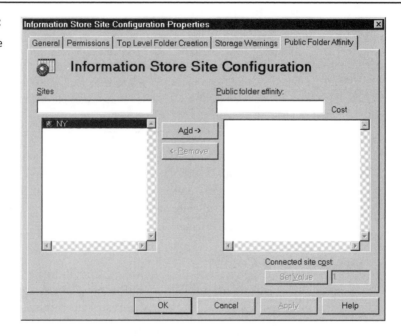

You set a cost for each site for which you have an affinity in the Connected Site Cost field in the lower right-hand corner of the Public Folder Affinity property page. Costs are used to determine which site to connect to when a specific public folder exists in more than one external site. This can happen when you replicate one site's folders to two or more other sites. (We'll get to public folder replication in just a bit.) You should set costs based on the available network bandwidth between your site and the other site. When a user needs to connect to a public folder in another site, the link is made to the site with the lowest cost. For now, accept the default cost value.

Now click OK in the Information Store Site Configuration Properties dialog box, and you're done.

## Did It Work?

To test out the affinity you set, open a client at your first site and then select a public folder from your second site. You should be able to open any of the messages in the folder. Select another public folder from your second site. Again, you should be able to view any of the folder's messages.

---

**NOTE**   Remember that although user mailboxes have home servers, they really live in sites, and public folders are stored on specific servers but really live in sites as well. This means that a user whose mailbox is in a specific site can access all unrestricted folders in that site without your having to do anything at all as an Exchange administrator. It's only when you want users in one site to access public folders in another site that you have to consider public folder affinity or replication.

---

At this point, if you were to open a client in your second site, you would see top-level public folders and all levels of subfolders from your first site, but you wouldn't be able to access the items inside those folders. That's because you didn't set public folder affinity with the first site at your second site. To do that, you'd have to repeat the process we just finished, except this time in your second site.

## Benefits and Costs

As you've seen, setting up public folder affinities is really easy. In one fell swoop you give all users in a site access to any unrestricted public folders in another site.

Another advantage of public folder affinity is immediacy. When you want to be sure that users are working with the latest view of a public folder, you'll usually want to pick affinity over replication. If all users connect to the one and only copy of a public folder, they know that whatever they (or others) put into or take out of the folder will be seen immediately by anyone connected to the folder. As you'll see in a bit, public folder replication is by contrast usually subject to at least small delays.

Nonetheless, two problems can occur with public folder affinity. First, users have to connect to intrasite public folders across the network to access them. If sites are connected by higher-bandwidth networks, that may be no big deal, depending on how many users try to access public folders at any given time. If network bandwidth is low or if cross-site public folder access is heavy, users connecting to intrasite public folders can bring a network to its knees.

The second problem with public folder affinity is that you can't select which public folders will be accessible. By default, all folders are available to users. If you want everyone in a public folder's home site to have access to the folder, but you don't want users in other sites to have such access, you have to remove any default access rights to the folder and assign such rights to a distribution list that includes all users in the home site. That's a lot of work, especially if you have more than a few public folders whose extrasite access you wish to restrict.

Both of these problems can be avoided with public folder replication. Let's move on to that option right now.

## Cross-Site Public Folder Replication

Public folders can be replicated between servers within a site as well as between servers in different sites. With public folder replication, users don't need to be directly connected to another site to access its public folders. Instead, they access synchronized replicas of the folders, which are stored on their home servers or at their home sites. Generally, you replicate public folders to make them available to users in other sites, to reduce cross-site network traffic, to distribute the load for heavily accessed folders across multiple servers in a site, and to create redundant copies of folders in one or more sites in case any single copy becomes unusable.

Public folder replication can be done at two levels: the server level and the folder level. Server-level replication lets you bring one or more folders *from* other sites *to* your site; you might want to think of it as a sort of *pull* process. Folder-level replication lets you replicate one folder at a time *from* your site *to* one or more sites; thus, you can think of it more as a *push* process. Regardless of which level you use, once replication is set up, all replicas of a given folder are automatically kept in sync with each other.

**NOTE**    Before we start, remove any public folder affinities you may have set up in the last section. There may be times when you want to set up affinities between two sites and at the same time replicate specific public folders between them; for the following exercise, however, we just want to replicate.

### Setting Up Public Folder Replication at the Server Level

Though public folders are treated as belonging to sites and even to an entire Exchange organization, their physical home is on Exchange servers. As you'll soon see, whether you replicate at the server level or folder level, there are times when you have to think in terms of servers.

In the left-hand pane of an Exchange Administrator window, select the container for the server to which you want to replicate public folders; let's call it the *target server*. I'm going to replicate a folder in my NY site (my *source site*) over to my LA site (my *target site*). The physical home for the folder will be the target server EXCHLA01. In other words, I'll pull a folder from my source site (NY) to my target server (EXCHLA01). Unless it carries specific restrictions, once the public folder has been replicated to EXCHLA01, it will be available to all users in my target site, LA. So I'll select the container for EXCHLA01 in the left-hand pane of the Administrator window.

Next, click Public Information Store once in the right-hand pane of the Administrator window and select Properties from Exchange Administrator's File menu. This brings up the Public Information Store Properties dialog box for the target server (see Figure 14.62).

**FIGURE 14.62:**

The Public Information Store Properties dialog box

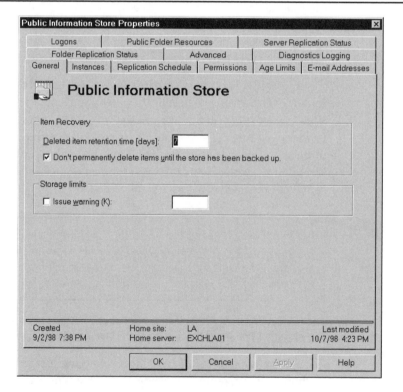

I already talked about the General property page of this dialog box back in Chapter 9. This is where you can set the number of days before items on the server are really deleted and enter serverwide parameters for maximum public folder size.

You set up public folder replication from the Instances property page. Tab over to it and you should see a page that looks something like the one in Figure 14.63.

**FIGURE 14.63:**

The Instances property page of the Public Information Store Properties dialog box

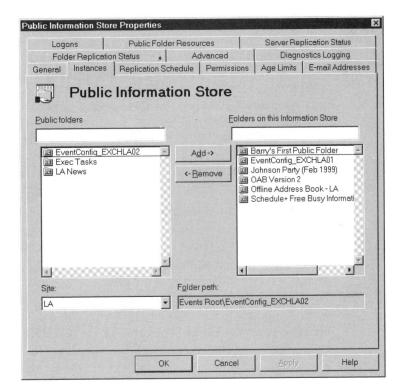

**Some Basics**   You're looking at information about public folders in the home site of the target server you just selected. (In my case, the site is LA and the target server is EXCHLA01. We know that it's LA because LA shows in the Site drop-down menu in the lower left-hand corner of the Instances property page. And we know that it's EXCHLA01 because that's the target server we selected earlier.)

Before I set up the replication of a folder in my NY site, we need to talk a bit about the Instances property page as it looks when you first tab over to it; that is, when it focuses on your target site and server. That'll put some basics under your belt that will come in handy as we actually replicate a folder in the next section.

First, let's look at the right-hand side of the Instances property page. The Folders on This Information Store box shows public folders and other items already in the target server's public information store. The folders Barry's First Public Folder and Johnson Party (Feb 1999) reside on my target server, EXCHLA01.

**NOTE**   Also on the target server are items that aren't public folders in the classic sense. Each is sitewide, as opposed to being only for the server you're working on at the time. The Offline Address Book and Schedule+ Free/Busy Information public folders support, respectively, remote Exchange client access and cross-site Schedule+ appointment scheduling. The OAB Version 2 public folder is a copy of the Offline Address Book for the newer Outlook clients that come with Exchange Server 5.5. The EventConfig_EXCHLA01 public folder holds information about programs that you design to run on public folders on a server. More about all of this in Chapter 17. For now, don't mess with these.

Now let's turn our attention to the left-hand side of the Instances property page. The Public Folders box shows the selected site's public folders that are available for replication to the target server's public information store. The three folders in my example are EventConfig_EXCHLA02, Exec Tasks, and LA News. These folders reside on the other server in my LA site, EXCHLA02. If I wanted to replicate the folder LA News to my target server, EXCHLA01, I'd select it and click Add, which would move it over to the Folders on This Information Store box. Remember, users in my LA site can open and use the folders on EXCHLA02, even if their mailboxes are on EXCHLA01. So, I'd only replicate folders from EXCHLA02 to EXCHLA01 to lighten network traffic or to improve folder access performance for users on EXCHLA01.

The Remove button is used here to turn off replication of public folders whose original home is another server in the site or another site altogether. Though the Remove button is enabled in Figure 14.63, I actually can't remove any of the six items in the Folders on This Information Store box, since this *is* the only server they are located on in their home site physical home and replication to this information store is, thus, a physical impossibility.

**Replicating a Public Folder at the Server Level**    We're now ready to replicate a folder in our other site. Open the Site drop-down menu in the lower left-hand corner of the Instances property page and select your other site from it (mine is NY). Your Instances page should now look something like the one shown in Figure 14.64.

I want to replicate the public folder Jolly Elves to my target server, EXCHLA01. To do so, I select the folder and click Add. As you can see in Figure 14.65, the folder moves over to the Folders on This Information Store box, indicating that it will be replicated to EXCHLA01 when you click OK.

That's it. It's that easy.

**FIGURE 14.64:**

Using the Instances property page to set up replication of a public folder from another site

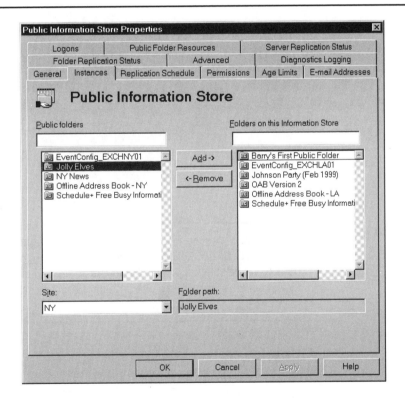

**FIGURE 14.65:**

The public folder will now be replicated.

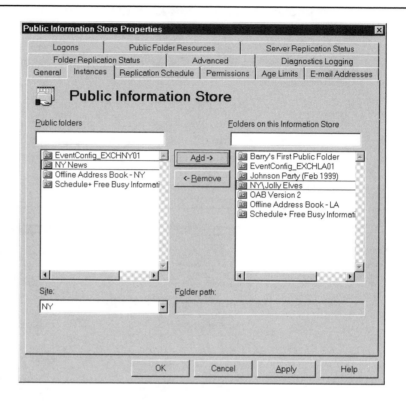

**NOTE**    I really don't want users in LA wasting their (and GerCom's) time reading the news meant for NY. By not replicating the folder NY News to my LA site, I ensure that LA users won't be able to open the folder and access items in it. If public folder affinity were in effect, I'd have to play with the folder's permissions to accomplish the same end.

**Did It Work?**    To find out whether the replication worked, simply open an Outlook client for a mailbox in your target site (LA in my case), then find the folder you set replication for (mine is Jolly Elves). Select the folder. You should be able to see what's in the folder, and you shouldn't be told that you can't access it. Now select the other folder in your second site that you didn't set replication for (NY News in my case). You should be told that the contents of the folder are unavailable.

Replication doesn't happen immediately. If everything isn't as expected, wait a reasonable time, depending on the replication schedule you set. If things still don't go as advertised, retrace your steps, following the example above.

### Administering and Managing Public Folder Replication at the Server Level

Let's take a quick look at some of the other property pages in the Public Information Store Properties dialog box. These pages let you administer and manage public folder replication at the server level.

**Replication Schedule (Figure 14.66)**    You use this property page to set timing for replications from the selected server to other servers. Generally, the preferred setting is the default, Always.

**FIGURE 14.66:**

The Replication Schedule property page

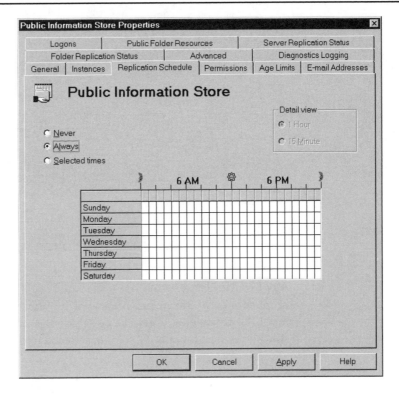

**Advanced (Figure 14.67)**    The Advanced property page allows you to set a time in minutes for the Always option in the Replication Schedule page and to specify the maximum size for each individual replication message the IS sends during public folder replication. The IS will not, however, break up a single message, so if it has to replicate a message larger than this size, the message will be replicated, and the replication message that gets sent will surpass the limit.

**Age Limits (Figure 14.68)**    Use the Age Limits property page to set the number of days after which messages in public folders that haven't been modified are deleted. Ages can be set for all folders in a public information store, as well as for specific folders (select a folder and click Modify).

FIGURE 14.68:

The Age Limits
property page

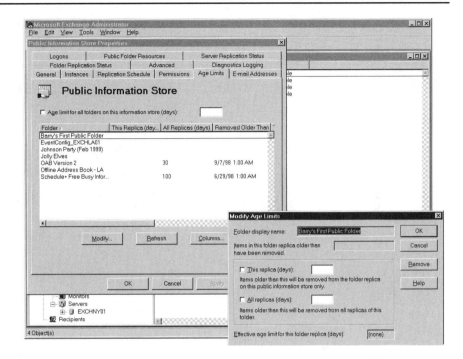

**Folder Replication Status (Figure 14.69)**   Use this property page to monitor the replication process for public folders and their hierarchy for the
organization. (Replicating the hierarchy gives each site a view of the public
folder tree structure. Only folder affinity settings or replication, however,
give users in one site access to the folders in another site.) Notice in the figure that my folder replicas are in sync. The Events Root folder holds the
EventConfig folder for each server in the organization.

**Server Replication Status (Figure 14.70)**   Use this property page to monitor the replication process for specific servers. The status Local Modified
means that there have been changes in the public folders that are to be
replicated to EXCHLA02 and EXCHNY01. If all changes had been replicated, In Sync would be displayed in the Replication Status column for
each server. Average Transmission Time is in seconds. It tells how long, on
the average, it takes to complete a replication cycle for the server in that
row. Hidden off to the right of the property page is another column, Last
Transmission Time, which reports the time in seconds required for the last

replication cycle. You can use these times to gauge the performance of your server. If replications are taking too long to a particular server, you might want to look into solutions like a faster site connector.

**FIGURE 14.69:**

The Folder Replication Status property page

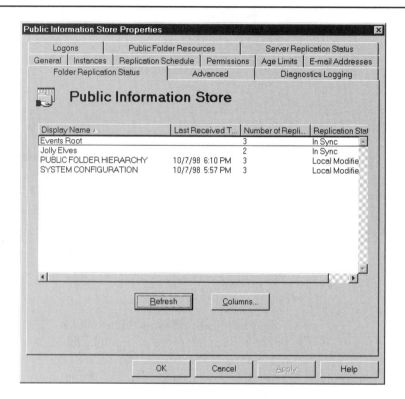

From your work with previous dialog boxes, you should be familiar by now with the remaining property pages in the Public Information Store Properties dialog box. The Logons page shows who's connected to the selected server's public information store, just like the Logons page for the Private Information Store dialog box that we discussed in Chapter 9. Among other things, the Public Folder Resources page shows you how much disk space each folder replica on the server currently consumes. And based on our discussions in earlier chapters, you should have no problems with the Permissions, E-Mail Addresses, and Diagnostics Logging property pages.

**FIGURE 14.70:**

The Server Replication
Status property page

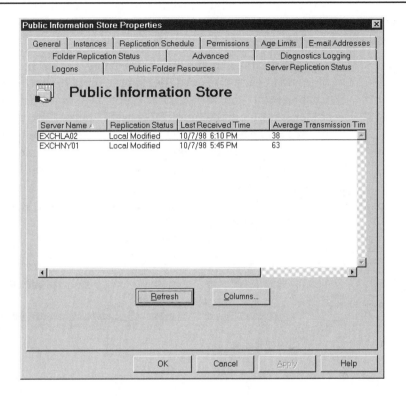

**FIGURE 14.70:**

The Server Replication
Status property page

## Setting Up Public Folder Replication at the Folder Level

Remember that configuring replication at the folder level is a *push* process. You
configure a public folder *from* one site (the *source* site) *to* a server (the *target*
server) in the same or another site. When the folder has been replicated to a
server in another site, it is available to users in that site—the target site.

> **NOTE**  You don't need to remove the server-level folder replication you set up in the last
> section. It will have no effect on what we do here.

**Replicating a Public Folder at the Folder Level**    In the Exchange Administrator, find one of the public folders in your first site. Look for the folder under the

organization-level Public Folders hierarchy near the top of the tree in the left-hand Administrator pane. (I'll use the folder Barry's First Public Folder; see Figure 14.71.)

Click the folder once and then select Properties from the Administrator's File menu. This brings up the Properties dialog box for the folder (see Figure 14.72). Since we already discussed the General property page for this dialog box back in Chapter 9, let's tab over to the Replicas page so we can set up replication for this folder. As you can see from Figure 14.73, the Replicas property page looks a lot like the Instances page in the Public Information Store dialog box we looked at in the last section. The rules here are pretty much the same as for the Instances page, too. The Servers box on the left-hand side shows available target servers, while the right-hand Replicate Folders To box shows which servers currently are receiving replicas of the folder. In the figure, we're looking at my source site, LA. If I wanted to replicate this folder to EXCHLA02 (the second server in my LA site), I would select it and click the Add button.

**FIGURE 14.71:**

Finding a public folder to replicate

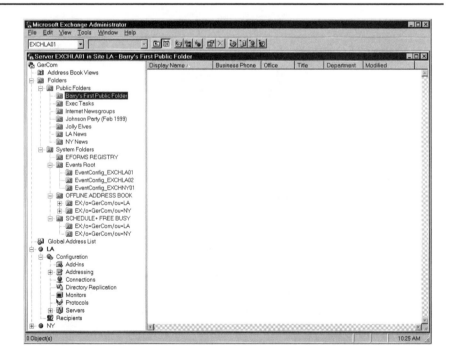

**FIGURE 14.72:**

The Properties dialog box
for the public folder to be
replicated

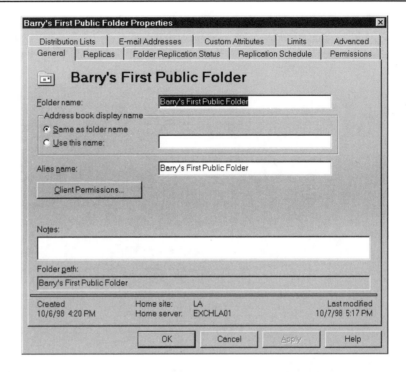

Use the Sites drop-down menu to move to your other (target) site, NY in my
case; see Figure 14.74. To set up replication of Barry's First Public Folder from my
LA site to the server EXCHNY01 in my NY site, I would select the server in the
Servers box and click Add.

This places the server in the Replicate Folders To box, indicating that the folder
will now be replicated to the target server. As you can see in Figure 14.75,
EXCHNY01 in my NY site will now receive a replica of Barry's First Public
Folder. That's it.

**Did It Work?**    Let's see if the replication worked. After waiting long enough to
allow replication—15 minutes if you chose the default replication schedule—
open an Outlook client whose home server is in your second site. (In my case,
that would be EXCHNY01.) Select the folder you chose to replicate. You should
be able to see what's in the folder, and you should not be told that the folder is
unavailable. If you can't access the folder, retrace the steps outlined above.

**FIGURE 14.73:**

The Replicas property page showing the source site

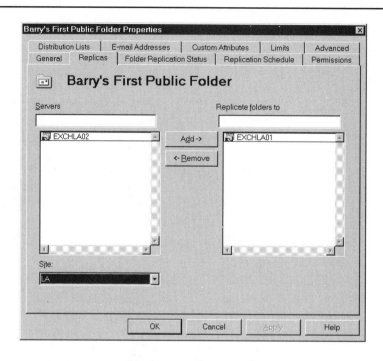

**FIGURE 14.74:**

The Replicas property page showing the target site

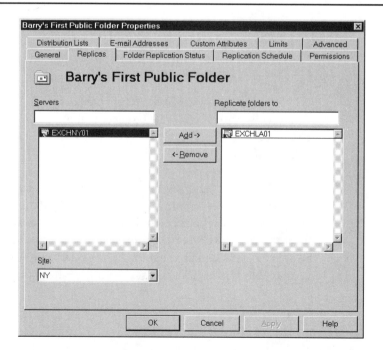

**FIGURE 14.75:**

The public folder will now be replicated to the target server.

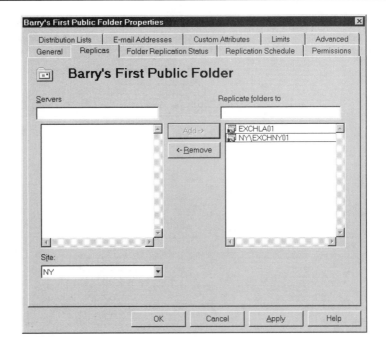

**Administering and Managing Public Folder Replication at the Folder Level**    Two property pages in the Properties dialog box for a public folder can help you administer and manage that folder's replication: Folder Replication Status and Advanced. Let's briefly look at these two pages.

**Folder Replication Status (Figure 14.76)**    Use this property page to monitor folder replication. The page works much like the same property page for server-level replication described above; however, since this page is for a single public folder, it shows status in terms of servers instead of specific public folders. As shown in Figure 14.76, my folder is in sync on both servers.

**Advanced (Figure 14.77)**    Use the Advanced property page's Trust Level list box to control whether the folder's address is included when the Exchange directory is sent to foreign e-messaging systems during directory synchronization. (We'll talk about directory synchronization in a later chapter.) Use the Replication Msg Importance drop-down list to set a priority for replication messages that are sent to the folder.

**FIGURE 14.76:**

The Folder Replication Status property page

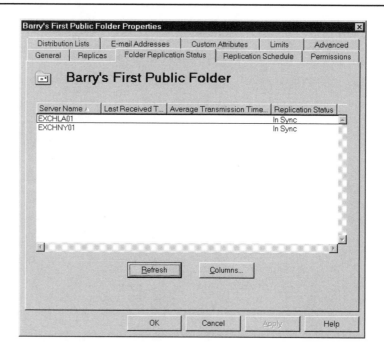

**FIGURE 14.77:**

The Advanced property page

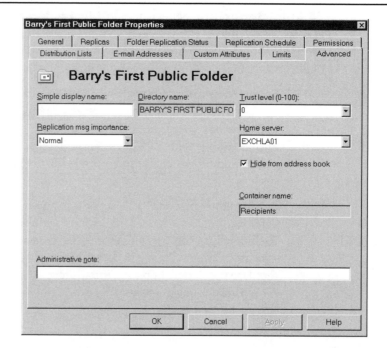

The rest of the fields on the Advanced property page—as well as the Permissions, Distribution Lists, E-Mail Addresses, Custom Attributes, and Limits property pages—should be old hat from your experience with other dialog boxes.

## Benefits and Costs

You have to set up public folder replication between each pair of sites on a folder-by-folder basis. This is more work than is required for setting public folder affinity, which lets users in one site connect to all unrestricted public folders in another site. However, replication is generally lighter on network bandwidth, since users access a local replica rather than connecting to the one and only copy of a public folder stored somewhere out there on a wide area network. With replication, bandwidth is required only to keep replicas in sync.

It's also somewhat easier to exclude public folders from intersite access with replication rather than with affinity. With replication, you replicate the folders you want people to see. With affinity, you have to mess with permissions on folders you don't want people to see.

One great advantage of replication is online redundancy. Even with just one replica of a public folder (that is, there are two instances of that folder), your risk of losing important information in the event of an Exchange server crash is cut in half. With two replicas (three instances), your risk is cut by two-thirds, and so on. And best of all, the public folders on a server will be automatically rebuilt when a crashed server comes back online. Sure, you should still back up your servers, but unless you back up every 15 minutes or so, you'll never capture that piece of newly folderized information to tape.

Replication does have one drawback: Each replica of a folder takes up disk storage space. Among the other issues mentioned above, in deciding whether to use affinity or replication, you should also consider the cost of bandwidth versus disk storage space.

# Site-Level Addressing and Routing Administration and Management

Look in the Configuration container for your site. Notice the Site Addressing object. This is where you deal with site addresses themselves and with message routing between sites. Since we already covered site addresses back in Chapter 8 when we installed our first Exchange server, we'll talk about intersite routing here.

Click the Configuration container in the left-hand pane of an Administrator window, then double-click Site Addressing. This opens up the Site Addressing Properties dialog box shown in Figure 14.78.

## General Properties

The Routing Calculation Server option on the General property page plays an important role in Exchange Server. One Exchange server in each site is designated as the routing calculation server, and the System Attendant on that server creates a routing table and replicates it to the other servers in the site. This table is used to send messages outside the site through Exchange connectors and gateways. A new routing table is calculated every time a change occurs that affects routing—for example, when a new connector is installed.

**FIGURE 14.78:**

The Site Addressing Properties dialog box

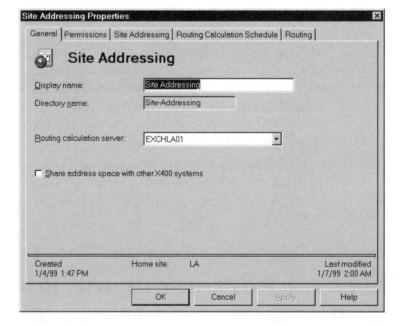

You can assign the task of calculating the routing table to any server in a site using the Routing Calculation Server drop-down list. Though routing calculation requires little CPU time, you might want to assign this task to the least busy of the servers in a site.

Use the Share Address Space with Other X.400 Systems option to let an Exchange server pick up and route messages for another system. It's most useful when you're making the transition from an X.400 system to Exchange. The other system doesn't need to be connected to the outside world; instead, it can send and receive messages through the Exchange server.

## Routing Calculation Schedule

Settings on the Routing Calculation Schedule property page determine when a new routing table is calculated. You've seen this page lots of times before, so I'll say no more about it here.

### Routing

The Routing property page shows all current routing table entries and lets you manually force a recalculation for the site's routing (see Figure 14.79). You can also save the routing table to disk as a comma separated values (CSV) file and view routing details for an entry. Routing Details include any connections (hops) between your site and the remote node; such information can be useful in tracing a downed link.

In Figure 14.79, you can see the routes in place from my LA site to my NY site. Each of my three Exchange connectors (DRAS, X.400, and Site) uses a standard Exchange-type address (/O=GERCOM/OU=NY) and a standard X.400 address (c=US;a= ;p=GERCOM;o=NY) to communicate with my NY site.

FIGURE 14.79:

The Routing property page
shows routing addresses
for all connectors in a site.

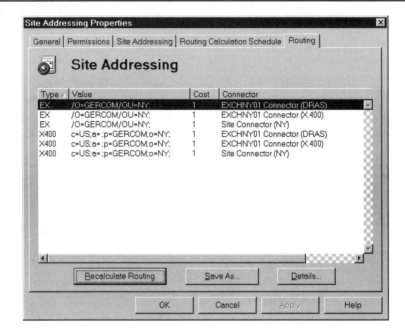

# Conclusion

You learned a lot in this chapter, including how to install an Exchange server in a new domain and site; how to connect two domains and sites; how to set up directory replication between two sites; how to add new servers and links to existing server and link monitors; how to give users access to public folders in other sites; and how to use tools for administering and managing intersite routing.

Now that you're an Exchange server connection wizard, you're ready to tackle connections to foreign e-messaging systems. Onward!

# PART VI

# Connecting to Other E-Messaging Systems

Now that you're an Exchange intrasite and intersite communications expert, it's time to focus on linking Exchange systems to other e-messaging systems. In Chapter 15 we'll talk about linking Exchange organizations to foreign X.400, Internet, and legacy Microsoft Mail systems and to Exchange gateways. We'll also cover indirect links between Exchange sites using X.400 and Internet mail.

In Chapter 16, we'll cover the synchronization of directories between Exchange and Microsoft Mail systems. At this point, you are pretty much an expert on a major portion of Exchange Server and Administrator. Given all this, I'll move through the remaining chapters of this book at a significantly greater speed. You're ready to fly on your own at this stage, and this chapter is a good first step out of the nest.

# CHAPTER
## FIFTEEN

# External Links Using Exchange Connectors

- Using the X.400 Connector

- Using the Internet Mail Service

- Using the Microsoft Mail Connector

- A brief overview of the cc:Mail Connector

- A quick look at Exchange gateways

**O**ne of the most exciting things about e-messaging is the ability it gives you to communicate with people outside your organization. Whether it's a friendly hello to a customer or a transfer of funds between trading partners, e-messaging makes interaction quick and easy.

Though the options for external connections have narrowed significantly over the last year or so, many remain. Exchange comes with four connectors for external systems:

- The X.400 Connector, which we put to use for site-to-site links in Chapter 14

- The Internet Mail Service, which supports the Internet's Simple Mail Transfer Protocol (SMTP) and MIME message–encoding standards

- The MS Mail Connector, which links Exchange and older Microsoft mail systems and lets you keep using MS Mail 3.*x*–compatible gateways with Exchange Server

- The cc:Mail Connector, which links Lotus cc:Mail to Exchange Server

We'll cover each of these options in order in this chapter.

# The X.400 Connector

As you'll remember from Chapter 14, an X.400 Connector must ride on top of a Message Transfer Agent (MTA) stack; check back there for your stack options. Either use an existing stack or create a new one, depending on how you'll configure this X.400 link.

Next, select the X.400 Connector option from the New Other menu on the Exchange Administrator's File menu. Fill in the General property page in the Properties dialog box that pops up for the new connector. You'll notice in Figure 15.1 that I've followed the naming conventions for the Exchange connectors I discussed in Chapter 14. Here, I'm setting up a link to a public X.400 service provider, Public X.400 Corp. Connecting to this provider will give GerCom's Exchange users direct access to external users of X.400 systems.

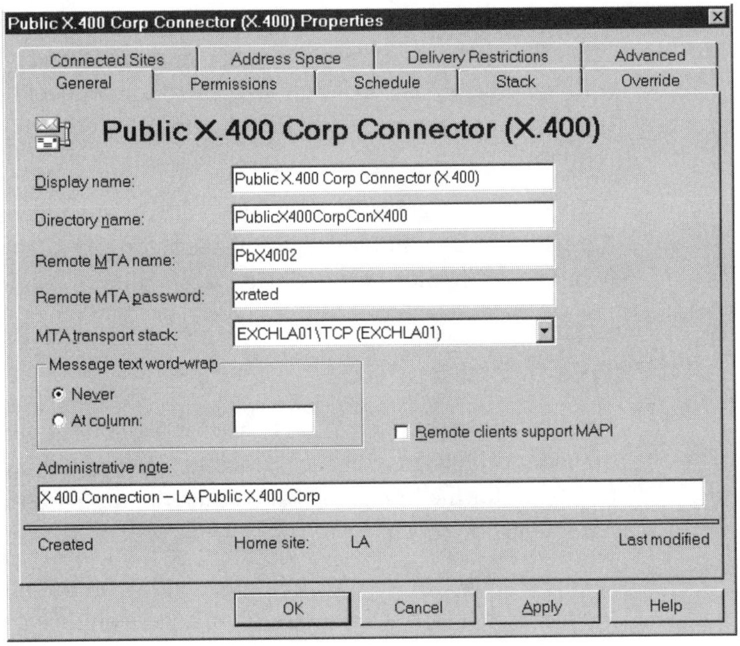

**FIGURE 15.1:**

Filling in the General property page for a connection to a public X.400 service provider

## General Properties

I obtained the correct MTA name and password for the target system from the X.400 service provider. I'm running my connection on top of a TCP/IP stack. I could have run it on top of any of the X.400-appropriate MTA stacks we discussed in Chapter 14. Because I can't be sure that users on the other side of GerCom's link to Public X.400 Corp will have MAPI-capable clients, I've deselected Remote Clients Support MAPI.

Both your server and the foreign system can contact each other to exchange messages, or one system can contact the other at all times for message exchange. If your server will be contacting the foreign X.400 system, then use the Schedule page to set that schedule. If the foreign system will contact your server exclusively, set the schedule frequency to Never.

Use the Override property page to enter an MTA name and password for your Exchange server. The name you enter overrides the MTA name specified on the General page of the server-level MTA object (which defaults to the Exchange server name). This is necessary only when the foreign X.400 system you're connecting to can't handle a name as long as the Exchange server's. We discussed the other Override page parameters in Chapters 13 and 14. Don't change any of these settings unless it is absolutely necessary for connecting to the X.400 site. Work with the manager of the foreign system to determine whether changes are required.

You'll need to get pertinent X.400 addressing information from the manager of the target system. Enter that information on the Address Space property page. (Check out Chapter 14 if you need a refresher on using this page.)

## Advanced Properties

The Advanced property page is used mostly to set parameters for X.400 conformance and links, message size, message body part, and the global domain identifier (GDI) for the foreign system. Follow along with Figure 15.2 as we cover the parameters on this page.

The default, 1988 normal mode, should work with most foreign X.400 systems; see the Exchange documentation for details on these options.

Public X.400 Corp Connector (X.400) Properties

| General | Permissions | Schedule | Stack | Override |
| Connected Sites | Address Space | Delivery Restrictions | Advanced |

**Public X.400 Corp Connector (X.400)**

MTA conformance
- ○ 1984
- ○ 1988 X 410 mode
- ● 1988 normal mode

X.400 link options
- ☑ Allow BP-15 (in addition to BP-14)
- ☐ Allow MS Exchange contents
- ☑ Two way alternate

Message size:
- ● No limit
- ○ Maximum (K): [      ]

X.400 bodypart used for message text:
[IA5                                   ▼]

- ○ Use the GDI from Site Addressing
- ● Use the GDI specified below:

Remote X.400 global domain identifier
- PRMD (p): [PubXCorp          ]
- ADMD (a):
  - ● Any
  - ○ Specific: [              ]
- Country (c): [US (United States) ▼]

[ OK ]   [ Cancel ]   [ Apply ]   [ Help ]

Choose from among the X.400 link options. Conformance with 1988 normal mode supports the Body Part-15 (or BP-15) standard, which includes specifications for such things as the encoding of binary message attachments and the handling of Electronic Data Interchange (EDI) body parts. The more limited BP-14 standard is specified in the 1984 X.400 standard and is supported in the 1988 X.400 standard. If you're sure the foreign system supports BP-15, then select this link option. If you don't select BP-15, binary parts will be sent in BP-14 format, which can still be handled by any X.400 system that conforms with 1988 normal mode.

Select Allow MS Exchange Contents if you're using this connection exclusively to link two Exchange sites indirectly or if you know that all users at the receiving foreign system (or systems) have Extended MAPI–compliant clients. (Check to be sure about the latter condition—you don't want those foreign users to be confused by an extra body part containing Exchange stuff that doesn't map to the X.400 standard.)

Under the Two-Way Alternate option, two X.400 systems take turns transmitting and receiving messages, speeding transmission somewhat. The X.400 Connector supports this option; if the foreign system also does, select the option in the X.400 Link Options area of the Advanced property page.

The Message Size option is just like similar options we've covered before. Use it to set the maximum size for messages that the connector will send or receive.

Leave the X.400 Bodypart Used for Message Text option set at IA5, unless you're communicating with systems that support foreign languages and their accents and other special characters. Other options on the drop-down list include versions of IA5 that are specialized for languages such as German, Norwegian, and Swedish, as well as some other standards.

The global domain identifier (GDI in Figure 15.2) is a portion of the X.400 address of the target system. It is used to prevent message transfer loops that involve outgoing messages. Check with your X.400 provider for help with these settings.

## Setting Up an Indirect Site Link

Indirect site link setup is a piece of cake: Just tab over to the Connected Sites property page and click New to bring up the Properties dialog box shown in Figure 15.3. (You saw this one back in Chapter 14, when we directly linked two sites with the X.400 Connector.) Type in the name of the site you want to link to—I'm linking to my Chicago site in Figure 15.3—and then tab over to the Routing Address property page, which is shown in Figure 15.4.

**FIGURE 15.3:**

Setting the name of
another Exchange site
for an indirect
X.400-based link

**FIGURE 15.4:**

Setting X.400 addressing
information for the
other site

By default, the X.400 organization name—the name of the Exchange site you want to connect to—is filled in, along with the Private Management Domain Name for your Exchange organization and the Country setting. As long as you created (or plan to create) a parallel X.400 Connector in your other site using default naming conventions, you can accept the defaults. The only thing you might have to change is the Country setting—and that's required only if the other site is located in another country.

Be sure to set the Cost parameter appropriately. If you've linked two sites with more than one connector pair, set the cost of this connection higher or lower, depending on the amount of bandwidth it has compared to the other links you've set up between the two sites. For example, if this is a low-bandwidth link based on an X.25 connection, set its cost higher than that of a full T1-based site link. If you set the cost of this link equal to the cost of one or more other connectors, the messaging load to the site will be balanced between the connectors with the same cost.

That's it. With the parallel X.400 Connector set up and running in the other site, your two sites will exchange user messages as well as directory and folder replication information through standard X.400 messages. The two sites don't even have to connect to the same public X.400 service provider. As long as the providers they connect to can communicate with each other, everything should work fine.

### Did It Work?

If you're establishing a link to a foreign e-messaging system, test the link first by sending a message to a user in an X.400 system. Then have the same user send a message back to you. If this link supports an indirect Exchange site link, first try the message exchange suggested above. Then, if you've got a Directory Replication connector in place, add a mailbox at one site and see if it is replicated at the other site. If that works, try the same thing from the other site.

# The Internet Mail Service

In Exchange 4, the connector that linked an Exchange server to the Internet was called the Internet Mail Connector or IMC. For Exchange 5, Microsoft decided to rename the IMC, calling it the Internet Mail Service, or IMS for short. The name was changed because the IMS does more than connect an Exchange server to

Internet mail resources. For example, it can route mail from non-Exchange clients—like the POP3 mail client Eudora—to the Internet. As with the X.400 Connector, you can use the IMS to connect an Exchange site or a whole organization to foreign e-messaging systems, as well as to link Exchange sites in the same organization.

## The IMS and TCP/IP

The IMS supports the Internet's Simple Mail Transfer Protocol (SMTP). It runs on top of TCP/IP. You don't have to create an MTA stack for the IMS; it uses NT's built-in TCP/IP networking.

The IMS is an SMTP mail host. A mail system must have access to an SMTP mail host to participate in the Internet mail system. The IMS communicates directly with other SMTP mail hosts to send and receive Internet mail.

The IMS can be used with a continuous or non-continuous connection to the Internet or to your organization's own TCP/IP local- or wide-area network. In continuous connect mode, the IMS assumes that any other SMTP mail host it needs to send mail to is available all the time. The IMS attempts to send outgoing messages whenever it has a spare moment. There is no fixed delivery schedule. If the receiving SMTP host isn't available, the IMS keeps trying to send a message until a preset timeout period is reached. If the message hasn't been delivered by the end of the timeout period, the IMS returns it to the sender as undeliverable. Other SMTP hosts treat the IMS in the same way when sending messages to it.

In non-continuous connect mode, the IMS sends and receives mail through a specific SMTP mail host, which might best be called an "Internet mail gateway." The gateway queues up messages for the IMS and the IMS queues up messages for the gateway. The IMS connects to the gateway by dialing up to it on some fixed schedule. Another IMS can serve as a gateway, as can an SMTP mail host supported by an Internet Service Provider (ISP). The IMS supports non-continuous connections using NT's Remote Access Service (RAS). If a dial-up–enabled IMS is unable to reach its gateway to send a message within the preset timeout period (after retrying several times at specified varying intervals), it returns the message to the Exchange user. Similarly, if the IMS doesn't contact the gateway to receive a message within the timeout period, the gateway returns the message to its sender.

In just a bit, I'll show you how to configure both continuous and non-continuous Internet connections.

# We Get Letters

You might have noticed that my e-mail address is included in the Acknowledgments section at the front of this book. Since the publication of the first edition of *Mastering Microsoft Exchange Server*, I've received hundreds of e-mail messages from readers. Most of those messages are about Internet access and most of the Internet access questions are about using SMTP mail. The rest are predominately about Outlook Web Access—getting to an Exchange mailbox with a Web browser. I'll talk about troubleshooting OWA in Chapter 18. Right now, if only to save a few million future electrons, I'll talk about the SMTP mail issues raised by readers.

Most reader problems with SMTP arise from a misunderstanding about the difference between Internet mailboxes and SMTP hosts, especially when it comes to non-continuous SMTP mail connections. An Internet mailbox—a mailbox on an Internet Service Provider's (ISP's) own SMTP host computer—usually holds messages for one user. To access those messages, a user runs a POP3 or IMAP4–compliant Internet e-mail client, connects to the ISP's SMTP host, and reads the messages. On the other hand, an SMTP host is a collection of Internet mailboxes. SMTP hosts connect to each other to send and receive messages and, as noted immediately above, users connect to their Internet mailboxes to access the messages in them.

Internet mailboxes are incapable of receiving or sending messages on their own. They require the services of an SMTP host to receive messages for them. Internet e-mail clients, not Internet mailboxes, send messages through SMTP hosts.

Some readers want to set up non-continuous connections, not between their Exchange server's IMS and an SMTP host but between their IMS and a specific Internet mailbox residing on an SMTP host. With one exception that I discuss immediately below, this isn't possible.

The exception? Microsoft, probably in response to messages similar to the ones I get, devised a way for Exchange Server to use one or more POP3 Internet mailboxes sort of like an SMTP host. However, this solution, called the *Microsoft Exchange Connector for POP3 Mailboxes*, is available only for Microsoft's Small Business Server version 4.5 or later, which supports up to 50 users. For more info on the Connector, check out `http://www.microsoft.com/smallbusinessserver/deployadmin`.

## Setting Up TCP/IP

If you haven't already done so, you'll need to set up TCP/IP on your Exchange server. This entails installing the TCP/IP software that comes with NT Server, assigning an IP address to your Exchange server, and providing information to your network's Domain Name Service (DNS)—which among other things equates hard-to-remember numeric IP addresses with the more common text-based host and Internet domain names.

TCP/IP setup is pretty simple. Be sure to set a domain name while installing TCP/IP. Mine's gercom.com. If you're going to use RAS for a non-continuous Internet link, don't forget to set up RAS with dial-out capabilities. Also, remember to create a RAS phone book entry for the ISP you'll be connecting to.

> **NOTE**
>
> You don't need to run DNS to run a TCP/IP network. However, if you're going to send SMTP mail to the outside world, your life will be far easier if you set up DNS. We mere mortals address SMTP mail using text-based host/Internet domain names (gercom.com, for example). But SMTP servers must send mail to IP addresses (such as 192.0.2.148), not to domain names. Without DNS, you'd need to manually maintain a HOSTS table of all the domains you want to communicate with, as well as their respective IP addresses. Without DNS or a HOSTS table, the IMS would have no way of translating domain names into IP addresses.

DNS is a client/server application. DNS client support is part of the TCP/IP services that come with Windows for Workgroups, Windows 95/98, and Windows NT. DNS server support comes with NT Server 4. There are some third-party vendors that sell NT DNS products. DNS services can also be provided by a UNIX system.

I don't have the space here to go into too much detail on TCP/IP or DNS, so I'll point you once again to the Sybex book *Mastering Windows NT Server 4*, by Mark Minasi, Christa Anderson, and Elizabeth Creegan. You can also take a look at the NT Server and Exchange Server manuals. Other sources of DNS information include the documentation that comes with your DNS software, and the books *sendmail, 2nd edition,* by Bryan Costales and Eric Allman (O'Reilly & Associates, 1997) and *DNS and BIND, 3rd edition,* by Paul Albitz and Cricket Liu, same publisher, 1998.

Back in Chapter 5, I touted the wonders of modern continuous connect technologies for linking to the Internet. I spoke especially fondly of Digital Subscriber Line,
or DSL, technology. It's fast (up to T1 speeds), reliable, and inexpensive (I pay less
than $200 for 384Kbps of DSL bandwidth). Setting up a continuous connect link
to the Internet is easier and, assuming a good provider, continuous links are less
prone to problems than non-continuous links. Higher speed continuous links buy
you quick and easy access to other Internet services like Web browsing, chat, and
FTP. I strongly suggest you go for a continuous link, unless you're really cost
constrained.

## Creating Key DNS Records for Exchange

Let's assume that your Exchange server is outfitted with TCP/IP and an IP
address and that you've got DNS running in your organization. You need to enter
a record in DNS for the Exchange server that's running the IMS. This is called an
*address record,* or simply an *A record.* Now let's say I want to do this for my LA
Exchange server. Imagine that I've given the server the Internet host name
EXLA01IP for DNS purposes, that my Internet domain name is gercom.com, and
that the IP address of EXLA01IP is 192.0.2.148. The A record would look like this:

```
exla01ip.gercom.com. IN A 192.0.2.148
```

The period after "`com`" in `exla01ip.gercom.com.`is *required*, as are all the periods in the DNS records listed in this chapter.

You don't have to give your server a different name for DNS purposes than for NT
networking; I just did it to show you that you can. You also need to set up at least
one *MX* (*Mail Exchanger*) record to tell DNS which computer (or computers) process
SMTP mail for your system. To keep with the naming conventions I used for SMTP
mail, my subdomain name here must be my site name—LA—and my domain name
must be gercom.com. Given all this, the MX record would look like this:

```
la.gercom.com. IN MX 10 exla01ip.gercom.com.
```

This record says that mail bound for the domain address la.gercom.com should
be sent to the DNS-defined host exla01ip.gercom.com. The *IN* means that this is
an Internet record, and the number *10* is a preference value. If there are multiple
MX records for mail delivery to a given domain, the delivering SMTP server will
first attempt a delivery to the host with the lowest preference value.

You can also use MX records to have mail for all your Exchange sites sent to the same SMTP host. In my case, I would just add a record like the one above for each site, substituting the name of the site for *la.gercom.com*.

There's one neat thing you can do with MX records: You can set up domain aliases. For example, if people in GerCom's LA sales department want to use the domain name la.sales.gercom.com on their business cards (instead of the simple la.gercom.com), you can add an MX record to direct mail sent to la.sales.gercom.com to exla01ip.gercom.com. The record would look like this:

```
la.sales.gercom.com. IN MX 10 exla01ip.gercom.com.
```

This record says that mail bound for la.sales.gercom.com should be sent to exla01ip at gercom.com.

## DNS Entries When Your IMS Picks Up and Delivers Messages Using Another SMTP Host

If your IMS is going to send and receive messages through another SMTP host using a non-continuous connection, special care is required in setting up DNS records. The DNS entries must be for that host and not for your Exchange server. For example, if your IMS is going to pick up and send messages through an SMTP host operated by your Internet Service Provider, the DNS entries must be for that host. Your ISP will make the DNS entries for you in its DNS. All you need locally is a DNS or hosts file entry for the IP address and the name of your ISP's SMTP host. I'll show you how to set up a non-continuous IMS connection a little later in this chapter.

I've gotten a number of e-mail messages on this one. It's a major stumbling block for non-continuous connection builders.

## Installing the IMS

In Exchange Server 4, you installed an Internet Mail Connector when you installed Exchange Server. With Exchange Server 5.*x*, you install an IMS using the New Other submenu of the Exchange Administrator's File menu (see Figure 15.5). Selecting this option brings up the Internet Mail Wizard (Figure 15.6), which helps you through IMS installation.

**FIGURE 15.5:**

Starting installation of the Internet Mail Service

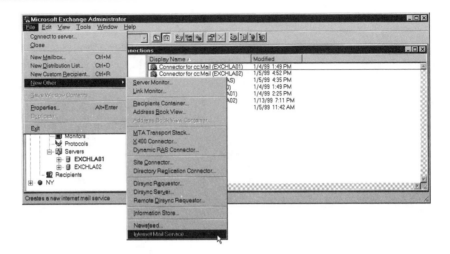

**FIGURE 15.6:**

The Internet Mail Wizard makes it easier to install the Internet Mail Service.

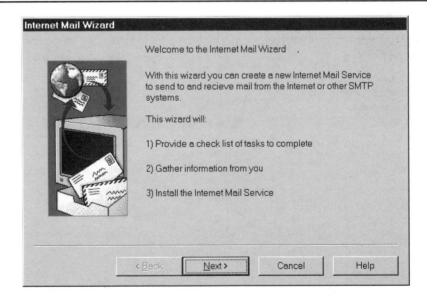

Click Next to display the next wizard page (Figure 15.7). This page reminds you to do the tasks we just discussed. Assuming you've completed these tasks, click Next to bring up the wizard's first configuration page (see Figure 15.8). Use this page to specify the Exchange server the IMS is to be installed on and to indicate whether the IMS will support dial-up non-continuous links.

**FIGURE 15.7:**

The Internet Mail Wizard lists tasks to be completed before moving on.

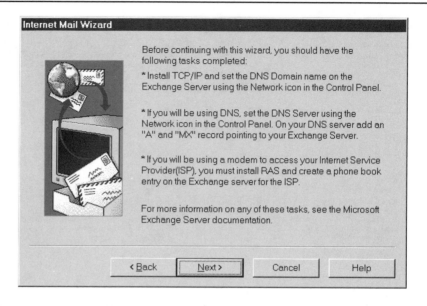

**FIGURE 15.8:**

Selecting the Exchange server to host the Internet Mail Service and the dial-up option

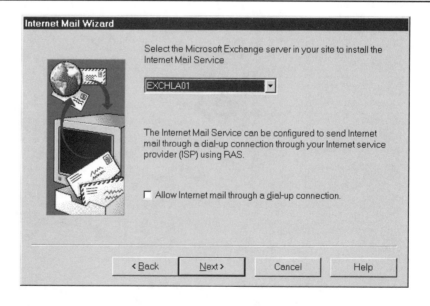

If you indicate that you want dial-up (non-continuous) connects, the next wizard page you'll see looks like the one in Figure 15.9. Here's where you tell the IMS where to get the telephone number and networking information it needs to access

the dial-up SMTP mail host that will serve as your Internet mail gateway. The dial-up information is entered into the RAS phone book. Use the Dial-Up Networking program in the Accessories program group to set up the phone book entry.

Telling the IMS where to find information for a RAS dial-up (non-continuous) connection

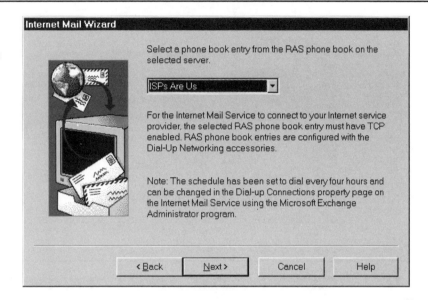

Figure 15.10 shows the next wizard page. This is where you tell the IMS whether you want it to send Internet messages to any and all SMTP mail hosts using your network's Domain Name System or to route outgoing messages to one SMTP mail host that will take care of sending them out to all other hosts. Choose the second option when you want to hide (firewall) your mail system from the outside world. You'll also find the second option attractive when your Exchange server is relatively low-powered hardware-wise and you've got a monster UNIX machine already functioning as an SMTP mail host. In this case, the monster may handle outgoing mail traffic better than your Exchange server. In Figure 15.11, I've chosen to have the IMS ship all its outgoing mail to GerCom's UNIX server, BIGUN. Choose the first option for sending mail if you don't need a firewall and you have an adequately powered Exchange server.

**NOTE**    Figures 15.10 and 15.11 show the way that the two options for sending mail from your IMS are displayed if you're using a continuous LAN or WAN connection. If you choose to set up a dialup connection, Route All Mail Through a Single Host is marked Typical.

**FIGURE 15.10:**

Setting the IMS to send messages directly to other SMTP mail hosts

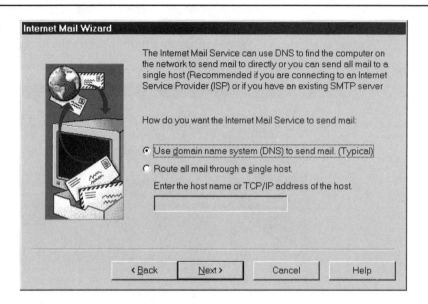

**FIGURE 15.11:**

Setting the IMS to send messages through another SMTP mail host

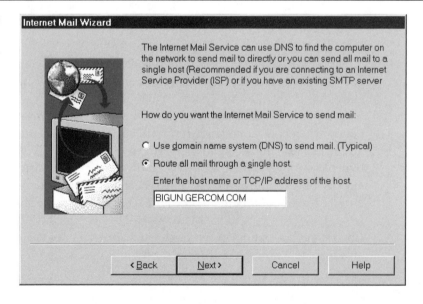

# Arranging for Dial-Up Internet Mail Gatewaying

Basically, whoever operates the SMTP mail host that will serve as your gateway will have to tell the world, through its Domain Name Service, that your domain can be reached for mail purposes through the gateway mail host. If you don't already have a domain name, you can work with the provider of gateway services to get one. Commercial Internet Service Providers (ISPs) are usually well set up to do this.

When all is set up, your IMS will connect to the gateway at set intervals. While connected, it will send outgoing Internet mail and pull down any incoming mail that is queued up on the gateway machine. After installation of the IMS, you'll need to make a few settings to assure that all this happens. I'll talk about these later in this chapter.

Use the next wizard page (see Figure 15.12) to tell the IMS whether you want it to send messages to all or selected Internet addresses. You can use the second option to distribute the load of sending mail over multiple IMSs on your Exchange servers, assigning responsibility for different sets of addresses to different IMSs. If you select the second option, you'll get a message warning you to configure the addresses after IMS installation is finished (see Figure 15.13).

**FIGURE 15.12:**

Telling the IMS to send messages to all or selected Internet addresses

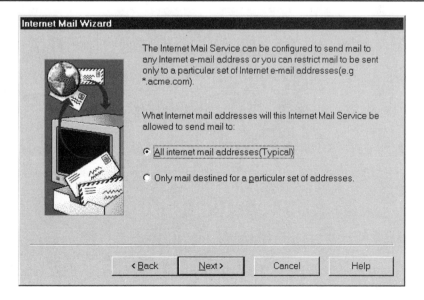

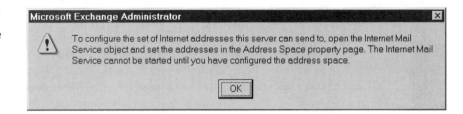

Next the Internet Mail Wizard asks you to enter the Internet address to be used for your Exchange site. The default is the address constructed from your site and organization name plus "com". As you can see in Figure 15.14, the default address offered by the wizard for GerCom is @LA.GerCom.com. You can change the default here or later by opening the site addressing object in the Exchange Administrator's Configuration container.

After you finish with your Internet site address, click Next to enter the name of a mailbox or distribution list that is to receive reports about non-delivered messages (see Figure 15.15). This is an important step. Non-delivery report notifications are one of the key ways you can monitor the health of your Exchange Internet link and, most importantly, keep your users happy.

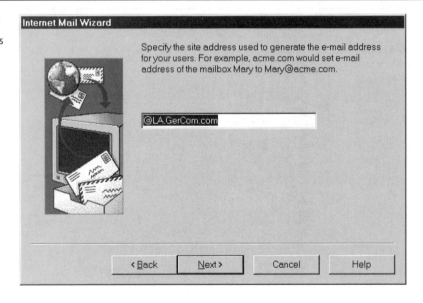

**FIGURE 15.15:**

Specifying a mailbox or distribution list to receive non-delivery report notifications for messages handled by the IMS

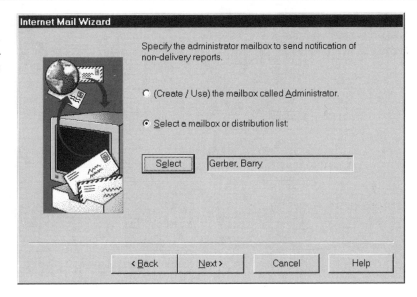

Hold on, we're almost done. On the next wizard page you enter the NT account and password for your Exchange Service Account. This is the account you set up and used when you installed your first Exchange server in the site (see Figure 15.16). Like all other Exchange services (the MTA, Information Store, Directory, etc.), the IMS will be installed to run under the authority of your Exchange Service account.

Finally, click Next and you'll see the final page of the wizard (see Figure 15.17). Click Finish and after a minute or so, you'll see the dialog box in Figure 15.18, telling you that the IMS has been installed and started. If you don't get that message, check out your TCP/IP configuration and take a look at the Application log in the NT Event Log for any IMS errors.

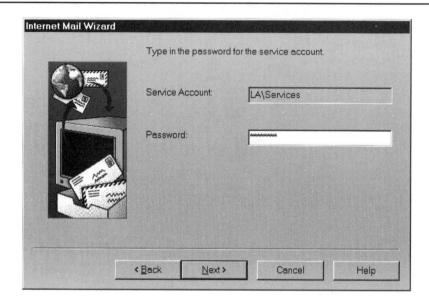

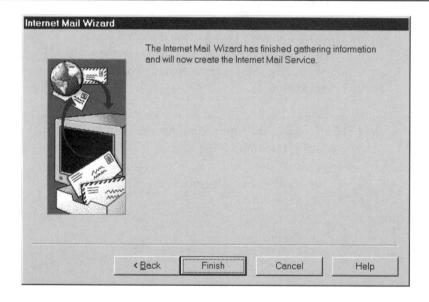

**FIGURE 15.18:**

The IMS has been success-
fully installed and started.

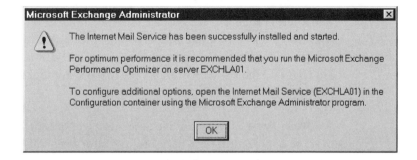

## Setting IMS Properties

At this point, your Internet Mail Service is ready to receive mail on a continuous Internet link without any special fancy settings like sending to only specific Internet addresses. To set your IMS to do more than the basics, you have to open and use the IMS Properties dialog box. You know I'm not going to let you off without a thorough lesson in this handy-dandy little gizmo, so let's go. Find the Internet Mail Service in your Connections container and double-click it. This brings up the Internet Mail Service Properties dialog box shown in Figure 15.19.

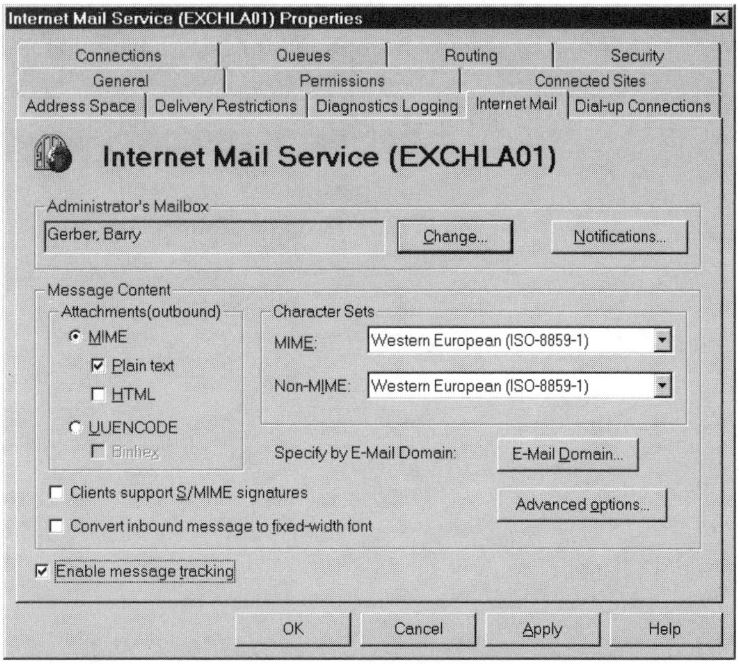

**FIGURE 15.19:**

The Internet Mail Service
Properties dialog box

## Internet Mail Properties

The Internet Mail Service Properties dialog box is a bit unusual in one regard: It opens on the Internet Mail property page rather than the General page (see Figure 15.19). Otherwise, it behaves pretty much like other Properties dialog boxes. Let's look at the Internet Mail property page in more detail. Follow along on Figure 15.19.

**Address Type**   When an Exchange user sends a message, it is directed to one or more e-mail addresses. Each of these addresses must be of an address type that has been defined in the Exchange system. Messages of a specific address type are handled by specific Exchange Server components. For example, messages with X.400-type addresses are handled by X.400 connectors. Messages with SMTP-type addresses are handled by IMSs.

**The Administrator's Mailbox**   When you ran the IMS installation wizard, you selected an Administrator's mailbox (or distribution list) to receive non-delivery report notifications. You can choose a different mailbox or list at any time by clicking the Change button.

**Notifications**   Click Notifications to set up the kinds of notifications that should be sent to the IMS administrator's mailbox; you can see the options in Figure 15.20. When I first set up an IMS, I like to see notifications for all non-delivery reports. Later, when I'm more comfortable with the way the IMS and addressing are set up, I select the option Multiple Matches for an E-Mail Address Occurred.

**FIGURE 15.20:**

Selecting the NDR notifications to be sent to the IMS administrator's mailbox or distribution list

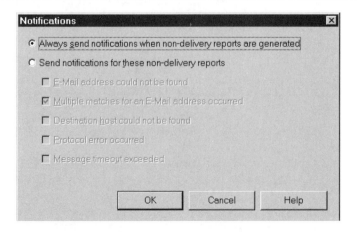

**Attachments (Outbound)**    Now let's go back to the Internet Mail property page (see Figure 15.19). In order to travel through the Internet, messages with binary attachments must be encoded to remove any 8-bit characters. Two encoding schemes are popular on the Internet: the newer MIME (Multipurpose Internet Mail Extensions) and the older uuencode (UNIX-to-UNIX Encode).

The Attachments (outbound) area is where you set the default encoding method for messages outbound from the IMS. As you'll see in just a bit, you can actually set different defaults on an outbound-domain–by–outbound-domain basis. Because it nicely supports a variety of message types and allows for the invocation of a supporting helper application, MIME is your best bet, unless you know you'll be sending exclusively to foreign systems where only the uuencode scheme is in use. Encoded message parts are decoded automatically by either the receiving SMTP host or by the user's e-messaging client. With some systems, automatic decoding isn't available. In this case, the recipient must manually decode the encoded message parts.

You can send MIME-encoded attachments as plain text and/or in HTML format. Plain text is straight 7-bit ASCII text, which is recognizable by any SMTP mail client. HTML encoding is now quite popular for Web browsers and growing in popularity for e-mail message content. Among other things, HTML supports such things as bold, italic, and colored text as well as different fonts. I'll talk more about HTML encoding in Chapter 18. Choose plain text unless you're sure recipient e-mail clients can handle HTML encoding.

**Clients Support S/MIME Signatures**    If your clients don't support S/MIME— the Exchange and Outlook clients for Exchange Server 4, 5, and 5.5 don't—disable this option. That way, messages will be converted into MIME messages that are unsigned and readable by your clients.

**Convert Inbound Messages to Fixed-Width Font**    If you want the IMS to convert all inbound messages into a non-proportional font, select this option. This is a useful option if the bulk of your inbound Internet mail depends on characters being aligned properly, such as tables and reports.

**E-Mail Domain**    You use the E-Mail Domain button to set different message-content parameters for specific domains with which your IMS will exchange mail. In Figure 15.21, I'm telling the IMS to uuencode messages with binary attachments that are sent to the domain msmail.davis.com. That's because Davis's Microsoft Mail SMTP gateway can decode only uuencoded messages. As you can see in the figure, you can set all the content parameters for the domain, including Advanced Options, which I talk about immediately below.

**FIGURE 15.21:**

Setting message size and content information for a specific e-mail domain

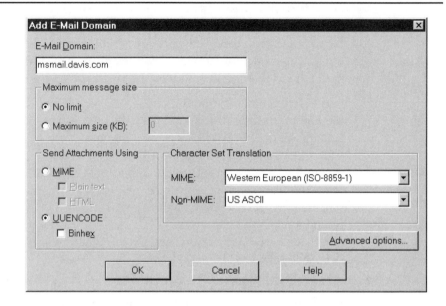

**Advanced Options**   Click the Advanced Options button (see Figure 15.21) to set message content parameters to ensure that your IMS sends messages in a format that is compatible with the SMTP hosts it will communicate with and that the IMS exposes only as much information to the Internet as your organization deems appropriate (see Figure 15.22).

**FIGURE 15.22:**

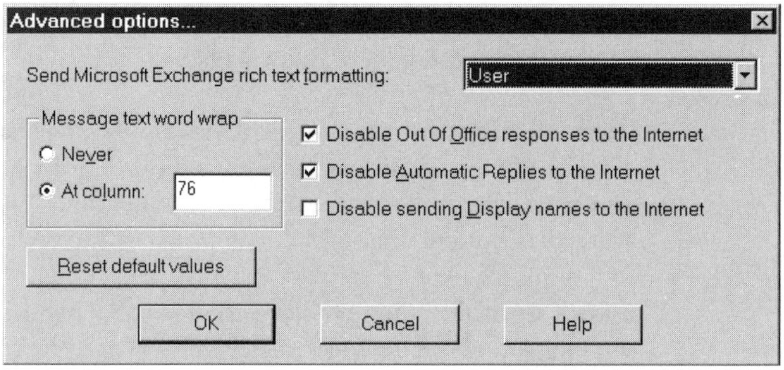

Selecting settings to ensure compatibility with other SMTP hosts

**Send Microsoft Exchange Rich Text Formatting**    You don't want to send messages in Exchange's rich text (bold, italic, underline, color fonts, etc.) to people who can't take advantage of it, because they'll often see a lot of meaningless junk when they open a message. Options for the Send Microsoft Exchange Rich Text Formatting field include User, Always, and Never. Unless you know for sure that all or no recipients in a foreign e-messaging system can handle rich text, User is usually your best option. When User is selected, the IMS sends in rich text only if that option has been enabled for the individual recipient. Administrators can enable rich text for custom recipients—the only Exchange Server recipients who might not be able to handle rich text—on the Advanced property page of the custom recipient's Properties dialog box. Users can do the same for addresses they create in their Exchange client personal address books.

**Word Wrap**    The proper word-wrap settings let recipient clients format message text into nice, word processor–like paragraphs. The default should work fine in most cases. You cannot alter this setting if you've selected MIME encoding.

**Disable Options**    You can disable the delivery of out-of-office messages and automatic replies to recipients reached through your IMS. You can also do the same for Exchange display names, which can be used by many SMTP systems to show more information about you than your simple Exchange Server alias name. Unless you've got some technical or policy reason for doing so, don't disable any of these options.

**Enable Message Tracking**    Let's go back to Figure 15.19. As you did in past chapters with your MTAs and information stores, you should enable message tracking here. This will let you check the status of messages sent out through and coming in from the IMS.

## General Properties

Use the General property page to set default message-size limits for the IMS; you can also enter an administrative note (see Figure 15.23). Notice that you have no control over the computer name given to the IMS; it's preset to the name of the Exchange server it runs on.

## Address Space

As with the X.400 Connector, you use the Address Space property page to set addresses that the IMS will send messages to (see Figure 15.24). These can be as specific as the address of a single recipient or as general as all SMTP recipients. If you have multiple IMSs, you can use the Address Space page to control which addresses a specific IMS sends messages to. For redundancy and load balancing, you can set up the same address space definitions on multiple IMSs.

The simplest approach is to create one address—a general SMTP address space for all recipients. The IMS installation wizard does this for you. So, if that's all you need, you're all set as far as the Address Space page is concerned.

**FIGURE 15.23:**

The General property page of the IMS Properties dialog box

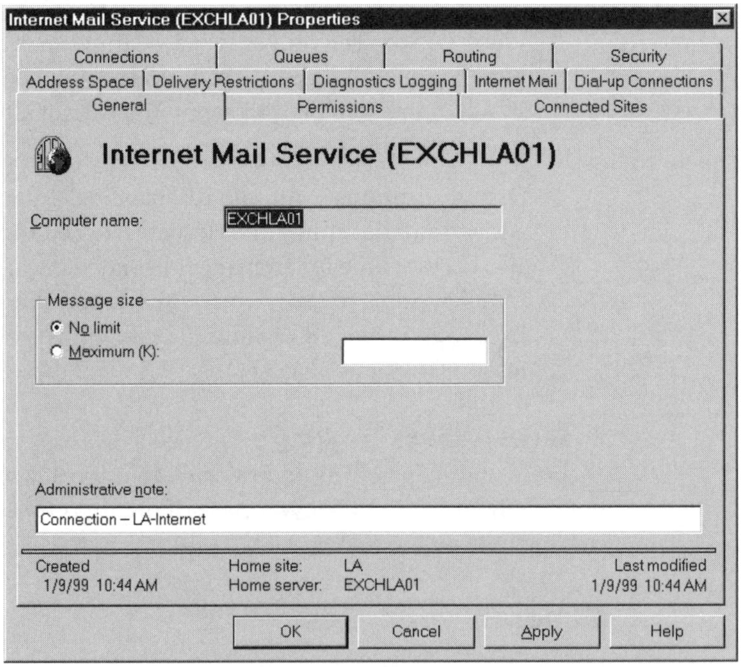

FIGURE 15.24:

Setting the addresses to
which the IMS will deliver
messages

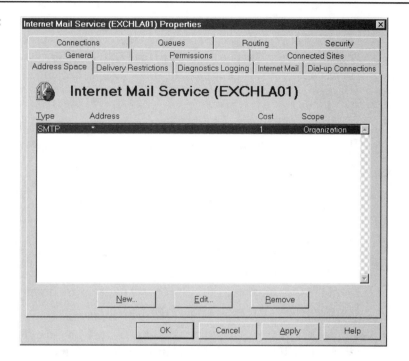

Let's say you want this IMS to handle only messages to the "com" and "gov"
Internet subdomains. Instead of the address space created by the IMS installation
wizard, you'd create two Internet address spaces—one for *.com and one for *.gov.
You don't have to limit yourself to these higher-level subdomains: You can set up
an IMS that just delivers mail to a specific company, university, or even individual.

## Dial-Up Connections

Here's where you set up a non-continuous connection to another SMTP mail
host—called an "Internet mail gateway" above—which your IMS will send and
receive messages through. Generally, this will be an SMTP mail host operated by
an Internet Service Provider. If you told the IMS installation wizard that you
wanted to do a dial-up connection, the wizard partially completed the entries on
the Dial-Up property page. If not, you can set up a dial-up connection from
scratch on this page.

Let's take a closer look at the options on the Dial-Up Connections property
page. Track along on Figure 15.25.

**Available Connections**   Make sure you pick the correct dial-up entry in your Remote Access Service (RAS) phone book. If you need to add a new entry, use the Dial-Up Networking program that's in the Accessories program group on your Exchange server. Then come back to the Dial-Up Connections page. Of course, you must have the proper modem and RAS installed and enabled for dial-out calls before you do all this.

**Mail Retrieval**   This is probably the most complex part of dial-up gatewaying. The IMS will send mail as soon as it connects to the gateway. But, to receive mail, you'll need to set some parameters for mail retrieval.

Click the Mail Retrieval button on the Dial-Up Connections property page. The button is partly visible in the upper-left quadrant of the property page in Figure 15.25. The Mail Retrieval dialog box pops up. If your ISP supports the relatively new ETRN protocol for retrieving mail from its mail host and its inbound and outbound mail hosts are on the same machine, select the Retrieve Mail Using ETRN option. You can specify the domains you want to retrieve mail for in the Domains area of this property page or use domain settings on the Routing page. I'll talk about that page soon.

If your ISP's inbound and outbound mail hosts are on different machines, select the Send ETRN to Specified Host Instead of Outbound Mail Host option as well as the Retrieve Mail Using ETRN option. Outbound messages will be sent through your dial-up host and the ETRN command will be sent to the host specified in the Send ETRN to Specified Host Instead of Outbound Mail Host field.

If your ISP doesn't support ETRN but does support the older TURN command for requesting inbound messages, check Issue TURN After Delivering Outbound Mail (Requires Outbound Authentication). If you select this option, be sure to set up proper security authentication information on the IMS Properties dialog box's Security property page.

Finally, if your ISP supports neither TURN nor ETRN, you'll have to enter a command in the Custom Command field (see Figure 15.25). Whatever command you type in the field is executed on your Exchange server after the connection is made to the provider's network. What you enter in this field depends on the kind of Internet mail gatewaying technology your provider has in place.

**FIGURE 15.25:**

Setting IMS Dial-Up Connections Mail Retrieval options

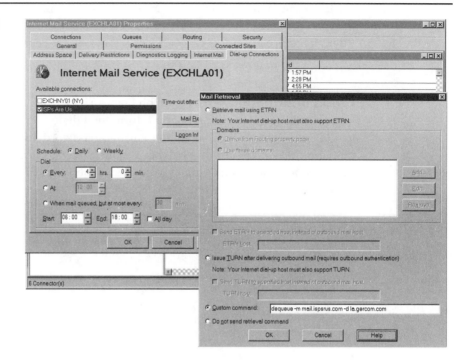

You can get up-to-date status reports on various gateway mail retrieval options for Exchange from a Web site operated by Simpler Webb Inc. Check it out at www.swinc.com. This site not only discusses the options, but it gives you specific instructions for retrieving mail using each option.

In Figure 15.25, I'm using the dequeue command, which is actually a program for Intel processor–based machines (DEQUEUE.EXE) that you can download free from the Simpler Webb site. This program works with Internet mail hosts running the program sendmail 8.8 or greater.

As you'll learn at the Simpler Webb site, typing dequeue -? gives you a list of command line options for the program. The name of the mail server acting as your gateway is -m. The name of the domain you want to retrieve mail for is -d.

For sites not running sendmail 8.8 or greater or using other Internet mail server packages, the Simpler Webb's Web site discusses a range of options other than the preferred DEQUEUE.EXE. These include the UNIX commands rsh, rexec, and finger.

All the command options require some level of cooperation from your provider. To the end of rewarding nice folks, www.swinc.com includes a list of Internet Service Providers who've gotten the message regarding dial-up connect.

If you select the Do Not Send Retrieval Command option, ETRN is disabled.

**Logon Information**    We're still on Figure 15.25. Click the Logon Information button and use the resulting Logon Information dialog box shown in Figure 15.26 to add the necessary username, domain, and password information for logging onto the SMTP mail host that will act as your gateway. You won't need domain information, unless you're going to connect to another NT server that provides the gateway service.

**FIGURE 15.26:**

Setting the IMS for dial-up connections

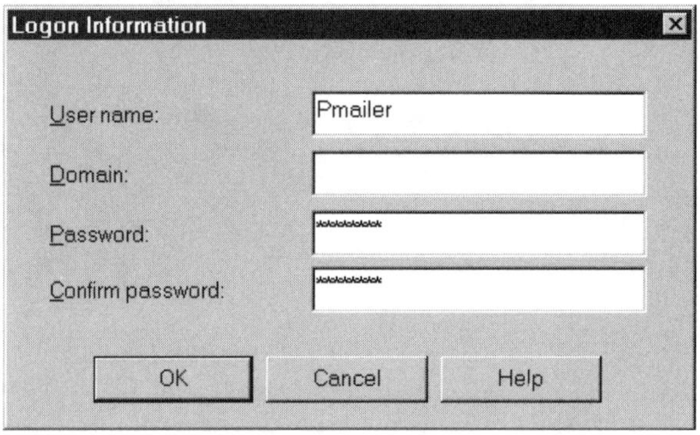

**Schedule**    As you can see in Figure 15.25, you have a wide range of options for scheduling connects to your gateway. What you set here depends on your organization's need for immediacy in its Internet mail communications. The default of every four hours is a good starting point. Adjust it as you work with the dial-up connect.

## Connections

Now let's go back to the Internet Mail Service Properties dialog box. The Connections property page provides a lot of tools for controlling your links to other SMTP systems (see Figure 15.27).

**Transfer Mode**    You set the send-receive functionality for the IMS in the Transfer Mode area of the Connections property page. Will your IMS both send and receive messages, only send or only receive messages, or do neither? You can accept the default to have the IMS both send and receive, or you can balance loads by having it send messages while another IMS receives them.

**FIGURE 15.27:**

Using the Connections property page to set several parameters that control links with other SMTP systems

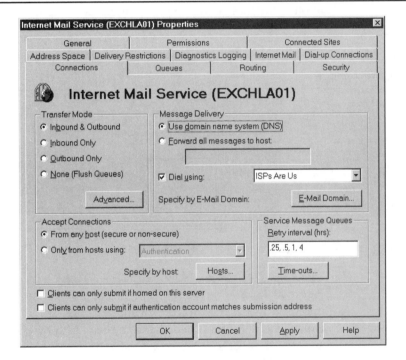

Select the None (Flush Queues) option to stop the IMS and have it deliver all messages in its queues. This is useful when queues are temporarily laden with messages due to such things as heavy internal message creation or when the IMS receives a lot of messages.

If queues back up regularly, then it may be time to change some Connections parameters or take even more drastic steps. You make parameter changes in the Advanced dialog box; to open it, click the Advanced button on the Connections property page. Here you can set the maximum number of inbound and outbound connections to the IMS, as well as the maximum connections to a single host and the maximum number of messages sent during one connection (see Figure 15.28).

Normally, sticking with the defaults is fine; you'd generally change them to fine-tune the IMS's message I/O performance. For example, if outbound message queues get backed up regularly, you might want to increase the number of outbound connections and reduce the other three parameters. The key to good performance is CPU power and the amount of memory in the Exchange server supporting the IMS. So if parameter adjustments don't help, consider adding another IMS or beefing up processing power and/or RAM.

**FIGURE 15.28:**

Setting advanced parameters for IMS connections to other SMTP hosts

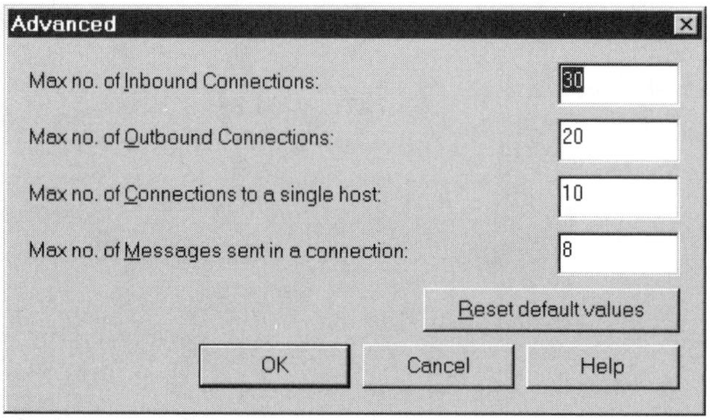

| Advanced | |
|---|---|
| Max no. of Inbound Connections: | 30 |
| Max no. of Outbound Connections: | 20 |
| Max no. of Connections to a single host: | 10 |
| Max no. of Messages sent in a connection: | 8 |

Reset default values

OK    Cancel    Help

**Message Delivery**    Now we're back on the Connections property page (see Figure 15.27). You can use DNS to resolve (that is, convert) text-based addresses into IP addresses or you can forward messages to another SMTP host for handling. Unless you're running a very small system, I strongly suggest that you develop and use DNS, NT's WINS, or at least a \WINNT\SYSTEM32\DRIVERS\ETC\ HOSTS file to resolve domain names into IP addresses. If you want to forward messages to another host that handles DNS, specify the name of the host or enter its IP address.

**Dial Using**    Check Dial Using to indicate that the IMS should connect by dialing to an SMTP mail host. Select the specific RAS phone book entry to be used when dialing from the drop-down list.

**E-Mail Domain**    If you wish, you can click the E-Mail Domain button and set different message-delivery parameters for different domains (see Figure 15.29). Notice that I'm going to queue up messages for keytop.com to pick up from my IMS using ETRN. That way, the IMS won't try to send the messages to that mail host.

**Accept Connections**    We're back on Figure 15.27. If you have a reason for doing so, you can specify only those SMTP hosts you'll accept mail from or those hosts you won't accept mail from. Select From Any Host (Secure or Non-secure) to accept connections from all servers. For more security, select Only from Hosts Using and then select Authentication, Encryption, or Auth and Encrypt. For even more security you can set a list of hosts that can connect to the IMS to deliver and pick up messages. To do this, click the Hosts button to bring up a dialog box that lets you enter specific host addresses. This is a nice way to restrict access to your Exchange system for security purposes or to prevent distracting messages from users of certain external e-messaging systems.

**FIGURE 15.29:**

Setting specific message-delivery parameters for a domain

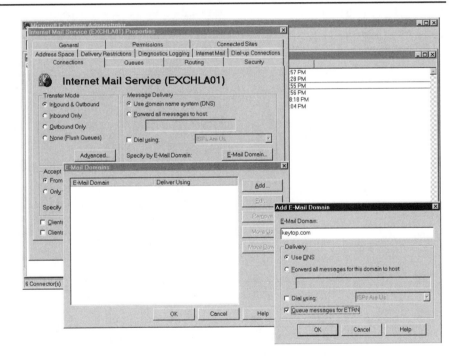

**Retry Interval**    As I noted back at the beginning of this section, the IMS continues trying to send a message until a timeout period is reached. Set the retry intervals in the Retry Interval (Hrs) field of the Connections property page's Service Message Queues area. In Figure 15.27, the defaults—.25, .5, 1, and 4—are in effect. So when the IMS first attempts to contact a host to send a message, if the connection is not made, it waits .25 hour before the second retry. If it receives no reply on the second retry, it waits .5 hour before the third retry. If it receives no reply on the third retry it waits 1 hour before the fourth retry, and if it receives no reply on the fourth retry it waits 4 hours before the fifth retry.

When it reaches the end of the string of retry wait times, the IMS retries connections at the last interval of time. It continues trying to send the message until a specific length of time passes. This time is set using the Message Time-outs dialog box that pops up when you click the Time-outs button on the Connections property page (see Figure 15.30). Timeouts are set for Urgent (24 hours), Normal (48 hours), and Non-urgent (72 hours); the default settings are in parentheses.

**FIGURE 15.30:**

Setting timeout parameters for messages to other SMTP hosts

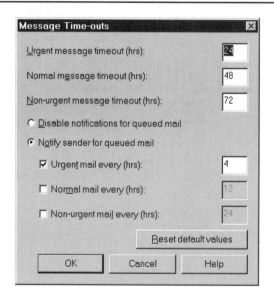

Another nice feature: There are also timeouts after which the sender is notified that a message is still waiting to be sent. These too are based on message urgency. Defaults are 4 hours (Urgent), 12 hours (Normal), and 24 hours (Non-urgent). However, notifications are only sent for Urgent mail by default. To send notifications for Normal or Non-urgent mail, select the check boxes next to those options.

**Clients Can Only Submit...** Back to Figure 15.27. These options are designed to prevent users from sending Internet messages that appear to have come from other persons. To choose either of these options, you must have chosen Only from Hosts Using Authentication or Only from Hosts Using Auth and Encryption. The

Homed on This Server option lets a client send a message only if the mailbox sending the message is located on the server supporting the IMS. The Authentication Account Matches Submission Address option allows a client to send a message only if the mailbox user's current NT account login is linked to the mailbox with the address that appears in the message's From field.

## Queues

You can check on and manipulate messages in the IMS's various queues. You can also watch over the IMS and other Exchange queues with the preset Performance Monitor applications that are installed when you install Exchange Server. You'll find these in the Microsoft Exchange program group on your Exchange server. For more on NT's Performance Monitor application, see Chapter 4.

## Routing

The IMS can route certain incoming SMTP messages back out to the Internet. Why, you might ask, would I want to do that? A good question, I might respond.

Let's say you've set up your Exchange server to support POP3 or IMAP4 mail service. (We'll get into that can of spaghetti in Chapter 18.) So now your users can get to their Exchange mail using a POP3 client like Qualcomm's Eudora or an IMAP4 client like Microsoft's Outlook Express. Great, but that only lets them get their mail. How do they send it out? The POP3 and IMAP4 protocol requires that, in addition to setting an incoming POP3 or IMAP4 mail host for your POP3 or IMAP4 client, you also set a specific SMTP mail host to handle outgoing mail from the client.

The same host can support both incoming and outgoing mail, but if your IMS is going to take outgoing client mail and ship it onto the Internet, you may have to set it up to do so. You don't want messages to Exchange users to be routed back to the Internet. You want them to be delivered into the Exchange system where they will be processed and sent to users. By default, incoming IMS messages addressed to the Internet domain name of the site where the IMS is installed (e.g., la.gercom.com) are routed right into the Exchange system. If your IMS supports other Exchange sites with their own Internet domain names, you'll need to tell the IMS to route messages addressed to those domains into the Exchange system. Here's how you do that.

Tab over to the Routing property page on your IMS properties dialog box (see Figure 15.31). Click the Add button. The Edit Routing Table Entry dialog box shown in Figure 15.31 pops up. In the E-Mail Sent to This Domain field, type the name of the domain, other than the already configured default domain, that you want to receive mail for. This is a domain that represents addresses inside your Exchange site or organization. In Figure 15.31, GerCom's Los Angeles domain is the default domain and I'm adding GerCom's New York domain to assure that messages addressed to that domain also are sucked into Exchange by the IMS. Of course, I had to enter correct settings in my DNS to ensure that Internet messages for my New York domain were delivered to my Los Angeles–based IMS. Next check the Should Be Accepted as "Inbound" option and click OK on the Edit Routing Table Entry dialog box. Repeat the above steps for each domain in your organization.

**FIGURE 15.31:**

Setting up inbound message routing for POP3 and IMAP4 clients

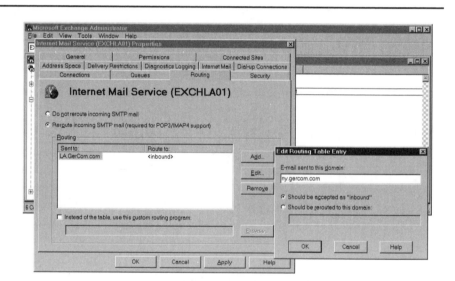

You can do lots of other things with this routing capability, like rerouting mail addressed to one domain to another domain. I'll leave all this to your imagination.

## Security

You use the Security property page (see Figure 15.32) to set up security for connections to other IMSs or other SMTP hosts. You can specify a range of security options from none at all to the Simple Authentication Security Layer/Secure Sockets Layer (SASL/SSL) Internet authentication and encryption protocols to the Windows NT–specific challenge response authentication and encryption protocol. You set security by e-mail domain. The host you're connecting to, of course, must support the protocol choice you make.

**FIGURE 15.32:**

The Internet Mail Service's Security property page

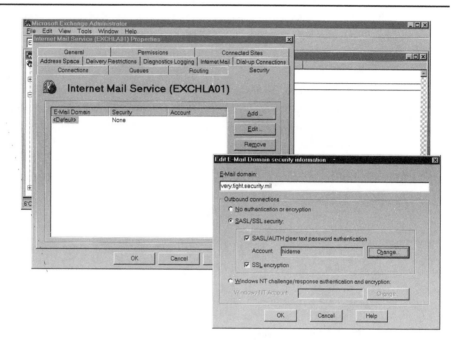

## Did It Work?

That's it—you're done. Click OK on the IMS Properties dialog box. Assuming that your TCP/IP and DNS configurations are set and you've got a connection to the Internet in place, your IMS started running when the Internet Mail Wizard finished. If you've made changes since using the Wizard, the IMS tells you when you'll have to restart the IMS service. Be sure to do so using the Services applet on the Control Panel.

Try sending mail to your Exchange mailbox from outside your Exchange system, for example, from an account you've set up with an Internet Service Provider. Use a POP3 or IMAP4 mail client. Next, ask someone on the Internet to send mail to your Exchange mailbox's Internet mail address. For the record, it does no good to send a message from your Exchange mailbox to your Exchange mailbox's Internet address. The address is resolved inside of your Exchange server and delivered. The message never gets out to the Internet.

**TIP**    I have an account with an Internet Service Provider. One of the main things I do with it is to test new IMSs. I use an IMAP4 mail client connected to the ISP's network to send messages to myself on a new IMS and to receive messages I send through the new IMS from an Exchange client. For more on using IMAP4 clients, see Chapter 18.

If everything works, you're home free. If you have problems, take a look at your DNS entries. If they look OK, be sure you've allowed enough time for those entries to find their way out to other DNS servers on the Internet. It can take several days before new DNS information is fully distributed across the worldwide hierarchy of DNS servers. If someone tries to send messages to your announced Internet address, and the DNS that person uses hasn't acquired your DNS information yet, the messages will be returned to the sender with a note indicating that your address couldn't be found.

## Exchange Server and Proxy Servers

Earlier in this chapter, I noted that I get lots of e-mail from readers. One question a number of readers ask is about putting an Exchange server running the Internet Mail Service behind a proxy server. Here's what I tell those readers.

A proxy server such as Microsoft's Proxy Server is designed to protect workstations and servers placed behind it from malicious Internet hackers. When your network is behind a proxy server, there are two ways to make an Exchange server's IMS accessible to e-mail clients and SMTP servers on the Internet. You can put the Exchange server on the same NT server as your proxy server or you can make the proxy server look to the outside world like it's an SMTP host.

Depending on the proxy server product you use, if you locate your Exchange server with IMS on a proxy server, make sure that packet filtering is set correctly or the IMS will still be invisible. For the details especially as they apply to Microsoft Proxy Server, see article Q176771, *Using Packet Filters with Exchange Server*, in Microsoft's Knowledge Base, accessible at `http://support.microsoft.com`.

If your Exchange server with IMS is behind a proxy server, you need to set parameters to support access by e-mail clients, from and to SMTP hosts. There are two Knowledge Base articles on this sort of configuration: article Q181847, *How to Configure Microsoft Exchange Server with Proxy Server* and article Q178532, *Configuring Exchange Internet Protocols with Proxy Server*.

## Setting Up a Site Link Using the IMS

As you did with the X.400 Connector, you can use the Connected Sites property page on the Internet Mail Service Properties page to start both direct and indirect links to other Exchange sites. You can even connect to sites running X.400 connectors, since you can specify an X.400 address in SMTP format.

A link is direct if the IMS talks to another Exchange server over the Internet or to your own internal TCP/IP network without the intervention of intermediate SMTP or X.400 systems. If intermediate systems are involved, then the link is indirect.

## Did It Work?

Take a look at the "Did It Work?" section for the X.400 Connector. You can perform the same tests here as I laid out there to determine if your IMS is functioning properly.

# The MS Mail Connector

If your organization is using Microsoft Mail (MS Mail) for PC Networks or AppleTalk Networks, you can transparently link MS Mail and Exchange users with the MS Mail Connector (MMC). Exchange also comes with software for migrating (moving) MS Mail users to Exchange; we'll discuss this software in the next chapter.

Migration is a pretty big move. As you start building your Exchange system, the MMC lets you maintain communications between Exchange users and MS Mail users. With Exchange-MMC links in place, you can then take a more leisurely approach to migration.

You can also use the MMC to let Exchange users take advantage of gateways not yet available for Exchange Server and to give MS Mail users access to Exchange's more powerful and stable connectors and gateways. For example, you can use Exchange's Internet Mail Service and the MMC to move SMTP mail in and out of MS Mail environments, dumping Microsoft's weak SMTP gateway for Microsoft Mail for PC Networks (MS Mail PC) in the process.

Because MS Mail PC is the more widely used of the two MS Mail products, I'll cover connectivity to it in detail here. I'm also assuming that you are familiar with the concepts and software behind MS Mail PC. (See the Exchange documentation for more information on using the MMC for linking Exchange systems and MS Mail for AppleTalk Networks.)

Whichever of the two MS Mail products you're connecting to, the MMC works in pretty much the same way. A shadow MS Mail PC network and post office are created on the Exchange server running the MMC. Then an NT service runs on the Exchange server that essentially emulates the functions performed by MS Mail PC's EXTERNAL.EXE program. This service moves messages between the Exchange shadow post office and the MS Mail PC post office, just as EXTERNAL.EXE does for a group of real MS Mail PC post offices. (For MS Mail for AppleTalk Networks, you connect the Macintosh mail side to the shadow post office and then run a connecting service on the Exchange server running the MMC.)

The MMC runs on top of standard NT local area network protocols or using NT's Remote Access Service (RAS) asynchronous or X.25 connections. You can use one or all of these links; network links should be set up before you configure the MMC. You can run only one instance of the MMC per Exchange server, but you can connect to multiple MS Mail PC post offices through a single MMC. And one MMC can serve some or all of the sites in an Exchange organization.

---

**WARNING**   You have to install the MMC before you can use it. If you installed it when you installed Exchange Server, you're ready to go. If not, you'll need to run the Exchange Server setup program and install the MMC. After that, you can move on to the configuration discussion below.

---

To start configuring the MMC, find and double-click the MS Mail Connector you want to run in the appropriate Connectors container of your Exchange Administrator. If you have multiple servers in a site and you've installed the MMC on each, you'll see multiple instances of the MMC, each marked for the server it resides on; make sure to pick the one for the server you want. The MS Mail Connector Properties dialog box will pop up (see Figure 15.33).

FIGURE 15.33:

The MS Mail Connector
Properties dialog box opens
on the Interchange prop-
erty page.

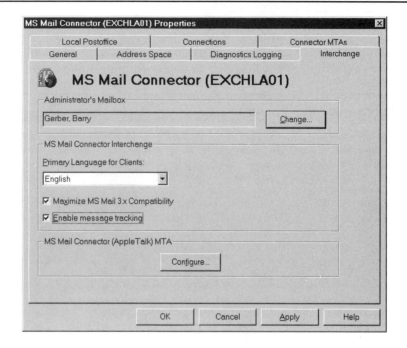

## Interchange

The MMC opens on the Interchange rather than the General property page. The first thing you need to do is add an administrator's mailbox. Click Change and select an Exchange recipient from the resultant address list dialog box.

If the primary language for clients isn't English, select the correct language from the drop-down list. Select the Maximize MS Mail 3.x Compatibility check box to let MS Mail users view and save OLE-embedded objects sent from Exchange clients. When this option is selected, the MMC creates a second version of the embedded object that's compatible with the earlier version of OLE supported by the MS Mail PC Windows client. Compatibility is costly in terms of storage, because the second version can be quite large—up to 1MB—so choose this option with care and forethought.

As usual, I strongly suggest that you enable message tracking. Though we're not going to get into it here, you use the Configure button to set up the MS Mail Connector for AppleTalk Networks.

# General Properties

Use the General Properties page shown in Figure 15.34 to set message-size limits and to enter an administrative note for the MMC. Notice that the note entered in Figure 15.34 follows the syntax I recommended earlier for Exchange connectors.

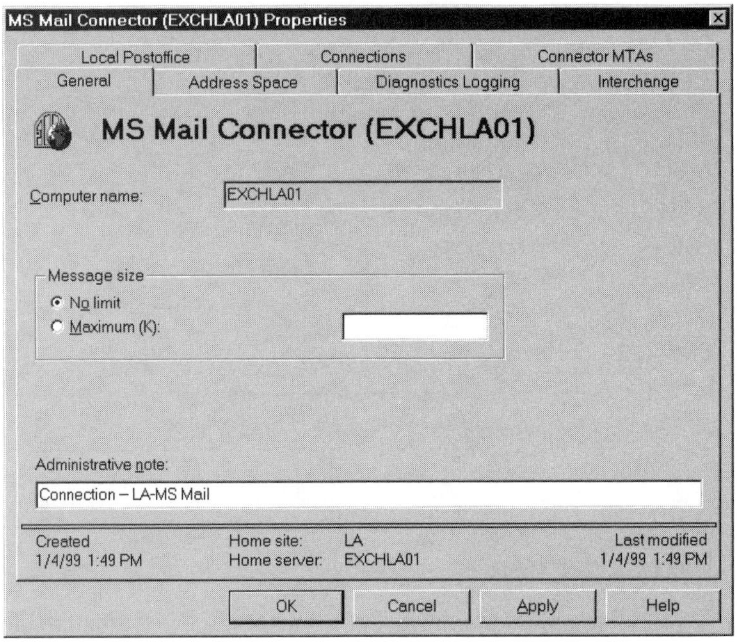

FIGURE 15.34:

The General property page
of the MS Mail Connector
Properties dialog box

# Connections

Tab over to the Connections property page (see Figure 15.35). This is where you add and maintain the MS Mail PC post offices serviced by the MMC. Notice in the figure that the connection to the Exchange shadow MS Mail PC network and post office—GERCOM/LA in my case—is already there; the link is created automatically. By the way, the MS Mail PC network is GERCOM and the post office is LA, both of which, of course, parallel the names of my Exchange organization and the Exchange site in which I'm creating the MMC.

**FIGURE 15.35:**

The Connections property
page of the MS Mail
Connector Properties
dialog box

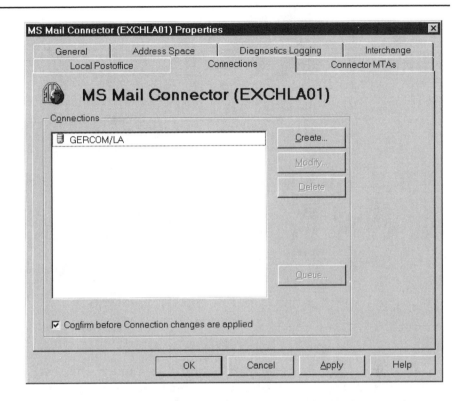

Now we have to create links to other real MS Mail PC post offices. From the
Connections property page, click Create to bring up the Create Connection dialog
box shown in Figure 15.36. We're going to create a local area network–based link,
so be sure that LAN is selected under Connection Parameters. Next, we have to
tell the MMC where the post office is located on the LAN.

---

**NOTE**    If we'd chosen the Async or X.25 option, we would have been asked for appropriate information to make the connection. If you've set up a modem connection
between two MS Mail PC post offices, you should have no trouble filling in the
info for Async or X.25 connections.

---

**FIGURE 15.36:**

Setting up a new connec-
tion to an MS Mail PC
post office

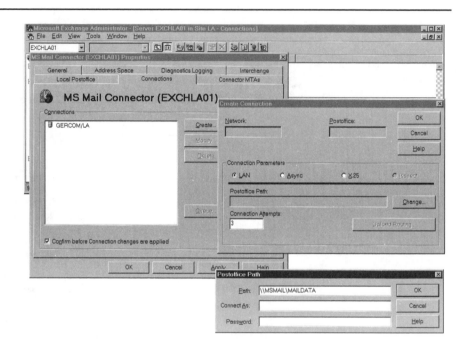

Click Change to enter the post office location. This brings up the Postoffice Path
dialog box shown in the lower right-hand corner of Figure 15.36. The path must
be entered in Universal Naming Convention (UNC) format, which doesn't use
disk drive letters and allows computers to connect without drive mappings.
Generically, the UNC format is \\Computer_Name\ShareName. My MS Mail
PC post office is on the NT computer named MSMAIL in the share MAILDATA.
(MS Mail PC administrators will immediately recognize MAILDATA as a standard data directory for MS Mail PC post office installations.) So the path shown
in Figure 15.36 is \\MSMAIL\MAILDATA.

---

**NOTE**    If your MS Mail PC post office is on a NetWare server, you must run the NT service
Gateway Service for NetWare. The UNC syntax for a NetWare server is \\NetWare
_Server_Name\NetWare_Volume_Name\Directory_Path.

---

Use the Connect As field to enter a network logon account name for the server
that's holding the MS Mail PC post office. Enter the password for the account in
the Password field. You need to fill in these fields only if the service account for the
MMC doesn't have standard domain-based security access to the MS Mail PC post
office server.

For NetWare-based post offices, create a NetWare user with the same name and password as the NT service account for Exchange. This is the account that will run the services that support the MMC on your NT/Exchange server. If you do this, you don't have to enter the NetWare account name and password in the Postoffice Path dialog box. The MMC will be able to connect to the post office just by virtue of the matching NT and NetWare account names and passwords.

Once you've entered the path to the MS Mail PC post office, click OK in the Postoffice Path dialog box. If you've entered the correct path and if security is properly set, you're returned to the Create Connection dialog box (see Figure 15.37). If something doesn't work, make sure the path and security are set correctly.

Notice that I didn't have to manually enter the names of the MS Mail PC network (GCMSMAIL) or post office (LA)—the Exchange server automatically retrieved this information from the post office.

Change the Connection Attempts default if you want the MMC to attempt to deliver messages more than three times before returning them to the sender on the Exchange side. Click the Upload Routing button to get routing information on MS Mail PC *indirect* post offices. These are post offices that have mail routed to them by the MS Mail PC post office you're connecting to now. This routing is set up at the MS Mail PC post offices. The MMC can reach indirect post offices through its connection to the routing post office. With routing in place, you don't have to create an MMC connection to each of the indirect post offices.

**FIGURE 15.37:**

The connection to the MS Mail PC post office has been established.

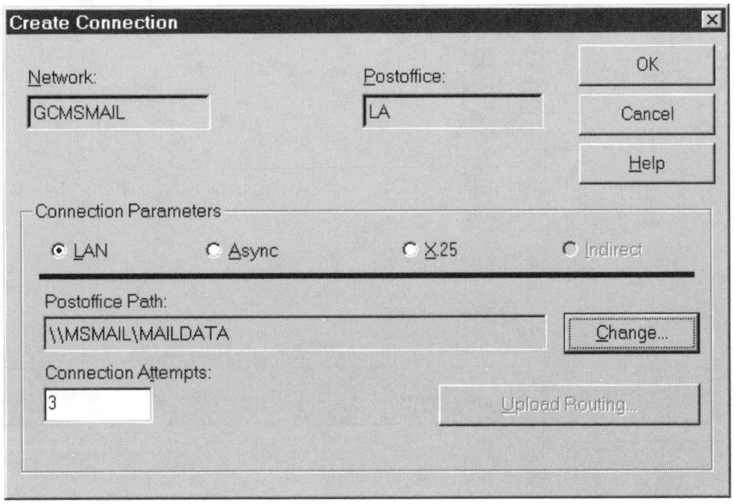

Click OK in the Create Connection dialog box when you're done, then click OK in the Apply Changes Now dialog box that pops up next. This finalizes the creation process and adds the newly created MS Mail PC post office link to the Connections area of the Connections property page.

Tab over to the Address Space property page. Notice that an MS Mail address type has been automatically added to the list for the MS Mail PC post office (see Figure 15.38).

## Connector MTAs

An MTA must be created to serve your newly established MS Mail PC post office connection. The MTA is an NT service. You manage it just like any other NT service—for example, the services for the four Exchange key components.

Tab over to the Connector MTAs property page and click New. This brings up the New MS Mail Connector (PC) MTA Service property page (see Figure 15.39). Give the service a name. You'll see this name when you run the NT Control Panel's Services applet.

**FIGURE 15.38:**

A new address space is added for the MMC connection.

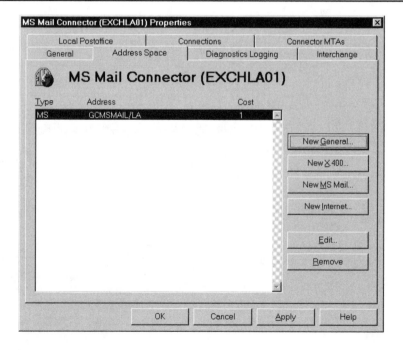

**FIGURE 15.39:**

Setting up an MTA to support connections to MS Mail PC post offices

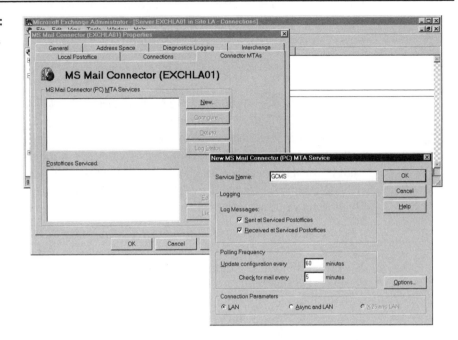

**FIGURE 15.39:**

Setting up an MTA to support connections to MS Mail PC post offices

## Log Messages

Indicate whether you want message traffic logged. Log files will be put into the shadow post office's LOG directory.

## Polling Frequency

Leave the polling frequency settings at their default levels. The value you set in the Update Configuration Every field determines how fast the MTA will get changes in parameters set in the Options dialog box. Remember, the default is 60 minutes. You can change the frequency at which the PC MTA checks for mail in the Check for Mail Every field.

## Connection Parameters

Use the Connection Parameters area to select the means by which the MTA will connect to the real MS Mail PC post offices it supports. Three options are available: LAN, Async and LAN, and X.25 and LAN. The Async and LAN option supports both asynchronous-modem and LAN connections, and the X.25 and LAN option supports LAN as well as X.25 connections. Put another way, all three options support LAN connections. More on this in a bit.

## Options

Click Options to bring up the MS Mail Connector (PC) MTA Options dialog box (see Figure 15.40). If you wish, you can use the Maximum LAN Message Size field in the Options dialog box to set a maximum size for messages moved in both directions by this MTA over a LAN-based link. If the space on a target MS Mail PC post office falls below the value in the Close Postoffice If field, the MTA will stop transmitting messages to the post office until the available disk space reaches the value set in the Open Postoffice If field.

Select NetBIOS Notification to have the MTA notify MS Mail PC users on the same LAN that they have new mail. Check Disable Mailer if you want to stop the MTA from distributing messages to the LAN-connected post offices it serves. Selecting Disable Mail Dispatch stops the MTA from distributing directory synchronization messages to LAN-connected post offices. (We'll discuss MS Mail PC directory synchronization in the next chapter.)

**FIGURE 15.40:**

Setting options for the MS Mail Connector (PC) MTA

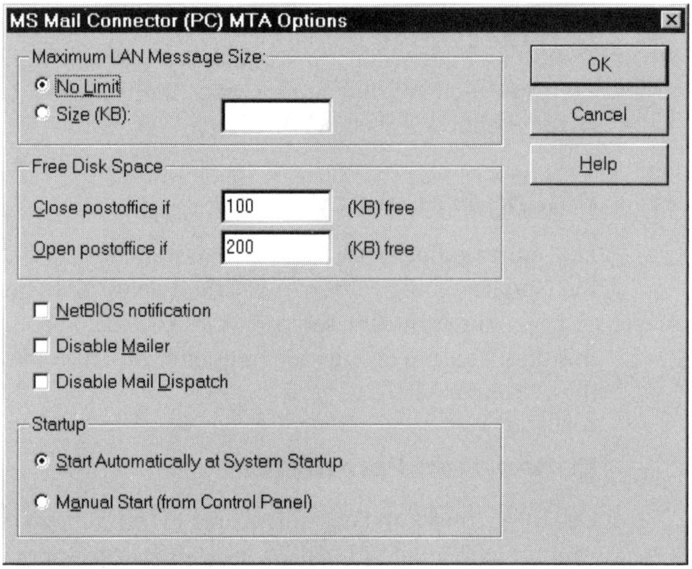

Finally, select the start-up mode for the MTA service from the Startup area of the Options dialog box. The default starts the service when NT starts. This is usually the appropriate choice. If you want to start the service manually using the Services applet on NT's Control Panel, choose that option.

When you're done configuring options, click OK to return to the New MS Mail Connector (PC) MTA Service dialog box shown in Figure 15.39.

Close the New MS Mail Connector (PC) MTA Service dialog box by clicking OK. Your Connector MTAs property page should look something like the one in Figure 15.41.

Now you can assign the post office you set up on the Connections property page to your new MS Mail Connector MTA. Click List in the MTA Service dialog box to bring up the Serviced LAN Postoffices dialog box (see Figure 15.42).

**FIGURE 15.41:**

A new MS Mail Connector MTA service has been created.

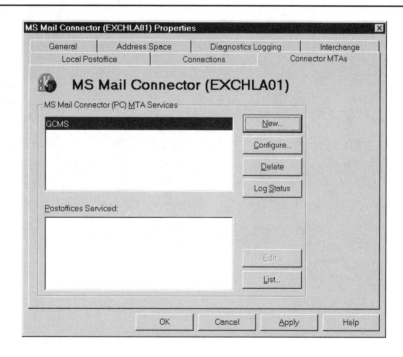

Select the post office you wish to service. Click Add and then click OK. Your Connector MTAs property page should look like the one in Figure 15.43.

If an MMC will be handling a lot of message traffic and will be using multiple connection methods (LAN, Async and LAN, X.25 and LAN), it's best to create at least one MMC MTA for each method. Just be sure to assign LAN-linked post offices only to the MTAs that support such links exclusively, not to MTAs that support Async and LAN or X.25 and LAN. This will leave the MTAs connected by the latter two methods free to handle only the message traffic that isn't based on LAN links.

**FIGURE 15.42:**

Adding a LAN-linked post office to the list of serviced LAN-linked post offices

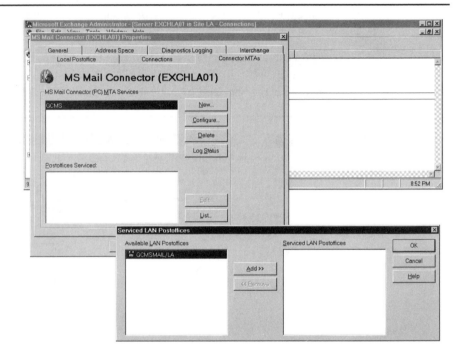

FIGURE 15.43:

The post office will now be
served by the newly cre-
ated MS Mail Connector
MTA service.

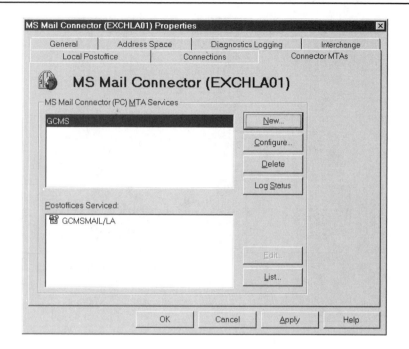

## Local Postoffice

The Local Postoffice property page shown in Figure 15.44 is for the MMC shadow post office. You can change the Sign-on Password as well as the network and post office names. You need a password for Async or X.25 connections only. If you change the shadow's network or post office name on this page, click the Regenerate button to re-create the site's MS Mail addresses to reflect your changes. Unless you have an excellent reason for doing so, don't change the network or post office name.

You'll need information on the Local Postoffice page when you set up one or more real MS Mail PC post offices, so that they can access the shadow post office. Write down the network and post office names as well as the Sign-on ID and, if you entered one, the Sign-on Password.

**FIGURE 15.44:**

The Local Postoffice property page shows information about the MMC shadow post office.

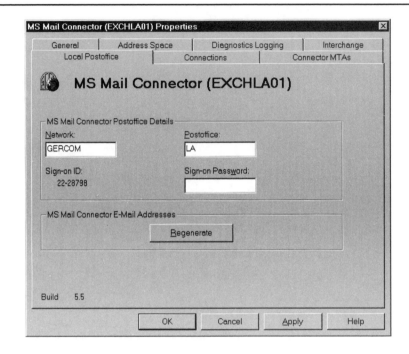

## Starting the MTA Service

Open the Services applet on the NT Control Panel. Find the new MMC MTA service you created. As you may remember, the service I created is called GCMS (for GerCom MS Mail). In Figure 15.45, you can see that I've located it on the Services applet. If you've indicated that you want the MMC MTA service to start automatically in the future, you won't have to do this again.

Click Start to bring up the service. Also, make sure the MS Mail Connector Interchange service is running.

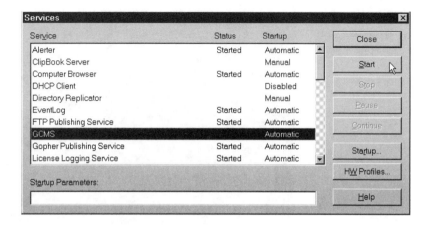

## MS Mail PC Post Office Setup

The next thing you need to do is tell the real MS Mail PC post offices about the shadow post office. In a DOS session, start up MS Mail PC's ADMIN program and log in as someone with MS Mail PC Admin rights. You or someone in your organization should know how to do this. When ADMIN is up and running, you'll see a DOS screen that looks something like the one in Figure 15.46.

Use the right arrow key to select External-Admin, then press the Enter key. This brings up the External-Admin screen shown in Figure 15.47. Make sure the Create option—on the menu at the top of the screen that starts out "Create Modify Delete"—is selected, and press Enter. Fill in the information about the MMC shadow post office here. Use the network and post office names you wrote down just a bit ago.

The route type should be Direct. Be sure to pick a connection type—MS-DOS Drive, Modem, or X.25—that matches the LAN, Async, or X.25 configuration for this post office on the MMC MTA that serves it. When you're finished entering the configuration information, you're asked if you want to create the post office. Be sure that Yes is selected and press Enter.

Your MMC's shadow post office and your real MS Mail PC post office(s) are now communicating with each other through the MMC MTA. All we need to do now is test the link.

**FIGURE 15.46:**

MS Mail PC's ADMIN program is up and running.

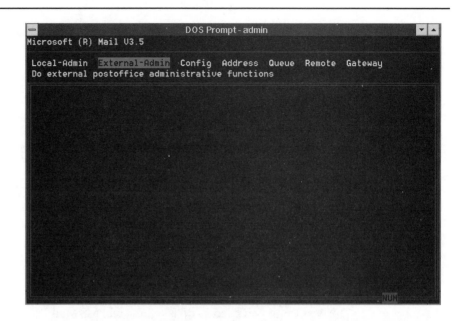

**FIGURE 15.47:**

Creating an external post office entry for the MMC shadow post office

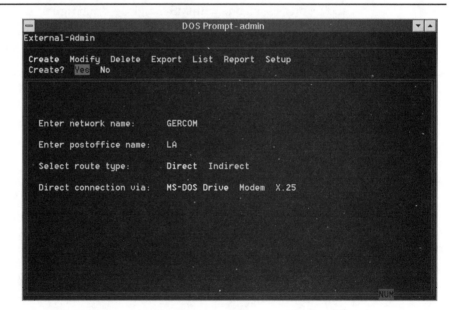

# Did It Work?

You test the MMC link by sending messages from the MS Mail PC side to the Exchange side, and vice versa. Addressing these messages will be a bit primitive, since we haven't yet synchronized directories between our MS Mail PC and Exchange systems. We won't be able to select the addresses from the address list, so we'll have to enter them manually.

Let's start on the MS Mail PC side. The following example assumes that you're using the MS-DOS MS Mail PC client. With the To field selected as you compose a new message, press Enter. This brings up the Postoffice Address List. Press the left arrow key to bring up the list of Address Lists, from which you select Postoffice Network List and press Enter. The Network List now pops up. Select the name of your MMC shadow post office's network (GERCOM in my case) and press Enter.

If there is more than one post office (that is, Exchange site) in your network (Exchange organization), a list of post offices will be presented. Pick the post office you want to send test mail to; you'll then see a little box for entering the mailbox's name (see Figure 15.48).

Here's where the magic happens. Notice that I'm addressing mail to GER-COM/LA, which is both the name of my Exchange organization and site and the name of the MMC shadow post office. The mailbox name I type in at this point is that of an Exchange mailbox, so the mail will be sent to that mailbox. To an MS Mail PC user, it looks as if the message will be sent to a real MS Mail PC post office on a real MS Mail PC network. Once we've got directory synchronization going, the illusion will be even better.

After you type in the Exchange mailbox name, press Enter, then compose the message and send it off. In a few minutes, the message will show up in the Inbox of the mailbox owner's Exchange client.

To send a test message from an Exchange client to an MS Mail PC network mailbox, start composing a new message. Click To and then click New in the Address Book dialog box. Select Microsoft Mail Address from the resultant New Entry dialog box and click OK. To enter the address, use the New Microsoft Mail Address Properties dialog box that pops up (see Figure 15.49).

When you're finished, click the little To button in the lower left-hand corner of the dialog box. The display name for the address will now appear in the To field of your new message. Complete the message and send it off. After the MMC MTA has done its thing, the owner of the MS Mail PC mailbox can access the message using any of the MS Mail PC clients.

If your test fails, go back and be sure you've done everything I've indicated above. This is one of the more complex Exchange connectors to set up, so it's not inconceivable that everything won't work the first time.

**FIGURE 15.48:**

Addressing an MS Mail PC message to an Exchange mailbox

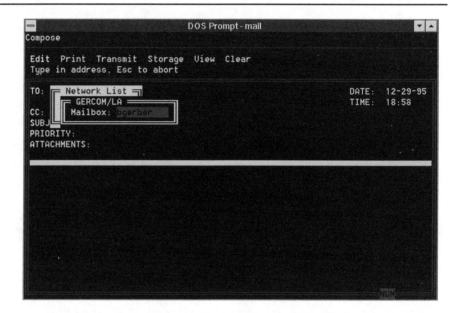

**FIGURE 15.49:**

Entering a new MS Mail PC address while composing an Exchange message

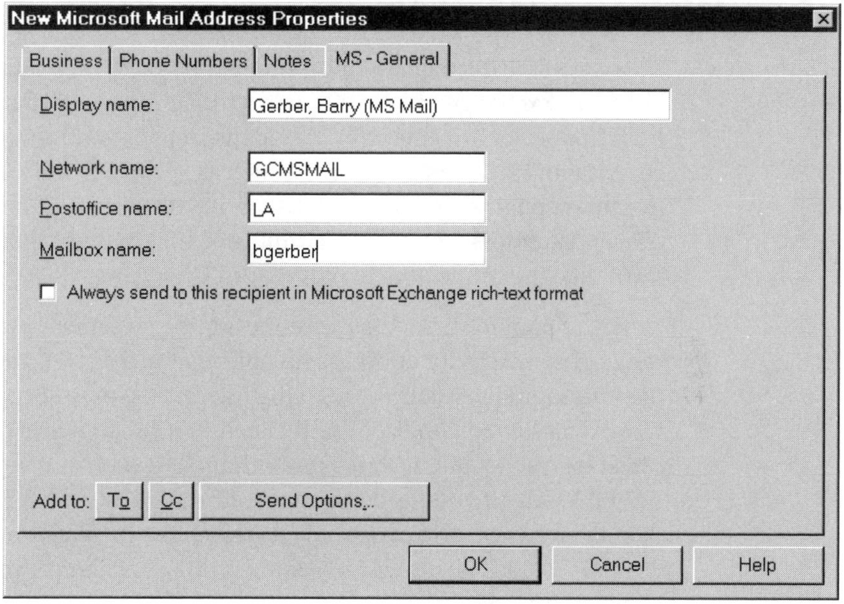

**New Microsoft Mail Address Properties**

Business | Phone Numbers | Notes | MS - General

Display name: `Gerber, Barry (MS Mail)`

Network name: `GCMSMAIL`

Postoffice name: `LA`

Mailbox name: `bgerber`

☐ Always send to this recipient in Microsoft Exchange rich-text format

Add to:  To   Cc          Send Options...

OK    Cancel    Help

# The cc:Mail Connector

If your legacy system is Lotus's cc:Mail, Microsoft has a way for you to link your users to Exchange Server. The cc:Mail Connector links cc:Mail post offices and Exchange Server sites. Like the MS Mail Connector, it passes messages between cc:Mail and Exchange Server and it synchronizes addresses between the two systems.

Conceptually, the cc:Mail Connector is much simpler. It's also considerably easier to configure, lacking things like shadow post offices. After all we've done with connectors, the Exchange Server docs for the cc:Mail Connector should be all you need to successfully set up and install the cc:Mail Connector.

# Exchange Gateways

Gateways link dissimilar e-messaging systems to each other. Though they're all built into Exchange, the X.400 Connector, Internet Mail Service, and Microsoft Mail Connector are gateways. A wide variety of vendors provide gateways for e-messaging systems and devices such as PROFS, SNADS, CompuServe, fax machines, pagers, and voicemail. Check with Microsoft for information on products and vendors. You install, administer, and manage these gateways pretty much like the connectors we covered in this chapter.

As you plan for links to other e-messaging systems, keep in mind the wide range of connectivity options available via the Internet. You can reach a number of e-messaging systems through the Internet—CompuServe and MCI Mail are two examples. So you don't really need special gateways to these systems. You can even reach X.400 systems through the Internet, making the X.400 Connector desirable only if you need to support functions like the X.400 flavor of electronic data interchange. You can, of course, reach the Internet through most X.400 systems. So if X.400 is your e-messaging protocol of choice, you can pretty much get along on it alone.

Exchange's Internet Mail Service is a powerful, robust, and stable link to the Internet. As a general rule, don't add gateways you don't need. Every gateway is another administrative and management headache. Save the gateways for e-messaging systems you can't readily reach through the Internet, such as fax, pagers, or voicemail. Even in this area, things are changing everyday. For example, faxing and paging are getting more Internet capable every day. Can voicemail be far behind?

Of course, there are times when specific gateways may be the best choice. If performance is key, a direct gateway between two disparate systems, such as Exchange Server and IBM mainframe–based SNADS systems, is your best choice. Without the conversion steps required by an Internet middleman, mail can move more quickly between different systems. Gateways can also make message tracking and directory synchronization easier because no Internet messaging baggage has to be taken into account.

# Conclusion

In this chapter you learned how to connect Exchange sites to foreign X.400, Internet, and MS Mail PC e-messaging systems to exchange messages and, where possible, to indirectly link Exchange sites. You also learned how gateways fit into the Exchange environment. Now you're ready to tackle directory synchronization between Exchange and Microsoft Mail PC systems.

# CHAPTER
## SIXTEEN

**16**

# Directory Synchronization with MS Mail PC Systems

- Understanding Dirsync

- Adding an Exchange organization to a Dirsync System

- Building a new Dirsync system that includes an Exchange organization

- Administering and managing the Exchange Server directory synchronization service

In the last chapter, using the Microsoft Mail Connector (MMC), we enabled mail interchange between our Exchange and Microsoft Mail for PC Networks (MS Mail PC) systems. As you'll recall, when we tested the MMC we had to enter addresses for the other system manually. In this chapter we'll use directory synchronization (*Dirsync*) to remove that annoying inconvenience. Using Dirsync, we'll import Exchange addresses into MS Mail PC, and vice versa. Then, when they compose messages, users of Exchange and MS Mail PC will be able to pick addresses for the other system from address lists just as they do for their own system.

> **NOTE**　You can also exchange addresses with Microsoft Mail for AppleTalk Networks systems and with any other e-messaging system that supports the Dirsync protocols. I won't cover these topics here because of the relatively limited installed base of the AppleTalk product and lack of demand for Dirsync with other systems. (See the Exchange Server docs for more on using Dirsync with MS Mail for AppleTalk Networks and other e-messaging systems.)

# Understanding Dirsync

Let's start by talking about Dirsync, which is a component of MS Mail PC. Each MS Mail PC post office has a directory database that includes those recipients whose mailboxes reside in the post office. *Dirsync* is the name of the process that keeps the recipient directories in a group of MS Mail PC post offices synchronized. This ensures that the address lists for any post office will include the current recipients at all of the post offices that participate in the Dirsync process.

One MS Mail PC post office is set up to be a *Dirsync server*. All other post offices that participate in the Dirsync process are set up to act as *Dirsync requestors*.

The Dirsync requestor in each post office sends directory change updates for its post office to the Dirsync server. Each Dirsync requestor asks the Dirsync server for directory updates for all of the other post offices, and the server sends them out. Requests and their responses are moved between MS Mail PC post offices as messages.

**WARNING**   The Dirsync server performs the equivalent of the Dirsync requestor functions for its own post office. So a post office that is a Dirsync server *cannot* also be a Dirsync requestor. This is a key piece of the Dirsync puzzle. Forget it and you'll do an Escheresque meltdown trying to figure out how the Dirsync server gets updates from and sends them to its own post office.

Dirsync is amazingly simple, yet when I incorporated my Exchange system into an existing MS Mail PC Dirsync process, I managed to do just about everything wrong in spite of having been involved with MS Mail PC and Dirsync for years and years. Why did I screw up? I had set up the Dirsync process on the MS Mail PC side eons ago, and I thought I remembered how it worked. I didn't. The consequences? The Dirsync-Exchange link failed, and it took hours to fix it.

To save you from the miseries I suffered, here's a list of several key rules of the Dirsync road, some of which I repeat for emphasis from the Dirsync basics above.

- A single MS Mail PC post office—including an Exchange Server shadow MS Mail PC post office—can function as either a Dirsync server or a Dirsync requestor. It *cannot and need not* function as both. The Dirsync server performs requestor duties for its own post office.

- There can be only *one* Dirsync server for a group of Dirsync requestors. One Dirsync server can serve multiple MS Mail post offices, whether they are on the same or different MS Mail PC networks. Here's where I went wrong in my first effort to include my Exchange system in the Dirsync process. I'd already established the Dirsync server on the MS Mail PC side. My one and only Dirsync server was already running on one of my MS Mail PC post offices. I then created a Dirsync server on one of my Exchange servers and all hell broke loose—or, more precisely, *nothing* broke loose. Trying to keep the requestors happy, the two Dirsync servers got into deadlock battles of epic proportions, and I never saw an updated address list on either side. Things returned to normal once I got rid of the Exchange Dirsync server.

- There can be only one Dirsync requestor per MMC and, you'll remember, only one MMC per Exchange server.

- Because Dirsync uses messages to exchange requests for updates and the updates themselves, the MMC must be installed and running between your Exchange and MS Mail PC systems.

- As is true without Exchange in the mix, you must run DISPATCH.EXE on the MS Mail PC side to perform whichever Dirsync server or requestor tasks are assigned to real MS Mail PC post offices. There is no need for (or equivalent of) DISPATCH.EXE on the Exchange Server side; these tasks are performed by the Exchange Server's directory synchronization service.

# Adding an Exchange System to Dirsync

Throughout this section, I'll assume that you've got Dirsync running on the MS Mail PC side. If not, the MS Mail PC *Administrator's Guide* provides detailed instructions. The Microsoft application note on Dirsync (WA0725.DOC) is also very helpful. You can view it at Microsoft's Knowledge Base Web site or download it from one of the company's many online libraries.

Since the Dirsync system is up and running on the MS Mail PC side, a Dirsync server is already in place. That means we need only to install a Dirsync requestor on the Exchange side.

To set up a Dirsync requestor on one of your Exchange servers, select Dirsync Requestor from the New Other submenu on the Exchange Administrator program's File menu. This brings up the New Requestor dialog box, where you select the Dirsync server that the requestor will use (see Figure 16.1). My Dirsync server is on the MS Mail PC network GCMSMAIL in the post office named LA, so I've selected the only MS Mail PC network/post office option, GCMSMAIL/LA.

Click OK in the New Requestor dialog box when you've chosen the Dirsync server post office. Next you'll see the properties dialog box for the requestor (see Figure 16.2).

## General Properties

The requestor is treated by Exchange Server as a connector, so I've named it EXCHLA01 Connector (Dirsync) GCMSMAIL. (You can't see the whole name in Figure 16.2, because the field box is too small.) If you want the name of the requestor to be appended to each imported MS Mail PC display name, check the box next to the Name field. Generally, however, you won't want to do this. It's usually better if MS Mail PC addresses look just like standard Exchange addresses.

FIGURE 16.1:

Selecting the Dirsync server
post office

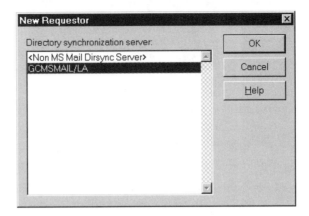

FIGURE 16.2:

The Dirsync requestor's
Properties dialog box

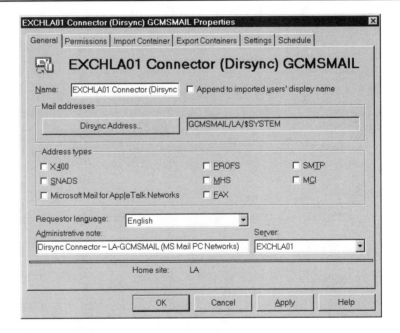

The Dirsync address is set automatically, based on the choice you made in the New Requestor dialog box; don't change it. Use the Address Types box to select the types of addresses you want to request from the Dirsync server. The Requestor Language drop-down list contains the primary language used on your mail system.

Use the Server drop-down list box to select the server that the requestor is assigned to.

## Import Container

Use the Import Container property page to tell the requestor where to put incoming address updates (see Figure 16.3). Click Container and pick the container you want from the list of Exchange Server recipients containers that pops up (see Figure 16.4). If you've added no new recipients containers, select the container Recipients, which holds all recipients for the site.

As you know, the contents of recipients containers in one site are replicated to other sites. Therefore, once MS Mail PC updates have been imported into a recipients container at one site, they will be replicated—along with whatever else is in the container—to all other sites. The addresses also get incorporated automatically into Exchange's Global Address List. Because MS Mail PC addresses are custom recipients, you can do anything with them that you can do with other custom recipients. For example, you can hide any address from the address book.

**FIGURE 16.3:**

The Import Container property page

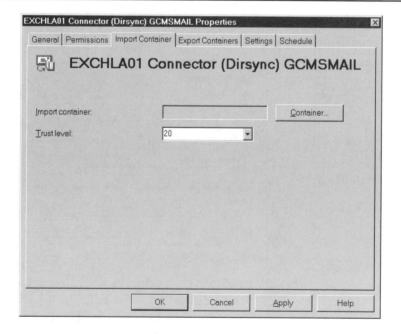

FIGURE 16.4:

Selecting the recipients
container to receive incoming MS Mail PC addresses

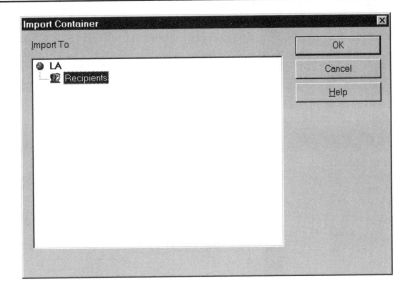

## Eliminating Your MS Mail SMTP Gateway

When it imports MS Mail mailbox addresses, Exchange treats them as custom recipients.
An Exchange custom recipient for an MS Mail mailbox is assigned MS Mail, cc:Mail, Internet, and X.400 addresses by default. So, using my fake company GerCom as an example,
a person with the MS Mail mailbox name bgerber will get an SMTP address of
bgerber@la.gercom.com. If someone on the Internet sends a message to bgerber@la
.gercom.com, the Microsoft Mail Connector that is running on my LA server, and I've set
my DNS to point to the Exchange server with the Internet Mail Service for all mail to
la.gercom.com, the mail will be received by the la.gercom.com IMS and magically transferred to bgerber's MS Mail mailbox. Ship outgoing MS Mail Internet messages to your
Exchange Server, and in one fell swoop you've eliminated your pesky MS Mail SMTP Gateway.

## Export Containers

Select the Exchange recipients containers whose addresses will be exported to the
MS Mail PC system using the Export Containers property page (see Figure 16.5).

The neat part of this process is that you can add any or all containers at any or all of your sites. (Notice the Site drop-down list in the lower left-hand corner of the page.) Thus, through one requestor, you can export all of the addresses in your Exchange organization.

Select the recipients containers you want to export from each site, then click Add for each one to add it to the export list.

**FIGURE 16.5:**

Selecting the recipients containers whose addresses are to be exported to the MS Mail PC side

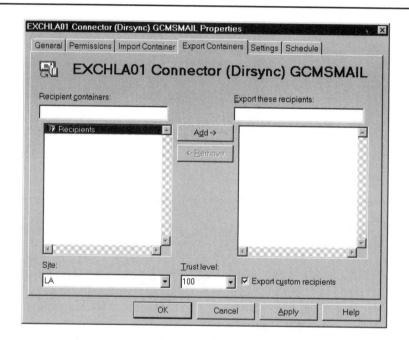

The Trust Level field controls which Exchange recipients—mailboxes, distribution lists, custom recipients, and public folders—get exported. On the Advanced property page of the dialog box for every Exchange recipient, you'll find a trust-level field. If the trust level set there is higher than the one set on the Export Containers property page, the recipient won't be exported. If the trust level set for the recipient is lower than or equal to the level set on this page, the recipient will get exported. Trust-level values can range between 0 and 100.

Because the trust level that's set on the Export Containers property page shown in Figure 16.5 is 100—the highest possible level—all recipients will be automatically exported, no matter what their trust-level setting.

If you want to exclude specific recipients from the export process, set the trust level on the Export Containers property page at a lower level—say, 80. Then set the trust level for those recipients you don't want exported to a value higher than the Export Containers page trust level—90, for instance.

Exchange's custom recipients are exported by default. You can deselect the Export Custom Recipients box to prevent custom recipients from being exported.

## Settings

If you want to add security to your Dirsync process, enter a password on the Settings property page (see Figure 16.6). This password is unique to Dirsync and has nothing to do with other passwords used with the MMC. In just a bit, we'll tell the Dirsync server about this password.

**FIGURE 16.6:**

The Settings property page

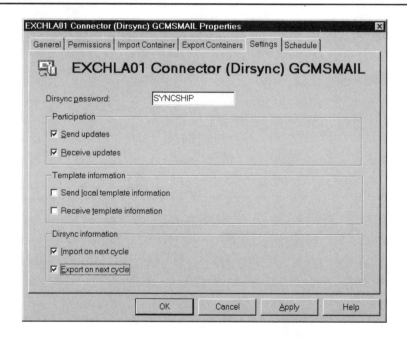

If you expect really heavy Dirsync traffic, you can set up two Exchange-based Dirsync requestors to the same Dirsync server. Each requestor must be on a different server and use a different MMC. If you do this, select Send Updates for one requestor and Receive Updates for the other. If you're going to have only one requestor, select both options.

If your MS Mail PC post offices use address templates, you can select to send Exchange templates to MS Mail and receive MS Mail templates in Exchange here. Check both Import on Next Cycle and Export on Next Cycle to force the requestor to perform both tasks on its next scheduled run.

## Schedule

Set the schedule for the requestor using the Schedule property page (see Figure 16.7). Notice that the page has no Always or Never options. This is because directory synchronization is generally run once a day; in fact, on the MS Mail PC side you can't schedule it to run more often than once a day. Leave the default schedule time as it is.

**FIGURE 16.7:**

Setting a schedule for the Dirsync requestor

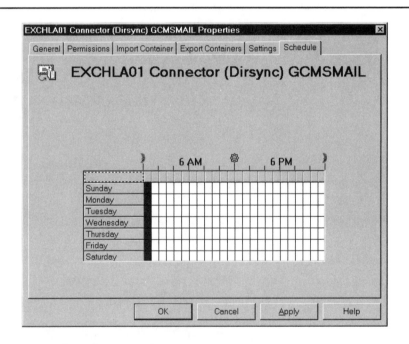

When you've finished setting the requestor schedule, you're done. Click OK to finalize the creation of the requestor. From now on, you'll find the requestor in the Connections container for the site where you created it.

Now you need to start the directory synchronization service using the Services applet on the Control Panel for the server on which you installed the requestor. While you're at it, be sure that directory synchronization is set to start automatically.

## Dirsync Server Settings

Now you need to tell the Dirsync server, which I'm assuming is already running on the MS Mail PC side, that it will be contacted by the Dirsync requestor you just set up. This is a security measure. Using MS Mail PC's DOS-based ADMIN.EXE program,

- Select Config from the first menu you see and press Enter.
- Select Dirsync from the next menu and press Enter.
- Select Server from the next menu and press Enter.
- Select Requestors from the next menu and press Enter.
- Select Create from the next menu and press Enter.

Use the resultant input screen to add the name of your Exchange MS Mail PC shadow network and post office (see Figure 16.8). If you've included a password in the Settings tab of the Dirsync Requestor object in Exchange for extra security, enter the same password you set up when creating the requestor.

Now simply restart DISPATCH.EXE. That's it.

**FIGURE 16.8:**

Giving an Exchange Server–based Dirsync requestor access to an MS Mail PC–based Dirsync server

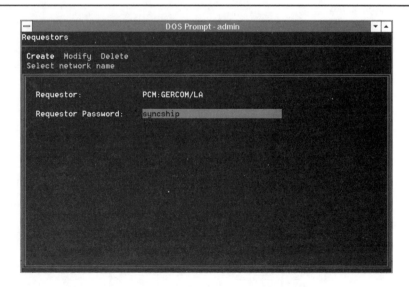

## Did It Work?

You'll have to wait until a full Dirsync cycle has completed to find out whether the process was successful. This can take a day or so. You'll know that everything worked as advertised when your Exchange recipients show up on the MS Mail PC side, and vice versa. Figure 16.9 shows the Open Directory and Address dialog boxes as they appear in the MS Mail PC client for Windows. In the Open Directory dialog box, my GerCom sites look like any other MS Mail PC post office. Note that the directory for LA (shown in the Address dialog box) even includes unhidden public folders, so MS Mail PC users can send messages to those folders just as Exchange users can. I turned on the Global Address List option on the MS Mail PC side (in MS Mail PC's ADMIN.EXE). So if we were to select the Global Address List from the Open Directory dialog box, shown in Figure 16.9, we'd see all of the MS Mail PC *and* GerCom addresses, just as we do on the GerCom side.

After the first Dirsync cycle, create a few new test mailboxes on both sides. If everything is okay, Dirsync will update the directory databases on the Exchange and MS Mail PC sides to reflect these additions.

**FIGURE 16.9:**

An Exchange site address list as it appears in an MS Mail for Windows client

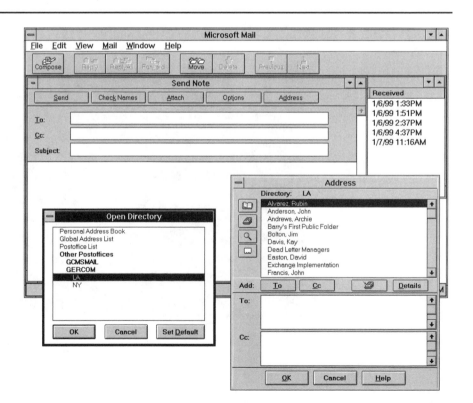

**NOTE**    When testing, you can speed up the Dirsync process on the MS Mail PC side by running a bunch of programs normally handled by DISPATCH.EXE. The *Administrator's Guide* for Microsoft Mail for PC Networks includes detailed instructions for doing this. On the Exchange side, you can schedule the requestor to run hourly (using the requestor's Schedule property page) and then select both the Send Updates and Receive Updates options on the requestor's Settings property page. This will force a full Dirsync cycle on the Exchange side at the top of the hour. If you don't want to wait until then, just reset the server clock to the top of the hour.

# Building a New Dirsync System That Includes an Exchange Organization

If, for whatever reason, you have one or more MS Mail PC post offices and have never installed Dirsync in the past but wish to add it now, you have two options. You can set up your system exactly as we did above, running your Dirsync server on the MS Mail PC side and running Dirsync requestors on all other MS Mail PC post offices, including any shadows on the Exchange side. Alternatively, you can run your Dirsync server on an Exchange server and run Dirsync requestors on all other post offices (and, if you have them, shadow post offices). Here's how to do the latter.

I'm assuming throughout the following discussion that you've already read the sections above that deal with setting up and running a Dirsync requestor on an Exchange server. I'm also leaving most of the setup on the MS Mail PC side to you. For help, check out the Microsoft Mail for PC Networks documentation.

## Setting Up a Dirsync Server on an Exchange Server

To begin setting up a Dirsync server on an Exchange server, select Dirsync Server from the New Other submenu on the Exchange Administrator's File menu. This brings up the Dirsync Server Properties dialog box (see Figure 16.10).

**FIGURE 16.10:**

Setting up a Dirsync server on an Exchange server

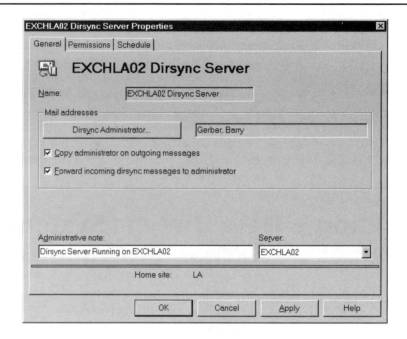

As you can see, Dirsync server setup is very easy. At this point you should be able to do it without any coaching from me. Go to it.

When you've finished setting up the Dirsync server, be sure to start the directory synchronization service on the Exchange server that the Dirsync server is running on. You'll find the service in the Control Panel's Services applet on the Exchange server. Also, make sure you set the directory synchronization service to start automatically when your Exchange server is rebooted.

---

**NOTE**

Remember, just as with a Dirsync requestor running on the Exchange side, the Microsoft Mail Connector must be running on the Exchange server supporting the Dirsync server. Remember, too, that you don't need a Dirsync requestor on the Exchange server running your Dirsync server. The Dirsync server handles requestor functions for its shadow post office.

---

## Setting Up a Remote Dirsync Requestor

Once you've set up the Dirsync server, you need to tell it which requestors will be contacting it, just as we did a bit ago for our MS Mail PC–based Dirsync server. (Refer back to Figure 16.8.) To do this, you must create a *remote Dirsync requestor* for each requestor that will contact the Dirsync server.

Things can get a little confusing here because, in spite of its name, a remote Dirsync requestor is *not* a requestor. Rather, it's two things:

1. An authorization for a real Dirsync requestor to contact the Dirsync server

2. A set of specs on, among other things, which Exchange Server recipient containers should be used for addresses imported from and exported to the real requestor's post office

So based on the terminology that's implied if not specifically used on the MS Mail PC side, a better name for the remote Dirsync connector would have been *requestor definition.*

To create a remote requestor, select Remote Dirsync Requestor from the New Other submenu. Select the Network/PO from the New Requestor dialog to get to the new Remote Dirsync Requestor's property page dialog box. The dialog box, shown in Figure 16.11, looks a lot like the one we used earlier to create an Exchange-based Dirsync requestor. For that reason, I won't go into any more detail here.

When all is set up and running on the Exchange side, you next have to set up Dirsync requestors in your other post offices. (See the Microsoft Mail for PC Networks *Administrator's Guide* for help on the MS Mail PC side.) If for some reason you have other Exchange-based shadow post offices, refer to the first section of this chapter for instructions on creating Dirsync requestors on the Exchange side.

Now start up DISPATCH.EXE on the MS Mail PC side; again, see the Microsoft Mail for PC Networks docs for details.

When everything is running properly, test your Dirsync setup by ensuring that addresses from the Exchange side show up in the appropriate MS Mail PC address lists, and vice versa. (For more on testing, see the "Did It Work?" section earlier in this chapter.)

**FIGURE 16.11:**

Creating a remote Dirsync requestor

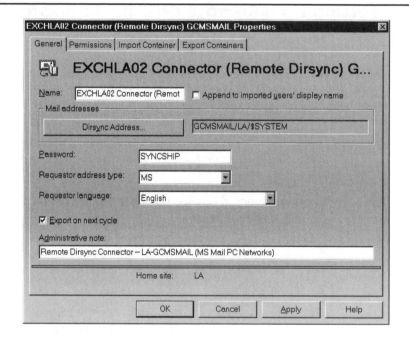

# Administering and Managing the Exchange Directory Synchronization Service

Whether you've installed a Dirsync requestor or server on your Exchange server, I've asked you to start the directory synchronization agent (DXA) service. The DXA is the real power behind Dirsync. It's similar to the program DISPATCH.EXE on the MS Mail PC side because it does a lot of the real work of directory synchronization.

You don't have to worry much about the DXA. Still, because the service is an Exchange object, there is a dialog box you can use to administer and manage it. The DXA object you want is in the container for the server on which you installed your Dirsync requestor or server. When you install the MS Mail Connector on a server, the DXA service is also installed; you need to use the one on the server that supports your Dirsync requestor or server. (In my case, it's EXCHLA01.)

Find the directory synchronization object in the correct server container and double-click it. You'll see a dialog box like the one in Figure 16.12.

**FIGURE 16.12:**

The dialog box for administering and managing the Exchange Server directory synchronization service

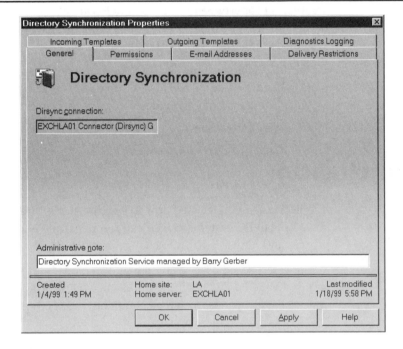

The only property pages that won't be familiar to you are those pertaining to Incoming Templates and Outgoing Templates. By default, only two pieces of information about each recipient are included in the Dirsync process: mailbox name or alias (JSmith, for example) and display name (Smith, John). As you'll remember, Exchange Server provides a large number of additional recipient information fields—including home address, office phone, fax, and department—and it lets you define up to ten additional custom attribute fields. To add recipient information fields on the MS Mail PC side, you must define a template that will hold that information.

Exchange users can view Exchange recipient information fields when running an Exchange client, and MS Mail PC users can see MS Mail PC recipient information when running an MS Mail PC client. So how do you allow users on one system to see information about recipients on the other system? You use the Incoming Templates and Outgoing Templates property pages.

Each Exchange Server recipient information field has a name, as does each field in an MS Mail PC template. You set up mappings or links between Exchange Server's and MS Mail PC's field names on the Incoming Templates and Outgoing Templates property pages. Mapped fields are exchanged along with the two standard recipient information fields and, voilà, information about recipients on both systems is available to users of either system.

Mapping is easy as long as you have the field names for your MS Mail PC template in hand. Setting up MS Mail PC templates is also a breeze; the Microsoft Mail PC *Administrator's Guide* provides very clear instructions. I'll leave the rest to you.

# Conclusion

In this chapter, you learned how to synchronize addresses between Exchange and MS Mail PC systems. Specifically, you learned about MS Mail PC's Dirsync process and how to add an Exchange organization to an existing Dirsync system.

You were also exposed to enough information about MS Mail PC–based Dirsync and Exchange-based Dirsync to build a new Dirsync system around your Exchange system. Finally, you learned a bit about the directory synchronization service and how to administer and manage it.

Now we're ready to move on to some heavy-duty advanced topics. First we'll explore all of those Exchange Administrator menu items we bypassed in earlier chapters. Then we'll tackle all those neat advanced Internet protocol-based goodies that come with Exchange 5.5. Finally, we'll build an Exchange electronic form and make it available to Exchange users.

# PART VII

# Advanced Topics

With this section, our tour of Exchange Server comes to an end. We've been over a lot of flat and gently sloping territory in the past 16 chapters. Now it's time to head up into the mountains for a look at some of the advanced features of Exchange Server. In Chapter 17 we move into the heights of advanced Exchange Server administration and management. We'll cover all those topics I earlier promised to get to. You're ready now, and we're gonna have fun! Chapter 18 takes us up pretty high into the world of some special Internet protocols that support Web browser access to Exchange Server mailboxes, POP3 and IMAP4 mail clients, Internet newsgroups, and LDAP access to Exchange Server's directory. In Chapter 19 we'll reach for the peaks of Exchange application development, focusing on one of the easier and most interesting options—Outlook 2000's Forms Designer.

# CHAPTER

## SEVENTEEN

**17**

# Advanced Exchange Administration and Management

■ Advanced IS administration and management

■ Advanced Exchange security

■ Migrating users from other e-mail systems

■ Advanced DS administration and management

■ Advanced folder management

■ Remote Exchange and NT Server administration

■ Basic Exchange Server troubleshooting

■ Advanced Exchange client support

■ Virus control

■ A quick look at Schedule+

**A**s you've probably realized, Exchange Server is loaded with fancy and fantastic features. Although we've covered a lot of these already, a rather diverse set of Exchange Server's more advanced features remains to be explored. We'll tackle these features in this chapter. Here's what we'll be covering:

- Creating new information stores

- Moving mailboxes

- Tracking messages

- Setting up advanced security

- Migrating users from other e-messaging systems

- Importing information into the Exchange directory

- Extracting information for the Exchange directory from other sources

- Exporting directory information from Exchange Server

- Moving mailboxes between Exchange sites

- Working with Address Book Views

- Folder scripting

- Other advanced Exchange Administrator options

- Remotely administering Exchange and NT servers

- Tips on troubleshooting Exchange Server

- Supporting remote users

- Supporting roving users

- Dealing with computer viruses

- A quick look at Schedule+

I think you'll be pleased to see that a number of these features are really quite easy to use. As with the last chapter, I'll respect your Exchange Server expertise and skip the detailed hand-holding of earlier chapters.

# Creating New Information Stores

There can be *one and only one* private information store and *one and only one* public information store on each Exchange server. These stores were created when you installed the server. Either, but not both of them, can be deleted at any time by locating the store in the appropriate Exchange Administrator server container and pressing the Delete key.

Why would you delete an information store? There are several reasons. To devote maximum computing resources to public folders on a server, you can delete the private information store on that server. Conversely, you can delete the public information store to increase the resources available for the support of private information store access.

To reduce the number of public folder servers and the amount of replication required, you can eliminate the public information stores on some servers, then have users access public folders on the remaining public information store servers. Do this with care, however, because the amount of traffic related to cross-network public folder access could be worse than that generated by public folder replication.

To make more computing resources available for Exchange connectors, delete the public information store from servers running connectors. Be careful about deleting private information stores on servers running connectors, though; except for those with X.400 and MS Mail connectors, servers running Exchange connectors (including the Internet Mail Service and any third-party gateways developed with the Exchange gateway development kit) must have a private information store.

But what if you later need to reinstall a deleted private or public information store? No problem. Let's say you need to add back the public information store on one of your Exchange servers. Just select Information Store from the New Other submenu on the Exchange Administrator's File menu. The New Information Store dialog box pops up (see Figure 17.1). Notice that the dialog box starts up assuming you want to create a new private information store. As you can see in the figure, I have private information stores on all the Exchange servers in the LA site I'm running from, so I'm not offered an opportunity to create private stores.

However, when I select Public under Information Store Type in the New Information Store dialog box, the server in my LA site that doesn't have a public information store—EXCHLA02—is shown (see Figure 17.2). To create the store, all I have to do is click the server name and click OK. That's it. The information store is automatically created.

**FIGURE 17.1:**

The New Information Store dialog box

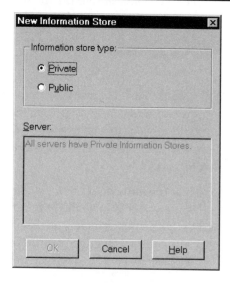

**FIGURE 17.2:**

Creating a new public information store

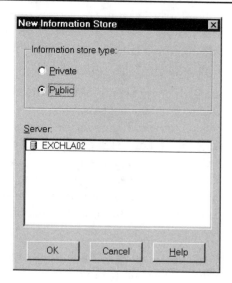

Now that you know how easy it is to delete information stores, be careful before taking that big step and make sure to preserve anything in the stores you want to keep. For public information stores, create a replica of the public folders you're going to delete on another public information store server. For private information stores, use the Move Mailbox option on the Administrator's Tools menu to move mailboxes to another private information store.

# Moving Mailboxes

You can change the home server of a mailbox, although the changes are limited to other Exchange servers in a site. In other words, you can't move a mailbox to an Exchange server in another site. I'll talk about how to move mailboxes between sites later in this chapter.

Why would you want to move a mailbox? One reason, as noted above, is you need to move mailboxes before deleting a private information store. Also, you can balance the loads on different servers in a site by moving mailboxes between them. And, of course, when you consolidate two or more servers, you'll need to move their mailboxes to your new megaserver.

To move a mailbox, select it in the Global Address List, site, or server recipients container using the Exchange Administrator. Next, select Move Mailbox from the Administrator's Tools menu and then select the server you want to move the mailbox to (see Figure 17.3). That's it. After a little cooking time, the mailbox is moved to the private information store on the selected server. You can select and move multiple mailboxes using the standard Windows item selection keys.

Once a mailbox has been moved, neither the Exchange administrator nor the mailbox's user has to do a thing. The Exchange system knows where the new home server is, and an Exchange client can find the mailbox without any alteration in the user's profile. Also, no mail is lost that comes in during the actual move—even if the user is connected to the mailbox when it is moved. In the latter case, the user does have to stop and restart the client, but that's it. All else is totally transparent, thanks to client/server technology and the creative way it was implemented by the Exchange development team.

FIGURE 17.3:

Moving a mailbox to
another server in a site

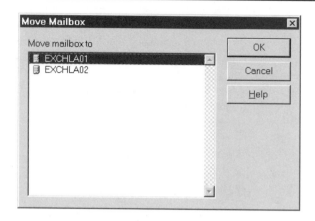

# Tracking Messages

One of the biggest pains in the management of e-messaging systems comes from lost (or *allegedly* lost) messages. With Exchange Server's message-tracking capability, you can get information on the status of messages in your Exchange system. This includes those between Exchange users, those generated by Exchange system components, and those originating in or destined for foreign e-messaging systems.

You'll remember that in earlier chapters I always suggested that you turn message tracking on for whatever information store or Message Transfer Agent we were working with. This is because Exchange Server's message tracking system relies on logs created when tracking is turned on. So if you haven't already done so, I suggest you go back and turn tracking on. The following objects can generate tracking logs:

- Information store in the site Configuration container
- Message Transfer Agent in the site Configuration container
- Internet Mail Service in the site Connections container
- MS Mail Connector in the site Connections container
- cc:Mail Connector in the site Connections container

You can track both user messages and system messages. Let's begin with user messages.

## Tracking User Messages

You can track user messages using two search modes: basic and advanced. We'll start with the basic mode.

### The Basic Search Mode

Start up Exchange's Message Tracking Center (or, as we'll call it here most of the time, the *tracker*). To do so, select Track Message from the Administrator's Tools menu. You'll first be presented with a standard server browser that allows you to select a server to connect to. Select the server where the message originated—the home server of the user who sent the message—and click OK.

Next, the Message Tracking Center dialog box shown in Figure 17.4 pops open. A second or two later, the Select Message to Track dialog box opens (see Figure 17.5). This is where you enter criteria for the messages you want to track.

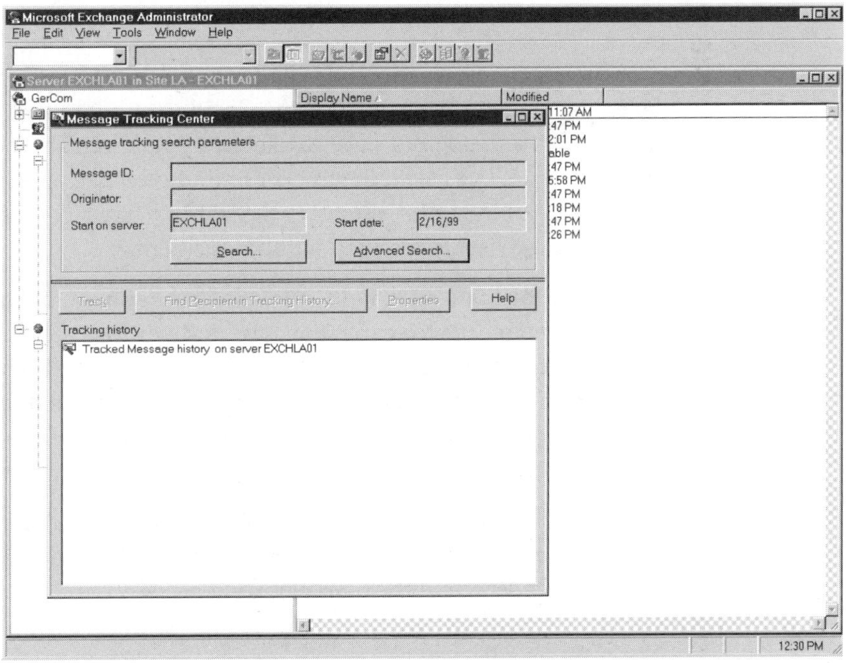

**FIGURE 17.4:**

The Message Tracking Center dialog box

**FIGURE 17.5:**

Looking at messages found after search criteria have been set

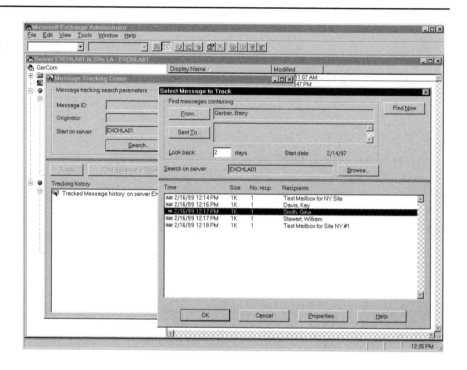

You can put information into the From field and/or the Sent To field in the Select Message to Track dialog box. Clicking either button brings up a standard address book dialog box. You can select a single sender and multiple recipients. In Figure 17.5, I've asked the tracker to find messages sent by me (my home server is EXCHLA01 in my LA site) over the last two days. For the record, I know that these messages were received without incident.

You use the Look Back field to tell the tracker how far back to search in the logs; an entry of 0 means to search the current day's logs. Click Browse to change the server whose message tracking logs will be searched. If you've selected a sender in the From field, the default search server is set to the home server of the sender. Otherwise, the default is the one you connected to with the server browser just before the tracker started up.

When you're done entering your search criteria, click Find Now in the Select Message to Track dialog box. When the tracker has finished searching, it lists the results of its search in the dialog box.

As you can see in Figure 17.5, the tracker found five messages sent by me on February 16, 1999. To find out more about a message, double-click it or highlight it and click Properties. This brings up the Message Properties dialog box shown in Figure 17.6. Notice that the message, which I sent at 12:17 P.M. on February 16, 1999, was transferred into the private information store on the Exchange server EXCHLA01.

**FIGURE 17.6:**

Viewing specific information about a message

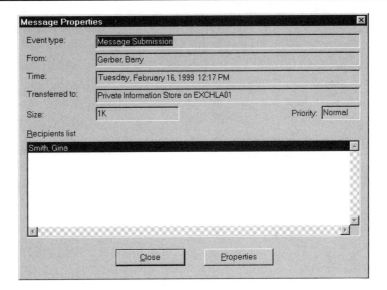

If you double-click a recipient listed in the Message Properties dialog box or click Properties while a recipient is selected, you'll see the full Properties dialog box for the recipient. So, for example, if I were to double-click "Smith, Gina," I'd get the full Mailbox Properties dialog box for Gina Smith's mailbox, complete with all of its property pages. This is the dialog box you use to administer and manage a mailbox in Exchange Administrator. Sometimes you'll find it useful to look at information in this dialog box; for example, you might want to check out the recipient's e-mail addresses (on the E-Mail Addresses property page) when trying to figure out why a message was lost.

Now let's look at the tracking history for a message. Select a message and click OK on the Select Message to Track dialog box (see Figure 17.7). Now you're returned to the Message Tracking Center dialog box (see Figure 17.8). Click Track, and the tracker goes to work. Soon you'll see a tracking history for the message (as shown in Figure 17.8). You can look at the properties of any item in the tracking history list. Notice in the figure how the message is fully tracked across my Exchange system right up to its delivery to Gina Smith's mailbox.

**FIGURE 17.7:**

Selecting a message for a detailed tracking history

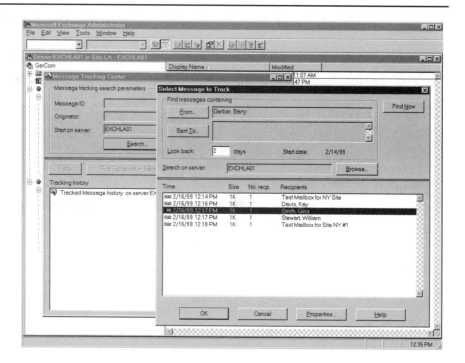

When you're done with the results of your search, close up all the windows related to the Select Message to Track dialog box; only the Message Tracking Center dialog box remains open. To do another basic search, click Search in this dialog box.

**FIGURE 17.8:**

Viewing the tracking history for the message selected in Figure 17.7

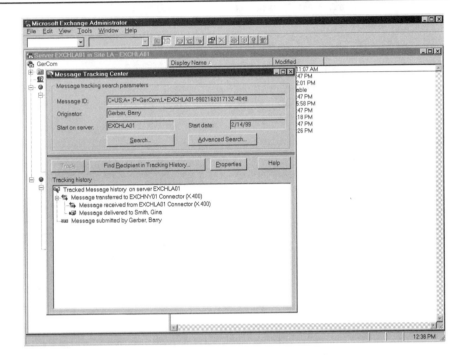

# Other Message Tracking and Management Tools

The message queues for such Exchange Server objects as Message Transfer Agents (MTAs), Internet Mail Services, and Microsoft Mail Connectors can also be useful in tracking a message. Even before you bring up a message tracker, check the queues for the appropriate servers in the site originating the message. If the message remains in a queue beyond a normally scheduled cycle of the MTA or connector, check to ensure that links and services in your messaging network are up. If they are, then be sure the receiving server or Internet mail host is running.

You can take a more proactive approach to link and server availability problems by running the Exchange link and server monitors we talked about in earlier chapters. You can also use NT Server's Performance Monitor (discussed back in Chapter 4) and the specific Performance Monitor setups that are installed with Exchange Server to warn you when queues exceed a specified length.

## The Advanced Search Mode

To track user messages using the advanced search mode, click Advanced Search in the Message Tracking Center dialog box (see Figure 17.8). The resultant Advanced Search dialog box, shown in Figure 17.9, gives you three search options. Only two of these—Transferred into This Site and By Message ID—apply to user messages. The third option, Sent by Microsoft Exchange Server, is used for tracking system messages; we'll get to it in just a bit.

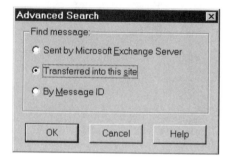

**FIGURE 17.9:**

Selecting an advanced search option

The Transferred into This Site option lets you track messages that came into the site through a particular Exchange connector or gateway—for example, an X.400, Internet Mail, or Microsoft Mail connector. The By Message ID option allows you to track messages by a unique system ID.

Select one of these two search options and click OK in the Advanced Search dialog box. You'll then see a dialog box that lets you set up and execute the option you chose.

**Transferred into This Site**    Let's start with the Transferred into This Site option. Figure 17.10 shows the Select Inbound Message to Track dialog box used for this option. As you can see, I've asked the tracker to find all messages that were transferred into my LA site (my search server is EXCHLA01) through the X.400 Connector that links my LA and NY sites. I've requested information only for the current day.

Since I entered no specific sender or recipients, the resulting list includes all messages transferred through the connector. This includes a system attendant message, directory update information from my NY site to my LA site, and one visible message from someone in the NY site to me.

**FIGURE 17.10:**

Tracking messages sent through an X.400 Connector from another site

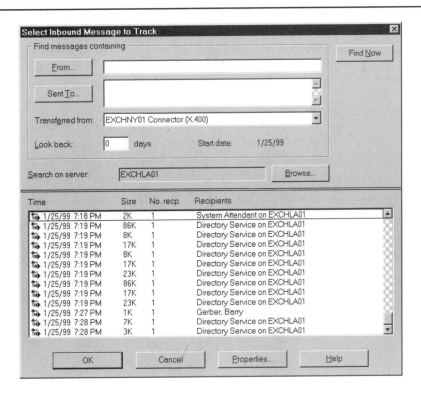

At this point, I could double-click any message to see some basic information about it (see Figure 17.6). I can also do a tracking history on any message, just as I did in the last section (see Figure 17.8). These options are available for any message search. So, I'll mention them from here on only when it's absolutely necessary.

**By Message ID**    Every Exchange message has a unique identifier that includes the address of the originating organization, the name of the originating Exchange server, the date, and a series of digits. When you track a message by its ID, you get the most complete and useful history of the message's progress through your Exchange system.

Here's an example of an Exchange message ID:

    c=US;a= ;p=GerCom;1=EXCHLA01-990110144428FK004600

Can you pick out the date 01/10/99 in the digits just after the server name?

The ID is one of the properties of a message; you use it to track a message using the Message Tracking Center. But how do you find the ID? First you have to find a copy of the message. If you're trying to figure out why a message never arrived at its intended location—which is generally why you'd use the tracker—you'll want the copy of the message stored in the Sent Items folder for the originating mailbox.

Using an Exchange client, find and open the message. Then select Properties from the message's File menu. Tab over to the Message ID property page in the resultant message Properties dialog box for the message. There in all its lengthy glory is the message ID (see Figure 17.11).

**FIGURE 17.11:**

Finding an Exchange message's ID

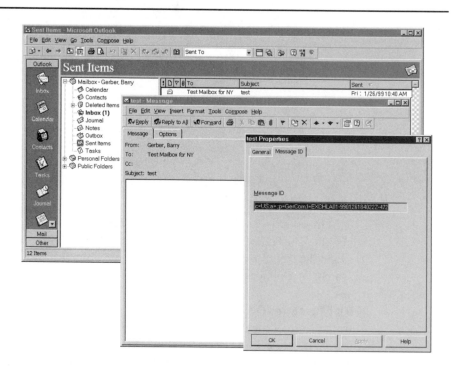

Once you have the message ID, go to the Exchange Administrator and select Advanced Search from the Message Tracking Center dialog box (see Figure 17.4). Then select By Message ID from the Advanced Search dialog box (see Figure 17.9). Next you'll see the Select Message to Track dialog box shown in Figure 17.12. Enter the message ID, set the search server and Look Back options, and click OK.

When the message is found, you're returned to the Message Tracking Center. Click Track to view the message history (see Figure 17.13).

**FIGURE 17.12:**

Entering the ID of a message to be tracked

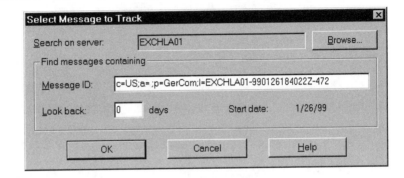

**FIGURE 17.13:**

The results of a tracking history request for a message found by its message ID

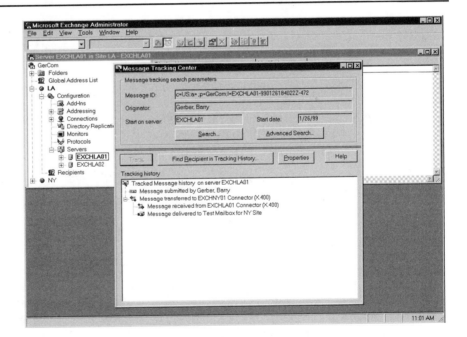

## Coping with Those Endless Message IDs

Worried about accurately typing in that long message ID? Relax. If you're running an Exchange client and the Administrator on the same machine, you can use Ctrl+C to copy the ID from the Message ID property page and then Ctrl+V to paste it into the Message ID field.

If you're running the client and the Administrator on different servers, you can paste the ID into a message and send it to yourself. Or you can drag the original message into a new message and send it to yourself as an attachment to the new message. When you open the attachment in the new message, you can look at all the properties, including the ID, just as if it were the original message. If you need to track the message for a user, this last approach is especially useful. Users don't have to know anything about message IDs—all they need to do is send you the message that needs to be tracked.

## Tracking System Messages

If you're interested in messages generated by key Exchange Server components such as the directory, information store, System Attendant, or directory synchronization, select Sent by Microsoft Exchange Server from the Advanced Search dialog box and then click OK (see Figure 17.9). This brings up the Select System Message to Track dialog box (see Figure 17.14). Use the From drop-down list box to select the Exchange Server component you're interested in, then set the search server and the number of Look Back days and click Find Now. Found messages will be listed in the box in the lower part of the dialog box.

Figure 17.14 shows the results of a search I did for the information store on the server EXCHLA01 in my LA site. As you can see, three messages were generated by EXCHLA01: two addressed to the EXCHLA02 server in my LA site and one for the server EXCHNY01 in my NY site. These are public information store messages that contain info used in public folder replication. Wow! Remember way back when we talked about how public folder replication was based on messages? Well, here they are.

As usual, you can see more detail about a message by double-clicking it in the list box or by selecting it and clicking Properties. To track one of the system messages, select it and click OK. When you're returned to the Message Tracking Center, click Track to view the message history.

**FIGURE 17.14:**

The Select System Message to Track dialog box

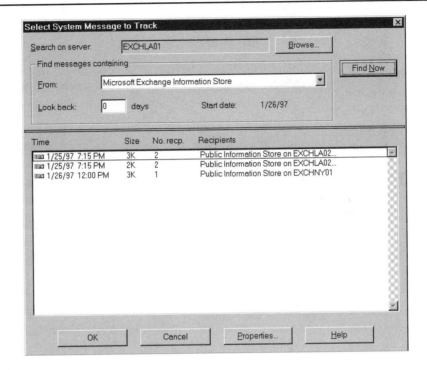

# Setting Up Advanced Security

Exchange Server is pretty secure in and of itself. User message stores and the use of the Exchange Administrator are protected by NT security. Also, the remote procedure calls (RPCs) that support some Exchange communications can be set to encrypt message data as it crosses network wires. Internet mail additionally has a range of security options.

In addition to all of the above, a level of advanced security is available in Exchange: digital signatures and data encryption based on the RSA public key cryptography system. A digital signature assures a message's receiver that the contents of the message haven't been altered since it was digitally signed and that the message was truly sent by the indicated originator. Data encryption with public and private keys virtually guarantees that only authorized recipients can read a message.

You have to enable advanced security on a mailbox-by-mailbox basis. Each enabled Exchange mailbox has two pairs of keys, each consisting of a public and a private key. One pair of keys is for digital signing, and the other is for encryption.

When a user chooses to sign an outgoing message, the user's Exchange client uses the private signing key of her or his mailbox to add a digital signature to the message. The message recipient's Exchange client verifies the signature using the public signing key of the sender's mailbox.

To encrypt an outgoing message, an Exchange client uses the unique public encryption key for the mailbox of each recipient of the message. When a user receives an encrypted message, the user's Exchange client uses the private encryption key for his or her mailbox to decrypt the message.

Public keys are stored in the Exchange directory as attributes of each advanced security–enabled mailbox. Private keys are stored on each user's private disk space in an encrypted file with the extension .EPF.

To run advanced Exchange Server security, you'll need to install a special *Key Management Server* program, or simply KM Server. Among other things, KM Server does the following:

- Certifies public signing and encryption keys to ensure their authenticity.

- Creates public and private encryption keys. (Public and private signing keys are created by Exchange clients.)

- Holds backups of private encryption keys and public signing keys.

- Generates tokens that are used only once to enable digital signatures and encryption or to recover lost or forgotten keys for a user.

- Maintains the original copy of the list of users whose rights to advanced security have been revoked.

The KM database itself is encrypted for additional security.

With the initial Exchange Server 5.5 release, you can enable advanced security within an Exchange organization. With Service Pack 2 for 5.5, you also can enable advanced security across Exchange organizations and you can even send secure messages to those in other organizations using Internet standard security algorithms.

No digital signature or data encryption system is perfect. However, the systems included in Exchange are about as good as they get. Two general digital signature/encryption options are available to Exchange Server clients: Exchange Server and S/MIME.

The Exchange Server encryption option uses standard encryption algorithms, but the option itself is unique to Exchange Server. The S/MIME option is based on the Secure MIME Internet standard. It too uses standard encryption algorithms. I'll discuss the S/MIME encryption algorithms here and I'll talk about the S/MIME standard in more detail later in this chapter.

The Exchange Server encryption option gives you a choice of three encryption algorithms: DES (Data Encryption Standard), CAST-40, and CAST-64. (*CAST* stands for the initials of *C*arlisle *A*dams and *S*tafford *T*avares, who developed the algorithm at Northern Telecom.)

Both DES and CAST-64 use 64 bits for keys, while CAST-40 uses only 40 bits. Because it produces a shorter and more easily broken key, CAST-40 is less secure than either CAST-64 or DES. Because the U.S. government allows exportation of 64-bit encryption only to Canada, however, only CAST-40 encryption is available for Exchange Server software shipped elsewhere. You can set the encryption algorithm used for each site separately and Exchange Server knows what encryption algorithm to use for messages to a site, so if you have sites both inside and outside of the U.S. and Canada, you don't have to use the less-secure CAST-40 algorithm across your entire organization.

Like the Exchange Server encryption option, the S/MIME option lets you choose from three encryption algorithms: 3DES (Triple Data Encryption Standard), DES, RC2-128, and RC2-40. (*RC* stands for either *R*on's *C*ode or *R*ivest's *C*ipher in honor of the inventor of the algorithm, Ron Rivest.)

3DES encrypts the regular DES key three times, meaning that there are really three keys. Microsoft's 3DES is a 112-bit implementation of the algorithm. RC2-128 encrypts at 128 bits. RC2-40 is the 40-bit algorithm for use outside the United States and Canada.

# Installing Key Management Server and Supporting Software

KM Server underwent an extensive overhaul for Exchange Server 5.5. The interface is new and the functionality behind it has grown. Several new KM Server features didn't make it into the first release of Exchange Server 5.5. Updates to both KM Server (part of Exchange Server Service Pack 1 and 2 or later) and the Outlook client (Outlook 98 or later) following the release of 5.5 include these missing features. In addition, starting with Exchange Server Service Pack 1, another Microsoft product, Certificate Server, is required to run KM Server.

So, if you want everything to operate as discussed and pictured here, after installing Exchange Server and KM Server, install Exchange Server Service Pack 2 or later, use the Outlook 98 or 2000 client, and be sure you've properly installed Certificate Server. We'll focus here on getting both KM Server and Certificate Server properly installed and set up.

## Installing KM Server

The KM server software is installed on an Exchange server. For maximum security, the server should be set up to use the NT File System (NTFS).

KM Server is at the heart of your advanced Exchange security system. Be sure to locate the computer that runs it in a physically secure place. KM Server access doesn't generate much network traffic, so it makes little difference which of your Exchange servers you put it on.

KM Server is installed using the Exchange Server SETUP.EXE program. You can find and run the appropriate SETUP.EXE for your operating system on the Exchange Server CD-ROM or you can use the installation and documentation menu that starts up when you insert the Exchange Server CD-ROM into your CD-ROM player. If you installed KM Server back when you first installed Exchange Server as I recommended in Chapter 7, then you're ready to go. If you didn't, rerun SETUP.EXE and install it before moving on.

Each time that KM Server starts up, you have to enter a special password or the program won't run. When you installed KM Server, you either chose to enter the password manually or to have KM Server look for it on special primary and backup diskettes that were created during the Exchange Server installation.

If you chose manual entry, the installation program gave you the password before it terminated. Be sure to store the password in a safe place.

If you chose to go the password-to-diskette route, the installation program created master and copy diskettes with the password on them. Whenever you need to start the service, one of the diskettes must be in the Exchange/KM server's A drive. Be sure to treat the diskettes with respect, and keep them under lock and key when not in use. The password is stored in non-encrypted format and can be read or copied by anyone. In addition to the master and copy diskettes created during installation, you should make your own copies of the diskette and store them in a safe and secure place.

---

**NOTE**     The KM Server that comes with the initial release of Exchange 5.5 allows you to install only one KM Server in your organization. Service Pack 2 and later updates to 5.5 allow you to install a KM Server in each of your sites if you wish. Multiple KM servers enhance security, performance, and reliability.

---

After installation, the KM Server service is set to start up manually. You can use the NT Services applet to set KM Server to start up automatically with the rest of the Exchange Server components. For auto-startup, you'll want to use the KM Server password diskette and to assure that your Exchange Server computer is set to attempt to boot from its hard disk drive before its diskette drive. That way, for unplanned reboots such as those initiated by Exchange Server's server or link monitors, the computer can boot with a copy of the password diskette in its diskette drive and KM Server will be able to start automatically.

Before we move on, open the Services applet on the control panel and start the Key Management Server. Then take a look in the Configuration container for the site where you installed KM Server. You'll see two new objects—one called *CA* and one named *Site Encryption Configuration*. We'll talk about these in just a bit.

## Installing Microsoft Certificate Server

Back in the days when Exchange Server 5.5 was first released, life with KM Server was relatively easy. KM Server was capable of issuing security certificates that allowed for encrypted and digitally signed messages within an Exchange organization. Exchange Server Service Pack 1 and later added significantly to both the range of organizations to which secure messages could be sent and the complexity of KM Server.

It is now possible for Exchange Server users to generate secure messages based on the Internet security standard S/MIME. These messages can be securely sent to recipients anywhere the S/MIME standard is supported, whether these recipients are in your own Exchange organization, in another Exchange organization, or even in an organization running an entirely different e-mail system.

The key to S/MIME is the X.509 V3 certificate. To support S/MIME security, Exchange Server must be able to provide users with X.509 certificates.

KM Server doesn't issue X.509 V3 certificates itself. Rather, it turns to Certificate Server for these certificates.

So, let's quickly cover Certificate Server installation. At this writing, installing Certificate Server is a rather convoluted process. Here's what you have to do:

1. Assure that KM Server is installed and updated to Exchange Server Service Pack 2 or later.

2. Obtain the NT 4 Option Pack on CD-ROM. Check with Microsoft on the details.

3. Install Internet Information Server 4 from the CD-ROM, but don't install Certificate Server.

4. Read the following two Microsoft Knowledge Base articles: Q184695 and Q192044. For more information on accessing the Knowledge Base, check out the section on troubleshooting Exchange Server near the end of this chapter.

5. Download the Certificate Server Update from the FTP site listed in Q192044.

6. Follow the directions in Q184695 for installing the Certificate Server using the update files.

7. Register the EXPOLICY.DLL file as instructed in Q192044.

That's it. Some fun, huh? Well, at least you're now ready to start using KM Server.

## Administering and Managing the Key Management Server

There are three distinct KM Server administration and management tasks:

- Setting encryption algorithms
- Setting KM Server's own security
- Enabling advanced security for mailboxes

We'll cover each of these tasks in order below. To start, be sure you're logged in as NT administrator for the domain where you installed KM Server. Then open the Exchange Administrator for the site where KM Server was installed.

## Setting Encryption Algorithms

You use a site's Site Encryption Configuration object to administer and manage KM Server settings. Open the Site Encryption Configuration Properties dialog box by double-clicking the Site Encryption Configuration object in the Configuration container for the site.

### General Properties

The General property page contains two alterable fields, the display name and the primary KM Server location. The second field will be included in an update to Exchange Server 5.5.

As I mentioned earlier, the initial release of Exchange Server 5.5 limits you to one KM Server per organization. The Service Pack 2 update lets you install one KM Server per site. With the updates in place, you can install a KM Server in any site you choose. If you don't install a KM Server in a site and you want to use Exchange advanced security in that site, you need to select an existing KM Server to support the site. To do that, again with the update in place, click Choose Site on the General property page of the Site Encryption Configuration Properties dialog box and pick the KM Server from the list that is presented. In Figure 17.15, this option is unavailable because the dialog box is being used in the site where the KM Server is installed, LA. I can't change the primary KM Server location setting in a site where KM Server is installed. However, when I open the Site Encryption Configuration Properties dialog box in my NY site, where no KM Server is installed, the Choose Site button isn't greyed out. Clicking it reveals that I may choose to use my LA site–based KM Server to support Exchange advanced security in my NY site.

**FIGURE 17.15:**

The General property page of the Site Encryption Configuration Properties dialog box

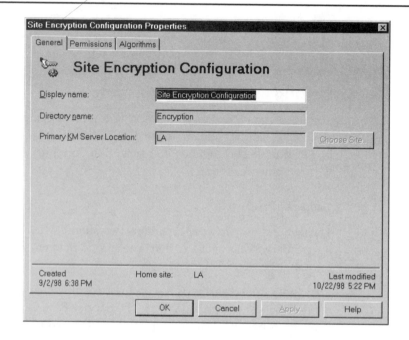

**Algorithms**  Tab over to the Algorithms property page (see Figure 17.16). Use the Select the Preferred Algorithms for Your Clients area to change the encryption algorithm used by clients in the site. You can change settings for North America where more secure encryption keys are permitted and for other geographic locations where the more secure keys can't be legally exported. Your two options for North America are CAST-64 and DES. If you change the encryption algorithm after enabling advanced security for specific mailboxes, the users of those mailboxes will still be able to read messages created under the previous algorithm. However, some reconfiguring will be required to enable the new algorithm for those mailboxes.

You can't change the encryption algorithm for messages addressed to Exchange sites outside North America. Even though a drop-down list is present for "other" sites, there is only one option on the list: CAST-40.

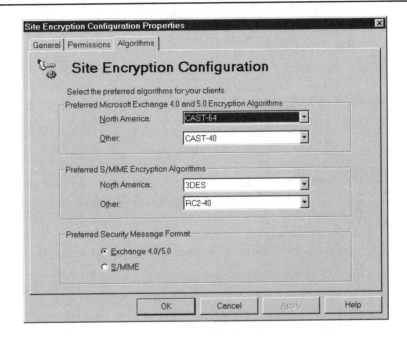

Service Pack updates to KM Server after the initial release of Exchange Server 5.5 added Secure Multipurpose Internet Mail Extensions (S/MIME) to security options available with Exchange Server. S/MIME is an Internet security standard for message encryption and digital signatures. Select the algorithm you want to use in the Preferred S/MIME Encryption Algorithms area on the Algorithms property page. S/MIME-compatible algorithms include: DES, 3DES, RC2-40, and RC2-128. As does the 40 in CAST-40, the numbers in the latter two standards refer to the length of the key used to encrypt messages under the standard. The longer the key, the more difficult it is to break the encryption.

Service Pack updates to KM Server also let you set the default format Exchange Server clients use for secure messages. With the updates in place, you do that in the Preferred Security Message Format area on the Algorithms property page. If all or most of your Exchange clients are 32-bit Outlook clients, go with S/MIME, the industry standard. If old Exchange clients or the 16-bit Outlook client that comes with Exchange Server 5.5 are in the majority in your Exchange system, select the Exchange 4/5 option. Users can change the default format in their mail clients.

## Setting KM Server's Own Security

If you have standard Exchange Permissions Admin rights on a site's Configuration container, you can change encryption options using the Site Encryption Configuration Properties dialog box shown in Figure 17.16. However, to change KM Server's own security, you must have some very special rights. You must be a Key Management Server Administrator (KMSA).

As a KMSA, among other things, you can change your KM Server password, add and remove other KMSAs, and enable and disable advanced security for mailboxes. Once you've enabled advanced security for a mailbox, the mailbox's owner can use digital signatures and data encryption. As you can see, KMSAs are very powerful, so you should assign KMSA rights with great care. To start with, the default KMSA is the account that installed KM Server. That is often the NT administrator account for the domain where KM Server was installed, but, for reasons of security, you can use any account you wish.

To modify KM Server's own security for the first time, be sure you're logged in under the account that installed KM Server. Then double-click CA in the Configuration container for the site. Before you can run CA, you need to enter the special KM Server password for the domain administrator (see Figure 17.17). This is not the password of the account that installed KM Server. It's a special password for use when the administrator runs CA. The default password is "password" in lowercase. In a bit I'll show you how to change the default.

**FIGURE 17.17:**

Entering the KM Server password for the administrator of the domain where KM Server is installed

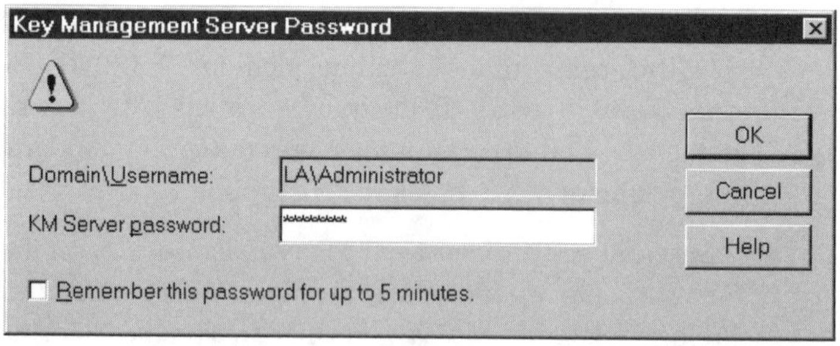

Every time you do an advanced security function, you're asked for that danged password. However, if you check Remember This Password for up to 5 Minutes, you can work for at least a little while without bother.

When you're done with the password dialog box, click OK to open the CA Properties dialog box shown in Figure 17.18.

**General Properties**    The name of the Certificate Server is shown on this page. You can't change it.

**FIGURE 17.18:**

The General property page of the CA Properties dialog box

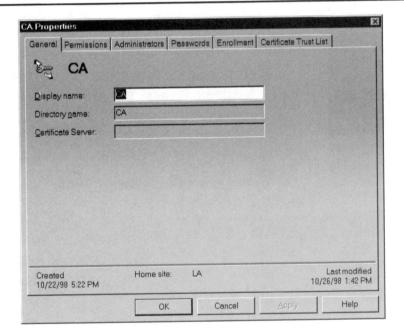

**Administrators**    If you need to add or remove KMSAs, use this page. In Figure 17.19, I've added the administrator in my New York site to the list of KMSAs. Each KMSA has its own special KM Server administrator password that can be changed by clicking Change My KM Server Password and filling in the information on the resultant change password dialog box. The currently logged on KMSA can only change his or her password. That's why it says Change *My* KM Server Password.

**Passwords**    If you want to increase security, you can use the Passwords property page (Figure 17.20) to require that multiple KMSAs authorize specific advanced security tasks. For example, if you've defined five KMSAs, you can require that any number of them from one to five must enter their NT usernames and KMSA passwords for the tasks shown in Figure 17.20 to complete.

The Add Administrators, Delete Administrators, or Edit These Multiple Password Policies option sets the maximum number of KMSAs that you can require to authorize the recovery and revocation of a user's security keys. (We'll talk about recovery and revocation of security keys, certificates from other Certification Authorities, and changing enrollment settings in a bit.) So, if you have three KMSAs and you require that all three authorize addition and deletion of administrators and editing of multiple password policies, you can require that one, two, or three KMSAs authorize recovery or revocation of security keys.

**FIGURE 17.19:**

The CA Properties dialog box's Administrators property page with a newly added KM Server administrator

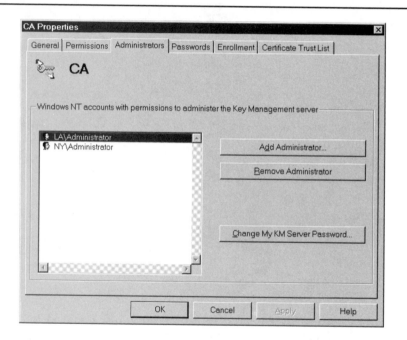

Be careful with all this multiple password authorization stuff. If you involve too many cooks in this particular concoction, the day might come when you find yourself in a bowl of alphabet soup without a spoon.

**NOTE**    You can't specify which KMSAs must consent to the completion of a task, just the number of them that must consent. If you have five KMSAs and require consent from three of them, any three of the five can authorize the task.

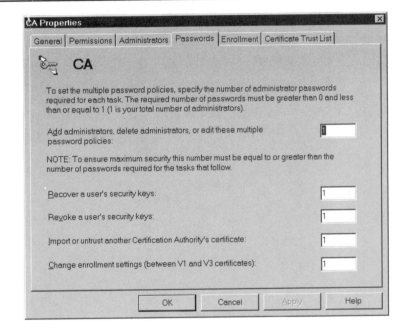

**FIGURE 17.20:**

Use the Passwords property page of the CA Properties dialog box to increase security when using Exchange Server's advanced security.

**Enrollment**    Use the Enrollment property page to set some policies to be applied when advanced security is enabled on an Exchange mailbox and to set up a group of users for advanced security. As Figure 17.21 notes, when advanced security is enabled for an Exchange mailbox, KM Server generates a temporary key. This key must be entered by the mailbox owner using an Exchange client as part of the process of enabling advanced security. I'll show you how the key is used a few pages down the road.

You can pass the key to the mailbox owner manually in a face-to-face meeting or you can have KM Server mail the key to the mailbox to be enabled. The e-mail option is disabled by default. For utmost security, leave the option disabled.

When the key is sent by e-mail, it is accompanied by a message. You can change the message by clicking Edit Welcome Message.

**FIGURE 17.21:**

Manage the security certificate creation and distribution process using the Enrollment property page of the CA Properties dialog box.

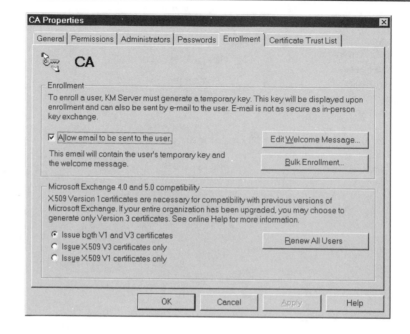

As you'll see in a bit, you can enable advanced security on each mailbox in your organization one mailbox at a time. If you've got to deal with lots of mailboxes, you can use bulk enrollment to enable all the recipients in a container. Click Bulk Enrollment and select the container you want to work with. You can only work in site recipients containers. You can't, for example, bulk enable advanced security for recipients in an address book view. If you've disabled the sending of keys to mailbox owners by e-mail, be sure to select the Save Results in a File option while setting up bulk enrollment. This file will include the key created for each mailbox. Use this information to let each mailbox user know what her or his key is.

All of what follows in the next three paragraphs works only if you've installed the Exchange Server Service Pack 2 updates to KM Server. Older Microsoft Exchange clients as well as Outlook 8.0x clients use version 1 X.509 certificates to bind a user's public key to their mailbox. S/MIME-compatible clients support V1 and V3 certificates. If your organization uses any of the Exchange or Outlook 8.0x clients, you must enable V1 certificates. If it uses only S/MIME clients, enable V3 certificates. If it uses both types of clients, either enable V1 or both V1 and V3 certificates. Though S/MIME clients can use V1 certificates, they won't use the S/MIME security format when using V1 certificates.

Click Renew All Users to initiate enrollment using the certificate type you've specified. This option should also be used to reset changes you make in X.509 certificate version handling or to the default security message format on the Algorithms page of the Site Encryption Configuration Properties dialog box.

**Certificate Trust List**    You can set things up so that your users can verify the digital signatures of messages sent by users in other Exchange Server organizations. You do this on the Certificate Trust List property page by importing a KM Server *.CRT file (see Figure 17.22). You can send *.CRT files to another organization for import into their advanced security environment. Use the Trust or Untrust button to enable or disable the trust for a specific organization.

**FIGURE 17.22:**

Enable Exchange Server advanced security across Exchange organizations on the Certificate Trust List property page of the CA Properties dialog box.

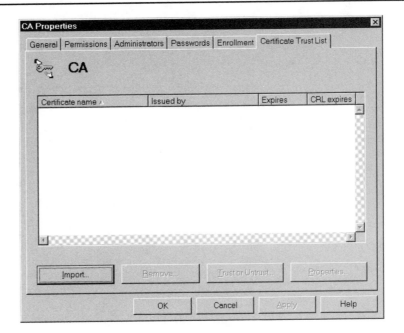

## Enabling Advanced Security for Mailboxes

Now we're ready to actually enable advanced security for mailboxes. This is a two-step process that's done partly on the Exchange Server side and partly on the Exchange client side. We'll start with Exchange Server.

## Enabling Advanced Security for Mailboxes: the Exchange Server Side

As a KMSA, you have two options when enabling advanced security for mailboxes: the mailbox-by-mailbox option and the bulk automated option. If you need to enable advanced security on only a few mailboxes, the mailbox-by-mailbox method is adequate. However, if you've got a bunch of mailboxes that need enabling, the bulk option is a better choice. I've already discussed the bulk method, so let's do the mailbox-by-mailbox option.

You can work on mailboxes in any recipients container, from the Global Address List to a server's recipients container. Using the Exchange Administrator, locate the mailbox for which you want to enable advanced security, and double-click it. This opens the standard mailbox properties dialog box. The box has a new tab on it named Security; tab over to it. The Security property page is protected by a KMSA password, which you'll be prompted for (see Figure 17.23).

Once you've entered the correct KMSA password, you'll see the Security property page for the mailbox (see Figure 17.24).

**FIGURE 17.23:**

Entering the KM Server password to gain entry to a mailbox's Security property page

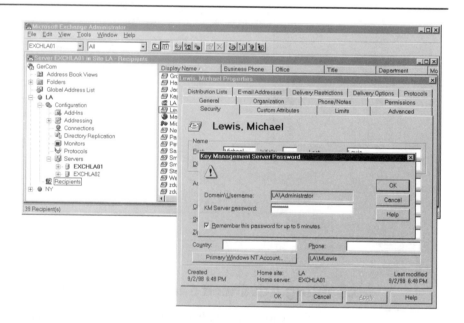

**FIGURE 17.24:**

The Security property page for an Exchange mailbox and some friends

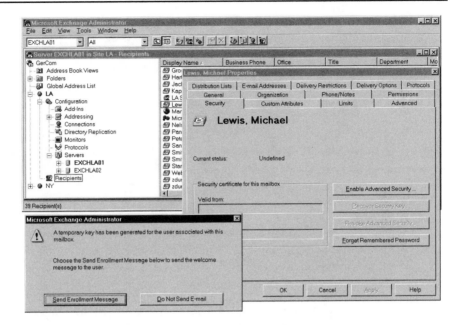

At this point, you can enable advanced security by clicking—you guessed it—Enable Advanced Security. Besides turning on advanced security, this option creates public keys for the mailbox and generates a code called an *advanced security temporary key*. The mailbox owner must enter this key to enable advanced security on the mailbox.

In a second or so, you'll see a dialog box labeled Microsoft Exchange Administrator (see Figure 17.24). If you want to send the token to the mailbox owner by e-mail, click Send Enrollment Message. If not, click Do Not Send E-Mail. You won't see this message if you didn't select the Allow E-Mail to Be Sent to the User option on the CA objects Enrollment property page.

Next you'll see a dialog box with the advanced security temporary key that was just generated (see Figure 17.25). If you sent the key to the mailbox owner, the dialog box tells you that the message with the key was sent to the mailbox and you can ignore the key. If you didn't send a message with the key to the mailbox, you'll need to write down the key so you can give it to the mailbox owner.

A dialog box showing the advanced security temporary key used to enable advanced security on a mailbox

Click OK in the Microsoft Exchange Administrator dialog box. The security property page now looks something like the one in Figure 17.26. You're through enabling advanced security for the mailbox.

Don't worry about the Recover Security Key and Revoke Advanced Security options right now; we'll talk about them later in this chapter. If you checked Remember This Password for up to 5 Minutes when entering the KM Server password (see Figure 17.23), clicking Forget Remembered Password forces the Exchange Administrator to forget the password before those five minutes pass.

### Enabling Advanced Security for Mailboxes: the Exchange Client Side

Open a client for the mailbox for which you want to enable advanced security. In the example presented here, I'm using an Outlook 2000 client. If you enabled the KM Server's Send E-Mail option, you'll find an e-mail message from the Exchange Server's System Attendant that includes your temporary security token. Open the message to see the token.

Next, select Options from the client's Tools menu to open the Options dialog box, then tab over to the Security property page (see Figure 17.27).

**FIGURE 17.26:**

The Security property page after advanced security has been enabled

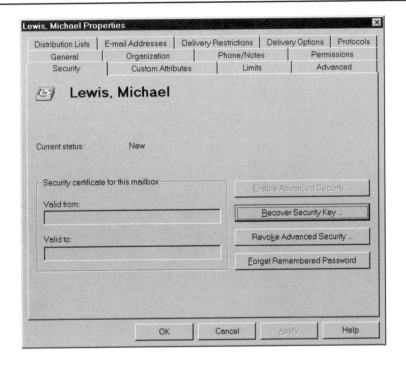

Then, click Get a Digital ID to bring up the Get a Digital ID (Certificate) dialog box (see Figure 17.27). As you can see in Figure 17.27, you can get an S/MIME certificate or an Exchange Server certificate. For now, select the Exchange Server option. This opens the Setup Advanced Security dialog box, which is also shown in Figure 17.27. Type in the token for the mailbox that was generated by the KMSA and click OK. When the Microsoft Outlook Security Password dialog box opens, enter and confirm an advanced security password that will be used when you generate or try to open a digitally signed or encrypted message. (The password must be at least six characters long.) When you're done, click OK.

Click OK in response to the next dialog box, which tells you that your request to enable security has been sent to the Key Management server and that you'll be notified when the request has been processed. This feature is pretty impressive. Communications between clients and KM Server are all by e-mail messages, so the client can be linked to the Exchange server environment by anything from a dial-up connection to a hard-wired WAN or LAN link.

**FIGURE 17.27:**

Use the Options dialog box to enable advanced security for a mailbox.

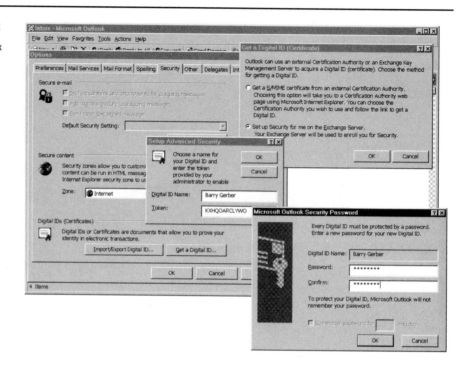

After the time required for a round-trip mail cycle, a message from the System Attendant will appear in your client's Inbox. The subject of the message will be Reply from Security Authority. This is a very special message. When you open it, you won't see a standard message window. Instead, you'll see the Microsoft Outlook Security Logon dialog box, which looks a lot like the Microsoft Outlook Security Password dialog box in Figure 17.27. Enter your password (the one you just created) and, if you wish, set the length of time in minutes that Outlook will remember the password after you've entered it. This is a nice feature. With it, you don't have to type in your password every time you create or open a secure message. When you're done with this dialog box, click OK.

Finally, you'll see the contents of the message from the Exchange System Attendant you just opened. The message tells you that security has been successfully enabled for your mailbox.

**NOTE**
After you've enabled advanced security for a mailbox, you can tell Outlook to digitally sign and encrypt **all** messages by selecting these two options on the Options dialog box (see Figure 17.28).

**FIGURE 17.28:**

Enabling digital signatures and encryption for all messages

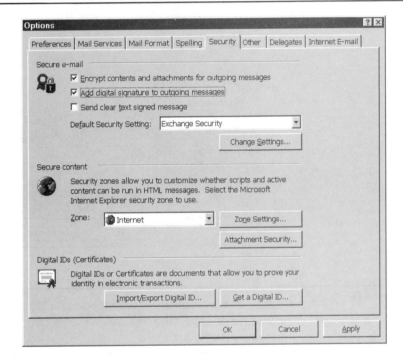

After a while, take a look in the Exchange Administrator at the Security property page of the mailbox for which you just enabled advanced security. Because the mailbox is now fully security-enabled, the Valid From and Valid To fields will be filled in (see Figure 17.29). By default, security keys are valid for a year and a half. New keys will be automatically generated at the end of this time period.

When a mailbox's Security property page looks like the one in Figure 17.29, advanced security is fully enabled, and the mailbox user can send and receive digitally signed and/or encrypted messages. The mailbox's public keys are part of the mailbox definition in the Exchange directory. Therefore, mailbox users in other sites will not be able to communicate with the mailbox using advanced security until a fully security-enabled replica of the mailbox has reached their sites.

**FIGURE 17.29:**

The valid life span of a
mailbox's security keys
has been set.

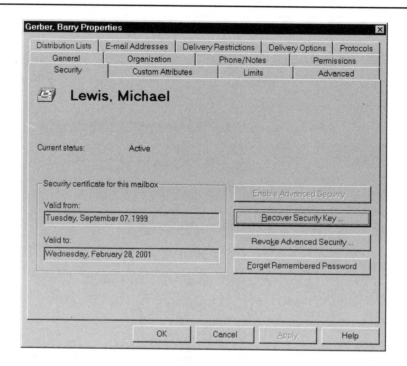

**FIGURE 17.29:**

The valid life span of a
mailbox's security keys
has been set.

**NOTE**    You can keep track of advanced security activity in Exchange by keeping an eye on
NT Event Viewer's Application log. You'll find the Event Viewer in the Administrative Tools program group.

## Sending and Receiving Digitally Signed and Encrypted Messages

Since this book doesn't focus on Exchange clients, I'll just give you a quick overview on the topic. If, when using the Options dialog box, you asked to have all
messages digitally signed and encrypted, you'll be led through any required steps
for each message. If you've chosen to sign or encrypt messages individually, then
while composing a message in your Outlook client, click Options on the message's
Standard toolbar. On the Message Options dialog box, select Encrypt Message Contents and Attachments and/or Add Digital Signature to Outgoing Message. When

you send the message, you'll be led through the steps required to give it advanced security.

**TIP**

You can also set security options for a message by selecting Properties from the message's File menu and then selecting Security from the resultant Properties dialog box. This option not only lets you select encryption and digital signing for the message, it also lets you pick from alternate security settings (S/MIME, as opposed to Exchange Server, for example) if alternative settings have been enabled.

# Additional Advanced Security Administration and Management Options

The Security property page for a mailbox has two options that we didn't talk about earlier: Recover Security Key and Revoke Advanced Security (see Figure 17.26). We're now ready to tackle these options.

## Recovering a Security Key

The Recover Security Key option on the Security property page is useful in the following situations:

- Users lose their temporary key before using it to set up advanced security on the client side.

- Users lose their advanced security password.

- Users corrupt or remove the local security file for their mailbox.

- You've changed the encryption algorithm for a site and need to update mailboxes that were enabled for advanced security before the change took effect.

Click Recover Security Key to start the recovery process. When it's finished, a Microsoft Exchange Administrator dialog box pops up to give you a new key. This key will be different from the original one; when the user reinstalls advanced security, whichever of the first three problems needed fixing will be fixed, or the new encryption algorithm will be enabled for that user.

### Revoking Advanced Security

Click Revoke Advanced Security to remove advanced security rights for a mailbox. If you ever want to re-enable these rights, just generate a new key for the mailbox and ask the mailbox user to enable advanced security on the client side.

# Migrating Users from Other E-Messaging Systems

You can move users from foreign e-messaging systems to your Exchange system. In some cases, Microsoft provides specific migration tools, while in others no tools are available. Even if there are no tools for migration, you can still automate at least part of it on your own.

Migration is a complex process. Rather than describe it here in detail, I just want to make sure you know it's available. Most of the documentation for migration is provided only on the Exchange Server CD-ROM, in the Migrate directory. Let's take a quick look at your options.

Exchange Server ships with migration tools for the following e-messaging systems:

- Microsoft Mail for PC Networks
- Microsoft Mail for AppleTalk Networks
- Lotus cc:Mail
- Novell GroupWise
- Collabra Share
- DEC All-In-1
- IBM PROFS
- Verimation Memo (for Memo/MVS only)

MS Mail for PC Networks, Lotus cc:Mail, Novell GroupWise, and Collabra Share migrations are done entirely using the Microsoft Exchange Server Migration wizard, which is installed along with Exchange Server. Both migrations move most available directory and message data to the Exchange environment, and both also assume a live network link between your Exchange system and your MS Mail PC or cc:Mail system. If everything is running properly, these two migrations are a piece of cake.

Migrating from the other four systems supported by Microsoft is a little more difficult. First you run what Microsoft calls a *migration source extractor,* which takes directory and message data from the foreign e-messaging system and writes it to a file that can be imported into Exchange. Once you have this file, you can import it into your Exchange environment using the Migration Wizard's Import from Migration Files option.

If Microsoft doesn't support migration from your current e-messaging system, you can still automate at least part of the process. If your e-messaging system lets you export directory and/or message data, and if you can get the data into a format acceptable to Exchange Server, you can then import it into Exchange Server using the Import from Migration Files option of the Migration Wizard.

If that's not possible, Microsoft provides information on building your own migration source extractor to produce data that can be imported into your Exchange Server directory using the Migration Wizard. And if you don't want to get that fancy, you can build user information files that can be imported into Exchange Server using the Administrator program's Directory Import option, which I'll discuss in a moment.

---

**NOTE**   Whichever route you take, be sure that someone on your migration team fully understands both the foreign e-messaging system you're working with and the computer operating system it runs on top of. Without this expertise, you can get into some very hot water. If no one in your organization qualifies for this distinction, consider getting help from the vendors of your e-messaging system and operating system, or think about hiring a knowledgeable consultant or two.

---

## Importing Information into the Exchange Directory

As I noted previously, you can build user information files that can be imported into an Exchange Server's directory. You create directory import files either manually or, preferably, using one or more computers. Let's start with a brief discussion of a directory import file's structure. Then we'll talk a bit about how to do a directory import.

## The Structure of an Exchange Directory Import File

Here's a portion of a simple directory import file:

```
Obj-Class,Common-Name,Display-Name,Home-Server,Comment
Mailbox,AAndrews,Archie Andrews,~SERVER,Comic Book Character
Mailbox,BGerber,Barry Gerber,~SERVER,
Mailbox,CPumpkin,"Pumpkin\, Charles",~SERVER,
Mailbox,Services,Exchange Services Account for Domain NY,
~SERVER,
```

The first line in a directory import file lists the names of the fields that are to be imported. Each following line lists the values of the import fields for a specific object. These must be listed in the same order in which the field names of the items themselves are listed in the first line of the file. A variety of field separation options can be used; the default is the standard comma-delimited mode.

The object class (*Obj-Class*) is set to Mailbox, meaning that, upon import, Exchange Server should create a new mailbox object for the row entry. Common object classes include *Mailbox* (mailbox), *dl* (distribution list), and *Remote* (custom recipient). *Common-Name* is the new object's name in the Exchange Server directory. Because Common-Name will become the mailbox's directory name, it must be unique from all existing directory names in the site. Common-Name also will become the new object's alias name.

You already know what Display-Name is. *Home-Server* is the Exchange server on which the new object should be created, and *Comment* is any text you want to add for the object.

*~SERVER* tells the Exchange directory import utility that the account should be created on the Exchange server the import runs on. (I could just as well have replaced each instance of ~SERVER with the name of a specific Exchange server.) And that backslash in old Charlie Pumpkin's name tells the directory import option that the comma is part of Charlie's display name, not a field separator.

The import file listed above will create four new mailbox recipient objects in an Exchange directory. If you just want to change some attributes of one or more existing recipients, you need to add a field called *Mode* and set the mode for any row with changes to Modify.

You can see how Mode is used in the import file below, which changes Charlie's display name from Pumpkin, Charles to Pumpkin, Charlie. Big deal, huh? Well, it's important to Charlie. Note that I've included Charlie's Common-Name; without it, the import option wouldn't know which recipient to modify. I deleted the Home-Server entry, since that was set when I ran the directory import file listed above.

```
Obj-Class,Mode,Common-Name,Display-Name
Mailbox,Modify,CPumpkin,"Pumpkin\, Charlie"
```

You may be wondering how to find the names of the fields you want to include in an import file. Short of asking Microsoft, there are four ways, which are listed below in increasing order of risk. The last option is for *certified* Exchange Server directory experts only.

- Use the Exchange Administrator's Export Directory option (discussed later in this chapter), which outputs a directory import file whose first line includes the names of several directory objects. This file also helps you become familiar with the general structure and format of import files.

- Check out the directory import and export documentation that comes with Exchange Server.

- Use the HEADERS.EXE utility that comes with the Exchange portion of the Back Office Resource Kit.

- Run the Exchange Administrator program in raw mode: Open a DOS command prompt, move over to the directory where the Exchange Server executables are stored (usually \EXCHSRVR\BIN), and type admin/raw. Once the Administrator is running, select an instance of the object you're interested in—say, a mailbox—and then select Raw Properties from the Administrator's File menu. Use the resultant dialog box to find the object names you need.

## Importing Directory Information

Once you've got a file to import, directory import is a piece of cake. Select Directory Import from the Exchange Administrator's Tools menu. Using the resultant Directory Import dialog box shown in Figure 17.30, select the NT domain, Exchange server, and recipients container you want to import to.

**FIGURE 17.30:**

Importing information to an Exchange Server directory

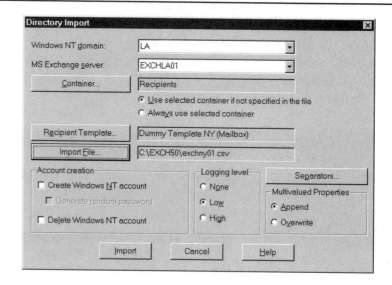

The Recipient Template is a useful gizmo—it's just an Exchange recipient that you create with some fields filled in. When recipient information is imported, Exchange Server uses the template to add any standard information for those recipients. For example, I created a mailbox in my NY site that I called Dummy Template NY (Mailbox) (see Figure 17.31). Into that mailbox I put such standard information as GerCom's New York address and company name. Now when I import directory information and specify the template, this information is automatically added for each recipient in the file. (Unique information like first name and last name is taken from the file, not the template.)

> **NOTE**    Notice in Figure 17.31 that my dummy mailbox has been associated with no NT account. This is perfectly permissible. There's no need for an NT account here, because the mailbox will never be opened by anyone. Similarly, when multiple Exchange users share a mailbox, while they all need permissions to use the mailbox (granted on the mailbox's Permissions property page), the mailbox doesn't have to have a *Primary* NT account.

You can get really fancy creating templates. For example, you can make a template for each department—or even for each supervisor in a department—because even information such as Manager (supervisor of the mailbox owner) on the Organization property page can be templated into a group of mailboxes.

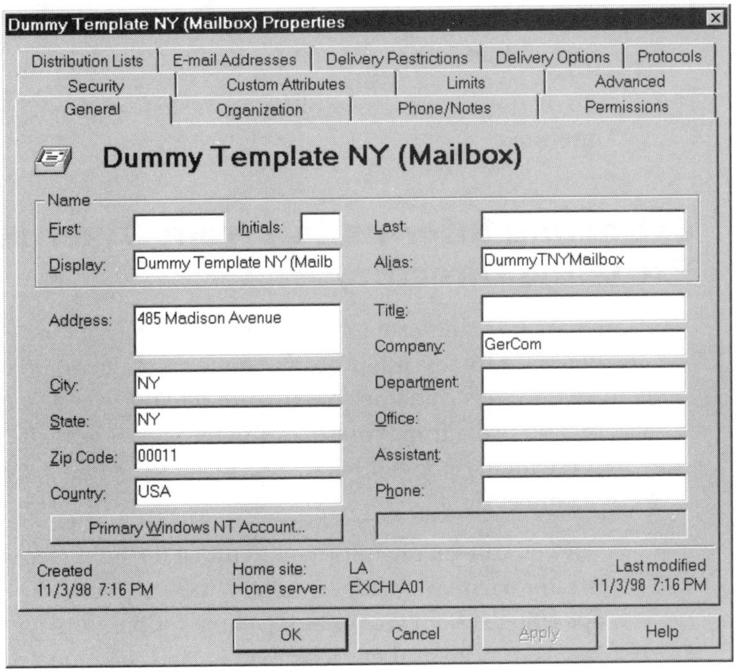

**FIGURE 17.31:**

A "dummy" mailbox template for GerCom's NY site

Of course, you'd have to set up a different directory import file for each template, but it might be worth it in terms of the hours of manual input saved. And remember, by using the Modify mode in a directory import you can change any templated information you want for a group of recipients. (For more about the Modify mode, see the section above on the structure of an Exchange directory import file.)

If you want to create an NT account for each newly created mailbox, check that option in the Directory Import dialog box, shown back in Figure 17.30. Select a logging level—Low is a good choice unless you are having trouble importing a file.

If your import file uses standard comma-delimited separators, don't worry about the Separators button. If it doesn't, use the button to set the correct separators.

The Multivalued Properties area of the Directory Import dialog box is very useful. If a directory import file contains values for an existing object—for example, recipients for a specific distribution list—and you select Append, the new values are appended to the old values (that is, the new distribution list recipients are added to the old ones). If you select Overwrite, the new values replace the old values (that is, the new recipients for the distribution list become the only recipients for that list).

When you've finished filling in the dialog box, click Import and the file will be imported.

## Extracting Information from Other Sources for the Exchange Directory

Often, migration isn't the problem—or at least it isn't your *only* problem. Perhaps you need to, say, pull information from some non-messaging source and use it to create a new directory or enhance one that already exists. Or maybe you want to grab users from your operating system's security database or even from some totally non-MIS database such as the one for your organization's human resources data.

If you can get the information into a format acceptable to the Exchange Administrator's Directory Import option, the rest is easy. The Administrator provides two operating system account-extraction options: one for NT systems and the other for NetWare systems. Let's look at these and then touch briefly on the extraction of directory data from non-MIS databases.

### Extracting a Windows NT Account List

Select the Extract Windows NT Account List option from the Exchange Administrator's Tools menu, then fill in the resultant Windows NT User Extraction dialog box. As you can see in Figure 17.32, you extract the accounts one domain at a time. When you're finished filling in the dialog box, click OK to begin the extraction.

The following is a portion of a file produced by an extraction from my NY domain:

```
Obj-Class,Common-Name,Display-Name,Home-Server,Comment
Mailbox,AAndrews,Archie Andrews,~SERVER,Comic Book Character
Mailbox,BGerber,Barry Gerber,~SERVER,
Mailbox,CPumpkin,"Pumpkin\, Charles",~SERVER,
Mailbox,Services,Exchange Services Account for Domain NY,~SERVER,
```

Surprise! You've seen this file before. It's the example I used earlier in this chapter when talking about the structure of Exchange directory import files. So it should be no additional surprise when I tell you that this file is ready to be imported into Exchange Server using the Directory Import option. If I wanted, I could enhance the individual data items or even add items; I just have to be sure that the file retains Exchange Server's directory import format.

FIGURE 17.32:

Preparing to extract a list of Windows NT accounts

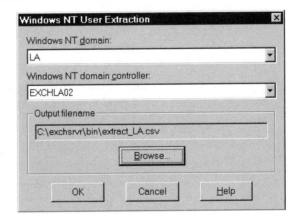

**FIGURE 17.32:**

Preparing to extract a list of Windows NT accounts

## Extracting a NetWare Account List

Select Extract NetWare Account List from the Administrator's Tools menu, then fill in the NetWare User Extraction dialog box that pops up (see Figure 17.33). Be sure to enter the name and password of a NetWare user with NetWare supervisory rights. When you're done, click OK to extract the user information.

**FIGURE 17.33:**

Preparing to extract a list of NetWare accounts

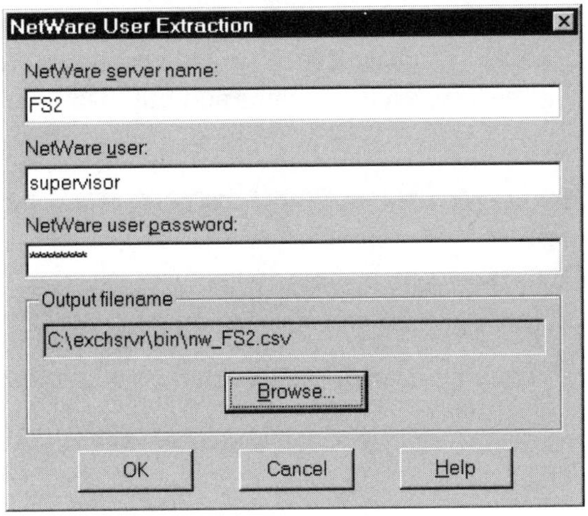

Here's the file I got when I extracted the four users on my test NetWare server:

```
Obj-Class,Common-Name,Display-Name,Home-Server
Mailbox,SUPERVISOR,,~SERVER
Mailbox,GUEST,,~SERVER
Mailbox,BARRYGNW,,~SERVER
Mailbox,ADMINISTRATOR,,~SERVER
```

In the revised export file listed below, I added "FS2" to Common-Names to ensure uniqueness. I also added display names for the four NetWare users. To indicate that a comma should be included in the display name for Gerber, Barry, I put a backslash before the comma. The file retains the Exchange Server directory import format.

```
bj-Class,Common-Name,Display-Name,Home-Server
Mailbox,SUPERVISORFS2,"Administrator (On FS2)",~SERVER
Mailbox,GUESTFS2,"Guest (On FS2)",~SERVER
Mailbox,BARRYFS2,"Gerber\, Barry (On FS2)",~SERVER
Mailbox,ADMINISTRATORFS2,"For NT Administrator",~SERVER
```

## Extracting from Non-MIS Databases

If programming resources are available, you can pull information from non-MIS databases and put it into Exchange Server's directory import format. This can be useful both for creating basic Exchange directory entries and for enhancing already existing entries.

For example, you could extract basic username information from your organization's human resources database and incorporate it into a directory import file. Or you could pull such items as the home address, fax and phone numbers, and even a supervisor's name and put them into a directory import file.

## Exporting Directory Information from Exchange Server

Let's start by looking at the reasons you might want to export Exchange Server directories. Then we'll look at the structure of an export file. Finally, we'll talk about how you do an export.

## Why Export?

There are a number of reasons why you might want to export your Exchange Server directories into files:

- When moving an Exchange Server mailbox to another site. (Remember, you can use the Move Mailbox option only within a site.) You can use directory export only to transfer Exchange directory information for the user; to move the actual mailbox, you or the user must temporarily move the contents of the server-based mailbox to a locally stored mailbox.

- To create a text file with selected properties for mailboxes, custom recipients, and distribution lists for some administrative use, such as generating a printed list of e-mail addresses of all or selected recipients for distribution to customers.

- To export all or part of a directory to another e-messaging system.

- To create a backup of at least a portion of the directory to be used in case of a catastrophic system crash in which—perish the thought—all tape backups of the directory are lost.

## The Structure of a Directory Export File

The following fields are included in an Exchange Server directory export:

- Obj-Class
- First Name
- Last Name
- Display Name
- Alias Name
- Directory Name
- Primary Windows NT Account
- Home-Server
- E-Mail Address
- E-Mail Addresses
- Members

- Obj-Container

- Hide from AB

This list doesn't represent everything, but it's certainly adequate for most of the reasons you might want to export a directory.

Recipient types are grouped in this order: distribution lists, mailboxes, custom recipients. So don't assume that custom recipients haven't been exported just because they don't show up in alphabetical order among the mailboxes (as they do in the recipients container). The following segment of a directory export file has been reformatted to make it easier to read:

```
Obj-Class,First Name,Last name,Display Name,Alias Name,
Directory Name,Primary Windows NT Account,Home-Server,E-Mail
address,E-Mail Addresses,Members,Obj-Container,Hide from AB

dl,,,LA Sales (Distribution List),LASales,LASales,,,,
MS:GERCOM/LA/LASALES%SMTP:LASales@LA.GerCom.com%
X400:c=US;a=p=GerCom;o=LA;s=LASales;,,Recipients/cn=BGerber%
Recipients/cn=RAlvarez%Recipients/cn=MLewis%
Recipients/cn=WPeterson,Recipients,0

Mailbox,Archie,Andrews,"Andrews\,Archie",AAndrews,
AAndrews,NY\Aandrews,EXCHLA01,,MS:GERCOM/LA/AANDREWS%
SMTP:AAndrews@LA.GerCom.com%X400:c=US;a= ;p=GerCom;o=LA;
s=Andrews;g=Archie;,,Recipients,0

Remote,Marsha,Franklin,"Franklin\,Marsha",MFranklin,
MFranklin,,,SMTP:mfranklin@keytop.com,
MS:GERCOM/LA/MFRANKLIN%
X400:c=US;a= ;p=GerCom;o=LA;s=Franklin;g=Marsha;
%SMTP:mfranklin@keytop.com,,Recipients,0
```

## Exporting a Directory

To export a directory, select Directory Export from the Exchange Administrator's File menu. This brings up the Directory Export dialog box shown in Figure 17.34.

Fill in the box, selecting the Exchange servers and recipients container(s) to be exported from. Specify an export file and indicate which of the three available types of directory objects you want to export: mailboxes, custom recipients, and/or distribution lists. Select a logging level and change the separators if necessary. In the Character Set section of the Directory Export dialog box, select Unicode if your directory entries contain special characters such as accents; otherwise ANSI is fine. If you want to include hidden directory objects, select that option.

When you're done filling in the information, click Export to create your export file.

**FIGURE 17.34:**

Setting up an Exchange Server directory export

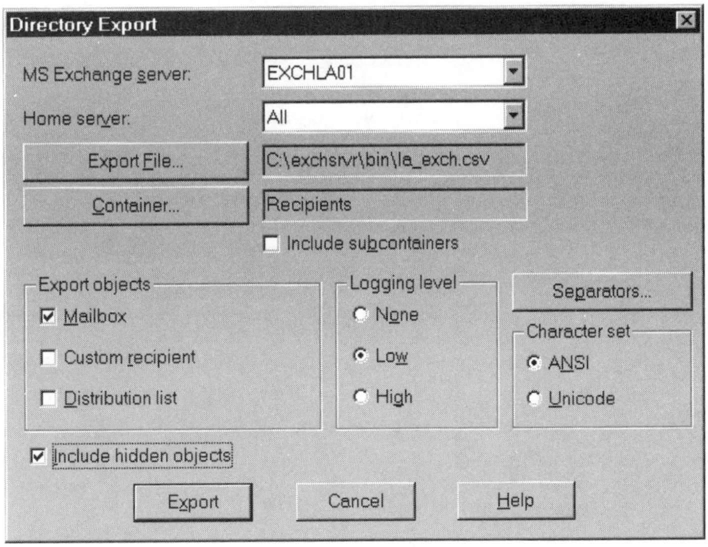

## Going Beyond the Basic Export

You can specify which directory fields Exchange Administrator should export. Just put the field names in the export file before requesting the export. For example, to export all the standard mailbox fields listed in the previous section, plus company, department, title, address, city, state or province, and phone number, enter the following header on a single line in the export file, then request a directory export to the file:

Obj-Class,First Name,Last Name,Display Name,Alias Name,Directory Name,Primary Windows NT Account,Home-Server,E-Mail address,E-Mail Addresses,Members,Obj-Container,Hide from AB,Company,Department,Title,Address,City,State-Or-Province, Phone number

You can use the somewhat misnamed Import Header Tool to automatically generate a file with the directory fields you want to import or export. See Appendix B for details.

# Adding Proxy Addresses to a Mailbox

Back in Chapter 8 we looked briefly at the E-Mail Addresses property page of the mailbox dialog box (see Figure 17.35). I promised then to talk more about how you can add new addresses for a mailbox. Well, you're now ready for all the gory details, so here we go.

**FIGURE 17.35:**

The E-Mail Addresses property page of the mailbox Properties dialog box

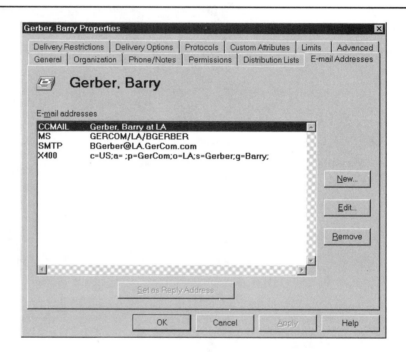

## Creating Proxy Addresses

First, why would you want to add a new address for a mailbox? Well, maybe your default Internet address is jjones@monster.com. Now, that's OK, if you don't mind getting lost among the millions of employees at good old Monster Corp. Let's say you're in Sales at Monster Corp. and you'd at least like to have that recognized in your e-mail address: jjones@sales.monster.com. The first step is to add what's called a proxy address to your mailbox.

Click New on the E-Mail Addresses property page. This brings up the New E-Mail Address dialog box shown in Figure 17.36. As you can see, you can create secondary proxies for all the address types supported by Exchange Server. Select Internet and click OK. The new Internet Address Properties dialog box pops up (see Figure 17.37). Type in the new address and click OK and, as you can see in Figure 17.38, the new address is created.

**FIGURE 17.36:**

Selecting the type of proxy address to create

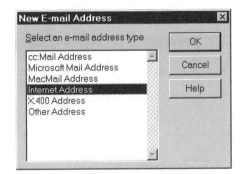

**FIGURE 17.37:**

Entering the new proxy address

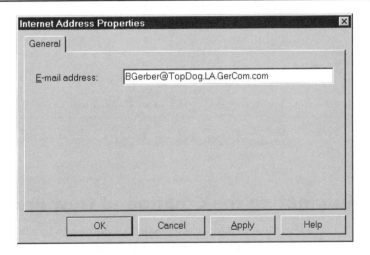

Notice in Figure 17.38 how "smtp" in the new address is in lowercase. That tells you immediately that this address is a secondary proxy address. You can make it the primary address by clicking the Set As Reply Address button. After you click Set As Reply Address, SMTP is displayed in lowercase for what was the primary proxy address (BGerber@LA.GerCom.com in my case), indicating that it has become a secondary proxy address for the mailbox.

New proxy addresses aren't limited to Exchange Server mailboxes. You can add a new proxy to any of the other Exchange recipient types: custom recipients, distribution lists, and public folders. Secondary proxy addresses can be very useful in a lot of places. Let your imagination roam. Once you get the basics down, you can both help your organization and have great fun with secondary proxies.

**FIGURE 17.38:**

The new proxy address is a secondary proxy address.

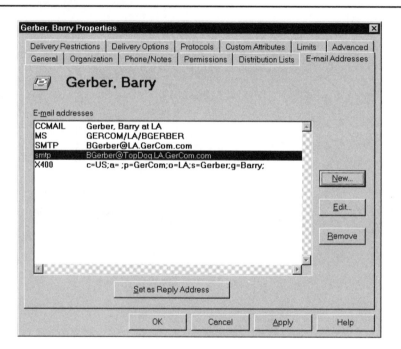

## Automating the Creation of New Proxy Addresses

If you have to add secondary proxy addresses to a bunch of mailboxes, you can use the directory import function I discussed earlier. The attribute name for secondary proxies is Secondary Proxy-Addresses. You'll have to do a bit of programming or make fancy use of a text editor on a directory export to create the import file to set up the secondary proxies, but it's still a lot easier than manually adding all those proxy addresses.

## Telling the Exchange Server IMS and DNS about New Proxy Addresses

Once you've created the proxy addresses, Exchange Server is ready to receive mail addressed to them. However, before the mail can be received, you might have to make some changes elsewhere in your Exchange Server and other environments. For example, for a new Internet secondary proxy, you'll have to be sure that the Exchange Server Internet Mail Service routes mail to the new address into Exchange. You'll also have to add MX records to your Domain Name Service, telling the world that your IMS is now handling messages addressed to the new proxy. See Chapter 15 for details on all this stuff.

# Moving Mailboxes between Exchange Sites

Back at the beginning of this chapter, I showed you what a no-brainer it is to move mailboxes between Exchange servers in a site. Moving mailboxes between containers in a site, sites, or organizations is a bit more of a challenge. There are two ways to do this. You can use a utility in the Exchange Resource Kit called the Mailbox Migration Tool or you can use a more manual technique.

With the Mailbox Migration Tool you provide a list of mailboxes to move, and the tool either moves the mailboxes in real time or exports the mailboxes to a disk file so you can use the tool to import them at a later time into the new server. The Mailbox Migration Tool can be used to move mailboxes between sites within the same Exchange organization or between Exchange organizations.

The more manual method works like this. Basically, you need to store a copy of your mailbox outside the Exchange information store. From the client's Tools menu, pick Services. Using the resultant Services dialog box, click Add and add a personal folder. Click OK your way out of the Services dialog box. You'll now see a new store in your Exchange client. Just drag and drop the folders and messages you want into the new store. You can't drag and drop either your Inbox or special folders. Just create new folders to hold the contents of these and drag and drop into them. Remember that you can mark and move or copy multiple messages and folders just by using the standard Windows item selection procedures; for example, Ctrl+click to select noncontiguous items.

When you're through filling up your personal folder, disconnect from your original mailbox and connect to the new one. Make sure your newly created personal folder file is available. Use the Services dialog box to add your personal folder to your client. Drag whatever you want from the personal folder to your mailbox. Voilà! You've moved your mailbox to a new Exchange site or organization.

# Working with Address Book Views

Address book views are one of the best features of Exchange 5. They're containers that hold specially grouped images of your Exchange global address book. Address book views can be organized by such directory fields as the geographical locations or the departments in which Exchange recipients in your organization are located.

Address book views add hierarchical structure to what are usually flat views of recipients in the Exchange global address book and in Exchange Administrator. They make it easier for users to find addresses and for you to organize and manage Exchange recipients in Exchange Administrator. Address book views are especially useful in large organizations.

> **NOTE**    Before Exchange 5, there was only one way to add structure to a global address book. You had to create a bunch of recipients containers and then create each recipient in the appropriate container. If you wanted to organize your global address book by department, you had to create a container for each department in your organization and then create each recipient in the container representing their department. Because it's difficult to move recipients to new containers after creating them—you have to export them to a file, modify the export file, and import the file—this method worked just fine until someone was transferred to a new department.

## Adding an Address Book View

To add an address book view, click the Address Book Views container (see Figure 17.39). Next, open Exchange Administrator's File menu and click New Other. Finally, select Address Book View from the menu that pops open. This brings up a dialog box for a new address book view as shown in Figure 17.40.

On the General property page, give the view display and directory names. Next, tab over to the Group By property page. As you can see in Figure 17.41, you use this page to set the directory fields that will be used to group recipient addresses. You can group to a depth of four levels. For example, if your organization is large, you might want to group by state, city, office building, and department. In Figure 17.41, I've set Department as the only grouping field.

On the Advanced property page (see Figure 17.42), you can set two options and perform one action.

**FIGURE 17.39:**

Preparing to create a new address book view

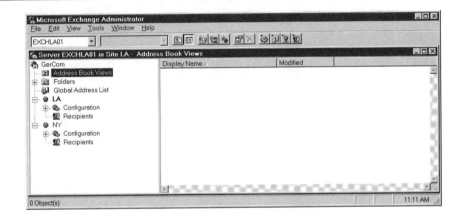

**FIGURE 17.40:**

The dialog box used to create new address book views

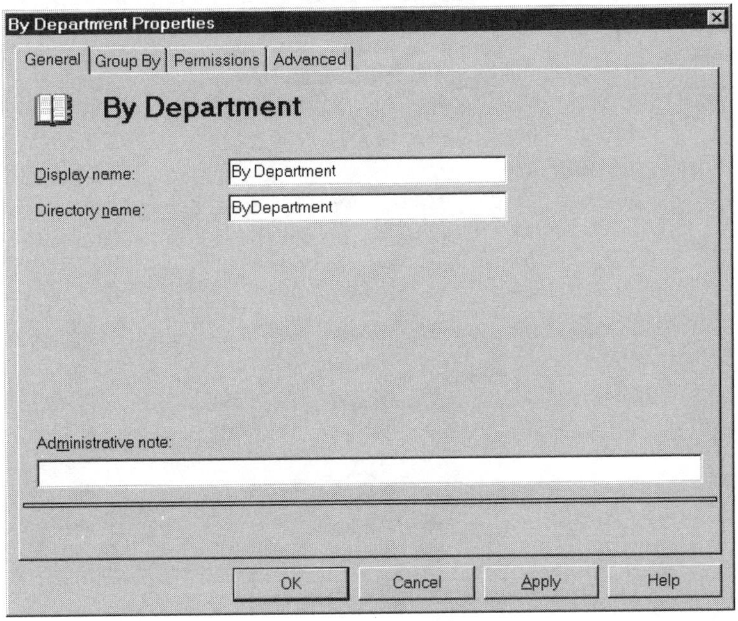

**FIGURE 17.41:**

Setting address book view grouping criteria

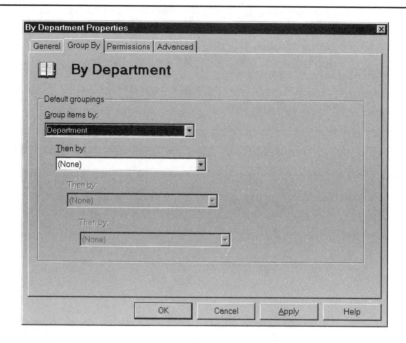

**FIGURE 17.42:**

The Advanced properties page for an address book view

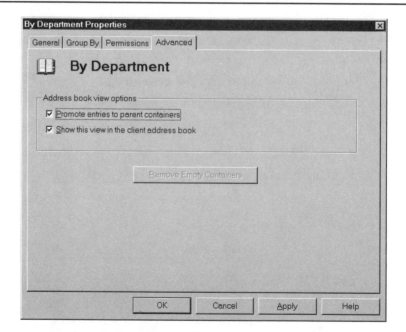

If you check Promote Entries to Parent Containers and your address book view is at least two levels deep, appropriate recipients will appear in all levels of the view but the top level. For example, if you create a view named Location grouped by state, then by city, and finally by department, recipients will show up in the appropriate state, city, and department container. No recipients will show up in the top-level container, Location. If you don't check Promote Entries to Parent Containers, recipients will show up only in the lowest-level container, which is Department in our example.

Check Show This View in the Client Address Book to make the address book view visible to Exchange client users. Click Remove Empty Containers to delete any subcontainers in the view that are empty, because all the recipients that belong in the container have been deleted.

When you're finished with the address book view dialog box, click OK to start a process that will create the view. How fast the view is created depends on how many objects there are in your global address book and on how busy your Exchange server is. When all is done, you'll see a new address book view in your Exchange server's directory. This view will, of course, be replicated to other Exchange servers in your organization.

Figure 17.43 shows how an address book view organized by department looks in Exchange Administrator. Figures 17.44 and 17.45 show how a user sees the same address book view within an Exchange client.

**FIGURE 17.43:**

An address book view as displayed in Exchange Administrator

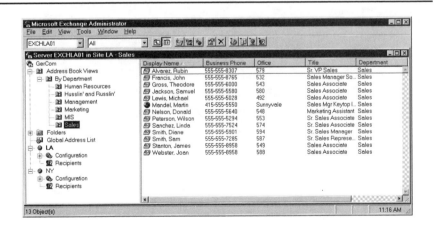

**FIGURE 17.44:**

Selecting a container from
an address book view
within an Exchange client

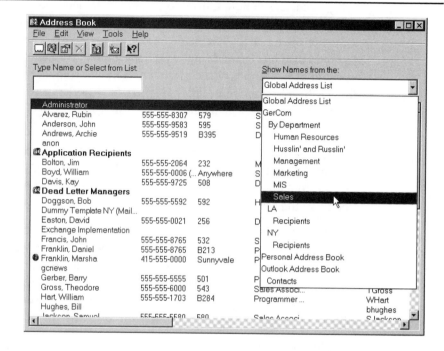

**FIGURE 17.45:**

Selecting a recipient from
an address book view con-
tainer within an Exchange
client

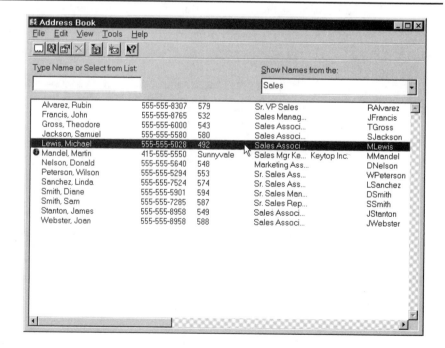

# Adding an Address Book View Container

As you've just seen, address book view hierarchies are normally built automatically. You can also manually add an address book view subcontainer to an existing address book view container. These specially added containers are useful where the standard groupings you've selected for a view don't work. For example, the grouping set country-city-state for a view called Location works fine for the United States, which has states. It doesn't work for countries such as Greece that don't have states but do have cities. For Greece, you need only country and city containers.

To create a new address book view subcontainer, click an appropriate address book view container or subcontainer. Then, select Address Book View Container from the New Other menu on the Exchange Administrator's File menu. When the dialog box for adding the container pops up, use the General property page to give the container display and directory names. Using our example, I'd use "Greece" for both names.

Next, tab over to the Group By property page. Here, you select the subcontainer you want to group by and a grouping value for the field represented by the container that will hold your new address book view subcontainer. This sounds a lot more complex than it is, so let's turn back to our example. In Figure 17.46, I'm adding the new subcontainer to the container that represents the field Country. I've requested that recipients be shown in the new subcontainer, if the value for the field Country is "Greece." I've asked that subcontainers be created within the container Greece based on the value of the field City. In Figure 17.47, you can see the fruits of my labor.

FIGURE 17.46:

Adding a new address book
view container

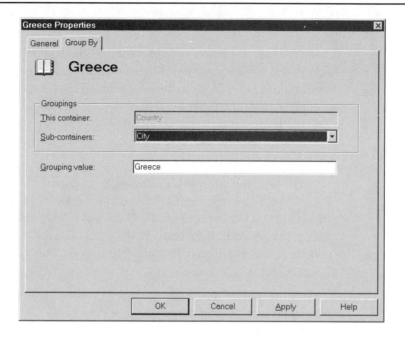

FIGURE 17.47:

A newly added address
book view container

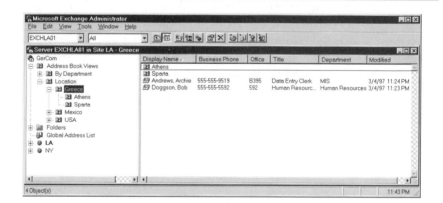

## Adding to an Address Book View

Let's say Alicia Jones, who used to work in the Los Angeles Sales department of
GerCom, is transferred to the Marketing department in LA. I can change her

department by opening a dialog box for her mailbox and editing the department field. I can also simply move Ms. Jones from the Sales to the Marketing department address book view container.

It's not quite as easy as dragging and dropping the object. Instead, I click Alicia Jones in the Sales container and select Add to Address Book View from the Exchange Administrator's Tools menu. Then I select the appropriate container from the little address book view tree that pops up.

> **NOTE**  *Add to Address Book View* isn't exactly the right term for what you're doing here. You're really moving a recipient from one view to another by changing some of its attributes. The recipient inherits the attributes of the address book view hierarchy it's moved to and can no longer be found in the old hierarchy. Check it out. Double-click the recipient after you've moved it to see its new attributes. Of course, you can quickly return to the old attributes by "adding" the recipient back to its old address book view hierarchy.

# Making Things Happen in Public Folders

You can build some really interesting groupware apps by triggering off various events in public folders. For example, a help desk public folder to which end users send requests for help could be set up to forward messages to specific technical personnel based on the subject line or another field in the message. If you use an Exchange or Outlook form (see Chapter 19), you can even protect the subject line or that other field to assure that a user doesn't change it. You could even send a reply to the sender thanking them and giving some estimate as to when staff will be getting around to their message.

There are several ways to trigger events in a public folder. You can use the public folder, Folder Assistant dialog box, to enable all the rules available with Inbox Assistant (see Chapter 12). To get to Folder Assistant, assuming you have all the requisite rights to a folder, right-click a public folder and select Properties from the pop-up menu. On the properties dialog box for the public folder, tab over to the Administration property page and click Folder Assistant. Use the resultant Folder Assistant dialog box to add a range of rules for the public folder.

If you need more programming flexibility than Folder Assistant affords, Exchange 5.5 adds server scripting. Using the Microsoft Visual Basic Script language, you can write code that performs virtually any task on schedule or when messages come into, are changed in, or are deleted from a public folder. We don't have time to get into Visual Basic scripting, but if you want to see what's up here, open the properties dialog box for a public folder (as indicated in the previous paragraph) and tab over to the Agent property page. Click New Agent and have fun shopping around. Be sure to take a look at the Visual Basic Script template that pops up when you click Edit.

You can also use server-scripting agents with private folders. As with public folders, scripting agents can only operate on private folders stored on Exchange server.

For some awesome server scripting samples, check out www.microsoft.com/ msdn/. For example, there's this fantastic expense report app that automatically sums an expense report and sends the result to the appropriate manager for approval. What's neat is that the whole operation is triggered when a new expense report is posted in or sent to the Expense Report public folder and the manager is selected using the supervisor/supervised information you enter on the Organization property page for a mailbox. (See Chapter 8 for more info on this page.)

# Other Advanced Exchange Administrator Options

The Exchange Administrator program provides a number of options I haven't covered yet. I don't have the time or space to go into great detail about each of them, but I do want to make you aware of what they are and, in general, what you can do with them. You'll find these options in the Configuration container for a site.

## Add-Ins

The Add-Ins container holds objects representing Windows dynamic link libraries (DLLs) that support one or another Exchange Server component. Add-ins include administrative components for the Internet Mail Service, the Microsoft Mail Connector, and the Free/Busy Connector that supports Schedule+. There is little you either can or need to do with these objects other than add an administrative note to them and change their permissions.

## Addressing

The Addressing subcontainer holds three subcontainers: E-Mail Address Generators, Details Templates, and One-Off Address Templates. *E-mail address generators* are objects representing the DLLs that actually generate addresses. As with objects in the Add-Ins container, there's little you can or have to do with these objects.

Exchange clients use *details templates* to display the properties of a recipient or for other Exchange client functions, such as a search for a specific recipient. *One-off address templates* are used when an Exchange client user generates an address for a foreign e-messaging system. You can modify the graphical user interface or the DOS version of either template type by opening the template, tabbing over to the Templates property page, and moving or editing old fields or adding new ones. When you choose to add new fields, a drop-down list shows you which ones are available. You can test changes you've made at any time without leaving Modify mode, and if you make a mistake, you can always revert to the original template.

In Figure 17.48, I'm modifying the details template for a mailbox by adding a new property page; in Figure 17.49, I'm testing my modifications. See the Exchange Server documents for more information on template modification.

**FIGURE 17.48:**

Modifying the details template for a mailbox

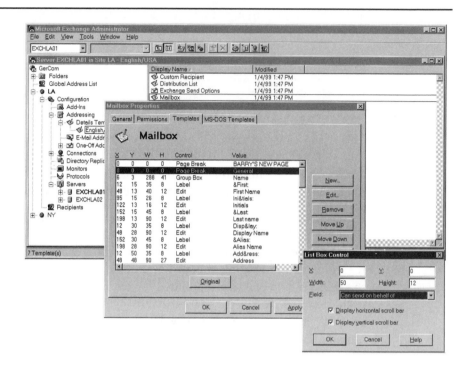

**FIGURE 17.49:**

Testing a modified details template for a mailbox

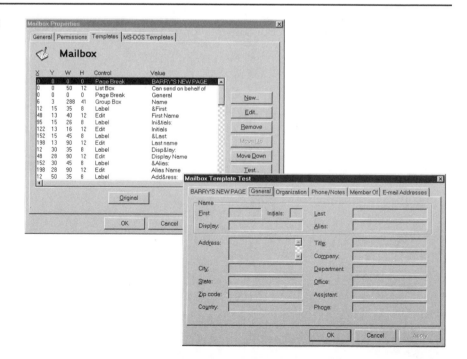

# Remotely Administering Exchange and NT Servers

Using a Remote Access Service connection, you can administer your Exchange organization from any place with a telephone. As I get deeper and deeper into Exchange administration, I am finding remote connects invaluable. In fact, if you've got the Exchange Administrator along with the full suite of NT Server administrative tools on your remote Window NT Workstation or Server machine, you can pretty much kick back and manage your NT network without leaving the comfort of your easy chair.

Remote administration is no special trick. With a RAS connection in place and assuming that your remote NT workstation or server has been properly admitted to an appropriate NT domain, all you have to do is fire up Exchange Administrator and point it at the right Exchange server. Things may be a bit slow for certain functions, but you can do anything remotely that you can do when connected to the network.

If you're running NT Workstation, you can copy the server administration tools, User Manager for Domains, Server Manager, etc., from an NT Server CD-ROM. With those tools in place, you'll add users and computers to your domains, start and stop Exchange and other NT services, and more, all without having to "go to the office."

Trust me: This is neat stuff. Try it; you'll like it. I promise.

# Tips on Troubleshooting Exchange Server

Sybex, the publisher of this book, recently released a great new book called *Exchange Server 5.5 24seven* (1999). The book's author, Jim McBee, is an Exchange professional with lots of experience fixing broken Exchange servers and clients. So, my first tip on troubleshooting Exchange Server is that you buy Jim's book.

My second tip is that you make Microsoft's Internet-based Knowledge Base your home away from home. As I noted earlier in this book, in a world paced by the clock of Internet immediacy, things change very fast. Microsoft's Knowledge Base does a respectable job of keeping up with the frenzied pace of the company's development teams.

As of this writing, you get can get to the Knowledge Base through the URL `http://www.microsoft.com/ms.htm`. On the site's homepage, select the Knowledge Base option from the Support menu (see Figure 17.50). Select Exchange Server from the My Search Is About drop-down menu. Then select from the available options and type in your question. Click Go and sift through the answers presented to you.

**FIGURE 17.50:**

Accessing Microsoft's Internet-based Knowledge Base

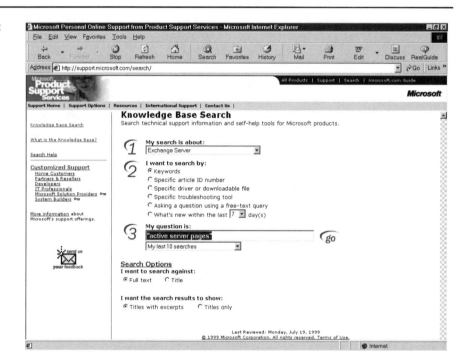

There's an art to posing Knowledge Base questions. Basically, you should keep your questions simple. If you are trying to solve a problem where you have an error message, search for all or part of the error message. If your question is really about another Microsoft product, select that product from the drop-down menu. Be sure to follow any promising links to other Knowledge Base articles. Finally, make sure you look for the latest and greatest info on any subject you're concerned about.

My third tip is that you get, test, and install all service packs for Exchange Server and Exchange clients. Many of the problems you'll experience with Exchange Server are recognized in Knowledge Base articles and, if they're deemed significant enough, are fixed in service pack releases.

Tip number four? Consider paid support from Microsoft and others. It can be pricey and the best support services cost the most. However, this is often the best way to get your problems solved fast. Check out `http://www.microsoft.com/support/supportnet/overview/overview.asp` for Microsoft's options. The Microsoft consulting operation can put you in touch with their own or independent consultants who can help.

Armed with Jim McBee's book, access to Microsoft's Knowledge Base, the latest Exchange Server and client service packs, and a modicum of paid support, your life as an Exchange administrator will be, if not a vacation in Maui, at least far less harried than it would be without these useful troubleshooting aids.

# Supporting Remote Users

Aside from ensuring that remote users install and set up their Exchange clients properly—as well as providing NT Remote Access Service (RAS) dial-in services and the modems and phone lines to support them—you don't have to do much else to support remote users on the server side. For more on the RAS, see *Mastering Windows NT Server 4* by Mark Minasi, Christa Anderson, and Elizabeth Creegan (Sybex, 1996).

On the client side, the client installation software specifically asks if the client will be used for remote access. If you answer yes, then each time you start up your Exchange client, you'll be asked if you want to connect to your Exchange server or work offline. Aside from a proper installation, the user needs to understand how to dial in to the network and use the Exchange client's folder synchronization capability.

## Linking Exchange Clients to Exchange Server over the Internet

You can connect Exchange clients to your Exchange Server without the benefit of RAS services. You can connect directly over the Internet through an Internet Service Provider (ISP). All you have to do is log into your ISP as usual. If your Exchange server is externally registered in the Domain Name Service so you can ping it by name, you're pretty much ready. If the server isn't registered, you'll have to create an entry for the server in the HOSTS file on the computer where you're running the client. For more on the HOSTS file, see Minasi, et al.

The Remote Procedure Calls that support Exchange client-server communications must be able to pass over the ISP-based link between your client and server. Technically, this requires that TCP/IP port 135 be enabled on all firewalls and routers between the client and server. You can test to see if this is the case by using a program developed by Microsoft called RPCPING.EXE. Check with the company for availability and source.

To connect your client to the server, get to the MS Exchange Settings Properties dialog box. In Windows 95 and NT, for older Exchange clients right-click the Inbox icon on your desktop and select Properties; for Outlook clients, open the Control Panel's Mail or Mail and Fax applet. Double-click Microsoft Exchange Server on the dialog box. Type in the name of your Exchange server as registered in the DNS or named in your HOSTS file. Then type in your mailbox's display name or alias and click Check Name. You'll know that all is well if the display name for your mailbox shows up underlined. OK your way out of the various dialog boxes and open your mailbox. It takes a while the first time, but once your client is able to talk to the server directly over the Internet you will be able to do virtually anything you can do locally or with a RAS connection.

# Supporting Roving Users

Some users sit at the same desk all day, every day. Others are moving around all the time, often not even having a computer of their own. These users are often referred to as *roving users*. Basically, you want each roving user to have a directory on a server where they can pick up their Exchange and other settings every time they log in to the network, whatever workstation they use to log in.

The Exchange settings you're interested in are those for home server and mailbox name. You want a roving user to get the same server and mailbox name no matter what workstation he or she chooses to log in on.

Supporting a roving Exchange user is no different from supporting a roving user who is working with any other software—Microsoft Word, for example. With Exchange you want to present the same server and mailbox name. With Word, your goal is for the user to get the same default template, window-size settings, etc. The specific procedures you must follow to support roving users depend on the workstation (and sometimes network) operating system you're using.

Fortunately, Microsoft has a tool for simplifying the job of setting up correct profiles for roving Exchange users. This tool (PROFGEN.EXE) can be found in the update to the Exchange Resource Kit. The update can be downloaded free from Microsoft's Exchange Web site.

The Outlook client's schedule information is stored directly on an Exchange server. Anyone connected to the server or another server in the Exchange organization can, if security is set to allow it, see and use schedule information to set up meetings.

Schedule+ schedules are stored in files outside the Exchange Server environment. The Schedule+ Free/Busy Connector brings at least a portion of Schedule+ data into an Exchange server database. This brings Schedule+ users into the meeting planning world of Exchange Server.

# Dealing with Computer Viruses

Nothing strikes terror in the heart of network administrators like computer viruses. Viruses are bad enough when carried from computer to computer on diskettes. But store files containing them on a network file system for all to access or send them to one and all by e-mail, and computer viruses become true threats to mission-critical systems. I've done quite a bit of work in public health and I can tell you there's more than a little similarity between computer viruses and those that cause influenza and other menaces to health.

There are two ways to deal with e-mail–borne viruses. You can catch them while the files that contain them are still inside your e-mail system or when users try to run the files containing them. I prefer to implement both options. However, if I had to make a choice, I'd rather shoot down viruses while they're still inside my e-mail system.

There are a number of third-party Exchange Server–based virus control products on the market. Appendix C lists several worthy products. My current favorite is Trend Micro's ScanMail for Microsoft Exchange.

ScanMail includes information on virtually all known viruses. The virus list can be updated automatically over the Internet on a regular schedule. The product also uses a set of rules and pattern recognition to help it find suspicious new viruses.

ScanMail operates on messages in both the private and public information stores of an Exchange server. It automatically scans messages as they come into the stores, and it can be scheduled to make regular passes on all Exchange folders. You can even scan all or selected mailboxes manually.

When ScanMail finds a virus, it can send notifications to the sender, the recipient, and the Exchange administrator. When ScanMail can't clean a virus, it can be configured to remove the infected file and send the virus to Trend Micro's *Virus Hospital* for further analysis and, hopefully, a virus-cleaning solution.

I use ScanMail in league with Trend Micro's network-aware, real-time, workstation-based virus product, Office Scan, and the company's server file scanner, Server Protect. I can say without fear of contradiction that my own and a number of clients' networks have been totally virus-free since I implemented this three-pronged virus management system. Check out Trend Micro's products at `http://www.antivirus.com`.

And, I should note, I'm not a cheerleader when it comes to computer and networking products. So these products must be good. Of course, there are products from other vendors that are also very good (see Appendix C). Let me know what you like. My e-mail address is `bgerber@bgerber.com`.

# A Quick Look at Schedule+

Users of Microsoft's Schedule+ have available (free) and unavailable (busy) times in their schedules. This *free/busy* information, which is used by Schedule+ to automatically set up meetings and appointments, is stored in special hidden public folders. When they need to access recipient schedules to set up meetings, Schedule+ clients go to these hidden folders. To support cross-site Schedule+ activity, the Schedule+ free/busy hidden public folder for each site is represented in the Exchange hierarchy (see Figure 17.51). At a minimum, these free/busy folders include information for connecting to the site they represent. If one site's free/busy folder is replicated to other sites, then the replicas include free/busy information for the site they represent.

When a user tries to include a recipient located in another site in a scheduling effort and the site's free/busy folder hasn't been replicated, the Schedule+ client uses the contact information to connect to the other site. It then gets the schedule information it needs directly from the hidden public folder in the other site.

If public folder replication delays between sites can be tolerated when scheduling meetings and appointments, you can replicate free/busy folders among the sites in your Exchange organization. (See Chapter 14 for more information on public folder replication.) With replication, Schedule+ clients can access free/busy information for other sites by looking in the free/busy replicas at their own sites. There's no need for these clients to contact the other sites directly.

**NOTE**  To connect to free/busy folders in other sites, the Schedule+ client must be able to establish an RPC-based session with the Exchange server in the other site. This requires a hard-wired or dial-up RAS link. If such a link isn't possible, cross-site folder replication is your only alternative, because it can be implemented on indirect links.

If you need to exchange free/busy information with older Schedule+ versions that are compatible with Microsoft Mail for PC Networks, you'll need to run the Schedule+ Free/Busy Connector, which is an extension of the Microsoft Mail Connector. See the Exchange docs for further information.

The Exchange hierarchy includes a Schedule+ free/busy public folder for each site.

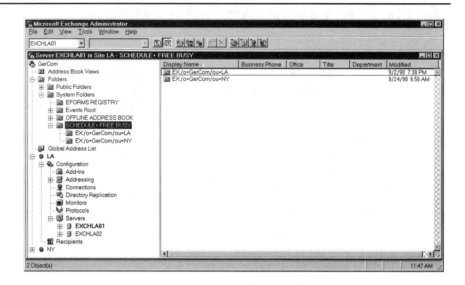

# Conclusion

Wow! What a trip. You've learned a lot in this chapter, including how to create new information stores, move mailboxes, track messages, set up the latest Exchange Server advanced security features, import information into the Exchange directory, extract information for the Exchange directory from other sources, and export directory information from Exchange Server.

By now you should also have a basic grounding in migrating users from other e-messaging systems, using Exchange add-ins and e-mail address generators, editing Exchange's details templates and one-off address templates, moving mailboxes between sites, using address book views, remotely administering your Exchange and NT servers, supporting remote and roving Exchange users, and working with Schedule+.

If that's not enough, you should now have some tools to guide you in troubleshooting Exchange Server and client problems and a basic understanding of Exchange Server virus control and the kinds of virus control tools available from third-party vendors.

Want more? Check out Appendices A, B, and C. Appendix A gives you some guidelines on daily maintenance activities. Appendix B is a quick overview of the neat support apps included in Microsoft's Exchange Resource Kit. And Appendix C lists some exciting third-party add-ons that extend the capabilities of Exchange Server.

I'd say that you're now almost an Exchange Server expert. All we have left is a set of exciting Internet protocols new to Exchange 5 and a tutorial on the use of electronic forms in the Exchange environment. Turn the page and we're off.

# Advanced Exchange Server Internet Protocols

- Setting up and using Exchange Server support for Post Office Protocol and Internet Message Access Protocol client-server messaging

- Setting up and using Web browser (Hypertext Markup Language) access to Exchange Server

- Setting up and using Exchange Server support for the Lightweight Directory Access Protocol

- Setting up and using Exchange Server support for the Network News Transfer Protocol

- Setting general parameters for more than one protocol

**T**his is one of the most exciting chapters in this book. Exchange Server 5 and later come with a set of Internet-based client-server protocols that, taken together, raise it from a fairly tightly controlled, proprietary client-server product to an open and flexible e-messaging system. Let's not waste any time. Onward into that rabbit hole again.

> **NOTE**      We're going to be looking at a ton of objects (tools) for managing and administering the Exchange advanced Internet protocols. As in earlier chapters, I'll skip over property pages on objects that have already been covered.

# The Post Office Protocol

Exchange Server includes full support for Post Office Protocol version 3 (POP3). POP3 is a simple but effective way for a client to pull mail from an e-mail server. There's no fancy support for access to folders other than your Inbox or all the fine bells and whistles you'll find in the Exchange and Outlook clients. But, if you're looking for a simple lightweight client that can function readily over the Internet, POP3 isn't a bad choice.

> **WARNING**      You set up the IMAP4 (for Internet Message Access Protocol version 4) in much the same way as the POP3 protocol. I'll cover IMAP4 in the next section. I strongly suggest that you read this section even if you're not planning to implement POP3 because, in the section on IMAP4, I'm only going to discuss the areas where POP3 and IMAP4 differ.

## POP3 Setup: The Exchange Server Side

The server side of POP3 protocol support is installed when you install Exchange Server. Once POP3 is installed on the server, your job is to set a few key parameters to customize your POP3 environment to the needs of your organization and users.

You can customize all POP3 parameters at both the Exchange site and server levels. This lets you set site-specific parameters and still have the flexibility to deal with special needs on one or more servers in the site. If that's not enough customization for you, you can even set some POP3 parameters at the individual mailbox level.

Let's get right to site level POP3 parameters.

## Setting Up POP3 at the Site Level

The first step is to find the Protocols container for your site. See Figure 18.1 if you're having trouble finding the container.

**FIGURE 18.1:**

The site Protocols container and its five advanced Internet configuration objects

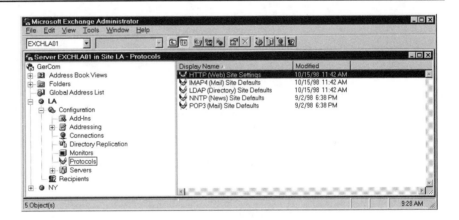

The Protocols container holds configuration objects for all five of the advanced Internet services supported by Exchange Server. Double-click the POP3 site defaults object to bring up the POP3 (Mail) Site Defaults Properties dialog box shown in Figure 18.2.

**General Properties**   You can enable or disable the POP3 protocol for the entire site on the General property page. The protocol is enabled by default. Deselect Enable protocol to turn off POP3 services for the site.

**FIGURE 18.2:**

The General property page
of the POP3 site configuration dialog box

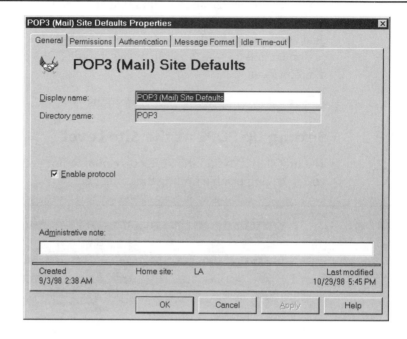

**Authentication**   Use the Authentication property page (Figure 18.3) to select
the security levels that your Exchange Server POP3 service will support. All three
of the authentication methods listed below are used to verify a POP3 user's account
name and password. They are listed in order of increasing security. Each can be in
its native format or its security can be enhanced by using the Secure Sockets Layer
(SSL), which adds its own level of client-server encryption. If you decide to use
SSL, be sure to read the Exchange Server documentation regarding setting up your
Microsoft Internet Information and Exchange servers to support it.

- Basic (Clear Text) authentication is the least secure but also the most ubiqui-
  tous security method available. All authentication is done in unencrypted text.

- Windows NT Challenge/Response uses standard NT account–based security and an encrypted password to authenticate users.

- MCIS Membership System uses the Microsoft Commercial Internet Server's
  Membership System account database.

All POP3 clients support clear text authentication. Windows NT Challenge/ Response without SSL is included in Microsoft's older Internet Mail 3 client. Microsoft Outlook Express adds SSL to its support for Windows NT Challenge/ Response authentication. MCIS Membership System authentication is available in the Microsoft Commercial Internet Server product that is available from Microsoft to commercial service providers. For the latest news on support for Windows NT Challenge/Response and SSL in other POP3 clients, check with their vendors.

**FIGURE 18.3:**

Setting the levels of authentication to be used by Exchange Server's POP3 service

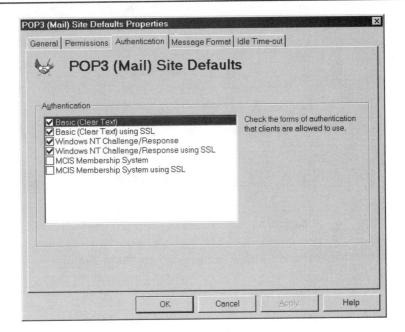

**Message Format**   You use the Message Format property page to set message-encoding parameters, the type of character set to be used in messages, and to tell Exchange Server whether to send documents in Exchange's rich-text format (see Figure 18.4).

**Message Encoding**   The Internet supports the transmission of messages and attachments in 7-bit characters. Formatted text (fonts, bold, italic, underlined, etc.) or binary attachments, both of which require 8 bits, must be coded into a 7-bit format to traverse the Internet.

**FIGURE 18.4:**

Setting parameters for message formatting

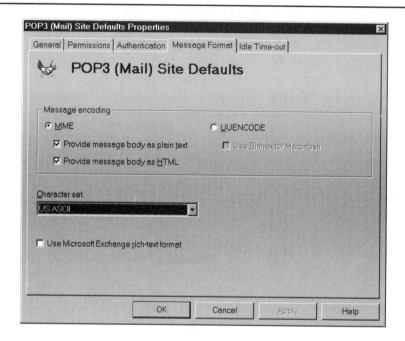

Like any single instance of the Internet Mail Service, an Exchange POP3 server can support either but not both of the two major encoding standards: MIME and uuencode. MIME is the newer and more popular encoding option. MIME can handle both formatted text and binary attachments. POP3 clients from Microsoft, Netscape, and Qualcomm (Eudora) all support MIME encoding.

If your POP3 client doesn't support MIME, you'll have to use uuencode, which does not support formatted text. It just handles binary message attachments.

**The Message Body**  MIME-encoded messages can support plain text and/or HTML message bodies. Plain text is just what you'd expect: simple 7-bit characters, nothing more. It will work with any MIME-compatible POP3 client. HTML (Hypertext Markup Language) is an Internet standard used in World Wide Web client-server systems. HTML supports fancy text formatting like different fonts, bold, italic, and color. The big three POP3 clients support HTML formatting.

If you choose both the plain text and HTML message body options, as I have in Figure 18.4, the MIME message will include versions of the message body in each format. The MIME-aware client will use the highest level format it can support.

If you pick the uuencode option, you can tell the POP3 server to use the Binhex encoding scheme for Macintosh POP3 clients. If you select Binhex, all messages will be sent in Binhex format. So you'd only want to use this option for an Exchange site dedicated to Macintosh POP3 clients.

**The Character Set**    Use the Character Set drop-down list to select the character set to be used in outgoing POP3 messages. The list includes the basic ASCII option as well as a wide range of character sets for other languages. The options available on your Exchange server will vary with the language or languages supported on the server.

**Microsoft Exchange Rich Text Format**    Microsoft rich text format is another way to get fancy text formatting to a POP3 client. Microsoft's Internet Mail 3 and Outlook Express can display rich text right in a message. Other POP3 clients will include rich text messages as attachments.

**Idle Time-Out**    Folks like to stay connected to their mail and Web servers. Each POP3 connection requires a little server overhead, especially if POP3 clients are periodically checking the server for new messages. Using the Idle Time-Out property page, you can set a time after which a POP3 connection will be closed. See Figure 18.5, which is all you'll need to figure out how to do this less-than-monumental task.

**FIGURE 18.5:**

Selecting a time-out period for POP3 connections

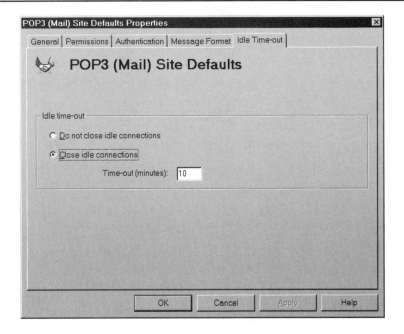

## Setting Up POP3 at the Server Level

POP3 is very server-centric. Users must specifically log into the server where their Exchange mailbox resides. You can modify the POP3 parameters you set for your Exchange site on a server-by-server basis. In this way, for example, you could set up an Exchange POP3 server to support users of Macintosh POP3 clients and Binhex encoding or users whose clients require binary attachments encoded in uuencode as opposed to MIME format.

To modify POP3 parameters on a specific server, use the server-specific POP3 setup object, which is located in the Protocols container for each server. As you can see in Figure 18.6, the server-based POP3 configuration object lets you set all the parameters you can set at the site level, as well as the logging levels to be used for server-based diagnostics.

**FIGURE 18.6:**

The server-level POP3 settings dialog box

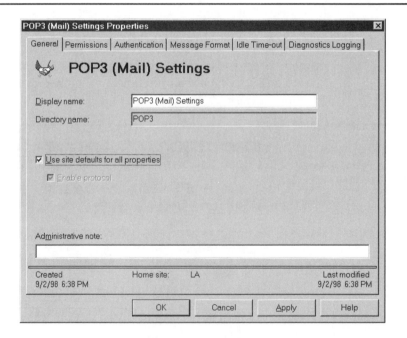

Since we've already talked about all the configuration options here, I'll leave it to you to make any server-based modification you need. Have fun.

**WARNING**     If POP3 services are turned off for a site, you can still turn them on for a server. You can also turn POP3 services off for a server if they are enabled at the site level.

## Sending Messages for POP3 Clients

POP3 clients pull their messages from POP3 servers. Simply put, POP3 servers are the source of incoming mail for POP3 clients. POP3 servers do not provide outgoing messaging services for POP3 clients. This service is provided by an Internet SMTP host.

Back in Chapter 15, I showed you how to use the rerouting capabilities of the Internet Mail Service to provide outgoing SMTP host services to POP3 clients as well as other servers. Check Chapter 15 for details on IMS routing.

### Customizing POP3 Support for a Mailbox

To customize POP3 support for a specific mailbox, find the mailbox in the appropriate recipients container in Exchange Administrator and double-click it. Tab over to the Protocols property page on the mailbox's properties dialog box (see Figure 18.7). Then double-click the POP3 (Mail) object.

**FIGURE 18.7:**

The Protocols property page of a mailbox Properties dialog box

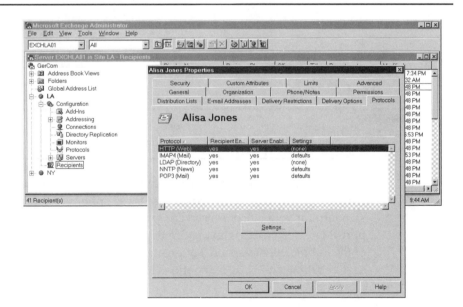

This brings up the Protocol Details properties dialog box shown in Figure 18.8. For a variety of reasons, security being a big one, you may not want all your Exchange mailbox users to access their mail using a POP3 client. To disable POP3 services for a mailbox, deselect Enable POP3 for this recipient.

**FIGURE 18.8:**

Customizing POP3 support for a mailbox

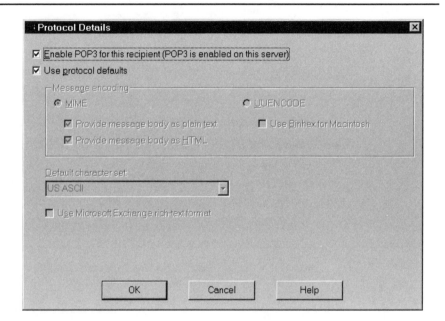

**WARNING**   If POP3 services are turned off for a server, turning them on for a mailbox on that server will not actually enable them until they are turned on for the server.

As you can see in Figure 18.8, you can set message formatting options on a mailbox-by-mailbox basis. You can use these options to support clients that aren't standard for your site or server. For example, say you've set up a server that supports Macintosh users who require Binhex encoding. You also can support users of the Eudora client version 3 or greater on that server by enabling MIME message encoding and body text options for the mailboxes of Eudora users.

## POP3 Setup: The Client Side

I've always thought of POP3 clients as one of life's little miracles. You set some basic parameters and tell the client to check for mail on your POP3 server, and your mail shows up. I'm sure that building sophisticated POP3 servers and clients is quite a task, but using them is a snap. Let's get some clients configured so you can experience the miracle.

### Start with Microsoft's Outlook Express Client

Though you can use any POP3-compliant Internet mail client to access your Exchange Server's POP3 server, you'll find that Microsoft's Outlook Express client is not only one of the best, but it's also enabled to support all five of the advanced Internet protocols I cover in this chapter. So I strongly suggest that you use the Outlook Express client for the exercises in this book, even if you plan to use another one later on.

The Outlook Express client comes with Microsoft Internet Explorer versions 4 and 5. You can download IE 4 or 5 from Microsoft's Web site, `www.microsoft.com`.

### Getting Connected to an Exchange Server–Based POP3 Server

First you need to set up your POP3 client to connect to an Exchange Server–based POP3 server. Before you start, you'll need to gather the following information:

- Your Exchange mailbox alias name
- Your NT account name if it's different from your Exchange mailbox alias name
- Your password for your Windows NT account
- Your Windows NT domain name (optional)
- Your POP3 e-mail address, which is your Exchange Server Internet mail (SMTP) address
- The IP address or name of your POP3 server (for incoming messages)
- The IP address or name of your SMTP server (for outgoing messages)

Let's take a look at how each of these is used to set up a POP3 client.

**The POP3 Account Name**    You'll use one or more of the first four items in the list above to set up your POP3 account name and password. When you're using Exchange Server's POP3 server, at the most basic level, the POP3 account name is the alias name of the Exchange mailbox you want to access with your POP3 client. My Exchange mailbox alias is bgerber, so my POP3 account name is bgerber.

Outlook Express makes it pretty easy to set up a POP3 client. Follow along on Figure 18.9. Open Outlook Express's Tools menu and select Accounts. On the resultant Internet Accounts dialog box, tab over to the Mail page and click Add. Select Mail from the little submenu that opens. This brings up the Internet Connection Wizard, which takes you through the steps of adding a POP3 or IMAP4 Internet mail account.

**FIGURE 18.9:**

Entering a name to be displayed in each sent message as the message's sender

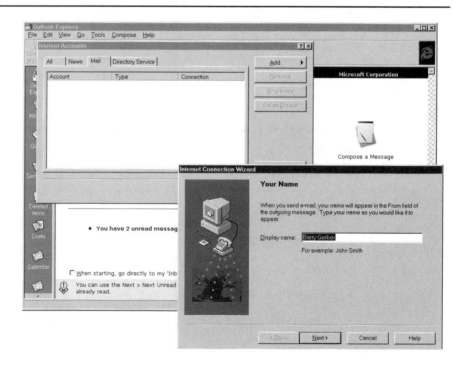

As you can see in Figure 18.9, the first thing you need to enter is the name of the sender that is displayed in the From field of each message you send. I've cleverly chosen "Barry Gerber". Click Next, and you're asked to enter your Internet

e-mail address. This is the Internet address for your Exchange server mailbox. Mine is bgerber@la.gercom.com.

Click Next to select the kind of incoming mail server you're setting up an account for (POP3 or IMAP4) and to enter names of the servers that will handle incoming and outgoing mail for your client (see Figure 18.10). Your incoming mail server name is the IP address or Internet domain name of the Exchange server where your mailbox resides. POP3 server services must be running on this server. Your outgoing mail server name is the IP address or Internet domain name of a server running SMTP mail services, a server that can send your mail out to the Internet for you. Though you could use any SMTP mail server, if you're running the Exchange Server Internet Mail Service, you need look no further.

**FIGURE 18.10:**

Selecting an e-mail server type (POP3 or IMAP4) and entering e-mail server names

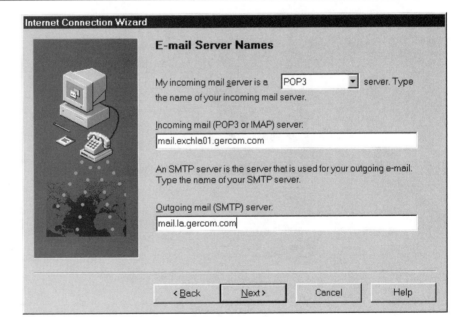

In Figure 18.10, I've entered special domain names for my Exchange server EXCHLA01 that runs both POP3 services and the Exchange IMS. The general convention with POP3 mail servers is to prefix incoming and outgoing server names with the word "mail"; hence, mail.exchla01.gercom.com for the incoming server. I put the name of the Exchange server, EXCHLA01, in there because POP3 users on EXCHLA02 will have to enter a domain name specifically for that server, mail.exchla02.gercom.com.

My Exchange Server IMS-based outgoing mail server was designed to be used by anyone in my LA site, so I chose to name it mail.la.gercom.com. I have another IMS for my NY site. Interestingly though, anyone in the GerCom organization or, to be more accurate, anyone in the world could use the IMS on my LA Exchange Server to send mail out to the Internet.

In Figure 18.11, I've moved on to the next Internet Connection Wizard page where I'm entering my POP account name and password. Why, you may be asking, is "la\" included in that account name, and what's my password? As it turns out, a lot happens on your Exchange and NT servers when you're authenticated to access your Exchange mailbox through a POP3 client. Let's take a look at the authentication process.

**FIGURE 18.11:**

Entering information to log on to a POP3 mailbox

You're authenticated to access your Exchange mailbox with a POP3 client in a number of ways. First, Exchange Server attempts to authenticate your use of your mailbox just as it would if you were using a standard Exchange or Outlook client. That is, it attempts to authenticate you through the Windows NT security system. It needs to find your NT domain and account name and finally to validate that you've entered the correct password for that account. Then Exchange Server needs to check to be sure that your NT account is authorized to access the mailbox. Finally, it has to verify that your mailbox is enabled for POP3 services.

Because my Exchange mailbox alias and my NT account name are the same, I only need to enter my mailbox alias in the POP Account Name field and my NT account password in the Password field. Exchange Server then uses the mailbox alias and password both to authenticate me in the NT security system and to locate my Exchange mailbox. If my mailbox alias were different from my NT account name, I'd have to enter both of these in the following format: NT_user _account_name\ mailbox_alias_name.

Now back to why "la\." "la" is the name of the NT domain where my Exchange Server LA site is located. As I mentioned earlier, NT security authentication starts at the domain level. Until your NT domain is known, it's not possible to begin authenticating your NT account name or password.

If I don't enter the name of my LA domain, Exchange Server will search through all known NT domains, attempting to find the one I'm in. If my NT environment includes lots of domains, that could take a long time. By entering the name of my domain, I shorten the time it takes to gain POP3 access to my Exchange mailbox.

**NOTE**    If you're a non–Exchange Server–based POP3 client user, all this may seem pretty complicated. After all, other POP3 servers don't require all this stuff. All you need enter in the POP3 Account field is your UNIX account name. If your Exchange mailbox alias and your NT account name are the same and you're willing to wait while Exchange Server searches for your NT domain, you can do exactly the same thing.

Some Internet Service Providers require that you log on using Secure Password Authentication, which adds a level of security to the clear text password you would normally pass to them. If you ever need to set up an Internet mail account with an ISP that uses SPA, you're all ready for it with Outlook Express.

When you finish entering the POP3 server and account information, click Next to move to the Wizard's Friendly Name page. Here you enter the name that is displayed in the list of mail accounts you've set up. As you'll see in a minute, the friendly name helps you quickly locate an account you want to modify.

The next Internet Connection Wizard page lets you tell Outlook Express how you'll connect to your POP3 server (see Figure 18.12). If by LAN or an already-established dial-up link to an ISP, select that option and click Next to move to the last Wizard page. If you want to dial up just before connecting to your POP3 server, select the first option and the Wizard will guide you through the process of setting up the parameters for your dial-up session. Finish that page and you're on to the last Wizard page.

Click Finish on the last Wizard page. Notice that your new account is now listed on the Mail page of the Internet Accounts dialog box. Leave the dialog box open. We'll get back to it in a minute.

**FIGURE 18.12:**

Selecting the type of connection to be used to access a POP3 server

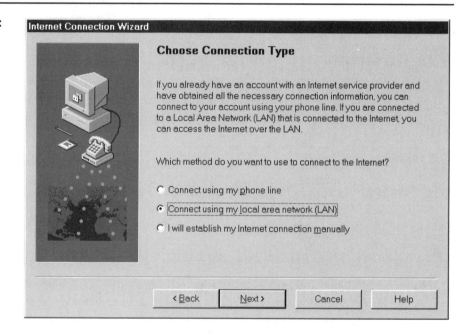

## Other POP3 Client Settings

Various POP3 clients allow you to set a range of other parameters. One of the most important involves whether you leave copies of your messages on the POP3 server. To better understand this option, you need to understand that POP3 clients download each message that is on the server. If you don't leave copies of messages on the POP3 server, they aren't available when you access them with a different client on the same or a different computer.

Your POP3 server is also your Exchange server. If you don't choose to leave a copy of all messages downloaded by your POP3 client on the server, you won't be able to access them with another POP3 client or with the Exchange or Outlook client. Whether you leave copies or not depends on how you work. If you're going to work from one place with the POP3 client, you can suck all your messages down into that client and deal with them there. If you're going to use a POP3 client when you're away from the office and an Exchange or Outlook client when in the office, you'll want to be sure to leave a copy on the server.

To leave a copy of messages on your Exchange server, you'll need to turn back to the Internet Accounts dialog box that you left open a bit ago (see Figure 18.13).

Highlight the friendly name of your account—mine's GerCom (POP3)—and click Properties to bring up the (POP3) Properties dialog box shown in Figure 18.14.

**FIGURE 18.13:**

The Internet Accounts dialog box with a newly created account listed

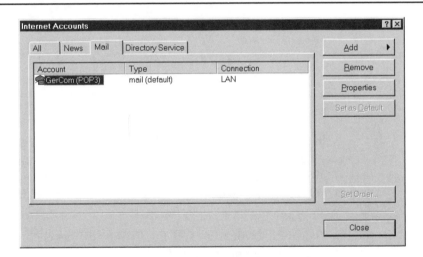

The first three pages of the dialog box contain information you entered with the Internet Connection Wizard. You use the Security page to obtain a digital ID from a third-party company called a "certifying authority" and to install the ID. A digital ID lets you digitally sign and encrypt messages with your Outlook Express client just like you can using KM Server with the standard Exchange and Outlook clients for Exchange Server. The Outlook Express docs do a pretty good job of explaining the digital ID game or directing you to Web sources for more information.

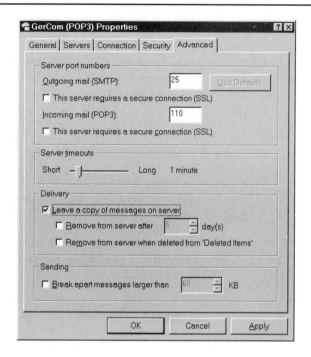

In Figure 18.14 down in the Delivery area, I've told Outlook Express to leave a copy of my messages on my Exchange server when it downloads messages to my POP3 client. Since I want to control what happens to my messages with my regular Outlook client when I'm connected in the office, I didn't check either of the Remove… options in the Delivery area.

I'll leave it to you to explore the above and other client settings offered by Outlook Express or your favorite POP3 client.

## Did It Work?

Figure 18.15 shows the rewards of all the server and client-side configuring we've been through. As you can see, we're looking at a message sent to me by GerCom's class clown, Rubin Alvarez. It was sent from his standard Outlook client and includes a couple of fonts that I can see in my Outlook Express client, because, in this case, my Exchange server's POP3 server is configured to send me messages in HTML format. Very nice.

| WARNING | Don't confuse the POP3 Sent and Deleted Items folders with the folders of the same name on your Exchange server. The POP3 versions of these folders contain only messages you've sent and received with your Outlook Express POP3 client. Since POP3 only lets you access your Inbox, messages sent with or deleted from your standard Outlook client don't show up in your POP3 client's Sent and Deleted Items folders. |
|---------|

I'm going to leave it to you to figure out how to send and retrieve messages with your POP3 client. It's easy and, hey, what's life without new things to learn?

## Troubleshooting POP3 Problems

Generally, I've found POP3 to be one of the easiest and least vexing protocols of all to use. If you do have trouble, ensure that your network connection is working and, if that doesn't fix things, retrace your steps through the process outlined above. If you still can't get POP3 to work, there are three major troubleshooting tools for POP3 connections: protocol logging, event logging, and counters for NT's Performance Monitor. See the Exchange Server documentation for help using these.

**FIGURE 18.15:**

Viewing an HTML format-
ted message with Microsoft
Outlook Express

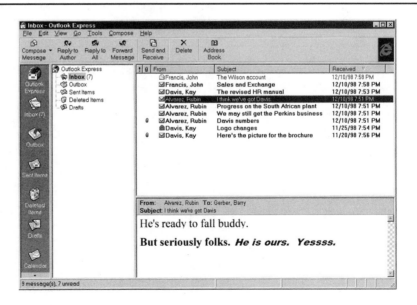

# The Internet Message Access Protocol

Exchange Server 5.5 adds support for the Internet Message Access Protocol version 4 (IMAP4). The major difference between IMAP4 and POP3 is that IMAP4 lets you access messages in folders in your Exchange mailbox and in Exchange public folders. With both protocols you can download messages to your local computer and view them. IMAP4 also lets you view messages without downloading them, much like the standard Outlook client. IMAP4 setup is very much like POP3 setup on the server and client sides. So, I'll just call your attention to the differences between the two protocols as I discuss IMAP4 below.

## IMAP4 Setup: The Exchange Server Side

As with POP3, we'll look at your IMAP4 configuration options at the site, server, and individual mailbox level.

### Setting Up IMAP4 at the Site Level

Using Exchange Administrator, find the IMAP4 (Mail) Site Defaults object in the site Protocols container and double-click it. Only three of the property pages on the resultant IMAP4 (Mail) Site Defaults Properties dialog box (see Figure 18.16) are different from the POP3 pages. Let's take a quick look at those three pages.

**FIGURE 18.16:**

The General property page of the IMAP4 (Mail) Site Defaults Properties dialog box, one of three pages that differ from the pages for POP3 setup

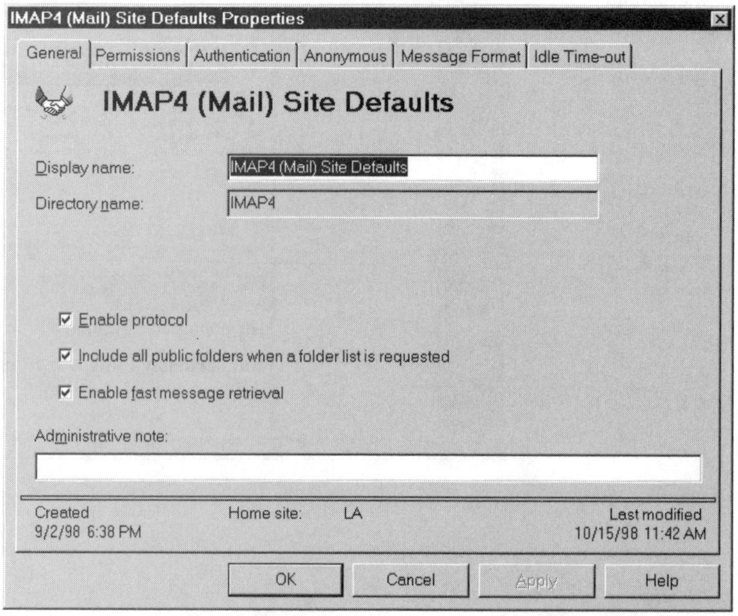

**General Properties**    The IMAP4 General property page lets you enable the IMAP4 protocol for your site, just like the POP3 page. Due to the nature of the IMAP4 protocol, however, the IMAP General page has two additional options.

Because they can access all the folders on an IMAP4-compatible server that a user has rights to, IMAP clients need information about available folders. To get this information, the clients make requests for lists of folders. Some IMAP4 clients suffer from performance problems when receiving lists with large numbers of public folders. If you're using such a client to access your Exchange server, deselect "Include All Public Folders When a Folder List Is Requested" to eliminate public folders from folder lists sent by the IMAP4 server to the client.

An IMAP4 server also sends information about messages in folders to its clients. To speed up this process, Exchange Server's IMAP4 server can estimate message size. Some clients require exact message size information. If your IMAP4 client is one of these, deselect Enable Fast Message Retrieval so that the IMAP4 server sends exact message sizes to its clients.

**Anonymous**    If you want to allow IMAP4 client users to access public folders anonymously, enable the Allow Anonymous Access option on the Anonymous property page (see Figure 18.17). You set anonymous access parameters for a public folder on the folder's Permissions property page as viewed from a standard Outlook client or Exchange Administrator.

**FIGURE 18.17:**

Enable anonymous access to public folders on the Anonymous property page of the IMAP4 (Mail) Site Defaults Properties dialog box.

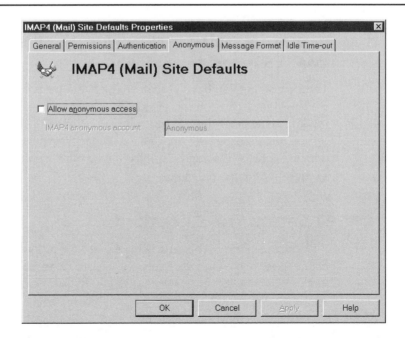

**Message Format**   IMAP4 only supports MIME encoding. Unlike POP3, it doesn't support the older uuencode standard. Hence the absence of the uuencode option on the IMAP4 Message Format property page (see Figure 18.18).

**FIGURE 18.18:**

The Message Format property page of the IMAP4 (Mail) Site Defaults Properties dialog box

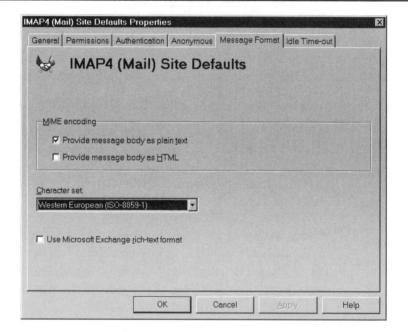

### Setting Up IMAP4 at the Server Level and Customizing IMAP4 Support for a Mailbox

There's nothing you haven't seen on the IMAP4 server or mailbox level. So, let me close this section on server side IMAP4 setup by noting that you can accommodate for some of the differences in IMAP4 clients I mentioned above at the server or mailbox level. For example, if specific users are running a client that demands precise message size information, you can deselect the Fast Message Retrieval option on the mailboxes of those users.

## IMAP4 Setup: The Client Side

With the exception of choosing IMAP4 in the drop-down list on the E-Mail Server Names page of the Outlook Express Internet Connection Wizard (see Figure 18.10), the initial setup of an IMAP account is no different from the setup of a POP3 account.

The only difference on the account properties dialog box is on the Advanced property page. As you can see in Figure 18.19, you can set a root folder path for the folders you access with your IMAP client and choose whether your client should show you all the folders you have access to or only the ones you've subscribed to.

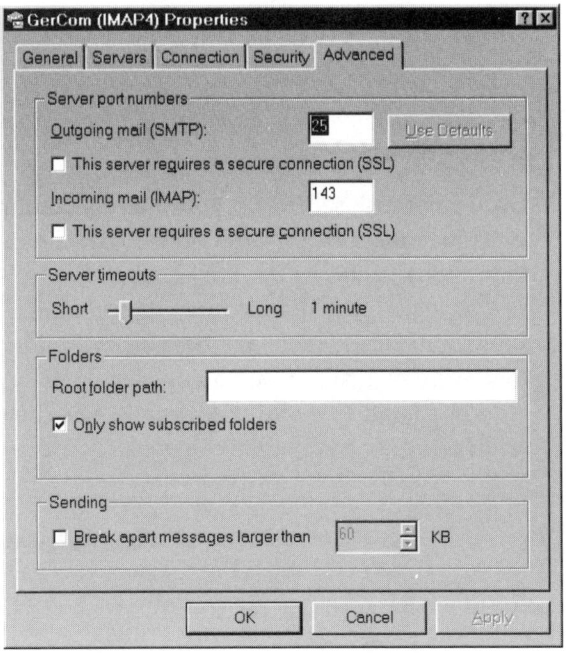

**FIGURE 18.19:**

Setting unique IMAP4 parameters on the IMAP4 Advanced Property page

An IMAP4 client can tell an IMAP4 server where in your folder hierarchy it should begin accessing folders. For example, if I entered **{mail.exchla01.gercom .com}INBOX** into the Root folder path field shown in Figure 18.19, Outlook Express would display only my Exchange Server Inbox, and I wouldn't even see any of the other folders on the server. If you want to see all those folders, leave this field blank.

The IMAP4 protocol lets you subscribe to specific folders on a server. This lets you limit the clutter in your client GUI and, if there are lots of folders, it also can improve IMAP4 client-server performance. By default, some IMAP4 clients, including Outlook Express, only display folders you've subscribed to. Deselect the Only Show Subscribed Folders option if you want Outlook Express to display all folders on your Exchange server. I suggest you do so, if only for the rest of this little IMAP4 tutorial. If you don't, only your Inbox will be displayed when your IMAP4 client starts up.

> **WARNING** A limitation in the IMAP4 protocol prevents you from accessing folders with forward slashes (/) in their names. The only fix is to rename any folders with the "offending" character.

That's it; you're ready to take a look at your folders and messages with your Outlook Express client.

### Did It Work?

Once you finish setting up your IMAP4 account, you'll be asked if you want to download the folder list for your IMAP4 link. Accept the offer and you should then see a new folder in your Outlook Express client. It'll have the friendly name you gave your IMAP4 account when setting it up with the Internet Connection Wizard. In Figure 18.20, my new IMAP4 folder is open and you can see all the folders in my mailbox and all the visible folders in my Exchange server's Public Folders container. As you can see, IMAP4 clients get their own master folder and set of subfolders in Outlook Express to display messages.

**FIGURE 18.20:**

Using the IMAP4 client support included in Outlook Express to view messages stored in Exchange Server folders

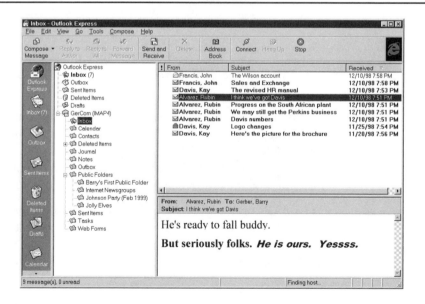

Now, go ahead and play around in your IMAP4 folders. Note that all the folders are a direct reflection of the folders on your Exchange server.

POP3 clients have to download messages to the machine you're running the client on before you can read them. IMAP4 clients don't have to do that. Like standard Outlook clients for Exchange Server, IMAP4 clients initially display folder and message header information. They pull message content down only when you open a message.

You can download the contents of your Exchange Server folders under the IMAP4 protocol. This lets you work with your folders and messages when you're not connected to your Exchange server, giving you the same functionality as the Synchronize option on the standard Outlook client's Tools menu.

If you have any problems with IMAP4, take a look at the little troubleshooting section in the discussion of POP3 clients above.

That's it for IMAP4. I leave the rest to you, your brain, your eyes, and your fingers. Have fun.

# Web Browser Access to Exchange Server

Microsoft has put together several components that let you access mailboxes and public folders on Exchange servers. The whole thing works pretty simply, although, as with POP3 and IMAP4, there's a lot of complexity behind the scenes.

At the center of Exchange Server Web access is "ActiveX Server" or just "Active Server" (AS). AS runs on Microsoft Internet Information Server and is the link between NT applications and Internet-based users of those applications. AS is a general-purpose server that can be used to bring applications and data to users over intranets and Internets. AS runs applications built to Microsoft's Active Server Pages standards. Active Server Pages applications are stored in files with the extension .ASP. Collectively, the Active Server Pages for Exchange Server–based Web access are referred to as Outlook Web Access (OWA).

Users access OWA through Internet Information Server using an Internet browser that is JavaScript and frames–capable. Both Microsoft Internet Explorer 3 and later and Netscape 3 and later meet this specification. OWA applications take data from Exchange servers, wrap it up in a nice user interface, and translate the whole thing into Hypertext Markup Language (HTML) and/or JavaScript, which is then sent to the browser through Internet Information Server.

You can install support for OWA either when you install Exchange Server itself or after that by running the Exchange Server setup program. If you need more information on OWA installation, check out Chapter 7. For more on Internet Information Server, see Chapter 6 of this book and Microsoft's docs for IIS.

## Outlook Web Access Setup: The Server Side

Outlook Web Access or HTTP (Hypertext Transfer Protocol) setup is pretty simple. You can configure HTTP at the site and mailbox levels. Unlike POP3 and IMAP4, no server-level configuration is available.

### Setting Up HTTP at the Site Level

Go to the site Protocols container and double-click HTTP to open the HTTP Site Settings dialog box (see Figure 18.21). If you need a re-orientation to the site Protocols container, take a look at Figure 18.1.

**FIGURE 18.21:**

The HTTP Site Settings dialog box

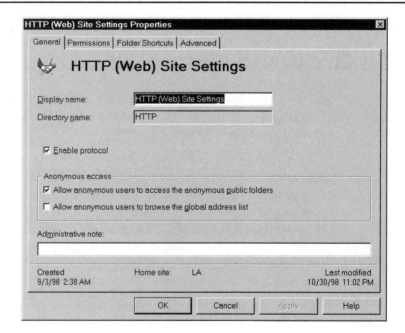

**General Properties**   As you can see in Figure 18.21, there's very little you need to do on the General property page. You can disable and enable the HTTP protocol and control anonymous user access to public folders and the global address list.

When you access your Exchange mailbox using the Outlook Web Access applications, Secure Sockets Layer (SSL) authentication is used. I discussed SSL in the section above on POP3. SSL authentication support for OWA applications is provided by the Internet Information Server.

---

**WARNING**   To access your Exchange mailbox with a Web browser, your browser must support SSL, as do the Microsoft and Netscape version 3 and later browsers. If you have trouble getting to your Exchange mailbox with your browser, be sure it provides this level of support.

---

Anonymous or unauthenticated users cannot access Exchange mailboxes. They can, however, access specific public folders and the global address list. As you can see in Figure 18.21, you can enable or disable public folder and global address list access separately. This makes good sense, since you might be more than willing to have others accessing marketing or other information you might want to publish through public folders but not getting into personnel information stored in your Exchange organization's global address list.

**Folder Shortcuts**   You use the Folder Shortcuts property page to specify which public folders are displayed to anonymous users (see Figure 18.22). Click the New button to bring up a dialog box to browse through your public folders and select the ones you want (see Figure 18.23). Select a folder and click OK on the dialog box. The folder now shows up in the folder shortcuts list (see Figure 18.24).

Click the Remove button on the Folder Shortcuts property page to delete public folders shortcuts from the list.

**FIGURE 18.22:**

The Folder Shortcuts property page

**FIGURE 18.23:**

Selecting public folders to be displayed to anonymous Exchange Server users

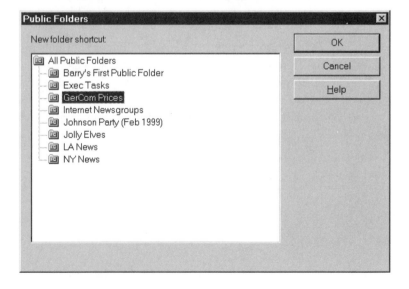

**WARNING**    The Folder Shortcuts page only specifies which public folders will be visible to
anonymous users. By default, anonymous users have no rights to a public folder
on the Folder Shortcuts list. To give them a level of access to a specific public
folder, the folder's owner needs to open the Properties dialog box for the folder
using a standard Outlook client. Specific rights are granted on the Permissions
property page of the dialog box (see Figure 18.25). You can also get to this dialog
box from Exchange Administrator by clicking Client Permissions on the General
Property page of the Properties dialog box for a folder. To get to this page, find
and click the folder in the Public Folders container in Exchange Administrator;
then select Properties from Administrator's File menu.

**Advanced Properties**    You can set a limit on the number of address book entries returned to an authorized user (see Figure 18.26). This helps limit server and network traffic.

---

**FIGURE 18.25:**

Setting anonymous user access rights for a specific Exchange public folder

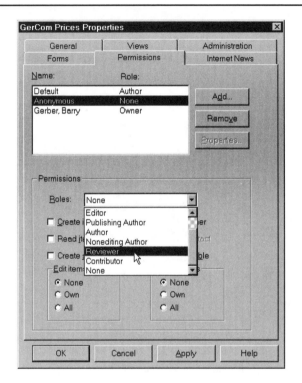

## Setting Up HTTP at the Mailbox Level

If HTTP access is enabled at the site level, you can disable it for an individual mailbox. That's it. For specifics on finding the mailbox-level Protocols container, check out the section of this chapter on customizing POP3 support for a mailbox.

FIGURE 18.26:

Setting limits on the
number of address book
entries returned to an
authorized user

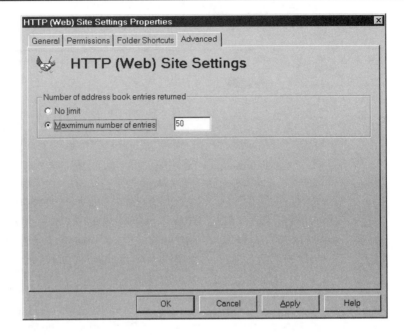

## Outlook Web Access (HTTP) Setup: The Client Side

Client side setup is a breeze. Just specify that you want to connect to the Internet
Information Server that supports your Exchange server plus "/exchange." In my
case I connect using the URL http://la.gercom.com/exchange.

In Figure 18.27, I entered my Exchange alias name in the Log On field on the
right-hand side of the screen. This opened the Enter Network Password dialog
box, where I've entered my NT domain name and account name and password.
When I captured the screen in Figure 18.27, I wasn't logged into a domain. So,
there is no Domain field on the Enter Network Password dialog box. I entered the
name of my NT domain as part of my User name, in the format DOMAIN
NAME\USER NAME.

The rules for logging into your Exchange mailbox through the Outlook Web
Access are pretty much the same as the rules for logging in using a POP3 or
IMAP4 client. The one very nice exception is that you don't have to specify the
server where your mailbox is stored. Since Microsoft controls this application,
they've set it up so that the app finds your mailbox wherever it is in your site.

That's why there's no server name in the URL I use to access the Exchange Outlook Web Access.

## It Doesn't Work!!!!!

I mentioned in earlier chapters that I've gotten lots of e-mail from readers of earlier editions of this book. My e-mail address is at the end of the Acknowledgments section way up front, and some readers are far from shy about asking questions.

OWA is a favorite topic of readers. The subject lines of messages about OWA generally contain the words *it doesn't work like you said*. So, let me save you some electrons with several tips that should help you get OWA up and working sooner rather than later.

1. A user who will access Exchange Server with a Web browser must be able to log on locally to the NT server running the Web server that supports OWA. On the server that supports OWA, create a Local Group using NT's User Manager for Domains. Then, in User Manager for Domains, give the group rights to log on locally to the server (Policies ➢ User Rights). Then add any user who will use OWA to the group.

2. If your Exchange Server organization crosses multiple domains, ensure users enter the correct domain name in the Domain field of the Enter Network Password box or use the *DOMAIN NAME\USER NAME* format shown in Figure 18.27.

3. Be sure you understand Internet Information Server's authentication options. Generally, NT Challenge/Response is used to support OWA. However, if all or some users access OWA through a proxy server like Microsoft's Proxy Server, you need to turn off NT Challenge/Response and turn on Basic Authentication. Yes, security is somewhat compromised, but that's the only way proxy server users can access Exchange Server using OWA.

4. If all this doesn't help, check out Microsoft's online Knowledge Base. See the section on Exchange Server troubleshooting in Chapter 17 for more on the Knowledge Base and accessing it.

In Figure 18.28 I'm using the Microsoft Internet Explorer Web browser to review the list of messages in my Exchange mailbox. In Figure 18.29 I'm looking at my favorite message from Rubin Alvarez complete with HTML text formatting. Figure 18.30 shows an anonymous view of a GerCom public folder showing various Enter key options. It is Internet publishing without our having written a bit of HTML code. Finally, Figure 18.31 shows an anonymous access to GerCom's global address list. Extremely nice.

**FIGURE 18.27:**

Entering authentication information for HTTP access to an Exchange Server mailbox

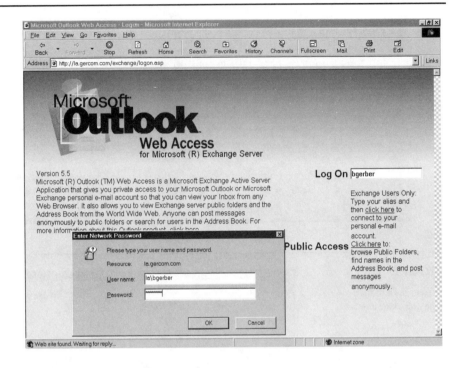

**FIGURE 18.28:**

Viewing a list of messages in an Exchange mailbox with Microsoft's Internet Explorer Web browser

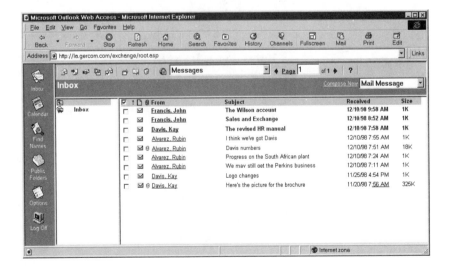

## OWA: Relief for Schedule+ Users

Outlook Web Access also lets you access your schedule and even set up meetings with your Internet browser. This may turn out to be the killer app part of OWA. A number of organizations still have many users on Windows 3.*x*, and that means they have to use Schedule+—which is called "Outlook Calendar" in Exchange 5.5—for scheduling, while the Win 95–enabled crowd can bop away on Outlook's Calendar. There's a lot of hand-wringing over who can see and do what in which client in organizations where Schedule+ and Outlook Calendar have to coexist. Web browser access to Exchange Server–based scheduling can pretty much put everyone on an even playing field or at least give more functionality to Windows 3.*x* folk whose only other option is Schedule+/Outlook Calendar.

**FIGURE 18.29:**

Viewing an Exchange message with a Web browser

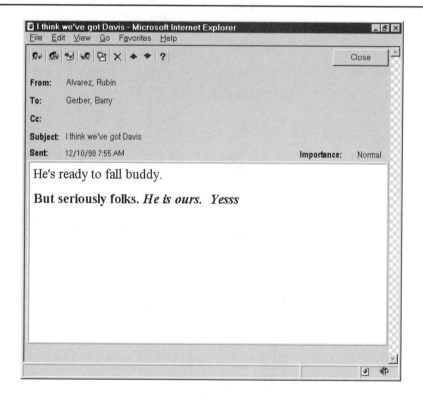

**FIGURE 18.30:**

An anonymous user views the contents of an Exchange Server public folder with a Web browser.

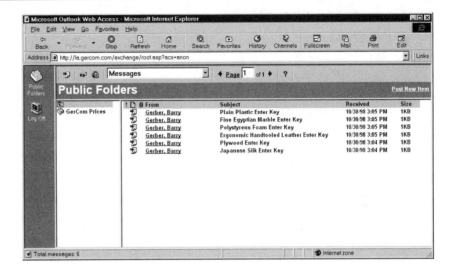

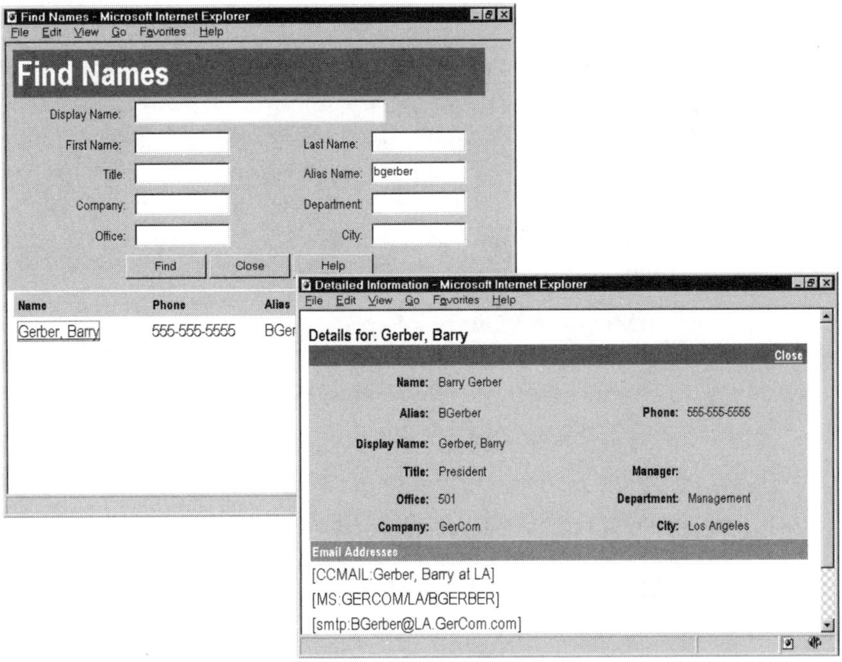

**FIGURE 18.31:**

An anonymous user views an entry in the Exchange Server global address list with a Web browser.

# The Lightweight Directory Access Protocol

The Lightweight Directory Access Protocol (LDAP) is a client-server protocol that lets you browse, read, and search for information stored in an electronic directory. It was developed at the University of Michigan to allow access to an X.500 directory without all the overhead required by the original X.500 Directory Access Protocol.

LDAP server support is installed when you install Exchange Server. Exchange Server's LDAP server accesses the Exchange directory database, which, as I'm sure you're aware by now, contains data attributes such as recipient display names, phone numbers, and e-mail addresses. Upon request, the LDAP server returns directory data to LDAP-compatible clients. Server-to-client data transmissions are limited by the user authentication rules and directory attribute permissions that are in place on Exchange Server for the LDAP server.

What I'm about to say is really neat, so listen up! One LDAP server can serve your entire Exchange organization. That's because there's a copy of the Exchange directory for your entire organization on each server in the organization.

There are basic LDAP clients that you can use to directly browse through an LDAP-compatible directory. But the real power of LDAP comes with its integration into e-mail clients, like POP3 or IMAP4 clients. A POP3 or IMAP4 client with integrated LDAP support provides not only access to a user's Exchange mailbox but also access to Exchange Server–based address books. And you're not limited to just Exchange Server address books. You can also search any LDAP server you have access to.

Microsoft's Outlook Express supports LDAP. Check with your favorite Internet e-mail client vendor to find out if its product is LDAP-compliant or, if not, whether there are plans to make it compliant.

Let's get our LDAP service up and running right now.

## LDAP Setup: The Server Side

You can configure LDAP parameters at the site and server levels only. There are no settings at the mailbox level. We'll start with site-level configuration.

## Setting Up LDAP at the Site Level

Find the LDAP configuration object in the Protocols container. Then double-click it to open the LDAP (Directory) Site Defaults dialog box shown in Figure 18.32.

**FIGURE 18.32:**

The LDAP Site Defaults
dialog box

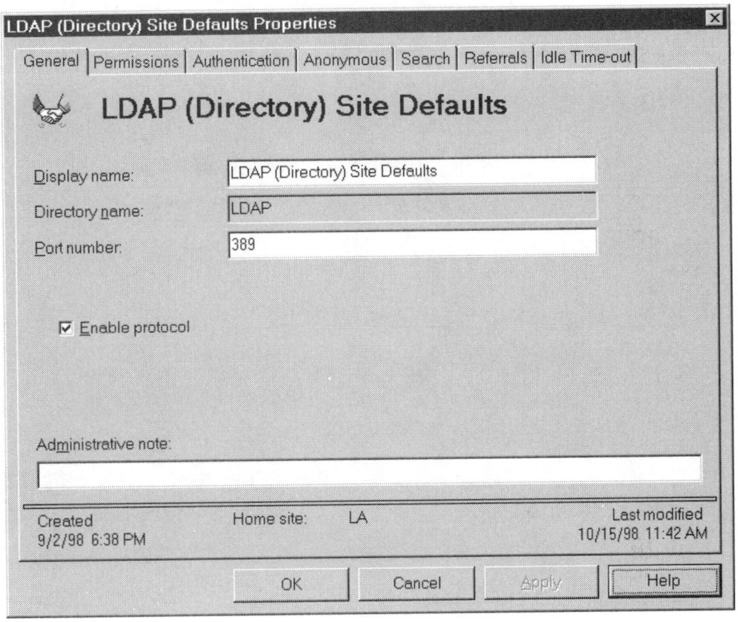

**General Properties**    As you can see in Figure 18.32, you know this page pretty well. Aside from the standard naming and note functions, you use the General property page to set the TCP/IP port number to be used for LDAP services by the server and to enable or disable LDAP for the site. Using a different port from the standard one, port 389, can help you enhance LDAP security. The port number on the LDAP client must be set to match the server's port number.

**Authentication**    Use the Authentication property page shown in Figure 18.33 to select the methods to be used for account name and password authentication. You have six options, all of which I discussed back in the POP3 section of this chapter.

You can choose none, one, some, or all of these authentication methods. If you choose no method, then only anonymous users will be able to access your

Exchange Server directory with an LDAP client. Let's move on to anonymous access right now.

**FIGURE 18.33:**

Setting authentication methods for LDAP connections to Exchange Server

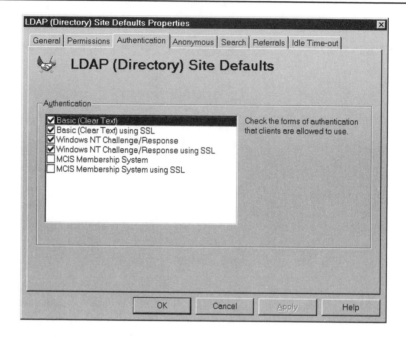

**Anonymous**    The Anonymous property page is used to enable or disable anonymous LDAP client access. See Figure 18.34. If you disable anonymous access, then users have to set their LDAP clients to log on using some form of authentication.

---

**NOTE**

You can limit what Exchange directory attributes are available to an anonymous or even an authenticated LDAP user. To do this, use the Exchange Administrator's Directory Service (DS) Site configuration dialog box (Attributes property page). See the previous chapter for more information.

---

**FIGURE 18.34:**

Enabling anonymous
access to an LDAP server

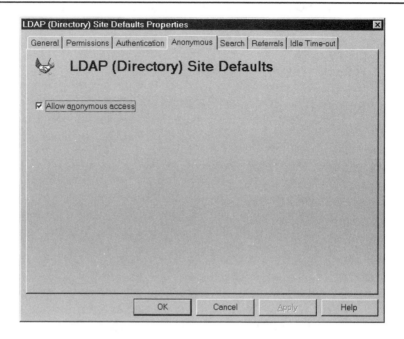

**Search**    You use your LDAP client to ask an LDAP server to search for a string
of characters in each entry in a specific directory field. For example, you might
request a search for all instances of "Smith" in the Exchange last name field. The
LDAP protocol allows a client to request that each search start at the beginning or
end of an entry or anywhere within an entry. For example, a search for the string
"jo," starting at the beginning of each last name entry in the directory, will return
all the *Jo*neses, *Jo*hnsons, and any other last name beginning with "Jo." A last
name search for "sky" starting at the end of each entry will return names such as
Per*sky*, Olin*sky*, and *Sky* itself. A search for "ro," starting anywhere within each
last name entry, will return names such as *Ro*wan, C*ro*w, and Domb*ro*.

When a search starts at the beginning of a directory entry, it's called an "initial
substring search" in LDAP parlance. A search that starts at the end of an entry is
called a "final substring search" and a search that starts anywhere within an entry
is called an "any substring search." Throughout the rest of this section, these
terms will be italicized to avoid confusion.

Initial substring searches are fast. Final substring searches are slower than initial substring searches, and any substring searches are the slowest of all. Slower
searches can eat up resources on an Exchange server, so don't think of them only

as inconveniences for LDAP client users. Any user of an Exchange server that is also an LDAP server could feel the impact of slower LDAP searches.

You use the Search property page shown in Figure 18.35 to tell your LDAP server how to deal with string searches. If you choose the first option, Treat "Any" Substring Searches as "Initial" Substring Searches, then final substring searches aren't done at all and any substring searches are converted to initial substring searches. This ensures fast searches but may result in incomplete information if the user submitted a *final* or *any* substring search.

With the second option, Allow Only "Initial" Substring Searches, any substring searches aren't even converted into initial substring searches. Only initial substring searches are honored. Running under this option, an LDAP server can easily match or exceed the search speed of the first option. If the final option, Allow All Substring Searches, is selected, the LDAP server is allowed to perform any of the three types of searches. This option will almost always result in slower searches.

Before we leave searches, note in Figure 18.35 that you can also specify how many search results your LDAP server returns to an LDAP client. The higher this number, the lower your LDAP server's performance is likely to be. A setting of around one hundred should be about right for light LDAP client access. Twenty-five to fifty is best if you expect your LDAP server to get heavy duty use.

**FIGURE 18.35:**

Selecting the method to be used for LDAP searches and the maximum number of search results to be returned

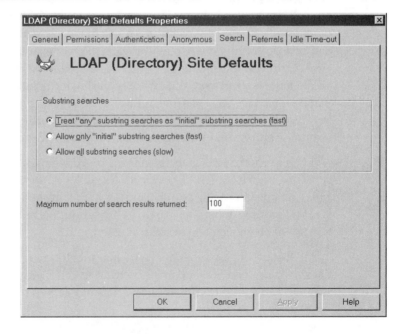

**Referrals**    In addition to providing a client with any appropriate information from particular entries in its own directory, an LDAP server can refer the client to other LDAP servers. In one scenario, you might refer LDAP clients to other LDAP servers in your business organization but outside of your Exchange organization, thus creating a sort of one-stop-shopping LDAP system.

You add referral servers on the Referrals property page (see Figure 18.36). Click New to get started. You'll need to know the LDAP server's IP address or Internet domain name; its directory name, which is in X.500 format such as ou=exchange,o=gercom2,c=us (see RFC 1779); and the port clients should connect on, if not 389.

**FIGURE 18.36:**

Use the Referrals property page to add other LDAP servers that users can search along with your own server.

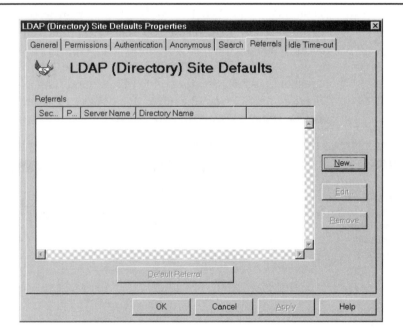

Take care here. You don't want to go into the business of supporting heavy LDAP referral loads on your Exchange server and, unless you're a sadist, you don't want to subject LDAP users to long waits as their LDAP clients plow through the up to 350 referral servers you can define.

You should know the Idle Time-Out page quite well by now. So, onward!

### Setting Up LDAP at the Server Level

Server-level LDAP configuration options are the same as for the site. I'll leave it to you to go ahead and make any custom server settings that you need.

# LDAP Setup: The Client Side

In this section, I'll show you how to set up and test LDAP functionality in Microsoft Outlook Express.

### Setting Up an Account for a Directory in Outlook Express

As with POP3 and IMAP4, we need to set up an account to access our Exchange server–based LDAP directory. So, select Accounts from Outlook Express's Tools menu. When the Internet Accounts dialog page opens, tab over to the Directory Service page (see Figure 18.37). As you'll notice, Microsoft has already set up a bunch of LDAP servers for you to play around with. Next, click Add and select Directory Service from the menu that pops up. This starts our old friend the Internet Connection Wizard, shown in Figure 18.38.

**FIGURE 18.37:**

The Directory Service property page of the Internet Accounts dialog box comes with a complement of preinstalled LDAP directory servers.

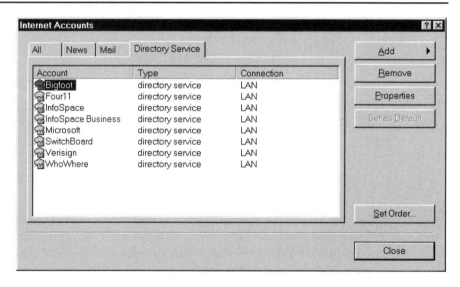

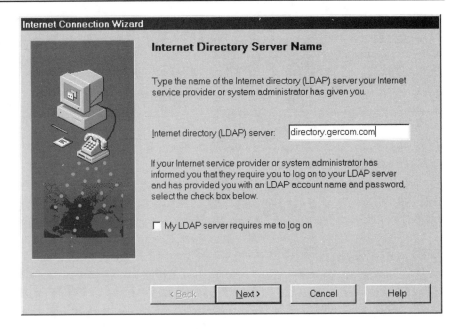

Fill in the IP address or Internet domain name of the directory server and, if
you have to log on to your LDAP server, check the box labeled My LDAP Server
Requires Me to Log On. Then click Next. If you didn't check the box, you move
on to the Check E-Mail Addresses page and you can move on to the next paragraph. If you checked the box, the Wizard presents a page that lets you enter
either an LDAP account name and password or indicate that you need to log on
to your LDAP server using Secure Password Authentication (see Figure 18.39).
As I noted above, if you've turned off anonymous access to your LDAP server,
you'll need to select some form of authentication. When using Basic Authentication (instead of SPA) for LDAP access, you enter the address name in the form
"cn=account;cn=Ntdomain". Quite intuitive, huh?

**FIGURE 18.39:**

Entering information
required for logging onto a
directory server

When you're using an LDAP-enabled e-mail client and you enter all or part of a
name into the To, Cc, or Bcc fields of a new message, your e-mail client's LDAP
client works with one or more LDAP servers to resolve the name into an e-mail
address. Beyond that, you can use your LDAP client to look in LDAP servers for
directory information. You'll want to use the LDAP account you're creating right
now to search for addresses on your Exchange server while you're composing
messages. So, be sure that Yes on the Check E-Mail Addresses page is selected.

Click Next to add a friendly name for your directory service. Click Next one
last time and then click Finish, and you're returned to the Internet Accounts dialog box shown back in Figure 18.37. The only difference you'll note at this point is
that your new directory service is nestled in alphabetical order among the other
directory services Microsoft was so kind to provide.

As with POP3 and IMAP4 accounts, you manage your LDAP account by opening the Properties dialog box for the account. I'll leave it to you to play with this
dialog box as need and whim move you.

## Did It Work?

First, let's try to find some names on our LDAP server using Outlook Express's basic Find function. Track along on Figure 18.40. On the Outlook Express main window, click Address Book on the Toolbar. This brings up the Address Book dialog box. Click Find to bring up the Find People dialog box. Select your LDAP account from the Look In drop-down menu at the top of the dialog box and type a name in the Name field. Click Find Now, and in a flash your Exchange server–based LDAP service returns information from the Exchange directory on all matching Exchange directory entries. In Figure 18.40, I've found all three of the Smiths who work at GerCom.

**FIGURE 18.40:**

A list of Exchange Server recipients and select attributes of each as returned in an LDAP search using an Outlook Express Client

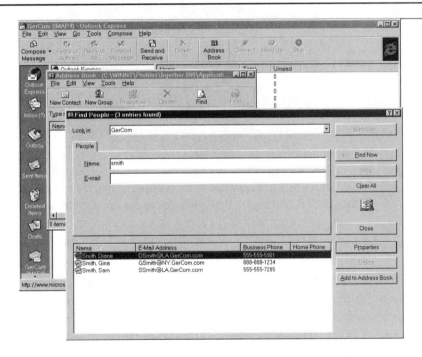

In Figure 18.41, I've opened the Properties dialog box for one of those Smiths, Gina. All those tabs on the dialog box open worlds of possibilities. If information is available and not security protected on an LDAP server, it will be displayed in appropriate fields on each of the six pages of the dialog box.

**FIGURE 18.41:**

Use the Properties dialog box for a returned directory entry to explore other information available in the LDAP directory.

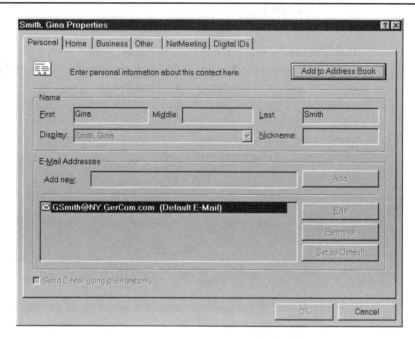

The Home and Business pages have room for lots of contact information, including business and personal Web site URLs. The Other page provides space for general notes and information about group memberships. The NetMeeting page is for information used in initiating network-based conferences, and the Digital IDs page contains information about the Digital IDs associated with this person.

This LDAP directory searching stuff is a lot of fun, especially on a cold winter night. If you're connected to the Internet, try some of the directory services that Microsoft provides with Outlook Express. See if you can find an old acquaintance, friend, or enemy.

Okay, now let's try composing a new message and using LDAP to find the e-mail addresses of the folks we want to send it to. Click Compose message on the Outlook Express Toolbar. This opens a new message window (see Figure 18.42). Type all or part of the name of one of your Exchange Server users into the To or Cc field and click the check names icon right next to the Address Book icon on the message's Toolbar. Assuming correct spelling and such, the names you typed in should be resolved into e-mail addresses by your LDAP client and server. You know an address has been resolved when the name is underlined in the To, Cc, or Bcc field. If you want to know more about this recipient, double-click one of the resolved addresses to open the Properties dialog box, shown back in Figure 18.41.

**FIGURE 18.42:**

A new message with e-mail addresses that have been resolved using an Exchange Server–based LDAP directory service

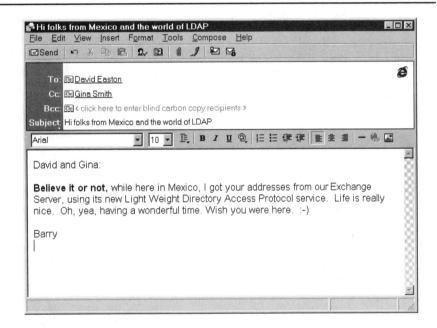

Go ahead and send your message. If it got through to the recipients you intended, all is well in the world and you can take a break or move on to the next section on the Network News Transfer Protocol and the newsgroups it supports. If nothing has worked, make sure your network connection is working, ensure that your network security settings are in sync on your LDAP client and server, and if that doesn't help, go back over the above steps. If things are still not working, take a look at the troubleshooting section under the section on POP3 above.

# The Network News Transfer Protocol

Aren't these advanced Internet protocols fantastic? Well, we're not finished with these wonders yet. We've got one more to go, the Network News Transfer Protocol (NNTP). NNTP supports those wild, woolly, and sometimes useful Internet newsgroups that are home to everything from the infamous and sometimes offensive *alt* to the fairly staid German language *zer* groupings. In between, you'll find lots of computer- and business-relevant groups, as well as enough other stuff to keep you (or people who work at your place of business) delightfully distracted from work for hours.

All of the above is to warn you that you should very carefully consider the consequences of giving your users access to the newsgroups. One argument in their favor, aside from the truly useful groups that are out there on the Net, is that you can use newsgroups for internal communications, too.

I'll leave it to you to ponder the business and social implications of NNTP. The good news is that, if you want newsgroups, Exchange Server 5 and later makes it about as easy as possible to set them up and make them available.

Once setup is done, your Exchange server acts just like any other NNTP server. Newsgroups from all over the world show up as public folders. Anyone who can get to those public folders by any of the means I've discussed in this and other chapters can get to the newsgroups on your Exchange server. In addition, your Exchange Server–based NNTP server fully supports standard newsreader clients like FreeAgent, WinVN, or the news client that's built into Microsoft's Outlook Express.

By whatever means someone gets to your Exchange NNTP server, if they have the rights to do so, they can post new or reply messages to any newsgroup or they can respond directly to the original sender of a news message by e-mail. Your server will see to it that those messages and postings are available not only locally but, if you want, to users of the newsgroup outside your Exchange site or organization.

If all this isn't enough, your Exchange NNTP server can also feed its newsgroups to other NNTP servers. Couple all of this good stuff with the kind of user-friendly interface you've come to expect from Exchange Server and you've got it all NNTP-wise.

As a protocol, NNTP isn't the most obvious thing you'll ever encounter. There are lots of terms and concepts to master. The best way to get a handle on all this is to jump in and get your hands dirty. So let's get to configuring and using NNTP on an Exchange server.

## What's a USENET Newsfeed?

You'll often read or hear the term "USENET" used in very close conjunction with "news-feed." A newsfeed is the regular transmission of a specific set of newsgroups from one computer to another. USENET is the network of computers that supports client and server Internet newsfeeds. One of your main tasks, should you choose to take your Exchange server into the NNTP world, will be to find a USENET newsfeed provider and subscribe to that provider's service.

# NNTP Setup: The Server Side

Your NNTP server can perform a range of tasks. It can get newsfeeds from other NNTP servers, send its newsfeeds—including new postings from its users—to other servers, and send newsgroup information and messages to NNTP clients. I'll cover the first two of these below. The third happens without any intervention on your part, although, as you'll see, you can limit the folders that differently authenticated NNTP clients can access in your newsgroups.

## The Newsfeed Configuration Wizard

Before you can actually set up a newsfeed, you'll need to make some arrangements with an Internet newsfeed provider. Many Internet Service Providers (ISPs) can supply you with a newsfeed. You should have the following in hand before you start the setup process:

- Your provider's USENET site name (which is an Internet domain name)

- The Internet domain names or IP addresses of your provider's host servers (which might be the same as the USENET site name)

- The username and password your Exchange NNTP server will use to log on to your provider's host computer (not all providers require these)

- Your provider's active file

If all this is new and strange to you, fret not. Your USENET provider will understand just what you need.

You can create as many newsfeeds as you like. To set up your first newsfeed, start from the Exchange Administrator's File menu and select New Other, then select Newsfeed. This brings up the startup page of the Newsfeed Configuration Wizard shown in Figure 18.43.

Click Next to move on to the Wizard's next page, which is shown in Figure 18.44. On this page you specify the Exchange server where the newsfeed will be installed and a *USENET site name*. The installation server must support public folders. The USENET site name is the domain name or, more specifically, the *fully qualified domain name* of the server the newsfeed will be installed on.

**FIGURE 18.43:**

The Newsfeed Configuration Wizard's startup page

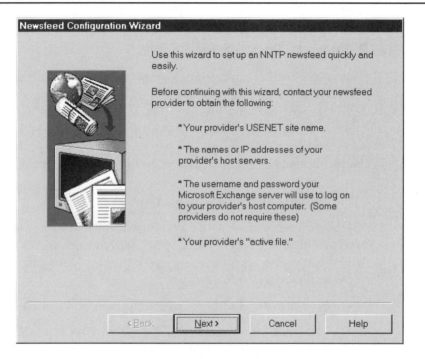

I'm sure you've gotten the hang of Wizards by now. So, I'm going to stop prompting you to click the Next button when you're ready to move on.

On the next Wizard page (see Figure 18.45), you set the type of newsfeed this is to be. Inbound newsfeeds are those where you get news from your USENET provider. Inbound feeds fill up those public folders on your Exchange server. Outbound newsfeeds send new newsgroup messages to other NNTP servers.

**FIGURE 18.44:**

Setting information about the Exchange server where a newsfeed will be installed

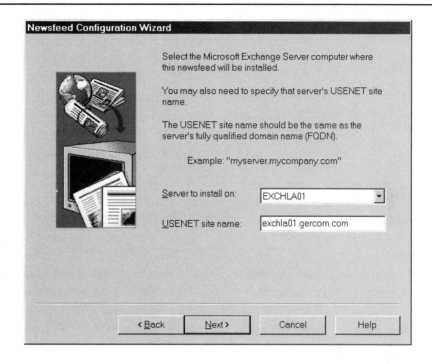

**FIGURE 18.45:**

Setting the type of newsfeed to be supported by an Exchange NNTP server

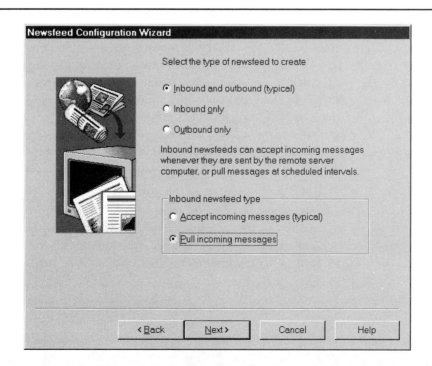

Outbound messages to your USENET provider reflect user postings in your server's copy of each newsgroup. The USENET provider's NNTP server adds these postings to its copy of each newsgroup. As one NNTP server passes its updates on to another, each server's copies of the newsgroups grow to include more and more of the messages posted by users in the wider USENET newsgroup community.

Outbound newsfeeds also let you become a USENET newsfeed provider in your own right. When your NNTP server sends newsgroup messages to non-USENET providers, you become their provider.

**NOTE**    In this section, I'm going to focus on getting a newsfeed from a USENET provider. I'll discuss the technical aspects of becoming a USENET newsfeed provider in a later section.

Generally, you'll want to configure an Inbound and Outbound newsfeed for feeds you get from a USENET newsfeed provider. Inbound-only feeds are fine where you don't want to send user postings back to your USENET provider. We'll talk about outbound feeds later. Outbound-only feeds are best when you don't want to get news messages from a provider but do want to send user postings to the provider.

Inbound newsfeeds can be of two types: push (Accept Incoming Messages in Figure 18.45) or pull (Pull Incoming Messages in Figure 18.45). In a push feed, your USENET provider sends news messages to your NNTP server on its schedule. In a pull feed, you go and get news messages from your provider on your schedule. Push feeds are best where you're after a large number of news messages and where a higher-speed network is in place between your server and your USENET provider. Pull feeds work best when you need to access smaller numbers of news messages over slower networks, especially those of the dial-up persuasion. Pull feeds are also useful when you want to control traffic on your network, because you can specifically schedule when pull feeds happen on your Exchange server.

Though push feeds are the most widely used, I, rebel that I am, like pull feeds. So, in Figure 18.45, I've chosen a pull feed. Depending on which kind of feed you choose, you'll be shown somewhat different options from this point on. I'll let you know when selecting a push feed would have yielded other options.

If you've selected any combination of push/pull and inbound/outbound newsfeed, with the exception of a push type, inbound-only feed, the Wizard next asks how you want to connect to your newsfeed provider (see Figure 18.46). Push type, inbound-only newsfeeds rely on another NNTP server to initiate the link and assume a LAN-based connection between your server and the remote server. So, if you're configuring a push type, inbound-only connection, you won't see this Wizard page.

**FIGURE 18.46:**

Setting the connectivity method for a newsfeed

As you can see in Figure 18.46, I've chosen a LAN-based connection. You can also use a dial-up link.

Before presenting the page in Figure 18.46, the Wizard checks to see if you've set up the Remote Access Service (RAS) and if you have a RAS phone book entry that might supply information for a dial-up. If you don't have any phone book entries, you'll see a rather scary message to that effect. Don't worry; unless you want to use RAS, you can ignore the warning. If you need RAS, you'll have to set it up and enter at least one number in the phone book. See Mark Minasi, et al., *Mastering Windows NT Server 4* (Sybex, 1996) for more on configuring RAS.

As with the previous Wizard page, you'll see the page shown in Figure 18.47 if you're configuring an inbound and outbound, pull type inbound-only, or outbound-only newsfeed. Use the drop-down list to tell your Exchange server how frequently it should connect to your newsfeed provider.

**FIGURE 18.47:**

Setting connection frequency for a newsfeed

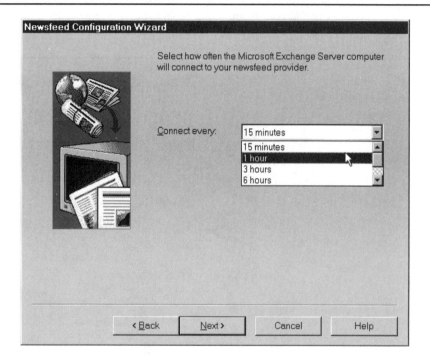

Now we're getting to some of that info I suggested you have close at hand when setting up your newsfeed. The next Wizard page is used to enter the USENET site name your newsfeed provider gave you. In Figure 18.48, I've entered the name of a USENET site Microsoft operated for the use of Exchange 5 pre-release users. My thanks to the good folks on the Exchange development team for giving me access to the site. By the way, this site ran on an Exchange 5 server and it worked very well throughout the period of my tests.

You enter the Internet domain name or IP address of your newsfeed provider's host computer or computers on the next Wizard page (see Figure 18.49). Remember back a bit, how I selected the Pull Incoming Messages option (see Figure 18.45)? I'm only offered an opportunity to enter one host. If you selected the Accept incoming messages option, the bottom of your version of Figure 18.49 will include fields to enter more hosts. For redundancy and better performance, some providers operate more than one outgoing host. If your provider has multiple hosts, you'd use these fields to enter the names of those hosts and to tell your NNTP service that it's okay to receive newsfeeds from them.

**FIGURE 18.48:**

Entering the name of the USENET newsfeed site

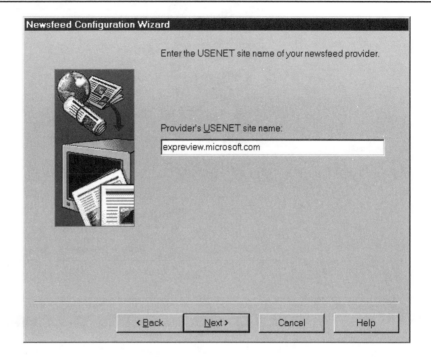

Next you need to enter some security information (see Figure 18.50). Enter any username and password information your USENET newsfeed provider gave you in the top two fields. The username in the Remote Servers Log In As field is actually the name of an Exchange mailbox or custom recipient. NNTP servers connecting to your server to push messages to it or pull messages from it will use this username and password. If it's a mailbox, the password is the password of an NT account linked to the mailbox. Click Change to open the Exchange address list. Then select the appropriate recipient from the list. If your provider requires Secure Sockets Layer security, check the box labeled Require Secure Connection (SSL).

.

**FIGURE 18.49:**

Entering identifying information for a newsfeed host

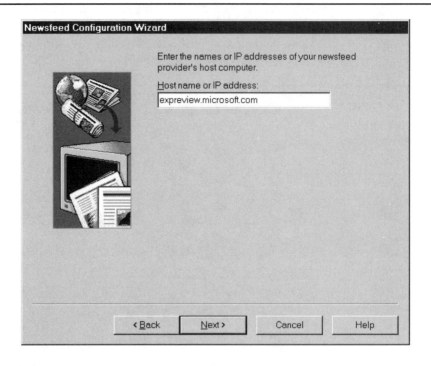

**FIGURE 18.50:**

Setting security information for a newsfeed

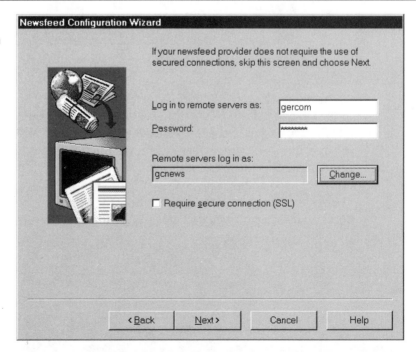

As you can see in Figure 18.51, the Wizard is now ready to install the Exchange Internet News Service. This is a standard NT service that supports newsfeeds. It's installed only once on an Exchange server. Since this is the first time I've installed a newsfeed on this server, the Wizard installs the Internet News Service. Click Next to start installation of the service and your newsfeed. (Woops! I promised I wouldn't tell you to click Next anymore. I just couldn't resist.)

At this point, you'll be asked to enter the password for your site services account. That's the one you created before you installed your first Exchange server.

If this is the first newsfeed on this server, you're next asked to set the mailbox of the Internet news administrator (see Figure 18.52). This mailbox owns all the Internet news public folders. Its user can do such things as modify access rights to newsgroup folders, move folders around, and delete them. To set the Internet news administrator's mailbox, click Change and select the mailbox from the address list that pops up.

**FIGURE 18.51:**

Exchange is ready to install the Internet News Service and a newsfeed.

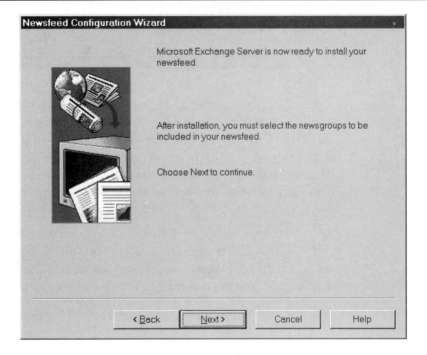

**FIGURE 18.52:**

Setting the Exchange mailbox of the Internet news administrator

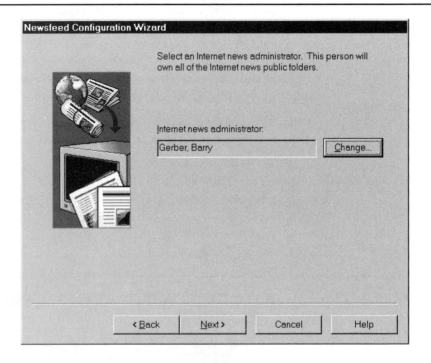

Your NNTP server needs a list of the newsgroups available from your USENET provider. This is called the "active list." You can get a copy of the file from your provider by e-mail or you can download it using the FTP protocol. Alternatively, your Exchange server can download the file for you right now. The next Wizard page, shown in Figure 18.53, is used to select the method you'll use to make the file available to the Exchange NNTP server. As you can see, you can even tell the Wizard you don't have the file right now and go on configuring your newsfeed.

If you chose either of the first two options on the Wizard page shown in Figure 18.53, the next Wizard page you'll see will look something like the one in Figure 18.54. You're shown a tree with the newsgroups that are available to you.

**FIGURE 18.53:**

Specifying how and when an Exchange server can access the active newsgroups file for the USENET newsfeed provider

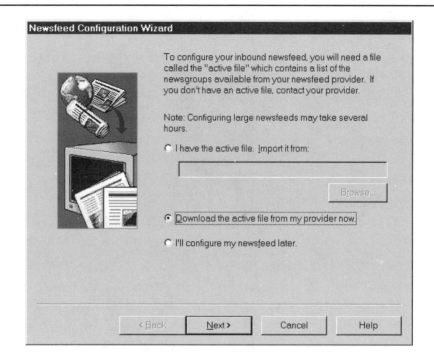

Newsfeed Configuration Wizard

To configure your inbound newsfeed, you will need a file called the "active file" which contains a list of the newsgroups available from your newsfeed provider. If you don't have an active file, contact your provider.

Note: Configuring large newsfeeds may take several hours.

○ I have the active file. Import it from:

[                                        ]

Browse...

◉ Download the active file from my provider now.

○ I'll configure my newsfeed later.

< Back    Next >    Cancel    Help

Click a folder and then click Include to add the folder and its folders and/or newsgroups to the list of newsgroups you want to receive. In Figure 18.54, I clicked the newsfeed itself (expreview.microsoft.com) and then the Include button. As you can see in Figure 18.55, my server will get all of the newsgroups in the feed.

In Figure 18.56, I clicked the newsgroup Migration and then the Exclude button to remove the migration newsgroup from the newsgroups my server will get.

**FIGURE 18.54:**

Preparing to select from a list of newsgroups available from a USENET newsfeed provider

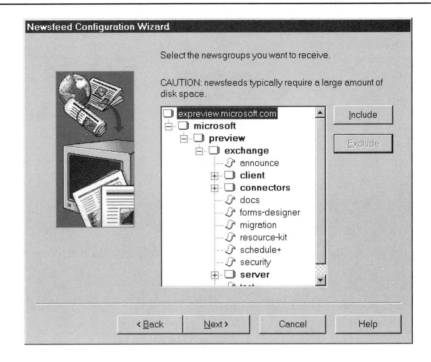

**FIGURE 18.55:**

Selected newsgroups are displayed.

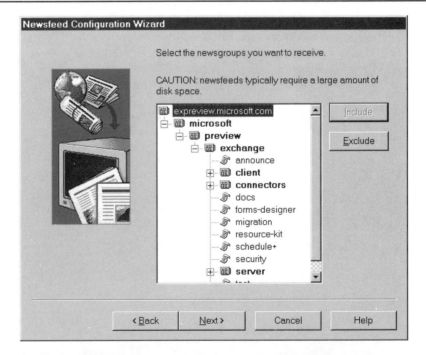

**FIGURE 18.56:**

Deselecting a newsgroup

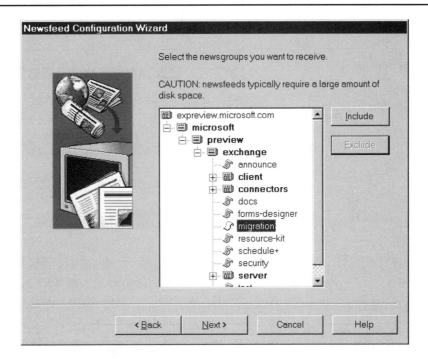

Before we go much further, I've got to talk to you about what I call *newsoverfeed-ing*. With millions of users hitting USENET newsgroups every day, it shouldn't surprise you that your collection of news messages is going to grow very quickly. There are two keys to sanity here. First, carefully select and limit the newsgroups you'll support. Second, use the message aging functionality built into public folders to ensure that messages are deleted from your newsgroup folders frequently. You now know how to select newsgroups from a newsfeed. I talked about public folder message aging back in Chapter 14. Set the public folder aging parameters based on how quickly a folder tends to grow in size. Some USENET news providers delete messages that are a day or two old from fast-filling newsgroups. So, don't feel bad if you have to wield a sharp, close-cutting razor.

When you click Next this time, your Exchange server starts creating the new public folders that will hold your newsgroups. To entertain you while it does its thing, the server shows you the little progress dialog box shown in Figure 18.57. Actually, if you're installing a lot of newsgroups, folder creation can take quite a while. You'll welcome that little dialog box, if nothing else than as an indicator that your Exchange server hasn't crashed.

**FIGURE 18.57:**

A dialog box showing an Exchange server's progress in creating new public folders to hold newsgroups

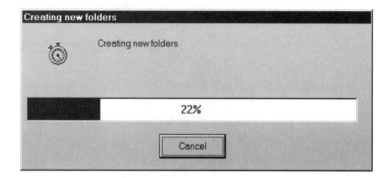

The Wizard page shown in Figure 18.58 tells you that you're finished at last. I won't bore you by repeating the important messages that are displayed on this final Wizard page. I'll just warn you to pay close attention to all the messages.

**FIGURE 18.58:**

A new newsfeed has been installed.

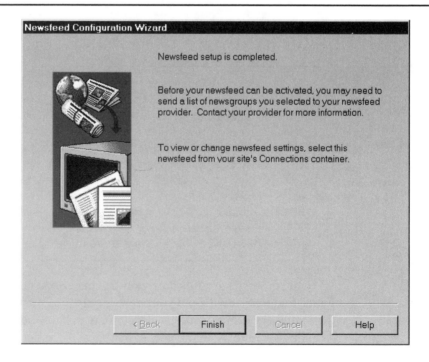

I can be pretty impatient at times. So, immediately after I clicked Finish on the Wizard, I fired up my Outlook client to see what my public folders looked like. Sure enough, there were all those newsgroup folders sitting in the Internet Newsgroups folder (see Figure 18.59).

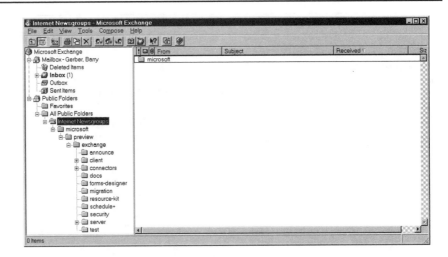

Imagine my disappointment when I found the folders themselves empty. They were empty, of course, because the time hadn't yet come for my first pull of newsgroup messages from my USENET provider. As you'll see later in this chapter, after an appropriate interval, my newsgroup folders did, indeed, fill with all the goodies from Microsoft's Exchange 5 preview newsfeed.

> **NOTE**  While you're thinking about those newsgroup public folders, don't forget about public folder replication. Because they're nothing more than public folders, you can wholly or selectively replicate newsgroups across your Exchange organization. Just keep in mind the traffic that can be generated during such replication. If network bandwidth is limited between those of your Exchange servers that need to support newsfeeds, it might make more sense to subscribe to separate newsfeeds for each server.

Before we move on, take a look in the Connections container for the site where you installed the newsfeed. There's now an object for the feed in that container. I'll talk about that object in just a bit.

## Administering and Managing the Exchange NNTP Service at the Site Level

Find the NNTP object in the site Protocols container and double-click it. This brings up the NNTP (News) Site Defaults Properties dialog box shown in Figure 18.60.

**FIGURE 18.60:**

The General property page of the NNTP (News) Site Defaults Properties dialog box

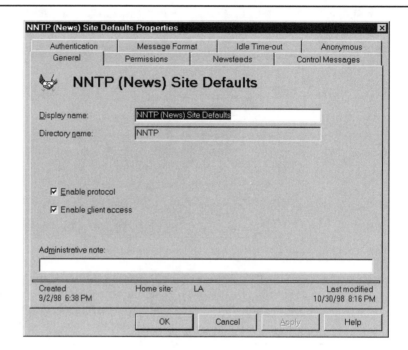

**General Properties**   You should be quite familiar with the General property page. It looks pretty much like the General pages for the three other advanced Internet protocols we've discussed in this chapter. You can disable and enable the NNTP protocol and client access for the site on this page. If client access is disabled, NNTP clients can't access the newsgroups on your Exchange server.

**Newsfeeds**   Tab over to the Newsfeeds property page. There's a lot behind that little newsfeed object in the list in Figure 18.61. Double-click it to bring up a whole new dialog box for administering and managing this particular newsfeed (see Figure 18.62). This is the same dialog box you'd get if you double-clicked the object for the newsfeed in the Connections container for the site where you installed the newsfeed.

**FIGURE 18.61:**

Preparing to open a newsfeed for administration and management

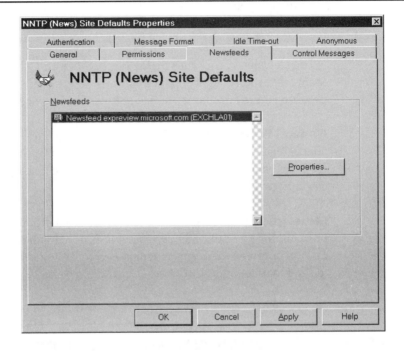

**FIGURE 18.62:**

The General property page of the Newsfeed Properties dialog box

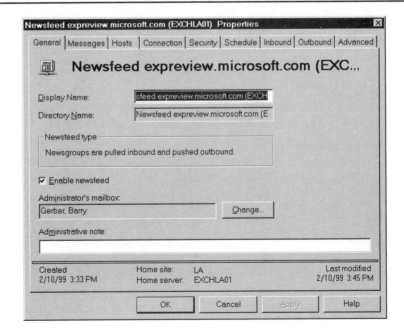

Until I tell you otherwise, we'll be looking at the property pages on the Newsfeed Properties dialog box shown in Figure 18.62. When we've finished with these, we'll return to the NNTP (News) Site Defaults dialog box in Figure 18.61.

The Newsfeed Properties dialog box is chock-full of property pages. Many of them are carbon copies of pages you saw on the Newsfeed Configuration Wizard. Because you're familiar with those pages I'll cover only the ones that are new.

**General Properties**   As Figure 18.62 shows, among other things, you can disable or enable the newsfeed and change the administrator's mailbox for the newsfeed. By default, this is the mailbox you set as the Internet news administrator. You can change it here for this newsfeed.

**Message Size Limits**   You use the Messages property page to set size limits on incoming and outgoing messages. Figure 18.63 shows the defaults. The 1MB max on outgoing messages is considered a fair limit on what users should be able to send to other newsgroups.

**FIGURE 18.63:**

Setting incoming and outgoing newsfeed message size limits

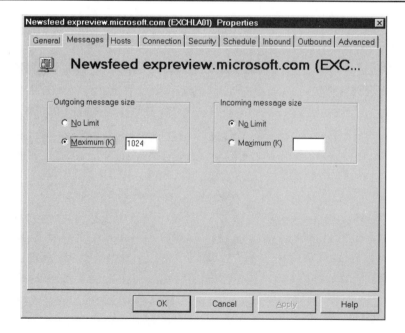

You can leave these settings as they are, unless you have a good reason for changing them. If you're worried about the disk space taken up by messages, it's better to limit the number of newsgroups you support, and/or use short public folder message aging settings, than it is to too narrowly limit message size. Small size limits could exclude messages that are key to understanding the conversational thread of a specific newsgroup.

**Hosts, Connection, and Security**    The Hosts, Connection, and Security property pages on the Newsfeed Properties dialog box contain pages you saw back on the Newsfeed Configuration Wizard. Check out the following figures and related text for details on these pages:

- Host: Figures 18.48 and 18.49

- Connection: Figure 18.46

- Security: Figure 18.50

**The Connection Schedule**    You use the Schedule property page on the Newsfeed Properties dialog box shown in Figure 18.64 to set how frequently your NNTP server will connect to your USENET provider in order to send and receive new messages. This schedule applies to outbound and inbound, pull type inbound-only, and outbound-only newsfeeds. Pick the schedule that works for your site's network traffic and your users' needs.

**Inbound Settings**    Here's another property page with contents you've seen before. Take a look at Figures 18.53 through 18.56 and the accompanying text for more information.

**Outbound Settings**    If your newsfeed is of the inbound and outbound or outbound-only variety, you can use the Outbound property page to specify the newsgroups for which you'll send postings by your users back to your USENET provider (see Figure 18.65). You'll remember that this is the way your users' postings get integrated into the image of the newsgroup beyond your Exchange environment.

**FIGURE 18.64:**

Setting a connection schedule for inbound and outbound, pull type inbound-only, and outbound-only newsfeeds

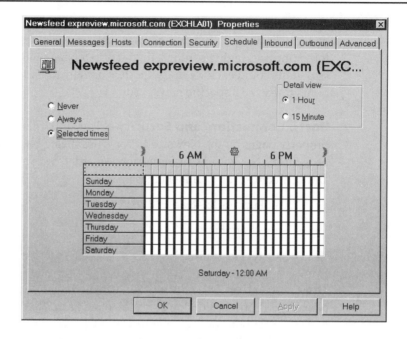

**FIGURE 18.65:**

Selecting the newsgroups to be included in outbound communications with a USENET provider

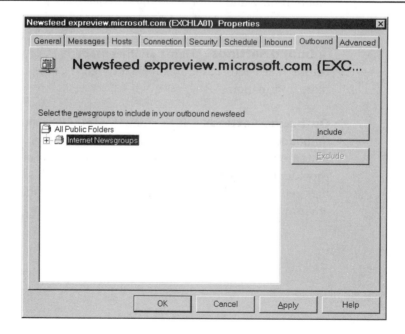

**Advanced Properties**   Your Exchange server can fall behind in processing messages from your USENET provider, whether your newsfeed is push or pull. This usually happens when a newsfeed includes a large number of messages. The server puts messages into a queue and then processes them in the order received. As the messages in a queue pile up, it takes longer and longer for the most current messages to find their way into the appropriate newsgroup.

To help speed things up, you can delete all unprocessed messages from their queue. The messages are lost, but, newsgroups being what they are, this is generally not considered a big deal. After all, you don't carefully preserve each daily edition of your newspaper as though it were a fine Moroccan leather–bound first edition of a literary classic.

You use the Advanced property page on the Newsfeed Properties dialog box to flush unprocessed newsgroup messages from their queues. To do this, click Mark All As Delivered (see Figure 18.66). This deletes all the messages in the queue and allows your server to catch up on its newsgroup message processing functions.

If you're getting a push newsfeed, all will be just fine after the flush. Each time your USENET provider connects to you, it sends only messages your server has not yet received. So, you'll get only messages that weren't sent to you before, not new messages plus a bunch of messages that you already deleted from the queue. If you're using a pull feed, when you flush the queue, the server resets the time base that is used to determine which messages your server needs from the USENET provider. The time base is set to the time when the queue was flushed. This assures that messages retrieved from your provider are no older than the time when the queue was flushed.

**FIGURE 18.66:**

Clicking Mark All As Delivered deletes all unprocessed newsgroup messages in this newsfeed.

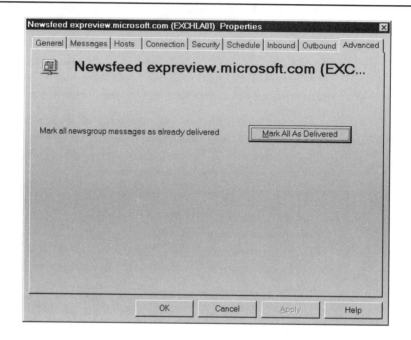

**Control Messages** Okay, we're done with the Newsfeed Properties dialog box and ready to return to the NNTP (News) Site Defaults Properties dialog box. Figure 18.67 shows the Control Messages property page.

NNTP control messages are generated for new and deleted newsgroups and when someone makes a request to delete a single message from a newsgroup. You have to process control messages for new and deleted newsgroups. If you trust the newsfeed providing the new newsgroup, accept the group by highlighting its control message and clicking the Accept button. If not, highlight the message and click Delete.

Your Exchange server processes requests to delete an individual message automatically if the person requesting the deletion is in your Exchange organization's global address list and the message originated from the organization. For other single item deletion requests, you get to accept or delete the control message.

**FIGURE 18.67:**

Use the Control Message property page of the NNTP (News) Site Defaults dialog box to accept or reject messages about certain changes in a newsfeed.

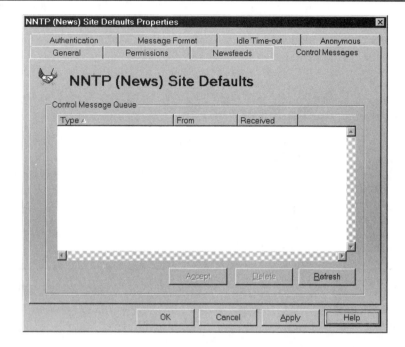

### Authentication, Message Format, Idle Time-Out, and Anonymous

You shouldn't have any trouble using the last four property pages on the NNTP (News) Site Defaults dialog box.

The Authentication page offers the usual three options for verifying account name and password: Basic (Clear Text) (with and without SSL), Windows NT Challenge/Response (with and without SSL), and MCIS Membership (with and without SSL).

Use the Message Format page to choose between the MIME or uuencode message encoding standards and to send message bodies in plain text and/or HTML format. As you'll remember, the HTML format preserves text formatting such as type of font, bold, italic, and color.

You can set a time after which idle NNTP client connections are closed on the Idle Time-out page.

If you wish, you can enable anonymous access to your NNTP server on the Anonymous page. If anonymous access is enabled, anyone who knows the Internet domain name or IP address of your NNTP server can connect to it and participate in newsgroups that are available to anonymous users. By default, anonymous users are given Nonediting Author access to newsgroup folders. In just a bit, I'll tell you how to change that.

## Administering and Managing the Exchange NNTP Service at the Server Level

To open the server-level object for administering and managing NNTP, double-click the NNTP object in the Protocols container on the server of your choice. As you can see in Figure 18.68, your NNTP server-level options are pretty much what they are at the site level, except for the absence of the Control Messages property page and the presence of the Diagnostics Logging page. Control messages are dealt with at the site level only, and diagnostic logging only makes sense at the server level.

**FIGURE 18.68:**

Use the server-level NNTP (News) Settings Properties dialog box to administer and manage newsfeeds on a server.

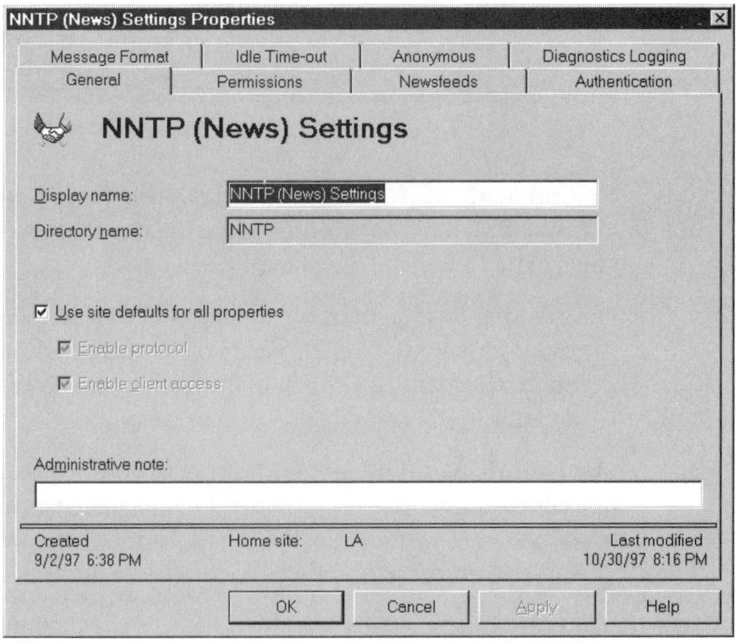

Aside from the fact that you'll only be able to work with newsfeeds on the specific server, you should have no problem using any of the property pages on the server-level NNTP (News) Settings Properties dialog box. Check the last section if you need a refresher on any of the property pages.

### Administering and Managing the Exchange NNTP Service at the Mailbox Level

As with other advanced Internet protocols I've discussed here, at the individual mailbox level you can disable or enable the NNTP protocol and set alternate message encoding options (see Figure 18.69).

**FIGURE 18.69:**

Setting NNTP protocol options for an individual mailbox

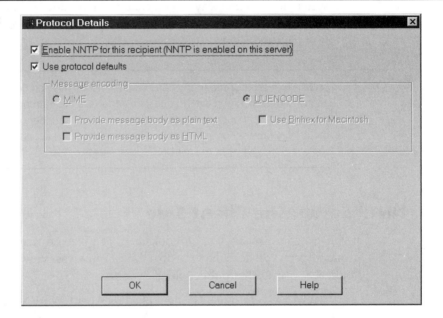

## Managing Newsgroups

You will need to manage newsgroups in your Outlook client. You must be an owner of the newsgroup folder or folders you wish to manage. Here's a quick list of key newsgroup management how-to's:

- Create new newsgroups by adding a new folder wherever you wish in the Internet Newsgroups hierarchy.

- Turn an existing private or public folder into a newsgroup by dragging it into the Internet Newsgroups hierarchy.

- Remove an existing newsgroup by deleting it from the Internet Newsgroups hierarchy.

- Change anonymous user access to a newsgroup by opening the properties dialog box for the newsgroup folder, tabbing over to the Permissions property page, and setting the role assigned to Anonymous users. This role can range from Owner (not a good idea) to None, which locks anonymous users out of a newsgroup.

- Change newsgroup access for users authenticated through the NT security system in the same way as you change anonymous user access—which, for the record, is the same way you change public folder access for any Exchange recipient.

---

**WARNING**     Be sure that settings for anonymous Web browser (HTTP) public folder access and anonymous newsgroup (NNTP) public folder access are harmonious. For example, you don't want to include a public folder in the list of folders available to anonymous Web browser users and then disable anonymous access to it, because, for some reason, you want to limit NNTP client access.

---

## NNTP Setup: The Client Side

If you use your Exchange or Outlook client or a Web browser to access newsgroup folders, you don't have to do a thing. You access newsgroup folders just as you'd access any other public folder.

If you use a standard NNTP client like FreeAgent, WinVN, or Outlook Express, you'll have to do a bit of configuring. You'll need to enter the Internet domain name or IP address of the Exchange server that supports your NNTP server. You'll also have to enter appropriate security information, if you've disabled anonymous access or if non-anonymous users have access to newsgroups not available to anonymous users.

Each NNTP client has its own unique user interface. All of these are pretty straightforward. So I'll leave it to you to figure out how to set up and use your favorite client. After configuring POP3, IMAP4, and LDAP clients, you should have no trouble setting up a news account in Outlook Express.

### Did It Work?

You can test your newsfeed in lots of ways. First, check it out through your Outlook client. After allowing sufficient time for newsgroup messages to populate your newsgroup folders, take a look at a couple of newsgroups. In Figure 18.70, I'm using a standard Outlook client to look at messages in the Microsoft Exchange preview newsgroup *nntp*. Open some messages and then take a shot at accessing your newsgroups with a Web browser through Outlook Web Access.

If all this works and your newsfeed supports outbound communications with your USENET provider, try posting a new message to a newsgroup. Be sure to label the message as a test message. After a reasonable waiting period, you should be able to see your message in the newsgroup when you connect to another NNTP server outside your Exchange organization, for example, to your Internet Service Provider's NNTP server.

**FIGURE 18.70:**

Viewing an Exchange server–based newsgroup with an Outlook client

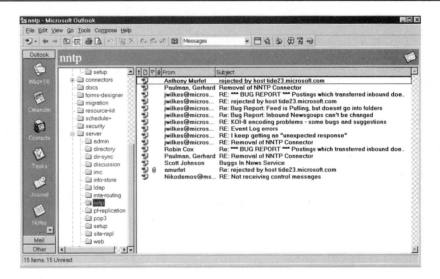

Finally, connect to your NNTP server with a standard NNTP client. In Figure 18.71, I'm using the WinVN NNTP client to access the nntp newsgroup on my Exchange server.

I've been working with NNTP Exchange style for some time now and haven't experienced any difficulties. If you have problems getting NNTP services to work, make sure everything is properly configured, including your TCP/IP setup, the information you've entered about your USENET newsfeed provider, and the permissions you've set on your newsgroup public folders. If none of this helps, check the Exchange documentation for troubleshooting tips.

**FIGURE 18.71:**

Viewing an Exchange server–based newsgroup and a message in the newsgroup using a standard NNTP client (WinVN)

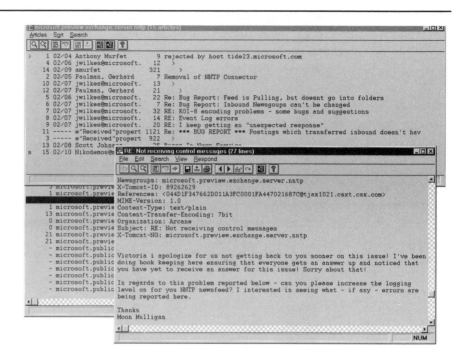

## Becoming a USENET Newsfeed Provider

By now you should be an expert at configuring, managing, and administering a newsfeed to receive newsgroup messages from a USENET provider. With the knowledge you already have, you'll find it very easy to set up a newsfeed that provides newsgroup messages to other NNTP servers. Basically, you have to think of everything you've just been through from the perspective of a USENET provider.

From a provider's perspective, a push newsfeed is an outbound feed. You need to connect to the NNTP server to transfer new messages to it. To do this you need basic NNTP access information about the recipient NNTP server: its USENET site and host names or IP addresses and, if one has been set, the username and password required to connect for NNTP client-server transactions. The person who is setting up a push feed on the recipient NNTP server needs the basic NNTP access information for your NNTP server.

To set up a pull newsfeed, the person at the recipient NNTP server needs the basic NNTP access information for your server. In a pull feed, the recipient NNTP server uses NNTP client technology to get newsgroup messages. So you don't have to do anything other than provide that basic NNTP access information.

---

**WARNING**    If you get into the newsfeed provider "business," be sure you protect the folders that shouldn't be seen outside your organization. Use the Outbound property page on the Newsfeed Properties dialog box (see Figure 18.65) to exclude those sensitive folders from your feed to the recipient NNTP server.

---

That's all I need to say about the technical aspect of becoming a USENET news-feed provider. Do remember to consider the kinds of loads that too many heavy-duty outbound feeds can put on your Exchange server. If you expect to get into this stuff big time, you should consider dedicating a pretty hefty chunk of computer to newsfeed provision.

# Configuring Protocols Containers

To wrap up this chapter, I'll talk briefly about site- and server-level Protocols containers configuration. The parameters you set for these containers apply to all the protocols in the container: HTTP, LDAP, NNTP, IMAP4, and POP3.

As you can see in Figure 18.72, which shows the site-level Protocols Property dialog box, there are three configuration options we haven't discussed, one item on the General property page and the Connections and MIME Types property pages. Enter the name of the Outlook Web Access server for the site on the General property page. This field is used to enable POP3 and IMAP4 clients to discover the name of their Outlook Web Access server so they can access it for calendaring and scheduling functions. Use the Connections property page to set the IP addresses your server will accept or reject connections from (see Figure 18.72). Use the MIME Types page (see Figure 18.73) to define how your Exchange server will map MIME content types to file extensions on inbound messages and vice versa on outbound messages. Most typical mappings are defaulted for you.

Setting the IP address of a server from which connections will not be accepted

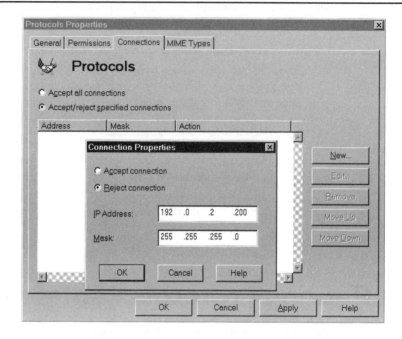

**FIGURE 18.73:**

Use the MIME Types property page to map MIME content types to file extensions.

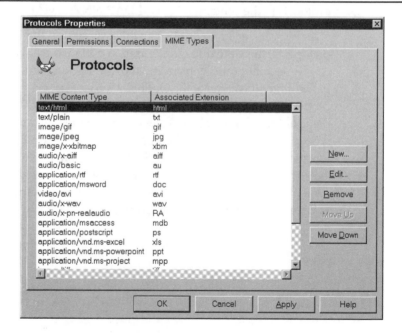

The server-level Protocol configuration dialog box is exactly the same as the site-level box, except that it lets you choose to use or not use site-level settings. Nothing more need be said.

## Protocol Policies

All the protocols I've discussed here can leave your organization's e-messaging system open to malicious intrusions. These intrusions can come from inside or outside your organization. For example, if you don't limit the data that an anonymous LDAP client user can access in your Exchange directory, competitors or headhunters could use the LDAP protocol to build a list of names and contact information to be used in recruiting away some of your organization's most valuable employees.

Protect your organization and yourself by encouraging the development of policies regarding these protocols. The source of this policy might be your organization's Human Resources department, a special committee, or executive management. Some issues that need attention include:

- Which of the protocols will we support?
- What kind of security do we want for authenticated users of the supported protocols?
- If we support them, will we allow anonymous access through the LDAP, HTTP, and NTTP protocols?
- What kinds of users will be allowed to use the different client options we choose?

# Conclusion

In this chapter you learned how to configure Exchange Server support for five advanced Internet protocols: the Post Office Protocol version 3 (POP3), the Internet Message Access Protocol (IMAP4), the Hypertext Transfer Protocol (HTTP), the Lightweight Directory Access Protocol (LDAP), and the Network News Transfer Protocol (NNTP). You also learned a bit about supporting clients for each of these protocols.

Now for something completely different. In the next and final chapter of this book, we'll take a look at the Exchange Outlook Forms Designer and how you can use it to develop forms for use in customized applications.

# CHAPTER

## NINETEEN

# Developing Forms with Outlook Forms Designer

- The Outlook application design environment

- Building an Outlook electronic form

- Publishing an Outlook electronic form for others to use

- Using a form

**N**obody likes filling in forms, right? Well, the answer probably seems obvious—until you consider the alternative: a blank piece of paper. Imagine doing your taxes without all those wonderful IRS and state forms. Imagine trying to process tax reports formatted every which way but clearly. Done right, forms—especially electronic forms—make it easier for users to get through complex or repetitive data-entry tasks with minimal pain. In addition, these forms help their creators collect data in a uniform manner and process it easily.

There are two major ways to create electronic forms for your Exchange Server environment: Microsoft Exchange Forms Designer (EFD) and Microsoft Outlook Forms Designer (OFD). EFD forms can be used with any Exchange or Outlook client for Exchange Server 4, 5, or 5.5. OFD forms can only be used with 32-bit Outlook clients. The 16-bit Windows 3.x Outlook client is really the old Exchange client in disguise, so you can only use EFD forms with it. So, your choice of forms design environments depends on the mix of Exchange Server clients in your organization.

EFD comes with Exchange Server. OFD is built into the 32-bit Outlook clients designed for Exchange Server. The two products offer very similar visual forms design environments. EFD forms are compatible with Microsoft Visual Basic. If you're familiar with VB, you'll find the EFD development environment familiar. OFD lets you use Microsoft Office's Visual Basic Scripting Edition, as well as ActiveX and OLE controls. So, Visual Basic skills are not wasted with OFD.

Overall, I find OFD a bit easier to use. Beware however, for you can't build very interesting applications without some form of programming whether in Visual Basic (EFD) or Visual Basic Scripting Edition (OFD).

Once you start working with EFD and OFD, you'll find yourself waking up at night with fantastic ideas for forms. Here are some examples:

**Request forms**    Used to ask for something:

> Purchase orders
>
> Computer program modifications
>
> Computer hardware maintenance
>
> Travel requests
>
> Vacation or sick-day requests

**Data collection forms**   Used to gather information:

> Input data for line-of-business applications such as patient management or product/services purchasing
>
> Employee feedback on health insurance plans
>
> User feedback on products or services
>
> Employee participation in company picnics

**Report forms**   Used to provide required information:

> Employee status reports to supervisors
>
> Employee travel and mileage reports
>
> Department head reports on success in staying within budget allocations

**Other forms**   Used for a variety of purposes:

> Standardized communications forms (for example, telephone notes, while-you-were-out memos)
>
> Forms for playing multiuser tic-tac-toe, chess, and other games

Your form making should be informed by a clear understanding of the process you're automating and the people involved in that process. If this is the case, you'll be a winner, reducing paper shuffling and increasing the productivity and satisfaction of everyone involved. On the other hand, if you don't study processes and people carefully, you'll frustrate your bosses and users alike to the point that your forms will hinder rather than help the workflow you're trying to automate.

# The Outlook/Exchange Application Design Environment

As I indicated way back in the first chapter of this book, EFD and OFD aren't the only way to design applications. The Exchange application design environment includes the following:

- Forms design tools
  - Exchange Forms Designer, used to make your own forms
  - Outlook Form Designer, used to make your own forms

- Folder design tools

  - The Exchange or Outlook client, used to create, organize, and set actions to take place within folders

- OLE-2–based applications

  - A word-processing document, a spreadsheet, or another element from an OLE-2–capable application such as Microsoft Word or Excel is pasted or inserted as an object into an Exchange message; the message becomes the application.

- Exchange Application Programming Interfaces (APIs)

  - APIs are used to develop custom-coded applications using Visual Basic, C++, J++, or any other compatible programming language.

Creating OLE-2 apps is just a matter of pasting or inserting the appropriate application object into an Exchange message. You don't need my help with that. To do justice to API-based application design, I'd need to write another book at least the size of this one. That's why I'm focusing this chapter on form design—and even then, as you'll see, we'll only be able to touch the surface of this fascinating topic.

I'll focus here on OFD. OFD and EFD are quite similar in a number of ways. If you need to use EFD, check out my *Mastering Exchange Server 5.5, Third Edition* (Sybex, 1998) for a detailed discussion of EFD.

Though OFD is fairly easy to use, it is a full-featured application, and I can't possibly teach you everything you need to know about using it. My goal here is to show you how easy forms design can be and get you started doing a simple form with OFD. For more details, you'll need to look at the OFD documentation and, if you want to get into serious programming, a good book on Visual Basic. In addition, take a look at *Mastering Microsoft Outlook 2000* by Gini Courter and Annette Marquis (Sybex, 1999) and Thomas Rizzo's *Programming Microsoft Outlook and Microsoft Exchange* (Microsoft Press, 1999). Both books provide an excellent grounding in OFD and Visual Basic.

# Installing Outlook Forms Designer

OFD is part of the Outlook 98 and 2000 client. The Outlook Visual Basic help files and Microsoft Script Debugger are part of the Outlook Development Tools package. Install these when you install Outlook on your computer or add them with the Add/Remove (*Microsoft Outlook 98* or *Microsoft Outlook 2000*) option on the Control Panel.

We'll start with a firm grounding in OFD basics. Then we'll actually build a form. Don't run too far ahead or you just might build a form that doesn't work very well, if at all.

# Outlook Forms Designer Basics

Begin by opening the OFD environment. In your Outlook client, from the Tools menu select Forms ➢ Design a Form. The Design Form dialog box opens (see Figure 19.1). As this figure shows, I've clicked the Details button to show information about each form type at the bottom of the dialog box.

As you can see in Figure 19.1, you can create a form using a variety of Outlook message types from appointments to tasks. You use the drop-down menu at the top of the form to select the container or location from which to choose forms. The Design Form dialog box opens with the Standard Forms Library selected. Forms can be stored in a personal forms library unique to each user, in any Outlook private or public folder, as well as in other special storage locations. Take a look at the drop-down menu for all the options.

## Outlook Message Forms

We're going to design a message form. So, double-click Message in the Standard Forms Library on the Design Form dialog box. This opens the Form Designer environment as shown in Figure 19.2. For all intents and purposes, the Form Designer environment is nothing more than an Outlook object, in this case a message. You can work on it; save it to disk, and come back and work on it some more at any time.

**FIGURE 19.1:**

The Outlook Forms
Designer Design Form
dialog box

Before we actually start developing a form, let's take a quick tour of the Outlook Forms Designer environment. Keep your eyes on Figure 19.2.

Notice the tabs on the form. They're labeled Message, (P.2) through (P.6), (All Fields), (Properties), and (Actions). These delineate specific property pages on the form. When a form's tab label is in parentheses, the property page is hidden when the end user opens the form. Generally, you'd hide unused property pages and pages where you don't want users to know what's going on. For example, if you don't want an end user to know where a reply to a form is being sent or to be able to change the subject of the reply, you'd hide the property page with the To and Subject fields on it.

**FIGURE 19.2:**

The Outlook Forms Designer environment editing a compose page

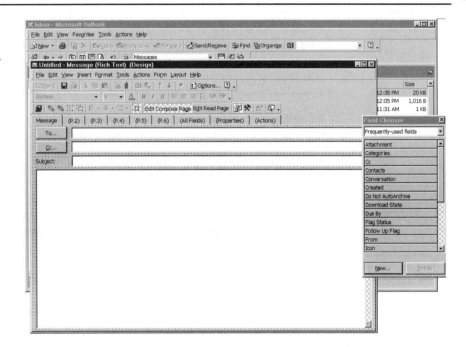

Messages have two basic kinds of pages: compose pages and read pages. Note the two buttons just above the property page tabs labeled Edit Compose Page and Edit Read Page. You use compose pages to create new Outlook items (messages, for example). You use read pages to view composed items that have been processed by Outlook and/or Exchange Server. Outlook e-mail messages offer a good example of these two types of pages. When you click the New message button in Outlook, a compose form opens. You enter addressing information, a subject line, and a message using the compose form. After you send the message, you can view it with a read form by double-clicking it in your Sent Items folder.

Any customizable page on a form can have compose and read pages. This option is enabled by default on the Message page. You must enable the option on all other pages by selecting Form ➤ Separate Read Layout when on the page. You can also use Form ➤ Separate Read Layout to disable the compose/read page option on the Message page. When a message form page has no separate read page, users see data in the same format whether composing or reading a message. If a field is editable, it can be edited whether the message is being read or composed.

**WARNING**    Create message pages without read pages with care. You could be courting disaster if you let readers edit the content of messages they receive. Be sure that recipients of filled-in forms without read pages are trustworthy and have no reason to alter the data in messages.

By default, you start out editing the compose page of the Message page (see Figure 19.2). Click Edit Read Page to see what a read page looks like (see Figure 19.3). Default read pages have From, To, and Cc fields that are read-only. Users can't enter data into these fields. The Subject and Message fields on a read page are editable.

**FIGURE 19.3:**

The Outlook Forms Designer environment editing a read page

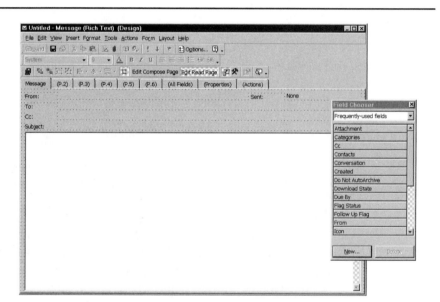

## The Field Chooser and Control Toolbox

You'll use two key dialog boxes when you design forms, the Field Chooser and the Control Toolbox. The Field Chooser is visible in Figure 19.2 and 19.3. You can drag and drop any Exchange Server field, including fields you design yourself, from the Chooser to your form. For example, if you wanted to include the size of your message on your form, you'd drag a message size field onto the form. You use the drop-down menu at the top of the Chooser to select the kinds of fields to be displayed. By default, you see the most frequently used fields. Among others, you can also see only address fields, only date/time fields, only the fields you created, or only the fields in other forms. Open the drop-down to see all your options.

We're done with the Field Chooser for now, so click the Field Chooser button to close the Chooser. Then click the Control Toolbox button to open the toolbox. See Figure 19.4 for the location of these buttons.

Figure 19.5 shows the Control Toolbox. With the exception of the button with an arrow on it, each of the buttons in the toolbox creates a different control for your form. You drag and drop controls onto your form.

Controls define data input and viewing fields or provide additional means for managing activity on the form. Figure 19.5 includes the names of each of the controls.

**FIGURE 19.4:**

The Outlook Forms Designer ready for action

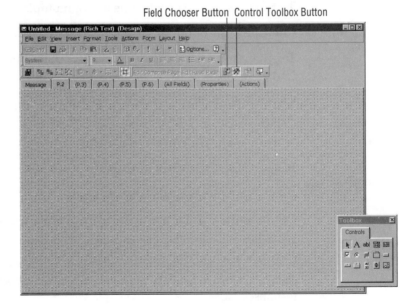

Field Chooser Button  Control Toolbox Button

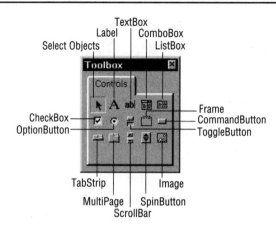

Figure 19.6 shows the key OFD controls as they appear in a real Outlook message. Here's what each is for:

**TextBox**   Is a place to enter one line or multiple lines of text

**CheckBox**   Is for options that can be toggled on or off

**ToggleButton**   Is similar to CheckBox, but the button is either pushed in (on) or not (off)

**ComboBox**   Lets you create a drop-down or droplist box where users can type responses or select from a choice of optional responses

**Frame**   Frames or groups other fields

**Image**   Displays a graphic image

**Label**   Provides text labels where needed

**OptionButton**   Is for multiple-choice options; users cannot select multiple option buttons on the same frame field

**ListBox**   Lets you create a drop-down or standard list box where users can select from a choice of optional responses but not type in their own responses

**TabStrip**   Is a multi-page control where you add additional controls; the controls on each page are the same

**MultiPage**   Is a multi-page control where you add additional controls; each page is a separate form with its own unique controls

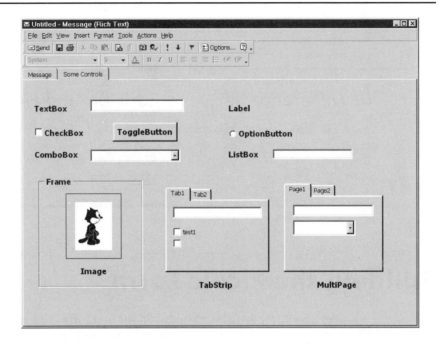

Other controls such as the CommandButton, ScrollBar, and SpinButton are
used to manage activities on the form. For example, to build a data input field
where the user can move through a set of numbers and select a specific number,
you'd use a SpinButton. We'll work with a SpinButton later in this chapter.

## Form and Control Properties

Forms and controls have properties. To look at the properties of a form or a control you have dragged onto your form, right-click anywhere on the form (the gray
dotted area of a form) and select Properties or Advanced Properties.

Take a look at the Properties and Advanced Properties of the To control on the
Message page of your form. You can change the properties of a To control to make
it read only or read/write. To do so, open the control's Advanced Properties dialog box as indicated above. Then find the Read Only property in the Properties
dialog box and click it to change the property from True to False, or vice versa. If a
control doesn't have a read only property, it is a fixed read/write control. The Subject control is a fixed read/write control.

By the way, the colors of a control have nothing to do with whether it is editable. Control colors are simply properties of the control. You change them like any other property.

## The Difference between Controls and Fields

What's the difference between controls and fields? You use most OFD controls to build fields for entering and viewing data. You can refer to a specific control on a form as a *field* when it has been bound to a data field in an Exchange Server database. Until then, it's only a control. We'll talk more about data binding in a bit.

# Building the Picnic Form

Okay, we're ready to begin building our first form. This form is to collect information from GerCom employees about an upcoming picnic, so we'll call it the *Picnic Form*. Be sure that the OFD environment is open and ready for you to create a message form. If you've closed the environment, refer back to the beginning of this chapter for details on opening it.

Among other things, you can customize the To and Subject fields for your message on the Message page. We're not ready for that yet. We need to start on one of the blank form building pages. So, tab over to page two (P.2) on your form.

## Working with Properties

First, let's change the form's background color. Right-click your form and select Advanced Properties from the pop-up menu. This opens the Advanced Properties dialog box for the form page (see Figure 19.7). You can use this dialog box to set all kinds of attributes for the window itself; I'll leave it to you to explore all of its great features. To change the background color, double-click the first item in the Properties dialog box, BackColor. Use the Color dialog box to select a new background color for your form page. In Figure 19.7, I'm choosing white as the background color for my page.

# Adding Controls

Now we're ready to add controls. As we move along, I'll show you how to do lots of neat stuff. Virtually everything you learn when adding one type of control can be used when you create other types. I'll tell you how to do a particular task as we set up a particular control; after that, I'll assume you know how and when to use what you've already learned in creating other controls. As we go along, refer back to Figure 19.5 if you need to look for the location of buttons on OFD's Control Toolbar.

**FIGURE 19.7:**

Changing a form's background color

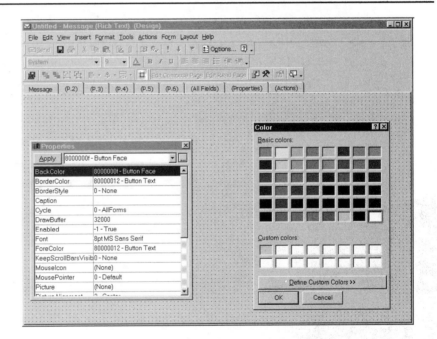

Let's start by adding a label that will serve as the title of our form. Click the label button on the Control Toolbox with your left mouse button. The label button is the one with the large capital letter *A* on it. Continuing to hold down your left mouse button, drag your mouse pointer over to the general location where you want the label to appear—I'm putting mine at the top of the message. Let go of the left mouse button. This brings up a little rectangular box with the word Label1 inside.

Click inside the box until it's surrounded by a dark rectangle with eight small white boxes and one large gray rectangle around it. You use the small boxes to change the size of the label control. Just put the pointer on one of the small white boxes, hold down the left mouse button, and drag the box to make the control larger or smaller. Resize your label control until it's about the size of the one in Figure 19.8.

To move your label control, put your mouse cursor anywhere on the control, hold down the left mouse button, and drag the control to the desired location on the form. By default, controls are snapped to a grid when they are moved. If you'd rather have very fine-grained control over where your control is placed, select Snap to Grid from the form's Layout menu. This toggles Snap to Grid off. Select Snap to Grid again to turn it on. Fine-grained control is great in some circumstances, but it can be a pain when you want to line up your controls in an aesthetically pleasing manner. You can use the Align options on the Layout menu to help tame unruly non–Snap to Grid controls.

Those little dots on your form show the grid that things are being snapped to. If they bother you, select Layout ➤ Show Grid to toggle grid visibility off.

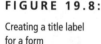

**FIGURE 19.8:**

Creating a title label for a form

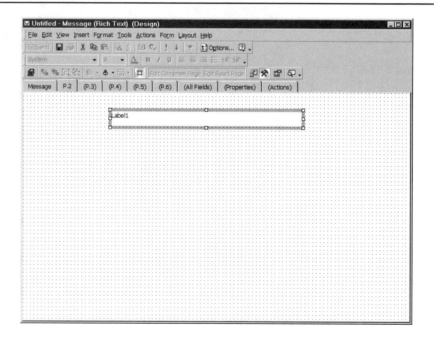

Next, right-click the label field and select Properties from the pop-up menu (see Figure 19.9). Type the text for your label into the Caption field on the Properties dialog box. My label is "The GerCom Picnic Is Coming Soon." Next, change the font size to 10 and make the text bold. Then click OK. If the field is too small for the text you've added, resize it and drag the label field around the form until it's attractively placed (see Figure 19.10). To make the rectangular box with the little resizing boxes disappear, simply click the form anywhere outside the field.

**FIGURE 19.9:**

Changing the text of a title label for a form

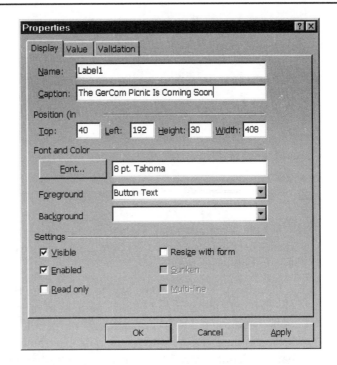

We took a lot of time fiddling around with sizing and placement on that first field. From here on, I'll leave it to you to do that kind of stuff on your own. Let's add another field.

---

**WARNING**    Be sure to save your form to disk on a regular basis. As with any other Windows application, use the File ➤ Save As and File ➤ Save options. To reopen your form to work on it at a later date, you have to use the Outlook main window Tools ➤ Forms ➤ Design a Form. Then select User Templates in File System from the Design Form dialog box that pops up and Browse to the location of your form.

---

**FIGURE 19.10:**

A label field resized to become the title of a form

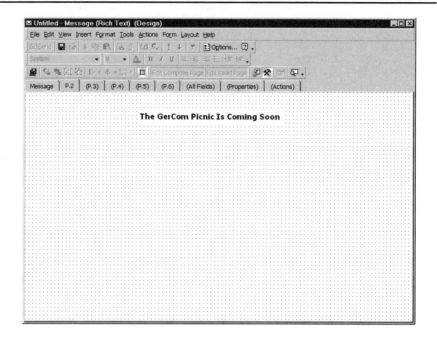

For planning purposes, we need to find out what people will want to drink at the picnic. So let's create a set of multiple-choice options and a control for people to enter other preferences.

Because people should be able to select more than one drink option, we'll use CheckBox fields grouped in a frame field to represent the options. (If we used options-button fields grouped on a frame, people would be able to select only one option in the group.) First, drag and drop a frame control from OFD's Control Toolbar; check out Figure 19.5 if you need a refresher on the Control Toolbar buttons.

We'll be offering four picnic drink options—coffee, tea, milk, and beer—so we'll need four CheckBox controls. Drag and drop four CheckBox controls onto the frame you just created. Place the four CheckBox fields in a vertical line (see Figure 19.11). Next, as shown in Figure 19.11, add a text box and label controls for users to enter drink preferences other than the four you offered in the CheckBoxes.

**NOTE**    Once you place fields on a frame field and then drag the frame, its associated fields stay in place and move with it. This makes it easy to properly locate a frame field and its associated fields.

Next you need to set the captions for each of the four controls. The captions on the four controls in Figure 19.11 are Coffee, Tea, Milk, and Beer. You set these captions just as you did for the title label you created. Right-click the first control and select Properties from the pop-up menu. The Properties dialog box opens on the Value property page. I'll explain why later. For now, tab over to the Display property page and type **Coffee** in the Caption field. Click OK and your first control now has the label Coffee. Go ahead and do the other three controls, then we'll move on.

**FIGURE 19.11:**

Creating a set of drink options for a company picnic

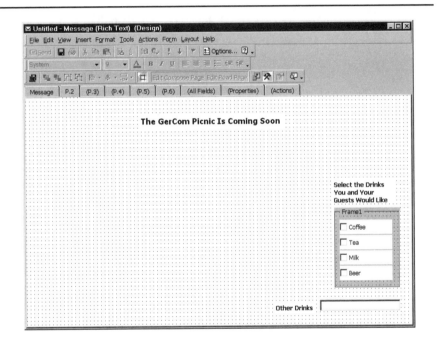

## Binding Controls to Exchange Server Data Fields

Now we're going to do something that is absolutely vital to the working of Outlook forms. We're going to bind each of the four data controls to a field in the Exchange Server database. If you don't do this, data entered into a form won't be available for viewing or manipulation after the form has been filled in and sent back to you. Think of it this way: Controls aren't data. They don't store data. They're just a way to enter data, but if they aren't bound to Exchange Server database fields, the data entered into them dies when a message containing an Outlook form is sent to someone or posted in a folder.

Remember the sidebar earlier in this chapter where I discussed the difference between controls and fields? Well, this is where a control earns the right to be called a field.

You can bind controls to standard Exchange fields or you can create new fields and then bind controls to them. We'll be binding our controls to new Exchange fields.

Here's how to bind the Coffee CheckBox to an Exchange database field. Open the Properties dialog box. The dialog box opens by default on the Value property page just as it did when you entered captions for the four drink controls. This is the cyber world equivalent of a nagging spouse. Microsoft doesn't want you to forget to bind each control to an Exchange Server database field. Until you do, the Properties dialog box always opens on the Value page.

Click New on the Value page. This opens the New Field dialog box. Type in a name for the new Exchange Server database field. I like to use a combination of the form name and a meaningful name for the field. In Figure 19.12, I'm using the name *PicnicCoffee*.

Before you close the Properties dialog box, you need to change the type for this field. Set the Type to Yes/No. CheckBoxes and ToggleButtons must be set to type Yes/No. If you don't do this, when people select a CheckBox or depress a Toggle-Button, values they check will not be in the form when they send it back to you. Once you've selected the Type Yes/No, notice that the format changes to an icon. Set the format to Yes/No or True/False. That way data from this field will be saved in the Exchange Server database in a format that is easy to manipulate.

While you're at it, take a look at the other Type options that are available. The lineup is very rich including (in addition to text), number, percent, currency, date/time, and formula. Each field includes formats appropriate to its content. For example, the date/time field includes a number of ways of displaying day of the week (e.g., Monday, Tuesday, etc.), month, day of the month (e.g., 1st, 20th, etc.), year, and time.

Now back to the task immediately before us. Click OK and you've created your new field and bound your control to it.

**TIP**

You're very likely to create a number of bogus fields while experimenting with Outlook forms. It's easy to get rid of unwanted fields, maybe too easy. To remove a field, open the Field Chooser, click the field you want to remove, and click Delete at the bottom of the Chooser. Then you need to delete the field from the current form. Tab over to the All Fields page on the form and delete the field. This probably goes without saying, but I'll say it anyway. Be careful not to delete valid fields, especially after lots of forms have been filled out and their fields are snugly stored in your Exchange Server database.

**FIGURE 19.12:**

Binding an Outlook form control to a new Exchange database field

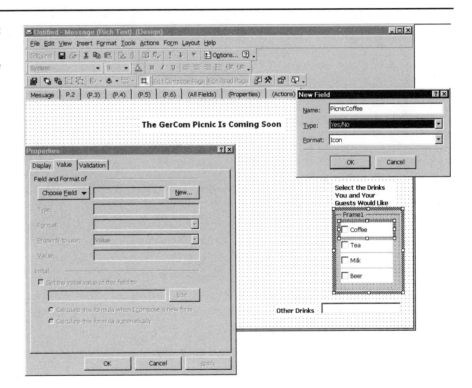

## Setting Initial Values for Controls

Figure 19.13 shows the Properties dialog box again. Notice the frame with the caption Initial at the bottom of the dialog box. This is where you set the value that will be seen by a user when the form is first opened. You don't need to set any initial values for a CheckBox. However, you might want to set a specific initial value for other fields. For example, you could set the initial value of a ComboBox to one of the possible values for the ComboBox. More about ComboBoxes, possible values, and such in a bit.

**FIGURE 19.13:**

Use the Properties dialog box to set the initial value of a field.

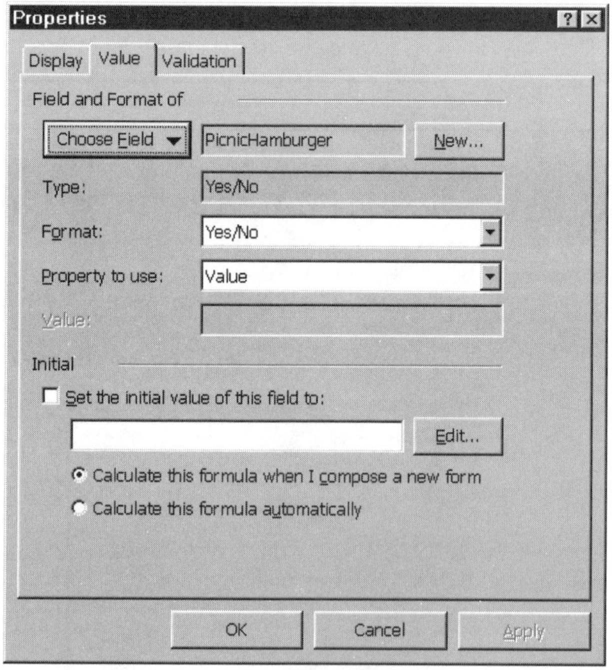

Now go ahead and create and bind new fields for the other three drink Check-Box controls. Don't forget to set the Type for each field to Yes/No. When you're done, we'll add some more controls to the form.

## Testing an Outlook Form

You can run a form anytime while you're creating it. Just select Form ➢ Run This Form on the form itself. In the case of a message form, a standard Outlook message is displayed that looks just like your form (see Figure 19.14). You can just look at the form to admire your work or you can fill in the form and send it to yourself to see how it works.

Woops! Notice that caption on the frame. It says Frame1. We really don't need a caption on the frame. To eliminate it, close the test message and go back to your form. Open the Properties dialog box for the frame and delete the caption. That's it.

The ability to run a form at any time is a fantastic capability of Outlook Forms Designer. As you can see, it makes format checking and debugging extremely easy.

**FIGURE 19.14:**

Testing an incomplete Outlook form

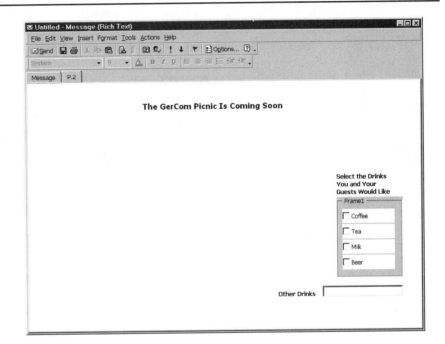

## Adding More Controls to the Picnic Form

Okay, we're ready to continue developing our Picnic form. I'm going to move much more quickly now that you have the basics of forms design under your belt.

Add a label above the frame for your Drinks CheckBox fields. "Select the Drinks You and Your Guests Would Like" seems to be a good choice for my form.

Now we need to add a control so people can type in other drink choices. Add a TextBox and label as shown in the lower-right corner of Figure 19.11.

Next we'll add a set of CheckBox fields so people can pick the main dish they want. We'll also provide an entry field to indicate a preference for other main-dish options.

Well, we're certainly not about to go through all the steps we just went through to create this new set of fields—we'll just copy and paste. Put your mouse pointer an inch or so to the left and above the Select the Drinks You and Your Guests Would Like label. Hold down the left mouse button and drag your mouse pointer until the select rectangle includes everything up to and including the Other Drinks control (see Figure 19.15). Release the left mouse button. All the controls within the rectangle should be highlighted. Select Copy from the form's Edit menu (or use the keyboard shortcut, Ctrl+C). Then choose Paste from the Edit menu (or press Ctrl+V).

**FIGURE 19.15:**

Selecting a set of controls that will be copied and pasted elsewhere in a form

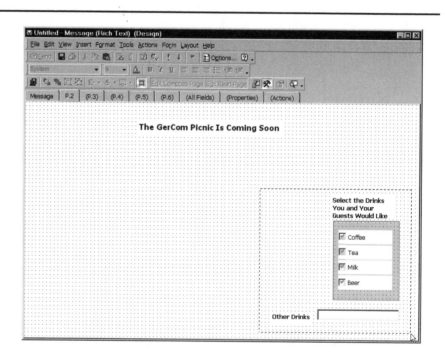

If you don't see the new frame and its associated CheckBox fields, they've probably been pasted right on top of the old frame. In that case, just move the top frame with your mouse and you'll see the original frame underneath. You now have two identical frames and CheckBox buttons. Move the copy to the left of the original.

Now edit the leftmost Drinks frame and its associated CheckBox fields. Change the Coffee, Tea, Milk, and Beer captions to Hamburger, Turkey Burger, Veggie Burger, and Hot Dogs. Next add new database fields for the four new controls and set their types to Yes/No. Then edit the Drinks label and the Other Drinks entry field so they are appropriate for a main dish. When you're done, your form should look something like the one in Figure 19.16.

**FIGURE 19.16:**

The picnic form with main-dish fields in place

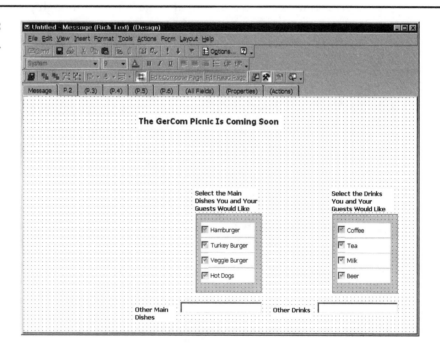

We'll need to know how many guests each person plans to bring and what kinds of games people will want to play. So, we need to add a TextBox for the number of guests, plus a label and two ComboBoxes for favorite games (see Figure 19.17).

We're going to set up a fancy TextBox for entering number of guests. Create the TextBox control and bind it to a new field, setting the Type for the Number of Guests TextBox to Number. Don't worry about the format. Next, drag and drop a SpinButton onto the right-hand edge of your TextBox just as you see in Figure 19.17. Then, bind the SpinButton to the same field as you bound the TextBox.

Run your form and you'll see that you can use the spin button to pick whatever numeric value you want. The problem is that you can spin up to some pretty grand numbers of guests or down to negative numbers of guests. We don't want to bankrupt GerCom, so let's set the minimum and maximum values you can spin to. Right-click the SpinButton and open the Advanced Properties dialog box. Find the Max and Min properties and set Min to 1 and Max to 8.

Now run your form. The initial value is 1, even though you didn't set an initial value. That's because you set Min to 1 for the SpinButton. And, you can only spin up to 8. Pretty nifty, huh?

## Validation

You've probably noticed the Validation tab on the Properties dialog box. You use this tab to require that users enter data into a field and/or to ensure that data entered by users meets a specific set of criteria. For example, we could have required that the value entered into our Number of Guests field be greater than 0 and less than 9. We could even have put in a message that would be shown to users if they put in a number outside the range of acceptable values. In this case, the SpinButton works much more elegantly than any set of validation checks. So, validation isn't needed here, but I'm sure you can imagine a number of scenarios where validation would help insure the quality of data entered into a form.

Now, go ahead and create the two ComboBoxes for favorite games. The ComboBoxes start out blank. At this point, if form users opened the drop-down list, they'd find nothing to select from. To add some options, right-click the first games ComboBox and select Properties from the pop-up menu. Then enter some games in the Possible Values field. If you want one of the values to show in the ComboBox when the form is first opened, type that value into the field named Set the Initial Value of This Field To. Check out Figure 19.18 for the details.

Notice in Figure 19.18 that I set the initial value for the ComboBox to Baseball. That way, the field shows the value Baseball when the form is initially opened.

**FIGURE 19.17:**

The picnic form now collects information on the number of guests and favorite games.

**FIGURE 19.18:**

Adding values to a ComboBox

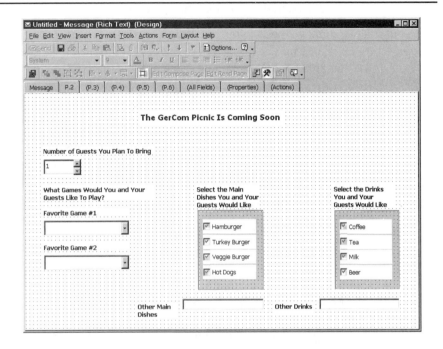

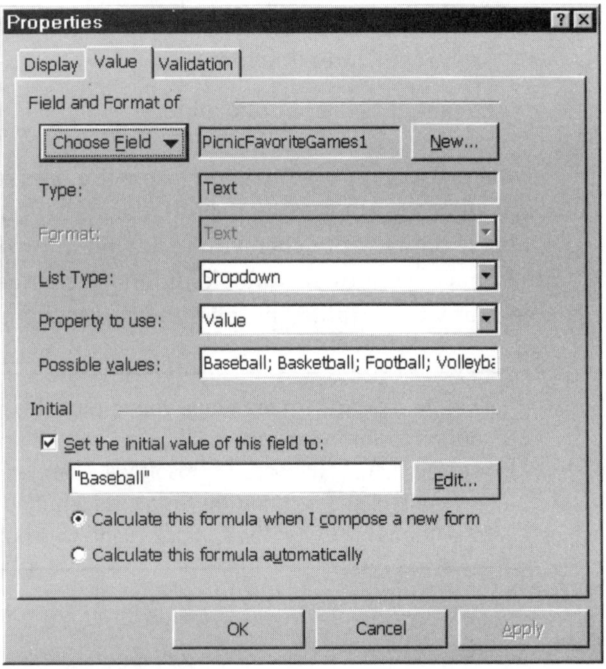

We need to do two more things before we finish.

First, we need to rename the second page on our form from P.2 to something else, like maybe Please Fill In Survey Here. Click the tab for P.2 and select Form ➤ Rename Page. Enter a new name in the Rename Page dialog box and click OK.

Second, we need to set a subject for our message. That way all messages sent to us will have a standard subject line. The initial value of my subject field is Survey for GerCom Picnic. Tab over to the Message property page of your form, right-click the form's Subject field, and select Properties. When the Properties dialog box for the field opens, tab over to the Value property page and type in an initial value.

That's it. We've finished creating our form. Be sure to save it.

Now we need to publish our form.

# Publishing a New OFD Form

You can publish an OFD form in a number of locations:

- An Exchange Server organization forms library
- Your own personal forms library
- Your own Outlook folders
- Exchange Server public folders

Exchange Server organization forms libraries reside on an Exchange server and are available to all users by default. Forms in your personal forms library are available only to you when you're logged into your Exchange Server mailbox, as are forms in your own Outlook folders. Exchange Server public folders are available to any user granted permissions to use them.

**NOTE**    If you're a stickler for grammar, you're probably cringing at the term "organization forms library." If you're like me, you can't help reading "organization" as "organizational." Perhaps Microsoft will change the name in Exchange 2000. For now content yourself that the library is identified to end users as the "organizational forms library" in the Outlook client. One out of two isn't bad.

As you'll see in a bit, the form we just created will be invoked when a user replies to a message from a specific individual. The user receives a message, opens it, and replies to it. The reply is the form. When the user is finished filling in the form, he or she sends the reply back to the original sender.

The form needs to be available to the recipient of the message so we can't publish it in a personal forms library or private folders. To accomplish the end outlined in the paragraph immediately above, the form must be published in an Exchange Server organization forms library. Even a public folder won't do. I'll show you why in a short while.

## Creating an Organization Forms Library

So, you're probably asking, where is this Exchange Server organization forms library thingie? Right now, it's nowhere. You have to create an organization forms library on one of your Exchange Servers. That means you have to shift gears, go over to your Exchange Server, and open the Exchange Administrator, your constant companion since way back in Chapter 8.

To create an organization forms library, select Forms Administrator from the Exchange Administrator's Tools menu. The Organization Forms Library Administrator dialog box pops up. Click New to bring up the Create New Forms Library dialog box. If this is your first organization forms library folder, just accept the default name, Organizational Forms, and click OK to return to the Organization Forms Library Administrator dialog box.

Now you need to give permission to one or more Exchange mailboxes or distribution lists to administer your new organization forms library. While you're still on the Organization Forms Library Administrator dialog box, be sure the library name is selected, and then click Permissions. Use the resulting Forms Library Permissions dialog box to give the Owner role to anyone who will be creating and installing forms in the library.

By default, the group Default has Reviewer permissions for the library. Reviewers have full read rights to the library and the forms stored in it. All Exchange mailboxes not explicitly specified in the permissions list belong to this group.

To publish your form, on the form itself select Tools ➢ Forms ➢ Publish Form or Tools ➢ Forms ➢ Publish Form As. Then select the location where you want to store your form from the drop-down list on the Publish Form or Publish Form As dialog box (see Figure 19.19). Zip up and down the options in the drop-down list. You'll see every private and public storage area available to you.

In Figure 19.20, I'm publishing my picnic form in the organization forms library (as noted above, called the "Organizational Forms Library" in Outlook). I've chosen to name the form GerCom Picnic Form.

Once the form is saved, we're ready to move on to the next step. Oh yes, there is a next step.

**FIGURE 19.19:**

Selecting the forms library where the form will be stored

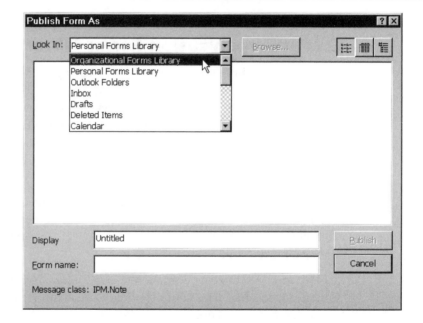

**Publish Form As**

Look In: Personal Forms Library

Organizational Forms Library
Personal Forms Library
Outlook Folders
Inbox
Drafts
Deleted Items
Calendar

Browse...

Display: Untitled

Form name:

Message class: IPM.Note

Publish

Cancel

Storing a form in the organization forms library

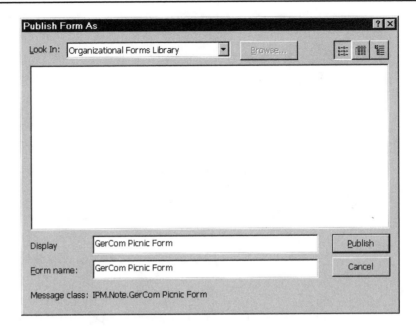

# Creating the Message Form Used to Send the Picnic Form

I'll bet you thought we were done. Nope. The form we just created is, for all intents and purposes, a reply form, not a send form. If you run the form, you get a Message tab to address the message and show its subject and you get the picnic survey tab. If you send this form to someone and they click the Reply button on the message, all they'll get is a standard reply message. The survey tab won't be there.

You can provide users with a reply version of the form in two ways:

1.  Attach your saved form to a message. In the message, tell users to double-click the attachment to open it and then to fill in the survey and send it back. In this case, you might want to make your mailbox alias or display name the initial value in the To field of the message. Then users won't have to enter your e-mail address to send the form back.

2.  Create a message with a reply that is itself your form.

While option number one is easier for you to pull off, it requires a lot more work for the user than option two. There's also more room for error. So, we're going to take the more elegant approach of option two.

Our second message is very simple. You've already done everything required to create it. Here's what to do:

1. Select Forms ➤ Design a Form from Outlook's Tools menu.

2. Select Message from the Design a Form dialog box.

3. Add the same subject line you created for the original message "Survey for GerCom Picnic."

4. On the Properties page of the form, click the CheckBox labeled Send Form Definition with Item.

5. On the Actions page of the form, double-click the row with the action name Reply.

6. On the Form Action Properties dialog box, on the frame labeled This Action Creates a Form of the Following Type, use the drop-down to change the form name from Message to the name of the form you just published in your organizational forms library (GerCom Picnic Form, in my case).

7. Repeat the above two steps for Reply to All.

8. Save your form and publish it in your personal forms library under a name such as Message with GerCom Picnic Form as a Reply.

Okay, that's it. Now, we're ready to put our forms to use.

---

**NOTE**　　When you selected the form GerCom Picnic Form in step six above, did you notice that you were only offered three containers to select the form from: Standard Forms Library, Organizational Forms Library, and Personal Forms Library? Those are all the choices there are. Now you see why a public folder wouldn't do here? Public folders are not a choice, because they might not have been replicated across an entire Exchange organization. Organization forms libraries are cross-organization by definition, meaning that they are replicated to all Exchange servers in an Exchange Organization.

---

**TIP**
Like fields, you just might wind up with a bunch of useless forms in a library or folder. You delete forms from folders just like any other item in a folder. To delete forms from libraries, from the Outlook main menu, select Tools ➢ Options ➢ Other. Next, click Custom Forms, then click Manage Forms and use the resultant Forms Manager dialog box to delete and otherwise manage your forms.

# Using Forms

To use the form we just created, select New ➢ Choose Form from the File menu of Outlook's main window. Use the Choose Form dialog box to find your personal forms library and double-click the form you created in the section immediately above (Message with GerCom Picnic Form as a Reply, in my case).

In Figure 19.21, I'm sending a message off to an Outlook distribution list that includes all GerCom staff. Note that there is no sign of the form at this point. In Figure 19.22, a member of GerCom's staff, me again, has clicked Reply on the original message and has just finished completing the picnic survey form that opened as part of the reply message. When I click Send, the message with the form is sent to the original sender, me yet again.

To be fancy, I could show you the form as it looks to the original sender when the reply is received. However, it would be anticlimactic, because the form looks just like it does in Figure 19.22.

**TIP**
Do you find the two-tab reply message annoying? I mean, why should someone have to tab over to the survey tab to fill it in? This little aesthetic nightmare is easy to fix. All you have to do is cut the To and Cc fields from the Message page and paste them on the survey page. Then, hide the Message page. Now your reply form is a beautiful single page. If you do make this change, be sure to save and republish your results.

**FIGURE 19.21:**

Sending a form to an
Exchange recipient

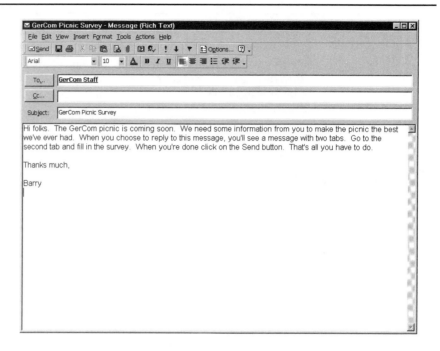

**FIGURE 19.22:**

The data in a completed
form ready to be returned
to the form's sender

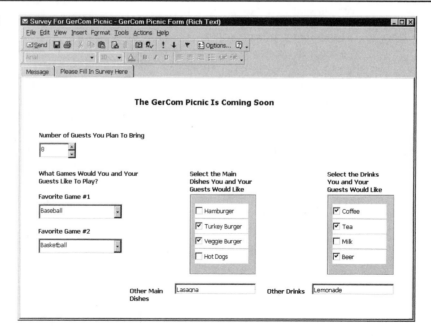

Just one thing before we conclude this section. All those fields that you created are available in the Outlook client. You can open the Field Chooser in the client and drag and drop any of these fields onto the field bar (the one with From, Subject, Received, etc. on it) in your Inbox. For example, if you drag the Number of Guests field to the field bar, you will then see in your Inbox, for every form that has been returned, how many guests the sender plans on bringing to the picnic.

## The Difference between Save, Save As, Publish, and Publish As

Outlook Forms Designer is chock-full of ways to save and publish your work. As you're building a form, it's a good idea to save or republish it frequently. Just be sure you know where things go when you use all the save and publish options OFD provides.

Save and Save As don't work like they do in other applications such as Microsoft Word. Save saves your form into your Outlook client's Drafts folder. Save As is more traditional and saves your work to a disk file of your choice. If you want to save or resave your form to a file, use Save As. Publish As lets you choose the forms library or folder where you want to publish your form. Publish republishes your form in the forms library or folder where you opened the form or anywhere you chose with Publish As.

# Don't Stop Here!

Unfortunately, we have to stop our exploration of OFD here, but don't let that stop you from exploring OFD further on your own. There are so many great things you can do with OFD, such as creating forms for posting in public folders, for setting group meetings, or for collecting key line-of-business information.

Also, look into and get into Visual Basic scripting. You'd be amazed at what you can do when you combine Outlook forms and VB scripting. You can do simple tasks like collating responses from Outlook forms all the way up to complex applications that help your organization sell its products or services; maintain its inventory; or manage its customers, clients, or patients.

OFD has a very good user interface. Combine that with its fine online help and you can usually have a project based on newly discovered OFD features up and running in minutes. As with any piece of technology—Outlook and Exchange Server included—your OFD watchwords should be *plan*, *do*, *test*, and *have fun*.

Also, please do check out Microsoft's Web Forms. Web Forms are built on one of the company's newer technologies, Collaborative Data Objects. Web Forms are Exchange Server–oriented Active Server Pages scripts, so you can think of them as part of Outlook Web Access. Web Forms are stored in the Web server environment and accessed with a standard URL. Outlook clients can be set up to access this URL and show a new Web Forms option on their Compose menu. So selecting a Web-based form is as easy as picking an OFD form.

## Where to Get Sample Forms and Help with Forms Development

Exchange Server comes with a number of sample forms-based applications and you can download more of both the EFD and OFD persuasions at Microsoft's Web site. These applications support such functions as customer tracking and help desks. They're worth looking at both because they may help you understand how to build multiform applications and because they use Exchange's public folders to organize applications, as well as deliver them to users throughout an Exchange organization.

Check the shelves of your favorite bookstore for weighty (five pounds at least) tomes on EFD and OFD. And take a look at Microsoft's Web site, which has some fairly good stuff. For example, a search for FORMSHLP.EXE on the site will reward you with a nice add-in help file on OFD for use with your Outlook client.

If you expect to get into forms programming, get ahold of one of the books out there on Office 97's or Office 2000's Visual Basic Scripting Edition. You might even want to buy Microsoft's Visual Basic learning package. It sells for under $100 and comes with a minimal feature set version of VB, a very nice introductory VB training manual, and lots of examples. This little gem will not only familiarize you with visual forms development, it will also give you some basic training in VB scripting.

Oh, yes, don't forget those books I mentioned way back at the beginning of this chapter.

# Conclusion

In this chapter you learned about the Outlook Forms Designer and how to use it to build, publish, and deploy simple electronic forms. You also found out where to go to learn more about OFD and its supporting programming language, Visual Basic Scripting Edition.

Well, folks, this is the last chapter of *Mastering Exchange Server 5.5*. For me, researching and writing the book has been a lot of fun and relatively painless. I hope that your experiences with Exchange Server are as positive and rewarding.

# APPENDIX

# A

# Suggested Microsoft Exchange Server Maintenance Activities

# Check Your Backups

Check to make sure that the last backup succeeded. If it hasn't, arrange to rerun the backup as soon as possible. It is generally not desirable to wait until the next backup cycle. Exchange backup employs a client-server backup mechanism, so, it's possible to safely and almost fully back up the Exchange databases while they are in use. The impact on end-user–experienced performance is minimal during backup, at least when Microsoft's NT Backup program or an Exchange-compatible third-party backup program is used.

# Check the Performance and Health of Your Exchange Server Using NT's Performance Monitor

For each Exchange server, it's a good idea to check at least the following Exchange Server Performance Monitor indicators at a minimum of twice a day. Build and save a Performance Monitor workspace file for each category of indicator. Also, build and save one workspace file to aggregate key cross-category indicators. This makes it easier to run one or more indicator sets as required. As user counts and loads on servers stabilize, accumulate typicality values for the indicators. Set up alerts through Performance Monitor using typicality values to trigger warnings. Use Performance Monitor reports, because they often make it easier to see key values than busy Performance Monitor graphic charts.

**MSExchange Internet Protocols:**

**Active Connections**    A sign of stress on the server

**Incoming Queue Length**    Possible indication of network problems

**Outgoing Queue Length**    Possible indication of network problems

**Peak Connections**    A sign of stress on the server

**Database (for Directory, Information Store, and Directory Synchronization Services):**

**Log Write/sec**    Slow writes could threaten integrity of data.

**Log File Operations Pending**    A larger number of pending file operations (reads and writes to the database cache manager) often indicates a bottleneck that can best be fixed with more CPU power or faster disk drives.

**Log Threads Waiting**    Too many log threads waiting for their data to be written to disk could cause loss of data.

**MSExchangeDS:**

**AB Browses/sec**    A relative indication of stress on the server caused by address book browsing

**Access Violations**    The number of directory services writes refused for security reasons

**ExDS Client Sessions**    Similar to AB Browses/sec, only for the entire directory service

**LDAP Searches and Searches/sec**    A good indication of the extent to which LDAP is used and its impact on the server

**Pending Replication Synchronizations**    A good sense of the state of directory replication across servers

**MSExchangeIMC (should be called "MSExchangeIMS," but it was not changed in either the v.5.0 or v.5.5 release of Exchange Server):**

**Connections Total Failed**    The failed connections to other hosts since IMS was started

**Connections Total Inbound**    The total number of connections to the IMS since it was started

**Connections Total Outbound**    The total number of connections made by the IMS since it was started; ratio of the total inbound to the total failed gives a sense of the health of IMS/network on the outbound side.

**Connections Total Rejected**    The total number of connection attempts IMS has rejected from other hosts since it was started; the ratio of the total rejected to the total inbound gives a sense of the health of the IMS/network on the inbound side.

**Inbound Bytes/hr; Inbound Connections/hr**    A good indication of the relative stress on IMS inbound activity

**NDRs Total Inbound; NDRs Total Outbound**   A good relative indication of the level of SMTP messaging problems (useful in determining when to turn NDR reporting to the Administrative team on and off)

**Outbound Bytes/hr; Outbound Connections/hr**   A good indication of the relative stress on IMS outbound activity

**Queued Inbound; Queued Outbound**   When high, a good indicator of network problems

**MSExchangeIS:**

**Active Anonymous User Count**   A good security check; if this gets too high, it also might indicate a need to either rethink policy on anonymous users or beef up computer and/or network hardware.

**Active Connection Count; Active User Count**   A good indicator of the extent to which Exchange is being used at any given time

**Maximum Anonymous Users; Maximum Users**   Another good indicator of the extent of Exchange usage

**POP3 Messages Sent (and IMAP Messages Sent in v.5.5)**   An indicator that is important to monitor as use of non-Exchange/Outlook clients rises

**MSExchangeIS Private:**

**Average Delivery Time; Average Local Delivery Time**   Respectively, the time to deliver an external message to the MTA and the time to deliver a message within a server; both are very helpful measures of performance.

**Messages Delivered**   The total messages delivered by and within the Private IS since IS startup

**Messages Sent**   The total messages sent to other storage providers through the MTA since IS startup

**Messages Submitted**   The total messages submitted by clients since IS startup

**Peak Client Logons**   The maximum number of concurrent client logons since IS startup; helpful for capacity planning

**Single Instance Ratio**    The average number of references to messages in the IS; the lower the number, the lower the average number of recipients per message sent to this server.

**MSExchangeIS Public:**

**Peak Client Logons**    Same as the indicator in MSExchangeISPrivate, above

Other indicators are useful only if experiencing problems with folder replication or newsgroups.

**MSExchangeMSMI:**

**Kilobytes Received/hr; Kilobytes Sent/hr**    Indicates amount of traffic on the MS Mail Connector Interchange

**MSExchangeMTA:**

**Disk File Reads/sec; Disk File Writes/sec**    A good stress indicator, this needs to be considered in light of the capacity of the disk and controller hardware being used.

**LAN Receive Bytes/sec; LAN Transmit Bytes/sec**    Virtually everything that moves between Exchange servers is standard messages or encapsulated in messages; thus, MTAs can send and receive heavy amounts of data; this gives a sense of the amount of stress the MTA is putting on a network.

**Work Queue Length**    Messages not yet processed by the MTA; this number should be relatively low.

**MSExchangeMTA Connections:**

Run the following measures at least for other Exchange servers the server communicates with, the Internet Mail Service, and the MS Mail Connector.

**Queue Length**    A quick indication of queue backups, which tend to indicate network health

**Receive Bytes/sec; Send Bytes/sec**    Quick indicators of traffic involving key MTA links to other services

**Processor:**

Run the following for each processor.

**Percent of Processor Time**    A very good indicator of the health of a server processor-wise, and it can be an early warning of the need to upgrade an existing server or to move some Exchange mailboxes to a new server.

**Percent of Interrupt Time**    This indicator is helpful in assessing the percentage of time that the processor is handling hardware interrupts (mostly disk I/O on an Exchange server); a high percentage of interrupt rates should trigger an assessment of disk hardware (if the high rates occur during backup hours, this may be less of a problem).

**PhysicalDisk:**

For each disk run the following.

**Avg. Disk Write/sec; Avg. Disk Write Queue Length**    Respectively, the average time in seconds to do a disk write and the average number of write requests in the queue during a sample interval; it's especially helpful in assessing problems getting logs written down to disk.

**Disk Read Bytes/sec; Disk Write Bytes/sec**    This indicator is helpful in tracking down performance problems.

# Check the Performance and Health of Your Exchange Server Using the Exchange Administrator

As a backup to the Performance Monitor checks discussed above, at least once a day check the following on each Exchange server, using the Exchange Administrator:

**The Internet Mail Service, MTA, and MS Mail Connector**    Watch queues for backed up messages.

**Server Logons and Mailbox Resources**    Sort Server Logons by Last Logon Time to get a sense of those users who haven't logged on for some time; sort Mailbox Resources by Total K to get a sense of who the high users of disk storage are.

**Non-Delivery Reports**    When major changes are made to one or more Exchange servers, activate more extensive NDR delivery to the Exchange Admins. distribution list, using Exchange Administrator (Internet Mail Service, Internet Mail property page). Monitor these reports to determine if changes lead to any problems.

**Exchange Server and Link Monitors**    Ensure that Exchange Server and Link monitors are in place and running for all Exchange servers.

# APPENDIX

# B

# Neat Tools in the Microsoft Exchange Server Resource Kit

B

The Microsoft Exchange Server Resource Kit contains a gaggle of exciting applications to make administering and managing Exchange servers easier. You can purchase the Exchange Server Resource Kit as part of the BackOffice Resource Kit series or you can download most of it at www.microsoft.com/exchange. The Kit is easy to install and comes with a nice set of docs. Here are some of the apps in the Exchange Resource Kit that I find especially useful along with a brief description of what each application does.

# Administrative Mailbox Agent

The agent runs on a Windows NT computer. You send it Exchange messages and it creates NT accounts and Exchange mailboxes. Of course, all the right permissions must be in place all around.

# Backup Tool for Microsoft Exchange

In Chapter 10, I showed you how to send yourself mail with the NT Backup program's log file attached. By examining the file, you can tell whether the backup worked or not. The Backup Tool for Microsoft Exchange checks the logs for you and reports any failures in an Excel spreadsheet that is mailed to you.

# Bulk Advanced Security Tool

If you or one of your users need to decrypt and then re-encrypt all of the messages in a folder or set of folders (for example, to move them), the Bulk Advanced Security Tool is for you. You can even re-encrypt only the messages that were previously decrypted by the tool.

# Cleansweep

Sometimes you need to remove forms, views, or rules from folders. You can also remove permissions settings. Use this one with caution. Its name says it all. For example, if you choose to remove the rules or permissions for a folder and you can't select which ones to remove, all of them are removed.

# Crystal Reports

The Exchange Server Resource Kit includes a limited functionality version of Seagate's Crystal Reports report generation application. Also included is a set of canned reports specifically for Exchange data. Data can come from Exchange Server message-tracking logs and an Exchange Server client's address books and messages. Among other things, you can use Crystal Reports to generate messaging statistics by an Exchange mailbox or, if you've entered the appropriate data into Exchange Server's directory, lists and labels for regular postal mailings.

# DL Import Tool

Do you maintain regular mail or e-mail list data in databases such as Access? Want to turn them into dynamic electronic mailing lists? All you need is the DL Import Tool, which creates Exchange distribution lists from such databases. This tool runs as a service on an NT server. On a daily basis, it uses Crystal Reports to extract data from the database and then automatically creates Exchange distribution lists from the data. I use the DL Import Tool to import data from e-mail directories that exist outside of the Exchange Server environment.

# Event Log Tools

Event Log Tools regularly scan NT Server event logs waiting for specific events to take place. When and if the events occur, these tools are able to notify a computer or send an e-mail message to a user or group or even restart or stop a service.

# Import Header Tool

In Chapter 17, I showed you how to manually set up a header file that you could then use to import or export items from the Exchange Server directory. I also noted that you could use the Import Header Tool to simplify this task. You just pick the fields you want and the tool copies their sometimes-esoteric names into a file.

# Mailbox Cleanup Agent

The Mailbox Cleanup Agent automatically deletes and moves outdated messages from Exchange Server mailboxes. The agent runs as an NT service and, with the other tools I discussed earlier, helps you keep Exchange Server information store disk space under control.

# Mailbox Migration Tool

I mentioned the Mailbox Migration Tool in Chapter 17. You can easily move mailboxes between servers in the same Exchange site with the Move Mailbox option on the Exchange Administrator's Tools menu. However, if you need to move mailboxes between sites or between Exchange organizations, you'll either have to do it manually, as I described it in Chapter 17, or use the Mailbox Migration Tool. I've used the tool to successfully move mailboxes between both sites and organizations. It's a godsend in the now-you-see-it-now-you-don't world of modern American corporate politics and economics.

# Mailbox Statistics Tool

Everything you've always wanted to know about your mailbox, but were afraid to ask. The Mailbox Statistics Tool tells you everything from the largest number of messages you sent in a day to the total number of bytes used by your mailbox in the information store. Each user runs the program and the tool generates a mail message with all this info, which it sends to a designated administrator's mailbox. In the past, I used the tool to get data out to users on total information store usage. The problem was that each user had to run the tool. There is an add-in for the Outlook client that solves the how-much-Exchange-Server-disk-space-am-I-taking-up dilemma for users. Now a user can find out how much space they're using in their mailbox, as well as in personal and public folders just by selecting Server Space from the Outlook client's Tools menu. Check with Microsoft on how to get the add-in.

# Management Chain List Tool

Remember the Organization property page of the Exchange mailbox dialog box? That's where you can show the display name of the mailbox user's manager and the display names of the people whom the mailbox user manages. If you issue the management chain list tool command with the alias name of a mailbox, you'll get back a nicely formatted little org chart segment showing the user, his or her manager, and subordinates.

# MAPIsend Tool

The MAPIsend Tool lets you send messages, even messages with attachments from a command prompt. I discussed this tool and its workings when I showed you how to send yourself a message with the previous night's NT backup log attached (see Chapter 10). You can use it for any situation where you want to send a message without using an Exchange Server client. For example, think what you could do with MAPIsend in a batch file that runs automatically just after month-end, and then sends a copy of the latest financials to a bunch of need-to-know management types in your organization.

# Microsoft Mail Tools

If you've got to integrate Microsoft Mail for PC Networks (MS Mail) with Exchange Server, you'll want to take a look at the MS Mail Tools in the Exchange Resource Kit. The Microsoft Mail Export Tool lets you move addressing information between MS Mail and the Exchange Server directory. With the Microsoft Mail Proxy to Microsoft Exchange Proxy Conversion Tool you can turn MS Mail SMTP, X.400, and MHS addresses into custom recipient addresses in the Exchange Server directory. The Microsoft Mail SMTP Gateway Proxy Migration Tool adds MS Mail SMTP addresses to Exchange mailboxes, making it easier for you to preserve your users' MS Mail SMTP addresses in the Exchange Server environment.

# Natural Language Support Configuration Tool

If you need to support multiple languages on your Exchange Server, the Natural Language Support Configuration Tool is just what the doctor ordered. This tool automates the process of installing code-page files for languages that Windows NT doesn't support by default.

# ONDL Tool

I really like this one. Issued at a command prompt, it returns either the members of an Exchange Server distribution list or the distribution lists a particular user belongs to. I'll spare you the sad tale of the programming hoops I had to jump through to get this info before ONDL arrived on the scene.

# PF TreeInfo Tool

The PF TreeInfo Tool is a confidence builder. It counts and displays the number of messages in a selected public folder and its subfolders. I sometimes use it early in the game to ensure that folder replication is working properly. I run the tool on each public folder replica. If the number of messages is the same for each replica, I can almost reasonably assume that replication is working. Almost. To enhance my confidence in the replication process, I also randomly check to ensure that specific messages in specific folders do indeed appear on each replica. Once you're comfortable that things are working well, you won't use this tool much. After that, you'll want to regularly run the Replver Tool, which I discuss below.

# Profgen Tool

The Profgen Tool, used in conjunction with the Newprof.exe tool, helps you set up Exchange Server clients for new users and roving users (users who don't always work at the same computer). Reading the Profgen Tool docs is worth the cost of admission, even if you don't use the tool. They'll teach you a lot about the things you have to consider when dealing with roving Exchange Server users.

# Replver Tool

As I mentioned above, when you want to be sure on a regular basis that public folder replication is running without a hitch, you'll use the Replver (for "replication verification") Tool. The tool does a comprehensive analysis of public folder hierarchy and content replicas to provide very good assurance that replication has indeed taken place.

# Cool Third-Party Applications for Exchange/Outlook Clients and Exchange Server

■ never appreciated the meaning of "cool" until I started playing with Exchange Server and its clients and some of the fantastic applications that third-party vendors have created to extend the reach of an already-great set of products. Here are some of my favorite products at the time of this writing. Products are listed by category along with information on how you can contact the vendors. Some vendors provide live demos or even trial versions of their products that you can download over the Internet.

Remember, I can't take responsibility for the workability of these products in your Exchange Server and organizational environments. That's up to you.

# Workflow

The great promise of e-messaging systems like Exchange Server lies in their ability to help manage the flow of documents to complete a specific task between the various persons who need to be involved in the task. Lotus Notes has long been considered one of the better workflow applications. As Exchange Server grows with each release, it gets closer and closer to Notes in its capabilities. The third-party products noted below help fill in the gaps that remain.

## Motiva

Motiva supports workflow, document management, and collaborative technologies in an Exchange Server environment. Contact: Motiva Software Corporation, phone (619) 481-4822; fax (619) 481-8482; e-mail info@motiva.com; World Wide Web www.motiva.com.

## PowerWork

PowerWork is nicely integrated with Exchange Server and its clients as well as Exchange Administrator. Contact: PC Konzepte GmbH, phone (49) 831-564-000 (yes just three zeros); fax (49) 831 564-0099; e-mail info@pck.allgaeu.org; World Wide Web www.pck.allgaeu.org.

## Sales and Project Tracking

Sales and Project Tracking uses Exchange Server public folders to support sales force automation and project tracking, especially for organizations with long sales and project development cycles. The product includes a searchable knowledge base; task assignment and monitoring capabilities; corporate calendaring; resource allocation; and contact information. Contact: PortalSoft Technologies, phone (505) 346-0507; fax (505) 346-0509; World Wide Web www.portalsoft.com.

## Transform Response

Transform Response is a tool for developing group inbox applications. The product can be used to support such applications as a customer service center for a Web site, an e-mail extension to a call center, or a corporate or customer help desk. Contact: Transform Research, phone (613) 238-1363; fax (613) 237-9221; e-mail info@transres.com; World Wide Web www.transres.com.

## Visual EDI Server

Visual EDI Server supports electronic data interchange, which is key to electronic commerce. EDI translators run as Exchange Mailbox Agents. Contact: Prospera, phone (800) 622-6118; fax (610) 993-0733; e-mail infobiz@prosperagroup.com; World Wide Web www.prosperagroup.com.

# Backup Software

The key here is support for Exchange Server. NT's own backup program backs up the Exchange private and public information stores as well as the directory while they're open and in use. That's really nice, but NT Backup isn't the most full-featured backup product around. For more features, turn to third-party backup solutions that include NT Backup's open info stores/open directory backup capability. The products listed below include this capability, though usually as an add-on.

## ARCserve

ARCserve has been around for a long time and is a good package. It has very good backup scheduling capabilities. Contact: Cheyenne, phone (800) 243-9462; fax (516) 484-3446; e-mail `sales@cheyenne.com`; World Wide Web `www.cheyenne.com`.

## Backup Exec

Like ARCServe, Backup Exec has been around for eons and is a good backup product with nice backup scheduling capabilities. Contact: Seagate Software, phone (800) 327-2232; fax (407) 531-7730; e-mail `sales@seagatesoftware.com`; World Wide Web `www.seagatesoftware.com`.

## CommVault

CommVault's focus is on backup and restoration of the contents of individual Exchange Server mailboxes. It also handles the full Exchange directory and information store. Contact: CommVault Systems, phone (650) 402-5800; fax (650) 401-5818; e-mail `west-region@commvault.com`; World Wide Web `www.commvault.com`.

# Exchange Server Administration and Management

Three of these products either display existing Exchange or NT monitor data in a different form or extend the range of monitoring options available. The fourth product adds list and reply server capabilities to Exchange Server.

## AppManager

AppManager has modules for the whole BackOffice suite. It lets you monitor the health and performance of an entire distributed Exchange system. Contact: NetIQ, phone (408) 556-0888; fax (408) 258-9118; e-mail `info@netiq.com`; World Wide Web `www.netiq.com`.

## EXMS

EXMS does such wonderful tasks as automatically maintaining distribution lists and synchronizing the Exchange directory with other databases. For example, the product can be used to create new Exchange mailboxes based on new or changed entries in an organization's human resources system. Contact: Discus Data Solutions, phone (212) 279-9090; fax (212) 290-8066; e-mail info@discusdata.com; World Wide Web www.discusdata.com.

## InforMe!

InforMe! adds list and reply services to Exchange Server. You can use it to create automatically maintained distribution lists and to deliver automated replies. Contact: NTP Software, phone (800) 226-2755; fax (603) 641-6934; e-mail info@ntpsoftware.com; World Wide Web www.ntpsoftware.com.

## List Manager

List Manager brings automatic list server capability to Exchange Server. Users can subscribe to and unsubscribe from lists. The product also includes an archive option that allows users to retrieve past postings. Contact NTP Software, phone (800) 226-2755; fax (603) 641-6934; e-mail sales@ntpsoftware.com; World Wide Web www.ntpsoftware.com.

## MailCheck

MailCheck does extensive end-to-end performance analysis and reporting for Exchange Server and other messaging systems. The product, which goes several steps beyond Exchange Server's own monitors, has some very nice graphical presentations. Contact: Baranof Software, phone (800) 462-4565; fax (617) 926-6636; e-mail info@baranof.com; World Wide Web www.baranof.com.

## Veranda

Veranda is a very cool product. Among other things, it lets you analyze Exchange Server message activity; plan for computer and network upgrades; audit for security problems; and charge back costs by sites, departments, and employees. Contact: Tally Systems, phone (800) 262-3877; fax (603) 643-9366; e-mail veranda @tallysys.com; World Wide Web www.tallysystems.com.

# Wireless Messaging

If your users need to stay in touch on the road when no phone line is available, these products are what you're looking for. Some support specific wireless options like packet wireless networks. Others support everything from standard cellular phone to satellite service links.

## Mail on the Run!

Mail on the Run! software adds very complete support for remote Exchange Server access, using wire-based, cellular, and wireless packet networks such as ARDIS. Contact: River Run Software Group, phone (203) 861-0090; fax (203) 861-0096; e-mail info@riverrun.com; World Wide Web www.riverrun.com.

## OnAir Mobile

OnAir Mobile software provides high data-throughput support for a range of wireless and wired options. Contact: Telsis North, phone (416) 229-9666; fax (416) 229-1396; e-mail info@onair.net; World Wide Web www.onair.net.

## Wireless Messaging Server

Use Wireless Messaging Server when you need to route Inbox messages to a pager or other wireless device. It's the coolest! Contact: IKON Office Solutions, phone (800) 916-2075; fax (520) 529-9517; e-mail Ceinfo@ikon.com; World Wide Web www.ikon.com.

## Wireless Extension for Microsoft Exchange

Wireless Extension for Microsoft Exchange is a client-server product. It supports packet wireless networks. Contact: Wynd Communications, phone (800) 549-9800; fax (805) 781-6001; e-mail info@wynd.com; World Wide Web www.wynd.com.

# Fax Servers

Generally, fax servers allow users to send and, in some cases, receive faxes through a central server, as opposed to their own workstations. Fax servers that integrate with Exchange Server add a new address type for faxing. To send a message to an e-mail user, select the user's e-mail address from the Exchange address book. To send a message to a fax user, select the fax "address" from the Exchange address book.

## FACSys Fax Connector

FACSys Fax Connector operates like any other connector on an Exchange server, but it sends faxes. Contact: FacSys, phone (732) 271-9568; fax (732) 271-9572; e-mail sales@facsys.com; World Wide Web www.facsys.com.

## Faxcom

Faxcom runs as an NT service and integrates with Exchange Administrator. Contact: Biscom, phone (800) 477-2472; fax (978) 250-1800; e-mail sales@biscom.com; World Wide Web www.biscom.com.

## Faxination

Faxination provides full Exchange Server integration and supports a range of languages. It allows for off-hours scheduling and least-cost routing. Contact: Fenestrae, Inc., phone (770) 622-5445; fax (770) 622-5465; e-mail info@fenestrae.com; World Wide Web www.fenestrae.com.

## FAXmaker

FAXmaker runs as an NT service and allows faxes to be sent from an Exchange/Outlook client. Includes call cost accounting. Contact: GFI Fax and Voice, phone (888) 243-4329; fax (919) 388-5621; e-mail sales@gfiusa.com; World Wide Web www.gficomms.com.

## Fax Resource

Fax Resource installs and works as an Exchange Server connector. Contact: Resource Partners, phone (800) 329-9099; fax (33) 1-30-64-1474; e-mail rpisales@faxresource.com; World Wide Web www.faxresource.com.

## LanFax

LanFax operates as an NT service, and supports Exchange and Outlook clients as well as other MAPI-compatible clients. Contact: Alcom, phone (415) 694-7000; fax (415) 694-7070l; e-mail sales@alcom.com; World Wide Web www.alcom.com.

## MsXfax

MsXfax also operates as an Exchange connector. Contact: TSG, Inc., phone (702) 746-0600; fax: (702) 746-9743; e-mail sales@tahoesolutions.com; World Wide Web http://www.bnsgroup.com.au/contents.html.

# Data Access through Exchange Server or Exchange/Outlook Clients

Many users live in their Exchange or Outlook clients. Some even use new messages to compose documents that would be better done in a word processor. So, why not give users access to the data they need through their Exchange and Outlook clients? Why not, indeed!

## Fulcrum Knowledge Network

With Fulcrum Knowledge Network you can issue a query in an Exchange or Outlook client and find information stored on Exchange servers, Web servers, file systems, databases, and more. Contact: Fulcrum, phone (617) 273-2680; fax (617) 273-2682; e-mail info@fulcrum.com; World Wide Web www.fulcrum.com.

## Replica-Action

Replica-Action lets you use Exchange or Outlook clients to access data in a wide range of supported databases. Also aids in migration of Lotus Notes users to Exchange or in synchronization of the databases of the two products. Contact: Casahl, phone (510) 736-7704; fax: (510) 736-3479; e-mail `casahl_sales@casahl.com`; World Wide Web `www.casahl.com`.

# Security, Virus Protection, and Anti-Spam

What scares users more than the boss? Security breaches, viruses, and junk mail! These products let you catch security breaches, mail-borne viruses, and spam messages in their natural habitat—your Exchange server. Most of these products automatically download and install virus updates.

## Antigen for Exchange Server

Antigen for Exchange Server does real-time virus scans and repairs of inbound and outbound messages. It also does scheduled scans and fixes. Contact: Sybari Software, phone (516) 630-8500; fax (516) 630-8550; e-mail `info@sybari.com`; World Wide Web `www.sybari.com`.

## Anti-Virus Software for Exchange Server

Anti-Virus Software for Exchange Server, like most of its competitors, scans mail on an Exchange server for viruses, including attachments and zipped files. Again, as do most similar products, this one sends notifications about found viruses. During virus outbreaks, the software's virus-scan frequency automatically increases. Contact: Nemx Software, phone (613) 831-2010; World Wide Web `www.nemx.com`.

## Global Virus Insurance

Global Virus Insurance does most of the Exchange Server-based virus scanning and cleaning tricks performed by its competitors. Contact: Panda Software, phone (415) 392-5850; World Wide Web `www.pandasoftware.com`.

## GroupShield

GroupShield includes a range of virus scanning and removal options. It is available as a stand-alone product or as part of Network Associates' Total Virus Defense package. Contact: Network Associates, phone (408) 988-3832; fax (408) 970-9727; e-mail sales@nai.com; World Wide Web www.nai.com.

## InocuLAN

InocuLAN includes an anti-virus agent for Exchange Server. Contact: Cheyenne, phone (800) 243-9462; fax (516) 484-3446; e-mail sales@cheyenne.com; World Wide Web www.cheyenne.com.

## Mail Essentials for Exchange/SMTP

Mail Essentials for Exchange is an all-in-one package that does virus and spam control. It also handles encryption, addition of disclaimers to outgoing messages, and automatic replies. Contact: GFI Fax and Voice, phone (888) 243-4329; fax (919) 388-5621; e-mail sales@gfiusa.com; World Wide Web www.gficomms.com.

## MIMEsweeper

MIMEsweeper checks for viruses on outgoing and incoming messages, controls large attachments that might clog your server, and prevents sending of confidential or sensitive material. Contact: Integralis in the UK, phone 44 (0) 118 930 1353; fax 44 (0) 118 930 1301; e-mail uk.sales@mimesweeper.com; World Wide Web www.integralis.com.

## Norton Anti-Virus for Exchange

The pioneering Norton line of anti-virus solutions now includes an offering for Exchange Server. The product provides full-service virus scanning and cleaning. Contact: Symantec, phone (408) 253-9600; World Wide Web www.symantec.com.

## Praetor

Praetor is one of that new breed of spam e-mail filters. It uses lists of banned or approved text as its first line of defense. The product also includes proprietary technology developed through the analysis of techniques used by spammers. Contact: Computer Mail Services, phone (800) 883-2674; fax (248) 352-8387; e-mail info@cmsconnect.com; World Wide Web www.cmsconnect.com.

## ScanMail

ScanMail looks for viruses on an Exchange server, even in encoded and compressed items. The product also handles spam e-mail. Contact: Trend Micro Inc., phone (800) 228-5651; fax (408) 257-2003; e-mail trend@trandmicro.com; World Wide Web www.antivirus.com.

## Virus Scanner

Virus Scanner does some neat virus control tricks, but its more interesting feature is its ability to help enforce organizational e-mail policy by assessing the content of messages and taking appropriate actions based on content. The product can be used to find security breaches in incoming and outgoing messages and to route questionable messages to appropriate personnel. Contact: Nexor, phone (301) 258-7000; fax (301) 258-7004; e-mail info@nexor.com; World Wide Web www.nexor.com.

# Exchange Server/Telephony Integration

Unified messaging, the linking of a variety of messaging tools from pagers to telephones to e-mail clients, has long been a dream of forward-looking communications types. As the products below indicate, the tools for accomplishing unified messaging are finally beginning to emerge.

## NTX

NTX is a client-server telecom manager. The server part runs as a service on NT Server. The client runs on a Windows workstation and lets you manage voice-mail, digital conferencing, phone switching, dialing, faxing, and even e-mail (using voice input). The whole product is integrated with Exchange Server. Contact: COM2001, phone (760) 431-3133; fax (760) 431-3141; e-mail sales@com2001 .com; World Wide Web www.com2001.com.

# Unified Messenger

Unified Messenger is an Exchange Server add-on that stores voicemail messages inside of users' Exchange mailboxes. You can reply to voicemail with e-mail and vice versa. More real coolness! Contact: Octel, phone (800) 444-5590; fax (408) 321-2100; e-mail address not available; send correspondence through the company's World Wide Web site, www.octel.com.

# INDEX

**Note to the Reader:** Throughout this index **boldfaced** page numbers indicate primary discussions of a topic. *Italicized* page numbers indicate illustrations.

# (

# E

# F

for servers, **312**, *313*
for X.400 Connector, 583
last names for mailboxes, 115, *115*
Launch a Process option, 280
Layout menu
   Align command, 830
   Show Grid command, 830
   Snap to Grid command, 830
LDAP (Lightweight Directory Access Protocol),
   **59, 772**
   attribute restrictions for, **335–336**
   client side setup for, **778–780**, *778–780*
   for mailboxes, 262–263, *263*
   for Outlook, 401–402
   server side setup for, **772–778**, *773–777*
   testing, **781–783**, *781–783*
LDAP Directory service, 401–402
LDAP (Directory) Site Defaults dialog box,
   **773–777**, *773–777*
legacy applications, 394
libraries for forms, **843–844**, *844*
License Manager, 162
licenses, 160
   for clients, 390
   Installation Wizard for, **162–163**
licensing modes, 208
lifetime parameter for Message Transfer Agent, 489
Lightweight Directory Access Protocol (LDAP), **59,
   772**
   attribute restrictions for, **335–336**
   client side setup for, **778–780**, *778–780*
   for mailboxes, 262–263, *263*
   for Outlook, 401–402
   server side setup for, **772–778**, *773–777*
   testing, **781–783**, *781–783*
Limit Administrative Access to Home Site
   option, **325**
Limits property page, **264–265**, *265*
link monitors, 55, **476–483**, *477–483*
   address books for, 479
   checking, 859
   for foreign systems, 479, 481, *481*
   General property page for, 477, *477*
   notifications for, **477–479**, *478–479*
   servers for, 479, *480*
   warnings for, **481–483**, *482–483*
links and connections
   for attachments, **9**, *10*

connectors for, **59–64**, *60*, *62*
external. *See* gateways; Internet Mail Service
   (IMS); Microsoft Mail Connector
   (MMC); X.400 Connector
monitoring. *See* link monitors
to multiple servers, **468–471**, *469–470*
to other systems, **138–141**, *140*
saving, 299
to servers, **243**
site-to-site. *See* site-to-site links
List Manager application, 873
ListBox control, 826, *826–827*
lists
   distribution. *See* distribution lists
   sorting, **293**
LoadSim monitor, 27, **95**, *95*, 131–132
Local Group Properties dialog box, 502, *502–503*
local names for Message Transfer Agent, 490
Local Postoffice property page, **629**, *630*
Locales property page, **312**, *313*
log files
   for link monitors, 477
   for Microsoft Mail Connector, 625
   in NNTP, 808
   in POP3, 755
   for server diagnostics, **318–319**, *319*
   for server monitors, 280
   server options for, 316–317
logging events, **93**, *94*
Logon Rights, 309
Logons property page
   for cross-site public folder replication, 564
   for information stores, **343–344**, *344*
lost messages, tracking, **666–676**, *667–675*
Lotus Notes, 29
low-battery signals, 173

# M

Mail Application Programming Interface
   (MAPI), 15
   conversions for, 54
   for X.400 Connector, **128**
Mail Essentials for Exchange/SMTP
   application, 878

# N

# O

# P

# Q

# R

# V

# W

#  Y

#  X

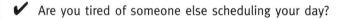

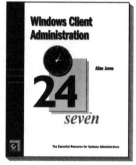

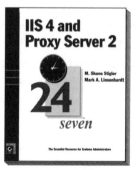

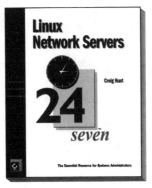

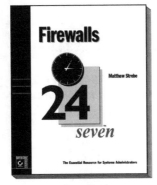

# NT IN THE REAL WORLD

## THE INFORMATION YOU NEED TO BUILD, SECURE, AND OPTIMIZE NT NETWORKS

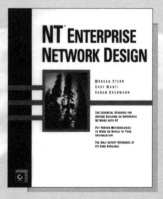

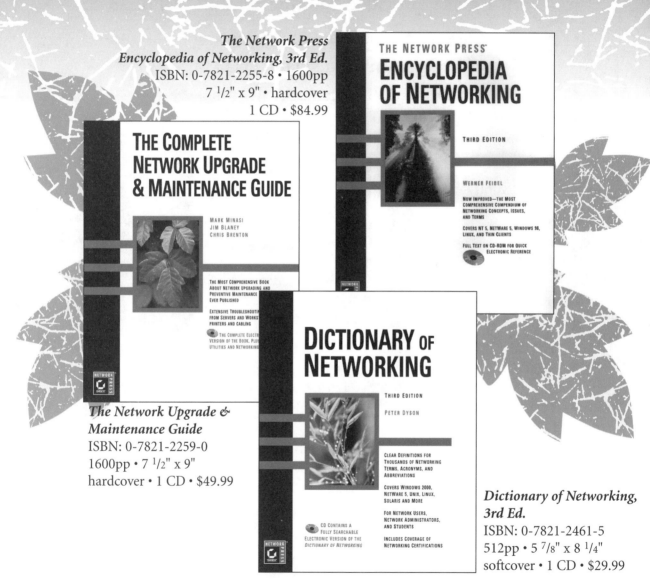

# MCSE ELECTIVE STUDY GUIDES FROM NETWORK PRESS®

Sybex's Network Press expands the definitive Study Guide series for MCSE and MCSE+I candidates.

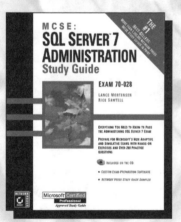

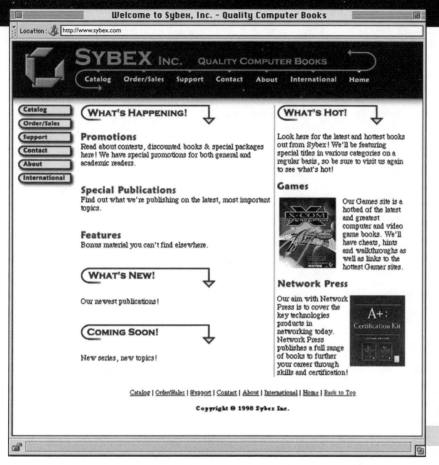

# How to: